RAF Bomber Command Profiles

61 Squadron

RAF Bomber Command Profiles

61 Squadron

Chris Ward

www.aviationbooks.org

This edition first published 2025 by Aviation Books Ltd., 25 Cromwell Street, Merthyr Tydfil, CF47 8RY.

Copyright 2025 © Chris Ward.

The right of Chris Ward to be identified as Author of this work is asserted by him in accordance with the Copyright, Designs and Patents Act 1988.

The original Operational Record Book of 61 Squadron RAF and the Bomber Command Night Raid Reports are Crown Copyright and stored in microfiche and digital format by the National Archives. Material is reproduced under Open Licence v. 3.0.

All rights reserved. No part of this publication may be reproduced, stored in a retrieval system, transmitted in any form or by any means, electronic, mechanical, or photocopied, recorded or otherwise, without the written permission of the copyright owners.

This squadron profile has been researched, compiled and written by its author, who has made every effort to ensure the accuracy of the information contained in it. The author will not be liable for any damages caused, or alleged to be caused, by any information contained in this book. E. and O.E.

Every effort is made to trace the copyright holders of photographs and we apologise in advance for any unintentional omissions. These and other errors brought to our attention will be corrected in subsequent editions of this Profile.

Cover design: Topics - The Creative Partnership www.topicsdesign.co.uk

Photos and captions: Clare Bennett

A CIP catalogue reference for this book is available from the British Library.

ISBN 9781915335470

Also by Chris Ward from Bomber Command Books:

Casualty of War: Letters Home from Flight Lieutenant Bill Astell DFC
Dambuster Deering: The Life and Death of an Unsung Hero
Dambusters : The Complete WWII History of 617 Squadron
(with Andy Lee and Andreas Wachtel)
Time Link

Other RAF Bomber Command Profiles:

IX Squadron
10 Squadron (with Ian MacMillan)
12 Squadron (with Pete Colley)
35 (Madras Presidency) Squadron
44 (Rhodesia) Squadron
49 Squadron
50 Squadron
57 Squadron
75(NZ) Squadron (with Chris Newey)
83 Squadron
90 Squadron (with Shannon Taylor)
101 Squadron
102 (Ceylon) Squadron
103 Squadron (with David Fell)
106 Squadron (with Herman Bijlard)
115 Squadron
138 Squadron (with Piotr Hodyra)
207 Squadron (with Raymond Glynne-Owen)
300 Squadron (with Grzegorz Korcz)
301, 304 and 305 Squadrons (with Grzegorz Korcz)
405 (Vancouver) Squadron RCAF
408 (Goose) Squadron RCAF
455, 458, 462,464 Squadrons RAAF
460 Squadron RAAF
467 Squadron RAAF
514 Squadron (with Simon Hepworth)
619 Squadron
630 Squadron

Contents

Introduction	9
Dedication	11
Narrative History	13
1940. The First Quarter	16
April 1940	17
May 1940	22
June 1940	30
July 1940	40
August 1940	45
September 1940	53
October 1940	61
November 1940	68
December 1940	75
January 1941	80
February 1941	83
March 1941	87
April 1941	92
May 1941	97
June 1941	101
July 1941	105
August 1941	130
September 1941	135
October 1941	140
November 1941	142
December 1941	144
January 1942	146
February 1942	150
March 1942	156
April 1942	161

May 1942	164
June 1942	167
July 1942	174
August 1942	179
September 1942	184
October 1942	190
November 1942	196
December 1942	200
January 1943	204
February 1943	210
March 1943	216
April 1943	223
May 1943	247
June 1943	252
July 1943	258
August 1943	266
September 1943	275
October 1943	280
November 1943	286
December 1943	291
January 1944	295
February 1944	301
March 1944	305
April 1944	312
May 1944	319
June 1944	326
July 1944	334
August 1944	361
September 1944	370
October 1944	377
November 1944	382
December 1944	387

January 1945 393
February 1945 397
March 1945 403
April 1945 409
Roll of Honour 416

61 Squadron 438
Stations 438
Commanding Officers 438
Aircraft 438
Operational Record 439
Aircraft Histories 440

Introduction

RAF Bomber Command Squadron Profiles first appeared in the late nineties and proved to be very popular with enthusiasts of RAF Bomber Command during the Second World War. They became a useful research tool, particularly for those whose family members had served and were no longer around. The original purpose was to provide a point of reference for all of the gallant men and women who had fought the war, either in the air, or on the ground in a support capacity, and for whom no written history of their unit or station existed. I wanted to provide them with something they could hold up, point to and say, "this was my unit, this is what I did in the war". Many veterans were reticent to talk about their time on bombers, partly because of modesty, but perhaps mostly because the majority of those with whom they came into contact had no notion of what it was to be a "Bomber Boy", to face the prospect of death every time they took to the air, whether during training or on operations. Only those who shared the experience really understood what it was to go to war in bombers, which is why reunions were so important. As they approached the end of their lives, many veterans began to speak openly for the first time about their life in wartime Bomber Command, and most were hurt by the callous treatment they received at the hands of successive governments with regard to the lack of recognition of their contribution to victory. It is sad that this recognition in the form of a national memorial and the granting of a campaign medal came too late for the majority. Now this inspirational, noble generation, the like of which will probably never grace this earth again, has all but departed from us, and the world will be a poorer place as a result.

RAF Bomber Command Squadron Profiles are back. The basic format remains, but, where needed, additional information has been provided. Squadron Profiles do not claim to be comprehensive histories, but rather detailed overviews of the activities of the squadron. There is insufficient space to mention as many names as one would like, but all aircraft losses are accompanied by the name of the pilot. Fundamentally, the narrative section is an account of Bomber Command's war from the perspective of the bomber group under which the individual squadron served, and the deeds of the squadron are interwoven into this story. Information has been drawn from official records, such as group, squadron and station ORBs, and from the many, like me, amateur enthusiasts, who dedicate much of their time to researching individual units, and become unrivalled authorities on them. I am grateful for their generous contributions, and their names will appear in the appropriate Profiles. The statistics quoted in this series are taken from The Bomber Command War Diaries, that indispensable tome written by Martin Middlebrook and Chris Everitt, and I am indebted to Martin for his kind permission to use them.

Finally, let me apologize in advance for the inevitable errors, for no matter how hard I and other authors try to write "nothing but the truth", there is no such thing as a definitive account of history, and there will always be room for disagreement and debate. Official records are notoriously unreliable tools, and yet we have little choice but to put our faith in them. It is not my intention to misrepresent any person or Bomber Command unit, and I ask my readers to understand the enormity of the task I have undertaken. It is relatively easy to become an authority on single units or even a bomber group, but I chose to write about them all, idiot that I am, which means 128 squadrons serving operationally in Bomber Command at some time between the 3rd of September 1939 and the 8th of May 1945. I am dealing with eight bomber groups, in which some 120,000 airmen served, and I am juggling around 28,000 aircraft serial numbers, code letters and details of provenance and fate. I ask not for your sympathy, it was, after all, my choice, but rather your understanding if you should find something with which you disagree. My thanks to you, my readers, for making the original series of RAF Bomber Command Squadron Profiles so popular, and I hope you receive this new incarnation equally enthusiastically.

My special thanks are due to Mike Connock and the 50 and 61 Squadrons Association for assisting with information and providing most of the photographs, and as always, to my gang members, Andreas Wachtel, photo editor, Clare Bennett, Steve Smith and Greg Korcz for their unstinting support, without which my Profiles would be the poorer. Finally, my appreciation to my publisher, Simon Hepworth of Aviation Books Ltd, for his belief in my work, untiring efforts to promote it, and for the stress I put him through to bring my books to publication.

Chris Ward. Skegness, Lincolnshire. March 2025.

Dedication

This WWII history of 61 Squadron is dedicated to the memory of Warrant Officer Allan Louis Knoke, who took part in nine operations as rear gunner in the crew of F/O Palmer between the 8/9th February and 25/26th April 1945. His name stands as representative of all who served in wartime 61 Squadron, whether in the air or in a support role on the ground. May they all rest in peace sure in the knowledge that they served their respective countries with honour.

Sergeant Peter Gore enlisted in the RAF in July 1942 as soon as he was eighteen and spent the next twelve months training to become a flight engineer. He considered himself fortunate to be assigned as a rookie to a crew of experienced men captained by F/O Alderdice. In July 1943 they were posted to 61 Squadron at Syerston and took off for their first sortie on the evening of the 25th bound for the Krupp armaments complex at Essen. They failed to return, and all lost their lives, Peter Gore at the age of nineteen years and one month.

Narrative History

61 Squadron first came into existence in the home defence role on the 24th of July 1917. In June 1919 it was disbanded, and remained on the shelf until the 8th of March 1937, when it was reformed as a bomber squadron. After operating Blenheims for thirteen months, the squadron re-equipped with Hampdens in line with the rest of 5 Group, receiving its first example of the type, L4103, on the 17th of February 1939, and a full complement of aircraft had been taken on charge at Hemswell by the 7th of March. When war arrived on the 3rd of September of that year, 61 Squadron's introduction to action was gentle, and like many squadrons in existence from the start of hostilities, short detachments to Coastal Command would interrupt its record of service with Bomber Command. Overseeing the transition from peace to war was W/C Brill, who had occupied the position of squadron commander since 1937, largely in the rank of squadron leader, but his tenure was soon to be over. His flight commanders were Squadron Leaders C M De Crespigny and J G MacIntyre, and their deputies, flight lieutenants Barrett and Lawrence. The squadron was informed of the mobilization of the RAF on the 1st of September, and in accordance with the scatter scheme, was sent north to Speke, near Liverpool, only to be recalled to Hemswell on the 2nd.

On the day of the declaration of war, Sunday, the 3rd of September 1939, Bomber Command was represented by 3, 4 and 5 Groups as its main offensive arm, equipped respectively with Wellingtons, Whitleys and Hampdens, while 2 Group operated Blenheim light bombers. 1 Group had been sent to France with its Fairey Battles on the 1st and 2nd of September to operate as the main component of the Advanced Air Striking Force (AASF) and would remain there until the fall of France in June. 5 Group, whose Air-Officer-Commanding was Air Commodore Callaway, organised its six front-line squadrons on three stations, 44 and 50 at Waddington, 49 and 83 at Scampton and 61 and 144 at Hemswell. 61 Squadron's pilot strength stood at twenty-seven officers, and ten NCOs, and as a two-flight unit, would have on charge sixteen Hampdens I.E. (Initial Equipment) and five I.R (Immediate Reserve).

Notification was received at all three operational stations at 17.50 to prepare nine aircraft each to attack enemy warships, which were reported to have sailed from Wilhelmshaven at 14.30. Hemswell's participation was cancelled later, and it would be left to Scampton and Waddington to undertake 5 Group's first operation activity of WWII. The destination for this armed shipping sweep was the Schillig Roads, located off the north-western corner of Jade Bay, some 350 miles distant, but darkness fell before the formation reached the target area, and they were still forty minutes short when adverse weather conditions effectively brought an end to proceedings. They returned to their respective stations at around 22.30 without having sighted their quarry and would have to wait a considerable time before next venturing into battle. Two of those taking part in this operation would achieve decoration and fame in the years ahead, 49 Squadron's F/O Learoyd, and 83 Squadron's F/O Guy Gibson.

Among a number of pilots posted to the squadron from Finningley on the 13th was Sgt John De Lacy Wooldridge, one of the great characters to serve in Bomber Command, a man of great intellect who would rise through the ranks eventually to command 105 Squadron of the Path Finder Force in 1943. An author, playwright and composer, his service would take him from 61 Squadron to 207 Squadron and later 106 Squadron to serve as a flight commander under W/C Guy Gibson, with whom he had a fractious relationship through constantly outwitting Gibson. Wooldridge would survive the war only to lose his life in a motoring accident in 1958. He married his second wife, the actress Margaretta Scott, in 1948, and she became best known for her portrayal of Mrs Pomfrey in the television series, "All Creatures Great and Small", while his daughter, Susan, has appeared in many theatre and TV productions including "Midsomer Murders".

On the 14th, Air Commodore Callaway was posted to HQ 18 Group to be succeeded as A-O-C 5 Group by Air Vice Marshal Arthur Harris, who would become a household name in the ensuing years of war and lead Bomber Command from February 1942 to the end of the war. On the 26th, W/C Brill was posted to Henlow, before eventually become involved in training in Canada, and was succeeded as commanding officer by S/L de Crespigny on promotion to wing commander rank.

On the 29th of September 5 Group sent eleven Hampdens from Hemswell in two sections to attack enemy warships in the Heligoland area, the 5 Group ORB specifying only the numbers and station, and as 61 Squadron was not involved operationally on this day, it must be assumed that all belonged to 144 Squadron. The two sections became separated, one of six carrying out an inconclusive attack on two destroyers, while the second section of five, including one containing the squadron commander and his crew, failed to return after all were shot down by fighters. Although one of 5 Group's front-line units, 61 Squadron was not called to action and occupied itself with training and frequent short-term visits to other stations under the "scatter" arrangement. It was while training that the squadron registered its first aircraft casualty, P1170 suffering an undercarriage collapse after landing at Doncaster on the 14th of October and running into a pile of cinders, before being consumed by fire.

There would be a number of further small-scale forays by the group, and some of a larger-scale by other groups, during which, the Command learned some expensive but valuable lessons about daylight unescorted incursions into enemy airspace. In fact, by the outbreak of war, 4 Group alone had trained its crews to operate by night, and for the remainder of 1939 and into early 1940, 4 Group Whitleys would roam far and wide over a blacked-out Germany, conducting reconnaissance and leafleting (nickelling) sorties, which condemned the crews to trips of up to twelve hours in the extreme discomfort of unheated aircraft. Most survived and learned a great deal about how to operate and navigate by night, while the rest of the Command clung to an as yet unproved theory.

In 1919, Italian air-war strategist, General Giulio Douhet, had propounded the idea that future wars would be fought by armadas of self-defending bombers, flying directly over the front lines in daylight to target the economic centres of the enemy, and, thereby, destroy its will and capability to continue the fight. This theory would gain support in a number of countries, in Britain with Arthur Harris, in America with Billy Mitchell and in Germany with Walther Wever. Fortunately for the conduct of WWII, Wever would lose his life in a flying accident in 1935, and the development of the Luftwaffe be put in the hands of army-minded strategists, who saw bombing as a tactical extension of artillery. This would prove to be an inspired decision in a short war, and Blitzkrieg would be highly successful in rolling up France and the Low Countries. However, an extended conflict required a strategic bomber force, and by the time Germany realised that fact, it would be too late to catch up. The main flaw in the Douhet theory concerned the suggested ability of bombers to get through in sufficient numbers in daylight to reach the target. During a shipping sweep in the Schillig Roads on the 14th of December, five of twelve Wellingtons would be lost, and twelve out of twenty-two on the 18th. This would force the air planners to take stock, and, ultimately, lead to all but 2 Group becoming a largely nocturnal force.

S/L Lee arrived on posting from Cottesmore on the 22nd of October to fulfil the role of flight commander, and this was at a time when the Germans were expending much effort in sowing magnetic mines in the sea lanes off the British coast, employing float planes for the task, and over the ensuing weeks, seventy-one security patrols were conducted by 5 Group Hampdens without loss over seaplane bases to prevent the use of lights to aid take-off. 61 Squadron was not involved and spent much of November on stand-by for operations against naval targets which never translated into action. Orders were received on the 23rd of November to load each of a dozen Hampdens with four 500lb semi-armour-piercing (SAP) bombs, and in company with a 50 Squadron element, send them north to Wick on the 24th to replace 144 Squadron and operate under the orders of Coastal Command against the German "pocket battleship", Deutschland, which was believed to be off the coast of Norway. Such was the state of the ground at Hemswell that one Hampden became bogged down in mud and required a tractor to extricate it, by which time the squadron had borrowed a replacement from 144 Squadron at Wick, and 144 Squadron claimed the rescued 61 Squadron aircraft on return to Hemswell.

The weather in northern Scotland was at its most inhospitable with gales and snowstorms, and on days when flying was possible, the squadron was on stand-by at one-hour's readiness that culminated each time in a stand-down. The Deutschland remained elusive and would soon be renamed Lützow to avoid the risk to national pride should she be lost in battle while bearing the nation's name, the original Lützow having been sold to the Russians even before her superstructure had been completed. The squadron returned to Hemswell on the 2nd of December and continued training for the ensuing three weeks, spending much time at Doncaster under the "scatter" arrangement, occasionally on stand-by for shipping sweeps that failed to materialise. Late on the evening of the 20th, Scampton and Waddington were alerted to prepare twelve aircraft each for an operation to seek out and attack the Deutschland, whose sister vessel, Admiral Graf Spee, had just been lost following the epic and tension-filled stand-off in Montivideo harbour, where she had sought sanctuary after the Battle of the River Plate. Wishing to avoid an unnecessary loss of life for no possible gain, Kapitän-zur-See, Hans Langsdorff, had scuttled her in the mouth of the river on the 17th of December, before committing suicide two days later.

Having waited for offensive action for almost four months, it was Christmas Day when orders were received for 61 Squadron to detail a dozen Hampdens for an armed shipping sweep in the North Sea and for any enemy surface vessels or U-Boots to be attacked. W/C De Crespigny and S/L MacIntyre were the senior pilots on duty as the formation departed Hemswell at 10.50, only to lose Sgt Emmanuel and crew to an early return almost immediately because of a broken oil pipe. The others ran into a cold front at the midpoint of the North Sea with cloud extending down to sea level, at which point they turned back also. A submarine was sighted off Skegness on the way out and off Spurn Head on the way back, and other vessels were spotted and identified as friendly, and no bombs had been dropped by the time they returned home at 15.00. The country was now in the grip of one of the harshest winters for years and temperatures would continue to plummet, freezing aircraft to the ground and restricting flying opportunities almost to nil.

1940. The First Quarter

What the American press dubbed the "Phoney War", was firmly established in January and was aptly described considering the reluctance of either combatant to attack the other's territory for fear of reprisals. It should be remembered that attacks on private property were still off-limits, which meant that the only legitimate targets were military ships at sea, where stray bombs could not hit land. On the 12th, the squadron prepared two sections of six Hampdens each, led by S/Ls MacIntyre and Lee, and dispatched them from Hemswell at 11.59 to search a square region of the North Sea beginning some 150 miles off Dundee at its northern extremity, extending eastwards some fifty miles and eighty miles off Newcastle-upon-Tyne as the southern-most point. All returned safely home between 15.10 and 15.40 after a fruitless search and no further operations would be mounted during the month. W/C de Crespigny relinquished command of the squadron on the 28th on posting to Pembury, where No 6 Bombing and Gunnery School was about to be formed. He was succeeded at 61 Squadron by S/L F M Denny, who was elevated accordingly to acting wing commander rank.

It would not be until the 23rd of February that the squadron was called next into action, when "nickelling operations, which had been ongoing in 5 Group since the turn of the year, were mounted. The destinations for the crews of F/O England and F/L Lawrence were Bremen and Hamburg, for which they departed Hemswell at 17.15 and 17.30 and returned after four-and-a-half and five hours respectively having successfully fulfilled their brief. At 00.30 and 00.45 on the 1st of March in this Leap Year, the crews of F/Os Fewtrell and Glover took off for nickelling sorties over Wilhelmshaven and Hannover respectively and were back home after four-and-a-half and six hours.

The crews of F/O England, F/Sgt Ross and Sgt Davis departed Hemswell at intervals during the evening of the 5th of March to conduct security patrols over seaplane bases at Sylt off the Schleswig-Holstein coast and the Frisian Islands of Borkum and Norderney, and F/O Clinkard and P/O How and their crews repeated the operation two nights later. On return at 05.30 after more than nine hours aloft, L4111 crashed on approach to Digby, killing F/O Clinkard and the other three occupants, and on examination of the bodies, one was found to have bullet wounds, suggesting an encounter in some form with the enemy. This was followed on the 12th by a training crash involving an Anson communications aircraft, which came down at 11.30 at Lechlade near the Oxfordshire-Wiltshire border, and P/O Hewitt and the other four men on board lost their lives.

At dusk on the 16th, fifteen enemy bombers carried out attacks on elements of the Royal Navy at Scapa Flow in the Orkneys, hitting HMS Norfolk and killing four of her officers. Bombs also fell close to Hatstone aerodrome and Bridge of Wraith on the road between Kirkwall and Stromness on the island of Hoy, and two cottages had been damaged, leading to the death of one civilian and injury to seven others. In retaliation for this, orders were issued on the 19th to carry out an attack on the seaplane base at Hörnum, located on the southern tip of the island of Sylt, off the western coast of Schleswig-Holstein. 4 Group made ready thirty Whitleys, which were assigned a four-hour slot in which to carry out their attacks, to be followed by twenty 5 Group Hampdens from Waddington and Hemswell during a two-hour window later in the evening. 61 Squadron provided the crews of F/L Lawrence and F/Os England, Fewtrell, Glover and Kydd, who departed Hemswell between 21.45 and 22.06 and all were back home by 04.03 to claim a successful outcome.

As events were to prove, this would be an undistinguished first deliberate attack on a German land target, despite the fact that the majority of returning 4 and 5 Group crews were enthusiastic about their part in the raid and were convinced that the base had been severely damaged. It was a claim that was splashed across the front pages of the daily newspapers, 5 Group recording that its aircraft had attacked between 23.45 and 01.50 from heights ranging from 1,000 to 10,000 feet and had delivered a total of sixteen 500 and forty-four 250-pounders along with 660 x 4lb incendiaries. The report added that the hangars had been hit several times and direct hits were observed on the living quarters and slipway. A cursory reconnaissance a day or so later failed to detect any signs of damage, which raised eyebrows in high places, and it was not possible to carry out a full reconnaissance until the 6th of April, which confirmed the worst fears. This would be the first of countless examples of overly enthusiastic claims of success by bomber crews, however, the propaganda value to the folks at home was massive. Only one aircraft failed to return, and all the Hampdens got back safely.

On the 24th the crews of S/L Lee, F/O Kydd, F/Sgt Ross and Sgt Emmanuel departed Hemswell between 19.05 and 19.33 on reconnaissance sorties, two bound for Kiel and two for Warnemünde situated some seventy miles further east along the Baltic coast. Heavy cloud made it impossible to navigate accurately, and S/L Lee and crew abandoned their sortie before reaching Kiel, while the others returned to claim a successful night's work, during which nickels had been dispensed over Kiel, Neumünster and Warnemünde. Thus ended the first quarter of 1940, during which the squadron conducted seven operations and dispatched thirty sorties for the loss of a single Hampden and crew in a crash on return and a second crew in the Anson accident while training.

April 1940

Training continued during the first week of the new month, and much time was spent at Ingham, the "scatter" aerodrome in use throughout March. The crews were unaware at this time that events further north would shortly increase the intensity of operations and that all of the training would stand them in good stead for what lay before them. The crew of a Hampden consisted of a pilot, a second pilot and two wireless operator gunners, the second pilot gaining experience before being allowed to captain his own crew. However, because of the Hampden's fighter style single-occupant cockpit arrangement, the second pilot acted as the navigator/bomb-aimer, perhaps for as many as a dozen sorties before being elevated to captain.

The first operation of the month was posted on the 6th and was a reconnaissance of the sea approaches to the naval and shipbuilding port of Wilhelmshaven located on the north-western coast of Jade Bight on the eastern side of Lower Saxony. The task was handed to the crews of F/Os Fewtrell and How, who departed Hemswell at 20.30 and 20.55 respectively carrying nickels only and proceeded eastwards at 10,000 and 8,000 feet to make landfall initially on the Schleswig-Holstein coast. After reconnoitering Brunsbüttel and Cuxhaven the Fewtrell crew progressed as far east as the Baltic coast at Kiel and dispensed nickels on the way back over the town of Neumünster. The How crew paid particular attention to the Kiel Canal, the waterway traversing the Schleswig-Holstein peninsula, through which U-Boots from the Kiel shipyards gained access to the North Sea. Both crews returned safely after six-and-a-half hours aloft and reported details of searchlights and flak and the imperfection of the blackout.

On the 8th, three Hampdens were loaded with six 250-pounders each for security patrols over the seaplane bases at Sylt, Norderney and Borkum, and the crew of Sgt Saunders took off first at 19.17, only to return three hours later after encountering cloud at between 1,000 feet and sea level that prevented any likelihood of observing the ground. F/O Kydd and crew departed Hemswell at 23.42 and F/O Glover and crew at 00.16, the latter to be recalled because of the conditions, while the Kydd crew pressed on with no prospect of fulfilling their primary brief, but through a gap from 10,000 feet spotted approximately thirty small vessels, probably a fishing fleet, under escort some fifty miles north of the central Frisians.

Suddenly, on the 9th, the entire tenor of the war altered when Germany invaded Denmark and Norway, and Bomber Command was thrust into the fray in an attempt to slow down the enemy advance into the latter. It brought an end to the shadow boxing that had characterised events since September, and it was the signal for the strategic bombing war to begin hesitantly, but in earnest. It took German forces just six hours to subdue Danish resistance after sending in forces by ground, sea and air, while the Norwegians would resist for two months, supported by British and French forces. 5 Group responded by sending twenty-four Hampdens in search of enemy warships and troop transports off Bergen on the 9th, and although twelve of the force were recalled, two of the remainder claimed hits on a cruiser.

61 Squadron entered the fray with a single sortie on the 10th conducted by F/O Kydd and crew, who departed Hemswell at 21.53 before setting course for the Baltic to conduct a special security and reconnaissance sortie. After crossing the Great Belt, cloud largely obscured the ground and Roskilde Fjord was mistaken for the Sound, the stretch of water between Copenhagen on Denmark's Zealand Island and Sweden's brightly illuminated western seaboard, but the Danish capital city was soon identified and the coastal region followed for some time. They returned after almost eight hours in the air and reported passing over Flensburg, the Baltic port close to the German/Danish frontier, and observing a column of motor transport heading north.

Elements of the Royal Navy and the Kriegsmarine came face-to-face on the 10th and would do so again on the 13th, and this would be followed by landings at Narvik involving British, French and Polish troops, which linked up with Norwegian forces. Bomber Command was prevented by the extreme range from directly supporting the landings and would focus instead on attacking enemy supplies of men and materials arriving by air on airfields at Oslo and Stavanger and by sea in the southern ports. On the 11th, squadrons across the Command were instructed to prepare for what would be the largest commitment of bombers since the war began. Eighty-three Wellingtons, Hampdens and Blenheims were assembled for the operation, which would take place on the following day, but in the meantime, six 61 Squadron Hampdens were loaded with four 500lb SAP bombs each and departed Hemswell at 11.27 with S/L Lee the senior pilot on duty. They were bound for Kristiansand Bay to search for enemy warships, including the Admiral Scheer, which was the third of the three Deutschland Class "pocket battleships", along with Graf Spee and Deutschland (Lützow). They crossed the North Sea at 6,000 feet over cloud, which broke up as the Norwegian coast came into view, at which point the formation climbed to 12,000 feet hoping to use high cloud as cover for an attack. In the event, a lack of cloud cover forced them to turn back, and all landed safely after sorties lasting a little under six hours. That night, twenty

Hampdens from other squadrons joined a contingent of Whitleys in a shipping sweep from Kiel Bay to Oslo, and at least one ship was hit.

The date of the arrival of S/L Sisson at 61 squadron as a flight commander does not appear to have been recorded, but he was the senior pilot on duty on the 12th, as six 61 Squadron Hampdens departed Hemswell at 10.07 to attack a battleship accompanied by destroyers. It was believed that the Scharnhorst and Gneisenau heavy cruisers had been spotted in the Skagerrac between Denmark and southern Norway. The flight out was conducted initially at between 1,000 and 2,000 feet, but the formation climbed later to 6,000 feet to be above the cloud and then descended on e.t.a to 500 feet, emerging into rain, at which point the two sections of three became separated and unsuccessfully searched independently for a target, before heading for home. Elsewhere, enemy fighters brought down six Hampdens and three Wellingtons at a cost of five of their number, and the lesson having been learned, there would be no further major daylight operations for Bomber Command's heavy brigade until the summer of 1944.

On the night of the 13/14th, 5 Group carried out the first mine-laying operation of the war, a task to which the Hampden was to prove itself eminently suited. This would represent the initial tentative steps in a new departure for Bomber Command operations, which would prove to be hugely successful, and by war's end, would have sunk or damaged more enemy vessels than the Royal Navy. The laying of parachute mines by air was given the code-name "gardening" and the entire enemy-held coastline from the Pyrenees in the south-west to the Baltic port of Königsberg in the north-east, and even the northern Italian coast, would be divided into gardens, each with a horticultural or marine biological name. The process of delivery was known as planting and the mines, themselves, were referred to as vegetables, and it would not be long before the other groups joined in to create a spiders' web of mines in chains across all of the sea-lanes employed by the enemy. There were no gardens allotted to the Kristiansand coastal region of south-western Norway at this early stage, and areas A and B were referred to in the ORBs, which would later become the Silverthorn and Hawthorn gardens off the North Sea and Baltic coasts respectively of Jutland.

On this night, Waddington, Hemswell and Scampton provided fifteen Hampdens between them for mining duties, for which the 61 Squadron crews of F/Os How, Kydd and Glover departed Hemswell in that order between 23.00 and 23.10, each sitting on a single 1,500lb parachute mine for delivery to the sea lanes between Denmark's main islands. Details were scant, but references were made to Nyborg, Knudshoved, Svendborg and Langeland as well as to German locations at Sylt and Flensburg. They were airborne for more than six hours, each aircraft calculated to have consumed seventy gallons of fuel per hour, and we are told only that each sortie was carried out satisfactorily. At 06.02, F/O Fewtrell and crew took off to conduct a sea search for a missing crew and returned at 10.32 with nothing to report.

On the 14th, all three 5 Group operational stations were notified of further mining operations that night off Denmark, for which twenty-eight Hampdens were made ready, seven of them by 61 Squadron. S/L Lee was the senior pilot on duty as they took off from Hemswell between 19.24 and 19.41 and lost the services of F/L Ross and P/O Davis to wireless failure within the first two hours. The weather conditions were unhelpful and persuaded the crews of S/L Lee and F/O Fewtrell to abandon their sorties, leaving the crews of F/L Lawrence and F/O England to persevere and reach their briefed target areas, where the former encountered low cloud and searched in vain to establish a pinpoint before giving up. The latter established a fix on the Hindenburgdamm, a seven-mile-long causeway joining Sylt to the mainland, from where a course was set for a timed run at 600 feet to the release point. Sadly, the target area could not be recognised, and the mine was withheld. They passed over Sylt in rain and were fired upon but made it home safely to land at Wattisham after more than eight hours in the air. On return to Hemswell they were greeted with the news that L4113 had failed to return with the crew of Sgt Emanuel, whose fate would never be established, and they became the first of many 61 Squadron crews to be reported missing from operations.

A crash during training on the 17th caused the demise of L4116, following an overshoot at Hemswell, but P/O Morley and his crew walked away unscathed. That night, thirty-three Hampdens were made ready for a return to the Baltic, to the Asparagus (Great Belt) and Carrot (Little Belt) gardens, for which 61 Squadron made ready six, which departed Hemswell between 21.29 and 22.00 with F/L Lawrence the senior pilot on duty and Sgt Wooldridge continuing his apprenticeship as second pilot to P/O Davis. On this occasion they benefitted from favourable weather conditions and a full moon and selected their own altitudes, crossing over Sylt at between 600 and 12,000 feet, some attracting the attention of searchlights and flak, and on reaching the Baltic coastline of Schleswig-Holstein, found Flensburg to be well-illuminated. All returned safely after sorties lasting six hours and more and reported a successful night's work.

5 Group detailed a dozen Hampdens each from Hemswell and Waddington on the 20th to operate in the Eglantine garden located in the Elbe Estuary, the vital waterway providing access to Germany's second city, Hamburg, and passage from there to the North Sea for its merchant, naval and U-Boot fleets. 61 Squadron made ready six Hampdens, which departed Hemswell between 19.15 and 19.36 with F/L Lawrence the senior pilot on duty and soon lost the services of F/Sgt Ross and Sgt Saunders to wireless failure. The weather conditions outbound were initially unfavourable but improved to five-tenths cloud at 4,000 feet by the time they pinpointed on the Frisian Islands of Norderney and Wangerooge and the uninhabited Trischen some five miles off the mouth of the Elbe. At this stage of the war, and until the roll-out of the H2S ground-mapping radar more than three years in the future, mining was conducted from low level, typically from between 500 and 800 feet, from where pinpoints could be established and accuracy guaranteed. The greatest danger during these operations came in the form of light flak from shore and ship-based batteries, and if brought down in an uncontrolled manner, survival by parachute was unlikely. P/O Davis and crew circled the Cuxhaven target area for thirty minutes before planting their vegetable and returning in bad weather conditions that persuaded them to head for Manston. As they passed close to the Norfolk coast two naval vessels opened fire and continued to do so even after the colours of the day had been fired, a not isolated incident.

5 Group launched a major mining effort on the 21st, detailing seventeen Hampdens each from Waddington and Scampton and a dozen from Hemswell to operate in the Baltic and in the Eglantine garden again. 61 Squadron made ready six Hampdens, which departed Hemswell between 19.04 and 19.13 with S/L Lee the senior pilot on duty and set course for landfall on the German coast over Sylt and Amrum Islands. S/L Lee and crew turned back seventy miles out after the IFF equipment blew, and Sgt Saunders and crew limped back to Waddington many hours later with an engine issue that prevented them from fulfilling their brief. The passage of the others across the Schleswig-Holstein peninsula was aided by bright moonlight, which facilitated map-reading to the Asparagus, Carrot and Daffodil gardens in the Baltic, and positions were established without difficulty. All returned safely after seven hours aloft, three to land at Bircham Newton and one at Mildenhall.

The 23rd brought further mining operations in the Baltic for twenty-seven Hampdens, ten based at Hemswell, five of them belonging to 61 Squadron. The crews learned at briefing that their destinations were on either side of the Schleswig-Holstein peninsula, including the previously visited Carrot garden in the Little Belt, and Hollyhock, located off Travemünde at the mouth of the waterway leading to the Hansastadt (ancient free trade city) and port of Lübeck. They took off between 18.43 and 18.54 with F/L Lawrence the senior pilot on duty, before setting course for landfall on the Schleswig-Holstein coast, which P/O Pascoe and crew crossed at Tonning and further east located a lake near the town of Schleswig to employ as the final turning point. They descended to 700 feet for the run to the release point only to suffer the frustration of a hang-up, and after three failed attempts to release the mine, they turned for home. P/O Davis and crew also brought their store home after being defeated by low cloud in their target area, but the crews of F/O How and S/L Lawrence pinpointed first on Stevns Klint lighthouse on Zealand Island and then on the Drogden Light for their successful runs to the release point. F/Sgt Ross and crew also fulfilled their brief after turning at Schleswig, but there is insufficient information to identify the precise drop zone. They returned safely to diversion airfields after uneventful round trips of up to eight hours duration.

Two nights later, 5 Group committed twenty-eight Hampdens to mining duties in the Forget-me-not garden, located on the approaches to Kiel Harbour, four of them to combine this with security patrols over Borkum and Sylt. The three-strong 61 Squadron element consisted of the crews of F/O Kydd, P/O Wyatt and Sgt Saunders, who departed Hemswell between 23.05 and 23.13 and began the North Sea crossing at Mablethorpe, losing the services of the last mentioned to W/T failure within the first hour. The others pressed on, flying blind all the way to the target area, where fog completely blotted out all ground detail and left them with no alternative but to abandon their sorties and return to land at Leuchars in Scotland.

Hemswell represented 5 Group on the 30, when five Hampdens were detailed to attack Aalborg aerodrome in northern Jutland, 61 Squadron contributing the crews of F/O Glover and P/Os England and Pascoe, who departed Hemswell between 19.20 and 19.24 each sitting on six 250-pounders. P/O Pascoe and crew turned back within ninety minutes because of wireless failure, while P/O England and crew crossed the North Sea at 6,000 feet and made landfall at Klitmøller on Jutland's north-western coast before heading south to Thyborøn, from where course was set eastwards to the target area. A mass of waterways lay beneath, compounding navigational difficulties, and it was necessary to orbit the aerodrome for forty-five minutes until the Islands of Oland and Giol were identified. A nest of twenty-five searchlights had to be negotiated during the north to south bombing run, and the glare prevented an observation of the outcome. The return journey was conducted in poor weather conditions, particularly over England, where the cloud was down in places to 600 feet, testing the already tired crew after seven-and-a-half hours aloft. We have no details of the sortie of F/O Glover and crew, who all lost their lives when L4119 crashed at 04.40 at Croxton Kerrial in Leicestershire, some six miles south-west of the 5 Group HQ in Grantham, after more than nine hours in the air.

During the course of the month the squadron took part in thirteen operations and dispatched fifty-seven sorties for the loss of two Hampdens and their crews.

May 1940

At this stage of the war there was no established procedure for the recording of events, as a result of which some Operations Record Books (ORBs) provide useful detail, while others are devoid of information, and most are reticent to name targets as if in fear of revealing secrets. This paranoia was made manifest from mid-1940 by referring to each individual target by a code, the prefix of which denoted the type of objective, as for example, A for oil refineries, C for factories and D for shipyards. It is, therefore, difficult to provide a detailed account of the squadron's activities as the intensity of operations increased, and what follows is the best that can be gleaned from the squadron and group records and other sources.

5 Group committed twenty-six Hampdens to mining duties on the 2nd, of which four were provided by 61 Squadron, which departed Hemswell between 21.10 and 21.25 with S/L Lawrence the senior pilot on duty bound for what would become known as the Onion garden in Oslo Fjord. F/O Fewtrell and crew were immediately afflicted with an engine issue and landed at Scampton, leaving the others to make their way via Jutland's western coast to the target area. F/O Kydd and crew ran into searchlights and flak and employed the city as cover before dropping down to low-level to release the mine and evade the light flak that chased them back out to sea. F/O How and crew observed the commotion caused by the Kydd crew and opted for a throttled-back glide approach, which proved initially to be successful, until a shell cut a hydraulics pipe and the bomb doors could not be closed. A tense return flight to Kinloss at a drag-reduced speed ended with use of the air bottle to deploy the undercarriage. Conscious of the flak, S/L Lawrence and crew approached the drop zone over land from the east, descending from 4,000 to 500 feet to plant the vegetable into the briefed location, before making their escape at 100 feet and climbing eventually to 12,000 feet for the return across the sea to Scotland.

The only activity on the following night involved ten Hampdens conducting mining sorties off the German and Norwegian coasts, for which 61 Squadron briefed the crews of F/O Baskett, P/O Morley and Sgt Saunders, before sending them on their way from Hemswell between 21.03 and 21.43. The Morley crew returned early with an intercom issue and took off again, while Sgt Saunders and crew abandoned their sortie within the hour because of wireless failure. We do not know to which garden the Morley and Baskett crews had been assigned but neither was able to identify the target area through cloud and both brought their mines back to base.

The 9th proved to be the last day of shadow-boxing, and the night was occupied by mining operations involving thirty-one Hampdens operating in the Eglantine garden in the Elbe estuary and off Kiel, Helsingborg (Sweden) Lübeck and Warnemünde in the Baltic. 61 Squadron made ready six aircraft, three each for the Forget-me-not and Nasturtium gardens located respectively in Kiel Bay and at the northern end of The Sound (Oresund) off Helsingborg and dispatched them from Hemswell between 20.00 and 20.40 with S/L Sisson the senior pilot on duty. The Nasturtium-bound F/O Baskett and crew were back on the ground within ninety minutes after experiencing excessive vibration, and F/O England and crew lost their artificial horizon as they crossed the Danish coast on course for the same location and had to turn back also. This left the crew of F/O Fewtrell to fulfill their brief in the Nasturtium garden, while the Forget-me-not trio were also successful and as they headed home in the early hours of the 10th, they were unaware that German forces were poised to launch an advance into the Low Countries at first light.

It was an event that signalled the beginning of the massacre of the Fairey Battle squadrons stationed in France as part of the AASF, and the Blenheims of 2 Group would also be thrust into the unequal fight against marauding BF109s, ME110s and murderous ground fire and suffer heavy losses over the succeeding weeks. On the 10th alone, twenty-four Battles and ten Blenheims were lost either during operations or destroyed on the ground and the figure for the 11th was nine and ten respectively.

Bomber Command was to play its part by attacking communications targets behind enemy lines, and in so doing, would bomb mainland Germany for the first time. The first raid of the war on a German urban target followed quickly on the 11th, for which nineteen Hampden and eighteen Whitley crews were briefed, four of the former from 61 Squadron. Their targets were road, rail and air communications in Mönchengladbach, a town located on the south-western edge of the industrial Ruhr Valley. The 61 Squadron crews of F/Os Baskett and How, P/O Kydd and F/Sgt Ross departed Hemswell between 22.41 and 22.59, each with four 500-pounders in the bomb bay, only for the Ross and How crews to return early, the latter with an unserviceable generator, which was fixed, enabling them to take off again at 00.27. The weather conditions were perfect as they set out from Mablethorpe via corridor G towards the enemy coast between The Hague and the Scheldt estuary, where they were greeted by intense searchlight activity. The target area was already on fire after being attacked by the Whitley element, and together with the glare from searchlights, this created challenging conditions in which to identify precise aiming points. A long line of transport was seen to be moving from north-east to south-west through the town, and it seems that this became the target for the 61 Squadron crews through patchy cloud from 10,000 to 12,000 feet, some observing their bombs burst on the road.

5 Group squadrons remained on the ground on the 12th, while the carnage at the battle front continued with the destruction of fourteen Battles and twenty Blenheims of the AASF and 2 Group. On the 13th, the squadron briefed four crews to attack road communications in the Aachen area, while the destination for S/L Lawrence and crew was the lettuce garden, located in a stretch of the Kiel Canal. They departed Hemswell first at 20.37, to be followed into the air between 22.47 and 23.59 by the bombing brigade led by S/L Sisson and crew, who were forced to abandon their sortie immediately because of intercom failure. The Lawrence crew established a fix on the Terschelling lighthouse before running into thick cloud, and on e.t.a. in the target area descended to 1,500 feet, searching in vain for twenty minutes without picking out anything recognisable. At this point they turned for home, while many miles to the south-west, F/L Barrett and crew had climbed to 18,000 feet in the hope of finding a gap in the cloud over Aachen, and on failing to do so, turned for home and jettisoned the bombs over the sea. P/O Morley and crew were more successful and dropped their four 500-pounders from 16,000 feet, observing them burst on the western side of the town. It seems that they were also carrying two wing-mounted 250-pounders, which they unleashed on Eindhoven aerodrome after finding it on fire as they passed by on the way home. F/Sgt Saunders and crew encountered intense searchlight and flak at Aachen, and when they caught a glimpse of railway sidings through the cloud, let their bombs go.

Meanwhile, the carnage at the battle front had continued on the 12th with the destruction of fourteen Battles and twenty Blenheims, and on the 14th thirty-three Battles and fourteen Blenheims were lost, which effectively knocked the Battle squadrons out of the fight. 5 Group detailed twenty-two Hampdens on the 14th for mining duties in the Baltic and a further twelve to attack road and rail communications in Holland, 61 Squadron supporting both endeavours. The crews of P/O Pascoe and F/O How were assigned to mining, the former in the Nasturtium garden off Helsingborg and the latter in Lettuce in the Kiel Canal, while the crews of S/L Sisson and P/Os Jones and Wyatt were to target moving motor columns on the road between Breda and Tilburg, a few miles inland from the Scheldt estuary in southern Holland. P/O Wyatt and crew turned back because of excessive airframe vibration, while the Sisson and Jones crews crossed the Dutch coast, noting The Hague to be burning, before turning to the south and easily locating the target area. S/L Sisson and crew attacked from 3,000 feet and P/O Jones and crew from an unspecified height, dropping four 250-pounders on the junction to the north of the town and two more on the road itself. Almost four hundred miles to the north-east, P/O Pascoe and crew had been unable to establish their position at the northern end of The Sound, and returned their vegetable to the station store, while F/O How and crew had located the Kiel Canal and had to run the gauntlet of searchlights and flak to plant their vegetable in the briefed spot.

Following the Luftwaffe's bombing of Rotterdam on the 15th, which caused an outcry across the world, the War Cabinet finally sanctioned operations against Germany proper, thus prompting the start of the strategic offensive for which the Command had been created. That night, ninety-nine assorted aircraft took off to attack sixteen industrial and railway targets in the Ruhr, while twelve Wellington crews were briefed to bomb communications in Belgium, and this was the first time that a hundred aircraft had been dispatched in a single night. 5 Group detailed a dozen Hampdens each from Hemswell, Scampton and Waddington to attack industrial and communications targets, and sent them on their way from Hemswell between 20.45 and 21 41 with S/L Lawrence the senior pilot on duty. He and his crew were hampered by ten-tenths cloud as they picked up the Rhine north of the Ruhr, before coming upon the town of Haltern, where, after stooging around for some time, they identified a blast furnace, bombed it and missed it by around one hundred yards. P/O Wyatt and crew also found a blast furnace near Recklinghausen, some eight miles south of Haltern, which may have been the same one attacked by the Lawrence crew. They descended from 16,000 to 6,000 feet and dropped two 250-pounders and a small bomb container (SBC) of incendiaries without observing the outcome, before heading for their briefed target at Ickern, a district of Castrop-Rauxel five miles further east, where the Klöckner Werke A.G synthetic oil refinery may have been the briefed objective. A further two 250-pounders and two SBCs were released, and a fire was reported to break out.

P/O Hall and crew found themselves south of their intended track and followed the Rhine to Cologne, where they released a parachute flare, and in its light, completed a circuit and attacked and overshot an objective from 5,000 feet. F/Sgt Saunders and crew were defeated by thick haze and were heading for the Scheldt on their way home when lights were spotted at two locations identified as railway stations at Boxtel and Gorinchem in southern Holland, both of which were attacked and bursts observed in close proximity. P/O Davis and crew found the town of Leeuwarden to be in flames as they crossed northern Holland towards Münster in Germany's flatlands to the north of the Ruhr, but haze prevented them from identifying their assigned target and when they attempted to bomb a railway station as a last resort target, only three 250-pounders fell away. F/O Basket and crew observed Rotterdam and The Hague to be burning as they passed by and picked up the Rhine from 8,000 feet, observing lights at their marshalling yards target, the location of which they did not specify. A stick of bombs fell across the yards before the local defences opened up and chased them out of the target area.

A major assault on Germany's oil industry was mounted on the 17th, when 5 Group detailed forty-eight Hampdens for targets in Hamburg, while twenty-four 4 Group Whitleys were assigned similar targets in Bremen and a handful of 3 Group Wellingtons went for railway installations in Cologne. As these raids were taking place over Germany, a force of forty-six Wellingtons and six Hampdens conducted tactical operations against a road and railway junction in Belgium, through which enemy troop columns were passing on their way to the front. 61 Squadron briefed eight crews, which departed Hemswell between 20.30 and 21.55 with S/Ls Lawrence and Sisson the senior pilots on duty and four 500-pounders in each bomb bay. Their targets were oil storage tanks coded A5 and A8, which, it is believed, were located on the northern bank of the River Elbe to the west of Hamburg city centre, while others from Waddington focused on A10, the Rhenania oil refinery at Harburg, situated on the southern bank. They exited the English coast between Mablethorpe and Skegness on a night of unlimited visibility enhanced by an almost full moon, which would enable them to map-read to the enemy coast via the lightship at Terschelling and the lighthouses at Westerhever and Heligoland. Those choosing to follow the course of the Elbe into the heart of the docks and industrial districts could expect an intense searchlight and flak defence from both banks of the river and a more prudent approach was from the south or the north.

At this stage of the war, routes, altitudes and timings were left very much to be decided at squadron level and crews could determine the details for themselves. F/L Barrett and crew were contending with wireless issues as they crossed the North Sea and turned back at the Terschelling light with a view to swapping aircraft. They took off again at 22.32, and returned within two hours, apparently having abandoned all thoughts of seeking out a target. Meanwhile, F/Sgt Ross and crew had dropped four 500-pounders from 16,000 feet aided by the perfect conditions, and a fire was observed to break out at the edge of the oil storage tanks. S/L Sisson and crew were over the target at 15,000 feet when the oxygen ran out, the wireless operator collapsed, and the second pilot (navigator) displayed signs of distress. The sortie was abandoned and altitude lost, and as they reached 6,000 feet homebound, the wireless operator recovered. P/O Pascoe and crew made two runs across the target at 10,000 feet, dropping two 500-pounders during each, and P/O Wyatt and crew followed the Elbe into the heart of the target area, both crews reporting fires resulting from the release of their payloads. F/O Kydd's four 500-pounders were observed to fall into the centre of the target and F/O How's on a corner of it in the light of a flare released by an aircraft ahead, and the result was an increase in the intensity of the fires. S/L Lawrence and crew watched their bombs fall directly onto a tank and set it ablaze, before joining the other participants on the ground after sorties of a little over six hours duration.

A similar pattern of operations against industrial targets in Germany and communications in Belgium and France occupied the following two nights, while the need to continue supporting tactical operations continued through to the fall of France in June. On the 18th, orders were received at Waddington and Hemswell to prepare six Hampdens each to attack road junctions and bridges in the battle area at Givet, located right on the Franco-Belgian frontier. 61 Squadron briefed the crews of P/Os Davis and Hall and Sgt Saunders for an attack on a crossroads at Dinant, and launched them from Hemswell between 21.05 and 22.10, only to lose the services of the last mentioned to engine trouble within the first hour. The Hall crew carried out four runs across the aiming point at 4,000 feet, dropping a total of six 250-pounders, observing one to burst on the road, and the Davis crew straddled the aiming point from a similar height.

On the 19th, W/C Denny relinquished command of the squadron and was succeeded by W/C Walter Sheen, who in April had concluded five months in command of 49 Squadron at Scampton, and before that had been a flight commander with 106 Squadron, the 5 Group pool training unit. He presided over his first briefing on the day of his appointment, when seventy-eight aircraft, including thirty-six Hampdens, were poised to carry out widespread attacks on German troop communications in France and Belgium and on railway and industrial targets in Germany. 5 Group detailed thirty-six Hampdens to attack a number of oil-related targets, including A21, a refinery at Salzbergen, situated on the River Ems in the Münsterland, north of the Ruhr and ten miles from the Dutch frontier. This Wintershall refinery was, in fact, the oldest in Germany, having been established in 1860, and was one of a number now run by the company at various sites across Germany, before being swallowed up by the I.G. Farben conglomerate. 61 Squadron briefed six crews and sent them off from Hemswell in two sections at 20.50 and 21.05 with S/L Sisson the senior pilot on duty and four 500-pounders in each bomb bay. The ORB provides no actual reference to a specific target but mentions that S/L Sisson and crew dropped a stick of bombs into a railway line at Salzbergen, which suggests that the others in his section, the crews of F/O Baskett and P/O Jones were close by. The latter attacked a railway junction from 7,000 feet, while F/O Baskett and crew arrived to find the target already on fire and believed that they had hit a large building, but when the bomb bay was inspected after landing, it was discovered that three 500-pounders had hung-up. The second section comprising the crews of F/L Barrett, P/O Morley and F/Sgt Ross identified their target, which may also have been the Wintershall refinery at Salzbergen, and bombed it from up to 10,000 feet, creating fires in storage tanks, the glow from which remained visible for a hundred miles into the return journey.

The need to hinder the enemy advance continued to draw elements of the Command's resources from strategic to tactical bombing, including, on the 20th, when ninety-two aircraft were detailed to attack troops and armoured columns that were breaking into northern France. 5 Group contributed six Hampdens each from Waddington, Hemswell and 83 Squadron at Scampton to attack road bridges over the River Oise, the 61 Squadron crews of F/O How, P/O Pascoe and Sgt Saunders departing Hemswell at 20.30 bound for one at Longchamps, located between the Belgian frontier and St-Quentin. The Saunders crew spent time searching for their target, and on locating it dropped six 250-pounders, but were unable to determine the proximity of the bursts. The How and Pascoe crews also experienced difficulty in identifying the objective as a low moon failed to reflect on the waterway, and when their loads eventually went down, they were observed to burst along the riverbank and not on the bridge.

The focus shifted to railways in Germany on the 21st, to attempt to stem the flow of troops and armour being fed into the battle area. 5 Group contributed twenty-five Hampdens to an overall force of 124 aircraft assigned to numerous aiming points on lines to the west of Cologne from Mönchengladbach in the north to Euskirchen in the south. The 5 Group effort was to be directed at a twenty-mile stretch of track between Cologne and Düren, situated to the south-west of the Rhineland capital, and the order was to attack any trains encountered. The 61 Squadron crews of S/L Lawrence, F/O Kydd and P/Os Hall and Wyatt departed Hemswell in that order between 20.47 and 21.19, each sitting on six 250-pounders, before setting course for the Scheldt estuary, from where they continued on a south-easterly track to the target area, which lay within Cologne's western defence zone. An initial reconnaissance revealed no moving rail traffic on the briefed stretch of line, but when P/O Wyatt and crew attacked a stationary train with a single 250-pounder, it prompted an intense and accurate searchlight and flak response. A large hole was punched in the port flap, despite which, the remaining bombs were delivered individually on junctions and stretches of a different track from 1,000 feet, before they headed home to land safely after five hours in the air. P/O Hall and crew eventually found a moving target just outside Baal station, located some fifteen miles south-west of Mönchengladbach, and carried out four runs across it before dropping a bomb that exploded alongside. The train stopped and another bomb wrecked the track in front of it, while others hit nearby sidings, and the gunners strafed the scene with nine hundred rounds. As F/O Kydd and crew reconnoitered the stretch of track from Aachen to Krefeld, P4346 was hit by anti-aircraft fire in the port engine, which sprang an oil leak, but marshalling yards at Eschweiler were located and a stick of bombs dropped across track and rolling stock. S/L Lawrence and crew missed one train by twenty yards, but wrecked two coaches at Baal station with two bombs, after which they headed north-east for four miles and attempted to hit a train at Erkelenz. The bursts of the bombs were not observed, and the scene was strafed for good measure.

It had been intended that the target for thirty-five Hampdens on the 22nd would be the oil refinery at distant Leuna, near Merseburg, one of many similar plants situated in an arc from north to south to the west of Leipzig. In the event, unfavourable weather conditions prompted a recall, which all but W/C Watts, the commanding officer of 144 Squadron, picked up and he went on alone to bomb and damage the target. Meanwhile, 5 Group contributed a dozen Hampdens from Waddington and 83 Squadron at Scampton to attacks on railway bridges and road targets in France, Belgium and Holland.

It was similar fare on the following night, when fifty Hampdens were among 122 aircraft sent to attack railway communications and trains in motion on either side of the Dutch/German frontier, southwards from Aachen in the Rhine-Palatinate region. 61 Squadron loaded each of its nine Hampdens with four 500-pounders and SBCs of incendiaries and dispatched them from Hemswell between 20.33 and 21.08 with W/C Sheen undertaking his first sortie since assuming command, backed up by S/L Sisson as the other senior pilot on duty. They flew out over Skegness in formation at between 4,000 and 6,000 feet, and within the first hour lost the services of F/O Baskett and crew to port engine failure and P/O Morley and crew to the loss of the artificial horizon. The others set course for the Scheldt estuary above a thick layer of cloud, and some elements of the 5 Group force were fired upon by a convoy. Once darkness closed in at the Dutch coast, the formations separated, and each crew proceeded independently to their respective targets, where rain-bearing cloud, thunderstorms and poor visibility hindered the search for trains in motion.

P/O Jones and crew were unable to find a train in their briefed area of Lissendorf, some forty miles south-east of Aachen, so bombed a junction there, before moving on to the railway station at Dorsel, where the incendiaries set fire to a warehouse. F/O Pascoe and crew found no moving train and instead attacked railway track five miles from Coblenz and at Bassenheim to the west of the town, while F/O Fewtrell and crew bombed the railway station at Wormersdorf, a dozen miles to the south-west of Bonn. W/C Sheen and crew had to contend with nine-tenths cloud with a low base as they sought out the railway line winding through hills but glimpsed a stretch of track at Gerolstein through a gap and attacked it with four 500-pounders without observing the result. P/O Davis and crew attacked a railway station at Braubach, a town on the eastern bank of the Rhine south of Coblenz, while S/L Sisson and crew were the only ones to catch a train in motion near Mendig, and bombed it from 2,000 feet, only to be denied a view of the outcome by fog. The return of F/Sgt Ross and crew in L4146 was awaited in vain, the last W/T contact having been received at about the time they should have been close to home. News was received eventually from the Red Cross that they had force-landed near Stuttgart after running out of fuel, having clearly been led astray by a wildly inaccurate compass to the extent that they believed themselves initially to be in Scotland. One can imagine their surprise and dismay when captured by jackbooted and hostile Germans to become the first from the squadron to end up in enemy hands.

Fifty-nine aircraft were made ready on the 24th for a repeat of the previous night's operations against enemy communications between Germany and the advancing battle front, for which 5 Group contributed eighteen Hampdens. 61 Squadron briefed the crews of F/L Barrett, F/O England and P/O Morley, before sending them on their way from Hemswell between 22.05 and 22.10 bound for railway targets in eastern Belgium. F/L Barrett and crew searched in vain for forty-five minutes for a moving train and turned their attention instead upon a junction at Libramont, which they attacked accurately from 1,500 feet and observed the incendiaries burning between the rails. P/O Morley and crew dropped an illuminating flare, and in its light released four 250-pounders and one SBC of incendiaries on rolling stock at a junction at Jemelle. One bomb burst among wagons and the others straddled the siding and set off an explosion. F/O England and crew were searching through fog for a reference on the ground and finally came upon a stretch of track between Liege and Tirlemont, which they bombed without observing the results, and on the way home over the Scheldt, dropped the incendiaries on Vlissingen (Flushing) aerodrome on Walcheren Island.

The British Expeditionary Force was now trapped with its back to the Channel in a reducing pocket at Dunkerque, while elsewhere the relentless round of operations continued on the 25th with further attacks on troop positions and communications. A total of 103 aircraft was involved, twenty-nine of them Hampdens, which, together with the Whitley element, focused on road and railway links to the battle front between Düren and Aachen in Germany and near Liege in Belgium, while the Wellingtons targeted troop concentrations. 61 Squadron briefed the crews of F/Os Baskett, How and Kydd, P/O Wyatt and F/Sgt Saunders and dispatched them from Hemswell at intervals between 20.57 and 22.20, losing the services of the Wyatt crew to wireless failure. They followed corridor "G", the standard route for making landfall over the Scheldt estuary, before heading towards their primary targets of railways near Liege, where F/O Baskett and crew failed to find a moving train and instead dropped four 250-pounders on a stretch of track near Hermalle, while F/O Kydd and crew attacked both ends of the Cochem-Bremm tunnel through fog and were confident that they had hit the southern end. Afterwards, they conducted a reconnaissance of hilly terrain south of the Ruhr in challenging visibility at 1,000 feet, before heading for Coblenz to bomb a marshalling yard, which could not be located, but their presence stirred up the flak defences. F/O How and crew were unable to locate a suitable target in the conditions and dropped their bombs on the outskirts of Binche as a last resort without observing the results. F/Sgt Saunders and crew located railway track and a crossroads at Neufchateau, and also failed to observe the outcome, and one remaining bomb aimed at a railway station near Gembloux was seen to overshoot.

The evening of the 26th brought the first evacuations from the Dunkerque beaches in a heroic campaign that would last until the 3rd of June and result in the rescue of 338,000 men. Meanwhile, operations continued against enemy communications and airfields in France, Belgium, Holland and Germany, for which forty-three aircraft were detailed, twenty-one of them Hampdens. 61 Squadron briefed the crews of F/O Fewtrell and P/Os Davis, Pascoe and Wyatt and launched them from Hemswell between 22.08 and 22.31 to head for the Scheldt estuary and onwards to areas north-east of Brussels and down to the Walloon region south-east of Charleroi. P/O Davis and crew chanced upon a moving train between Diest and Aaschot and attacked it with four 250-pounders, but while jinking for position failed to observe the fall and outcome. After searching for some time, P/O Pascoe and crew dropped a flare over a mainline railway bridge near Mettet and followed it up with bombs and incendiaries, the smoke and glare from which masked the result. F/O Fewtrell and crew spotted an embankment on the line between Cochem and Clotten (untraced) and delivered four 500-pounders from 4,000 feet, which appeared to burst where intended. On the way home they observed considerable motor transport activity in the Coblenz area. P/O Wyatt and crew brought their bombs home after a compass error led them astray and they were unable to establish a pinpoint on the ground by which to navigate.

His Majesty King George visited a number of 5 Group stations on the 27th, including Hemswell, and at each a parade was held and an investiture. During the course of the day, 120 aircraft were detailed for a busy night of operations, for which 5 Group assigned forty-nine Hampdens to a variety of targets, twenty-four to oil refineries, one in the Altona district of Hamburg, situated on the northern bank of the Elbe to the west of the city centre, the Rhenania plant on the opposite bank in Harburg (A10) and the Korff A.G site in Bremen. The remaining twenty-five Hampdens, including six representing 61 Squadron, were to attend to communications targets, principally trains in motion in the area between Cologne and Leuven in Belgium or other targets of opportunity. They departed Hemswell between 22.06 and 22.34 with S/L Sisson the senior pilot on duty and Sgt John "Dim" Wooldridge operating as crew captain for the first time. F/Sgt Saunders and crew had been assigned to a railway junction at Libramont, where the illumination flare failed to ignite and searchlight glare hampered sight of the bursts, which were believed to have straddled the track. P/O Morley and crew aimed their bombs at a train in a siding at Bertrijk (untraced) but hit sheds some fifty yards away causing explosions and fires. P/O Jones and crew were escorted from Flushing to the target by three enemy aircraft, which signalled continuously but did not attack, and delivered their bombs on what they identified as a railway station at Hildesheim. Sgt Wooldridge and crew were defeated by thick cloud and ended up bombing an aerodrome at Schellingwoude on the north-eastern outskirts of Amsterdam, while F/L Barrett and crew also found an aerodrome as a last resort target south of Delmenhorst and dropped a long stick across the flying field. S/L Sisson and crew searched in vain for an hour before turning for home with dawn approaching so fast that it was daylight when they crossed the Dutch coast.

5 Group detailed six Hampdens from each station on the 30th to attack the Rhenania-Ossag oil refinery at Harburg, for which 61 Squadron briefed the crews of F/L England and F/Os How and Kydd and dispatched them from Hemswell between 20.57 and 21.11. The How crew returned after forty-five minutes with a defective wireless and took off again at 21.50, only to be recalled. F/L England and crew ran into very bad weather and electrical storms over the North Sea, a regular feature of the conditions in this area, and followed the River Elbe to the target, where an illuminating flare from another aircraft proved to be of no assistance in the face of low cloud, and the sortie was abandoned. F/O Kydd and crew broke cloud over Hamburg at 500 feet, but during a thirty-minute search, recognisable ground features remained elusive, persuading them to backtrack to the Frisian Island of Langeooge, where the bombs were dropped on the aerodrome from 1,200 feet and observed to fall on Hangars and the flying field.

During the course of May, the squadron took part in eighteen operations and dispatched eighty-two sorties for the loss of a single Hampden and crew.

June 1940

If May had been seen as a busy month, then June would be considerably more so as French resistance crumbled in the face of the irresistible "Blitzkrieg" machine and British forces scrambled to evacuate the beaches of Dunkerque. 61 Squadron was in action on the first night of the new month, when supporting 5 Group operations against oil targets and marshalling yards in Germany, Hemswell supporting the latter with twelve Hampdens, while Waddington and Scampton put up twelve aircraft each to attack the previously targeted A7 oil plant in Harburg and A19, a refinery at Ostermoor, a location between the western end of the Kiel Canal and the North Bank of the River Elbe. Neither the squadron nor 5 Group ORBs provide details of the precise locations of the marshalling yards to be targeted, but it seems that the region south of the Ruhr between Aachen in the west and Coblenz in the east had been assigned to the six 61 Squadron participants, which departed Hemswell between 22.02 and 22.50 with S/L Lawrence the senior pilot on duty. F/O Fewtrell and crew brought their bombs home after circling the target area for thirty minutes over impenetrable fog, which even thwarted the light from their illuminating flare. P/O Wyatt and crew were attracted by the glow of searchlights in cloud, but unable to see the ground, headed for the Frisian Island of Borkum, where four 500-pounders were deposited on the aerodrome. F/O Baskett and crew were guided by the glow of many searchlights as they made their way from Aachen to Düren, where the marshalling yards remained concealed beneath ten-tenths cloud and rain, and it was Euskirchen that received the bombs from 3,000 feet. P/O Hall and crew located their target near Coblenz in the light of a parachute flare, and in the face of an intense searchlight and flak response delivered four 250-pounders and incendiaries without observing the results. S/L Lawrence and crew were unable to find their objective on e.t.a., but chanced upon a train between Mendig and Kottenheim, and after three 250-pounders had hung-up, attacked it with a single bomb and incendiaries, again without observing the outcome. P/O Davis and crew, meanwhile, had returned with their bombs after encountering low cloud and haze that obscured the ground from view.

A proposed operation by elements from Waddington and Scampton against the Ostermoor oil plant on the 2nd was cancelled in the face of an unfavourable weather forecast, and it was left to Hemswell to provide six Hampdens to attack Ruhr marshalling yards. The 61 Squadron crews of S/L Sisson, P/O Pascoe and F/Sgt Saunders took off between 21.25 and 21.31 and immediately lost the services of the Saunders crew to a wireless issue. P/O Pascoe and crew spent an hour searching for their target, but even with the aid of flares were unable to identify a suitable recipient for their bombs. On the way home, shortly after crossing the Belgian/Franco frontier they were attracted by fires and came upon oil storage tanks at Saint-Laurent, where they dropped four 250-pounders and incendiaries from 2,000 feet, the detonations of which were lost in the glare from the existing conflagration. S/L Lawrence and crew also failed to locate their briefed target, but on the way home chanced upon a motor transport convoy, which they strafed and attacked with four 250-pounders and incendiaries, concluding from the resulting explosions that they had hit fuel or ammunition supplies.

The Dunkerque evacuations ended on the 3rd, and that night, Bomber Command launched 142 sorties, the largest number in one night to date, to target German industry, particularly oil plants at various locations between Hamburg in the north and Frankfurt in the south. 5 Group committed forty-eight Hampdens to the fray, six of them made ready by 61 Squadron and assigned to an oil refinery in Düsseldorf coded A24. F/L Barrett was the senior pilot on duty as they departed Hemswell between 21.47 and 21.59 and lost the services of Sgt Wooldridge and crew to engine trouble after around ninety minutes. P/O Jones and crew were contending with the failure of their generator as they became attracted to the target by fires already burning in its vicinity. With no electrical power they were forced to release the bombs manually, and from 8,000 feet watched them burst on the western edge of the target. P/O Morley and crew were also experiencing difficulties, in their case with the bomb sight gyro, and on the fourth runs across the aiming point the bombs and incendiaries were jettisoned "live" in a salvo employing the bomb sight as a fixed sight. P/O Hall and crew carried out two dummy runs over the target to establish identification, during which, bombs from another aircraft started a large fire. They dropped their own stick across the target, setting off another fire that remained visible for 120 miles into the return journey. F/Sgt Saunders found their aiming point with ease and dropped their load from 11,000 feet onto the north-western corner, while F/L Barrett and crew were challenged initially by searchlight glare before establishing a pinpoint and releasing four 250-pounders, which also created a fire.

Later, on the 4th, an assessment by the government of Germany's oil industry suggested that a concerted effort against it could reduce its output by half a million tons over the summer period. In the light of the massive offensive by four-engine aircraft in 1944, this was a wildly optimistic view, and, although a sizeable proportion of the Command's effort would be directed against oil refineries and storage sites, the effect on Germany's war effort during this early stage of the war would be negligible. That night, twenty-four Hampdens were among fifty-eight aircraft returning to Germany, Scampton sending eleven from 49 Squadron back to A161, the oil depot located on the River Main in the Offenbach district to the south-east of Frankfurt city centre. Waddington and Hemswell, meanwhile, provided six Hampdens each to attack an oil production and storage plant at Mannheim some forty-five miles to the south. The 61 Squadron crews of F/L England, F/O Fewtrell and P/O Wyatt departed Hemswell between 21.00 and 21.09 and the numbers were reduced to two as the Fewtrell crew returned within ninety minutes because of W/T failure. S/L England and crew were defeated by searchlight glare and thick haze and brought their bombs home, while, unaccountably, the Wyatt crew found good visibility over the target and released four 500-pounders on the first run, observing two to burst on the north-western corner.

5 Group stations were busy on the 5th preparing thirty-six Hampdens for an attack on A22, an oil refinery and storage facility at Schulau/Wedel, situated on the North Bank of the River Elbe a dozen miles downstream from Hamburg city centre. The Group would also be providing six Hampdens to resume the mining campaign, focusing on this night on the western Baltic, and 61 Squadron would support both undertakings, providing six aircraft for bombing and three for mining. The latter departed Hemswell first, the crews of F/Sgt Saunders, P/O Davis and F/O Baskett between 20.52 and 21.00 before setting course for the Quince garden located off the southern tip of Langeland Island in Kiel Bay. The sound of their engines was still heavy in the air as the bombing brigade followed them away between 21.04 and 21.25 with S/Ls Lawrence and Sisson the senior pilots on duty and set course for the coast at Mablethorpe to begin the North Sea crossing to north-western Germany. On arrival at the mouth of the Elbe, S/L Lawrence and crew experienced difficulty in establishing their position in the midst of intense searchlight and flak activity, particularly from Brunsbüttel, and the Hampden was rocked by the burst of shells at 16,000 feet as the bombs were released over Wedel, to the west of the target. P/O Jones and crew suffered a hang-up over the target but eventually managed to release two 250-pounders and one SBC of incendiaries, before persuading the rest of the load to leave the bomb bay at 2,000 feet over Heligoland and hit buildings. P/O Morley and crew followed the Elbe into the heart of the

city and dropped their six 250-pounders in a stick across what appeared to be a power plant, but was later believed to have been a dummy site. The crews of F/O Fewtrell and P/O Pascoe delivered ten 250-pounders between them from around 10,000 feet without observing the results in the glare of searchlights and the flashes from flak guns. S/L Sisson and crew made landfall at Sylt, well to the north, before heading south to the target and failing to locate it or a suitable alternative and landed with their bomb load intact. The gardeners, meanwhile, benefitted from excellent conditions and all planted their vegetables according to brief during uneventful sorties of six-and-a-half hours duration.

During the 6th preparations were put in hand for a return to north-western Germany that night by eighteen Hampdens from Hemswell, Scampton and Waddington, to take another swipe at the previously attacked oil refinery coded A7. At the same time a further six Hampdens took advantage of the main event to sneak in under cover and plant mines in the Eglantine garden in the Elbe estuary. 61 Squadron briefed the crews of F/Os How and Kydd and P/O Hall for the main event and sent them on their way from Hemswell between 21.32 and 21.37, all to arrive in the target area to begin their search for the briefed aiming point. P/O Hall and crew circled Hamburg for fifteen minutes and having failed to locate A7 through the thick haze, followed the estuary back out and identified and bombed the Ostermoor oil plant (A19) with six 250-pounders, hitting the south-eastern corner of the site but not causing any fires. F/O How and crew did manage to identify the primary target, and after several runs to confirm it, delivered six 250-pounders in a stick, which burst about fifty yards wide. F/O Kydd and crew were confounded by the haze but timed a run after pinpointing on the Aussen Alster Lake and dropped their load from 10,000 feet, only to watch it undershoot by some two hundred yards.

The main battle for the next week would be the vain attempt to rescue France from impending occupation, as German ground forces consolidated their hold on the country and prepared for the assault on Paris. However, it was oil that continued to be the focus for 5 Group on the 7th, as the hectic start to the month continued with the launching of twenty-four Hampdens to attack A17, the Deutsche Erdölraffinerie, also known as Deurag-Nerag, a synthetic oil refinery at Misburg, situated east-north-east of Hannover. 61 Squadron was in the middle of a run of operations on thirteen consecutive nights, an intensity, which would not be repeated, even during the cauldron of July 1944, when Bomber Command was prosecuting four separate campaigns. The crews of F/Ls Barrett and England, P/O Webster and Sgt Wooldridge attended briefing on the 7th to learn of their part in the night's activities and departed Hemswell between 21.00 and 21.12, only to lose the services immediately of F/L England and crew to excessive vibration. By the time that the Wooldridge crew arrived in the target area, the oil plant was already partially obscured by smoke, through which the bombs fell from 12,000 feet and the incendiary content was observed to set off explosions. F/L Barrett and crew released their bombs in a stick and were rewarded with a fire in the western corner of the site, while P/O Webster and crew failed to locate the primary target or a suitable alternative, and having lost the use of their wireless, jettisoned the bombs in anticipation of a forced landing. P4349 eventually ran out of fuel and was put down in a fog shrouded field six miles east-south-east of King's Lynn, never to fly again, while the Webster crew emerged unscathed and continued their operational careers.

5 Group issued orders for a number of operations on the 8th, one of them by twelve crews from Scampton to attack enemy communications in the Amiens area of north-eastern France, while other elements from Hemswell and Waddington attended to marshalling yards in the Ruhr. 61 Squadron called upon the services of the crews of F/O Baskett, P/O Morley, F/Sgt Saunders and

Sgt Blakemen to operate against the Uerdingen marshalling yards at Krefeld, M401, and another railway target involving a tunnel coded AM5, but so scant was the detail from all sources at this stage of the war, and so numerous the marshalling yards, junctions and other railway infrastructure, that we can only guess the precise location of the latter. The 61 Squadron quartet departed Hemswell between 21.18 and 22.08 and was soon reduced to a pair as the crews of F/O Baskett and P/O Morley returned with artificial horizon issues. The Blakeman crew was blinded by searchlights over Krefeld, a city located on the western fringe of the Ruhr, and dropped their bomb load in a stick without observing the results, while the Saunders crew located AM5 and unleashed a 500-pounder on a hillside at the eastern end of the tunnel and three others on a bridge over a canal a mile-and-a-half west of the target.

Forty-two Hampdens were detailed for operations on the 9th, thirty-six of them to continue the previous night's assault on marshalling yards in and around the Ruhr, which for the nine 61 Squadron participants involved a return to the Uerdingen yards at Krefeld, while other targets coded M405 and M470 were located at Aachen and Rheydt, the latter a town on the western edge of the Ruhr as a twin to Mönchengladbach. They departed Hemswell between 21.35 and 21.42 with S/L Lawrence the senior pilot on duty, only for F/O Baskett and crew to drop out immediately when an engine failed. Poor visibility to the west of the Rhine thwarted F/L England and crew and they dropped their load on Flushing aerodrome on the way home. It was a similar story for F/O Kydd and crew at Aachen, and they unloaded the contents of their bomb bay on a searchlight concentration at what they believed to be Hamborn, an aerodrome to the north of Duisburg. P/O Pascoe and crew managed to locate Aachen but could not hold the marshalling yards in the bomb sight and ended up over Düren, some fifteen miles to the east, where they released their bombs on a bunch of incendiaries from another aircraft. P/O Jones and crew found a flare path as a last-resort target after failing to locate the Uerdingen yards, while the Wooldridge crew identified that they were over Langerwehe, between Aachen and Düren, and came upon a railway junction as they navigated back towards Aachen. They unleashed two bombs from 1,500 feet, claiming a direct hit, and in the process were hit in the port wing by a flak shell that also smashed the rear gunner's window. The remaining two bombs were dropped on another junction at Distalrath, located on the north-eastern outskirts of Düren. P/O Hall and crew bombed Flushing aerodrome on the way home after failing to locate Aachen, and F/O Fewtrell and crew attacked a "flyover" road junction between Mönchengladbach and Neuss. S/L Lawrence DFC and crew failed to return in P4336 after the Hampden was brought down by flak without survivors while attacking the Uerdingen yards. This was the first of a spate of losses involving experienced crews during what remained of the month.

The priority on the 10th, the day on which Italy declared war on Britain and France, was to try to stem the tide of the German advance into Northern France, for which 5 Group committed twenty-nine Hampdens to attacks on railway yards, junctions and bridges over the River Meuse at Sedan. 61 Squadron briefed five crews, those of P/O Webster and Morley to attack a railway junction at Libramont in south-eastern Belgium, while F/O Baskett and Sgt Blakeman and their crews were assigned to the marshalling yards at Euskirchen, fifteen miles west-south-west of Bonn. The destination for Sgt Wooldridge and crew was unrecorded as their sortie was terminated by engine failure as they climbed away. The others departed Hemswell between 21.50 and 22.29 to follow the usual route out via corridor "G" to cross the enemy coast over the Scheldt estuary and encountered the most challenging weather conditions of towering cloud with magnetic storms, which compromised accurate navigation. Neither of the Libramont-bound crews succeeded in locating their target, the Webster crew bombing what appeared to be aerodrome boundary lights on the way home, while the Morley crew found a road and railway junction at Herentals much further north to the east of Antwerp. Sgt Blakeman and crew were thwarted by the conditions and found no suitable target, and only F/O Baskett and crew located their briefed target at Euskirchen, after establishing pinpoints based on searchlight and flak activity at Aachen and Cologne. The incendiaries went down from 9,000 feet and straddled the track, and the bombs were released from 6,000 feet, missing the target and falling into a nearby wood.

The need to slow the German advance demanded further attacks on communications targets in France, in response to which, 5 Group detailed thirty-six Hampdens for operations on the 11th, thirty-one of them to return to the Sedan area and five for mining duties. At the same time, eighteen Wellingtons of 3 Group were to attack the Black Forest in south-western Germany with incendiary devices known as "deckers" or "razzle" in an attempt to cause widespread fires, and thirty-six Whitleys would carry out the first attacks on Italy with a raid on Turin. In the event, only nine would actually bomb at Turin, while the ill-conceived policy of setting fire to forests, which would be played out over the ensuing months, would prove to be a monumental waste of resources at a time when the Command had more important matters to focus on. Eight 61 Squadron crews attended briefing, when five found themselves assigned to bombing and three to mining duties, and it was the latter, the crews of P/O Jones, F/Sgt Saunders and Sgt Wooldridge, who departed Hemswell first between 21.19 and 21.24 bound for the Baltic gardens of Wallflower in Kiel Harbour and Radish in the Fehmarn Belt, the stretch of water that connects Kiel and Mecklenburg Bays. They were followed into the air by the bombing brigade between 21.47 and 22.08, and each element was depleted by one crew as those of F/Sgt Saunders and P/O How returned early because of engine and wireless issues respectively.

F/L Barrett and crew crossed the enemy coast at Zeebrugge bound for Sedan, which they identified in the light of incendiaries from another aircraft and bombed from 7,000 feet, only to be prevented by poor visibility from observing the outcome. The others arrived over the Ruhr, where P/O Hall and crew identified their target with the aid of parachute flares and lights from a nearby marshalling yard. The code, AX5, is not a standard code for marshalling yards, and we cannot, therefore, be certain of its location, but we are told that the first bomb went down from 3,500 feet and was seen to burst in the centre of the yards, and the remaining three 500-pounders were dropped during a second run, by which time the flare had burned out and the bursts could not be plotted. F/O Fewtrell and crew were unable to locate Hamm marshalling yards to the north of the Ruhr, but found a square of lights nearby, upon which the incendiaries were released with no effect, suggesting that they were dummies, and this persuaded them to withhold the bombs. Flying on a north-easterly track towards the Dutch frontier homebound they came upon the aerodrome at Metelen and bombed the beacons. P/O Pascoe and crew identified the Nippes marshalling yards to the north-west of Cologne city centre, but during the bombing run mistook another set of lights as the target and bombed them from 2,000 feet in the face of intense light flak and searchlights, at which 1,500 rounds were fired. Their attention was captured by fires and explosions at the location of their bomb bursts and these were plotted later to be at the Ehrenfeld gasworks. Meanwhile, Sgt Wooldridge and crew had been unable to locate the Wallflower garden in thunderstorms and poor visibility, but P/O Jones benefitted from more favourable conditions and planted their vegetable according to brief from 800 feet.

A reduced effort on the night of the 12th saw thirty Hampdens and eight 4 Group Whitleys detailed for a return to the same general area of north-eastern France, but further west in the Hauts-de-France region, to attack road and rail junctions and marshalling yards, while five other Hampdens were assigned to gardening duties. 61 Squadron briefed five crews and sent them on their way from Hemswell between 21.59 and 22.44 with F/L Kydd the senior pilot on duty, and he and his crew spent almost two hours searching at various heights without success for the bridge over the River Aisne at Rethel, a town twenty-five miles north-east of Reims. F/O Baskett and crew also failed to locate their target in continuous rain, and on the way home identified Brugges with the aid of flares and bombed a stretch of railway track to the west of the town. F/Sgt Saunders and crew came home empty-handed citing rain and mist as the reason for failing to identify their assigned target or suitable alternative. The Blakeman crew were searching for their target in the Hirson area, close to the Belgian frontier, and dropped incendiaries in a wood, before bombing the most northerly set of crossroads without observing the outcome. F/O How and crew dropped flares in the same area on e.t.a., before releasing incendiaries and bombs, again without observing the results.

163 aircraft were prepared for operations on the 13th, their crews briefed to attack a wide variety of communications targets in France, Belgium and Holland, 5 Group calling for a maximum effort from its three operational stations at Scampton, Hemswell and Waddington. Sixty-four Hampdens answered the call, a dozen of them provided by 61 Squadron, the crews of which were assigned to targets in and around Reims and Soissons to the north-east of Paris and Les Andelys further to the west. They departed Hemswell between 22.02 and 22.38 with W/C Sheen the senior pilot on duty and each loaded with four 500-pounders, but the ORBs do not provide us with details of their precise destinations. It seems that the crews of F/L Barrett, P/Os Jones, Webster and Wyatt and Sgts Blakeman and Wooldridge were bound for the Reims area, while the crews of F/L Kydd, F/O How and P/O Hall headed for Soissons, thirty miles to the north-west, and those of W/C Sheen and F/O Fewtrell for Les Andelys some eighty miles further west. They faced moderate weather conditions over the North Sea with six-tenths cloud, which would disperse over northern France to leave haze. The target for F/Sgt Saunders and crew has not been determined because they abandoned their sortie within minutes of taking off and landed at Marham.

The Wyatt crew ran into intense anti-aircraft fire north of Lille but evaded it and made their way south to come upon a stationary train north of Reims, which became engulfed in flame after being bombed. In the same area, the Wooldridge crew found a railway station and dropped incendiaries and a single bomb from 2,000 feet, the latter overshooting and causing a series of explosions in a cutting beyond. The remaining bombs were delivered in a stick during a second pass conducted in the face of intense opposition, two falling into the station and the third causing a vivid flash followed by a large explosion, presumed to be from an ammunition train. P/O Webster and crew ran into intense searchlight and flak activity at 2,000 feet and their Hampden was flipped onto its back during violent evasive action, before control was regained and the bombs dropped from low level. Sgt Blakeman and crew attacked clearly defined crossroads from 900 feet, while F/L Barrett and crew circled Reims for forty minutes without identifying their target in poor visibility and eventually bombed a bridge and rail junction to the south-west of the town. P/O Jones and crew had been contending with a dodgy throttle control, which the pilot had to hold throughout the flight, and after circling the target area for thirty minutes and failing to locate something worthy of their bombs, they headed home.

Meanwhile, to the west, F/O Baskett and crew had identified Soissons by means of a flare from another aircraft and dropped their bombs and a flare of their own on a road to the west of the town near a bridge. P/O Hall and crew also identified Soissons, but according to their report dropped two bombs on a rail-over-road junction in Faubourg-de-Reims, a district of Reims itself, before delivering incendiaries on the railway station during a second pass and the remaining bombs also on the station during a third. F/L Kydd and crew dropped their incendiaries on a railway bridge over the Aisne on the eastern side of the town, before bombing a crossing on the main road leading south from the town. At Les Andelys, F/O Fewtrell and crew dispensed their incendiaries on the western side of a bridge and set off a fire, while the bombs fell near the bridge head on the eastern bank and caused another fire. W/C Sheen and crew delivered the entire contents of their bomb bay on the bridge at Les Andelys from 10,000 feet and failed to observe the results through the haze. At some time on the 13th, P4339 collided with an OTU Hampden seconds after take-off from Cottesmore, and two crewmen were killed in the ensuing crash, while the pilot, P/O Helsby, and one other survived with injuries.

After thirteen consecutive nights of operations since the start of the month, 61 Squadron was allowed to rest on the 14th, while 4 Group prepared its Whitleys to continue the losing battle to save France from occupation and Wellingtons and Hampdens from 3 and 5 Groups were detailed to attack targets in Germany. In fact, only five Hampdens were mobilized, three by 144 Squadron at Hemswell, one from 83 Squadron at Scampton and one from 50 Squadron to represent Waddington. There were no operations for 5 Group on the 15th, the day on which the last of the battered remnant of the Advanced Air Striking Force arrived back from France with what remained of their Fairey Battles. 12 Squadron settled in at Finningley and 142 Squadron at Waddington, both temporarily, and 103 and 150 Squadrons found a home at Newton in Nottinghamshire. They would become part of the newly reconstituted 1 Group, which, after continuing briefly with Battles, would convert to Wellingtons later in the year. Adverse weather conditions on the 16th kept most of the Command on the ground during the night, while 3 Group Wellingtons went to Italy, and Waddington detailed three Hampdens each from 44 and 50 Squadrons to carry out mining duties in the Radish garden in the Fehmarn Belt.

Forty-six Hampdens were made ready for operations on the 17th, six from Scampton to continue the mining campaign, while a further twenty-one from there and nineteen from Waddington were assigned to attack the oil refineries coded A3, A7 and A10, respectively at Dollbergen, east of Hannover, and at Harburg on the South Bank of the Elbe and marshalling yards M107 and M434 at Coblenz and Hamm. On the 18th, 5 Group detailed five Hampdens to seek out and destroy trains in motion north of the Ruhr in the area from Wesel on the Dutch frontier as far east as Hamm, and south of the Ruhr between Düren and Coblenz. The 5 Group ORB makes no mention of a sortie by 61 Squadron's P/O Morley and crew to attack the marshalling yards at Rheydt, for which they departed Hemswell at 21.46 and landed at Abingdon at 03.30, having fulfilled their brief.

On the following night, 112 aircraft from 3, 4 and 5 Groups were detailed to attack oil and railway targets between Hamburg in the north and Mannheim in the south. 5 Group contributed fifty-three Hampdens, some to attack H150, Handorf aerodrome, located north-east of Münster, with the purpose of dissuading the Luftwaffe from interfering with a simultaneous attack on M25A, a newly built aqueduct next to an old one (M25) carrying the Dortmund-Ems Canal over the River Ems between Gittrup and Fuestrup to the north of the city. Ten crews were briefed for M25A, while P/O Wyatt and crew were to join in on the diversionary raid on Handorf aerodrome, and all departed Hemswell between 21.45 and 22.12 with W/C Sheen and the recently promoted S/L England the senior pilots on duty. It seems that the attack on the aerodrome proceeded as planned and there were claims of strikes on hangars, but there is no mention of the aqueduct, and it must be assumed that it was not attacked for whatever reason, perhaps poor visibility or the intensity of the defences. There would be further attacks on this target later in the summer, one in particular resulting in the award of a Victoria Cross.

On the 20th, 4 and 5 Groups were notified of operations in the Ruhr and in the Münsterland region to the north, 5 Group responding with orders, among others, to Waddington and Scampton to prepare six Hampdens each to attack an aircraft park, K9, at Paderborn, situated some forty miles to the east of Hamm. The 61 Squadron crews of F/O Smith and P/O Morley were briefed for railway disruption sorties in the Borken area to the north of the Ruhr, and also to see if they could confirm damage to the aqueduct resulting from the previous night's efforts. They departed Hemswell at 22.02 and 22.13 respectively, and only P/O Morley and crew returned five-and-a-half hours later to report that ten-tenths cloud had prevented any sight of railways and the Dortmund-Ems Canal region. It was learned later that P4355 had been brought down by flak near the town of Rheine located to the north of Münster, and there had been no survivors from the crew of F/O Smith.

Forty-two Hampdens were among 105 aircraft from 3, 4 and 5 Groups detailed on the 21st to carry out operations in northern and central Germany and the Ruhr in-between, for which 61 Squadron was called upon to provide eleven aircraft, one for a reconnaissance of M25A and then to bomb a target of opportunity, two for mining duties in the Yam garden in Jade Bay, two to target the marshalling yards at Schwerte at the south-eastern corner of the Ruhr and six to attack A17, the Deutsche Erdölraffinerie (Deurag-Nerag) synthetic oil refinery at Misburg near Hannover. They departed Hemswell between 21.01 and 21.55, last away F/L Kydd and crew, whose brief was to reconnoitre M25A, and they were trailed by three enemy aircraft, which failed to engage. They flew as close to the aqueduct as the searchlight and flak defence would allow and confirmed an apparent absence of damage, before heading northwards and bombing a railway siding at Emsdetten. S/L Sisson had concluded his tour and had been succeeded by S/L Golledge as a flight commander, and he and his crew were eased gently into operations with a mining sortie in company with Sgt Blakeman and crew. In the event, the Golledge crew was unable to locate the target area in the prevailing conditions and returned their mine to the station store. Of those assigned to the oil plant, one bombed an aerodrome south-east of Lingen as a last resort target, and the others succeeded in fulfilling their briefs, although they were prevented by the hostility of the defences from determining the outcome. F/L Barrett and crew failed to return from Schwerte in P4346, having had their tailplane shattered by flak, and only F/L Barrett survived to fall into enemy hands.

Bomber Command stayed at home on the 22nd, after forty-four consecutive nights of operations since the balloon went up in May. This was the day on which the French authorities signed the instrument of surrender at Compiegne, to leave Britain standing alone against a seemingly unconquerable enemy. Unfavourable weather conditions were to blame for the brief break in bombing operations, but orders were issued on the 23rd to resume the fight and 5 Group detailed fifty-three Hampdens for that night's activities. Thirty-eight of them from Scampton and Waddington were to attack F74, the Horten aircraft factory at Wismar on the Baltic coast, and F49, the Hamburger Flugzeugbau aircraft works belonging to Blohm & Voss at Wenzendorf, south-west of Hamburg, which was building subassemblies on a contract basis for Messerschmitt, Dornier, Heinkel, Junkers and Focke-Wulf.

There is a discrepancy between the Forms 540 and 541 in the 61 Squadron ORB, the former recording thirteen crews taking part in the night's activities, while the latter lists just ten. Trusting in the accuracy of Form 540, the 61 Squadron crews were briefed for a variety of targets, railway and canal traffic north of the Ruhr for F/O Fewtrell and P/O Hall, the marshalling yards at Hamm, on the northern rim of the Ruhr, for P/O Pascoe and Sgt Wooldridge, marshalling yards at Wanne-Eickel in the heart of the Ruhr for Sgt Blakeman, F/Sgt Saunders and F/O How and the Kalk-Nord marshalling yards in Cologne for F/L Kydd, F/O Baskett and P/O Morley, while the crews of S/L England and P/Os Gould and Jones were to mine the waters of the Yam garden at the mouth of the rivers Jade and Weser, where the sea-lanes served the ports of Wilhelmshaven and Bremen. The bombing brigade departed Hemswell between 21.58 and 22.18 and the gardeners between 22.29 and 22.35, and according to Form 541, three of the former turned back early with engine or wireless issues, while S/L England and crew had to curtail their sortie after the mine broke loose in the bomb bay. Form 540 states that the crews of P/O Pascoe and Sgt Wooldridge were unable to locate Hamm marshalling yards and attacked alternative yards at Dalen and Coesfeld, respectively on the Dutch and German sides of the frontier. The Blakeman and Saunders crews located their briefed target, while the How crew failed to do so and bombed a blast furnace somewhere nearby, before dropping their incendiaries on Schiphol aerodrome at Amsterdam. P/O Morley and crew were successful at Cologne, but failed to observe the results, while the crew of F/O Baskett attacked Waalhaven aerodrome as a last-resort target and F/L Kydd and crew brought their ordnance home. Finally, the gardening duo reported fulfilling their brief, leaving us with the imponderable contradictory claim in the Form 541 that the How, Morley and Blakeman crews along with that of S/L England had all landed back at Hemswell by 23.05, little more than an hour after taking off.

Bomber Command detailed 103 aircraft on the 24th for operations against twenty-one targets between Hamburg in the North and Mannheim in the south, 5 Group detailing twenty-four Hampdens, nine from Hemswell to target marshalling yards at Wanne-Eickel and Kalk-Nord, of which six belonged to 61 Squadron. Form 540 of the 61 Squadron ORB makes no mention of the operation, while Form 541 lists the six crews, which departed Hemswell between 22.15 and 22.37 with F/L Kydd the senior pilot on duty. We are not told their specific target or what the outcome was, but all returned safely after sorties lasting little more than five hours.

Forty-eight aircraft were detailed for operations against twenty-one targets on the 25th, and half of them were Hampdens, assigned to attack oil plants, marshalling yards and individual factories. 61 Squadron briefed the crews of S/L Golledge and Sgt Wooldridge for L82, an aluminium foundry at Grevenbroich, located between Mönchengladbach to the north-west and Cologne to the south-east, and the crews of P/Os Pascoe and Wyatt for the marshalling yards at Hamm. They departed Hemswell between 22.00 and 22.45 and the Wooldridge crew landed five-and-a-half hours later with the bombload intact having failed to locate the primary or suitable alternative target. Alternative targets fell into two categories, MOPA, military objective previously attacked, and SEMO, self-evident military objective, and after these came last-resort targets, which could be anything that might be of value, however small, to the enemy. S/L Golledge and crew also failed to locate the aluminium foundry and dropped their bombs on a stretch of railway track between Roermond and Weert in Holland, clearly as a last resort. P/O Wyatt and crew were defeated by poor visibility and brought their bombs home, while P/O Pascoe and crew apparently flew all the way up to Harburg 160 miles away to attack a MOPA, the oil plant A10 on the southern bank of the Elbe. They encountered barrage balloons at 12,000 feet over Hamburg and a hostile searchlight and flak welcome, which dissuaded them from loitering to ascertain the result of their effort.

On the 26th 5 Group detailed thirty-four Hampdens for operations against marshalling yards, aerodromes and railway and canal traffic in north-western Germany, and seven for a special mining/reconnaissance operation in the Lettuce garden in the Kiel Canal, (Kaiser Wilhelm Kanal) a sixty-one-mile-long vitally important waterway that traversed the Schleswig-Holstein peninsula and provided access for U-Boots from Kiel's construction yards to the North Atlantic via the Elbe estuary at Brunsbüttel. There were no senior pilots on duty among the seven 61 Squadron participants departing Hemswell between 22.17 and 22.57, P/O Gould and F/Sgt Saunders seemingly assigned to aerodromes in Holland, H173 (untraced) and Schiphol, while the remaining five were to focus on railways and canals. P/O Gould and crew were unable to locate their briefed target and dropped their bombs on docks on the northern bank of a canal in Rotterdam as a last resort, while F/Sgt Saunders and crew returned their ordnance to the station dump. Sgt Blakeman and crew also brought their load home having failed to find a suitable target, but the remaining four crews found unspecified objectives to attack, for which no detail was recorded. 50 Squadron lost two crews, including that of its commanding officer, W/C Crockart, who had been in post for just two weeks and would be succeeded by S/L Golledge on his posting from 61 Squadron and promotion to acting wing commander rank on the 27th.

On the 27th, 5 Group detailed a dozen Hampdens from Waddington to attack an oil-tankerage site at Nyborg on the eastern coast of Denmark's Fyn Island, and eleven from Hemswell to target railway and canal traffic north and south of the Ruhr and conduct mining sorties in the Forget-me-not garden in Kiel Bay. The six 61 Squadron crews were divided between bombing and mining, those of F/L Kydd, P/O Wyatt and Sgt Wooldridge taking off between 22.15 and 22.19 with bombs on board and following in the wake of the gardening crews of F/O How and P/Os Morley and Pascoe, who had departed thirty minutes earlier. P/O Wyatt and crew scored a direct hit on a barge and apparently blew it out of the water, before dropping the remaining bombs on Nordhorn aerodrome close to the Dutch frontier. F/L Kydd and crew dropped bombs on a road bridge over the River Ems south of Rheine and on lock gates, but then had to jettison the remainder of their load after flak punched a hole on the port mainplane and destabilised the aircraft. Sgt Wooldridge and crew attacked a lock gate in the canal between Meppen and Lingen and scored a direct hit, before returning home after a five-hour round-trip. P/O Morley and crew failed to return after L4112 was brought down by flak and crashed in Kiel Bay, killing one member of the crew. The pilot and two others were picked up and taken into captivity, while the body of Sgt Anderson was recovered for a local burial.

While twenty Hampdens were being prepared at Scampton and Waddington on the 28th for operations against a Bayer explosives and chemicals factory at Dormagen, a town on the Rhine between Düsseldorf and Cologne, ten others were being bombed up at Hemswell for an attack on M25A, the Dortmund-Ems Canal at its junction with the River Ems. The six 61 Squadron participants took off between 22.26 and 22.35 with F/O Baskett the senior pilot on duty, and all arrived in the target area, where five attacked the lock gates at the southern end of the aqueduct section, and the sixth joined in on a diversionary raid on nearby Handorf aerodrome.

On the following day 5 Group detailed ten Hampdens each from Hemswell and Waddington for an operation against the Düneberg gunpowder factory at Geesthacht, located on the Elbe to the south-east of Hamburg, and nine others, mostly from Scampton, to attack marshalling yards in the Ruhr. 61 Squadron briefed five crews for the former and dispatched them between 21.00 and 21.04 with F/L Kydd and the newly promoted F/L How the senior pilots on duty, leaving P/O Pascoe and crew on the ground until their departure at 22.20 for the Ruhr. F/L Kydd and crew reached and attacked the primary target without observing the outcome, while the crews of F/L How, F/O Fewtrell and Sgt Wooldridge were driven off by intense and accurate anti-aircraft fire and sought out alternative targets. The Fewtrell crew bombed the aerodrome on Norderney Island, but the others failed to identify a suitable target and brought their bombs home, P4298 running out of brake pressure on landing in the hands of Sgt Wooldridge and crashing into the boundary fence. There were no casualties, and the Hampden would be returned to flying condition. Sadly, F/O Wyatt and crew failed to return in P4356 after falling victim to flak in the general target area, and information from the Red Cross would confirm that the pilot and one other had lost their lives, and that the two survivors were in enemy hands. The return from the Ruhr of P/O Pascoe and crew was also awaited in vain, and it was established eventually that P4341 had crashed into the sea off the Dutch coast and took with it the four occupants.

The final operations of the month for 61 Squadron involved mining duties for the crews of P/Os Gould and Hall and F/Sgt Saunders in the Endive garden, located in the Little Belt between Jutland and Fyn Island, for which they departed Hemswell between 21.26 and 21.30. The crews of S/L England and P/O Webster had been briefed to attack marshalling yards at Osnabrück, a city to the north-east of Münster in the flat agricultural land between the Ruhr and north-western Germany, and they took off at 22.09 and 22.13 respectively. P/O Webster and crew brought their bombs home after failing to locate the primary or a suitable alternative target, while S/L England and his crew fulfilled their brief, as did the gardeners to bring an incredibly busy month to an end.

During the course of the month the squadron took part in thirty-one operations and dispatched 152 sorties for the loss of six Hampdens and crews, five of the crews highly experienced and all keenly missed by the squadron and station communities.

July 1940

The new month began for 5 Group with a busy night of operations involving all three operational stations, Waddington providing six Hampdens each for mining and the bombing of marshalling yards at Osnabrück, Scampton a dozen to target the heavy cruiser Scharnhorst, which was believed might be in a dry dock in the Deutsche Werke shipyard in Kiel and twelve also from Hemswell to attack the Rheinpreussen (Meerbeck) synthetic oil plant at Moers/Homberg on the western bank of the Rhine opposite Duisburg. 61 Squadron briefed six crews for the last mentioned and sent them on their way between 22.22 and 22.33 with F/Ls How and Kydd the senior pilots on duty. The visibility at the western edge of the Ruhr was poor and only the crews of F/O Baskett, P/O Jones and Sgt Wooldridge succeeded in locating and bombing the primary target, setting off fires, while the crews of F/Ls How and Kydd found alternative targets, the former a blast furnace in Essen and the latter the aerodrome at Venlo. F/O Aldridge and crew failed to find a suitable alternative target and brought their ordnance home.

On the 3rd the stations of Binbrook and Newton were transferred to 1 Group, which had reformed on the 1st of July with the remnant of the squadrons from the AASF, and while 103 and 150 Squadrons remained at Newton, 12 and 142 Squadrons, which had been lodging at Scampton and Waddington, moved into Binbrook. 5 Group operations for that night required Waddington to take care of mining duties with six aircraft, while Scampton targeted marshalling yards at Osnabrück with a further six and Hemswell detailed three to attack the embankment containing the Dortmund-Ems Canal at its junction with the River Ems (M25). The 61 Squadron crews of P/Os Hall and

Gould took off at 22.26 and 22.29 and ran into poor conditions in the target area, which prevented the Hall crew from identifying the primary or a suitable alternative target, and they returned their bombs to the station dump. The Gould crew was able to carry out an attack and claimed the result to be satisfactory, but we know from subsequent events that the embankment remained intact.

Among 5 Group operations on the 4th was a return to Kiel by a dozen Hampdens from Scampton and four from Hemswell to attack a floating dock, this time in the Krupp-Germania shipyard at Kiel, in the continuing search for the under-repair cruiser Scharnhorst. The crews of P/O Webster and Sgt Wooldridge were the first of six from 61 Squadron to become airborne at 21.15 and 21.19 respectively, bound for Kiel docks, and they were followed off the end of the runway by the crews of S/L Kydd, F/Sgt Saunders and P/O Aldridge, whose destination was the Dortmund-Ems Canal, leaving S/L England and crew to complete the night's departures at 21.46 to head for the Forget-me-not garden in Kiel Bay. The Wooldridge crew was beaten back by intense searchlight and flak activity and witnessed the destruction of a 144 Squadron Hampden from Hemswell, before heading back towards the west and dropping their bombs in the Weser estuary. P/O Webster and crew negotiated the defences by gliding down to 300 feet to drop their bomb, in their estimation close to Scharnhorst. Meanwhile, S/L Kydd and crew carried out an attack on M25 without observing the results, but the Saunders and Aldridge crews were hindered by engine issues and the former jettisoned their bombs. S/L England and crew were the last to land after seven hours in the air and reported a successful conclusion to their sortie.

On the 5th, 5 Group detailed a dozen Hampdens from Waddington to continue the assault on Scharnhorst at Kiel, while Scampton took care of mining duties and three crews from Hemswell were briefed to attack the embankments of the Dortmund-Ems Canal. The 61 Squadron crews of F/O Baskett and F/L How took off at 22.34 and 23.05 respectively but soon lost the services of the latter to W/T failure, leaving the Baskett crew to negotiate thunderstorms and seek out a suitable area of the canal to attack. What they found was a long, straight stretch of around twenty-five miles running from the River Ems south of Lingen and passing through the town of Nordhorn and across the Dutch frontier to Almelo. Direct hits were claimed on two lock gates and barges in a sortie lasting five-and-a-half hours.

Adverse weather conditions on the 6th restricted 5 Group operations to mining by eleven Hampdens from Waddington, but thirty would be active on the 7th, a dozen at Hemswell assigned to mining duties, while three others were to attack the embankments of the Dortmund-Ems Canal. On a busy night for the group, nine Scampton crews were briefed for an operation against an oil refinery at Offenbach near Frankfurt, and six from Waddington were handed marshalling yards in the Ruhr. The six-strong 61 Squadron mining element departed Hemswell between 20.53 and 21.19 with F/L How the senior pilot on duty, bound for the Hollyhock garden located off Travemünde, the estuary leading to the Baltic port-city of Lübeck. They were well on their way across the North Sea by the time that F/L Fewtrell and crew took off at 22.19 to attack the Dortmund-Ems Canal and failed to return after P4390 was brought down by flak at Nordhorn. The pilot and two others survived to fall into enemy hands, and this was the sixth experienced crew to be lost in a month, five of them in the last sixteen days. The gardeners, meanwhile, enjoyed favourable conditions and all completed their sorties according to brief during sorties of six to seven hours duration.

50 Squadron was stood down from operations on the 8th while the move took place to a new home at Hatfield Woodhouse, located across the county line in Yorkshire, five miles north-east of Doncaster. This was a brand-new airfield completed in June, and 50 Squadron would be its first

resident unit. To prevent confusion with the Hatfield in Hertfordshire, which was home to the de Havilland aircraft factory, Hatfield Woodhouse would be renamed in August to become Lindholme, after a country house and hamlet on the eastern boundary of the airfield.

It was reported that the battleship Tirpitz, the sister ship of Bismarck, was at berth in Wilhelmshaven, where it had been built between 1936 and 1939 and was still in the process of being fitted out. In fact, the Kriegsmarinewerft shipyard in Wilhelmshaven had built much of Germany's fleet of warships, including the Deutschland class "pocket battleships", Admiral Scheer and Admiral Graf Spee, launched in 1934 and 1936 respectively, the Scharnhorst heavy cruiser in 1939 and now the mighty Bismarck-class Tirpitz in addition to Type VII U-Boots. Eleven Hampdens from Scampton and three from Hemswell were detailed to attack Tirpitz on the 9th, the 61 Squadron crews of S/L Kydd and P/O Jones taking off at 22.27 and 22.30 respectively and arriving in the target area to find low cloud and intense searchlight and flak activity. S/L Kydd and crew attacked what they believed was the target vessel without observing the results, but the Jones crew were defeated by the conditions and bombed the aerodrome on the Frisian Island of Borkum on the way home.

The Dortmund-Ems Canal and industrial targets occupied seventeen 5 Group Hampdens on a night of reduced activity on the 11th, 61 Squadron briefing the crews of F/L How and P/O Gould for the Krupp Treibstoffwerke synthetic oil plant at Wanne-Eickel in the Ruhr and those of S/L England, the newly promoted F/L Baskett and P/O Hall to target a stretch of the Dortmund-Ems Canal coded M24. The former departed Hemswell first at 22.02 and 22.04 only to lose the services of P/O Gould and crew to an issue with their radio, while F/L how and crew were persuaded by the conditions to attack the alternative target of Waalhaven aerodrome at Rotterdam. The second element took off between 22.22 and 22.50 and lost the services of P/O Hall and crew to instrument failure, while S/L England and crew failed to locate the target in the prevailing conditions and jettisoned their bombs over the sea on the way home after losing brake pressure. The departure of F/L Baskett and crew had been delayed by an instrument issue and once airborne they headed directly for the alternative target at Waalhaven.

Another busy night for 5 Group on the 13th involved fifty-seven Hampdens from all four of its operational stations as Hatfield Woodhouse launched its first sorties. Hemswell detailed a dozen Hampdens for mining duties and three to target the Dortmund-Ems Canal, Scampton contributed fifteen to an attack on the Blohm & Voss shipyard on Finkenwerder Island on the southern bank of the Elbe in Hamburg, Waddington fourteen for the Weser Flugzeugbau airframe factory at Deichshausen/Lemwerder to the north-west of Bremen and Hatfield Woodhouse thirteen for a return to the gunpowder factory at Geesthacht near Hamburg. 61 Squadron briefed its eight crews for mining duties in the Eglantine garden in the Elbe estuary and sent them on their way from Hemswell between 21.53 and 22.13 with W/C Sheen the senior pilot on duty. F/Sgt Saunders and crew turned back with engine trouble over the North Sea, leaving the others to arrive in the target area and encounter low cloud and rain, which prevented all but the crews of W/C Sheen and P/Os Hall and Jones from fulfilling their briefs.

One of the targets for 5 Group on the 14th was the Hamburger Flugzeugbau aircraft factory, a subsidiary of the Blohm & Voss company, located at Wenzendorf to the south-west of Hamburg, for which the 61 Squadron crews of F/L Baskett, F/Sgt Saunders and Sgt Massey departed Hemswell between 21.22 and 21.26. They were forced to run the gauntlet of anti-aircraft fire all the way to the target area from Borkum and the coastal regions of Cuxhaven and Wilhelmshaven, and F/L Baskett and crew were forced to jettison their bombs after sustaining damage. Cloud prevented any from locating the target and the Saunders and Massy crews returned their bombs to the station dump.

The 17th brought a night of little activity and 5 Group detailed just three Hampdens for mining duties in the Undergrowth garden in the Kattegat off Frederikshavn in north-eastern Jutland. 61 Squadron had briefed the crews of S/L England and F/L Baskett, but engine trouble prevented the former from taking off and the latter took to the air alone at 21.06, only also to suffer engine issues and have to return early after jettisoning the mine "safe".

Ninety-five aircraft were detailed by Bomber Command for operations on the 20th against six targets in Germany, aerodromes in Holland and for mine-laying. 5 Group was called upon to support an operation against the Tirpitz and the "pocket battleship" Admiral Scheer, which were at berth at Wilhelmshaven and were to be attacked with a special weapon, possibly a type of mine. 61 Squadron briefed the crews of S/L England, P/O Webster and Sgt Wooldridge to carry out mining sorties and act as a diversion for the bombing element, which included five other 61 Squadron crews, those of F/Sgt Saunders and P/Os Davis and Jones to target Tirpitz and Sgt Massey and P/O Gould Admiral Scheer. They departed Hemswell between 22.02 and 22.19, and S/L England returned at 05.07 with a full bomb load after failing to locate the target area. The others had to face an intense searchlight and flak response, which persuaded F/Sgt Saunders and crew to pull away and drop their bombs on a group of ships lying off the mole. P4343 crashed into the Grosser Haven close to the Kaiser Wilhelm Bridge and only P/O Davis escaped with his life to fall into enemy hands, while P4344 and P4358 crash-landed with flak damage, the latter burning fiercely on mudflats on the outskirts of the town. The body of the rear gunner was found with an unopened parachute, and he was the only fatal casualty among the eight crewmen, the surviving seven soon finding themselves in captivity. At 06.26, P/O de Mestre took off for the first time as crew captain to conduct a search over the North Sea for 144 Squadron's F/L Edwards and crew, who had sent an SOS message. Sadly, nothing was found, and no trace of the Hampden and its crew ever came to light. There were no claims of hits on the warships and the loss of five aircraft and crews was a high price to pay for failure.

Bomber Command committed eighty-one aircraft to operations on the night of the 21/22nd, 5 Group detailing twenty Hampdens from its four operational stations for an attack on the Dornier aircraft factory at Wismar, a Hansastadt (ancient free-trade city) on the Baltic coast. 61 Squadron supported the operation with four Hampdens containing the crews of F/L How, F/O Aldridge, P/O Gibson and Sgt Blakeman, who departed Hemswell between 21.31 and 21.37 for what would be a round-trip of more than six hours. P/O Gibson and crew abandoned their sortie immediately on the failure of their a.s.i., leaving the others to press on across the North Sea and Schleswig-Holstein to find patchy cloud in the target area, where each carried out an attack without observing results. A number of fires were reported but it is unlikely that any serious damage was achieved.

On the 22nd, 5 Group detailed twenty-three Hampdens for a variety of targets including the Nordstern (Gelsenberg A.G) synthetic oil refinery in the Horst district of Gelsenkirchen in the Ruhr and the aircraft park at Eschwege, located some one hundred miles east of the Ruhr. Others were assigned to mining duties and among these was another 61 Squadron second pilot, New Zealander P/O Arthur Paape, who had completed his apprenticeship and was allowed at last to captain his own crew. They departed Hemswell in company with the crew of P/O Tunstall at 21.30 bound for the Nasturtium garden, which lay at the northern end of The Sound (Oresund), the channel between Helsingborg in Sweden and Denmark's Zealand Island. When the Tunstall crew turned back early because of a W/T problem, the Paape crew continued on and fulfilled their brief during an uneventful, if sometimes wet sortie lasting seven hours and fifteen minutes. They had been preceded into the air at 21.22 by the crew of P/O Gibson, whose destination was the aircraft park at Eschwege, but cloudy conditions concealed it and an aerodrome near Detmold, near Bielefeld, was attacked instead.

Hemswell sat out a return to the Hamburger Flugzeugbau aircraft factory at Wenzendorf on the 23rd, but the same target was posted for nine Hampdens from the station on the 24th, while Hatfield Woodhouse provided four for another shot at the Dornier works at Wismar. 61 Squadron made ready four of its own containing the crews of P/Os Hall, Tunstall and Webster and Sgt Massey, who took off between 22.30 and 22.49 and headed out over the North Sea, from where the Tunstall crew turned back after around ninety minutes because of an engine issue. The others ran into one of the frequent electrical storms acting as north-western Germany's gate-keeper, and icing conditions in thick cloud at 6,000 feet created challenges, particularly for target identification. P/O Webster and crew gave up their search and turned for home with their bomb load intact, while Sgt Massey and crew headed north and bombed Emden docks as an alternative. Only P/O Hall and crew made a positive identification of the primary target after pinpointing on Sinstorf, an urban area south of Hamburg, and carried out an attack without observing the outcome.

The night of the 25/26th was a busy one for 5 Group, in which forty-one aircraft from Hemswell, Waddington and Hatfield Woodhouse were sent to attack oil refineries in the Ruhr, while Scampton's eighteen aircraft focused on the Dortmund-Ems Canal. This was an important component in the German communications system, through which raw materials were imported into the industrial Ruhr and finished products exported to wider Germany to assist the war effort. There were two stretches of the canal which featured a twin aqueduct section, the already mentioned and attacked M25 and M25A at the junction with the River Ems and another some six miles further north, near Ladbergen, which carried the waterway over the Ibbenbürener Aa River. The canal would develop a close association with 5 Group and, along with the nearby Mittelland Canal, would continue to be a target for it for the remainder of the war. The target for seven 61 Squadron crews was the Krupp-Treibstoff synthetic oil plant at Wanne-Eickel, although to be accurate, it would be early 1941 before the Krupp organization was handed controlling interest in most of Germany's vital industrial companies. They departed Hemswell between 22.01 and 22.58 with F/L How the senior pilot on duty, but on a night of poor visibility over the Ruhr, only F/Sgt Saunders and crew succeeded in locating and bombing the primary target, without observing the results. The crews of Sgts Harrison and Wooldridge found alternative factories nearby, while P/O Paape and crew attacked the marshalling yards, and the others brought their bombs home. It was standard practice on all operations to carry nickels (propaganda leaflets), and each crew dispensed bundles at various points over enemy territory.

Reduced activity on the 27th saw just nineteen Hampdens representing 5 Group, a dozen of them at Hemswell prepared for mining duties in the Endive garden located between Jutland's Baltic coast and Fyn Island. The six-strong 61 Squadron element took off between 21.58 and 22.10 with F/O Aldridge the senior pilot on duty, but he and his crew turned back early because of intercom failure, leaving the others to fulfil their briefs. In addition to their single 1,500lb parachute mine, Hampdens engaged in gardening also routinely carried two wing-mounted 250-pounders for use against targets of opportunity, and on this night the crews of P/Os Hall and Webster dropped theirs on the Island of Sylt, attracting intense anti-aircraft fire in the process.

Hemswell sat out operations on the 28th, when thirty-six Hampdens from the other stations targeted oil refineries in Hamburg and Bremen and conducted mining operations. It was the turn of Hatfield Woodhouse and Waddington to remain inactive on the 29th, while Hemswell prepared a dozen Hampdens for mining duties and three to attack the Dortmund-Ems Canal, while Scampton put up eighteen to target oil tanks in Frankfurt. 61 Squadron briefed the crews of F/L How, F/Sgt Saunders and Sgts Blakeman and Oakley for the Daffodil garden located at the southern end of The Sound (Oresund) between Zealand Island and the Swedish coast, and the crews of P/Os Gibson and de Mestre and Sgt Harrison for Sweet Pea, situated in the bay of Mecklenburg to the south of Denmark's Lolland Island. They took off in two sections between 21.28 and 21.35 and 21.44 and 21.50, leaving the crew of P/O Paape on the ground until their departure for M25 at 22.35. All of the gardeners succeeded in fulfilling their brief, but on the way home a deviant compass took Sgt Oakley and crew off track and into a severe storm off the northern coast of France and by the time the English coast appeared on the horizon, the Hampden was flying on fumes. A course was set for Shoreham on the Sussex coast, but both engines cut out during the final approach, and Sgt Oakley had the presence of mind to raise the undercarriage before carrying out a belly-landing on the side of a hill. There were no crew casualties and P4398 would be returned to flying condition. P/O Paape and crew, meanwhile, had encountered ten-tenths cloud with a very low base and had been forced to abandon their attempt to bomb the Dortmund-Ems Canal.

The last night of the month brought mining operations for a dozen Hampdens from Hatfield Woodhouse, while Waddington and Hemswell contributed a dozen and four Hampdens respectively to an attack on the Deurag-Nerag synthetic oil refinery at Misburg near Hannover with oil storage tanks at Emmerich on the Rhine north of the Ruhr as an alternative. 61 Squadron was represented by the crews of F/O Aldridge and Sgt Wathey, who took off at 22.20 and ran into such adverse weather conditions that neither target could be attacked, and they returned their ordnance to the station dump.

During the course of the month the squadron took part in twenty-four operations and dispatched eighty-four sorties for the loss of three Hampdens and crews.

August 1940

August's operations would follow a similar pattern to those of July as the Battle of Britain raged overhead and invasion fever increased. 5 Group divided its effort on the 2nd between the oil refinery at Misburg near Hannover for the Hemswell crews and mining for the 83 Squadron boys at Scampton. 61 Squadron made ready six Hampdens and sent them on their way between 21.17 and 22.04, but on a night of poor serviceability, the crews of P/O de Mestre, P/O Gibson and Sgt Harrison returned early with W/T, R/T and engine issues respectively, and of the others only Sgt Blakeman and crew attacked the primary target without observing the results. Sgt Oakley and crew went for the briefed alternative, oil storage tanks in the town of Emmerich on the frontier with Holland, which they bombed from 12,000 feet but overshot and caused a dull red glow as evidence that they had hit something combustible. F/Sgt Saunders and crew found a stretch of the Weser-Elbe Canal to attack from 8,500 feet, and despite circling twice to ascertain the outcome, they were prevented by searchlight glare.

5 Group operations on the 3rd called upon the services of fourteen Hampdens from Scampton to attack the heavy cruiser, Gneisenau, at berth in the Germania Werft shipyard at Kiel and a dozen from Waddington to take care of mining duties. At Hemswell, 61 and 144 Squadron's made ready three Hampdens each to send against the Dortmund-Ems Canal at its junction with the River Ems. The crews of P/O Hall, S/L Kydd and P/O Hall took off in that order between 21.25 and 21.35, P/O Hall carrying four 500-pounders to drop on the southern lock gates of the new aqueduct section, while the others were to target barges in the old one. The Hall crew was defeated by searchlight glare and haze and after abandoning the attempt to hit the primary target, sought out an alternative on the way home, finding De Mok seaplane base at The Hague, where the burst of bombs was observed but no detail. S/L Kydd made five passes over M25 at 300 feet and spent fifty minutes searching in vain through intense searchlight glare for the aiming point. A similar story was recounted by F/L Baskett and crew at debriefing, and all were adamant that the searchlight and flak defences had been substantially increased since the last visit.

According to the 5 Group ORB operations planned for the night of the 4/5th were cancelled, but the 61 Squadron ORB records that six 61 Squadron crews departed Hemswell between 20.56 and 21.09 bound for the Eglantine garden in the Elbe estuary with F/L How the senior pilot on duty. Sgt Harrison and crew returned early because of an R/T issue, leaving the others to press on across the North Sea and run into low cloud and haze in the target area that provided challenging conditions. Only the crews of Sgt Wooldridge and P/O de Mestre succeeded in planting their vegetable in the briefed location, the former also dropping the two wing-mounted 250-pounders on searchlights on Wangerooge on the way home. The de Mestre crew were followed out of the target area by a single-engine enemy aircraft, which the gunners engaged, and although they did not observe it crash, they watched it fall vertically towards the ground as if fatally damaged. Mist had descended over much of Lincolnshire by the time of their return, which resulted in diversion orders, and while force-landing near Boston, P4400 caught a wheel in a ditch and, according to the squadron ORB, was wrecked, but without injury to P/O de Mestre and his crew. This incident is not mentioned in Bomber Command Losses, probably because the Hampden was restored to flying condition and was transferred eventually to 25 O.T.U.

At 10.00 on the 5th, P4357 crashed into the sea off the Yorkshire coast near Skipsea while on a training flight, and one of Sgt Blakeman's crew lost his life, while the pilot and the other occupant sustained injuries. Briefings for that night's operations revealed that nine Hampdens from 83 Squadron at Scampton and eight belonging to 50 Squadron at Hatfield Woodhouse were to seek out the battleship Bismarck, which was under the final stages of fitting-out in Hamburg. Hemswell remained dormant on this night and the next, when Scampton provided a dozen Hampdens for mining duties in the Kattegat off north-eastern Jutland, and it was the 7th before 61 and 144 Squadrons were next alerted. They were called upon to provide four Hampdens each for mining duties in the Quince garden, situated south of Langeland Island in the Bay of Kiel, which would provide a diversion for the main event, another attempt to hit the cruiser, Gneisenau, at Berth in a Kiel shipyard. S/L England was the senior pilot on duty among the 61 Squadron quartet as they departed Hemswell between 19.57 and 20.04 and headed for the North Sea, where they lost the services of P/O Paape and crew after an hour when their oxygen supply failed and Sgt Wathey and crew soon afterwards because of an intercom issue. S/L England and Sgt Harrison and their crews were unable to locate the garden in conditions of low cloud, but the former found a flare-path north of Kiel, which they took to be Holtenau aerodrome, and attacked it with their wing-mounted 250-pounders, observing bursts but no details.

Hemswell and Hatfield Woodhouse represented 5 Group on the 10th, when providing nine Hampdens each for a raid on the Rheinpreussen (Meerbeck) synthetic oil refinery at Moers/Homberg on the western bank of the Rhine opposite Duisburg. 61 Squadron briefed the crews of Sgt Massey, P/O Paape, F/O Tunstall, Sgt Wathey and F/O Aldridge and sent them on their way in that order between 22.50 and 23.41, only to lose the services of the Massey crew within minutes because of a jammed rear door. F/O Tunstall and crew were misled by a faulty compass and spent two hours wandering over England before landing at Cranfield. The others were hampered by poor visibility and only the Wathey crew came close to the target, when attacking a fire at Moers, which may have been in the refinery site. P/O Paape and crew bombed an aerodrome at Krefeld, while the Aldridge crew found a last resort target in the Ruhr, probably a factory.

Scampton represented 5 Group on the 11th when sending nine Hampdens from each of its squadrons to operate against A108, an oil refinery in Dortmund at the eastern end of the Ruhr and to employ the previously mentioned "razzle" incendiary device to attempt to set fire to a heavily wooded region from Cologne eastwards as far as Herborn. The same responsibility was handed to Hemswell twenty-four hours later, when the oil target was the Wintershall refinery, situated at Salzbergen on the River Ems in the Münsterland, north of the Ruhr, ten miles from the Dutch frontier. The region selected for "razzling" was Schwarmstedt-Soltau-Uelzen, a wooded area between Hamburg to the north and Hannover to the south to which 61 Squadron dispatched the crews of W/C Sheen, F/O Tunstall and P/Os Cundill and Sheldon between 20.52 and 21.08. They flew out in formation as far as the Dutch coast before separating north of the Zuider Zee and proceeding independently to their briefed beats to carry out the plan to "razzle" first and then head home via the oil plant. Having identified their target area, they were to fly up and down thirty-mile stretches of forest dispensing fifty tins each, but on a disappointing night for the squadron, only W/C Sheen and crew are known to have completed the "razzle" component of their brief. They descended to 1,500 feet, guided by lights from what they discovered later to be the town of Verden, located south-east of Bremen and west of Soltau, and dispensed all fifty tins, but made no mention in their debriefing report of Salzbergen. F/O Tunstall and crew failed to locate either target and dropped their bombs on an aerodrome at Lastrup, some fifteen miles from the Dutch frontier. P4335 disappeared without trace with the crew of P/O Cundill, and P4379 was brought down somewhere in the Hamburg defence zone with no survivors from the crew of P/O Sheldon. This was the night on which Hampdens of 49 and 83 Squadrons carried out a low-level attack on the twin aqueduct section of the Dortmund-Ems Canal at its junction with the River Ems, M25 and M25A, and F/L Learoyd of 49 Squadron earned a Victoria Cross for flying into the teeth of a light flak defence that had already brought down two 83 Squadron aircraft. He and his crew caused a breech, which would affect navigation for weeks, and he was the first member of Bomber Command to receive the ultimate recognition of gallantry.

On the 13th, all four operational stations were alerted to operations that night against Junkers aircraft factories at Dessau and Bernburg, situated some twenty miles apart in east central Germany, south of Magdeburg. 61 Squadron provided five of the twenty-eight Hampdens and sent them on their way from Hemswell between 21.10 and 21.19 with P/Os Gibson and Paape the only commissioned pilots on duty and the Hugo Stinnes-Riebeck oil plant at Dollbergen near Hannover as the designated alternative target. Ten-tenths cloud from the Dutch coast all the way to the target area ruined any chance of locating the primary and alternative targets, and the crews of P/O Paape and Sgt Wathey brought their bombs back to base. Last resort targets were any aerodromes being used by the enemy, and Sgt Massey and crew bombed one at Oldenburg, to the west of Bremen and observed two bursts but no detail. Sgt Oakley and crew found another to attack at Osnabrück, while P/O Gibson and crew dropped their load on marshalling yards thirty miles west of the Dümmer See, which means that they must have been very close to Hamburg.

A change of focus on the 14th would pitch 5 Group against marshalling yards in Cologne and Hamm and oil production and storage facilities in the Gironde estuary to the north of Bordeaux in south-western France. Bordeaux was an important port and U-Boot base on the Garonne River from where the Gironde estuary provided access to the Atlantic, in addition to which, the oil facilities at Pauillac, Bec-d'Ambes, Blaye and Bassens were of interest to Bomber Command, although it would be the summer of 1944 before a concerted effort was mounted against these targets. The target for the crews of Sgt Wooldridge, F/Sgt Saunders and P/O Webster was the highly important marshalling yards at Hamm, a major railway hub in the communications system in and out of the Ruhr. They departed Hemswell between 22.42 and 22.55 and set course via Mablethorpe for the Dutch coast but were hampered by eight to ten-tenths cloud and rainstorms, which prevented the Wooldridge and Saunders crews from identifying the primary or suitable alternative target. The Webster crew dropped one bomb, precisely where is not recorded, and returned the others to the station dump.

The 15th was the day selected by the Luftwaffe as "Adlertag", Eagle Day, which was intended to be the opening salvo in the destruction of the RAF's ability to defend Britain. It began the most intense four weeks of the Battle of Britain, and its outcome could possibly determine the course of the war. Bomber Command's attention switched to the Ruhr that night, when 5 Group operated alone, sending thirty-three Hampdens from Scampton and Hemswell to a variety of targets. The destination for five 61 Squadron crews was the Rhenania-Ossag synthetic oil refinery at Reisholz, a south-eastern district of Düsseldorf, for which they departed Hemswell between 23.18 and 23.26 with F/O Tunstall the senior pilot on duty. Sgt Oakley and crew lost their intercom shortly after taking off and were back on the ground within ninety minutes, leaving the others to benefit from favourable weather conditions and an almost full moon. Sgt Wathey and crew were twenty minutes short of the target when engine trouble forced them to jettison their bombs and turn for home, while the others pressed on and bombed the primary target, which was already partially concealed by smoke by the time they arrived.

Waddington and Hatfield Woodhouse were back in harness to join Hemswell and Scampton on the 16th, when A77, the I G Farben-owned oil refinery at Leuna, near Merseburg, was posted as the target. As previously mentioned, it was one of many oil production and storage sites situated in an arc to the west of Leipzig from north of the city to the south, in a region that would increase in importance to Bomber Command from mid-1944 onwards. That was in the distant future, however, when a thousand sorties might be launched in a single night, while on this night, the commitment of 150 sorties to targets in the Ruhr and eastern and southern Germany represented a major effort. S/L Kydd was the senior pilot on duty among the seven 61 Squadron participants, which took off between 20.20 and 20.45, having been briefed specifically to attack blocks 2 and 3 within the plant. Only F/L How and crew failed to locate the target and brought their bombs home, while the others carried out attacks on the designated aiming points in the face of an intense searchlight and flak defence. S/L Kydd and crew were blinded by searchlight glare and had to make three passes over the target before being satisfied, and F/L Baskett and crew claimed to have attacked the site's power station. All were short of fuel as they reached England, but landed safely after what was reported to be a particularly effective night's work.

On the 17th, Hatfield Woodhouse underwent the change of name described earlier and would now be known as Lindholme. That night, 102 aircraft took part in wide-ranging operations, 61 Squadron preparing eight Hampdens to attack the Krupp complex in the Ruhr city of Essen. The name Krupp conjures up a vision of a massive factory, but this is far from what actually existed. The Krupp organisation had been the largest manufacturer of weapons in Europe since before the Great War and had a hand in all aspects of German war production from tanks to artillery and ship and U-Boot construction and was given a controlling share in all major heavy engineering companies in Germany and the Occupied Countries. It also built manufacturing sites in other parts of Germany, many situated close to concentration camps, and employed vast numbers of forced workers in all of its factories. Once known as "Die Waffenschmiede des Reichs", the weapons-forge of the realm, its manufacturing sites in Essen included among others the Friedrich Krupp steelworks, the Friedrich Krupp locomotive and general engineering works, six coal mines and ten coke-oven plants, the Altenberg zinc works, the Presswerk plastics factory and the Goldschmidt non-ferrous metals smelting plant, all situated either within or close to the four Borbeck districts in a segment radiating out from near the city centre to the Rhine-Herne Canal on the north-western boundary on the banks of the Emscher River. The steel and engineering works alone employed in the region of eighty thousand workers, and the company's sites covered an area of more than two thousand acres, of which three hundred acres were occupied by factories and workshops. All of that required massive rail and canal access in the form of marshalling yards and its own harbour, and energy from at least four nearby power stations.

They departed Hemswell between 22.39 and 23.06 with S/L England the senior pilot on duty and each crew sitting on four 500-pounders and lost the services of P/O Gibson and crew to engine trouble after ninety minutes. The others all arrived over the Ruhr to find favourable conditions, a full moon, a hostile defence and barrage balloons tethered at heights of between 7,000 and 12,000 feet. The crews of F/Sgt Saunders and Sgts Oakley and Wathey identified and bombed the briefed target, E8, while the crews of S/L England and Sgts Blakeman and Harrison went for an alternative, E4, the identity of which is not known. Sgt Wooldridge and crew found a self-illuminating objective somewhere in the Ruhr, and all returned safely from another apparently successful night's work.

5 Group was given the night off on the 18th as adverse weather conditions prevailed, but it was back in harness on the 19th with nineteen Hampdens, seven each from Hemswell and Scampton assigned to a petrol refinery at Bec-d'Ambes, located on the point of the confluence of the Garonne and Dordogne Rivers in the Gironde estuary fifteen miles north of Bordeaux. The 61 Squadron crews of F/O Tunstall, P/O de Mestre and Sgts Massey and Wooldridge took off between 20.51 and 21.01, and after contending with engines that refused to be synchronized, the Tunstall crew turned back, leaving the others to reach the target after a long outward flight and deliver what they claimed was a successful attack that left the plant burning from end to end. P2089 sustained damage to a fuel tank over the target and was flying on fumes as P/O de Mestre and crew approached the south coast of England, where a forced-landing at Lyme Regis wrote off the Hampden without injury to the crew. By the time that the Massey and Wooldridge crews landed at base, they had been airborne for more than eight hours.

The German synthetic oil industry relied on two main production methods, the Bergius process, which involved the hydrogenation of highly volatile bituminous coal to manufacture high-grade petroleum products like aviation fuel, and the Fischer-Tropsch process, which produced lower-grade diesel-type fuels for vehicle, Tank, U-Boot and shipping requirements. The dual targets for forty-four Hampdens on the 21st were a ship lift at the eastern end of the Mittelland Canal at its junction with the River Elbe, and the Bergius-process Braunkohle A.G (Aktien Gesellschaft or production company) synthetic oil refinery (hydrogenation plant) coded A78, both located in the same Rothensee district to the north of Magdeburg city centre. Also, on the target list and assigned to five Hampdens of 49 Squadron was M44, a second ship lift located at Hohenwarthe, close by to the north-east, which, in reality, had not been built, and as a result of the war, would not be. The seven-strong 61 Squadron element departed Hemswell between 20.43 and 21.30 with S/L Kydd the senior pilot on duty and met with unfavourable weather conditions, including severe icing, rain, snow and almost continuous electrical storms, which prevented all but the crews of S/L Kydd and P/O Webster from delivering an attack. Both dropped bombs in the canal short of the ship lift in the face of a spirited searchlight and flak defence, and F/Sgt Saunders and crew, having failed to locate the primary target, released theirs over the seaplane base on Texel on the way home.

Hemswell, Lindholme and Waddington received orders on the 22nd to prepare between them twenty-three Hampdens for an operation that night against an aircraft components factory (G82) in Frankfurt, while a dozen from Scampton took care of mining duties in the Artichoke garden off the Biscay port of Lorient. 61 Squadron briefed six crews and launched them into the air between 21.54 and 22.20 with F/L Baskett the senior pilot on duty and immediately lost the services of P/O de Mestre and crew to a W/T issue. The others again had to contend with adverse weather conditions including icing, but all reached the target area, where F/L Baskett and crew carried out an attack on the factory but failed to observe the results. The crews of Sgts Blakeman and Wathey bombed the briefed alternative target, the nearby Chemische Fabrik Griesheim-Elektron factory, while the crews of P/O Langford and Sgt Harrison were unable to locate a suitable target and brought their bombs home.

On the following night, 5 Group launched forty Hampdens to conduct mining sorties in the Jellyfish garden off the port of Brest, for which 61 Squadron briefed six crews and dispatched them from Hemswell between 23.26 and 23.44 with S/L England the senior pilot on duty. They began the Channel crossing at the Dorset coast, heading for landfall on the French side of the Channel somewhere to the west of St-Malo, and lost the services of F/O Tunstall and crew to engine trouble on the way. The others arrived in the target area to find excellent conditions with bright moonlight and the defences already stirred into action by earlier arrivals. The pinpoints for the timed runs, among them Pointe-Sainte-Mathieu on the northern headland, were easily established, but S/L England and crew could not find a way through the curtain of light flak and were unable to plant their vegetable. The crews of P/Os Gibson and D'Arcy-Wright fulfilled their briefs and then dropped their two wing-mounted 250-pounders on flak batteries near the port.

It was similar fare on the following night for twenty-nine 5 Group Hampdens, only this time in the Beech and Cinnamon gardens off the ports respectively of St-Nazaire and La Pallice/La Rochelle. F/Ls Baskett and How were the senior pilots in the five-strong 61 Squadron element that departed Hemswell between 22.00 and 22.38 bound for the former. They benefitted from excellent conditions and bright moonlight, and all were able to plant their vegetables in the briefed locations and the crews of F/Ls Baskett and How attacked targets of opportunity with their 250-pounders on the way home, the latter hitting the southern edge of the Luftwaffe aerodrome on the Channel Island of Jersey.

In retaliation for the inadvertent bombing of London on the night of the 24/25th, the War Cabinet sanctioned the first raid of the war on Berlin by around fifty aircraft to take place on the 25th. 5 Group contributed forty-six Hampdens for this and other operations, thirty-four from Scampton, Waddington and Lindholme to attack an electrical power station, B57, one of five serving the city, while twelve from Hemswell targeted Tempelhof aerodrome to the south. Germany's capital lay at the limit of endurance for Hampdens carrying a load of four 500-pounders and they might have to rely on perfect weather conditions to complete a round trip, which for some would exceed eight hours. The six 61 Squadron crews took off from Hemswell between 20.31 and 21.00 with S/L England the senior pilot on duty, before setting course via the Lincolnshire coast for the target, six hundred miles away. P/O Paape and crew were back home within the first hour after experiencing aileron vibration, while the rest adopted a route that would take them close to Hannover and Braunschweig. A blanket of cloud stretching across northern Germany largely denied them a sight of the ground, and the unfavourable conditions persisted in the target area, where the cloud base was down to 2,000 feet and only the crews of S/L England and F/O Aldridge carried out an attack from 14,000 and 16,000 feet respectively, without being able to see any results. Others among the Berlin force found alternative objectives in the form of a marshalling yard, factories and flak concentrations, and Sgt Harrison and crew an aerodrome at Langsdorf, which they attacked from 14,000 feet while heading home into a headwind, the very worst prospect for fuel management. Four Hampdens ran out of fuel over the North Sea, and three of the crews were picked up safe and sound. Local sources confirmed that most of the bombing had missed the city to the south and that the only building destroyed was a summerhouse, but it was an unsettling experience for the Nazi leadership and gave further lie to Göring's boast that no enemy aircraft would fly over the Reich.

Another busy night of operations on the 26th saw the preparation of twenty Hampdens from Hemswell and two from Waddington to attack A77, the Leuna (Merseburg) oil refinery near Liepzig, while six others from Waddington were assigned to a gas production plant in the city itself. Eight 61 Squadron crews were briefed, before taking off between 20.52 and 21.24 with F/L Baskett the senior pilot on duty, and by the time that they were over enemy territory, P/O Gibson was contending with an engine problem, and after failing to find a suitable last resort target, brought their bombs home. The outward route was attended by a layer of seven to ten-tenths cloud with haze below, and after descending through cloud to 1,200 feet, P/O Paape and crew found themselves right over Leipzig and the target for every flak battery that could be brought to bear. They were forced down to 400 feet as they raced westwards across the city, and found themselves on a direct course for the refinery, which they bombed from 1,200 feet, reporting large explosions on their return after almost eight hours aloft. P/O Webster and crew made three runs across the target before releasing their bombs and incendiaries from 9,000 feet and observing a vivid green flash and a fire break out in the powerhouse block, and Sgt Blakeman and crew hit the same building from 12,000 feet and increased the area of fire. P/O Langford and crew also claimed to have started a fire, while F/L Baskett and crew were unable to locate the primary target and attacked an aerodrome at Nordhausen in the Harz Mountains on the way home. Sgt Oakley and crew failed to locate either the primary or a suitable alternative target and returned their ordnance to the station dump. The return of F/O Tunstall and crew was awaited in vain, and news soon arrived to reveal that they had run out of fuel and had force-landed P4324 on the Frisian Island of Vlieland and were now guests of the Reich.

Orders were received on all 5 Group stations on the 28th to prepare thirty Hampdens for an operation that night against the Siemens and Halske A.G factory in the Siemensstadt district of Spandau, north-west of Berlin city centre. This site produced components for aero-engines and would be found after the war to have employed slave workers from concentration camps. The five 61 Squadron Hampdens each received a load of four 500-pounders and departed Hemswell between 21.15 and 22.00 with S/L England the senior pilot on duty. An hour later, F/L How and crew took off on a special sortie to bomb M25, the Dortmund-Ems aqueduct, with four 250-pounders, and photograph the results, but poor visibility prevented them from locating the target and they attacked an aerodrome eight miles south-west of Lingen as a last resort. Of the Berlin-bound element, Sgt Harrison and crew dropped out immediately because of engine trouble, and S/L England and crew were eventually forced to abandon their sortie after the heating system and the artificial horizon let them down. The crews of F/O Aldridge and F/Sgt Saunders attacked the primary target causing an explosion and fires, while P/O de Mestre and crew were unable to locate it and bombed a flak concentration as a last resort.

On the 29th, Hemswell and Waddington were called upon to provide twenty Hampdens between them to attack the Scholven-Buer synthetic oil refinery, situated north of Gelsenkirchen city centre in the Ruhr, 61 Squadron responding with seven aircraft, which took off between 21.05 and 21.21 with P/Os Gibson, Langford and Webster the commissioned pilots on duty. The weather conditions in the target area were not ideal, with seven to ten-tenths low cloud with haze below, and searchlight glare added to the challenge of locating the primary target. Despite the difficulties, five returning crews claimed to have attacked the refinery without observing the results, while Sgt Wathey and crew located the briefed alternative target, the city's power station, and caused a fire to break out. This left just the crew of P/O Langford to come back empty-handed after failing to identify a suitable target.

Hemswell sat out returns by Scampton and Lindholme crews respectively to the Bergius-process hydrogenation plants at Magdeburg and Scholven-Buer on the 30th, but was back in action on the last night of the month for an operation against the BMW aero-engine works at Spandau located in Berlin's western suburbs. Waddington aircraft were also assigned to the Berlin area to target Tempelhof aerodrome, while Scampton and Lindholme sent fifteen aircraft between them back to Magdeburg. Seven 61 Squadron crews took off between 20.26 and 20.40 with F/L How the senior pilot on duty and "Dim" Wooldridge resplendent in his new pilot officer's uniform. P/O Earl and crew returned shortly after midnight after losing their intercom, by which time the others had reached their destination to encounter weather conditions that again proved to be challenging with ten-tenths cloud down to 2,000 feet. Crews were reduced to spotting the ground through occasional chinks, despite which all delivered an attack, largely on estimated positions after briefly glimpsing what appeared to be the primary target, but none observed the results. P/O Wooldridge and crew dropped only their incendiaries at Berlin, and the four 250-pounders went down onto the flare-path at Lastrup aerodrome on the way home.

During the course of another busy month the squadron took part in twenty-two operations that generated 116 sorties for the loss of five Hampdens, three complete crews and one other crew member.

September 1940

While the Battle of Britain was reaching a crescendo overhead, and invasion fever gripped the nation, the overriding priority for the Command in September was the destruction of the invasion craft assembling in ports along the occupied coast. That said, the new month began for 5 Group on the 1st with small-scale attacks on industrial targets in Germany, Hemswell providing six Hampdens to attack the Bosch electrical components factory in Stuttgart, Scampton two for marshalling yards in Mannheim, and Waddington two for a dehydrogenation plant at Ludwigshafen. 61 Squadron briefed six crews and sent them on their way between 20.35 and 21.00 with P/Os Earl, Gibson and de Mestre the commissioned pilots on duty, and would lose two to technical problems within the first two hours. Sgt Cooper and crew were the first to return after an engine overheated, and soon afterwards P/O Gibson and crew landed having bombed the aerodrome at Knokke on the Belgian coast while contending with an oxygen shortage and unserviceable W/T. The others reached the target area, where P/O Earl and crew were unable to establish the location of the primary target in conditions of thick haze and bombed marshalling yards, probably at Böblingen to the south-west of Stuttgart. The others carried out an attack and observed bomb bursts and a few explosions and fires but no detail to pass on to the intelligence section at debriefing.

On the following night, Scampton provided six crews from each squadron for the first of many future raids on U-Boots at berth in ports, on this occasion at Lorient, while Hemswell's ten Hampdens were assigned to the dehydrogenation plant in Stuttgart targeted by two Waddington crews on the previous night. This site would soon fall under the umbrella of the infamous I G Farben chemicals and pharmaceuticals company, or to give it its full name, Interessen-Gemeinschaft Farbenindustrie, in English, Common Interest Conglomerate of chemical dye-making corporations. It was formed in 1925 as a merger between BASF, Bayer, Hoechst, Agfa, Chemische Fabrik Griesheim-Elektron and Chemische Fabrik vorm Weiler Ter Meer and was heavily involved in the development and production of synthetic oil and numerous bi-products. It would employ slave labour at all of its factories across Germany, including 30,000 from the Auschwitz concentration camp, where it would build a plant. One of the company's subsidiaries manufactured the Zyklon B gas used during the Holocaust to murder millions of Jewish victims. Other targets on this night were the Bosch electrical components factory at Stuttgart for three crews from Waddington and marshalling yards at Hamm and the Dortmund-Ems Canal for four from Lindholme. The 61 Squadron crews of P/O Langford and F/Sgt Saunders took off at 21.44 and 21.46 in company with eight from 144 Squadron, and arrived at the target to find favourable conditions, the Langford crew bombing from 9,000 feet and observing the plant to be in flames, while the Saunders crew attacked to the strains of "God Save The King", which had been picked up on the TR9 radio equipment.

Berlin was the destination for a dozen Hampdens on the 3rd, nine of them provided by Scampton, while nine from Hemswell and Waddington returned to Magdeburg to attack the Braunkohle hydrogenation plant in the Rothensee district. The crews of P/O Massey and Sgt Blakeman took off at 21.11 and 21.16 respectively and in the absence of a moon flew out in extreme darkness, and from 8° East patchy cloud added to the difficulty of identifying ground features. Sgt Blakeman and crew were fortunate to be in the wake of 144 Squadron's S/L Lovell and crew, whose bombs started fires and provided a reference for the 61 Squadron crew, although searchlight glare prevented an assessment of the outcome. P/O Massey and crew had no such assistance and returned their bombs to the station dump having failed to locate either the primary or suitable alternative target.

Another distant target was posted on the 4th, for which twenty-three Hampdens were detailed and sent to forward bases at Mildenhall and Stradishall for bombing up and launching. Crews learned at briefing that their primary target was the I G Farben-owned Wintershall synthetic oil refinery at Politz to the north of the Baltic port city of Stettin, for which 61 Squadron briefed the crews of Sgts Wathey and Oakley. They took off from Stradishall at 20.50 and 21.01 for what would be an eight-hour round trip and exited the English coast over Mablethorpe on course for Heligoland and landfall on the Danish coast north of Sylt. A clear, starlit night provided conditions sufficiently favourable for crews to map-read their way across southern Jutland and the Baltic to the target area with a tailwind to speed them on their way and horizontal visibility of ten miles. Both arrived in the target area under continuing clear skies but extreme darkness, and each delivered an attack resulting in explosions, before turning for home with the impression that the raid had been effective.

On the following day, Scampton, Hemswell and Waddington were alerted to a return to Politz that night, for which eighteen Hampdens were made ready, two of them belonging to 61 Squadron. Hemswell was also to provide five Hampdens to attack A8, the oil refinery at Wilhelmsburg located to the south of the Elbe in Hamburg, and two to disrupt and delay the repairs to the M25 section of the Dortmund-Ems Canal. 61 Squadron briefed the crews of F/L How and P/O Wooldridge for Politz and those of P/Os Earl and Gibson and Sgt Cooper for Hamburg and assigned the crew of F/L Baskett to M25, sending them on their way over an extended period between 20.32 and 21.45. The Baskett crew failed to locate their target in conditions of haze and extreme darkness and bombed an aerodrome at Twente in eastern Holland as an alternative. The Hamburg-bound trio reached their target and carried out attacks that left fires burning, and on return and contending with engine trouble and a jammed, partially deployed undercarriage, P/O Earl crash-landed X2893 in a field at Burton, on the outskirts of Lincoln. P/O Wooldridge and crew landed at Marham short of fuel after more than eight hours in the air and they were able to report bombing the target and leaving fires in their wake. F/L How and crew had been unable to locate their target and jettisoned their bombs on the way home to save fuel, but even so, as they approached Marham flying on fumes after more than nine hours aloft, X2894 hit a tree near Stradsett and came down tail-first, killing the lower rear gunner, Sgt Knight, and severely shaking the other occupants.

The intensive period of back-to-back operations continued on the 6th, when a dozen Hampdens were detailed, eight at Scampton and four at Hemswell, to attack an oil refinery in Dortmund, and while we are provided with the code A108, we do not know whether it referred to the Hoesch-Westfalenhütte A.G, the Hoesch-Benzin GmbH in the Wambel district or the Zeche Hansa coking plant. In addition, nine Hampdens from Waddington were to target marshalling yards at Hamm, Krefeld, Trier and Mannheim. The 61 Squadron crews of F/Sgt Saunders and Sgt Harrison departed Hemswell at 20.03 and 20.05 and encountered eight-tenths cloud over the Dortmund area with thick haze below that rendered target recognition something of a challenge. The Harrison crew bombed a pear-shaped factory with shaded lights in the vicinity of A108, and on return commented on the paucity of the searchlight and flak defence. F/Sgt Saunders and crew were unable to locate the primary target and bombed the aerodrome at Arnhem on the way home.

The anti-invasion campaign continued on the night of the 7/8th, with operations against concentrations of barges in the occupied ports and aerodromes. Ninety-two aircraft were committed to the night's endeavours, most of them against barges, and they included Fairey Battles operated by a number of 1 Group squadrons. 5 Group detailed twenty-nine Hampdens to attack Ostend, 61 Squadron responsible for five of them, which departed Hemswell between 20.28 and 20.36 and set course via corridor "G" towards the mouth of the Scheldt, before turning to the west and running in on the target. A mist lay over the area, and light from a quarter moon reflected upon it to decrease visibility, but the main impediment to target identification and assessment of results was the hostility of the flak and searchlight defences. Although the searchlight glare blinded the attacking crews, the beams did, at least, provide an indication of the whereabouts of the target, and the crews of P/Os Paape and Stewart and Sgt Blakeman dropped their bombs among harbour buildings without identifying barges or any other specific features, and were able to report fires. P/O Langford and crew carried out a successful run across the target only to suffer the frustration of a hang-up.

For the eighth day in a row, 61 Squadron crews were called to briefing on the 8th to learn of their part in the night's activities, which were to involve 133 aircraft attacking ports, and were told that they would be going to Hamburg in company with forty-two others to attack a specific dockyard installation, D2, possibly a capital ship, located some 500 yards from the Blohm & Voss shipyards on a heading of 120° from its centre. For any unable to locate the primary target, the alternative was invasion barges in the port of Delfzijl on Holland's north-eastern coast. Eight Hampdens were loaded with either four 500-pounders or six 250-pounders plus incendiaries and dispatched from Hemswell between 20.29 and 20.49. The standard route to Germany's second city involved skirting the chain of the Frisian Islands to make landfall on the Schleswig-Holstein coast, before running in from the north. An alternative was to pinpoint on Scharhörn island north of the mouth of the Elbe, thence to follow the river's course into the heart of the city, usually under the constant attention of searchlights and flak from both banks. P/O Gibson and crew turned back from a position over the North Sea after a member of the crew became unwell, leaving the others to locate the primary target and carry out an attack on the general area in the face of an intense searchlight and flak defence. Some crews observed bomb bursts through the glare and others not, and having fulfilled their brief, they had to contend with an electrical storm as they made their way home over the North Sea. At debriefing, P/O Wooldridge and crew reported that they had shot up an aerodrome located to the north-west of Hamburg, probably at Fuhlsbüttel.

The operation was repeated on the following night by twenty-one Hampdens, including four representing 61 Squadron containing the crews of F/Ls Baskett and How, P/O Langford and F/Sgt Saunders. They departed Hemswell between 20.03 and 20.10 and flew initially into challenging weather conditions, which improved as the target drew near, but intense and accurate anti-aircraft fire accompanied the force from the coast to Hamburg. This may have been responsible for the loss of an engine, which persuaded F/L Baskett and crew to drop their bombs on Cuxhaven as they headed home. The others reached and bombed the target and dispensed "razzle", although in the cramped crew positions in the Hampden fuselage, F/L How's rear gunner was too big to be able to release all of his tins through the chute. For the second night running, returning crews had to negotiate electrical storms, which affected radio communications and made it difficult to obtain navigational fixes.

All four 5 Group operational stations were called into action on the 10th to provide between them twenty-one Hampdens for operations against invasion barges at Calais and Ostend, while

Hemswell also provided three to conduct mining sorties in the Deodar garden in the Gironde estuary. The 61 Squadron crews of P/Os Gibson and Stewart took off at 19.50 and 19.52 bound for the Bassin-Carnot at Calais, and they were followed into the air at 20.02 and 20.06 by the crews of P/O Paape and Sgt Blakeman with a much longer round trip ahead of them. Two layers of cloud over Calais separated the crews from the target, one at 2,500 feet and the other at 6,000 feet, which tempted P/O Stewart and crew to descend to 1,200 feet, from where they had a clear view of the barges and the shower of debris, explosions and fires that followed the burst of their bombs. P/O Gibson and crew also delivered an attack but from a height that prevented an observation of the outcome. Meanwhile, more than four hundred miles to the south, the crews of P/O Paape and Sgt Blakeman planted their vegetables from below broken cloud at 1,500 feet and returned from uneventful sorties lasting eight-hours-forty minutes and seven-hours-twenty minutes respectively.

Hemswell, Lindholme and Scampton detailed twenty-one Hampdens between them on the 11th to return to D2 in Hamburg, 61 Squadron briefing six crews and dispatching them between 19.12 and 19.21 with W/C Sheen and S/L England the senior pilots on duty. The latch on S/L England's sliding hood would not engage and although he battled on towards the target, the icy blast created intolerable cold for the crew and on reaching the Frisian Island of Wangerooge, the bombs were dropped on the aerodrome and a course set for home. The others were able to deliver an attack and observed fires breaking out, before heading for areas east and north of the city to dispense "razzles".

The weather caused 5 Group operations on the 12th to be cancelled, and this was the first time since the start of the month that 61 Squadron remained entirely on the ground. On the 13th Hemswell and Scampton were called upon to provide ten Hampdens each for operations against invasion craft at Boulogne and Ostend respectively, for which 61 Squadron responded with five for the crews of F/L How, P/Os de Mestre and Langford, F/Sgt Saunders and Sgt Harrison. They took off between 21.00 and 21.13 and all reached the target to find low cloud and intense searchlight activity accompanied by a hostile flak defence, through which four crews were able to deliver an attack and observe bursts all across the port area. X2922 failed to return with the crew of F/L How DFC after crashing in the sea with no survivors, and the loss of this highly experienced crew would be felt keenly by the squadron and station communities. One of the gunners, Sgt Dickenson, was a holder of the coveted DFM.

It was similar fare on the following night when the ports of Calais, Ostend and Dunkerque were the targets for thirty Hampdens from all four operational stations. While each of their aircraft were being loaded with six 250-pounders and two anti-submarine bombs, 61 Squadron briefed the crews of S/L England and P/Os Earl, Webster and Wooldridge for Calais and those of S/L Kydd, P/Os Gibson and Massey and Sgts Blakeman, Cooper, Oakley and Wathey for Dunkerque, before sending them on their way between 20.25 and 21.22. Bright moonlight prevailed in the target areas, but searchlight glare, intense anti-aircraft fire and icing conditions contributed to the challenge of locating the aiming points. At Calais, S/L England was blinded by an iced-over windscreen and searchlight dazzle, and after four unsuccessful runs across the target took his bombs home. P/O Webster lost his instruments, which robbed him of control of the Hampden at 5,000 feet, and before it could be regained, the navigator, Sgt Bissett, baled out. The rear gunner took over navigation duties as they jettisoned the bombs into the sea and limped home. The crews of P/Os Earl and Wooldridge carried out accurate attacks, hitting barges as light flak shells burst all around them, and each returned with splinter damage. The Dunkerque element faced similar challenges, but all came through the cauldron of fire and made it home.

The Battle of Britain reached its climax on the 15th, and although skirmishes would continue into October, the decision had already been taken by Hitler to abandon Einsatz Seelöwe, Operation Sealion, and prepare instead for an assault on Russia in the coming summer. That night, thirty-three Hampdens from Scampton and Waddington were detailed for an operation against invasion barges at Antwerp, while 61 Squadron made ready three, two for mining duties in the Eglantine garden in the Elbe estuary and one to target the marshalling yards at Osnabrück. The gardening crews of F/Sgt Saunders and P/O de Mestre were first away at 20.00 and 20.04 respectively and were followed into the air at 20.21 by Sgt Harrison and crew, by which time F/Sgt Saunders and crew were back on the ground because of engine failure. It seems that the Harrison crew reached their destination but were thwarted by ten-tenths cloud and dropped their bombs on railway installations at Rheine, some twenty miles to the west, as they headed for home. P/O de Mestre and crew fulfilled their mining brief and reported flak from the Frisian Islands and Scharhörn, which was in contrast to the experience of the Harrison crew, who reported much reduced defensive activity at Osnabrück.

The 17th brought Bomber Command's greatest commitment of aircraft to date in a single night of 197, approximately two-thirds of them assigned to operations against invasion craft in the occupied ports. The 5 Group ORB is unclear, but it seems that Scampton's effort was directed at port facilities and invasion craft in the Scheldt ports, while the other stations focused on Antwerp. 61 Squadron contributed five crews, that of P/O Stewart to attack vessels in the inner town quays, while Sgt Blakeman and crew went for basins to the north of the town and the crews of F/Sgt Saunders and P/Os Massey and Paape concentrated on Z11, Antwerp docks. They departed Hemswell between 22.57 and 23.08 and all reached the target area, where they met unfavourable weather conditions in which precision was not possible, and although four reported bombing in the general area, the number of barges destroyed could not be ascertained. P/O Stewart and crew could not identify Antwerp, and their bombs were dropped without effect on the mole at Zeebrugge.

Another busy night for the Command on the 18th involved 174 aircraft, the majority to target Channel ports and the rest to attack railway installations in Germany. Hemswell launched seventeen Hampdens, eight of them belonging to 61 Squadron, which took off between 19.30 and 19.46 with no senior pilots on duty. All reached the target and carried out attacks, which caused fires and a number of explosions, but it proved impossible to assess the level of damage through the glare and smoke. On return, four crews managed to land before a warning was issued for others to remain airborne because of enemy intruder activity in the area, and it was some ninety minutes before the all-clear was given to enable them to land safely.

5 Group detailed thirty-seven Hampdens on the 19th to send against the Dortmund-Ems Canal, shipping and barges at Ostend and Flushing and for mining duties in the Deodar garden in the Gironde estuary. Ostend was the destination for five 61 Squadron crews, which departed Hemswell between 01.00 and 01.36 with S/L England the senior pilot on duty, only for P4401 to crash on take-off in the hands of Sgt Harrison. Apparently, the aircraft and crew suffered only superficial damage, and Sgt Blakeman and crew were drafted in to make up the numbers. They arrived in the target area to encounter adverse weather conditions in the form of thick cloud between 2,000 and 8,000 feet, with mist below and persistent drizzle. and only the crews of P/Os de Mestre and Stewart were able to carry out an attack. They chanced upon breaks in the cloud and delivered

their bombs from 3,500 and 1,000 feet respectively, the latter during their third pass, while the former reported their incendiaries causing fires along the new tidal harbour.

The Hemswell squadrons detailed ten Hampdens each for operations on the 20th, 61 squadron assigning four to mining duties in the Beech garden off St-Nazaire and six to an attack on Antwerp docks. The former element, consisting of the crews of P/Os Massey and D'Arcy-Wright, F/Sgt Saunders and Sgt Harrison took off first between 21.00 and 21.07 and all reached the target area, where three planted their vegetables according to brief, while the Saunders crew accidentally dropped a 250-pounder instead. There is no mention of a second attempt to release the mine, leading to the conclusion that an electrical fault in the circuitry was responsible. The bombing section departed Hemswell between 23.01 and 23.19 and soon lost the services of P/O Earl and crew to a wireless issue, leaving the others to complete the short hop across the Channel and, in unhelpful weather conditions of heavy cloud, carry out an attack on dock installations, basins and vessels.

Berlin had been posted as the main target for forty-five Hampdens on the 21st, but adverse weather conditions caused a cancellation and the 5 Group effort was reduced to eight Hampdens from Scampton and seven from Lindholme with Ostend as their destination and an alternative of Dunkerque. On the following night, thirty Hampden crews were briefed for operations against the ports of Ostend, Boulogne, Le Havre, Flushing and Antwerp, and it was to Ostend docks that the 61 Squadron crews of P/Os Earl and Wooldridge were assigned with the nearby aerodrome and Flushing docks as alternative targets. They departed Hemswell at 02.20 and 02.35, each carrying six 250-pounders and incendiaries, and found conditions in the target area to be ideal with moonlight streaming from clear skies. Although the barges themselves were not visible, the outline of the harbour provided a strong refence and the Wooldridge crew reported debris, presumably from barges, being catapulted into the air.

The Berlin operation was reinstated on the 23rd and a force of 129 Hampdens, Wellingtons and Whitleys assembled to attack eighteen specific targets, made up of seven railway yards, six electrical power stations, three gasworks and two aero-engine and aircraft component factories. It was unique at this stage of the war to focus the entire strength of an operation on a single city, but in time it would become clear that such a concentration of bombing was the most effective way to achieve the desired results. 5 Group contributed forty-five Hampdens from all four operational stations, 61 squadron launching seven into the night sky between 21.25 and 21.38 with P/Os de Mestre, Langford and Paape the commissioned pilots on duty. Their objective was the electrical power station at Klingenburg, a south-eastern district, but first they had to find Berlin through the heavy cloud that persisted for the entire outward flight. Sgt Cooper and crew became hopelessly lost over enemy territory and abandoned their sortie, while P/O Langford and crew were in a brand-new aircraft, X2912, which consumed far too much petrol, and with no prospect of completing the round-trip, bombed Delmenhorst aerodrome to the west of Bremen. Over Berlin itself, the cloud prevented light from the waning moon from getting through and P/O Paape and crew were unable to pick out the power station, locating instead the aerodrome at nearby Tempelhof and bombing the hangars. The others claimed to have attacked the primary target and P/O de Mestre's gunners silenced three flak guns in the Berlin defence area, while Sgt Harrison and crew strafed a searchlight on Schiphol aerodrome on the way home and knocked it out. They also carried "razzles", which were dispensed over an area to the north of Hannover and Magdeburg.

A return to the anti-invasion campaign on the 24th called upon 5 Group to detail thirteen Hampdens from Scampton and Hemswell to attack the harbour lock, barges and shipping at Le Havre, while ten others from Hemswell and Lindholme targeted Calais. 61 Squadron briefed the crews of Sgts Hills and Oakley for Calais, and the latter took off safely at 23.03, while the former, in X2911, collided with P/O Stewart's P4397, presumably during the take-off run, and crashed in flames, killing the pilot and slightly injuring the other crew members. The accident left just the crews of P/Os Massey and D'Arcy-Wright to take off for Le Havre at 23.50 and 00.22, and they returned safely along with the Oakley crew to report fulfilling their briefs. P4397 would be returned to flying condition and continue serving as training aircraft with 14 O.T.U.

The Berlin power stations B56 and B57 were briefed out as the targets for twenty-one Hampden crews from Lindholme, Scampton and Waddington on the 25th, but in the event, the Lindholme element of four was prevented from taking off because of enemy intruders operating near Bircham Newton, the forward base in use. Hemswell detailed two Hampdens from each squadron to attack marshalling yards at Osnabrück and Trier, 61 Squadron's P/Os Wooldridge and Young assigned to the former and taking off at 00.25 and 00.29. The Wooldridge crew arrived on target first and watched as their bombs fell in a stick across the yards, flinging debris into the air, setting off explosions and bringing down a tall chimney. The Young crew followed up, noting the effect of the Wooldridge crew's attack, and flew across the aiming point in the opposite direction to add to the destruction.

5 Group divided its forces on the 25th, sending eight Hampdens from Hemswell and four from Waddington to attack the heavy cruiser, Scharnhorst, which was at berth in the Krupp-Germania shipyard in Kiel. This magnificent vessel, which entered service in January 1939, displaced 38,700 tons fully loaded, and boasted a length of 771 feet, with an armament of nine eleven-inch guns arranged in three triple turrets. During an engagement in June 1940, in which she sank the aircraft carrier, HMS Glorious, she was damaged by a torpedo from the sinking destroyer, HMS Acasta, and would spend the next six months at Kiel under repair. Another 5 Group effort on this night involved six more Hemswell crews taking another swipe at M25A, the newer of the twin aqueducts of Dortmund-Ems Canal north of Münster, while seven from Lindholme continued the anti-invasion campaign at Calais. Finningley in Yorkshire had now become an operational station after Operational Training Units (O.T.Us) took responsibility for training, allowing 106 Squadron to be reassigned from a Group Pool training function to the front-line, and on this night would take care of gardening duties.

61 Squadron divided its eight participants equally between the two targets, sending them on their way together between 20.02 and 20.34 with S/L Kydd the senior pilot on duty and leading the M25A section. The ORB is not clear as to which target individual crews were assigned but specifically links S/L Kydd and crew to M25 and P/O Stewart and crew to Scharnhorst. Clues suggest that P/Os Langford and Earl and Sgt Cooper were also Kiel-bound, while P/Os Gibson and D'Arcy-Wright and their crews had M25A as their destination. The Gibson crew returned early because of a gyro issue, the same problem that would prevent P/O D'Arcy-Wright and crew from delivering an attack, despite probably reaching the target. The weather conditions over Kiel were unhelpful with ten-tenths cloud topping out at 6,000 feet and penetrated by intense but inaccurate flak, and only P/O Stewart and crew appear to have carried out an attack, the Form 541 suggesting that they probably hit the Scharnhorst with a single bomb. P/O Langford and crew brought their bombs home after failing to locate the target, Sgt Cooper and crew returned but nothing about their sortie was recorded and Australian, P/O Earl, and crew failed to return in

P2090. Eventually, the Swedish authorities revealed that the Hampden had been damaged by flak and destroyed in an attempted crash-landing at Oresund on Sweden's western coast with no survivors. S/L Kydd and crew reported straddling the Dortmund-Ems Canal and Sgt Harrison and crew dropped their bombs on the nearby town of Rheine as a last resort target.

The anti-invasion campaign continued on the 27th, when twenty-five Hampden crews were briefed at Scampton, Hemswell and Lindholme to target barges, motor torpedo boats and U-boots at Lorient, which, early in the coming year, would be the site of a massive civil engineering project to construct three huge concrete U-Boot facilities. The 61 Squadron crews of P/O Gibson and Sgts Cowan, Oakley and Wathey were briefed for an aiming point on the eastern bank of the River Scorff between Pont de Caudan and the railway bridge and departed Hemswell between 18.52 and 19.04, each carrying eight 250-pounders. The night was very dark, but clear, and the water in the inlet was easily discernible as all four dropped their bombs on dockside installations and left fires burning to give the impression of a successful attack.

Hemswell, Scampton and Waddington were in action on the 28th, detailing between them six Hampdens for M25A, thirteen for anti-invasion operations at Fecamp and Le Havre and six for marshalling yards at Hamm and Mannheim. The crew of P/O Massey was the sole 61 squadron representative and was briefed at Scampton before taking off at 00.45 bound for Hamm, the highly important and well-defended railway hub on the north-eastern fringe of the Ruhr. Weather conditions over the Continent were unhelpful and the Massey crew was unable to see the ground at any point until homebound, when a gap in the cloud cover revealed a stretch of railway track near Ommen in northern Holland, which was bombed as a last-resort target. The intention had been to land at Hemswell, but the starboard undercarriage leg would not lock and it was decided to return instead to Scampton. P/O Massey carried out a masterful landing, keeping the starboard wing level until the last minute, when it scraped the ground causing minimal damage.

The operation against the Hamm marshalling yards was to be repeated on the 29th and to it were added the Eifeltor and Gremberg marshalling yards situated respectively on the western and eastern sides of the Rhine to the south of Cologne city centre. 61 Squadron briefed the crews of P/Os de Mestre, Stewart and Young and Sgt Harrison for Hamm, P/O Paape and Sgt Cooper for Gremberg and P/O D'Arcy-Wright for Eifeltor and dispatched them from Hemswell between 19.57 and 22.00 on another night of unfavourable weather conditions and extreme darkness. The de Mestre crew was back on the ground within forty minutes because of W/T transmitter failure, while, in the darkness, P/O Young and crew mistook a junction a mile north of the main yards for the target and hit it with their bombs. Sgt Harrison and crew searched in vain for the primary target, before giving up and seeking out an alternative, which they found in a large factory at Kamen, some eight miles to the south-west. Only P/O Stewart and crew found the target in the light of flares dropped by a 144 Squadron aircraft, and they watched their bombs impact the eastern edge of the yards. Sgt Cooper and crew failed to reach Gremberg because of an engine issue and P/O Paape and crew searched for an hour before abandoning the sortie and bringing their ordnance home. P/O D'Arcy-Wright and crew enjoyed the greatest success among the 61 Squadron participants, attacking the vast spread of the Eifeltor yards in company with a 144 Squadron aircraft in the face of a hostile flak defence, and leaving fires raging.

On the last night of the month, seventeen Hampdens from Hemswell, Lindholme and Scampton were detailed for a raid on the Chancellery building in Berlin, identified in the 61 Squadron ORB as H41, which was, in fact, the Air Ministry building situated in Wilhelmsstrasse. 61 Squadron briefed the crews of Sgt Oakley and the newly promoted F/O de Mestre, and they were preceded into the air at 20.03 and 20.05 by the crews of Sgt Cowan and P/O Gibson, bound for mining duties in the Eglantine garden in the Elbe estuary. The Berlin duo departed Hemswell at 21.35 and 21.43 respectively and after around two hours the Oakley crew turned back and bombed the docks at Antwerp as a last resort target. F/O de Mestre and crew were among ten to reach Germany's capital city, but in cloudy conditions and extreme darkness, they failed to identify the briefed aiming point and attacked the Klingenburg electrical power station as an alternative. On return, P4396 struck the boundary hedge and tore off an undercarriage leg and the landing was a repeat of P/O Massey's of two nights earlier.

During the course of the month the squadron took part in operations involving thirty-seven targets undertaken on twenty-seven nights, and in the process dispatched 131 sorties for the loss of four Hampdens, two crews and two other crew members including a pilot.

October 1940

Ninety-nine aircraft were detailed by the Command to open the new month's account on the 1st and among 5 Group targets was the synthetic oil refinery at Wesseling, or to give it its full name, the Union Rheinische Braunkohlen-Kraftstoff A.G, situated on the west bank of the Rhine in the southern reaches of Cologne, for which Scampton and Waddington provided fifteen Hampdens.

The target for nineteen crews from Hemswell, Lindholme and Waddington on the 2nd was an oil refinery in Hamburg (A8), and as often was the case at this early stage of the war, an operation might be spread over an extended period with individual squadrons deciding for themselves routes and timings. On this night, the arrival in the target area of the Waddington Hampdens would be some five hours after the Lindholme crews had attacked and two behind those from Hemswell. Barrage balloons were reported to be tethered at 6,000 feet over Wilhelmshaven, and this inconvenience had to be added to the eight to ten-tenths cloud with haze below, and the usual intense searchlight and flak activity along the course of the Elbe leading towards the heart of Germany's second city. 61 Squadron briefed seven crews for the night's action, three to learn that they would be undertaking mining duties in the Quince garden, which encompassed the northern reaches of Kiel Bay from the southern tip of Langeland Island, while the remaining four would be targeting Hamburg's Wilhelmsburg oil plant. The crews of P/Os Massey, Langford and Stewart departed Hemswell in that order between 19.01 and 19.21, and all were successful in planting their vegetables in the allotted positions. On the way home, the Massey and Stewart crews dropped their wing-mounted 250-pounders on aerodromes on Fohr Island, Schleswig and another unidentified location. Meanwhile, the Hamburg-bound crews of the newly promoted F/O Paape, P/Os D'Arcy-Wright and Young and Sgt Cooper took off between 21.06 and 21.21 on a night of challenging weather conditions and those reaching the target area found it to be cloud-covered. P/O D'Arcy-Wright and crew returned early because of a W/T issue, while the others reached Hamburg but were unable to see the ground and withheld their bombs. On the way home F/O Paape and crew jettisoned theirs into the North Sea, Sgt Cooper and crew brought theirs home and P/O Young and crew attacked Borkum aerodrome, where night flying was in progress.

In a low-key start to the month, the Hampden brigade was employed sparingly over the ensuing nights as 2 Group took the strain, and it would be the 5th before 5 Group ventured forth again with thirty Hampdens distributed between the Nordstern oil plant at Gelsenkirchen, marshalling yards north and south of the Ruhr and gardening duties. This was the day on which Sir Charles Portal relinquished his post as Commander-in-Chief of Bomber Command and took up his new appointment as Chief of the Air Staff. He was succeeded by ACM Sir Richard Peirse, whose tenure was to be dogged by the inadequacies of the equipment available to him and the increasing and often unrealistic demands from on high. The 61 Squadron crews of S/L Kydd, P/Os Gibson and D'Arcy-Wright and Sgts Cowan and Harrison departed Hemswell between 18.55 and 19.09, and to reach the Elbe estuary had to pass through ice-bearing low cloud and negotiate gale-force winds. The crews of S/L Kydd, P/O Gilbert and Sgt Cowan succeeded in planting their vegetables in or close to the allotted area, but the Harrison crew was unable to establish a pinpoint after a considerable effort and jettisoned theirs. On return, some aircraft were diverted away from Hemswell because of mud, and X2920 crashed on the Yorkshire Moors near the 4 Group station at Leeming, killing P/O D'Arcy-Wright and his crew.

On the 7th, 5 Group issued orders to Hemswell, Scampton and Waddington to prepare nineteen Hampdens between them for operations against marshalling yards at Osnabrück, Soest and Hamm located north of the Ruhr, and Gremberg in Cologne to the south and Mannheim and Ehrang further south still. The 61 Squadron crews of P/Os Langford and Stewart and Sgt Cooper were assigned to the last-mentioned, situated in the Rhineland-Palatinate region in west-central Germany close to the Luxembourg frontier, and took off between 19.32 and 19.38 with a standard bomb load and in accordance with standard practice at the time, tins of "razzles" to dispense over wooded areas, of which there are many in Germany. Only P/O Stewart and crew were able to identify and bomb the target, while the others attacked Diest aerodrome in Belgium on their way to exit enemy territory over the Scheldt.

Orders were received at Waddington and Scampton on the 8th to prepare for an operation that night against the Bismarck-class Battleship Tirpitz, which was in the final stages of fitting-out at a floating dock in Wilhelmshaven. The Admiralty was acutely conscious of the threat posed by Germany's mighty battleships Bismarck and Tirpitz, and there was a constant pressure on Bomber Command to deal with them before they began their careers as surface raiders. Laid down in the Kriegsmarinewerft yards in 1936, Tirpitz had been launched in the spring of 1939, and, once ready for sea trials in early 1941, she would be two thousand tons heavier than her sister ship. Despite a gallant effort by all involved in the face of an intense searchlight and flak defence, the attacks failed to result in damage to the vessel.

The following night brought focus upon the Krupp empire, which at this stage of the war was centred upon the Ruhr city of Essen and would feature prominently in Bomber Command's target list, particularly from early 1942. 5 Group detailed nineteen Hampdens from Hemswell, Lindholme and Scampton, 61 Squadron contributing six of its own, which took off between 18.17 and 18.42 with F/Os de Mestre and Paape the senior pilots on duty. They flew out, initially, into fine weather conditions and soon lost the services of F/O de Mestre and crew to W/T failure, while the others pressed on in excellent visibility that enabled them to pinpoint on Vlieland and map-read inland to Elburg on the eastern shore of the Ijsselmeer. Shortly afterwards, however, they ran into a bank of ten-tenths ice-bearing cloud some fifty miles west of the target, which persuaded the crews of P/Os Gilbert and Young to turn back and jettison their bombs. The crews of P/O Massey and Sgt Harrison were contending with a snowstorm when they opted to bomb alternative targets, the former a searchlight concentration at Rheinberg and the latter Haamstede aerodrome on Zeeland Island in the Scheldt. P/O Paape and crew, meanwhile, overcame the challenges, making five attempts to push through the ice-belt near Utrecht, before reaching Essen to deliver an attack through partial cloud from 6,500 feet and observe bursts but no detail.

The promise of bright moonlight on the 10th may have been a consideration in scheduling another assault on the battleship Tirpitz at Wilhelmshaven, for which thirteen Hampdens were made ready, nine at Waddington and four at Lindholme. A simultaneous operation would be conducted against the Krupp-Germania shipyard in Kiel by eleven 49 Squadron Hampdens from Scampton, probably with the intention of hitting the heavy cruiser, Scharnhorst, while Hemswell attended to mining duties in the approaches to the port in the Forget-me-not garden. The 61 Squadron crews of Sgts Cowan and Cooper and P/Os Stewart and Gibson took off in that order between 00.32 and 01.08 and lost the services of the Gibson crew to intercom failure. The others benefitted from favourable conditions, but Sgt Cowan and crew were late arriving in the target area and with daylight approaching dropped their mine early in the Endive garden at the southern end of the Little Belt. The crews of P/O Stewart and Sgt Cooper planted their vegetables according to brief and the former dropped their two 250-pounders on an aerodrome seven miles east-north-east of Husum.

There is no mention in the ORB that W/C Sheen was succeeded as commanding officer on the 11th by S/L George Valentine, who, in time, would be elevated in rank to acting wing commander. The pursuit of Tirpitz continued on the 11th at the hands of five Hampdens from Lindholme, while another one joined five from Hemswell to target the Blohm & Voss shipyards at Hamburg. Under cover of this, three Finningley crews conducted mining sorties in the Eglantine garden at the mouth of the Elbe estuary, while on the eastern side of Schleswig-Holstein, a dozen Hemswell Hampdens were to attack the Germania Werft shipyard in Kiel, a few miles south of the Kiel Canal, where nine Scampton crews were to carry out mining duties in the Lettuce garden. 61 Squadron briefed the crews of P/Os Clemerson, Gibson, Gilbert and Young and Sgt Oakley for Hamburg and those of F/O Paape and P/O Massey for Kiel and dispatched them from Hemswell between 19.06 and 20.10. They encountered challenging weather conditions outbound, with ten-tenths cloud and icing above 5,000 feet, and this persuaded the crews of P/O Clemerson, who were on their maiden sortie, and P/O Gibson to attack Borkum aerodrome as a last-resort target. The crews of P/Os Gilbert and Young and Sgt Oakley bombed the Hamburg area in the face of intense anti-aircraft fire, but saw little of the impact, and P/O Gilbert's P2082 was thrown into a spin and plummeted from 7,500 down to 3,000 feet, during which the order to bale out was issued. Only the navigator had time to comply before control was regained and one of the gunners took over his duties for the homeward flight. At Kiel the Massey crew mistook Eckernförde Fjord for Kiel Fjord, while the Paape crew bombed Wilhelmshaven on the way home.

The final operations against invasion craft were notified to stations on the 12th and this night would also see the final deployment in Bomber Command service of the Fairey Battle. Elsewhere, sixteen crews at Scampton and two at Hemswell were briefed for an operation that night against an aluminium factory producing aircraft components in the Herringen district of Hamm, which is referred to in the 61 Squadron ORB as the Wintershall A.G Magnesium works. In addition, ten crews at Waddington were informed that they would be attacking the Krupp complex at Essen. The crews of Sgt Harrison and P/O Stewart took off at 18.40 and flew out in generally reasonable conditions to arrive at the target over six-tenths cloud with haze below. The Harrison crew descended to 3,000 feet and although unable to identify the specific factory buildings, pinpointed on the road-rail crossing at Herringen and delivered an attack that set off many small fires and probably damaged the railway. P/O Stewart and crew attacked from 4,000 feet and the rear gunner reported a large, white explosion apparently emanating from the works and followed by fires.

The Admiralty continued to obsess about Tirpitz, in response to which, 5 Group detailed thirty-five Hampdens from Hemswell, Lindholme, Waddington and Scampton on the 13th, and briefed their crews for a return to Wilhelmshaven. 61 Squadron briefed seven crews, those of Sgt Loadman and P/O Webb for their first sorties and sent them on their way from Hemswell between 20.36 and 20.47 with F/O Paape the senior pilot on duty. Having reached the mid-point of the North Sea crossing, they ran into one of the enormous fronts that frequently barred the route into north-western Germany, characterised by ice-bearing and storm-laden towering cumulonimbus cloud, which were a nightmare to negotiate and often too enormous to circumnavigate or climb over. The icing layer on this night extended from 6,000 to 12,000 feet, with rainstorms from 1,000 to 12,000 feet, which prevented most crews from reaching the target. Only the freshman crew of P/O Webb of the 61 Squadron element managed to locate and bomb the primary target in company with just five crews from other squadrons, but it was not possible to ascertain where the bombs fell. A few of the other 61 Squadron crews stooged around in the target area for a considerable time without locating the aiming point, and these either jettisoned their bombs or dumped them on targets of opportunity on the way home.

5 Group detailed twenty Hampdens on the 14th for another shot that night at H41, the Air Ministry building in Berlin's Wilhelmsstrasse, on a night when cities in eastern Germany were targeted by fifty aircraft from other groups. 61 Squadron contributed three Hampdens containing the crews of P/Os Massey and Young and Sgt Cooper, which departed Hemswell between 22.40 and 22.46 in surprisingly favourable weather conditions with brilliant moonlight. However, fog was encountered at the German coast, which caused P/O Massey and crew to lose their bearings and stumble around the Schleswig-Holstein coastal region until running out of time to continue, at which point they unloaded the contents of the bomb bay in a stick across the aerodrome on the Island of Sylt. The Young and Cooper crews reached the target area to carry out an attack, encountering up to ten-tenths cloud and haze, which required them to spend time either circling or making dummy runs from a variety of directions in order to familiarise themselves with the lay of the land and to establish the best method of attack. They had to face intense searchlight and flak activity, and one shell exploded so close to the Cooper crew's Hampden that it rotated through 360 degrees. They arrived back at Hemswell after sorties lasting seven-and-a-half to more than eight hours, and among debriefing reports was mention of barrage balloons tethered at up to 15,000 feet.

Germany's oil industry featured prominently on the 15th, when 134 aircraft were detailed for wide-ranging targets in Germany and the Channel ports, 5 Group directing the bulk of its effort of thirty-three Hampdens against oil targets in Magdeburg, principally the Rothensee plant that they had attacked last in early September and another unidentified one coded A160. 61 Squadron briefed six crews and dispatched them from Hemswell between 17.36 and 17.56 with F/O de Mestre the senior pilot on duty and four 500-pounders in each bomb bay. All reached the target area to find ten-tenths cloud with haze below and only the crews of P/O Gilbert and Sgt Loadsman identified the briefed aiming point to carry out an attack, observing bursts but no detail. The crews of F/O de Mestre and P/O Stewart backtracked to the German/Dutch frontier and attacked the Salzbergen oil refinery, while Sgt Oakley and crew bombed marshalling yards in Hannover and P/O Gibson and crew the seaplane base at De Mok in The Hague.

Twenty-four Hampdens were made ready at Hemswell and Waddington on the 16th for an operation that night against the oil refinery at Leuna, near Merseburg, west of Leipzig, while Scampton prepared a dozen to mine the waters of the Deodar garden in the Gironde estuary and then to attack U-Boots in their base a few miles further south in Bordeaux itself. Eight of Hemswell's fourteen Hampdens belonged to 61 Squadron, and they took off between 17.58 and 18.50 with no pilots on duty above the rank of pilot officer as the senior officers continued to take a back seat. P/O Langford and crew were back on the ground after thirty-seven minutes because of engine trouble, leaving the others to press on in reasonable weather conditions across Holland and northern Germany to the target, at which Sgt Harrison and crew were the first to arrive. After several passes, the four 500-pounders went down from 7,000 feet and were seen to burst on the north-western corner of the buildings. Sgt Cowan and crew had lost their intercom by the time that they reached the target, and this, along with the need to take evasive action, resulted in the bombs bursting some five hundred yards west of the oil plant. P/O Webb and crew failed to identify the target and found an alternative at Zeitz, situated some twenty miles to the south, while P/O Massey and crew bombed an Autobahn near Halle ten miles to the north.

Sgt Cooper and crew attacked a power station near Leuna and P/O Young and crew a factory at Markranstädt, and as for P/O Clemerson and crew, who were on just their third operation together, we will never know if they found a target. Most crews met appalling conditions as they fought their way home, and the Clemerson crew were attempting an emergency landing when X2979 crashed near Swaffham in Norfolk at 02.45 after more than eight-and-a-half hours in the air, and all on board lost their lives. Meanwhile, the Cowan crew had reached Zwolle on their way to the Ijsselmeer, when the pilot began to smell cordite, and only then, having no intercom, did he realise that they were under attack by an aircraft recorded as a ME10. Whether this is in error for 109 or 110 is uncertain, but after the gunners had emptied ten magazines each at it, it broke off the engagement, allowing the Hampden to continue its journey home. One gunner had sustained a wound to a foot and the other had the water bottle in his Mae West punctured but was not himself touched. X2989 crashed before reaching Hemswell, but the crew scrambled clear and carried their wounded crew mate to a neighbouring house where they telephoned for an ambulance.

There was little activity generally on the 18th, but 5 Group detailed nineteen Hampdens from Scampton and Lindholme to target the Bismarck at berth in Hamburg. They had to battle through ice-bearing cloud over the North Sea, and on arrival over the Elbe estuary, they encountered eight to ten-tenths cloud that severely inhibited their attempts to locate the aiming point. Only eight crews were able to release their loads on estimated positions, and it was a typically indeterminate operation at this stage of the war. The briefing of crews on the 19th came to nothing after the intended operations against the Air Ministry building in Berlin and the Aluminium works at Lünen were cancelled because of adverse weather predictions.

The operation was rescheduled for the following night and thirty Hampdens detailed, with the Air Ministry building the primary target and the M499 marshalling yards the designated alternative for the Scampton crews, while the others, including six from 61 Squadron, targeted the Lehrter railway station to the west of the city centre and the Siemens & Halske A.G works. These were, of course, a euphemistic cover for an area raid on the city centre in retaliation for German attacks on British cities, as, according to pre-war principles, it was still morally unacceptable to specifically target civilian areas, despite the fact that the Luftwaffe had bombed Warsaw and Rotterdam indiscriminately and was currently engaged in a fifty-seven-consecutive day and night assault on London. As far as the British public was concerned, the RAF was retaliating by attacking military and war-production targets, which, in reality, was beyond its capability and it would be a further seventeen months before the pretence officially ended.

Thirty Hampdens were made ready, while the Whitley boys of 4 Group were briefed to venture across the Alps into Italy and to Pilsen in Czechoslovakia. The 61 Squadron element departed Hemswell between 23.59 and 00.13 with pilots of pilot officer rank taking the lead and all reached the target area, where only the crews of Sgt Oakley and P/Os Langford and Stewart were able to identify and bomb their assigned aiming points and observe nothing more than bursts and a fire or two. P/O Gilbert and crew dumped their bombs in the Ijsselmeer on the way home, while Sgt Loadsman and crew bombed Neuruppin aerodrome to the north-west of Berlin and Sgt Harrison and crew went for Hamburg docks. Weather conditions on return were appalling and required the Hemswell crews to divert, and as the crew of P/O Stewart came in over The Wash with X2906 flying on fumes, both engines cut and an outstandingly good wheels-up landing was carried out in a field near King's Lynn without damage to the aircraft or crew.

5 Group airfields were largely fogbound over the ensuing two days, and the local watering holes did good business until the 23rd, when Lindholme, Waddington and Scampton were alerted to that night's operation against the Rothensee oil refinery in Magdeburg, while Hemswell targeted the Deurag-Nerag plant at Misburg near Hannover with ten aircraft. The names of two senior 61 Squadron officers appeared on the order of battle for this operation, S/L England and the newly-arrived S/L Oldfield, who were accompanied by the crews of F/O Paape and Sgt Cowan as they departed Hemswell between 00.56 and 01.15. All reached the target area to encounter ten-tenths cloud concealing the ground, but the flak barrage guided most to the approximate location of the refinery and only S/L England and crew failed to locate it. "Razzles" were dispensed over parts of northern Germany from Hannover to the Steinhuder Lake and Dümmersee and S/L England and crew bombed an unidentified aerodrome on the way home, enduring extreme discomfort after their heating system failed. In general, on this night, conditions proved too testing for most to locate their primary targets and a variety of alternative targets of opportunity received the bombs.

Orders arrived at Hemswell and Scampton on the following day to prepare twenty-two Hampdens for a return to the Misburg oil plant, and 61 Squadron responded with six of its own, some, if not all, including a 1,000-pounder in the bomb load. They departed Hemswell between 00.40 and 01.07 and encountered conditions similar to twenty-four hours earlier with ten-tenths low cloud over northern Germany preventing all but the crews of P/Os Gilbert and Langford from identifying and attacking the primary target. The others found alternatives in the form of Cloppenburg aerodrome for P/O Young and crew, a factory at Wietmarschen to the west of Lingen for Sgt Harrison and crew, a railway crossing south of Bremen for P/O Webb and crew and railway track near Sulingen for P/O Massey and crew.

The main focus on the 25th was Germany's oil industry and shipbuilding, and 5 Group sent out orders to Hemswell, Lindholme and Scampton to prepare eighteen Hampdens to attack the Germania Werft shipyard at Kiel, while Waddington took care of the gardening requirements. 61 Squadron briefed the crews of Sgts Loadsman and Cowan and F/O Paape and dispatched them from Hemswell in that order between 17.18 and 17.35 on a night of extreme cold and severe icing conditions over the North Sea and northern Germany. The Paape crew returned after four-and-a-half hours having been defeated by icing, and two hours later the Cowan crew landed to report attacking the target in the face of a flak barrage so intense that the flashes blinded them to the fall of the bombs, and all they could report was a large fire, for which they may have been responsible.

The return of Sgt Loadsman and crew was awaited in vain, and a sea-search on the following morning by the crews of P/Os Langford and Massey and S/L England revealed no trace of X2971 and its occupants. They were among many hundreds of airmen to find a final resting place at the bottom of the Baltic and North Seas and their names are now commemorated on the Runnymede Memorial.

During the course of the 26th, nineteen Hampdens were made ready at Hemswell, Scampton and Waddington to be sent against multiple targets in Berlin, the 61 Squadron crews of P/Os Webb and Young and S/L Valentine handed a choice of targets, the Lehrter railway station, the Tempelhof station and marshalling yards, the Moabit electrical power station and the Air Ministry building. They departed Hemswell between 23.15 and 23.30 and the Webb crew was deep into enemy territory when it was discovered that they had strayed off track and now had insufficient fuel to complete the Berlin round trip. After turning back, they attacked the aerodrome at Menzendorf to the east of Lübeck and then the docks at Hamburg. P/O Young and crew reached Berlin but were unable to locate any of the assigned targets and instead bombed the BMW engine works at Spandau. S/L Valentine and crew were sitting on an extra fuel tank, which allowed them the luxury of spending thirty minutes searching for the Lehrter railway station, which they bombed successfully.

On the 27th, Scampton, Lindholme and Waddington were ordered to prepare for an attack that night on A10, the Harburg oil plant situated on the southern bank of the Elbe, while five Hemswell crews attended to mining duties in the Artichoke garden off the port of Lorient. 61 Squadron launched the crews of Sgts Harrison and Cooper and F/O Powdrell off the end of the runway in that order between 17.27 and 17.38 and lost the services of Sgt Cooper and crew after around two hours when severe icing conditions froze the artificial horizon, and the automatic pilot, "George", ceased working. The Powdrell and Harrison crews reached the target area to find ten-tenths cloud at 3,000 feet and rain below, through which they descended to plant their vegetables respectively south and west of the briefed locations in the face of a spirited flak response from shore and ship-based batteries.

Twenty-four hours later, Hamburg hosted another visit from 5 Group, ten Hampdens from Hemswell and Lindholme assigned to the Harburg oil refinery, while ten others from Scampton and Waddington targeted dock installations. The 61 Squadron crews of P/O Massey, S/L Oldfield and Sgt Cowan departed Hemswell in that order between 16.33 and 16.50 in company with three from 144 Squadron and all reached the target to encounter extreme darkness rent by the usual hostile searchlight and flak welcome. S/L Oldfield and crew made two runs across the aiming point and picked up a shrapnel splinter for their pains, and all returned safely to report bombing but, apart from fires, no detail.

On the 29th, 5 Group detailed twenty Hampdens from Scampton, Hemswell and Lindholme for a variety of targets in Berlin, including the Danziger Strasse Gas Works situated to the north-east of the city centre, the Lehrter railway station, the Klingenburg electrical power station and an oil production site at Tegel. The Berlin-bound 61 Squadron crews of P/O Webb and Sgts Harrison and Cooper departed Hemswell over an extended period between 21.37 and 00.14, while F/O Powdrell and crew took off at 23.55 for a mining sortie in the Baltic in the Daffodil garden at the southern end of The Sound. Inhospitable weather conditions prevented any from reaching their assigned targets, so Sgt Cooper and crew brought their bombs home, while those of P/O Webb and Sgt Harrison diverted to Hamburg and bombed the docks. F/O Powdrell and crew were unable to establish a pinpoint on the Drogden Lighthouse and also returned their ordnance to the station dump.

During the course of another busy month the squadron undertook twenty-two operations on nineteen nights and dispatched ninety sorties for the loss of three Hampdens and their crews.

November 1940

By the onset of November, the Battle of Britain had run its course, and the fear of invasion had been banished for the time being at least. Industrial Germany would now become the main focus of attention as the winter took hold, with oil related targets at the head of an impressive list drawn up by the Air Ministry in a new directive issued three weeks after the enthronement of C-in-C Sir Richard Peirse. 5 Group hoped soon to have a new weapon in its armoury, the Avro Manchester, a twin-engine replacement for the Hampden, which would soon be delivered to Waddington and into the hands of 207 Squadron for introduction into operational service. The squadron was reformed officially on the 1st under the command of W/C "Hettie" Hyde, who had spent August with 44 Squadron to gain operational experience. In the coming February, F/O Arthur Paape and P/O Blakeman, who had now completed their tours and were O.T.U.-bound as instructors, would be recruited, and while the Manchester proved to be hugely disappointing, its failure resulted in the development of its offspring, which became by far the war's most successful bomber.

The trend of sending small forces to wide-ranging targets continued in November, and this diluting of the effort would render the operations ineffective and of little more than nuisance value. The first targets of the new month for 5 Group were two of Berlin's many electrical power stations, for which seventeen Hampdens were detailed from Hemswell, Lindholme and Waddington on the 1st, while Scampton and Finningley took care of mining duties in the Jellyfish garden off Brest. 61 Squadron briefed the crews of P/Os Stewart and Webb and Sgts Cooper and Cowan for B58 and sent them on their way from Hemswell between 23.05 and 23.50. *(There were now two Sgt Coopers serving as pilots with the squadron, J.F, and the newly posted-in K.G.)* When P/O Webb and crew arrived at the target, the power station appeared to be already in a state of collapse and on fire, and deeming it wasteful to bomb it further, it was decided to attack the Lehrter railway station instead. The others all attacked the briefed target through haze and in the face of an intense flak barrage, which P/O Stewart described as the most ferocious he had ever faced, and the consensus among returning crews was of a successful operation.

The weather continued to challenge the raid planners, and most of the Command remained on the ground for the ensuing few nights. 5 Group detailed ten Scampton Hampdens on the 3rd and briefed their crews for a raid on the Germania Werft shipyard at Kiel, after cancelling the participation of the Lindholme and Hemswell elements, but few reached and attacked the primary target in adverse weather conditions.

It was the 5th before the other groups stirred into life again to join with 5 Group in detailing ninety-seven aircraft for operations over Germany, Italy and the occupied countries. The target for eighteen Hampdens was A78, the Braunkohle A.G oil refinery in the Rothensee district of Magdeburg, while five others from Lindholme and Hemswell were assigned to a shipyard in

Bremen and seven to gardening duties in the Willow garden off the Baltic port of Sassnitz on the island of Rügen. The Deutsche Schiff und Maschinenbau A.G shipyards in Bremen, the name of which was abbreviated to Deschimag, had been formed in the mid-twenties as a co-operation of eight shipyards to compete with Blohm & Voss in Hamburg and the Bremer Vulkan yards situated at Vegesack on the northern bank of the Weser some ten miles north-west of Bremen. The largest was the A.G Weser company, which, after six of the others had fallen by the wayside before the outbreak of war, was partnered now only by the Seebeckwerft, the entire organisation soon to become part of the Krupp empire in early 1941. 61 Squadron briefed the crew of Sgt K G Cooper for Bremen and dispatched them from Hemswell at 03.02, having already sent the Baltic-bound crews of S/L Oldfield and P/O Langford on their way at 00.14 and 00.28. The gardeners encountered adverse weather conditions and an intense defence over Schleswig-Holstein, and the Langford crew planted their vegetable in an alternative garden in Kiel Bay, probably Forget-me-not, while S/L Oldfield and crew all lost their lives when P2082 crashed in the Kiel Canal. The Cooper crew returned in broad daylight with their bomb load intact after failing to locate the designated shipyard.

The prospects for decent weather conditions were again bleak twenty-four hours later, when 5 Group dispatched twenty-five Hampdens to the twin cities of Mannheim and Ludwigshafen, which face each other from the East and West Banks respectively of the Rhine in south-central Germany. On this night, marshalling yards and a power station were the designated targets, for which the six 61 Squadron participants departed Hemswell between 01.16 and 02.09 with F/O de Mestre the senior pilot on duty. Unpleasant weather conditions in the form of sleet and snow and electrical storms over France gave way to an improved situation in the target area, despite which only the crews F/O de Mestre and P/Os Stewart and Webb identified and attacked the primary targets through cloud with indeterminate results. P/O Young and crew attacked marshalling yards at Mainz as an alternative, while the crews of P/O Gilbert and Sgt Harrison jettisoned their loads into the sea.

On the 7th, 2, 3 and 5 Groups combined to send sixty-three Blenheims, Wellingtons and Hampdens to attack the Krupp works at Essen in the heart of the Ruhr, 5 Group contributing thirty aircraft, of which just three belonged to 61 Squadron. The crew of F/L Moncrief were on their first operation since joining the squadron and they were joined by the crews of F/O Powdrell and Sgt Stevenson in the departure from Hemswell between 19.41 and 19.54. All reached the target area after crossing the North Sea and Holland over cloud, and, although Essen also lay under a protective blanket, crews were able to pick up a distinctive bend in the Rhine to the south of the target area and plot a course from there. Some were guided by fires already burning as a result of the 3 Group attack, and the 61 Squadron crews added their bombs during uneventful sorties lasting six to seven hours.

5 Group notified its four main stations of an operation on the 8th against the Pasing marshalling yards and engine sheds in the western suburbs of Munich, for which twenty-three Hampdens were made ready, while others, including the 61 Squadron crews of Sgts J F Cooper, Cowan and Harrison, were assigned to the Siemens-Schuckert electrical engineering works in Nuremberg, for which they took off between 18.35 and 18.53. A fourth 61 Squadron crew, that of P/O Hall, was briefed to attack the Eifeltor marshalling yards in Cologne and departed Hemswell at 19.28, and all reached their respective targets in favourable weather conditions to carry out an attack. Sgt Cowan's rear gunner reported direct hits on the factory, achieved through a curtain of anti-aircraft fire, some of which struck home, and when they passed over Scampton on their way back to Hemswell, the port wheel fell off, forcing Sgt Cowan to carry out a belly landing from which all

occupants walked away. A strong wind encountered on the way home blew some aircraft south of track, and when the Cooper and Harrison crews strayed over the Thames estuary, they were fired upon by the London defences, which punched a hole in each of P2144's wings. After nine hours in the air and in conditions of haze, an exhausted Sgt Harrison allowed P4399 to stall from 50 feet and land heavily, causing substantial damage to a wing but no crew casualties.

On the 10th, 5 Group ordered twenty-eight Hampdens to be made ready for a number of long-range operations that night, with destinations from Mannheim in the south to Danzig in the north-east and Merseburg (Leuna), near Liepzig, in the east. Three crews at Scampton and two at Waddington were briefed to attack military objectives in distant Danzig on the Baltic coast (now Gdansk in Poland) and to dispense nickels to the natives in celebration of Polish Independence Day on the 11th. This daunting task required a round trip of some sixteen hundred miles, a somewhat ambitious undertaking for a winter's night in 1940, although the Whitleys of 4 Group had been the first to undertake such operations a year earlier, the crews sometimes enduring sorties lasting twelve hours and more in unheated aircraft. In the event on this night, only one crew would press on to the target area, where, in the face of poor visibility, they were unable to locate either the primary or alternative targets and dropped their bombs on a railway some two-and-a-half miles away, while dispensing nickels (leaflets) over an area between Danzig and the River Vistula. They returned from their epic flight of ten hours and twenty minutes to report enduring the most difficult conditions of severe icing and a snow-covered landscape that created challenges for navigation.

Bomber Command continued to mark Polish Independence Day by sending a small but indeterminate number of aircraft to attack targets in Poland as a morale-booster for the many Poles in England, particularly those serving in the four Polish squadrons in 1 Group, which were currently in the process of converting from their Fairey Battles to Wellingtons. 61 Squadron was represented by the crew of P/O Langford, who departed Hemswell at 21.34 only to be thwarted by an oil pressure issue and have to return early.

The 5 Group targets for eighteen aircraft on the 12th were much closer to home and were oil refineries in the Ruhr, A80, the Krupp Treibstoffwerke at Wanne-Eickel, north-east of Gelsenkirchen for the Scampton and Lindholme crews, and A108, one of the Dortmund sites further to the east for Hemswell and Waddington. 61 Squadron briefed the crews of Sgt Harrison, P/O Webb and Sgt Cowan, sending them on their way from Hemswell in that order between 01.59 and 02.06 only to run into heavy cloud over the North Sea that extended beyond the target area and prevented any from positively identifying the oil plant. Sgt Harrison and crew dropped four 500-pounders on a railway track south of the Ruhr and narrowly missed, while the others jettisoned their ordnance into the North Sea on the way home.

Seventy-two aircraft took off for various targets in Germany on the night of the 13/14th, twenty-two of them Hampdens detailed for operations over Hamburg after the Lindholme element of five had been cancelled by the station commander because of poor visibility. The primary target for the 61 Squadron crews of F/L Moncrief, F/O Powdrell, P/Os Hall and Langford and Sgt K G Cooper was marshalling yards in Hamburg, and it was already the 14th by the time that they began to take off, F/L Moncrief and crew starting the ball rolling in X3006 at 00.27, but crashing into a hut, killing the pilot and navigator and injuring the other two occupants. The incident delayed the departure of the others, who finally got into the air between 02.39 and 02.57 only to be thwarted by adverse weather conditions that extended from the North Sea to the target area. Sgt Cooper and crew had to jettison their bombs as ice-accretion began to affect the stability of his aircraft, and the others were unable to locate the primary objective, the Hall crew reduced to bombing a flak concentration at Brunsbüttel to the north of the city. F/O Powdrell and crew were attacked by three Spitfires as they crossed the coast homebound, and on landing at Leconfield the undercarriage collapsed. Worse by far, the highly experienced crew of P/O Langford failed to return in P4396 having been hit by flak, it is believed, from Heligoland, and there were no survivors. Not mentioned in the 5 Group record was an operation on this night by three 49 Squadron aircraft against A108, the Dortmund oil refinery targeted on the night before by 61 Squadron, but the outcome was the same.

On the following night, more than five hundred Luftwaffe bombers attacked the city of Coventry over a period of many hours and left the central districts in ruins and unrecognisable. While this was in progress, 5 Group dispatched seventeen Hampdens to target an oil refinery and the Blohm & Voss shipyards in Hamburg, and ten to attack an electrical power station in Berlin's south-western suburb of Wilmersdorf. 61 Squadron briefed the crews of P/Os Young and Stewart for Berlin and dispatched them from Hemswell at 23.03 and 23.11 respectively, each carrying the new Imp mines designed for urban targets. P/O Stewart and crew were met at the target by heavy and intense anti-aircraft fire, which dissuaded them from loitering after delivering their bombs, but they did register that a fire had been started. They escaped to return home, but it was a different story for P/O Young and crew, who had to abandon X2967 after it was hit by flak, and they soon found themselves in enemy hands. Their loss, coming on the heels of that of the Langford crew twenty-four hours earlier, was a bitter blow that would be felt keenly by the squadron and station communities.

The night of the 15/16th brought a two-wave attack on Hamburg separated by eight hours, for which the twenty-five-strong Hampden element took off after midnight in the second phase to target a number of aiming points including the power station at Altona on the northern bank of the Elbe to the west of the city centre. The 61 Squadron crews of S/L England and Sgts Clarke and Stevenson departed Hemswell at roughly thirty-minute intervals between 01.28 and 02.30 having been briefed to attack A366, which the 49 Squadron ORB described as a small gas works in a populated area of the city. After facing the challenges of ice-bearing cloud at between 1,500 and 11,000 feet and driving rain during the North Sea crossing, crews were greeted over north-western Germany by excellent conditions with a full moon enhancing the visibility. S/L England and crew believed that they had successfully attacked the primary target, the rear gunner watching the fall of bombs but observing no bursts, while the Stevenson crew also claimed that their bombs had found the mark and started a large fire. This was the first operation as crew captain for Sgt Clarke, and he was determined to make the most of the occasion. On reaching the mouth of the Elbe he descended to 50 feet to follow it into the heart of the city, the gunners strafing flak positions on both banks, but blinded by searchlight glare, he overshot the target and the next positive pinpoint was over Buchholz, some fifteen miles south of the city centre. He climbed to 1,500 feet to drop two 250-pounders and then sank back down to 50 feet to allow his gunners to strafe a stationary train, before turning north towards Hamburg, only somehow to find that they were at the Baltic end of the Kiel Canal, where two 500-pounders were aimed at the wharf. On the way home they attacked two lines of E-Boots at 20 feet and rounded off the night's work with a dive attack on the waterfront at Wesermünde (Bremerhaven). They landed in broad daylight after seven hours and forty minutes aloft and with flak damage that included a smashed compass in the navigator's compartment. The attacks on Hamburg by the relatively modest number of sixty-seven aircraft produced probably the most successful raid of the war to date, after which the Hamburg authorities reported sixty-eight fires and substantial damage in the Blohm & Voss shipyard.

For the third night running, Hamburg was posted as the destination for a force from Bomber Command on the 16th, this time of 130 aircraft including thirty-four Hampdens of 5 Group. 61 Squadron briefed six crews, four for A10 at Harburg, believed to be the Rhenania-Ossag refinery, and two to attack Altona power station on the northern bank of the Elbe. In addition, the Waddington crews had been briefed to target the industrial areas of Veddel and Peute, located on the islands in the Elbe in the heart of the city, but the weather would have its say and most of the carefully laid plans would come to nothing. The 61 Squadron crews departed Hemswell between 01.18 and 01.49 with F/O Powdrell the senior pilot on duty and a time-on-target of 04.25 and 05.00. P/O Webb and crew turned back early because of an oil pressure issue, while the others headed into a weather front over the North Sea that contained all kinds of unpleasant surprises. In the face of low cloud and severe icing conditions the crews of Sgts J F Cooper and Hopkins abandoned their sorties, leaving just P/O Gilbert and crew to attack A10, which they did through ten-tenths cloud with a base at 2,000 feet and were unable to report on the fall of their bombs. F/O Powdrell and crew spent forty minutes searching in vain for the Altona power station, and on the way home bombed Meldorf railway station in Schleswig-Holstein, observing five bursts and explosions in adjoining buildings. Despite the loss of his automatic pilot and being forced to run the gauntlet of heavy flak near Cuxhaven, P/O Hall and crew delivered the four 500 and two 250-pounders on Altona power station from 12,000 feet and watched them fall in a stick from north-east to south-west.

Adverse weather conditions at home and over Germany caused the cancellation of 5 Group operations on the following two nights, and when orders were received on its stations on the 19th, they contained details of that night's long-range operations, by eight aircraft to the Skoda armaments works at Pilsen in Czechoslovakia and by thirteen to A74, a Bergius-process Wintershall oil production site at Lützkendorf near Leipzig, with the nearby A77 Leuna refinery as the designated alternative. 61 Squadron briefed the crew of W/C Valentine for Pilsen, his acting rank having now caught up with his status as squadron commander, while the crews of P/O Webb and Sgt Harrison were assigned to Lützkendorf. This was one of many oil refineries on the western side of Leipzig in a semi-circle from north to south, but the location no longer exists on a map and is now known as Mücheln of Krumpa. W/C Valentine's X2906 was fitted with an extra fuel tank for the thirteen-hundred-mile round trip, which was some 180 miles shorter than that for the others, and took off at 22.42, only for the feed from the additional fuel tank to fail after forty minutes. Undaunted he and his crew pressed on to reach the target area, where fog prevented them from locating the factory complex. On the way home they found a factory or power station between Plauen and Chemnitz and bombed it, before arriving home after almost nine-and-a-half hours in the air. The other two had departed Hemswell at 23.52 and 00.07 and landed at 07.58 and 08.40 to report fulfilling their brief and leaving fires burning.

The target for eighteen Hampdens on the 20th was much closer to home, requiring a trip to the East Bank of the Rhine at Duisburg in the Ruhr, where Germany's largest inland docks, Duisburg-Ruhrort, lay to the south of the city centre. 61 Squadron sat this one out and the entire group remained at home on the 21st. It was on this day that S/L Cecil Thomas Weir was posted in from 5 Groups pool training unit, 106 Squadron, having spent the war to date as an instructor, firstly at a bombing and gunnery school, before being appointed A Flight commander with 106 Squadron at Finningley in December 1939. As Operational Training Units took over the training function, 106 Squadron's A Flight was declared operational under S/L Weir, but by the time of his posting to 61 Squadron he had not seen action.

On the 22nd, AVM Sir Arthur Harris left 5 Group on his appointment as second deputy to the Chief of the Air Staff, Sir Charles Portal, and he was succeeded by AVM Bottomley. Fifteen months hence to the day, Harris would return to lead the Command and rescue it from the brink of disbandment. That night, 5 Group sent seven Hampdens back to Duisburg-Ruhrort and a further fourteen to destroy hangars on Merignac aerodrome near Bordeaux. 61 Squadron contributed the rookie crew of Sgt Ivatt to the Ruhr along with the crews of Sgts Clarke and Hopkins, and they took off between 17.02 and 17.09, leaving the crews of Sgt Stevenson and P/O Hall on the ground until their departure for south-western France at 23.51 and 23.55 respectively. The Hall crew was actually late in taking off after becoming bogged down at their dispersal, but they made up time, and although not locating Merignac, bombed the harbour at Bordeaux as an alternative and set off five fires. The Stevenson crew also failed to locate the primary target but bombed a seaplane base at St-Nazaire as they headed home and started a violent fire in a hangar. On return from the Ruhr at 23.15, Sgt Ivatt undershot the runway and X2897 crashed into the bomb dump, killing him and his navigator and injuring the other two crew members. It is believed that they had reached and bombed the target, as did the Clarke crew in a run from east to west at 9,000 feet, which resulted in five bomb bursts. Sgt Hopkins and crew were unable to locate the target and jettisoned their bombs on the way home.

The 5 Group targets for twenty-four hours later were Duisburg Ruhrort again for ten crews from Hemswell and an oil refinery in Gelsenkirchen for five from Scampton, 61 Squadron providing the crews of Sgt Oakley and P/Os Gilbert and Stewart for the former, for which they took off at intervals between 16.55 and 17.52. P/O Gilbert and crew must have been close to enemy territory when engine trouble ended their interest in proceedings, and Sgt Oakley and crew were some ninety miles out from the English coast when confronted by three black-painted Ju88s with no discernible markings. During the ensuing engagement, the Hampden was forced down from 9,000 to 2,000 feet and the bombs jettisoned to aid manoeuvrability, while the gunners expended eight hundred rounds, which resulted in one of the enemy night-fighters crashing into the sea with its cockpit ablaze and the others breaking off the attack. This left just P/O Stewart and crew to fulfil their brief, and they reported setting off several fires.

On the 24th, Lindholme and Scampton put up a dozen Hampdens between them to target the Blohm & Voss shipyards at Hamburg, but they soon ran into six to ten-tenths cloud with tops at between 4,000 and 6,000 feet, which prevented all from identifying the primary target. On the following night, Hemswell and Lindholme joined forces to send nine Hampdens to attack the Deutsche-Werke shipyard at Kiel, where the Scharnhorst-class heavy cruiser, Gneisenau, had been built between 1935 and 1938. The 61 Squadron crews of Sgts Hopkins and Clarke should have been accompanied by the crew of S/L Weir, but his Hampden became unserviceable at the last minute, and he would have to wait to undertake his first operational sortie. The others got away at 17.22 and 17.46 respectively and initially good weather conditions over the sea gave way to a layer of nine to ten-tenths cloud over the target area with a base at around 1,500 feet, which prevented them from locating the target. The Clarke crew dropped their four 500-pounders on the Island of Heligoland in the face of a hostile flak reception and returned safely, but as Sgt Hopkins and crew were on final approach to Hemswell at 01.40 after more than eight hours in the air, X3064 crashed with no survivors. We do not know whether or not they reached and bombed the target and the reason for the crash remains a matter of speculation, with fuel starvation, damage and fatigue all possible causes.

It had been decided to deploy Hampdens in an air defence role, to patrol the skies over major cities expecting a visit from the Luftwaffe, and three crews from each Hemswell squadron were put on stand-by in full flying kit to await the call. In the event, adverse weather conditions kept them on the ground on this occasion, but the experiment would continue.

Cologne was posted as the destination for sixty-two aircraft on the 27th, which would be assigned to five separate aiming-points within the city. Ten 5 Group Hampden crews were briefed to attack what was described as a "land armament factory", which was, in fact, the Klöckner-Humboldt works in the Deutz district on the eastern bank of the Rhine, which manufactured aero-engines and heavy and tracked vehicles for the Wehrmacht. However, Hemswell was also in action on this night in the same general area with five crews, and S/L Weir would finally launch his operational career in company with the crews of Sgt J F Cooper and P/O Hall, who took off between 02.31 and 02.38 bound, it is believed, for the Quadrath power station located outside of the city to the west. They set course to make landfall over the Scheldt estuary, where they found their way inland barred by a bank of towering, ice-bearing cumulo-nimbus cloud, extending from 6,000 up to 15,000 feet. Despite the challenges, they arrived in the target area, where P/O Hall and crew are credited with starting a large blaze which acted as a beacon to their squadron colleagues and all successfully attacked the target before returning home safely to make their reports. Crews at Hemswell were again on stand-by for four hours for possible deployment as night-fighters but were stood down shortly after 22.00.

Hemswell and Lindholme were the stations called upon on the 28th to provide aircraft for operations against a naval store at Mannheim and the inland port on the other side of the Rhine at Ludwigshafen. Among six Hemswell crews briefed for the former were those of the newly posted-in S/L Sidney Misselbrook and Sgt Cowan representing 61 Squadron, while the crews of Sgts Hughes and Stevenson were to attack the docks at Le Havre. They took off together between 17.11 and 17.15 and arrived over the French coast to encounter cloud that would prevent the latter from locating the port and the Hughes crew flew back along the coast to the north-east to bomb the harbour at Fecamp. The Stevenson crew flew inland in search of an alternative target, crossing Belgium and entering Germany to the north of Luxembourg and eventually coming upon the marshalling yards at Coblenz. As the bombs fell away, they entered cloud and were unable to report on the outcome. By coincidence, Sgt Cowan and crew attacked a road, rail and canal junction also in Coblenz after failing to locate their primary target, and they observed three bursts. S/L Misselbrook and crew alone found and bombed their briefed target and were able to report bomb bursts but no detail.

The Le Havre operation was rescheduled for the 29th and both Cooper crews were briefed to represent 61 Squadron before departing Hemswell at 17.25 and 17.27, only for K G Cooper and crew to experience W/T issues that prevented them from leaving the English coast and kept them airborne for five hours. Sgt J F Cooper and crew arrived over the Normandy coast to find six-tenths cloud but fair visibility and delivered an attack from 8,000 feet, which, according to the rear gunner, resulted in one huge burst.

During the course of the month the squadron operated on eighteen nights against twenty-three targets and dispatched sixty-two sorties for the loss of six Hampdens, four complete crews and four other crew members including two pilots.

December 1940

The new month began for 5 Group with the new air-defence role still in force, and although twenty Hampdens per night had been on stand-by, none had yet been deployed as night-fighters. The content of the operational order received on 5 Group stations informed the resident squadrons that they were *"to provide four aircraft to take part in an experiment to be carried out as to the possibility of intercepting and destroying enemy bomber aircraft over their target, by concentrating twenty Hampden aircraft in a stepped-up patrol over the area being attacked. The patrol would operate if large-scale enemy formations attacked either Coventry, Birmingham, Derby, Manchester, Sheffield, Bristol, Liverpool or Wolverhampton."* Each aircraft was to be given a sky-layer of five hundred feet within a defined four-thousand-foot height band and would be working in co-operation with the searchlight and flak defences and must not arrive in their patrol area until "zero-hour" or remain in it once the four-hour patrol time had elapsed. Each aircraft was to carry maximum ammunition and an additional gunner to man the midships guns.

During the afternoon of the 1st, ten Scampton crews were briefed for an operation that night against shipbuilding yards at Wilhelmshaven, which, as events turned out, was conducted in unfavourable weather conditions that prevented any from fulfilling their orders and sent them in search of alternative targets. The weather continued to be unfavourable, causing the cancellation of bombing operations planned for the 2nd and 3rd, but apparently relented sufficiently on the 4th to allow an operation involving twenty Hampdens from Hemswell, Lindholme and Scampton to go ahead against multiple targets in Düsseldorf. 61 Squadron briefed six crews to attack the city's gas works, and they had to wait until the early hours of the 5th before taking off between 03.12 and 03.52 with S/L Misselbrook the senior pilot on duty. In the event, the weather conditions proved to be as challenging as those leading to cancellations on the two previous nights, with severe icing and ten-tenths cloud over the target in a band between 1,600 and 4,000 feet. The crews of Sgts Clarke and Williams failed to locate the target and jettisoned their loads "safe", while the others carried out an attack but had no clue as to the fall of their bombs.

On the 6th, fifty-five Hampden crews were briefed for intruder sorties over Luftwaffe bomber aerodromes in the occupied countries, while twenty others from Scampton, Hemswell and Waddington stood by for the first offensive patrols. The departure of the bombing element was spread over many hours between 17.00 and the early hours of the 7th, while the 61 Squadron crews of S/L Weir, P/O Gilbert and Sgt Harrison and three representing 144 Squadron waited on the ground at Hemswell to be launched into the fray against the Luftwaffe in the skies over Bristol. They took off between 21.12 and 21.40 on a night of extreme cold, during which temperatures at operating altitude plummeted to minus 33 degrees and caused cases of frostbite. They arrived at the end of the raid and began to fly diagonal courses, and with the exception of the Harrison crew, who caught a fleeting glimpse of another aircraft, no contact was made with the enemy and a similar story was told by the other squadrons involved. What also became clear at debriefing was that provisions for crew comfort were seriously lacking and all complained of inadequate heating.

On the 7th, Hemswell and Lindholme provided ten Hampdens between them to attack a "land armaments factory" in Düsseldorf, almost certainly the Mannesmann Rohrenwerke, which manufactured heavy gun barrels. While that was in progress, the 61 Squadron crews of F/O Frutiger and Sgt Hughes took off at 02.10 and 02.15 bound for the Jellyfish garden off the port of

Brest. The ORB is horribly confused and talks of vegetables in use against target E6, the above-mentioned arms factory, which could not have been the case. Sgt Hughes and crew turned back within two hours after losing their intercom, while the crew of F/O Frutiger, who was operating as crew captain for the first time, encountered icing conditions in a bank of cloud over the French coast extending from 1,000 to 16,000 feet. Despite the challenges they planted their vegetable according to brief but failed to find a suitable target for their wing-mounted 250-pounders.

On the 8th, Hemswell and Lindholme joined forces to send fourteen Hampdens back to Düsseldorf, this time to attack L12, which is described in the ORB as a basic steel furnace, which may have been attached to the Mannesman Rohrenwerke. While this operation was in progress nineteen aircraft from Hemswell, Scampton and Waddington were to rendezvous in the Oxford area and wait to be directed to where-ever the Luftwaffe raid was taking place. The bombing quartet took off first between 17.01 and 17.07 with F/L Powdrell the senior pilot on duty, and they were followed into the air eventually by the crews of P/O Webb and Sgt Cooper at 18.52 and 19.01 only for them to be recalled after orbiting the Oxford area for two hours. It is believed that all four 61 Squadron crews reached their primary destination, and in favourable weather conditions, carried out attacks that left fires burning, but only three returned to Hemswell to make their reports. It would be learned in time that X2975 had been shot down by flak and had crashed at Grevenbroich, a dozen or so miles south-west of Düsseldorf, and that only the pilot, Sgt Williams, had survived to fall into enemy hands.

On the 10th, Scampton and Lindholme sent six Hampdens each to target the inland docks on the Rhine at Mannheim, while three 44 Squadron crews and two from Hemswell attended to mining duties in the Deodar garden in the Gironde estuary. S/L Misselbrook and crew alone represented 61 Squadron, taking off at 01.16 and returning almost nine hours later with the mine still in the bomb bay having failed to locate the drop zone in conditions of extreme darkness and poor visibility. It was not an entirely wasted night, however, as on the way home they were intercepted by a BF110 night-fighter, at which rear gunner, Sgt Wiltshear, fired four hundred rounds in a long burst and had the satisfaction of watching it crash into the sea.

A return to security patrols awaited six crews each from Hemswell and Waddington on the evening of the 11th, despite the fact that the 5 Group ORB records that all operations were cancelled because of the weather. The 61 Squadron crews of Sgt Harrison, P/O Gilbert and Sgt K G Cooper took off in that order between 19.06 and 19.22 and headed for the skies over Birmingham, where they encountered icing conditions but fair visibility. For the first time during this type of operation, enemy aircraft were spotted and attempts made to engage them, and thousands of incendiaries were observed being released from lower altitudes, while a German transmission was also picked up from what was believed to be a Luftwaffe commander directing his crews. No contact was made with the enemy and the 61 Squadron trio landed between 23.10 and 00.39 having not fired a shot.

A dozen Hampdens were detailed on the 12th to attack the Ruhrort docks complex and the Thyssen steelworks in the Ruhr city of Duisburg, and this was a figure reduced by 50% because of concerns about the weather. Five 61 Squadron crews were briefed and took off between 16.30 and 16.37 with F/O Frutiger the only commissioned pilot on duty, and all but Sgt Cowan and crew picked up a recall signal at 17.00 and responded accordingly. The Cowan crew continued on and reached the docks to carry out an attack in excellent conditions, before returning safely after almost five hours in the air.

Thirty Hampden crews at Hemswell, Lindholme, Scampton and Waddington were briefed to attack a variety of objectives in Berlin on the 15th, while other elements of the Command targeted Frankfurt and Kiel. The target for five 61 Squadron crews was an electrical power station in Berlin, for which they departed Hemswell between 23.28 and 23.47 with S/L Misselbrook the senior pilot on duty. They all arrived in the target area to find moonlight, which they described as illuminating the city below as bright as day and revealing the pattern of streets and major landmarks. This enabled them to identify the aiming point with ease and carry out their attacks in the face of a surprisingly modest flak defence, which was in contrast to reports from some other squadrons of patchy cloud and intense and accurate anti-aircraft fire. This suggests that the 61 Squadron target was in the suburbs rather than more central districts, and as the operation was conducted over a period of hours, the cloud conditions may have altered.

Orders were received on all 5 Group stations on the 16th to prepare fifty-eight Hampdens between them to attack various targets in Mannheim that night as part of a major operation under the code name Operation Abigail Rachel in retaliation for recent devastating raids on English cities, particularly Coventry and Southampton. The Abigail part of the plan called for eight of the most experienced 3 Group Wellington crews to open the attack on the centre of the city with all-incendiary loads to start fires that would act as a beacon to the Rachel force following behind. As the day drew on, it became clear that the weather conditions over the bomber stations might cause problems, and the force was cut from an original two hundred aircraft to 134, which was still the largest force yet committed to a single target. 61 Squadron briefed the crews of P/Os Hall and Webb and Sgts Cowan and Oakley and launched them from Hemswell between 21.45 and 21.56 in company with five belonging to 144 Squadron, all as part of the Rachel second wave. According to a number of official records, twenty-nine Hampden crews had been given the Motorenwerke Mannheim in the northern outskirts of the city as their aiming point, which is curious, as the purpose of the raid was to cause as much damage as possible to the central districts in what was the first officially sanctioned area attack. The same official records suggest that some of the second wave crews were to target Mannheim's Rhine docks, and this D55, was indisputably the target for the Hemswell elements.

The weather conditions outbound persuaded perhaps a quarter of the force to turn back, but those reaching the target area found largely clear skies and a bright full moon, with only a modest defence in operation to repel the raiders. There are no details of the part played by the 61 squadron participants, but any success was marred by the failure to return of Sgt Cowan and crew in X3128, which disappeared without trace. With this operation, Sgt Cowan would have amassed the two hundred hours necessary to complete a tour and his loss came just four days after he was awarded a highly coveted DFM. Returning crews largely reported a successful outcome, but post-raid reconnaissance revealed that the operation had not produced the desired results, after the "path finder" element had missed the city centre and the subsequent bombing had been scattered. Even so, local reports provided a figure of 240 buildings either destroyed or seriously damaged, with more than a thousand people bombed out of their homes at a cost to the Command of just three aircraft. On the following afternoon S/L Misselbrook led a sea search by four crews in the hope of locating the Cowan crew in a dinghy, but nothing was found.

The weather kept 5 Group at home on the ensuing two nights, while very small forces returned to Mannheim, and when the teleprinters on 5 Group stations burst into life on the 19th it was to reveal plans to attack the Union Rheinische Braunkohlen-Kraftstoff A.G synthetic oil refinery at

Wesseling on the west bank of the Rhine south of Cologne. Forty Hampdens were made ready across the group, while eight others, five from Waddington and three from Finningley, took care of mining duties in the Jellyfish and Artichoke gardens off Brest and Lorient respectively. What is not mentioned in the 5 Group ORB is an operation by a dozen Hampdens from Hemswell against the Knapsack power station located on the south-western outskirts of Cologne and the Gereon marshalling yards, which served the central goods station. They departed Hemswell between 03.26 and 04.09 with S/L Weir the senior pilot on duty and ran into ten-tenths ice-bearing cloud on the far side of the North Sea, which persuaded the crews of P/O Street, Sgt J F Cooper and P/O Webb to turn back in that order and land between 05.00 and 06.39. Only P/O Hall and crew caught a glimpse of a suitable target through a momentary break in the cloud, and this was a railway junction some five miles south-east of Cologne, which they hit with five bombs. P/O Parry and crew dropped their load on e.t.a. from 10,000 feet and saw nothing of the result and S/L Weir and crew returned their bombs to the dump after finding nothing of value to attack.

The 20th would mark the resurgence of 1 Group, which had been reconstituted on return from its role as the major component of the AASF in France for the first nine months of the war. The Fairey Battles of 12, 103, 142 and 150 Squadrons had been replaced, and with four squadrons of fanatical Poles added to its ranks and working towards operational status, this night would see the first six operational sorties in Wellingtons. Tragedy struck 61 Squadron on this day, when X2981 exploded over the Theddlethorpe bombing range while testing an Imp mine, and the recently posted-in F/L Cooper and the two other occupants lost their lives. 5 Group detailed a dozen Hampdens on this night to attack the Schlesischer railway station located south-east of Berlin city centre, thirty-one others for a return to the Wesseling synthetic oil refinery at Cologne and five from Hemswell for mining duties in the Baltic's Forget-me-not garden on the approaches to Kiel. P/O Stewart and crew took off first at 00.14 bound for Berlin, and they were followed into the air between 01.38 and 01.58 by the gardening trio consisting of the crews of S/L Misselbrook, P/O Gilbert and Sgt Clarke, and finally by the Cologne-bound crews of F/L Powdrell and Sgts Harrison and Stevenson between 03.10 and 03.15.

Quite why some of the Berlin crews had been released so late is unclear, particularly as the 83 Squadron element had taken off either side of 17.00. As a consequence, they would be under time pressure throughout, conscious that they would struggle to vacate enemy territory before the arrival of daylight. They exited the English coast at Skegness, and adopted a direct course for the target, P/O Stewart and crew arriving at their destination having benefitted from clear skies most of the way, and the favourable conditions persisted as they carried out their attack and observed one burst which resulted in a large fire. The Cologne trio all delivered their bombs according to brief and returned with enthusiastic reports of explosions, one large fire and many small blazes. After planting their vegetable in the briefed location, S/L Misselbrook and crew dropped their wing-mounted 250-pounders on the causeway between Nordstrand and the mainland. The crews of Sgt Clarke and P/O Gilbert also fulfilled their briefs, and the former scored two direct his on a factory on the southern outskirts of Meldorf, a town near the western coast of Schleswig-Holstein.

The target for twenty-four Hampdens from Hemswell, Lindholme and Scampton on the 21st was a power station at Zschornewitz, a village to the south-east of Dessau and north-east of Halle, north of Leipzig. When it was built during the Great War, it was the world's largest brown-coal-fired power station and by the early 1940s it had upgraded its turbines and with its thirteen huge chimneys was a major landmark. 61 Squadron briefed the crews of F/O Frutiger, P/O Street and Sgts Hughes and Oakley, before sending them on their way between 21.39 and 22.17, and it is believed that all reached the target area to be confronted by impenetrable ten-tenths cloud, which had them seeking out alternative objectives. Sgt Hughes and crew headed towards the north-west to Magdeburg, where they attacked the Braunkohle A.G synthetic oil refinery without observing the results. The Oakley crew attacked a railway station west of Hannover, while P/O Street and crew found a railway junction at Osnabrück and F/O Frutiger and crew bombed the town of Lingen, all observing bursts but no detail.

The second wartime Christmas came and went, and it was Boxing Day when Hemswell was next called into action, briefing six crews from each squadron for an operation against Merignac aerodrome, located on the western fringe of Bordeaux, with the nearby U-Boot pens designated as the alternative target. They were to operate out of a forward base at St Eval in Cornwall and were in transit when Sgt J F Cooper and crew were forced to drop out with an issue affecting the artificial horizon. It was the early hours of the 27th when S/L Misselbrook took off at 01.40 to be followed eventually between 02.20 and 02.23 by the crews of F/L Powdrell and Sgts Hughes and Oakley, leaving P/O Stewart and crew on the ground with a recalcitrant engine. They passed to the west of the Channel Islands to make landfall over the Finistere peninsula, and by the time of their arrival in the target area the weather conditions created challenges for target identification. The crews of S/L Misselbrook and Sgt Oakley attacked the primary target and Sgt Hughes and crew the alternative, while F/L Powdrell and crew were unable to locate either and brought their bombs home.

The operation was to be repeated on the following night, with S/L Misselbrook again taking the lead and P/O Street and crew substituting for the Oakley crew, and this time they departed St Eval between 00.30 and 01.51 with F/L Powdrell and crew bringing up the rear and taking off a full forty-five minutes after the last of the others. As they made their way across the Channel, Sgt K G Cooper and crew took off from Hemswell at 02.20 for mining duties in the Beech garden off St-Nazaire, where ten-tenths cloud prevented them from establishing a pinpoint. The cloud also interfered with the Bordeaux-bound element, and Sgt J F Cooper and crew returned their bombs to the station dump after failing to locate either the primary or alternative target, while P/O Street and crew jettisoned theirs before landing at St Eval. P/O Stewart and crew located the primary target but failed to observe the burst of their bombs, and F/L Powdrell and crew attacked the seaplane base at St-Nazaire with a similar outcome. S/L Misselbrook and crew attacked the U-Boot pens and were the only ones to observe their bombs actually burst. On return and short of fuel they force-landed in a field near Grantham without damaging X3140 or its occupants, and this brought an end to the first full year of war.

During the course of the month the squadron took part in seventeen operations, which generated sixty-six sorties for the loss of three Hampdens and crews. It had been a backs-to-the-wall year, and one of presenting a defiant face to an as-yet all conquering enemy. 1941 was not destined to bring more than a slight increase in effectiveness, and it would be a case of treading water for the foreseeable future. Some new aircraft were emerging to offer a degree of hope for the future, but the problems arising from pressing them too soon into service would result in a painfully slow development, and the existing types were to bear most of the burden for the next twelve months and even beyond.

January 1941

A second successive severe winter restricted operations at the start of the year, when most of the effort would be directed at French and German ports, beginning on New Year's Night, when a force of 141 aircraft was assembled for an operation against targets in Bremen. 5 Group detailed ten Hampdens each from Scampton, Lindholme and Waddington and briefed their crews for two targets, the Korff A.G oil refinery, which the ORB suggested was also a depository for food stocks, and, it is believed, the Focke-Wulf aircraft factory in the south-eastern district of Hemelingen. Some described the conditions as good, while others complained of a snowstorm over eastern England that extended as high as 11,000 feet, and severe icing as they climbed over the North Sea. Those reaching the target area found that the cloud had built to between eight and ten-tenths, despite which, some were able to locate their aiming points, aided in part by the intensity of the flak, which was bursting at around 9,000 feet.

5 Group signalled a return to Bremen twenty-four hours later with eight Hampdens from Hemswell and Scampton on a night, as events were to prove, of technical failures and wasted effort. The target for the five 61 Squadron crews was the Atlas Werke shipyard, for which they took off between 03.01 and 03.16 with F/L Powdrell the senior pilot on duty and lost the services of Sgt J F Cooper and crew to engine failure almost immediately. F/L Powdrell and crew were some seventy miles short of the target when they turned back also because of an overheating port engine. They were over the Hemswell threshold when both engines cut and X3126 crashed some five hundred yards from the officers' mess at 07.36, the pilot sustaining leg injuries and the navigator a broken wrist. Almost four hundred miles to the north-east Sgt Clarke and crew alone of the 61 Squadron element attacked the primary target in a glide approach from 10,000 down to 2,000 feet, and although they observed two bursts, they were unable to determine the result. This left the crews of P/Os Hall and Webb to attack the port of Wilhelmshaven and the town of Oldenburg respectively as alternatives after failing to locate the primary target.

On the 3rd, the new bomber station at Coningsby was declared open on a Care and Maintenance basis and would shortly welcome 106 Squadron as its first resident unit. Also, on this day, the decision was taken to draft all Rhodesian aircrew into 44 Squadron as they became available. This would lead, ultimately, to the adoption of the title, Rhodesia, to be inserted after the squadron number, once Rhodesian aircrew predominated. That night, Scampton sent fifteen Hampdens back to Bremen as part of an overall force of seventy-one aircraft, which benefitted from improved weather conditions and inflicted further damage that was confirmed by local sources.

It had been intended to send a 5 Group force of thirty Hampdens from Hemswell, Lindholme and Waddington to Hamburg on the 4th, and having been briefed accordingly, some crews at Hemswell were already in their aircraft when a change of orders was received to prepare instead for an operation against an unnamed Hipper class German cruiser at berth in No 1 dry dock at Brest. A process of elimination suggests that it was the Admiral Hipper herself, which had been raiding in the Atlantic following her part in the Norwegian campaign. Laid down in the Blohm & Voss shipyards in 1935, she had a length of 673 feet and displaced 18,500 tons, and was one of three of her design, including Prinz Eugen, which entered service in August 1940. The 5 Group contingent was part of an overall force of fifty-three aircraft, while others, four from Finningley and two from Waddington, were to take care of mining duties in the Artichoke garden off Lorient. The seven 61

Squadron participants took off between 17.51 and 19.24 with F/O Frutiger the senior pilot on duty and flew out over the Dorset coast at Chesil Beach in good conditions, until encountering a layer of eight-tenths cloud over the Channel at between 3,000 and 6,000 feet, which persisted all the way to the French coast and beyond. The target was easily identified on approach by the reflection of the searchlights in the cloud, and the volume of tracer breaking through it to reach 12,500 feet. Crews spent up to seventy-five minutes orbiting the target area and running across the estimated position of the aiming-point, seeking one of the few gaps in the nine to ten-tenths cloud cover. Eventually, all but one of the 61 Squadron crews delivered their bombs in the general area of the vessel's location and some bursts were observed. Only Sgt Stevenson and crew actually saw the aiming point and watched their incendiaries overshoot, but during a further circuit they could see that they had set fire to a long factory-type building. F/O Frutiger and crew failed to identify the target and returned their bombs to the station dump.

It was left to 49 Squadron to represent 5 Group on the 5th with a dozen Hampdens detailed for mining duties off the Biscay coast, ten in the Jellyfish garden off Brest and one each in Artichoke (Lorient) and Beech (St-Nazaire). The naval shipbuilding yards at Wilhelmshaven and the battleship Tirpitz were posted as the targets for thirty-two aircraft on the 8th, ten provided by 5 Group from Lindholme and Waddington, while sixteen other aircraft were assigned to Emden, some forty miles to the west. Nine further Hampdens were required for mining duties in the Eglantine garden in the Elbe estuary, and these were also provided by Lindholme and Waddington.

The Commander-in-Chief, Sir Richard Peirse, had decided upon launching one major raid each month on an important industrial city, for which Gelsenkirchen was selected on the 9th, and a force of 135 aircraft assembled. 5 Group called upon Hemswell to provide ten crews from each squadron and briefed them to attack the Gelsenkirchener Bergwerke synthetic oil refinery, known to the Germans as Gelsenberg A.G and to the RAF as Nordstern, located in the Horst district to the north-west of the city centre. While this operation was in progress, four Finningley crews would be taking care of mining in Kiel Bay. The 61 Squadron element took off between 19.00 and 19.34 with W/C Valentine and S/L Weir the senior pilots on duty and a 1,000-pounder and two of 500lbs in each bomb bay. Sgt Clarke and crew found themselves being stalked by enemy aircraft and jettisoned the two 500-pounders to aid their escape but retained the 1,000-pounder for future employment. Both of the Cooper crews attacked the primary target along with P/O Street and crew and all observed bursts, while P/O Hall and crew found a SEMO (self-evident military objective) to bomb in the Ruhr and Sgt Hughes and crew a railway junction at Gladbeck. W/C Valentine and crew spent two hours searching for the primary target before giving up and heading for home and bombing a factory in Duisburg based on a fleeting glimpse. S/L Weir and crew attacked Haamstede aerodrome on Zeeland Island at the mouth of the Scheldt and this left the crew of P/O Parry to jettison their load over Germany and Sgt Glover and crew, for which nothing was recorded. An analysis revealed that fewer than half of the force reached the assigned target area, and local sources reported bombs falling in various parts of Gelsenkirchen and its environs.

Scampton took care of 5 Group business on the 11th, when sending sixteen Hampdens to attack Tirpitz in its berth at Wilhelmshaven. There was cloud over the target and only two crews ducked beneath it to catch sight of the vessel, while eight others bombed from estimated positions above cloud. Hemswell and Lindholme were notified on the 12th that they would be responsible for 5

Group bombing operations that night and were to provide ten and five Hampdens respectively for a second shot at the Hipper class cruiser at Brest. The six 61 Squadron Hampdens took off between 16.48 and 17.09 with S/L Misselbrook the senior pilot on duty and Sgt K G Cooper and crew stepping up at the last minute as a reserve for a 144 Squadron crew that was unable to take-off. The bomb load for most consisted of four 500 and two 250-pounders, but three aircraft in the force had a single 2,000-pounder in their bomb bay, and it is likely that at least one was in a 61 Squadron aircraft. They climbed away into nine to ten-tenths cloud that persisted all the way out over the Dorset coast and the Channel, and it was only as the French coast drew near that the cloud began to disperse. By the time that Brest appeared on the horizon, the skies were clear and the target area visible under the light of the moon. An intense searchlight and flak defence awaited them as they focused on the dock layout, which could be identified, but only P/O Gilbert of the 61 Squadron element picked out the target vessel, while the others bombed the general area. A large fire was reported close to the warship, but on landing at St Eval, none could confirm a direct hit.

In a directive issued on the 15th, the Air Ministry revealed its belief that an all-out assault against oil related targets would eventually take its toll on the German war effort, and operations from now on would reflect this. A list of seventeen sites was drawn up, the top nine of which represented 80% of Germany's synthetic oil production, and of these, Scholven-Buer and Gelsenkirchen were in the Ruhr, Leuna, Zeitz, Böhlen and Lützkendorf were in the east near Leipzig, Magdeburg and Ruhland were north and east of Leipzig respectively and the other was at Politz close to the Baltic coast, but it would be February before Peirse was able to comply. In the meantime, a force of ninety-six aircraft was assembled that night to target the dockyards at Wilhelmshaven, for which Hemswell provided the seventeen Hampdens. The eight-strong 61 Squadron element took off between 02.30 and 02.56 with S/L Weir the senior pilot on duty and lost the services of Sgt J F Cooper and crew early on for an undisclosed reason. Six of the others carried out an attack and several fires were reported to be burning between the Bauhafen and Grosserhafen along with others in the town that remained visible for thirty miles into the return flight. Local sources confirmed damage to the main post office, the police HQ, army barracks, dock offices and seven commercial buildings.

Waddington and Scampton detailed a further fifteen Hampdens on the 16th to return to Wilhelmshaven to target Tirpitz as part of an overall force of eighty-one aircraft, on a night when the weather conditions proved to be inhospitable. Thereafter, twelve consecutive nights of operations were cancelled because of severe weather conditions, which rendered airfields frozen under a blanket of snow, and then left them waterlogged as a thaw set in. When operations finally resumed for 5 Group on the 29th, Wilhelmshaven, or more specifically, the Tirpitz, was posted as the target yet again, for a force this time of nine Hampdens from Lindholme and twenty-five Wellingtons. The Tirpitz remained elusive, and those locating the target area mostly bombed the town, according to local sources inflicting a degree of residential damage.

During the course of the month the squadron took part in just five operations and dispatched thirty-six sorties for the loss of a single Hampden in a landing crash, but there were no missing crew members or fatalities.

February 1941

February got off to a bad start for 61 Squadron, when AD725 was involved in a ground accident involving a snow-covered dispersal pan on the 1st, which resulted in the deaths of the pilot, Sgt Lloyd, and the only other occupant of the Hampden, a Sgt Guest. In other respects, February began as January had ended, with ports occupying the bulk of the Command's attention, although the accent shifted from Germany to those in France and Belgium. 5 Group dispatched thirteen Hampdens from Hemswell to attack the Admiral Hipper in Brest on the night of the 2/3rd, and also to lay mines in the Artichoke garden off Lorient. In the absence of clarity from the ORB, it is concluded that the four participating 144 Squadron crews were responsible for gardening duties, while the nine representing 61 squadron targeted the warship. They took off between 02.45 and 03.48 with S/L Weir the senior pilot on duty and ran into unfavourable weather conditions in the form of ten-tenths ice-bearing cloud containing electrical storms. This prevented any from identifying the target, and while seven crews released their bombs in the general area of the vessel more in hope than in expectation, one jettisoned and one returned the bombs to the station dump.

In a new departure for night raids, the Command assigned a specific target to each of 2, 3, 4 and 5 Groups on the 4th, aerodromes for the Blenheims, French ports for 3 and 4 Groups and the Ruhr city of Düsseldorf for 5 Group. Thirty Hampdens were made ready at Scampton, Hemswell and Lindholme, while Waddington remained off the order of battle and 61 Squadron also sat out this night's activities. The moon was waxing towards full and clear weather conditions prevailed up to within about ten minutes of the target, when eight to ten-tenths cloud obscured the ground. However, an intense searchlight and flak defence left them in no doubt that they were over the target, whether or not they caught a glimpse of it through small gaps in the cloud. The weather deteriorated again to keep 5 Group on the ground on the next two nights, but the Group Meteorological Section staff managed to find a window of acceptable weather across the Channel on the north-eastern coast of France on the 7th. This was sufficient to allow an operation by a dozen Scampton crews and fifteen from Lindholme against shipping and dock installations at Dunkerque. On the 8th, Hemswell and Waddington were ordered to prepare nine and six Hampdens respectively for an operation that night against a specific target in Mannheim. Most reached the target area after flying south-east across Belgium and entering Germany via Luxembourg, but two layers of cloud blotted out the ground, forcing crews to descend in an attempt to break into clear air to establish their whereabouts and all would be forced to bomb from estimated positions on e.t.a.

On the following day, twenty-three Hampdens were detailed at Hemswell and Scampton to be sent against the Tirpitz at Wilhelmshaven, and 61 Squadron responded with ten of its own, which took off between 02.20 and 02.31 with S/Ls Misselbrook and Weir the senior pilots on duty. Sgt J F Cooper and crew signalled that they were returning early, and Sgt Stevenson and crew took off in the reserve aircraft at 03.05 to fill the gap. They were met by heavy ice-bearing cloud that obscured the target, even from the eyes of P/O Hall and crew who descended to 500 feet without breaking into clear air. and only one crew claimed to have attacked the primary target. F/O Frutiger and crew sent a distress message that fixed them some sixty miles out from the English coast, and the next news came with a report that P4405 had crashed near Oulton in Norfolk at 06.50, shortly after crossing the coast and that none had survived.

While 5 Group conducted the two above-mentioned operations, the rest of the Command had stayed on the ground, and C-in-C Peirse had not yet implemented the January directive against Germany's synthetic oil industry. First, he would launch his monthly "big" effort against a major industrial city, and orders went out across the Command on the 10th to prepare a force, which, at take-off time, would number 222 aircraft, a record for a single target. At briefings, the crews learned that the northern city of Hannover was to be their destination, and that they were assigned to attack one of a variety of aiming points in the industrial sector. The city was a major centre of war production, the home among others to the Accumulatoren-Fabrik A.G factory which manufactured lead acid batteries for U-Boots and torpedoes, the Continental tyre and rubber factory at Limmer, the Deurag-Nerag synthetic oil refinery at Misburg, the VLW (Volkswagen) metalworks, and the Maschinenfabrik Niedersachsen Hannover and Hanomag factories, which were producing guns and tracked vehicles. A second operation was also planned for this night involving forty-three aircraft in an attack on oil storage tanks in Rotterdam, and in a demonstration of the burgeoning power of the Command, the contribution by 3 Group of 119 aircraft would be the first time that any group had exceeded one hundred aircraft. Among them, as part of the Rotterdam force, would be the first three sorties by the new four-engine Short Stirling in the hands of 7 Squadron.

5 Group notified all of its operational stations to prepare for the main event, and forty-six Hampdens were made ready, those of the newly elevated F/O Stewart, P/O Noble and Sgts K G Cooper, Glover and Hughes representing 61 Squadron and departing Hemswell between 23.15 and 23.27 with the main post office building as their aiming point. This was, of course, a euphemism for an area attack on the city generally, which benefitted from ideal weather conditions of clear skies and bright moonlight to assist navigation and map-reading. Four of the 61 Squadron participants reached the target area, pinpointing, initially, on the Steinhuder Lake to the west, and then the Maschsee to the south of the city centre. Over the target itself, around three-tenths cloud was reported at 7,000 feet, but it would have no influence on the course of the raid, which attracted what appeared to be only a limited and inaccurate light flak defence. This emboldened crews to circle, if necessary, to establish their positions and decide on a method of attack, and in a number of cases, to descend to a fairly low level. Some adopted a glide approach, while most favoured a higher-level attack from between 10,000 and 14,000 feet. We are told only that the 61 Squadron crews bombed the target and contributed to fires, while P/O Noble and crew attacked the town of Hildesheim to the south-east, for which no explanation is forthcoming.

On the 11th, a force of seventy-one Hampdens, Wellingtons and Whitleys was made ready to attack Bremen, while eighteen Wellingtons and eleven Hampdens returned to Hannover, five of the former belonging to 61 Squadron, which departed Hemswell at 17.45 with S/L Misselbrook the senior pilot on duty. Sgt J F Cooper and crew came under attack by an enemy night-fighter and jettisoned the bomb load during the successful evasion, leaving the others to locate the target, where fires were reported to be still burning from the previous night. Eight-tenths cloud prevented them from observing the results of their efforts and it is unlikely that significant damage occurred, but at least, no aircraft were lost.

The oil directive was finally implemented on the night of the 14/15th, when the Nordstern (Gelsenberg A.G) refinery at Gelsenkirchen was earmarked for an attack by Wellingtons, while Wellingtons and Blenheims tried their hand at a similar target, the Rheinpreussen (Meerbeck) synthetic oil plant at Moers/Homberg, situated on the west bank of the Rhine opposite Duisburg. Both of these massively important plants were vital to the German war effort and employed the

Bergius process to refine high-grade petroleum products such as aviation fuel. It was on this night that 207 Squadron had hoped to launch its maiden sorties, but the modifications to the Manchesters had taken twice the time planned for, and the aircraft had not been tested. According to the 49 and 61 Squadron ORBs, they launched eleven and six Hampdens respectively on this night against the Homberg oil plant, while all other squadron records suggest that 5 Group did not operate. The Hemswell element took off between 02.54 and 03.38 and arrived at the western edge of the Ruhr to find six to ten-tenths cloud that hampered target identification, and four bombed without observing the outcome, while two attacked Düsseldorf as an alternative.

On the following night, thirty-three Hampdens and thirty-seven Blenheims were sent against the Homberg plant, while seventy-three Wellingtons and Whitleys targeted the Hydrierwerke-Scholven refinery at Sterkrade-Holten. 61 Squadron briefed seven crews for the operation, which would be spread over many hours, some of the 5 Group elements taking off as early as 18.00, when conditions were quite favourable, and 61 Squadron was among these, departing Hemswell between 18.36 and 19.08 with S/Ls Misselbrook and Weir the senior pilots on duty. S/L Misselbrook and crew were contending with an engine issue and turned back from Geldern, just a few miles short of the target and on the way home bombed a flare-path near the Dutch frontier. Four of the others attacked the primary target but only one observed bomb bursts, and two others found last resort targets in nearby Duisburg. In contrast to the experiences of the early shift, by the time that the last 5 Group crews took off from Scampton either side of 03.00, they climbed into rain and only broke cloud at 7,500 feet over the North Sea. Ten-tenths cloud accompanied them all the way to the target, and few if any managed to locate the primary target.

On the 20th, Finningley was transferred out of 5 Group to be taken over by 7 Operational Training Group, and the evicted 106 Squadron moved south to take up residence at Coningsby. Small-scale operations against Channel and North Sea ports had occupied the week following the Homberg operation, as low cloud and rain kept 5 Group stations effectively closed for business. It had been planned to send a minelaying force to Brest on the night of the 19/20th, with the intention of sinking the Hipper-class cruiser, should it try to venture out into open water. In the event, the operation was cancelled, but forty-four 5 Group crews were called to briefing on the afternoon of the 21st, to be told that it was on again for that night. It was recorded in ORBs as a mining operation in the Jellyfish garden, for which the 61 squadron crews of F/O Stewart, P/O Gilbert and Sgt K G Cooper departed Hemswell between 18.41 and 18.59. They began the Channel crossing at the Dorset coast and set course for the target area in predominantly favourable conditions, encountering cloud over the sea, which had dispersed to five-tenths at 2,000 feet by the time that the target area drew near. Pinpoints were established with ease in good visibility, most employing Pointe-Saint-Mathieu on the headland west of the port, where searchlights ensnared some of the attackers and flak ships took pot-shots at them as they made their timed runs. The 61 Squadron trio all fulfilled their brief before returning safely, the Stewart and Gilbert crews to report attacking Lanvéoc aerodrome with their 250-pounders.

5 Group would spend the next two nights on the ground, while a small force of Wellingtons targeted enemy warships at Brest on the 22nd and the docks at Boulogne twenty-four hours later. When orders arrived on 5 Group stations on the 24th, they signalled the introduction to operations of a new squadron and aircraft type. 207 Squadron had completed its working-up programme with the Manchester at Waddington and would contribute six of the type to this night's raid by fifty-seven aircraft on enemy warships at Brest. It had been a difficult gestation period for the squadron, and the coming operational career of the Manchester would be dogged by grounding orders caused

largely by the unreliability of its Rolls-Royce Vulture engines. Despite this, and ignorant of the full extent of the problems that would occur, orders would be issued on the following day to reform 97 Squadron at Waddington as the second Manchester unit. The Manchester would bring a massive increase in bomb-carrying capacity, and on this night, each would be loaded with a dozen 500-pounders to drop on the cruiser, Admiral Hipper, as part of an overall force of fifty-seven aircraft, eighteen of them Hampdens.

Düsseldorf was posted as the target on the 25th, for which a force of eighty aircraft was assembled, Hemswell and Scampton providing the 5 Group contribution of twenty-two Hampdens. The six 61 Squadron crews were briefed to attack the Rhine docks and took off between 18.54 and 19.25 with W/C Valentine and S/L Misselbrook the senior pilots on duty. They encountered poor weather conditions and ten-tenths cloud over the entire Ruhr area, and this would result in only around seven bomb loads falling within the city. W/C Valentine and crew descended to 1,500 feet in the hope of securing a better view of the ground and ultimately bombed what appeared through the mist to be a factory from 1,800 feet. The others stooged around with only searchlights, flak and an occasional barrage balloon as a reference, and delivered their bomb loads indiscriminately in the vicinity of Düsseldorf from 8,000 to 10,000 feet, observing the flash of bomb bursts but no detail.

Briefings on the 26th revealed Cologne to be the target for a force of 126 aircraft, for which Hemswell, Lindholme and Scampton made ready twenty-eight Hampdens and Waddington five Manchesters. 61 Squadron briefed the crews of Sgts Clarke, Cooper and Glover and P/O Street for one of two designated targets and launched them off the end of the runway between 19.14 and 19.32 in favourable weather conditions. They set course for the English coast at Orford Ness and reached the target under clear skies, guided to the aiming point by the many fires already burning and huge pillars of smoke rising from the centre of the target area. Numerous searchlights ringed the city, but the flak was remarkably light for such a well-defended target, and this emboldened some crews to take their time to ensure accuracy. Most picked up the Rhine to the south of the city, suggesting, perhaps, that the Wesseling oil plant was the specific target, and crossed from east to west to deliver their bombs from between 7,000 and 14,000 feet. Returning crews reported numerous explosions and fires and were confident of a highly successful raid, while local reports mentioned only ten high-explosive bombs and ninety incendiaries falling on the western edge of the city, with more hitting three villages.

The Admiralty continued to maintain pressure on the Command to deal with the enemy's capital ships, and it was the Tirpitz at Wilhelmshaven that featured in briefings on the 28th, for which 116 aircraft were made ready across the groups, 5 Group contributing twenty-three Hampdens from Scampton and Waddington. In the event ten-tenths cloud obscured the target area, only four aircraft bombed the position of the vessel, while others sought out alternative targets.

Ten months after it had begun, an assessment of the efficacy of mining operations revealed that seventeen enemy vessels had been sunk in the Baltic's Great and Little Belts and eighteen damaged. It was believed that a further eighteen had probably been sunk and it was considered safe to estimate that for every known case of a sinking or damage, another would have occurred without news of it reaching England. Among the known sinkings was that of a troopship carrying three thousand men, of whom fewer than four hundred survived.

During the course of the month, 61 Squadron took part in nine operations and dispatched fifty-five sorties for the loss of two Hampdens, one complete crew and an additional airman.

March 1941

The new month began with a return to Cologne on the night of the 1/2nd by an initial force of 131 assorted aircraft, of which forty-four Hampdens were provided by 5 Group from its stations at Coningsby, Hemswell, Lindholme and Scampton. The eight 61 Squadron crews took off between 19.58 and 20.15 with S/L Misselbrook the senior pilot on duty and the favourable weather conditions over the North Sea enabled them to establish their positions as they made landfall over the Scheldt estuary and headed across Holland. They arrived in the target area to find clear skies and easily identifiable ground features, predominantly the distinctive bends in the River Rhine, which provided most with the necessary references required to run in on the briefed aiming point. S/L Misselbrook and crew were guided by the fires already burning and added to them from 7,000 feet in the face of an intense defensive response, and the other 61 Squadron participants also attacked the target, but as a result of the tragic events on their return, few details were recorded. As they approached their stations in deteriorating weather conditions after up to eight hours in the air, some received diversion signals, but P1253 ran out of fuel before reaching Stradishall and crashed at 03.20 at Great Wratting in Suffolk, killing the second pilot, mortally injuring one of the gunners and leaving P/O Noble and one other with survivable injuries. Fifty-five minutes later X3147 came down six miles west-north-west of Fakenham in Norfolk with fatal consequences for Sgt Clarke and crew and at 05.00 the crew of Sgt K G Cooper perished in the wreckage of AD723 near Caistor in Lincolnshire. These were among thirteen aircraft to either fail to return or crash in England on a night when total crew casualties amounted to more than forty killed or seriously injured. At debriefings most crews reported an apparently successful operation, and this was confirmed by local sources, which reported extensive damage in central districts, particularly in the docks areas on both banks of the Rhine.

The threat of adverse weather conditions caused a reduction in the 5 Group force briefed to attack the Admiral Hipper at Brest on the night of the 2/3rd, and, ultimately, it was left to eight crews from 44 Squadron to carry out the operation. A force of seventy-one aircraft was assembled later on the 3rd to send once more against Cologne, for which Coningsby and Scampton provided the 5 Group element, while Waddington made ready three Hampdens and two Manchesters for a return to the Admiral Hipper at Brest. Thereafter, the weather took a hand to keep most of the Command on the ground for the next week, and it was during this period, on the 8th, that a new shape landed at Hemswell, Manchester L7307, which was to be used for crew familiarisation in preparation for the squadron to become the third unit to receive the type after 207 and 97 Squadrons. L7315 would arrive on the 18th, but conversion would be a slow process occupying three months, before the first tentative sorties could be launched.

On the 9th, the Air Ministry responded to the urgent and burgeoning threat posed by U-Boots, which were claiming a massive tonnage of shipping crossing the Atlantic in convoys with vital war supplies. A new Directive was issued, which would unleash a concerted campaign against this menace and its partner in crime, the Focke-Wulf Kondor long-range maritime reconnaissance bomber. These two threats were to be attacked where-ever they could be found, at sea, in their bases in the occupied ports, and at their point of manufacture in the shipyards and in the assembly and component factories. A new target list was drawn up, which was headed by Kiel, Hamburg and Vegesack (Bremen), all of which were home to U-Boot construction yards, and Bremen itself, which also boasted a Focke-Wulf aircraft factory in its south-eastern Hemelingen district. Other related targets included the diesel engine plants at Mannheim and Augsburg, aircraft factories at Dessau, and, of course, the U-Boot bases at Brest, Lorient and St Nazaire. Until otherwise instructed, this was to be the focus of Peirse's efforts, and, only occasionally, would he be able prosecute the oil campaign.

When 5 Group resumed operations on the 10th, only Hemswell and Waddington were involved in sending nineteen Hampdens back to Cologne, the 61 Squadron element of five taking off between 18.58 and 19.01 with S/L Misselbrook the senior pilot on duty. All arrived at the target area to benefit from favourable weather conditions, in which seventeen aircraft delivered an attack and according to debriefing reports, left many fires burning. On the way home, Sgt Hughes and crew came upon a Luftwaffe aerodrome with aircraft in the circuit and engaged three of them in quick succession, shooting down a BF110 from 300 feet with the fixed forward guns and damaging a Ju88, before exchanging fire with three others with indeterminate results.

The new directive was implemented first on the night of the 12/13th, at the end of a day of hectic activity across the Command as aircraft were made ready for three major raids to be conducted that night. Eighty-eight aircraft were to attack the Blohm & Voss shipyards at Hamburg, while eighty-six other crews were briefed for the Focke-Wulf factory and the city of Bremen, and, finally, seventy-two aircraft were prepared for the long slog to Berlin to target two aiming points. 5 Group supported the first-mentioned with forty Hampdens and four Manchesters, and the last-mentioned with thirty Hampdens, and, with the addition of a single freshman crew on gardening duties, this represented the largest effort undertaken by the group thus far in the war. The four Manchesters and three 4 Group Halifaxes at Hamburg were the first of their type to operate over Germany. 61 Squadron briefed the crews of P/O Street and Sgts Glover, Hughes and Metcalfe for Hamburg, those of S/L Weir and P/Os Parry and Webb for Berlin and P/O Pritchard for mining duties in what the ORB refers to as the Free Area north of the Frisian Island of Ameland. The Nectarine region encompassed the entire Frisian chain and was divided into three gardens, Nectarine I from Texel to the eastern tip of Ameland, Nectarine II from east of Ameland to Memmert, and Nectarine III, Juist to Wangerooge.

The Hamburg-bound trio of P/O Street and Sgts Glover and Metcalfe and their crews departed Hemswell first, between 18.53 and 19.03, and they were followed into the air at 19.12 by P/O Pritchard and crew and finally between 21.39 and 21.57 by the crews of S/L Weir, P/Os Parry and Webb and Sgt Hughes with the long slog to Germany's capital city ahead of them. Hamburg was basking under what were described as perfect weather conditions, which allowed easy identification of the aiming point once the crews had run the usual gauntlet of intense searchlights and flak as they approached from the north and north-west. The 61 Squadron crews all attacked the Blohm & Voss shipyard, the Glover crew from a lowly 5,000 feet, and one of the resultant fires remained visible for forty miles into the return journey. With the whole of northern Germany under clear skies, those heading for Berlin also experienced no difficulty in navigating across Holland on course for the gap between Bremen and the Hannover/Braunschweig area. All identified the target area, if not necessarily the designated aiming point, and delivered their attacks, P/O Webb and crew from 13,000 feet as the only ones with a recorded bombing height and observed bursts one mile west of the aiming point. The crews of S/L Weir and P/O Parry also attacked, but no details of bombing altitude were recorded, and neither observed any bursts, while Sgt Hughes and crew bombed a railway junction in Hamburg as a last-resort target and observed one burst between the track and a large factory building.

The 5 Group ORB expressed disappointment that despite the unusually favourable conditions only a modest nineteen of its crews reported bombing the primary target. Local sources in Berlin reported sixty buildings damaged, mostly in southern districts, while, at Hamburg, twenty high-explosive bombs and up to four hundred incendiaries had inflicted significant damage on the Blohm & Voss U-Boot construction yards and four other shipyards. Meanwhile, Wellingtons had attacked the Focke-Wulf factory at Bremen, and a number of hits had been scored there also. P/O Pritchard and crew planted their vegetable into the briefed location from 800 feet and were back home before midnight to enjoy a full night in bed.

Weather conditions remained favourable as preparations were put in hand on the 13th to return to Hamburg that night with a force of 139 aircraft, including a contribution from 5 Group of thirty-four Hampdens and five Manchesters. The 61 Squadron crews of P/O Pritchard and Sgt Glover were Hamburg-bound as they departed Hemswell at 19.10 and 19.18 respectively, and they were followed into the air at 19.35 by the crew of F/O Glennie, whose destination was the same Nectarine I garden as on the previous night. F/O Glennie was operating as crew captain for the first time having completed his apprenticeship as second pilot/navigator. They crossed the Lincolnshire coast in the region of Skegness, before making their way independently of each other, as was the practice at this stage of the war, towards the enemy coast. Moonlight helped with identification of the aiming-point, and the bombing took place in the face of accurate searchlights and heavy and light flak. The general consensus among returning crews was of an effective raid, which local sources and post-raid reconnaissance confirmed had inflicted further damage on the Blohm & Voss shipyards and caused 119 fires in Hamburg generally, thirty-five of them classed as large. The Glennie crew returned four hours before the others and reported planting their vegetable according to brief from 600 feet.

A raid on the Hydrierwerke-Scholven synthetic oil refinery at Gelsenkirchen was briefed out to twenty-one Hampden crews on the 14th, as part of an overall force of 101 aircraft assigned to a number of similar targets in the city. The 61 Squadron crews of P/O Street and Sgt Hughes departed Hemswell at 18.50 and 19.00 respectively and made landfall over the Scheldt estuary, observing large fires from the oil storage tanks at Rotterdam to the north, which had just been attacked by Whitleys and Blenheims. The glow was still visible from the Ruhr as they closed on the target, where fires were also already burning and smoke beginning to drift across to obscure ground detail. P/O Street and crew claimed a direct hit on the oil plant, while the Hughes crew's bombs impacted the north-eastern corner of the plant and a dull, orange fire was observed to emit a column of black smoke rising through 11,000 feet as they turned for home. Shortly before they arrived in the circuit, W/C Valentine and crew took off at 23.47 to conduct a security patrol, which was not recorded in the 5 Group ORB and may have been to seek out and attack Luftwaffe intruders, which were dropping incendiaries in the vicinity of Hemswell. Whatever the reason for the sortie, it lasted only a little over an hour and no report was forthcoming. Local reports suggested that this had been the most destructive raid yet on Gelsenkirchen, where some useful damage had been inflicted on the Scholven-Buer refinery after some sixteen bomb loads hit the oil plant, causing a total loss of production for a brief spell, and adjacent workers housing had also been hit. It was, however, still pinprick stuff, and it would be a further two years before this and other Ruhr production centres felt the full force of a Bomber Command attack.

Hemswell, Lindholme and Waddington were notified of a return to the Ruhr on the 15th, this time to attack a specific target in Düsseldorf, for which 61 Squadron briefed the crews of P/O Pritchard and Sgt Metcalfe and sent them on their way at 19.14 and 19.16 respectively. After experiencing haze over base, they enjoyed good visibility with cloud east of the Trent all the way to the Dutch coast, where the skies cleared, and when ten miles from the target they hit a wall of searchlights, but surprisingly little or no flak. The moon had risen during the outward flight, and its light glinted off the Rhine to offset the effects of the industrial haze and provide a firm pinpoint for some, while the 61 Squadron pair described fog as an impediment to target identification and they were unable to observe the fall of their bombs. Fog over Lincolnshire for the return meant a busy night for the fighter station at Tangmere in Sussex, which acted as host to many of the bombers.

It fell to Scampton and Coningsby to provide eighteen Hampdens on the 17th for a force of fifty-seven aircraft targeting shipyards in Bremen. The raid took place in excellent conditions in the presence of the first Stirling to operate over Germany, and returning crews claimed a successful outcome. Thirty-eight Hampdens and two Manchesters were detailed by 5 Group on the 18th for an operation that night against the Deutsche Werke U-Boot construction yard at Kiel in company with fifty-seven Wellingtons and Whitleys. 61 Squadron dispatched eight Hampdens from Hemswell between 18.18 and 18.22 with W/C Valentine and S/L Weir the senior pilots on duty. The information provided by the squadron ORB is typically scant and we are told only that the night was extremely dark and the skies clear. In contrast other accounts report cloud all the way to the target and haze that prevented identification of the aiming point. However, local reports claimed this to be the heaviest raid yet on Kiel and mentioned an increase in the number of incendiaries, while confirming damage to the U-Boot yards.

On the 20th, 5 Group committed forty-two Hampdens to an extensive programme of mining off the Biscay ports of Brest, Lorient and St-Nazaire, while three Manchesters and twenty-one Whitleys turned their attention upon U-Boots at the base being built on the Keroman peninsula on the southern extremity of Lorient. The first phase of the massive construction project had begun just weeks earlier, and would continue until January 1942, by which time K1, K2 and K3 would be completed and capable of sheltering thirty vessels and their crews under cover. The complex would boast a revolutionary lift system, which could raise U-Boots from the water and transport them across the facility to repair and servicing bays. The thickness of the concrete rendered the structure impervious to the bombs available to Bomber Command at the time, and attacks would be directed predominantly at the town and its approaches to prevent access by road and rail, while extensive minelaying compromised access by sea. The Jellyfish garden off Brest provided the destination for six 61 Squadron crews, which departed Hemswell in two phases, the first between 18.54 and 18.56 led by F/L Aldridge and the second, consisting of the crews of Sgt Stevenson and P/O Pritchard, unexpectedly and at short notice at 02.09 and 02.40, after the others had landed. Those on the early shift reported challenging conditions in which to establish a pinpoint, despite which the crews of F/L Glennie and Parry and Sgt Johnston planted their vegetables in the briefed area, while F/L Aldridge and crew were unable to identify the drop zone and jettisoned their mine. The latecomers benefitted to a small degree from faint moonlight and also fulfilled their brief.

Twelve Hampden crews at Hemswell and Scampton were briefed to return to Lorient on the night of 21st, while a handful of others were sent mining in the Deodar garden in the Gironde Estuary on the approaches to Bordeaux, 144 Squadron taking care of business at Hemswell while 61 Squadron took the night off. With the moon out of commission for a period, and weather conditions over northern Germany unfavourable, 5 Group sent thirty Hampdens to Kiel on the 23rd, while Berlin played host to a force of sixty-three Wellingtons and Whitleys. The 61 Squadron crews of Sgt Johnston, P/O Pritchard and F/O Glennie departed Hemswell in that order between 18.40 and 18.42 and lost the services of the Glennie crew to low oil pressure when over the North Sea. The others encountered heavy cloud, which persisted all the way to the Danish coast, but it thinned sufficiently over Schleswig-Holstein to allow them to identify pinpoints, and by the time that they reached the western Baltic, the horizontal visibility was adequate for their purposes. Both bombed the target and observed bursts, but X3005 was hit by flak and on the way home the port engine seized, causing the Hampden to sink towards the waves and the crew to systematically jettison all removable equipment in an effort to remain airborne. That was sufficient to enable them to gain the Yorkshire coast near Bridlington, but shortly afterwards, at 01.30, they were forced to abandon the Hampden to its fate and landed safely by parachute near Driffield.

Düsseldorf was posted as one of the targets on the 27th, for which a force of thirty-nine aircraft was made ready, consisting of twenty-two Hampdens from Hemswell, Scampton and Waddington, four 207 Squadron Manchesters and thirteen Whitleys from 4 Group. 61 Squadron continued to be employed sparingly and only the crews of F/O Glennie and Sgts Hughes and Hodgkinson were briefed, before being sent on their way between 19.23 and 19.26. All reached the target area to be greeted by the expected industrial haze and intense searchlight and flak defence, the glare from which, bouncing off the haze, produced challenging conditions for target identification. It took time for crews to establish their positions, assisted to some extent by the distinctive reversed S-bend in the River Rhine to the west of the city centre, which proved to be the only identifiable ground feature. By the time that they released their bombs from estimated positions a number of fires were observed to be developing. No detailed assessment was possible, and an absence of post-raid reconnaissance and local reports left the crews uncertain as to the effectiveness of their work.

On the 29th, the German cruisers Scharnhorst and Gneisenau were reported to be off Brest, and 50 Squadron was ordered to dispatch six Hampdens from Lindholme to carry out a cloud-cover daylight attack, a type of operation that would come to be known as "moling". The arrival of the vessels must have been expected, because Lindholme had been standing-by at two-hours readiness for seven days when the order was received. They flew out in two vics over the Lizard, until insufficient cloud cover over the Channel forced them to turn back. That night, twenty-five Hampdens were dispatched from Scampton, Waddington and Coningsby to mine the waters of the Jellyfish garden on the approaches to the port.

Hemswell and Lindholme joined forces on the 30th to send six Hampdens each on another daylight foray to Brest, the crews of F/O Glennie and Sgts Glover and Metcalfe representing 61 Squadron and taking off at 14.12. They flew out in a stepped-down echelon with a minimum requirement at the target of seven-tenths cloud cover to provide protection, but when thirty miles out over the Channel they were recalled and returned to Hemswell. That night, a force of 109 aircraft was assembled for a return to the port, and this number included fourteen Hampdens and four Manchesters representing 5 Group, while ten others from the group attended to gardening duties in the approaches. The crews of F/O Glennie and Sgt Hodgkinson took off at 19.32 and 19.40 and reached the target area to find clear skies but extreme darkness, which, typically, was at variance with other participants, some of which reported the target vessels to be obscured by cloud. Most, however, found the target to be easily identified and attacks were carried out in the face of an intense flak defence from the vessels themselves and batteries around the port. This was the opening phase of a saga that would endure until the following February and during that period call upon massive Bomber Command resources and act as a major distraction. The British press managed to derive some fun from the situation by dubbing Scharnhorst and Gneisenau "Salmon

& Gluckstein", in a comic reference to the country's largest tobacconist, established in London 1873 by a German Jewish émigré and his English partner.

During the course of the month the squadron took part in sixteen operations, a number involving just one crew, and dispatched fifty-three sorties for the loss of four Hampdens in crashes at home and two complete crews and two members of another.

April 1941

The first week of the new month was reserved exclusively for operations on and around Brest with the intention of disabling its lodgers, the heavy cruisers, Scharnhorst and Gneisenau. The assault on Brest began with 5 Group launching a dozen Hampdens from St Eval in Cornwall for a daylight attack on the 1st, 61 Squadron represented by the crews of F/L Aldridge and Sgt Metcalfe, who departed Hemswell at 12.32, with orders to observe a minimum cloud cover at the target of seven-tenths. When the cloud disappeared completely thirty miles from the target all but one turned back, and the one that continued on, a 144 Squadron aircraft from Hemswell, failed to return. 49 and 83 Squadrons sent six Hampdens each from their Scampton base to St Eval for another attempt on the 3rd, for which the details are omitted from the ORBs of 5 Group and both squadrons. We are told only that one crew dive-bombed the vessels with indeterminate results, while the others involved in this action had turned back in the face of insufficient cloud cover and a second attempt launched in the afternoon was also recalled. Ninety other aircraft were made ready during the course of the afternoon to return to Brest that night, while fifteen Hampdens were to sneak in under cover of the main event to mine the approaches in the Jellyfish garden and also the waters of the Cinnamon garden off La Rochelle. 61 Squadron contributed the crews of P/O Pritchard and Sgts Hodgkinson, Johnston and Stevenson, who departed Hemswell between 19.37 and 19.47 bound for the Jellyfish garden, where they faced accurate light flak from flak ships, but avoided damage as they planted their vegetables according to brief. Sgt Johnston and crew dropped their two wing-mounted bombs on one of the flak ships before returning with the others to land at St Eval.

On the 4th, Gneisenau entered a dry dock, which was to be drained on the following day for an inspection of the vessel, while 5 Group detailed eleven Hampdens and four Manchesters for yet another attempt on the enemy cruisers that night as part of a force of fifty-four aircraft. Five of the eleven participating Hampdens carried out low-level attacks, and one went in at 1,000 feet at 22.55 to score a direct hit on Scharnhorst, which was recognised in the flash as being in a dry dock precisely as depicted in the reconnaissance photos shown to the crews at briefing. The rear gunner confirmed the success, but it was impossible to determine which part of the vessel had been hit. Another of the low-level attackers was the 106 Squadron commanding officer, W/C Polglase, whose Hampden was seen to be shot down. The Continental Hotel in the town was also struck by bombs just as dinner was being served, and a number of naval officers were killed. While the above was in progress, the 61 Squadron crews of Sgt Woodley and F/O Parry departed Hemswell at 19.20 and 19.27 respectively, and in favourable conditions planted their vegetables according to brief. On the way home the Parry crew attacked Lanveoc aerodrome with their wing bombs and both returned safely to land at diversion aerodromes.

When Gneisenau's dry dock was drained on the following day, the 5th, a single unexploded 500lb bomb was found nestling at the bottom, and the ship's captain, Kapitän-zur-See Otto Fein, decided to move his vessel out into the harbour while it was dealt with. The dock was refilled to allow Gneisenau to vacate it, and she was spotted by a reconnaissance aircraft at some point, which led to an operation being planned by Coastal Command to be carried out at first light on the 6th. In the meantime, still on the 5th, 44 and 50 Squadrons were ordered to prepare for another daylight operation to be launched from St Eval, concerning which, the 5 Group record mentioned only that the weather conditions were inhospitable with ten-tenths low cloud. By the time that they had passed south of the Isles of Scilly, they were in rain at 500 feet, and although a number of Lindholme crews reached the target, only one carried out an attack on estimated position with no hope of hitting anything of value.

The Coastal Command operation on the 6th took place in poor weather conditions, which led to the six Beauforts becoming separated while outbound, and F/O Kenneth Campbell and his crew alone pressed home an attack, which caused damage to Gneisenau that would require six months to repair. In the face of the most concentrated anti-aircraft fire, the Beaufort stood little chance of getting away with it and was shot down without survivors. F/O Campbell was posthumously awarded a Victoria Cross for his actions. That evening, while Hemswell and other stations remained inactive, fifteen Hampdens were made ready at Scampton for mining duties in the Jellyfish garden off Brest, while four others were to ply their trade in the Nectarine garden around the Frisian Islands.

When Kiel shipyards were posted as the primary targets on the 7th, a new record force for a single target of 229 aircraft was assembled, among which were sixty Hampdens, six of them representing 61 Squadron. They departed Hemswell between 19.53 and 19.59 with F/L Aldridge the senior pilot on duty and crossed the English coast near Skegness, before setting course for Rømø Island on Denmark's western coast, where they would turn east to a position north of Flensburg to approach Kiel from the north. They encountered cloud at 6,000 feet for the first fifty miles of the North Sea crossing and then benefitted from clear skies for the remainder of the outward flight, overflying the enemy coast at around 10,000 feet before map-reading their way across Schleswig-Holstein and arriving in the target area to find the defences had already been stirred into action. The bright moonlight helped to tone down the glare from dozens of searchlights, which were co-operating with the medium calibre flak batteries hosing shells up to 12,000 feet, while heavy flak reached as high as 18,000 feet and the light stuff awaited any crew foolhardy enough to try to sneak in lower down. The 61 Squadron crews bombed from an average of 9,000 feet, and noted many fires, which remained visible for up to eighty miles into the homeward leg. Returning crews were confident that the raid, which had taken place over a period of almost five hours, had struck a major blow against this important target, and this was confirmed by local reports of widespread damage to housing in the town, and to port facilities and the eastern docks area. The nightshift workers at the Germania Werft and Deutsche Werke U-Boot construction yards had been sent home, causing a number of days' loss of production.

A force of 160 aircraft was made ready during the following day to return to Kiel that night, and among them were twenty-nine Hampdens and twelve Manchesters, four of the latter belonging to 5 Group's latest addition, 97 Squadron at Coningsby, which would be operating for the first time. 61 Squadron briefed the crews of F/O Glennie and Sgts Hodgkinson, Metcalfe and Woodley for the main event and those of the newly posted-in S/L Newall and Sgt Johnston for mining duties in the Jellyfish garden. They departed Hemswell together between 19.45 and 20.00, the bombers carrying either a single 1,900lb bomb and incendiaries or a mixture of 500 and 250-pounders, also with incendiaries, and followed the same route as on the previous night, once again meeting a band of cloud over the Lincolnshire/Yorkshire coasts that extended from 3,000 to 6,000 feet. Climbing through it they encountered severe icing conditions, which, once negotiated, gave way to clear skies, bright moonlight and excellent visibility, enabling crews easily to establish the aiming point and deliver an effective attack. Returning crews reported a very large explosion that was followed by a column of black smoke, and they described the target area as a mass of flames as they retreated to the west. Absent from debriefing was the crew of F/O Glennie, who all lost their lives when AD827 was shot down by flak in the target area. Meanwhile, the gardening duo had fulfilled their briefs, and the Johnston crew attacked a flak ship with their 250-pounders without observing the result. Local sources in Kiel confirmed another damaging raid, which had fallen more into the town than the docks and seafront area and some eight thousand people had been bombed out of their homes.

The main operation on the 9th was directed at Berlin and was prosecuted by eighty aircraft, including twenty-four Hampdens, while 61 Squadron remained at home. Berlin was found to be under largely clear skies and the bombing of the main railway station and its marshalling yards took place in almost perfect conditions. Orders were received on some 5 Group stations on the 10th to prepare for a joint 4 and 5 Group effort against Düsseldorf involving fifty-three aircraft, for which twenty-nine Hampdens were detailed. 61 Squadron briefed five crews and sent them on their way from Hemswell between 20.00 and 20.15 with S/L Newall the senior and only commissioned pilot on duty and lost the services of Sgt Metcalfe and crew to wireless failure during the North Sea crossing. The crews of S/L Newall and Sgt Harris attacked the primary target through industrial haze, but despite the otherwise favourable conditions, the crews of Sgts Hodgkinson and Woodley failed to locate it and bombed last resort objectives at Hilden and Coblenz respectively. The other operation on this night was another assault on Brest and its guest enemy warships involving fifty-three aircraft, including five Manchesters of 97 Squadron to represent 5 Group. Four bombs hit the under-repair Gneisenau on the starboard side of the forward superstructure, and, although only two detonated, seventy-two men were killed and ninety injured, sixteen of which would not survive.

It was the turn of Lindholme to stay at home on the 12th, while 5 Group split its forces to cover two bombing operations and mining. The main event would be played out once more at Brest, for which a force of sixty-six aircraft included a dozen Hampdens and six Manchesters, while other Hampdens from Scampton mined the approaches in the Jellyfish garden. A second force of fifteen Hampdens and nine Wellingtons bypassed the Brest area on its way further south to attack Merignac aerodrome near Bordeaux.

On the 13th, B flight was detached to Watton in Norfolk under the command of S/L Newall and his deputy, F/L Aldridge, and took up residence on its satellite aerodrome at Bodney, from where it would operate under the orders of 2 Group and conduct daylight cloud-cover operations referred to as "moling". The Manchester's Rolls Royce Vulture engines were proving to be problematic, with overheating and component failures seriously affecting the type's rate of serviceability, as a result of which, the first of a number of grounding orders was issued, also on the 13th, while investigations were carried out into the engine-bearing problem and modifications put in hand. This meant that no further operations would be undertaken by the type during what remained of the month. That night, seventeen Hampdens were dispatched for mining duties in the Cinnamon garden off the port of La Rochelle, the crews having been briefed to drop their wing-mounted bombs on a hotel south of Quiberon, which, presumably, was home to U-Boot personnel.

The pattern of operations was now set for the remainder of the month, in which Brest and Kiel would continue to be the principal objectives, the former posted as the primary target for a force of ninety-four aircraft on the 14th. 5 Group contributed twenty-five Hampdens for what turned into an ineffective raid, for which a post-raid analysis blamed low cloud. Kiel was posted as the target for ninety-six aircraft on the 15th, 5 Group contributing nineteen Hampdens on a night when cloud was again the decisive factor and returning crews were unable to offer an assessment of the outcome, while local reports suggested an ineffective raid that had caused little damage. The destination for 107 aircraft on the 16th was Bremen, where the shipyards were the aiming points, and the bombers ran into thick cloud at the Dutch coast that persisted all the way to the target area. The only clue to their whereabouts for most crews was the flak coming up from Delmenhorst and Oldenburg and it was this that provided the reference for most crews to bomb on estimated positions after searching for up to ninety minutes. Berlin provided the target for 118 aircraft on the 17th, thirty-nine of them Hampdens, which had two aiming points to aim at in the city centre, including the telephone exchange building. There were clear skies over the border region between southern Denmark and Germany, but haze blotted out ground detail, and those reaching Berlin would find it difficult to locate the planned aiming points. Most crews carried out their attacks on estimated positions and none was able to offer an assessment either because of cloud or the glare from searchlights.

61 Squadron's first operation from Bodney was posted on the 18th and involved all six Hampdens in a cloud-cover raid on the docks and shipping at Cherbourg, for which they took off between 15.10 and 15.50. Sgt Glover and crew turned back early because of engine trouble, and S/L Newall and P/O Pritchard ran out of cloud cover with the French coast twenty miles ahead on the horizon and also curtailed their sorties. The crews of F/L Aldridge and Sgts Metcalfe and Hodgkinson opted to press on despite the lack of cloud, and while the Hodgkinson crew somehow got away with it and delivered their bombs unopposed, the Aldridge and Metcalfe crews came under heavy fire and sustained damage, which in the case of AD732 proved to be terminal. The Hampden crashed in the target area killing F/L Aldridge DFC and two of his crew and delivered the sole survivor into enemy hands. Meanwhile, Sgt Metcalfe had sustained leg and arm wounds and ordered the bombs to be jettisoned while he focused on bringing AD825 and its occupants home. By the time that they arrived over the Wiltshire/Berkshire border between Hungerford and Swindon, Sgt Metcalfe feared he would not be able to land safely and ordered his crew to bale out, leaving the Hampden to crash in open country. The experiences of the above crews demonstrated the utter madness of "moling" operations, which had obviously been devised by someone who did not have to put his life on the line. The crews of 2 Group were accustomed to operating in daylight, it was their "raison d'etre", but their Circus and Ramrod operations had purpose and were organised under a strong fighter escort, while to sacrifice the lives of brave men purely for nuisance value was unforgiveable and wasteful.

Eleven Hampdens joined fifty other aircraft to raid Cologne on the 20th and a further nine were detailed for mining duties in the Jellyfish garden off Brest. 61 Squadron dispatched the crews of Sgts Johnston and Woodley at 12.10 on the 21st to test the water for "moling" raids on Rotterdam and Antwerp, but an absence of cloud had them turn back and the operations were scrubbed. At Bodney on the 23rd, six crews were briefed for "moling" sorties against the Frisian Island of Borkum and the town of Emmerich situated on the Rhine north of the Ruhr. The crews of P/O

Pritchard and Sgt Glover were sent ahead at 10.00 to report on cloud conditions, and before they were able to do so, the crews of S/L Newall and Sgts Harris, Johnston and Woodley also took to the air, only to turn back in the absence of cloud, the Harris crew actually making landfall over the Scheldt estuary before abandoning their sortie. Later ten Hemswell Hampdens of 144 Squadron attempted to maintain the pressure on the German warships at Brest, but the crews failed to identify the location of the vessels and bombed on approximate positions. In addition, fourteen Hampdens were assigned to gardening duties and were divided equally between Quiberon Bay, off the Biscay coast, and the Frisians. It was left to ten Hampdens from Scampton to represent 5 Group in an overall force of sixty-nine aircraft with Kiel as their destination on the 24th, after which local sources confirmed the scattered nature of the raid, and the small amount of damage achieved.

A follow-up raid by sixty-two aircraft twenty-four hours later involved ten Hampdens from Coningsby and Hemswell and developed into a scattered affair that caused modest damage. Hamburg would be a frequent destination throughout the war and would receive its own mini campaign of six raids between the end of April and the middle of May, but in the meantime, twenty-eight Hampdens and twenty-two Wellingtons were prepared for an operation against it on the 26th, although, at this stage of the war, it is unlikely that they would have been over the target at the same time. The presence of ten-tenths ice-bearing cloud over Germany's north-western coast created challenges for navigation and local sources reported no more than sixteen bomb loads falling, no fires and only minor damage.

Six crews were called to briefing at Bodney on the 27th and learned that they were to be organised in three pairs to carry out "moling" raids on Cologne, Münster and Osnabrück, for which they took off between 15.25 and 15.50. The crews of P/O Pritchard and Sgts Harris, Hodgkinson and Johnston all turned back before reaching the enemy coast, while the crews of Sgts Glover and Asson pressed on to attack De Kooy aerodrome and the docks at Ijmuiden respectively, the latter under heavy fire. The operation was repeated on the following day with a departure between 09.40 and 10.05, and although all reached enemy territory, cloud conditions precluded deep penetration, and alternative targets were sought out. P/O Pritchard was intercepted by a BF109 over the fishing port of Harlingen and was forced to dump his 1,900-pounder before escaping into the small amount of available cloud. The crews of Sgts Glover and Johnston respectively attacked marshalling yards and a factory in the Dutch town of Meppel, while Sgt Hodgkinson and crew went for the docks at Den Helder, Sgt Harris and crew a 2,000-ton cargo vessel off the Dutch coast and Sgt Asson and crew the aerodrome at De Kooy near Den Helder. After bombing, two BF110s latched on to the Asson crew, who took advantage of the available cloud to evade their would-be assailants.

On the 30th, six crews were again briefed for "moling" duties, this time with the port of Emden as their destination. The crews of Sgts Glover and Hodgkinson were sent out at 10.25 ahead of four other crews to report on cloud conditions, and when they returned three hours later to advise that little or no cloud was evident, the operation was cancelled, bringing to an end B Flight's time at Bodney.

During the course of the month the squadron took part in thirteen operations and dispatched fifty-three sorties for the loss of two Hampdens and one crew.

May 1941

B Flight returned to Hemswell on the 1st to find that there had been a further influx of Manchesters, L7279, L7281 and L7304 having been collected from 207 Squadron for crew training on the 15th, while L7292 arrived on the 22nd to be followed by L7387 and L7388 on the 24th and L7294 on the 27th. The new month began with the posting of an operation to Hamburg on the 1st, but this was subsequently cancelled, only to be reinstated on the following day and a force of ninety-five aircraft assembled. The grounding order on the Manchester had been lifted, and three of the type representing 207 Squadron joined nineteen Hampdens as the 5 Group contribution. The weather for the outbound flight was fairly good with just a little low cloud, but this increased over Germany and combined with haze to create challenging conditions for some crews. Most crews found the target without difficulty and would comment at debriefing on the intensity of the searchlights and flak that welcomed them to Germany's second city. They attacked either their briefed aiming point or an alternative within the city and according to local sources set off twenty-six fires, half of them large, but caused no significant incidents.

5 Group put up twenty-seven Hampdens and two Manchesters on the 3rd, in an overall force of 101 aircraft bound for Cologne, while a predominantly Wellington force of thirty-three aircraft continued the assault on Brest and its lodgers. On the following day, 5 Group contributed twenty-one Hampdens to an overall force of ninety-seven aircraft to take part in the next attack on the cruisers at Brest, the Group ORB offering the thought that the warships must be crippled by now following repeated attacks. Certainly, damage had been inflicted, but effective camouflage and smoke screens ensured that the British authorities actually had no clear picture of the vessels' state of serviceability, and the raids would continue. The teleprinters on 1, 3, 4 and 5 Group stations began churning out the orders of the day on the 5th, to reveal that Mannheim was to be the destination for a force of 141 aircraft, of which 5 Group's contribution amounted to thirty-three Hampdens and four Manchesters. The outward flight was attended by ten-tenths cloud, which persisted in the target area, and despite the claim by 121 crews that they had attacked the city, local sources reported some twenty-five bomb loads falling and causing only minor damage. A force of 115 aircraft was assembled for an attack on the Blohm & Voss shipyards in Hamburg on the 6th, an operation supported by 5 Group with twenty-seven Hampdens and four Manchesters.

The eighteen Hampdens detailed for a raid on Brest on the 7th represented a reduced figure in the light of a forecast of adverse weather conditions. In the event, the weather turned out to be more favourable than expected, and those reaching the target area found moonlight that enabled some to identify the dry dock occupied by one of the vessels, while others were blinded by searchlight glare. Some bursts were observed in the docks area but claims of direct hits remained unconfirmed. All 5 Group operational stations received orders on the following day to prepare aircraft for what would be a record-breaking night of activity involving 364 sorties. 188 aircraft were to attack Hamburg, 119 of them assigned to the Blohm & Voss shipyards and sixty-nine to target the city, while 133 Whitleys and Wellingtons attended to the A.G Weser U-Boot construction yards in Bremen. 5 Group contributed a record seventy-eight Hampdens and nine Manchesters to the Hamburg forces, nine of the former representing 61 Squadron as it resumed operations after its long lay-off. They had been briefed to target the shipyards and departed Hemswell between 22.10 and 22.31 with S/L Newall the senior pilot on duty as they flew out over the Lincolnshire coast on course initially for Jutland, losing the services of the crews of Sgts Glover and Sleight on the way to engine issues. Conditions over north-western Germany promised a reasonable chance of identifying the aiming points and this proved to be the case as the bombers made landfall at various points on the Danish and German coasts, some roaming far and wide over Schleswig-Holstein as far as Kiel and Lübeck to the north and north-east of Hamburg. Sgt Johnston and crew ended up over Lübeck after being led astray by a navigational error, while the others mostly pinpointed on the town of Neumünster as the starting point for their bombing run and found the target city laid out beneath them and throwing up an intense but inaccurate defence. Six 61 Squadron crews claimed to have attacked the primary target, but no details were recorded, and we must trust in the reports coming out of Hamburg that an accurate and effective raid had taken place and resulted in eighty-three fires, thirty-eight of them large, and the highest death toll yet in a German city of 185 people. Many of these may have resulted from the demolition of ten apartment blocks by a single 4,000-pounder.

While the Scampton squadrons were rested, a force of 146 aircraft was assembled on the 9th for that night's operation against the twin cities of Mannheim and Ludwigshafen, for which 5 Group made available twenty-four Hampdens and eleven Manchesters. The aiming point for the 5 Group element was the Badische Anilin & Soda-Fabrik (BASF) works in Ludwigshafen, which was part of the infamous I G Farben company, the largest manufacturer of chemicals and synthetic oil products in the world and major employer of slave workers. 61 Squadron prepared six Hampdens for the main event and another to take the freshman crew of P/O Casement to one of the Nectarine gardens off the Frisians. The bombing element departed Hemswell between 21.59 and 22.10 and the sound of their engines had barely faded by the time that the Casement crew took off at 22.18, returning a little over five hours later to report a successful outing. Meanwhile, the bombers were benefitting from favourable conditions, which sadly, was of no help to Sgt Glover and crew, who made repeated passes over the aiming point in vain attempts to release their bombs, and it would be only after landing that an electrical fault was found to be the cause. Most crews avoided being targeted by flak by conducting a throttled-back glide approach, and the impression at debriefings was that the raid had been effective, local reports confirming that some useful industrial damage had been inflicted on both cities, and that more than 3,500 people had been left homeless.

61 Squadron was not called into action when Hamburg was posted to face its fourth major operation of the month on the 10th, for which a force of 119 aircraft was assembled and the crews briefed to aim for shipyards, the Altona power station (Tiefstack) and the general city area. 5 Group put up thirty-five Hampdens and a 97 Squadron Manchester for the main operation, and six Manchesters for Berlin as part of a force of twenty-three aircraft. Crews returning from Hamburg were enthusiastic about the outcome, and local sources confirmed that 128 fires had broken out, forty-seven of them classed as large, and that extensive damage had been inflicted upon the city centre.

There would be no respite for Germany's second city as plans were already in hand to send ninety-two aircraft back there twenty-four hours later, while eighty-one others, including thirty-one Hampdens and two Manchesters, sought out one of the Deschimag shipyards in Bremen. Nine 61 Squadron Hampdens were made ready before departing Hemswell between 22.46 and 23.09 with P/O Pritchard the senior pilot on duty, but as he and his crew entered the Bremen defence zone, something persuaded them that they had been hit by flak and the bomb load was jettisoned. The others enjoyed favourable conditions as they carried out their attacks and observed bursts but no detail, and Sgt Glover and crew were on their way out of the target area having bombed the docks, when fired upon by two BF109s and sustaining a number of hits before making their escape.

Returning crews hailed the operation as a success, and local sources confirmed that many bombs had fallen in the docks area, where a floating dock belonging to the A.G Weser Company had been sunk. The main damage, however, was inflicted upon the city, where housing was the principal victim. The Hamburg operation had also been effective, causing eighty-eight fires and damage mostly to residential property.

61 Squadron was excluded from the order of battle when Mannheim and Ludwigshafen were posted again as the primary targets on the 12th, for which a force of 105 aircraft was divided 65/40 between the two cities and would involve forty-one Hampdens and four Manchesters. They crossed the North Sea over ten-tenths cloud, which diminished as they traversed Belgium and some were able to pick up the Rhine and follow it to the target, where thick haze obscured ground features, and this combined with intense searchlight and flak activity to prevent some crews from identifying the aiming point. Any failing to establish their position in relation to the primary target turned to the north-west to head the 120 miles to the designated alternative target of Cologne.

The weather precluded operations on the following two nights, and it was the 15th when the northern city of Hannover was posted as the target for 101 aircraft, for which 5 Group detailed twenty-seven Hampdens, while a simultaneous raid on Berlin involved eight Manchesters and six 3 Group Stirlings. 61 Squadron was not invited to join in on the night's activities, which were compromised to an extent by ten-tenths cloud obscuring the ground and rendering accurate navigation something of a challenge. The cloud had reduced to five-tenths over Hannover, which was identified by the River Leine to the north-west and the Maschsee to the south-east, but, despite the improving conditions, only a handful of crews observed the burst of their bombs, and as usual at Hannover, no local report was forthcoming to confirm the level of damage.

Cologne would be the object of Bomber Command's attentions on the following two nights, on the first occasion, the 16th, again in the absence of a 61 Squadron presence when 5 Group contributed twenty-four Hampdens to a force of ninety-three aircraft. They adopted a new route in an attempt to avoid searchlights when making landfall on the enemy coast, and this involved Aldeburgh in Suffolk as the starting point for the North Sea crossing and Nieuwpoort on the Belgian coast as the point of entry into Fortress Europe. They were then to head for Ghent before swinging south of Antwerp to approach Cologne from the south-west, which proved to be a successful ploy for the time being at least, and only those straying north over the Scheldt estuary found themselves in searchlights. Crews encountered ground haze and were guided to the target area by searchlights and flak, and although some picked up the Rhine as a reference, they were largely blinded by searchlight glare, and none was able to identify the planned aiming point even after flares had been deployed. Most remained in the target area for a considerable time searching for a recognisable ground feature but ultimately bombed the general area or found an alternative on the way home. Returning crews were of the opinion that they had bombed within the city, while local sources suggested that, in fact, the majority of bomb loads had missed the city, and just eleven houses had been damaged.

After six nights on the sidelines, 61 Squadron resumed operations on the 17th to participate in the second of the Cologne raids, for which a force of ninety-five aircraft was assembled, among them twenty-three Hampdens. The nine-strong 61 Squadron element departed Hemswell between 22.41 and 22.56 with S/L Newall the senior pilot on duty, only for him and his crew to return early after experiencing excessive engine vibration. Sgt Glover and crew were also concerned about the state of their starboard engine and opted to bomb the docks at Ostend as a last-resort target. The others approached the Rhineland capital city in conditions of extreme darkness in the absence of a moon, and at debriefing all claimed to have attacked the primary target while providing no details of bomb bursts, explosions and fires.

A force of seventy aircraft set off for Kiel's shipyards on the 18th, eighteen of them 5 Group Hampdens, and managed to produce only light, scattered damage. Earlier in the day, S/L Paape had been posted to 408 (Goose) Squadron Conversion Flight. He would return to operations as a founder member and flight commander in 467 Squadron RAAF, but sadly, lose his life during a raid on Essen on the night of the 3/4th of April 1943. On the 22nd, five 49 Squadron Hampdens were loaded with four 500-pounders each and put on stand-by at Scampton along with others at Waddington for a possible operation against German surface raiders, which, although not named, were the battleship Bismarck and heavy cruiser Prinz Eugen, which had put to sea on operation "Rheinübung". This was Bismarck's first offensive action and was under surveillance by Coastal Command aircraft as she and her consort slipped out of Bergen, heading for the Denmark Straits between Greenland and Iceland. In the event, the 5 Group aircraft were not called into action, but on the 24th, the shocking news came through that the mighty HMS Hood had been blown out of the water in an engagement with Bismarck with just three survivors from a complement of more than 1,400.

The belief that Bismarck was now racing for sanctuary at Brest with the Royal Navy snapping at its heels in a vengeful mood prompted the cancellation of a raid on Hamburg and the detailing of forty-eight Hampdens on the 25th for mining duties in the Jellyfish and Beech gardens off Brest and St-Nazaire respectively. After a week away from the operational scene, 61 Squadron was back on the order of battle and made ready nine Hampdens, which departed Hemswell between 22.21 and 23.10 before climbing into adverse weather conditions as they set course for Chesil Beach. The Channel crossing was undertaken in conditions of ten-tenths cloud, rainstorms and static, and a 600-foot cloud base would prevent most from establishing a pinpoint once in the target area. S/L Newall and crew were thwarted by a navigational error and had no choice but to return home, In the event, only five of the 61 Squadron crews succeeded in planting their vegetables in the briefed locations, while Sgt Harris and crew dropped theirs in an alternative location in the mouth of the River Rance off St-Malo, Sgt Johnston and crew jettisoned theirs and Sgt Donovan and crew brought theirs home.

In fact, the Bismarck's rudder would be crippled by a Fleet Air Arm torpedo during the 26th, rendering the vessel unable to manoeuvre other than in circles and restricted to a top speed of ten knots. Later that night, 5 Group sent thirty-eight Hampdens to continue mining the approaches to Brest while 61 Squadron remained on the ground. At first light on the 27th, multiple units of the Royal Navy closed in on the helpless Bismarck, and from 08.47, engaged her with guns and torpedoes until she slipped beneath the waves at 10.39. This left her consort, Prinz Eugen, at large, and the mining at Brest would continue over the succeeding nights in case she put in an appearance. Six 61 Squadron Hampdens were among thirty-six detailed for mining duties in the Jellyfish and Beech gardens on the evening of the 27th, and they departed Hemswell for the latter between 22.07 and 22.18 with P/O Pritchard the senior pilot on duty. He and his crew were beaten by the conditions, while Sgt Johnston and crew were forced to abandon their sortie when the navigator became unwell, leaving just four crews to fulfil their brief.

61 Squadron had now completed its month's account, during which it had taken part in seven operations and dispatched forty-nine sorties without loss.

June 1941

June and July were to be significant months for the Command, as its performance began to be monitored in order to provide an assessment of its effectiveness for the War Cabinet. The project was initiated by Churchill's chief scientific advisor, Lord Cherwell, who handed the responsibility to David M Bensusan-Butt, a civil-servant assistant to Cherwell working in the War Cabinet Secretariat. The new month would be dominated by operations against Cologne, Düsseldorf and Bremen, with Kiel and Brest also receiving their share of attention. During the second half of the month Cologne and Düsseldorf would be attacked simultaneously on no fewer than eight nights by forces of varying sizes, and Bremen, including the shipbuilding yards at Vegesack, would host six raids. On, or soon after the 1st, the Hipper Class cruiser Prinz Eugen, which had been acting as consort to Bismarck, arrived at Brest having evaded detection by the Royal Navy following the sinking of the battleship. She would now join Scharnhorst and Gneisenau to form a powerful battle group that would continue to be a threat to the Admiralty and, at its urging, a distraction for Bomber Command.

The month began for 5 Group with an operation against Düsseldorf on the night of the 2/3rd, for which forty-three Hampdens were detailed in an overall force of 150 aircraft, 61 Squadron contributing nine, which departed Hemswell between 22.39 and 23.04 with S/L Newall the senior pilot on duty. After exiting the English coast at Orford Ness, most set course for Brussels, while a few headed directly for the southern Ruhr, all having to contend with far from ideal weather conditions. A layer of ten-tenths cloud stretched along the entire route at 2,000 feet, with broken medium cloud at 9,000 feet and another band at 17,000 feet, but this dispersed sufficiently to leave six to eight-tenths in the target area, through which glimpses of the Rhine provided an indication of the location of Düsseldorf. Even so, bombing took place on estimated positions mostly from between 9,000 and 17,000 feet in the face of considerable searchlight and flak activity, but P/O Casement and crew came down to 3,500 feet and dropped their bombs slightly to the south of the city. Sgt Woodley and crew were unable to locate the primary target and unloaded their bombs on Aachen on the way home. Sgt Sleight and crew were flying on fumes as they crossed the Norfolk coast and when both engines cut they force-landed in a field near Dereham at 04.45, writing off P2144 but avoiding crew casualties. At debriefings, crews reported fires in the centre of the target area, but no precise results were observed, but absent from the process was the crew of Sgt Asson, who, it is believed, ran out of fuel on the way home, and having ditched and vacated X3120, drifted into the arms of the enemy.

Thereafter, the group, and, in fact, most of the Command, was kept on the ground by an unprecedented period of adverse weather conditions during the best part of the moon period. This was a source of monotony and massive frustration, until, finally, on the 10th, Brest was posted as the target for thirty-nine Hampdens in company with sixty-five Wellingtons and Whitleys, which would not have been over the target at the same time. 61 Squadron was not called into action on this night, and when Düsseldorf and Duisburg were posted as the primary targets on the 11th for forces of ninety-eight and eighty aircraft respectively, there were no 61 Squadron representatives among the thirty-five Hampdens in the 4 and 5 Group force assigned to the latter. Instead, seven of the squadron's crews were briefed for mining duties in the Forget-me-not and Nectarine gardens respectively in Kiel harbour and off the Frisians. The ORB provides no clear indication as to which garden was the destination for individual crews as they departed Hemswell between 22.39 and

23.01 with S/L Newall the senior pilot on duty, but the crews of Sgts Harris and Sleight and F/O Pritchard were definitely bound for the Baltic.

All encountered ten-tenths cloud in their target areas, despite which six crews are known to have planted their vegetables according to brief and Sgt Sleight and crew dropped their wing-mounted 250-pounders on the seaplane base at Sylt, while P/O Casement and crew narrowly missed a ship close to the drop zone. At debriefing Sgt Harris and crew reported being stalked by a twin-engine aircraft with a powerful searchlight in its nose, but a well-aimed burst of fire from the Hampden caused the light to be doused and the enemy to break away. The return of AD727 with the crew of F/O Pritchard was awaited in vain, and it was left to the Red Cross eventually to confirm that none had survived after the Hampden was brought down by flak in the area of Lolland Island, where the remains of the pilot alone were recovered for burial. No reports came out of either city to shed light on the effectiveness of the bombing raids, but a proportion of the predominantly Wellington force assigned to Düsseldorf strayed over Cologne and caused damage to the main railway station, the Rhine docks and housing.

The following night was devoted largely to attacks on railway yards at four locations in Germany to the east and north of the Ruhr, with 5 Group committing most of its available Hampden force, amounting to ninety-one aircraft, to attack the important hub at Soest, situated a few miles north of the Ruhr. 4 Group was to target the yards at Schwerte, south of Dortmund, while 1 and 3 Groups were handed those at Hamm and Osnabrück, and a small Halifax element was assigned to the I G Farben-owned "Buna" works, a chemicals and synthetic rubber plant at Marl-Hüls. Five 61 Squadron Hampdens departed Hemswell between 22.25 and 22.55 with W/C Valentine the senior pilot on duty and a 2,000-pounder in each bomb bay and flew out over the Humber on course for Den Helder. Having reached the Dutch coast, they turned to the south-east to bypass Zwolle, where a few selected crews from other units dropped boxes of tea donated by the Dutch East Indies Company as a boost to morale for the beleaguered populace, each teabag bearing the imprint of a message from Britain that the Netherlands would rise again. Pressing on into Germany, many crews employed the one-day-to-be-famous Möhne reservoir and its dam as a pinpoint for the six-mile run north to the target. A layer of cloud at 2,000 to 3,000 feet obscured Soest and many bombed on the evidence of a large fire surrounded by flak batteries, probably at nearby Hamm. W/C Valentine made two runs across the target before bombing from 3,000 feet, while P/O Bill Deas and crew attacked from 4,500 feet and watched their bomb detonate among buildings.

A major assault on the enemy warships at Brest was notified across 1, 3 and 5 Group stations on the 13th, and resulted in the assembly of a force of 110 aircraft, of which, thirty-seven were Hampdens, although none represented 61 Squadron. However, when twenty-nine Hampdens were detailed on the 14th for a 5 Group operation that night as the first of four raids on consecutive nights against Cologne, 61 Squadron briefed the crews of S/L Newall and Sgts Donovan, Harris and Sleight and sent them on their way from Hemswell between 22.57 and 23.04. They ran into ten-tenths low cloud with broken medium cloud at up to 9,000 feet over the entire route, and not one crew was able to positively identify the briefed aiming point, which was probably one of the marshalling yards. Sgt Donovan and crew came down to 1,500 feet and found themselves in the teeth of a flak barrage, which left them blinded to ground features as they delivered their attack. Most of the bombing took place from between 5,000 and 15,000 feet on estimated positions based largely on searchlight and flak activity and there was little to pass on to the intelligence sections at debriefings.

The rest of the month would be devoted largely to eight simultaneous raids on Cologne and Düsseldorf, the first of which was posted on the 15th, and involved forces of ninety-one and fifty-nine aircraft respectively. 5 Group contributed forty-two Hampdens to the night's operations, with just two belonging to 61 Squadron containing the crews of P/O Casement and Sgt Johnston, who departed Hemswell at 22.45 bound for Cologne. Which of the many marshalling yards in Cologne was the specific aiming point is not recorded, but both bombed on estimated positions guided by evidence of searchlights and flak. It soon became clear to those attacking Düsseldorf that the prospects of locating the Derendorf marshalling yards through dense cloud at between 3,000 and 8,000 feet were nil, and most headed south down the Rhine for twenty miles to join their 5 Group colleagues at Cologne.

In the absence of a 61 Squadron contribution Cologne and Düsseldorf were the principal targets again on the following night, for which 5 Group put up forty-seven Hampdens in an overall force of 105, all bound for the former. Bombing was scattered and local sources reported only fifty-five high explosive bombs and three hundred incendiaries falling within the city and causing no significant damage. Forty-three Hampdens and thirty-three Whitleys took off to return to Cologne on the 17th, while fifty-seven Wellingtons were dispatched to Düsseldorf. 61 squadron made ready five Hampdens and dispatched them from Hemswell between 23.03 and 23.15 with S/L Newall the senior pilot on duty, but poor visibility caused by thick ground haze prevented most crews from locating their respective targets. P/O Casement and crew bombed a built-up area to the east of the Rhine, which bombing photos revealed to have been Düsseldorf, but neither operation produced meaningful results. Sgt Sleight and crew dropped two flares, illuminating a built-up area which they bombed from 6,500 feet, discovering later on the basis of bombing photos that they had been over the city of Bonn, while Sgt Johnston and crew bombed what appeared to be a factory on the eastern side of Cologne, but their bombing photos depicted only open country. This was typical for the period and similarly ineffective operations would continue throughout the year.

The country was now basking in a spell of very hot weather, which began on the 19th, and would continue through the 23rd. A force of 115 aircraft set off for Kiel on the 20th in search of the battleship Tirpitz, and among them were twenty-four Hampdens, three of them taking off between 22.35 and 22.37 and bearing aloft the 61 Squadron crews of P/O Casement and Sgts Donovan and Sleight. The Casement crew returned early because of a wireless issue, leaving the remaining pair to encounter ten-tenths cloud, which completely obscured the ground in the target area and prevented any hope of locating Tirpitz. On e.t.a., and guided by evidence of flak, they bombed from estimated positions and returned with no confidence in the outcome.

It was not until the 21st that the Manchester was once more declared fit for operations after almost five weeks on the side lines and during the course of the day, a record number of eighteen was made ready to target the docks at Boulogne, this figure including a contribution of six from 61 Squadron for its maiden operation on the type. The main operations on this night were against Cologne and Düsseldorf, the former the target for sixty-eight Wellingtons, while twenty-eight Hampdens and an equal number of Whitleys attended to the latter. The crews and aircraft selected at Hemswell for this momentous occasion were those of W/C Valentine in L7387, S/L Weir in L7388, F/O Parry in L7389, F/O Webb in L7304, F/O Hall in L7307, and F/L Riley in L7315, which took off between 22.59 and 23.29 each carrying an impressive bomb load of fifteen 500-pounders. Last away and slightly delayed by an engine issue was the Parry crew, who, despite the risk, refused to be sidelined for such an important operation and were rewarded for their press-on spirit with a completed sortie during which they bombed the docks from west to east. A thin layer of stratus cloud at 3,000 feet provided poor visibility, but five crews identified the target, W/C Valentine and crew gliding down from 9,000 to 500 feet to deliver their attack. S/L Weir and crew made two passes, dropping a stick on each, F/O Hall and crew ran in from the south-east and bombed along the north bank of the River Liane south of the railway bridge and the Webb crew released their load during a second pass. F/L Riley and crew bombed Le Touquet in error, but that apart, it was a satisfactory beginning to what would be a testing time on Manchesters.

Bremen's dockyard was the destination for forty-five Wellingtons and twenty-five Hampdens on the 22nd, when conditions were generally favourable, but thick haze obscured the ground to create challenges and even the River Weser proved difficult to identify, leaving the crews reliant again upon searchlights and flak to point the way. Most crews bombed on estimated positions from between 10,000 and 14,000 feet, some after searching for more than an hour, and a few were rewarded with the sight of bursts but no detail. Kiel, Cologne and Düsseldorf were the destinations for modest forces on the following night, the last-mentioned a 5 Group effort against railway yards involving thirty Hampdens and eleven Manchesters. 61 Squadron contributed five Manchesters and five Hampdens, loading the former with six 1,000-pounders each and three small bomb cases (SBCs) of incendiaries, before sending them on their way from Hemswell between 22.52 and 23.25 with W/C Valentine and S/L Weir the senior pilots on duty. The crews of Sgts Hodgkinson and Johnston turned back early with engine issues leaving just three Hampdens to continue on, and when W/C Valentine had to bring his load home after losing the hydraulics system and finding himself unable to open the bomb doors, he landed at Waddington without flaps. S/L Weir and crew bombed on the reflection of a large fire, while F/L Riley and crew failed to locate the primary or an alternative target and also returned their bombs to the station dump.

Yet again, Kiel, Cologne and Düsseldorf were selected as the targets on the 26th, and on this occasion it was for the important naval stronghold on the eastern side of Schleswig-Holstein that eighteen Manchester crews were briefed, while thirty Hampden crews learned of their part in the operation against marshalling yards at Düsseldorf. The Manchester crews were told that they would have fifteen Stirlings and eight Halifaxes for company, although, not necessarily over the target at the same time, and the Hampden crews would share their target with 1 Group Wellingtons. It was a night on which cloud, snow, electrical storms and icing conditions played their part and persuaded many crews to turn back from Düsseldorf or seek out alternative targets. 61 Squadron's six Manchesters and six Hampdens departed Hemswell between 22.52 and 23.20 with W/C Valentine and S/L Weir the senior pilots on duty and lost the services of F/O Hall and crew to an issue with a propeller. The Manchesters were each carrying six 1,000-pounders and three SBCs, and those from the aircraft of W/C Valentine, S/L Weir and F/L Stewart and the 500-pounders from the Hampdens of P/O Deas and Sgts Harris and Johnston all fell in the general target area, while Sgt Donovan attacked Duisburg and Sgt Hodgkinson and crew brought their bombs home. F/O Webb and crew became the first in the Manchester era to fail to return from an operation, L7304 crashing without survivors near Brunsbüttel at the mouth of the River Elbe.

The night of the 28/29th was devoted to mining operations by thirty-four Hampdens in the Eglantine and Rosemary gardens, respectively in the Elbe estuary and the Heligoland Bight, for which 61 Squadron made ready six and dispatched them from Hemswell between 23.02 and 23.45 with P/Os Casement and Deas the commissioned pilots on duty. They crossed the Humber before setting course for their target area off the island of Heligoland, located some thirty-five miles north-west of Cuxhaven and found it under ten-tenths cloud with a base sometimes as low as 500 feet.

Despite the challenges all were able to establish a pinpoint on the island from which to make a timed run and plant their vegetables as briefed from below 1,000 feet.

On the 29th, L7315 suffered an engine fire while on a training flight, and crashed near Grantham killing P/O Colborne, the only other occupant, the wireless operator, having baled out and landed safely. Bremen was chosen to be in the firing line again that night, when thirty Hampdens were detailed to join seventy-six other aircraft, while six of the group's Manchesters took part in a small raid on Hamburg. Following a spate of engine failures, particularly some afflicting 61 Squadron aircraft, another Manchester grounding order was issued on the 30th and in a conference held at 5 Group HQ on this day, it was decided that each Manchester squadron would select four aircraft for intensive flight testing. That night, in the absence of a 61 Squadron contribution, 5 Group detailed fourteen Hampdens to attack a railway station in Düsseldorf.

During the course of the month the squadron took part in twelve operations that generated fifty-one Hampden and sixteen Manchester sorties for the loss of three Hampdens and two Manchesters, three crews and one other pilot.

July 1941

Having been prominent during the final few days of June, it fell to Bremen to open the Command's July account on the night of the 2/3rd, while smaller forces targeted Cologne and Duisburg. The last-mentioned was an all-Hampden affair involving thirty-nine aircraft and focused on the marshalling yards with Cologne and Düsseldorf as alternative targets. They found seven-tenths cloud hanging over the Ruhr at 6,000 feet, with thick industrial haze lurking beneath, and this left the crews with no prospect of identifying the briefed aiming point. Searches were carried out, some aided by flares, but it was a futile exercise, and only a small number of crews would claim to have bombed the estimated location of Duisburg.

Scampton and Hemswell combined on the following night to send twenty-three and seventeen Hampdens respectively to join Wellingtons in attacking the Deschimag shipyards at Bremen, while ninety Wellingtons and Whitleys attempted to hit the Krupp complex and railway installations at Essen. The six-strong 61 Squadron element took off between 22.44 and 22.56 with P/Os Casement and Deas again the senior pilots on duty and adopted a variety of courses. Some intended to pinpoint on Heligoland and others on the uninhabited Scharhörn Island located nine miles north of Cuxhaven or on the mainland coast itself, but all encountered the same conditions of ten-tenths cloud over the sea and the additional challenge of haze over land. The cloud was estimated to be at between 8,000 and 15,000 feet, which completely obscured all ground references and left the crews reliant on evidence of flak to guide them to the general area of the primary target and the briefed alternatives at Bremerhaven and Wilhelmshaven. Some Scampton crews stooged around for an hour and more, before mostly abandoning their sorties and bringing their bombs home in accordance with instructions, while, curiously, all sixteen of the Hemswell crews to make it back reported carrying out an attack, mostly on Bremen city and the town area of nearby Bremerhaven. It all became clear later when the Hemswell brigade revealed that they had been searching at around 5,000 feet, while the Scampton crews had remained at 11,000 feet or above.

The Hemswell and Scampton squadrons were not involved on the 4th when twenty-five Hampdens were detailed to attack U-Boots at Lorient, where construction of the major new concrete structure was well under way on the Keroman peninsula. The operation took place in perfect weather conditions and, while no U-Boots were evident, the raid hit the general port area and was hailed as most successful. Marshalling yards in the cities of Münster and Osnabrück were the targets for two forces on the 5th, the former facing the larger one of sixty-five Wellingtons and twenty-nine Whitleys, while the latter would host an initial thirty-nine Hampdens. Just thirty miles apart and located between the Ruhr and Bremen, Münster was more militarily significant as home to the HQ of the 6th Military District of the Wehrmacht and its extensive barracks accommodated infantry and armoured (Panzer) Divisions. Preceding the bombing element into the air at Hemswell at 22.38 and 22.45 were the freshman crews of P/O Braithwaite and Sgt Baker, but the latter was forced to return early with engine trouble, leaving the former to benefit from perfect moonlit conditions and easily establish their pinpoints on Pointe-Saint-Gildas before planting their vegetable according to brief from around 500 feet.

The bombing brigade departed Hemswell between 22.52 and 23.12 with P/Os Casement and Deas the senior pilots on duty and set course for the Dutch coast in ideal conditions, some employing the beacon on Texel as a guide to navigation before turning toward the south-east to run in on the target. Flares assisted crews to pick out the numerous waterways and railway tracks leading to the city, but searchlight glare played a part in preventing some from identifying the briefed aiming point and most, including three from 61 Squadron, bombed the general built-up area. Only P/O Deas and crew picked up the briefed aiming point, while Sgt Johnston and crew attacked the docks at Den Helder on the way home as a last-resort target. AD806 did not return with the others and was lost without trace with the crew of Sgt Holden.

On the 6th, a 5 Group force of eighty-eight Hampdens was assembled for a raid on the German warships at Brest in company with twenty-one Wellingtons. Among the Hampdens were five 44 Squadron aircraft loaned to 207 Squadron crews to enable them to "keep their hand in" while their Manchesters were grounded. As the situation dragged on, they would continue to borrow from 44 Squadron, until receiving six Hampdens of their own as a stopgap measure. 61 Squadron supported the operation with seven aircraft, which departed Hemswell between 22.20 and 22.56 with S/L Riley the senior pilot on duty and began the Channel crossing at Chesil Beach. They crossed the French coast under clear skies and a full moon, which enabled them to map-read their way to the target area, where they encountered the usual intense searchlights and flak defence. Initially at least, the smoke generators were not active, allowing those in the vanguard a clear run, but when P/O Hughes and crew arrived at the head of the 61 Squadron element, they reported eight smoke generators starting up to provide a highly effective screen that completely obscured Scharnhorst and Gneisenau.

It must have been a chaotic scene above Brest as aircraft approached the aiming point from a variety of headings from east to west, north-east to south-west and south-west to north-east at altitudes of between 7,500 and 12,000 feet, dodging not only the searchlights and flak but also the bombs falling from as high as 17,000 feet. Searchlight glare and the need to take evasive action prevented any from observing more than bomb bursts and it was just another inconclusive raid during which 5 Group delivered over three hundred high explosive armour-piercing and semi-armour piercing bombs into the target area, sixty-seven of them 2,000 pounders. Returning crews reported fires in the town centre, in the northern outskirts and near the seaplane base, and a number also reported an aircraft being hit at around 3,000 feet and crashing into the sea in flames. Despite the best efforts, the warships remained a threat as a "fleet in being", and the strategists at Bomber Command HQ continued to seek a solution.

Four main targets were posted on stations across the Command on the 7th, Cologne, Osnabrück and Münster for Wellingtons and or Whitleys, while forty Hampdens were to target marshalling yards in the town of Mönchengladbach, located on the south-western rim of the Ruhr. The seven participating 61 Squadron aircraft departed Hemswell between 22.52 and 23.13 with P/Os Braithwaite and Casement the commissioned pilots on duty, and in accordance with the practice of the day, some adopted the northerly route via Skegness and Enkhuizen, while others preferred Orford Ness and the Scheldt. Whichever track was chosen, the outward flight took place under clear skies with a full moon to aid map-reading in coastal areas, until thick ground haze blotted out detail over land. Sgt Donovan and crew were over Holland when attacked by a BF110, which the Hampden's gunners sent spinning towards the ground, but not before it had inflicted severe damage to the port engine, wing and wheel and the tailplane. The navigator was wounded in the leg but assisted the pilot in bringing AD963 back to a crash-landing at Coningsby, from which they walked or hobbled away. Meanwhile, a number of lakes to the north-west of the town were of benefit to those approaching from the north, as were the railway lines running into the town, but, ultimately, most crews turned their attention upon alternative targets at Düsseldorf, Neuss and Duisburg. Absent from debriefing was the crew of P/O Braithwaite, and news eventually arrived via the Red Cross that AD937 had been shot down by the night-fighter of Lt Reinhold Knacke of I./NJG1 and only the pilot had survived to be taken into captivity.

Taking advantage of the daylight extending into the late evening, F/O Street and crew took off at 20.52 on the 8th to conduct a sea-search in response to a report that a dinghy had been sighted in the North Sea but returned within three hours having found nothing. 5 Group was handed marshalling yards again that night, when forty-five Hampdens were detailed at Scampton, Waddington and Lindholme to target the northern half of those at Hamm, while twenty-eight Whitleys attended to the southern half.

A new Air Ministry directive was issued on the 9th, which alluded to the German transportation system and the morale of its civilian population as the enemy's weakest points. The C-in-C, Sir Richard Peirse, was consequently ordered to concentrate his main effort in these areas, which meant that from now on during the moon periods he was to target the main railway centres ringing the Ruhr, to isolate it from the other regions of Germany, thus preventing the movement in of raw materials and the export of finished goods. On dark nights, the Rhine cities of Cologne, Duisburg and Düsseldorf would be easier to locate for area attacks, and, when unfavourable weather conditions prevailed, operations were to be mounted against more distant urban centres in northern, eastern and southern Germany.

That night, thirty-nine Hampdens joined forces with forty-three Whitleys and Wellingtons to target the Nazi Party HQ at Aachen, the first time that Germany's most westerly city had faced a major attack. The choice of aiming point meant, in reality, that it was intended as an area raid, for which 61 Squadron's element of seven departed Hemswell between 22.50 and 23.19 with F/Ls Paape and Stewart the senior pilots on duty, the former having returned to the squadron to begin a second tour of operations. The weather conditions were favourable as the bombers approached the target, and shortly before arriving F/O Gascoyne-Cecil and crew were set upon by a night-fighter with a headlamp. The wireless operator sustained a wound to his hand, but remained at his post as violent evasive action and accurate return fire from the Hampden persuaded the enemy to break off the engagement, allowing them to continue on to the target and observe their bombs burst close to a railway junction. F/L Paape and crew ran into a concentration of searchlights, and having struggled to escape them, failed to re-establish their position despite a forty-minute search and demolished a house while attempting to bomb a bridge. The crews of P/O Hughes and Sgt Woodley attacked the city from 7,000 and 10,000 feet respectively, the former on their fourth pass, but no results were observed and the remaining three crews also bombed in the target area. F/O Hall and crew returned with battle damage to the port mainplane after an encounter with a night-fighter, which was hit by Hampden's return fire. Local sources reported much damage to commercial and residential property, particularly in central districts, and 3,450 residents were bombed out of their homes.

On the 10th 5 Group detailed thirty-two Hampdens to join ninety-eight Wellingtons for an attack on Cologne, where one of the 5 Group targets was the Klöckner-Humboldt mechanical engineering and armaments works in the Deutz district, situated on the east bank of the Rhine. 61 squadron was not called into action but was alerted on the following day to a 5 Group operation that night against Wilhelmshaven, where the main railway station was designated as the aiming point for thirty-six Hampdens. The seven-strong 61 Squadron element departed Hemswell between 22.54 and 23.38 with F/L Stewart the senior pilot on duty and reached the port to find generally favourable conditions, but haze to inhibit the vertical visibility. Only the crews of F/L Stewart and Sgt Baker identified and attacked the railway station, while the others bombed the general town area and returned to report what they deemed to have been an effective operation. In fact, according to local sources, most of the bombing had fallen into open ground and in the harbour, where a fishing vessel was damaged, and a barrack hut burned down.

Scampton and Lindholme were called into action on the 12th to provide thirty-four Hampdens between them to target the main railway station in Bremen with Wilhelmshaven as the designated secondary target. Seven 61 Squadron crews were called to briefing on the 14th, to learn of that night's operation to the northern city of Hannover, where the railway station and main post office building were designated as the aiming points for a force of eighty-five aircraft, forty-four of them provided by 5 Group from Coningsby, Hemswell and Waddington. Based on past performances, the choice of aiming points was somewhat optimistic, and in reality disguised the actual intention to destroy the city centre. The 61 Squadron element departed Hemswell for the final time in anger between 22.12 and 22.50, the latter time that of P/O Fraser and crew, who were delayed by the need to swap aircraft at the last minute and then found themselves to be off track at the enemy coast. By the time that they established their position it was too late to continue to the primary target, and as they were close to Emden, bombed it from 8,000 feet and observed one burst on railway sheds. P/O Graham and crew had also passed this way and had been caught in the searchlight and flak belt, which persuaded them to abandon all thoughts of Hannover and attack Wilhelmshaven as an alternative target. The others found the primary target, some after pinpointing on Steinhuder Lake, and Sgt Johnston and crew carried out a glide attack from 10,000 down to 5,000 feet taking advantage of the light from flares dropped by other aircraft, as did Sgt Sleight and crew, who went in low and released their load in the middle of the built-up area.

Hamburg was posted as the target for 107 aircraft on the 16th, of which thirty-two Hampdens from Scampton and Lindholme represented 5 Group, but almost half of the force attacked alternative targets in the form of flak concentrations and aerodromes and Wilhelmshaven also attracted attention. Local sources in Hamburg reported four fires and no significant damage. 61 and 144 Squadrons had spent the day preparing for a change of address to be completed on the 17th with the move to North Luffenham, a station located between the cities of Leicester to the west and Peterborough to the east in England's smallest county of Rutland. It had been built in 1940 as a training station, and when taken over by 5 Group, 61 and 144 Squadrons became its first resident bomber units. The squadrons were still settling in when twenty-five Hampdens and fifty Wellingtons targeted the Gereon marshalling yards in Cologne that night, and it was the 19th before the first offensive sorties were launched from the new home. Five 61 squadron Hampdens each had a single mine winched into its bomb bay before taking off between 23.03 and 23.10 to join thirty others of the type bound for the Eglantine and Yam gardens that encompassed the Elbe, Jade and Weser estuaries. P/O Deas, the only commissioned pilot on duty, was forced to return early after the loss of the intercom prevented him from communicating with his crew, but the others benefitted from favourable conditions and planted their vegetables according to brief. While this operation was in progress, a dozen other Hampdens were included in a force of forty-nine aircraft assigned to Hannover.

A force of 113 aircraft was assembled on the 20th for a return to Cologne for another swipe at marshalling yards, for which 5 Group contributed thirty-nine Hampdens from Scampton and Swinderby, the latter the new home of 50 Squadron after its move from Lindholme. The operation was a failure caused largely by unfavourable weather conditions but also by the inadequacies of the equipment available to bomber crews at the time. Frankfurt and Mannheim were named as the targets for a mini-campaign on three consecutive nights from the 21/22nd, and it would be the former's first taste of a major Bomber Command assault. Thirty-seven Wellingtons and thirty-four Hampdens were made ready, the latter at Coningsby, North Luffenham and Waddington, while thirty-six Wellingtons and eight Halifaxes were prepared to attack Mannheim city centre some forty-five miles to the south. At 5 Group briefings crews were instructed to aim for the post-office and main telephone exchange buildings, or in other words, the city centre, for which the 61 Squadron element of five took off between 22.26 and 22.32, each with an officer pilot at the controls. The first task was to reach the target and P/O Fraser and crew failed in that regard after an engine issue curtailed their sortie when roughly an hour out, leaving the others to arrive in the target area at around 01.00 to be greeted by favourable conditions with haze. P/O Hughes and crew carried out a glide approach from 11,000 down to 5,000 feet, where the bombs were released and set off fires. The glare from an accurate searchlight and flak defence largely concealed the results of the efforts of the crews of F/Os Parry and Gascoyne-Cecil, who had located the city and marshalling yards in the light of flares from other aircraft. F/O Street and crew pinpointed on the Rhine but lost the city twice before bombing a factory somewhere nearby. A number of bursts were observed along with fires, but the local reports spoke of minor damage, and the city of Darmstadt, situated some ten miles to the south, sustained a greater level of destruction.

On the following night thirty-four Hampdens from North Luffenham, Coningsby and Swinderby joined twenty-nine Whitleys and Wellingtons in a return to Frankfurt, while a small force of Wellingtons attended to Mannheim. Nine 61 Squadron aircraft were made ready for an operation that brought out the senior officers, W/C Valentine and S/Ls Riley and Weir and their crews among those taking off between 22.31 and 22.58, only for S/L Riley to turn back with engine trouble. The others pressed on to the turning point at Namur in Belgium, from where they encountered severe icing conditions and during the leg from Aachen to Frankfurt dispensed tins of "razzles", which together with "nickels" were standard cargo on each operational sortie. Most gained a brief glimpse of the River Main on the southern outskirts of Frankfurt, but that was as good as it got in the face of eight-tenths cloud, and, with no prospect of identifying the briefed aiming-point the bombing was carried out predominantly on estimated positions. W/C Valentine and crew, however, descended to 4,000 feet for a better view of the target and sank even lower to bomb the centre of the city from 2,600 feet in the eye of the searchlight and flak defences. The crews of P/O Graham and Sgt Woodley attacked from 8,000 and 10,000 feet respectively, while those of Sgts Donovan and Hodgkinson and P/O Deas all carried out glide attacks starting from heights of 12,000 down to 6,500 feet and releasing their bombs from 4,000 to 7,000 feet. The crews of P/O Casement and S/L Weir were unable to identify the primary target and bombed alternatives at Coblenz and Cologne from 6,000 and 11,000 feet respectively.

The final raid of the series on Frankfurt on the 23rd involved thirty-one Hampdens from Scampton and Swinderby for the all-5 Group show, while fifty Wellingtons tried their hand at Mannheim. The results in keeping with most operations at this stage of the war were indeterminate, but at least no aircraft were lost. While the above was in progress, thirty Whitleys were sent to attack the dry dock at La Pallice, the deep-water port located west of La Rochelle on the Biscay coast between St-Nazaire to the north and Bordeaux to the south. It was home to the 3rd U-Boot Flotilla that was feeding wolfpacks into the Atlantic to savage Allied convoys bringing vital supplies to Britain. However, the objective for this operation was the cruiser Scharnhorst, which had slipped away from Brest unnoticed and was feared to be about to break out into the Atlantic for a campaign of surface raiding. Her disappearance from Brest had also caused a change of plans for a major raid on Brest due to take place on the following day.

Preparations and formation flying training had been ongoing for a number of weeks to carry out an audacious attack by daylight on the German warships at Brest under the codename Operation Sunrise. Scheduled for the 24th, as mentioned above, it had been discovered at the last minute that Scharnhorst had slipped away to La Pallice, some two hundred miles further south, and this required an adjustment to the original complex plan of attack. The intention had been to send three 90 Squadron Fortress Is in to bomb from 30,000 feet to draw up enemy fighters, while 5 Group Hampdens performed a similar function at a lower altitude under the umbrella of a Spitfire escort. While this distraction was in progress, it was hoped that Halifaxes and Wellington from 1, 3 and 4 Groups could sneak in unopposed to target the ships. However, now that Scharnhorst had moved, it was decided to send the Halifax element to deal with her, while the rest of the original plan went ahead at Brest. 5 Group detailed six Hampdens each from Waddington, Coningsby and North Luffenham, the last mentioned represented by 144 Squadron, and they had congregated at Coningsby on the previous day for the briefing, before taking off at 10.45 to proceed to Predannack in three boxes with Coningsby leading. They collected the Spitfire escort provided by 10 Group over Cornwall and were shepherded all the way to the target, which they reached at 14.15, seven minutes after the Fortresses had bombed. The enemy flak and fighter defences were more fierce than anticipated, and the Hampdens found themselves in a hornet's nest of single and twin-engine fighters. Ten of the seventy-nine Wellingtons were shot down by flak and fighters, along with two Hampdens, in return for six unconfirmed hits on the Gneisenau. The Halifaxes had also suffered the loss of five aircraft at La Pallice, and the ten survivors all sustained damage to some extent, while scoring five confirmed hits on Scharnhorst to necessitate her return to Brest, where superior repair facilities existed.

The Deutsche Werke and Krupp Germania shipyards were the aiming points in Kiel for that night's main event, for which a force of thirty-four Wellingtons and thirty Hampdens was made ready, the latter on the stations at Coningsby, North Luffenham and Waddington. It was 61 Squadron's turn to represent North Luffenham, from where it launched seven Hampdens between 22.30 and 23.04 with S/L Riley the senior pilot on duty, leaving P/O Hughes and crew on the ground contending with a technical issue. When they eventually took off at 00.07 it was too late to reach Kiel and they left with orders to attack the shipyards at Wilhelmshaven instead, a task they fulfilled despite the presence of thick haze. The others benefitted from favourable weather conditions with visibility clear enough for ground features to be identified during the run in as they ran the gauntlet of an intense searchlight and flak barrage. S/L Riley's AE235 was damaged in an encounter with an enemy night-fighter over Kiel Fjord, but he and his crew carried on to bomb the target from 7,000 feet and observe two explosions. Approaching the Lincolnshire coast at 1,500 feet in fog on the way home, they were fired upon by a convoy some twenty miles off Skegness but survived to land safely after seven hours in the air. Three attacks were carried out in a glide, P/O Fraser and crew from 7,000 feet after negotiating balloons tethered at between 7,000 and 10,000 feet, F/O Gascoyne-Cecil from 7,500 feet and Sgt Woodley and crew from 9,000 feet, while Sgt Sleight and crew made two passes during which they captured excellent photographs of the docks and observed a large fire that remained visible for forty miles into the return journey. AE189 failed to return with the crew of F/O Parry, who all lost their lives when shot down by a night-fighter to crash off the Dutch coast at Den Helder. Despite the enthusiastic claims of some crews at debriefings, the bombing was scattered and inaccurate, and local authorities reported only a few bombs falling in the shipyards or the town.

Orders were received at Scampton and Swinderby on the 25th to provide thirty Hampdens to join forces with twenty-five Whitleys for an attack on Hannover, where the crews were to aim for the main railway station and post office. Returning crews were unable to offer any information on the outcome of the raid, which cost four Whitleys and a Hampden, and as usual at this target, no local report was forthcoming. The 27th and 28th were devoted to mining operations off the Biscay ports and in the Baltic respectively, and then on the 30th, after five nights without action, 61 Squadron was called upon to provide eleven Hampdens as part of a North-Luffenham contribution of twenty-six in company with sixteen from Waddington for a raid on marshalling yards in Cologne by an overall force of 116 aircraft. The 61 Squadron element took off between 23.00 and 23.32 with no pilots above pilot officer rank on duty, and encountered appalling weather conditions, which prevented many crews from identifying the primary target. Six 61 Squadron crews were among twenty-two claiming to have bombed on estimated positions based on searchlight and flak activity, P/O Casement and crew dropping incendiaries first in the hope that they would set off a fire to reveal ground features and then letting the high explosives go over the same spot. Sgt Sleight and crew circled a large fire for forty minutes before bombing from 9,000 feet, while six others from the squadron targeted Aachen or its approximate position. P/O Metcalfe and crew were thwarted by the conditions at Cologne, Aachen and finally Dunkerque, at the last mentioned because it was under an electrical storm, and having exhausted all reasonable possibilities landed at Harwell with the bombs still on board. Sgt Harris and crew had similar experiences at Cologne and Aachen and eventually came upon a flare path in Belgium as a last resort target. On return, P4399 crashed at Deast Hill in Kent at 04.00 after Sgt Baker lost control in the midst of an electrical storm, and he alone was able to parachute to safety. Fifty minutes later, AE266 crashed while trying to land at Upwood, and only one man survived from the crew of F/O Adshead, who was on his maiden bombing operation. Sgt Durtnall DFM had survived a crash in early January while flying with F/L Powdrell but lost his life on this occasion when tantalisingly close to the end of his tour.

During the course of the month, the squadron took part in fourteen operations and dispatched eighty-seven sorties for the loss of five Hampdens and crews. F/L Stewart was posted out to pass on his skills as an instructor at 25 O.T.U at Finningley, and P/O Stevenson went to 90 Squadron to train for operations in the Boeing B17C, designated in the RAF as Fortress I.

61 Squadron Ansons at RAF Hemswell c. 1937

61 Squadron Handley Page Hampden P4379, RAF Hemswell July 1940. Lost 12/13th August 1940 during "Razzling" operation on Salzbergen, Germany. The four-man crew were all lost - P/O Harry Sheldon, F/Sgt Wilfred Ward, Sgt Robert Morrison and Sgt Douglas Aldom.

Mining (Gardening) area code names (Aircrew Remembered)

The Synthetic Oil Plant at Homberg, before attacks by the RAF

Misburg Oil Plant (1946) - Attacked in 1940 by 61 Squadron

12/13th August 1940. The original shot of the destruction of the Dortmund-Ems Canal for which F/L R A B Learoyd was awarded the VC.

Modern views of the Dortmund Ems canal which was attacked by F/L Learoyd

Present day parts of the Dortmund Ems Canal which had been attacked in 1940. (Andreas Wachtel)

'Sticky target tonight boys'. Probably 61 Squadron Hampden Crew.

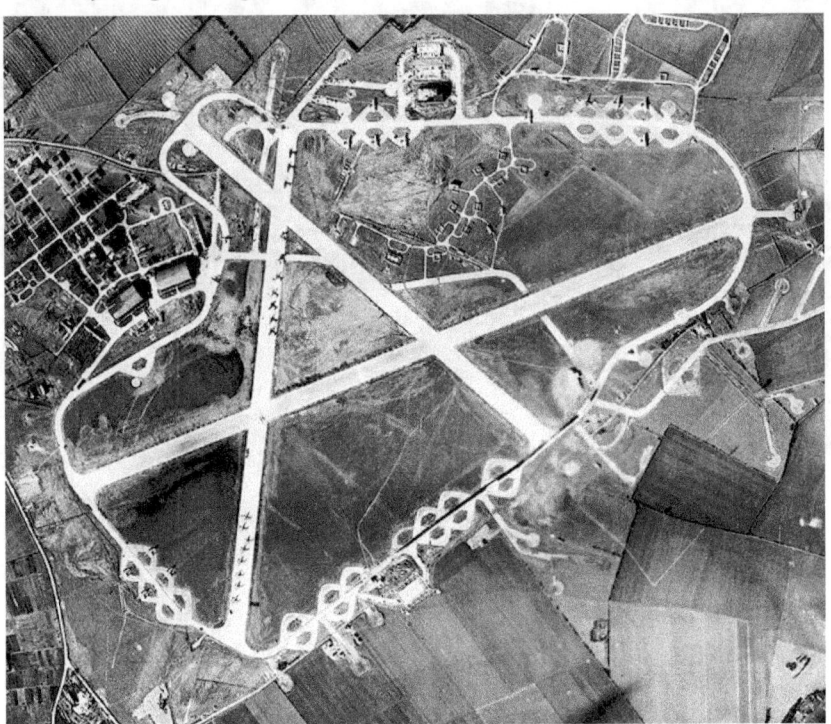
RAF North Luffenham (1944) Home to 61 Squadron 1941

Lancaster R5724 QR-F with unknown crew. Crashed at Wittering 25th September 1942. No injuries reported.

Sgt Eric Booth. Shot down over Bremen in September 1942 and became PoW in Lamsdorf.

Consolidation Benzol plant at Gelsenkirchen (Schalke district). Attacked by 61 Squadron 1941.

Lancaster QR-O, R5679, after its encounter with the Altmark tanker.

Lancasters parked near bomb dump RAF Syerston

F/L Harry Charles Shaw Page, pictured shortly after receiving his DFC. KIA 31st January 1942 on Brest operation.

*Sgt Alexander Cormack
Bomb Aimer (and Navigator)*

*Sgt Lewis H. Morrison
Pilot*

*Sgt John Duffield (Jack)
Navigator*

Sgt Thomas Bevan (always known in his family as Ralph) Rear Air Gunner.

All killed on a mine-laying operation on 25th September 1942. Sgt Bevan baled out but too low for the parachute to deploy. Their Lancaster (below) exploded on impact. Also lost were Sgt C N Coldicott and Sgt E Dyson. All lie in Frederikshavn Cemetery, Denmark.

*Sgt William Emerslund
RCAF – Mid Upper Gunner*

Lancaster W5679 with its damage from the tanker August 1942

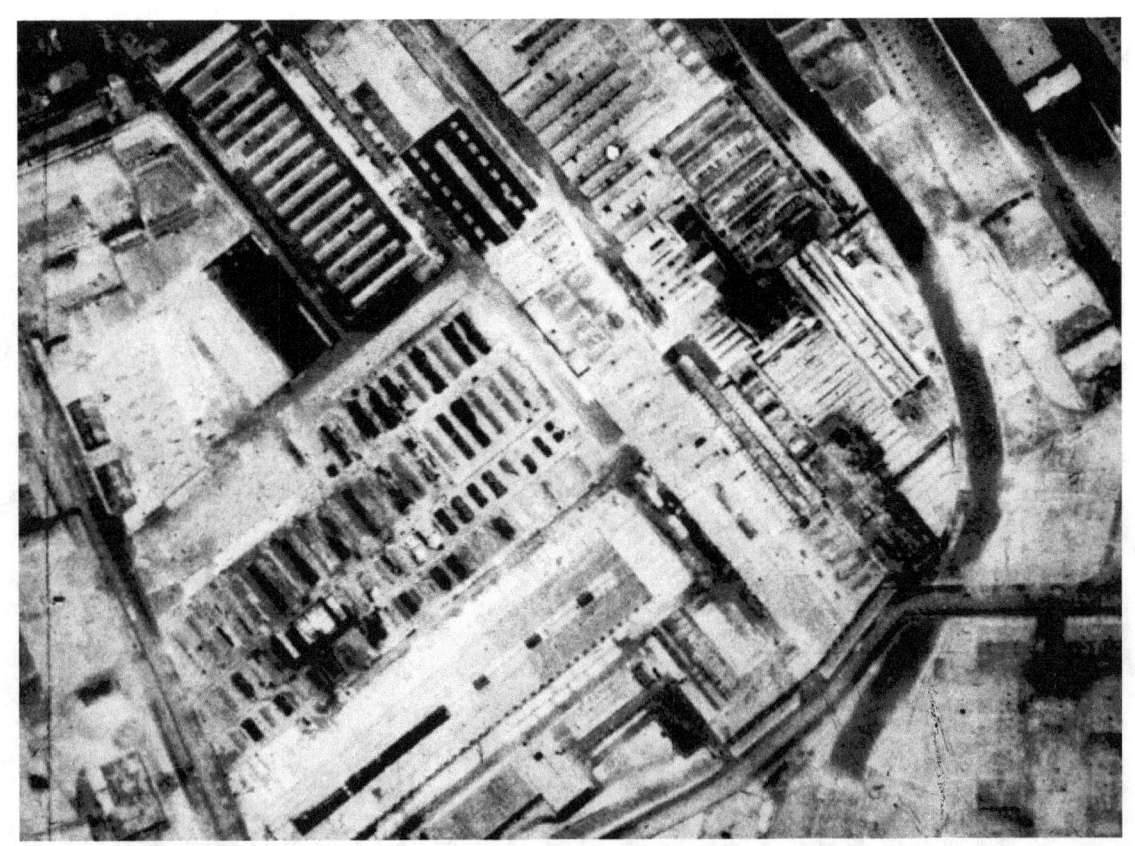
Augsburg raid target, post operation photograph of the MAN factory.

Avro Manchester

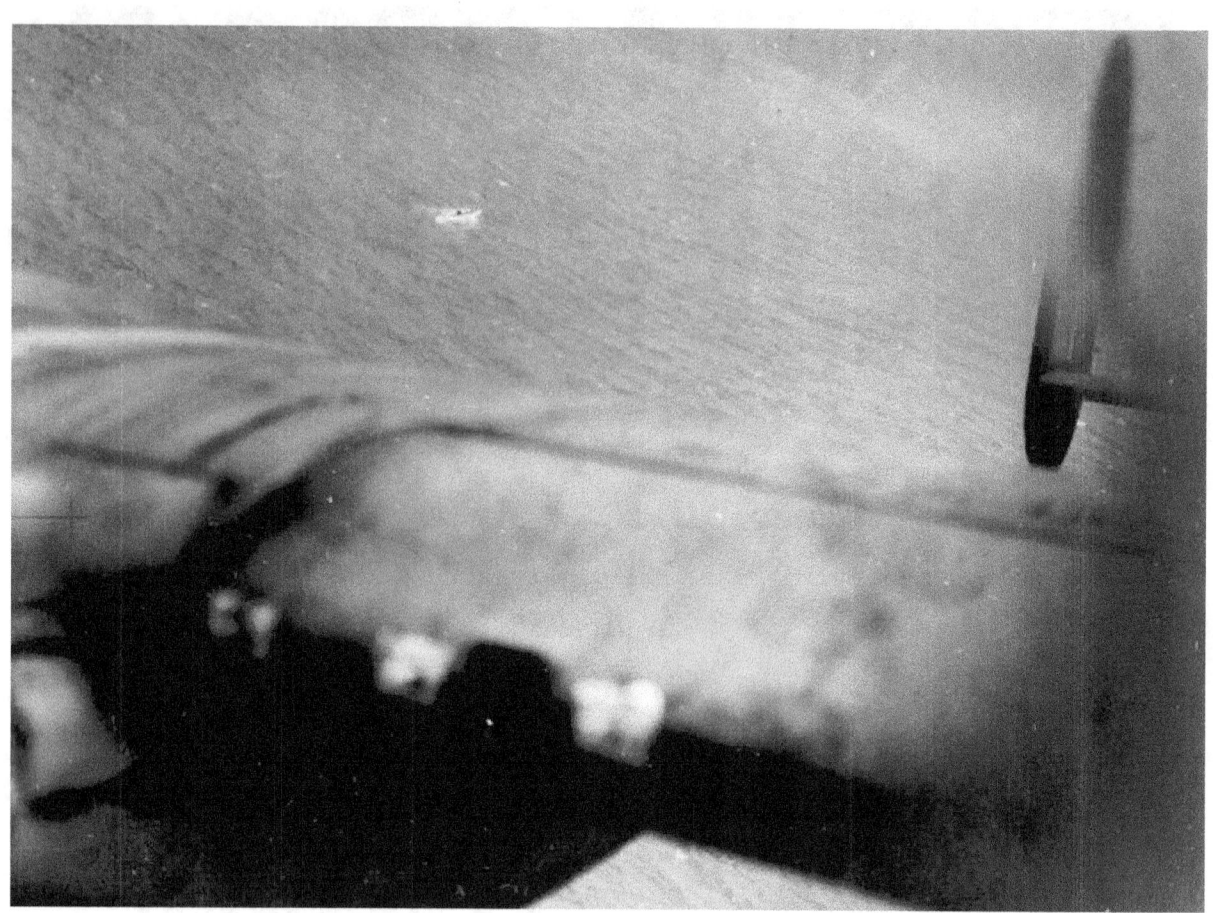

View looking backwards from 61 Squadron Lancaster R5724, showing U-751 under attack, July 1942.

Lancaster Mark II DS604 QR-W of 61 Squadron at RAF Syerston

Saarbrucken, Germany

29th July 1942. Two 4,000lb high capacity blast bombs exploded in a residential area in an attack during the night of 29-30th July. two points of impact can be seen clearly marked "A" and "B" in the photograph.

Below: RAF Syerston

Frankfurt before and after attacks by RAF Bomber Command

*Pilot Officer John Underwood
KIA 31st May 1942*

*A damaged Manchester, flown by P/O Underwood
but not on the fatal night.*

The Burns Crew
L to R: Standing; F/Sgt William Dixon. Bob Wake. F/L Bill Burns (Pilot). F/O Tom Croally. and F/Sgt Len Taylor. Sitting: F/Sgt George Wilkie and F/Sgt Graham Stokes.

W/C William Penman DFC AC MiD CO of 61 Squadron from February to October 1943. KIA 3rd October 1943.

Sgt Richard Stuart. KIA 30th December 1943. Rear gunner in Harvey Crew below.

The Harvey crew
Back row from right: F/Sgt R W Carver (Nav), F/L George Harvey (Captain), Sgt Noel "Ginger" Meehan (W/Op), P/O Don Thomas (MUG) (PoW) and Sgt Stuart Kennedy (F/E). The four ground crew are not identified, but are thought to include 'Oscar' and 'Geordie'. All aircrew, except P/O Thomas, were killed on a Berlin operation 30th December 1943.

F/L William Reid VC

*W/C Reginald Stidolph DFC
Commanding Officer 61 Squadron
September 1943- June 1944*

Lancaster B. MkII, with Hercules VI engines, of 61 Squadron. January 1943

P/O Ian Robertson RAAF (navigator) on Lancaster W4898. The Lancaster was presumed lost on 28th April 1943 while carrying out mine laying duties over the Baltic Sea.

F/O Colin Godley RAAF died on 3rd August 1943, when his Lancaster JA837 with a crew of nine was shot down near Luneburg, Germany and crashed near Wolfenbüttel, Germany.

61 Squadron Crews after Berlin Raid, November 1943. Reg Stidolph at microphone.

Warrant Officer Reg Freeth
The first Bomb Aimer to fly in 'Just Jane'.

F/O W H McDowell
KIA 22nd October 1943.

Lancaster JB138 QR-J. The original ' Just Jane'

S/L G S Paape AM, DFC and Bar
KIA 3rd of April 1943, aged 24 years.

August 1941

The policy of dispatching small numbers of aircraft to various targets simultaneously had rarely produced effective results, but it would be persisted with throughout the remainder of the year, and, in fact, until a new Commander-in-Chief arrived in 1942 to provide a different direction. 5 Group was informed that it would open its August account on the 2nd and sent instructions to Scampton and Coningsby to make ready twenty-nine and twenty-one Hampdens respectively to attack the town of Kiel and its shipyards, while larger forces attended to Hamburg and Berlin. Three operations were planned for targets in south-central Germany on the 5th at Mannheim, Karlsruhe and Frankfurt, for which forces of sixty-five Wellingtons and thirty-three Hampdens, fifty Hampdens, twenty-eight Wellingtons and nineteen Halifaxes and Stirlings, and eighty-eight Whitleys and Wellingtons respectively were assembled.

The same three targets were posted on the following night for smaller forces in the hope of building on the significant damage achieved at Mannheim and Karlsruhe in particular, and thirty-eight Hampdens were detailed to return to the latter for another shot at the railway workshops. A further thirty-eight aircraft were detailed for freshman crews to employ against the docks and shipping at Calais, and Scampton provided the ten 5 Group representatives. The Karlsruhe operation was to be launched from North Luffenham, which provided thirty-five of the participating Hampdens, while three flew over from 50 Squadron at Swinderby to take part. 61 Squadron had been inactive for a week by this time and was able to prepare a record seventeen Hampdens, which took off between 22.10 and 22.48 with S/Ls Riley and Weir the senior pilots on duty. They exited the English coast over the Essex resort of Frinton-on-Sea, before setting course for the Mons region of Belgium, and although encountering cloud and electrical storms as they made their way eastwards, they found the target at times to be under clear skies. Not all from the squadron reached the primary target, but those that did attacked from between 4,500 and 7,000 feet mostly after carrying out a glide approach. S/L Weir and crew did not bomb on their first pass, which turned out to be a mistake after cloud slid beneath them and left them searching for an hour before releasing their load and observing four large, smoking fires. By this time they had attracted the attention of flak batteries and a shell burst under the tailplane causing minor damage. F/L Sooby and crew had lost thirty minutes at the Norfolk coast through navigational issues, and unable to reach the target in time, bombed the marshalling yards at Charleroi in Belgium from 4,000 feet. P/O Metcalfe and crew bombed Mannheim in error, while difficulties with navigation left S/L Riley and crew with no choice but to seek out an alternative target, for which the frontier town of Rastatt offered itself. Sgt Craven and crew experienced severe icing after crossing the enemy coast and when the a.s.i failed, the Hampden fell out of control, losing three thousand feet of altitude before the fall was arrested at 7,000 feet and they were then able to continue on to bomb the primary target. Returning crews reported many fires but no meaningful assessment was carried out and local sources made no comment on the outcome.

The troublesome operational career of the Manchesters got under way again on the night of the 7/8th, after the grounding order had been lifted earlier in the day and three from 207 Squadron and fifty-four Hampdens were made ready to join forces with forty-nine other aircraft to attack the mighty Krupp manufacturing complex in Essen. The bombers adopted a course via the Scheldt estuary, pinpointing on Tilburg as they crossed Holland to enter Germany near Wesel, a region criss-crossed by waterways, including the Rivers Rhine, Ruhr and Lippe, that provided strong navigation references through the industrial haze once the cloud dispersed as the target area drew near. The density of Krupp buildings in the Borbeck districts should have guaranteed that some would be hit, if only the crews could pinpoint on that segment of the city. Bombing was carried out on a variety of headings and altitudes in the belief that Essen lay below, but local sources would report only thirty-nine high explosives bombs and two hundred incendiaries falling in the city, while other Ruhr locations received the rest.

61 Squadron was not involved in the above and its first Manchester sortie on the morning of the 8th took W/C Valentine and crew on a sea-search for a dinghy spotted to the north-east of Mablethorpe, from which they returned after six hours and fifteen minutes without having located anything. Later in the day fifty Hampden crews at North Luffenham, Swinderby and Coningsby were briefed for an attack on the U-Boot construction yards at Kiel in company with four Whitleys. The 61 Squadron element of fifteen took off between 22.08 and 22.41 with S/L Riley the senior pilot on duty flew out over Mablethorpe on course for Rømø Island to approach the target from the north. They found cloud increasing as they headed across Schleswig-Holstein and three layers of five-tenths lay over the target, which amounted to a total cover of up to nine-tenths. Some crews were able to identify the aiming-point through gaps, while others contented themselves with bombing the town, all in the face of a fairly intense searchlight and flak defence, and on the strength of reports from other squadrons, it seems that the bombing was carried out from between 13,000 and 16,000 feet. Fires were reported to be taking hold as the aircraft retreated to the west and one very large fire appeared to be oil-related, emitting a column of black smoke, which remained visible for eighty miles into the return flight. On return, AE259 was serenely approaching the Lincolnshire coast off Spurn Head, when it fell foul of the famed poor aircraft recognition skills and the "fire-first, consider-the-consequences-later philosophy of an Allied convoy. The starboard engine was put out of action, and it became necessary for P/O Metcalfe to carry out a crash-landing at 05.30 near Boston, which resulted in terminal damage to the Hampden. Less fortunate were the crews of P/O Graham in X3127 and Sgt Craven in AE263, who failed to return, the latter without trace, while the former came down in the target are with fatal consequences for a Kiwi gunner, while the others were taken into captivity.

Poor weather conditions kept 5 Group on the ground for the ensuing two nights, and it was the 11th when the next batch of orders was received, detailing an operation against marshalling yards in the Ruhr city of Krefeld for twenty Hampdens from North Luffenham, and docks in occupied ports for thirty freshman crews. The 5 Group ORB mentioned only Rotterdam as the target, but Calais was referenced in the ORBs of the Scampton squadrons. 61 Squadron detailed ten Hampdens, which took off from the satellite station at Woolfox Lodge, located some six miles to the north, between 23.41 and 23.56 with S/L Weir the senior pilot on duty. They encountered unfavourable weather conditions over enemy territory, including heavy ice and static-bearing cloud, which prevented all but S/L Weir and crew from locating the target city. Unable to identify the marshalling yards, they attacked the general built-up area and when a flak shell exploded nearby, it left S/L Weir almost blinded with Perspex splinters in his face, despite which he was able to bring the aircraft and crew home to a safe landing. Seven crews sought out alternative targets in the Ruhr and aerodromes on the way home, and the crews of F/L Paape and F/Sgt Sleight brought their bombs home.

A plan to support the beleaguered Russians by persuading the Luftwaffe to withdraw fighters from the Russian front to protect economic targets in the west resulted in a number of daylight operations involving 5 Group Hampdens on the 12th. Waddington sent six to attack Longueness aerodrome at

St-Omer in support of a 2 Group raid on Cologne's power stations at Knapsack and Quadrath and Coningsby dispatched a similar number to Gosnay power station, also in France, both elements protected by a fighter escort. The Waddington element encountered ten-tenths cloud with tops at 8,000 feet, which thwarted any hope of identifying the briefed target and the bombs were dropped on a stretch of railway track some two-and-a-half miles south of St-Omer.

The night of the 12/13th was to be a busy one for the Command, and, throughout the day, aircraft were made ready for attacks on Berlin, Hannover, Magdeburg and Essen. 5 Group detailed thirteen Hampdens to join sixty-five Wellingtons for Hannover, and thirty-six to operate on their own at Magdeburg, while a force of seventy aircraft assigned to the capital included nine Manchesters. Together with minor operations, the night's activities involved a total of 234 aircraft. Hannover lay on the route to both Magdeburg and Berlin, and the three forces would fly out together until reaching it, at which point the Berlin element would continue straight on for the 150 additional miles, while the Magdeburg element peeled off to the south-east with eighty miles still ahead of it. 61 Squadron initially detailed fourteen Hampdens for Magdeburg, but doubts about the weather reduced the number by 50%, and ultimately six were assigned to the main event and one to Hannover. They departed Woolfox Lodge in extremely cloudy, wet and misty conditions between 21.02 and 21.36 with S/L Riley the senior pilot on duty, but he and his crew made it only as far as the Dutch coast before turning back as a result of excessive flame issuing from the starboard engine exhaust. The entire outward route was accompanied by ten-tenths cloud that topped out at between 12,000 and 15,000 feet, and crews decided for themselves whether to fly above or below. The cloud dispersed to a large extent some twenty miles from the target, which enabled the River Elbe and other ground features to be identified, and the bombing took place in the face of intense accurate flak. The 61 Squadron ORB is devoid of information, and we are not even informed as to which crew went for Hannover, only that fires were evident at both Magdeburg and Hannover and no report emerged from either to shed light on the outcome.

Orders were received across the Command on the 14th to prepare for operations that night against railway targets in three major cities in northern Germany to the north of the Harz mountains, Hannover the most westerly, Magdeburg the most easterly and Braunschweig (Brunswick) in-between. 5 Group detailed eighty-one Hampdens to operate alone against the main railway station in Braunschweig, while seven Manchester crews were briefed for Magdeburg as part of an overall force of fifty-two aircraft. 61 Squadron made ready eleven Hampdens and a single Manchester for W/C Valentine and sent them on their way from Woolfox Lodge between 21.04 and 21.40 with F/Ls Paape and Sooby the senior Hampden pilots on duty. Having made landfall on the Dutch coast between Amsterdam and Den Helder, five of the Hampden crews abandoned their sorties because of excessive exhaust flames advertising their presence to the enemy. F/L Sooby and crew bombed Texel, F/O Gascoyne-Cecil and crew De Kooy aerodrome, F/L Paape and crew Rotterdam docks and F/O Street and crew Handorf aerodrome near Münster, while P/O Fraser and crew brought their bombs home. The rest of the force pressed on over a blanket of medium-level cloud to arrive in the target area at altitudes up to 17,000 feet with little prospect of identifying the aiming point. Most delivered their bombs in the general area of Braunschweig, while some backtracked to Hannover and others found alternative targets. Meanwhile, W/C Valentine and crew had bombed Magdeburg from a perilously low 1,500 feet, and that was the most detailed report to find its way into the squadron ORB. No report came out of Braunschweig to provide details of damage, and the likelihood is that very little occurred. The city would prove to be elusive, and it would be a further three years before it succumbed to a devastating Bomber Command attack.

Railway objectives featured again on the 16th, when orders went out to stations across the Command to prepare for attacks on installations in the Ruhr cities of Düsseldorf and Duisburg and nearby Cologne. Düsseldorf was to be a 5 Group show involving fifty-two Hampdens and six Manchesters to which 61 Squadron contributed six Hampdens. Five of them took off between 23.00 and 23.08 with F/Os Gascoyne-Cecil, Hall and Street the senior pilots on duty, leaving Sgt Hodgkinson and crew on the ground while a technical issue was rectified, and by the time that they took off at 00.17 it was far too late to proceed to the primary target and they set course instead for Rotterdam to bomb the docks. Four crews identified Düsseldorf and bombed the general area through cloud and industrial haze in the face of a spirited searchlight and flak defence, and although many fires were reported, no detail was gleaned, and no report came out of the target city. P/O Deas and crew attacked Bonn as an alternative target on another night of underachievement and disappointment, the full extent of which was about to be revealed with the publication of the assessment of the Command's performance during the summer.

North Luffenham (Woolfox Lodge) was not called into action on the 17th, when thirty-nine Hampdens were assigned to the main goods railway station in Bremen, while twenty 4 Group Whitleys targeted the city's Focke-Wulf factory in the south-eastern district of Hemelingen. Some hits were claimed on the aircraft factory but again no local report emerged to confirm the level of damage, if any.

On the 18th, the Butt Report on the Command's operational effectiveness was released, and it sent shock waves reverberating around the War Cabinet and the Air Ministry. Having taken into account around four thousand bombing photographs produced during night operations in June and July, it concluded that only a fraction of bombs had fallen within miles of their intended targets, and the poorest performances had been over the Ruhr. It was a massive blow to morale, and demonstrated that thus far, the efforts of the crews had been almost totally ineffective in reducing Germany's capacity to wage war. The claims of the crews were shown to be wildly optimistic, as were those of the Command, and Sir Richard Peirse's tenure as Commander-in-Chief would forever be blighted by the report's revelations. The report also provided ammunition for those, principally at the Admiralty, who were calling for bomber aircraft to be diverted to other theatres of operation.

While the report was being digested that evening, 5 Group sent forty-two Hampdens from North Luffenham and Coningsby to attack the West Station at Cologne in company with twenty Whitleys and Wellingtons. 61 Squadron's ten participating aircraft took off between 22.53 and 23.17 with F/Ls Paape and Sooby the senior pilots on duty and headed for the Scheldt estuary, Sgt Donovan and crew the latest to be afflicted by excessive exhaust flame, and as soon as they reached enemy territory, they bombed the flare-path at South Beveland aerodrome on Walcheren Island. Despite favourable conditions only the crews of F/L Sooby and P/O Deas located and bombed the railway station, while seven others hit the general built-up area and P/O Gilpin and crew attacked marshalling yards in the town of Düren located between Cologne and Aachen. Returning crews reported many fires on the western side of the Rhine, but local reports of nothing more than superficial damage suggested that a decoy fire site had attracted the main weight of bombs.

61 Squadron was not called into action for the following week, during which Scampton and Waddington sent twenty-six and sixteen Hampdens respectively to join sixty-seven other aircraft for an operation against a railway junction at Kiel on the 19th. This was followed by a series of three operations against Mannheim beginning on the night of the 22/23rd, for which 5 Group

provided forty-one Hampdens from Coningsby, Syerston and Waddington, which were to join forces with fifty-six Wellingtons. Returning crews reported bomb bursts and fires, but local sources claimed that only one house had been destroyed and five others lightly damaged. It was left to Scampton to provide a dozen Hampdens to represent 5 Group at Düsseldorf on the 24th, when 4 Group Whitleys and Halifaxes completed the force of forty-four aircraft. Six additional Hampdens were assigned to searchlight suppression duties in the Wesel defensive belt, their task to attack with 40lb bombs and guns any battery holding a bomber in its beams.

A 5 Group attack on Mannheim by thirty-eight Hampdens and seven Manchesters was briefed out on all stations on the 25th, and the main post office specified as the aiming point for an assault on the city centre. 61 Squadron's eight Hampdens took off between 20.14 and 20.31 with F/Os Casement, Hall and Street the senior pilots on duty and they undertook the outward flight in conditions of cloud and icing. Over the target gaps began to appear through which some crews were able to identify the city if not the briefed aiming point, and in fact, only F/O Casement and crew of the 61 Squadron element would claim to have aimed for the post office building. The others, with the exception of P/O Deas and crew, who attacked the town of Germerheim to the south, bombed the general target area and along with the rest of the force claimed a moderate success, when, in reality, it was another inconclusive affair.

A familiar face returned to the squadron on the 26th to begin a second tour, P/O John "Dim" Wooldridge having completed his instructional duties at 16 O.T.U. He had time to reacquaint himself with any former colleagues still on the squadron as the experienced crews at North Luffenham sat out a raid that night on Cologne, while seven freshman crews were assigned to mining duties in one of the Nectarine gardens. A force of ninety-nine aircraft was made ready for the main event, which included twenty-nine Hampdens and a single Manchester drawn from Coningsby, Scampton and Syerston, while six other Hampdens were to carry out flak suppression sorties to the west of the city. Conditions in the target area were good, despite which, most of the bombing fell harmlessly to the east of the city and only around 15% of bomb loads were recorded within the city boundaries. Meanwhile, the gardeners had all reached their target area in extreme darkness and having encountered electrical storms en-route, each planted their vegetable according to brief.

Orders arriving on 5 Group stations on the 27th revealed a return to Mannheim for ninety-one aircraft, including thirty-five Hampdens from North Luffenham, Waddington and Swinderby. They were to attack the main railway station, while elements of 1, 3 and 4 Groups focused on other aiming points within the city and seventeen Hampdens from the same stations mined the waters of the Nectarine gardens around the Frisians. The six-strong 61 Squadron element took off between 22.18 and 22.27 with F/Os Casement and Street the senior pilots on duty and lost the services of P/O Fraser and crew straight away after a piece of radio equipment fell off and jammed the elevator controls. The others found clear skies over Mannheim, but the benefits were nullified by extreme darkness and haze, and many crews were prevented by searchlight glare from identifying the aiming point. The crews of F/O Casement and P/O Hughes positively identified the briefed aiming point, but five bombed the built-up area generally and P/O Deas and crew attacked the nearby city of Mainz as an alternative target on the way home. There was some optimism among returning crews concerning the effectiveness of the raid, but local sources reported no significant damage.

The main event on the 28th was an attack on marshalling yards in Duisburg, for which an overall force of 118 aircraft was assembled, which included a 5 Group contribution of thirty Hampdens and six Manchesters, while 61 Squadron remained off the order of battle. Good bombing results were claimed, but local sources reported only sixty-three high explosive bombs and five hundred incendiaries, which caused no significant damage. The final raid of the Mannheim series was posted on Wellington stations on the 29th, while Frankfurt was notified as the destination for a 4 and 5 Group force of 143 aircraft for what would be the first attack on this city by a hundred-plus aircraft, the crews of which had been briefed to use the inland docks as the aiming point. 5 Group contributed seventy-three Hampdens and three 207 Squadron Manchesters, 61 squadron dispatching its ten participating Hampdens between 21.40 and 22.02 with F/Os Casement, Gascoyne-Cecil and Street the senior pilots on duty. Some crews adopted the briefed route from Orford Ness to make landfall south of Ostend and bypass Namur, while others opted to fly directly to the target from the English coast, which meant landfall over the Scheldt estuary and skirting northern Belgium to pass south of Cologne. Cloud lay over most of the route, and icing became a problem, but all of the 61 Squadron crews reached the target area, where the crews of F/O Street and P/Os Fraser and Searby bombed the briefed aiming point, and the crews of F/O Gascoyne-Cecil and Sgt Donovan went for the general built-up area. The crews of F/O Casement and P/Os Deas, Gilpin and Raw failed to identify the primary target and sought out alternatives on the way home. Sgt Richmond and crew failed to return in AD247, and were lost without trace, presumably in the Channel or North Sea on the way home. They would prove to be the last crew to be lost in a 61 Squadron Hampden.

The final operation of the month was notified to thirty-nine Hampden and six Manchester crews at briefings on the 31st, when railway targets in Cologne were revealed as the targets for an overall force of 103 aircraft. The bombers arrived in the Cologne area largely on the basis of dead-reckoning (DR) and evidence of searchlights and flak and were prevented by ten-tenths cloud from obtaining more than a fleeting glimpse of the ground. Most searched for a time before bombing the approximate location of the city and a few noted the glow of fires reflected in the cloud. Local sources reported a few bombs falling and no damage in what had been another ineffective and wasteful use of resources.

During the course of the month the squadron took part in thirteen operations and dispatched 102 Hampden sorties and one by a Manchester for the loss of four Hampdens and three crews.

September 1941

5 Group was in action on the first night of the new month, when twenty Hampdens joined forces with thirty-four Wellingtons for yet another attack on the city of Cologne in what turned out to be favourable weather conditions. 61 Squadron briefed six crews to aim for the main railway station, located in the shadow of the cathedral on the western bank of the Rhine, before sending them on their way, according to the blanket departure time recorded in the ORB, at 20.15, with F/L Sooby the senior pilot on duty. The crews of F/O Wooldridge and P/O Fraser identified and bombed the target, the latter having been forced down to below 1,000 feet by searchlights and flak, which inflicted minor damage. In revenge, his wireless operator/gunner, Sgt Hadley, shot out a searchlight on the outskirts of the city. The crews of F/L Sooby, F/O Gascoyne-Cecil and Sgt Donovan bombed the general built-up area and F/O Casement and crew attacked a railway junction fifteen miles to the south. Despite the claims of many fires, local sources reported only thirty-five

bombs of all calibres hitting the city and causing damage to one house, and the likelihood is that decoy fire sites attracted the rest.

Briefings took place across the Command on the 2nd for two operations to be carried out that night, both supported by 5 Group. The main operation by 126 aircraft, including eleven Hampdens, was to be against the inland docks at Frankfurt, while a force of forty-nine aircraft targeted the Schlesischer (Berlin-East) railway station on the northern bank of the River Spree in Berlin, some 260 miles to the north-east. The bulk of the latter force, thirty-two Hampdens and four Manchesters, was provided by 5 Group, with a handful of 3 Group Stirlings and 4 Group Halifaxes in attendance. 61 Squadron prepared Manchester L7388 for W/C Valentine and crew to take to Berlin with the station commander, G/C Barrett DSO and Bar, DFC, on board as a guest, and dispatched it from North Luffenham at 20.30. The crews of P/O Beard and Sgt Furby had been assigned to gardening duties in one of the Nectarine gardens off the Frisians, and no take-off time was recorded for them. The Berlin element set a course from the Lincolnshire coast to the east Frisians and were dogged by ten-tenths cloud at 6,000 to 8,000 feet, which prevented many from establishing their position at the Dutch and German coasts. Not all of those reaching the German capital found a gap to confirm their arrival, some glimpsing the River Spree or other ground features to provide a reference, and it was over the target that flak found L7388 and sent it crashing to earth with no survivors from the crew of W/C Valentine DSO. The navigator, F/L Harrison, was also a holder of a DSO, and the loss of the station and squadron commanding officers and experienced crew would be felt keenly by the station community. While the above was in progress, the gardeners fulfilled their briefs in conditions, according to the 5 Group ORB, of seven to ten-tenths cloud and mist and returned safely, but as 5 Group squadron ORBs at this stage of the war were lacking in detail, that of 61 Squadron particularly so, there is nothing more to add.

The enemy warships at Brest returned to the spotlight on the 3rd after a respite in recent weeks, and a force of 140 aircraft was made ready to attack them. 5 Group contributed thirty Hampdens and two 207 Squadron Manchesters from North Luffenham, Coningsby and Waddington, 61 Squadron putting up six Hampdens led by the crews of F/Ls Paape and Sooby. No take-off time was recorded in the ORB, but conditions as they got away were favourable with clear skies and a full moon, despite which a recall signal was issued shortly afterwards to 1, 4 and 5 Group aircraft in anticipation of deteriorating weather conditions for the time of their return. In the event, 3 Group and four other aircraft that had failed to pick up the signal carried on and fifty-three returning crews claimed to have bombed the estimated positions of the warships through an effective smoke screen, claiming no hits.

The vacancy for a commanding officer was filled from within by the promotion of S/L Weir on the 5th, and he would have a short time to get to grips with his new role before presiding over his first briefing. In the meantime, on the 6th, 5 Group detailed eighteen Hampdens from Coningsby to join with sixty-eight other aircraft to target the I G Farben-controlled chemicals/synthetic rubber factory at Marl-Hüls on the northern edge of the Ruhr. Known locally as the "Buna" works because of the chemicals butadiene and natrium employed in the manufacturing process of synthetic rubber for tyres, the Chemische Werke-Hüls GmbH had been formed in 1938 after its acquisition by the I G Farben company in association with the Bergwerkgesellschaft Hibernia A.G. Whether or not it was using slave workers at this time is uncertain, but the I G Farben company would become infamous for drawing its labour force from concentration camps and forcing tens of thousands of foreign workers to toil under the harshest conditions at its many manufacturing sites across

Germany. *(In some of my previous books I have mistakenly located this factory in the Hüls district of Krefeld in the western Ruhr).*

Berlin was posted as the night's main target on the 7th, for which a force of 197 aircraft was made ready, while the Deutsche Werke U-Boot yards and the town of Kiel would occupy the attentions of a further fifty-one aircraft. 5 Group supported both operations, with eighteen Hampdens for the latter and forty-three Hampdens and four 207 Squadron Manchesters for Germany's capital city. 61 Squadron briefed five crews for Berlin and those of P/Os Beard and Gilpin and Sgt Donovan for Kiel and dispatched them from North Luffenham at a blanket time of 20.40 with S/L Riley the senior pilot on duty. The crews of S/L Riley and F/L Sooby returned early because of engine and intercom issues respectively, and while the crews of F/L Paape and F/Os Casement and Gascoyne-Cecil continued on towards the "Big City", the Kiel-bound crews arrived in the target area to find favourable conditions with up to three-tenths cloud, and, according to most, good visibility. At debriefing, no claims were made of direct hits on the shipyard, but local sources reported damage in a number of locations to warehouses and housing and to two passenger vessels.

Meanwhile, the Berlin force had also passed this way and had employed the Baltic coast as a strong navigation pinpoint that would aid them to reach the target area some 180 miles to the south-east. Clear skies prevailed in the Berlin area and a hostile flak defence greeted the force, the searchlights to an extent nullified by the brightness of the moon. The crews of F/L Paape and F/O Casement bombed the built-up area generally, while F/O Gascoyne-Cecil and crew found an alternative target in the form of something of military importance at an unrecorded location. Many crews ran into the defences at Hamburg and Bremen on the way home, before arriving in English airspace with diminishing fuel reserves. Two-thirds of crews reported successfully bombing in the Berlin area, and the effectiveness of the attack was partly borne out by local descriptions of damage to several war-industry factories, housing, utilities and communications, mostly in the north and east of the city. Fifteen aircraft failed to return, and when added to three losses from crashes at home, two involving Hampdens from North Luffenham's 144 Squadron, this represented the highest number of bomber casualties in a single night.

The first large Bomber Command attack on the city of Kassel, located some eighty miles to the east of the Ruhr, was briefed to crews of all groups on the afternoon of the 8th, and would involve ninety-five aircraft, including twenty-seven Hampdens. There were to be two aiming points, both of them belonging to the Henschel Company, the presence of whose numerous manufacturing sites dominated the city and employed eight thousand workers in addition to a large number of slaves. Aside from building the Dornier Do17Z bomber under license, Henschel was the main producer of the Panzer III tank and the Tiger I and II, as well as narrow-gauge locomotives. The force was to be divided, sixty-eight aircraft assigned to the tank works, and twenty-seven to the locomotive workshops, with the crew of P/O Searby the sole 61 Squadron representatives assigned to the latter. They flew over to Waddington and took off from there at 20.40, before adopting the briefed route from Orford Ness to Dinant in Belgium, benefitting once over enemy territory from the fine weather conditions, which aided them in their search for the target. Kassel lay beneath clear skies, the excellent visibility enhanced by bright moonlight, which enabled crews to pinpoint on the River Fulda running from north to south through the city. The Searby crew experienced no difficulty in identifying and attacking the target and reported fires, while others observed bursts and a particularly large conflagration at the main railway station to the west of the aiming point, smoke rising through 5,000 feet and light flak reaching 10,000 feet. Local sources in Kassel reported serious damage to two industrial concerns and the destruction of eleven houses with more than seventy others requiring repair. This was a poor return for the size of the force operating in favourable conditions, but at least no aircraft were lost.

Orders were received on the 11th to prepare for an attack on the A.G Neptun shipyards at Rostock, while the rest of the force targeted the nearby Heinkel factory and the town itself. A total force of fifty-six aircraft consisted of thirty-nine Hampdens and five 207 Squadron Manchesters from Coningsby, North Luffenham and Waddington, and a dozen Wellingtons. This was one of three Baltic coast targets for the night, the others at Kiel and Warnemünde, having been assigned to Wellingtons and Whitleys respectively. Other operations on this night involved eight freshman crews to attack the docks and shipping at Boulogne and twenty Hampdens mining off the Frisians, Heligoland and Warnemünde. 61 Squadron briefed six crews for Rostock and sent them on their way with a blanket take-off time of 21.10 and S/L Riley the senior pilot on duty. The ten-tenths cloud present from the start began to thin to eight-tenths by the time that the target area drew near, and ground features could be identified by some through a large gap at around 8,000 feet. There were no searchlights and only a small amount of light flak as they carried out their bombing runs, typically from around 14,000 feet either side of 01.30, and bursts and fires were reported across the harbour area. The apparent success of the operation was observed by some crews in the gardening element, who described buildings flung into the air and flames reaching 500 feet. The crew of F/O Gascoyne-Cecil joined in on the raid at Warnemünde, while F/O Casement and crew bombed a built-up area on the southern coast of Fehmarn Island. On return, Sgt Donovan crash-landed X3138 at Dunholme Lodge after both engines cut out, and two members of the crew sustained slight injury.

On the 12th, Scampton, Swinderby and Waddington were notified of an operation that night against marshalling yards in Frankfurt, for which 5 Group detailed thirty-one Hampdens in an overall force of 130 aircraft, and then it was time for another attempt on the German warships at Brest on the 13th, for which a force of 147 aircraft of six different types was assembled across the Command. 5 Group contributed thirty-eight Hampdens and four Manchesters from North Luffenham, Coningsby and Waddington, the seven representing 61 Squadron given a blanket take-off time from North Luffenham of 01.00, with S/L Riley the senior pilot on duty. The crews of P/Os Beard and Tofield returned early for unspecified technical reasons, and Sgt Huband and crew had the target in sight when they too were forced by the failure of their intercom to abandon their sortie. Sgt Furby and crew jettisoned their load over the target as they were unable to maintain height, and this left just the crews of S/L Riley, F/L Paape and Sgt Gilpin and the rest of the force vainly to attempt to locate the vessels through the extreme darkness, ground haze and smoke screen.

On the 14th the former 61 Squadron pilot, the now F/L de Mestre DFC was posted from 44 (Rhodesia) Squadron to fulfil the role of deputy flight commander with 49 Squadron. Hamburg was posted as the destination for a force of 169 aircraft of six different types, of which 5 Group contributed fifty Hampdens to target the city's Blohm & Voss shipyards in company with more than a hundred others, and four Manchesters to attack a railway junction.

While North Luffenham remained inactive on the 15th, Hamburg was posted as the destination for a force of 169 aircraft of six different types, of which 5 Group contributed fifty Hampdens to target the city's Blohm & Voss shipyards in company with more than a hundred others, and four Manchesters to attack a railway junction. A layer of ten-tenths stratus cloud at 5,000 feet hid the North Sea and the German coastal region from view, but it dispersed sufficiently to allow some a sight of the Elbe Estuary, from which point, they would have to run the gauntlet of searchlights and flak all the way to the aiming points. According to most crews, the skies over the city were clear, but searchlight glare proved to be a serious impediment to aiming point identification and some crews turned their attention upon Wilhelmshaven, Bremerhaven and Bremen. Light flak was reaching 10,000 feet, with searchlights co-operating with night-fighters to create the usual hostile environment for the attackers, and those that returned reported the glow of fires visible for eighty miles. A post-raid analysis and local reports confirmed that Hamburg had sustained quite severe damage in various residential districts with seven large fires and more than fourteen hundred people bombed out of their homes, while a 4,000lb blockbuster had destroyed a block of flats in Wandsbek, killing sixty-six residents.

The 16th was a momentous day in the history and fortunes of Bomber Command, with the arrival at Waddington of the first prototype Lancaster, BT308, for crew familiarisation, in preparation for 44 (Rhodesia) Squadron to introduce the type into squadron service. This early Lancaster retained the three-fin configuration tailplane and narrow elevator span common to the Manchester, but, in time, would be replaced with the iconic two large fins, some of which would also be fitted to modified Manchesters. That was for the future, however, and, in the meantime, operations would continue with the magnificent and trusty, but increasingly obsolete Hampden.

On the 17th, North Luffenham was called upon to provide fourteen Hampdens for gardening duties in the Eglantine and Rosemary gardens at the mouth of the River Elbe and in the Heligoland Bight respectively. 61 Squadron briefed the crews off F/O Gascoyne-Cecil and P/Os Beard and Gilpin and dispatched them from North Luffenham at 17.55 on a night of ten-tenths cloud with a base over the North Sea at between 1,000 and 2,000 feet and in the target areas 500 feet. We are not told as to which garden each crew was assigned and know only that all three successfully fulfilled their brief and the Gilpin crew dropped their wing bombs in the direction of what was believed to be a flak ship.

Adverse weather conditions began to play a part in proceedings at this stage, and 5 Group squadrons were put on stand-by for a number of operations that were subsequently cancelled. Orders were received at North Luffenham, Swinderby and Waddington on the 20th to prepare for operations that night against Berlin and Frankfurt, and there would be more than an element of chaos surrounding the Berlin endeavour, when the force of seventy-four aircraft was recalled because of deteriorating weather conditions. 5 Group had sent thirty-six Hampdens to forward bases at Horsham-St-Faith and Swanton Morley, the crew of F/O Gascoyne-Cecil to represent 61 Squadron, but ten of these were cancelled when they could not be refuelled in time. The Gascoyne-Cecil crew took off for Berlin at 19.15, the same time recorded for the departure from North Luffenham of the Frankfurt-bound crews of Sgts Huband and Williams, and the first mentioned was recalled at some point and bombed Wilhelmshaven as a last-resort target. By this time Sgt Huband and crew had jettisoned their bombs in the face of inhospitable weather conditions and landed at Scampton, while the Williams crew attacked Ostend docks on estimated position through ten-tenths cloud and observed nothing of the result.

Following a layoff from the 21st to the 27th caused by the weather, 5 Group detailed forty-eight Hampdens from Coningsby, Scampton, Swinderby and Waddington for an attack that night on the main railway station at Frankfurt. However, continuing bad weather caused the withdrawal of the less experienced crews, and, together with accidents and incidents, this reduced the numbers to thirty Hampdens from Scampton, Coningsby and Waddington. On the 29th, crews were called to briefing to be told that a force of eighty-nine aircraft was being assembled to attack the Hamburger

Flugzeugbau aircraft factory, a subsidiary of the Blohm & Voss company, situated on Hamburg's Finkenwerder Island in the Elbe to the west of the city centre. 5 Group's contribution would be thirty-eight Hampdens and four Manchesters, while ten others attempted to hit the Admiral Scheer pocket battleship moored nearby. Nine fires were reported by local sources, forty-eight people lost their lives and more than a thousand were bombed out of their homes, but no significant damage was inflicted upon the aircraft factory.

Hamburg was posted as the destination again on the following night, this time for eighty-two aircraft again targeting the Blohm & Voss aircraft factory after the previous night's failure. 5 Group put up forty-eight Hampdens from Coningsby, Scampton, North Luffenham, Syerston and Swinderby, while sixteen freshman crews were briefed to bomb the docks and shipping at Cherbourg. 61 Squadron briefed seven crews for the main event, dispatching them from North Luffenham at 17.55 with W/C Weir the senior pilot on duty, and all reached the target area after negotiating icing conditions. Despite encountering heavy, low cloud and mist, the crews of W/C Weir, F/L Sooby and Sgt Williams picked out the factory and carried out an attack, observing a number of explosions where the incendiaries fell. The other four crews bombed the built-up area having been hampered by varying amounts of cloud and intense searchlight and flak activity, through which few ground references were established. The operation proved to be another unsatisfactory endeavour, which caused fourteen fires and some housing damage, but nothing commensurate with the effort expended. This was the final sortie of Sgt Donovan's first tour, and he could now look forward to at least six months away from the operational scene.

During the course of the month, the squadron took part in thirteen operations and dispatched fifty sorties for the loss of a single Manchester, which claimed the lives of the commanding officer and his crew and the station commander.

October 1941

From this point until the end of the year 61 Squadron was effectively stood down from operations to focus in earnest on the Manchester conversion programme, and only one sortie would be undertaken in October, none in November and four on a single night in December. The squadron became the chief beneficiary of an influx of brand-new Manchester IAs during October, as these began to exit the factories in numbers and the venerable old Hampden finally ended its association with 61 Squadron, the final sortie carried out by P/O Parsons and crew against the docks and shipping at Dunkerque on the 10th. It was his first sortie as crew captain, and the purpose of the sortie was simply so that he could be retained by the squadron as a Manchester captain. He and his crew took off at 18.58 and in conditions of extreme darkness and haze, bombed the target from 6,500 feet without observing the results and landed at 22.45 to bring the Hampden era to an end.

Elsewhere, the adverse weather conditions would continue to disrupt operations at the start of the new month, and the forty-four Hampdens dispatched to Karlsruhe on the night of the 1/2nd were recalled because of the risk of fog at the time of their return. There were no operations for 5 Group and most other elements of the Command between the 2nd and 9th as the weather took a hand, and this would pave the way for a busy and record-breaking night of operations on the 12th. In the meantime, on the 10th, an overall force of seventy-eight aircraft was assembled for an operation against the Krupp complex in the Borbeck districts of Essen. Sixty-nine others were assigned to attack Cologne, thirty-five miles away to the south, while eighty mostly freshman crews cut their teeth on occupied ports from Rotterdam to Bordeaux. 5 Group detailed forty-six Hampdens and ten Manchesters for Essen, six Hampdens for searchlight suppression duties in the Bocholt-Borken area on the northern approaches to the Ruhr and twenty-three freshmen for Dunkerque. Cloud and industrial haze created difficulties at both main targets and neither operation was effective.

The first major night of operations in the month was notified across the Command on the 12th, when a number of targets were posted in northern and southern Germany and the Ruhr in-between, which would require the highest number of sorties yet in a single night. The largest effort, for which 152 aircraft were detailed from 1, 3 and 4 Groups, was the first major assault of the war on the southern city of Nuremberg, the site of massive Nazi rallies during the thirties. The other targets were the Deschimag shipbuilding yards at Bremen, for which ninety-nine aircraft were detailed, including twenty-two Hampdens, and the Buna works at Marl-Hüls on the northern rim of the Ruhr, which was to be a 5 Group show involving seventy-nine Hampdens and eleven Manchesters. The total number of sorties for the night was 373, which included eight Hampdens to carry out an intruder role in the searchlight belt in the Bocholt area. The Ruhr-bound 5 Group force ran into nine to ten-tenths cloud over the Dutch coast at 7,000 to 10,000 feet, which extended past their pinpoint at Enkhuizen on the eastern side of the Den Helder peninsula and all the way to the target, testing their ability to establish a position. Some dropped flares and all stooged around for up to fifty minutes searching for some kind of reference, which was provided generally by searchlight and flak batteries, many of which became last-resort targets. The Nuremberg and Bremen raids were equally disappointing and the gloom and frustration at Bomber Command HQ deepened further.

Thirty Hampdens and nine Manchesters eventually made their way to take-off from 5 Group stations in the early hours of the 14th, after a number had been withdrawn for technical reasons. The target for this 5 Group operation was the main railway station in Cologne, situated in the shadow of the cathedral on the west bank of the Rhine, while twenty miles to the north, elements of 1 and 3 Groups attended to Düsseldorf. Both operations were ineffective, as was the one launched later that night involving a force of eighty aircraft assembled from 1, 3 and 4 Groups in a return to Nuremberg. It was compromised largely by adverse weather conditions during the outward flight, and only a single 78 Squadron Whitley crew managed to identify and hit the Siemens factory and destroy a workshop. 3 Group sent thirty-four Wellingtons and Stirlings to Cologne on the 15/16th, and returning crews claimed large fires, while local sources reported only a few bombs and no damage.

On the 16th, while 61 Squadron's Conversion Flight took up residence at Woolfox Lodge, 5 Group contributed twenty-six Hampdens from Scampton and Syerston to a force of eighty-one aircraft sent to attack railway yards at Duisburg, while others operated as intruders in the searchlight belt in the Wesel-Borken-Bocholt area to the north. The intruders were successful in disrupting searchlight activity, but hardly any of the bombers were able to establish a position over Duisburg through the ten-tenths cloud and most attacked from estimated positions. The weather intervened to keep the bomber force on the ground on the following three nights, until orders came through on the 20th to prepare for operations against the ports of Bremen, Wilhelmshaven and Emden in north-western Germany and Antwerp in Belgium for freshman crews. A force of 153 aircraft assembled for Bremen included a 5 Group contribution of eighty-two Hampdens and eight

Manchesters, but the operation produced scattered and ineffective bombing and the results at the other targets were equally disappointing.

Bremen was posted as the destination again on the 21st for a force of 136 aircraft, including eighteen Hampdens and two Manchesters, whose crews were briefed to attack shipyards. Conditions were similar to those of twenty-four hours earlier and local sources reported another scattered attack which hit largely housing but landed one bomb in the Vulkan shipyard. Mannheim was selected as the target for 123 aircraft on the 22nd, for which 5 Group put up forty-five Hampdens, but thick cloud, electrical storms and icing conditions up to 15,000 feet made life difficult during the outward flight, particularly as they crossed Belgium to pinpoint on Brussels on their way to the German frontier north of Luxembourg and the operation was another failure. The main operation on the night of the 23/24th was a two-wave attack on the shipyards in Kiel involving 114 aircraft, including thirty-eight Hampdens from Swinderby and Coningsby and six Manchesters from 97 Squadron. The two waves were widely separated, and it was the second one that gained some success by hitting the Deutsche Werke U-Boot construction yards. Orders were received across the Command on the 24th to prepare for that night's operation against railway workshops and marshalling yards in Frankfurt-am-Main, which would involve a force of seventy aircraft. They ran into ten-tenths cloud at around 8,000 feet shortly after crossing the enemy coast, and this persisted all the way to the target, which was located by just a fraction of the crews taking part. The dismal failure of the operation was typical for the period, and the situation continued to heap frustration on C-in-C, Sir Richard Peirse.

Hamburg was posted as the target for 115 aircraft on the 26th, for which 5 Group contributed an unknown number of Hampdens and six Manchesters, briefing the crews of the former to aim for the Blohm & Voss shipyards and the latter the main railway station. Those reaching the target area found good bombing conditions under moonlight and delivered a sharp and effective attack. Following two nights on the ground because of continuing adverse weather conditions, 5 Group detailed forty Hampdens and five Manchesters on the 29th to target the aerodrome at Schiphol, situated to the south-west of Amsterdam. It became another operation beset by the most difficult conditions of ten-tenths thick cloud and rain, and only six crews reported locating and bombing the primary target. The month ended with a return to the Blohm & Voss shipyards at Hamburg on the 31st, for which a force of 123 aircraft was assembled. 5 Group called upon the services of Syerston, Coningsby and Swinderby to prepare forty-two Hampdens and five Manchesters, while a further eighteen Hampdens and a single Manchester were assigned to gardening duties in northern waters in the Forget-me-not garden in Kiel Harbour and Nectarine II off the central Frisians.

November 1941

On the 1st, preparations were put in hand to send a force of 132 aircraft to attack the Deutsche Werke shipyard and harbour installations at Kiel, for which 5 Group detailed thirty-two Hampdens from Scampton, North Luffenham and Waddington. The weather kept most aircraft on the ground on the 2nd, but while training on this day, 61 Squadron's L7520 suffered the failure of its port engine and had to be crash-landed near Roxton, seven miles north-east of Bedford, when the propeller could not be feathered to reduce drag. The Manchester was notoriously reluctant to maintain height on one engine and this one was damaged beyond repair, while, happily, P/O Searby and crew emerged from the wreckage unscathed. Only minor operations were mounted on the 3rd, among them an anti-shipping patrol by six Hampdens off the Frisians. While the rest of the bomber force remained on the ground, a busy night awaited 5 Group on the 5th, the programme of operations involving six Hampden "sneakers", five on anti-shipping sorties, twenty-four gardeners and twenty-two freshmen to bomb the docks at Cherbourg.

No doubt still frustrated by his inability to deliver a telling blow on Germany during the extended period of unfavourable weather, and almost certainly eager to rescue the besmirched reputation of the Command after the damning Butt Report, Peirse planned a major night of operations for the night of the 7/8th. The original intention had been to send over two hundred aircraft to Berlin, but continuing doubts about the weather prompted the 5 Group A-O-C, AVM Slessor, to question the wisdom of going ahead with that plan, and he was allowed to withdraw his force and send it instead to Cologne. A third operation, involving fifty-three Wellingtons and two Stirlings from 1 and 3 Groups was also to take place with Mannheim as the target. 169 aircraft eventually took off for Berlin, while sixty-one Hampdens and fourteen Manchesters set off for the Rhineland capital and other small-scale operations raised the number of sorties to 392. 5 Group crews returning from Cologne claimed to have observed the flashes as their bombs hit home and evidence of many fires, but local reports mentioned just eight high-explosive bombs and sixty incendiaries falling into the city, causing minor housing and no industrial damage. The only positive from this was the absence of casualties from among the 5 Group participants on a night when a new record loss would be established.

Once every aircraft from the night's endeavours had landed, it became clear that a record thirty-seven were missing, more than twice the previous highest loss in a single night. An analysis revealed that fewer than half of the Berlin force had managed to reach their objective, and twenty-one had failed to return. The Mannheim contingent missed its target altogether and suffered the loss of seven Wellingtons in the process, and this disastrous experience proved to be the final straw for the Air Ministry. Sir Richard Peirse was summoned to an uncomfortable meeting with Churchill at Chequers on the 8th to make his explanations and on the 13th, he would be ordered to restrict future operations while the future of the Command was considered at the highest level. The need for an independent bomber force was to be keenly questioned in high places during this period, most notably at the Admiralty, where it was felt that bomber aircraft could be more profitably employed to combat the huge losses to U-Boots in the Atlantic, while others wanted them to help redress reversals in the Middle East.

In the meantime, on the 8th, 5 Group detailed twenty Hampdens for an attack on the Krupp complex at Essen in company with thirty-four other aircraft, ten Hampdens and five Manchesters for freshman sorties over Dunkerque and six for searchlight suppression duties in support of the Essen force. Hamburg was posted as the main target on the 9th, the aiming point for which was the Blohm & Voss shipyards on Finkenwerder Island and included in the force of 103 aircraft were thirty Hampdens and six Manchesters provided by 5 Group. According to local sources, the operation achieved only modest success, and just three large fires had to be dealt with. Adverse weather conditions kept the bulk of 5 Group on the ground for the ensuing two weeks, and the group's only operational activity involved small numbers against Emden on the night of the 15/16th. On the 23rd orders were received on all 5 Group stations to make ready fifty-one Hampdens and two Manchesters for an all-5 Group attack on the docks and U-Boots at Lorient, while 3 Group focused on Dunkerque.

Most 5 Group stations were alerted on the 27th to prepare for a raid that night on marshalling yards in Düsseldorf in company with elements of 3 Group in an overall force of eighty-six aircraft. Thirty-four Hampdens and six Manchesters were made ready, and their crews found the southern Ruhr to be largely cloud-free, although some reported up to eight-tenths of the white stuff and the usual blanket of industrial haze to create poor vertical visibility. Despite claims of large fires in the railway yards, local reports detailed only light damage, while nearby Cologne attracted plenty of attention and recorded damage to 119 houses. On the last night of the month, a force of 181 aircraft was assembled that included forty-eight Hampdens and four Manchesters, whose crews had been briefed to aim for the Blohm & Voss shipyards in Hamburg. Local sources confirmed twenty-two fires but only two classed as large, and there was sufficient housing damage to deprive 2,500 people of their homes.

December 1941

The dominant theme during December would be the continuing presence at Brest of Scharnhorst, Gneisenau and, sometimes, Prinz Eugen, and no fewer than fifteen operations of varying sizes would be mounted against the port and its guests during the month, some by daylight. The weather kept the entire Command on the ground for the first six nights of the new month, and it was not until the 7th that a posted operation actually went ahead. The target for a force of 130 aircraft was Aachen, Germany's most westerly city, perched on the frontiers with both Holland and Belgium. A second target on this night involved 3 Group Wellingtons and Stirlings against Brest, during which the Stirling element conducted the first operational trials of the Oboe blind bombing device, a game-changing system not destined to enter service for almost thirteen months.

Almost unnoticed on this night was an operation by four 61 Squadron Manchesters against the docks and shipping at Boulogne, for which the crews of W/C Weir, S/L Riley, F/L Sooby and F/O Gascoyne-Cecil were briefed and dispatched from Woolfox Lodge between 17.14 and 17.48. As usual, details in the ORB are scant, but we can assume that each had been loaded with around sixteen 500-pounders, and it seems that those beneath the feet of W/C Weir and crew contained delayed-action fuses. He and his crew were the first to bomb, from 12,000 feet, and, of course, observing no bursts, circled the target to watch the results of the others with non-delayed-action bombs. F/O Gascoyne-Cecil and crew attacked from 6,000 feet and did not observe the outcome, while F/L Sooby and crew released their load from 10,000 feet, and although seeing bursts, could not be certain whose bombs they were. L7494 was seen to explode on the run in to the target, the victim of a direct hit by a flak shell, and there were no survivors from the crew of the A Flight commander, S/L Riley. This was the final loss of a frustrating year for the squadron, which had seen only limited operational activity with the troublesome Manchester, to the tune of a paltry twenty-three sorties, despite having received the first examples for crew familiarisation back in March.

The briefed aiming point at Aachen was the Nazi Party HQ, which had no special significance other than the fact that it was situated in the city centre, at a time when it was still not admitted publicly that population centres were being bombed. 5 Group detailed fifty Hampdens and a dozen Manchesters, and they flew out initially in fair weather conditions with isolated clouds, which built up to nine to ten-tenths in the target area with tops at 15,000 feet, off which bright moonlight reflected to create an impenetrable visual barrier. It became clear at debriefings that barely half of the force had attacked the city, and local sources estimated a raid by sixteen aircraft, causing minimal damage and no casualties.

On the 14th, Scampton, Syerston and Waddington made ready twenty-two Hampdens to attack Scharnhorst and Gneisenau at Brest on a night of extremely unfavourable weather conditions including ten-tenths ice-bearing cloud at between 1,500 and 3,500 feet over the sea, which persuaded most to turn back after reaching a position west of the Channel Islands. A dozen Hampdens targeted the docks at Ostend on the 15th, and fourteen from Scampton were made ready to represent 5 Group at Wilhelmshaven on the 16th, while five others joined a contingent from Coningsby to take care of mining duties in the Jellyfish garden off Brest. Another major assault on Brest was notified across the Command on the 17th, for which a force of 121 aircraft was assembled, among them twenty-five Hampdens from Waddington, Scampton and Syerston. Eleven Manchesters took part in the next attempt on Brest, by daylight on the 18th, when claims were made of at least one hit on Gneisenau. On the 19th, 5 Group added a new squadron to its strength with the formation of 420 (Snowy Owl) Squadron RCAF at Waddington under the command of W/C Bradshaw. A dozen daylight intruder ("moling") sorties by Hampdens over north-western Germany on the 21st came to nothing, after sufficient cloud failed to materialise to protect them.

The third wartime Christmas passed peacefully, and operations resumed on the 27th, when 50 Squadron supported the epic and successful Vaagso raid by Royal Marines off the Norwegian coast on the 27th, before Düsseldorf was posted as the target for 132 aircraft later that night. 5 Group contributed thirty Hampdens and seven Manchesters, whose crews were briefed to aim for the main marshalling yards, in what turned out to be another ineffective attack on a Ruhr target, which caused little damage at a cost of seven aircraft and crews. The two main operations on the 28th involved eighty-six Wellingtons at Wilhelmshaven, while eighty-one Hampdens returned to the synthetic rubber factory at Marl-Hüls on the northern edge of the Ruhr. The target area lay under clear skies, and bright moonlight glinted off the snow-covered landscape to provide perfect visibility, which enabled navigators to map-read their way to the aiming point. Seventeen crews carried out an attack on the primary target from between 6,500 and 17,000 feet, observing bursts and fires, black debris flying into the air and a fire described by some as the largest they had witnessed. Many crews watched their bombs fall on or close to the factory and returning crews were confident of a successful outcome, although no local report emerged to confirm or deny.

During the course of the month the squadron carried out a single operation involving four sorties and lost one Manchester and crew. It had been a disappointing year for the Command, and despite the best efforts of the crews, one of under-achievement, with little to show in terms of an advance on the performance of 1940. The new aircraft types, the Stirling, Halifax and Manchester, introduced into operational service early in the year, had each failed to meet the requirements expected of them and had undergone long periods of grounding while essential modifications were carried out. 1942 would bring changes, however, chief among which were the arrival on the operational scene of the war-winning Lancaster, and a new Commander-in-Chief, who would know how to exploit it.

January 1942

As far as most crews were concerned, the incoming year would look and feel exactly like the outgoing one, and still under the restrictions of the November directive, the Command's activities reflected the continuing obsession with the German raiders at Brest, against which a further eleven operations would take place during January. 5 Group would be without 44 (Rhodesia) Squadron until early March as it worked towards operational status on the Lancaster. 5 Group's first operational activity of the year involved four Hampdens each from 49, 106 and 144 Squadrons conducting daylight "moling" sorties over Holland and north-western Germany, three of which turned back because of a lack of cloud cover.

5 Group detailed a dozen Manchesters for a raid that night on St-Nazaire, and thirty-six Hampdens for gardening duties off the Biscay ports and the Frisian Islands. in cloudy conditions that prevented them from establishing whether they were over sea or land. Small-scale mining operations occupied elements of the group on the 3rd, and there were further daylight "moling" operations on the 4th. Twenty-seven Hampdens and twelve Manchesters took off on the evening of the 5th as part of a force of 154 aircraft targeting the Scharnhorst and Gneisenau at Brest and the naval docks area. Many crews were thwarted by an effective smoke screen and eight to ten-tenths cloud at around 10,000 feet, and despite claims of large fires by some returning crews, no accurate assessment of results could be made. On the 6th, nineteen Hampdens were committed to roving commission sorties against targets of opportunity at specific locations in northern Germany, which were referred to in the 5 Group ORB as "Scuttle A" and appear to differ from "moling" only by relying on the cover of darkness rather than cloud.

AM Sir Richard Peirse left his post as C-in-C Bomber Command on the 8th to be succeeded temporarily by AVM Baldwin, the A-O-C 3 Group. In February, Peirse would take up a new appointment as C-in-C Allied Air Forces in India and South-East Asia, but the sense that he had been "sacked" from Bomber Command would linger, and perhaps unjustly tarnish his legacy. Brest was posted as the target for a force of 151 aircraft that night, reconnaissance having revealed that Scharnhorst and Gneisenau had been joined by Prinz Eugen. 5 Group contributed thirty-seven Hampdens and ten Manchesters to the main event and six Hampdens and seven Manchesters for the use of freshman crews against the docks and shipping at Cherbourg. After more than a month on the sidelines, 61 Squadron briefed six crews for Cherbourg and as Woolfox Lodge was temporarily out of commission because of a crashed aircraft, they departed North Luffenham between 04.35 and 05.00 with S/L Paape the senior pilot on duty. P/O Matthews DFM and his crew were outbound over Wiltshire when the starboard engine burst into flames and the fully laden R5789 began to lose height. Reluctant to jettison the bombs over a potentially populated area, P/O Matthews ordered his crew to bale out, which they accomplished safely, while he and second pilot, P/O Wilson, attempted an emergency landing. In the extreme darkness, they failed to notice a line of trees across their path and crashed with fatal consequences at 06.20 at Wiltshire Cross near Tidworth. The others all arrived in the target area to find ten-tenths cloud with a base at 2,000 feet, a fact discovered by S/L Paape and crew when they broke cloud at that height after circling above it for forty-five minutes. They were scraping the cloud base as the bombs were dropped, while two thousand feet above, P/O Tofield and crew spotted a gap and let theirs go immediately. The crews of P/Os Gilpin and Hubbard and Sgt Webster stooged around at between 3,500 and 5,000 feet until giving up and returning their bombs to the station dump.

A force of eighty-two aircraft was assembled for a return to Brest on the following night, for which 5 Group put up twenty-seven Hampdens and six Manchesters, while 61 Squadron remained on the ground. The weather in the target area continued to be unhelpful with eight to ten-tenths cloud and poor visibility, and many crews brought their bombs home, while others attacked last-resort targets. Thirty-four Hampdens and nine Manchesters were detailed by 5 Group on the 10th to contribute to an overall force of 124 aircraft bound in the early evening for Wilhelmshaven to attack the main railway station on what was the final night of Hampden operations for 83 Squadron, which was in the process of converting to the Manchester. The operation was another inconclusive affair, during which bombing took place through cloud and the outcome could not be determined. 61 Squadron was not involved in the main event, but dispatched the crew of F/Sgt Noble from Woolfox Lodge at 17.25 to join with other freshmen to bomb the docks at Emden, where, barely forty miles to the west of Wilhelmshaven, the cloud was only six-tenths and the target more easily identified. With their destination in sight, the Noble crew was forced to abandon their sortie when the port engine had to be shut down because of high oil pressure. Unable to maintain height, they set course for the Frisian Island of Terschelling and bombed the seaplane repair base from 5,000 feet.

Adverse weather conditions kept 5 Group on the ground for the next three nights, and when the faithful were called to prayer on the 14th, it was to reveal Hamburg as the destination for an overall force of ninety-five aircraft. The targets were the Blohm & Voss shipyards situated on the Kuhwerder Island opposite the Sankt Pauli district to the west of the city centre and the nearby Hamburger Flugzeugbau airframe factory located on Finkenwerder Island. 5 Group was to have supported the operation with thirty-five Hampdens and fifteen Manchesters, but four of the former from 61 Squadron could not be made ready in time and three from 49 Squadron were cancelled after one crashed on take-off and prevented the other two from getting away. The remaining three 61 Squadron crews of F/Ls Sooby and Page and F/Sgt Noble departed Woolfox Lodge between 17.35 and 18.05 and lost the services of F/L Page and crew to engine failure during the climb-out, while F/Sgt Noble and crew again experienced oil-pressure problems and bombed Emden from 5,000 feet before heading home. Those reaching the target were challenged by extreme darkness and thick ground haze, which created challenging conditions for aiming point identification. That said, crews could always rely on the searchlight and flak batteries to guide them into the heart of the city, where large ground features like the Binnen and Aussen-Alster Lakes on the north-western edge of the centre were a good guide for non-precision bombing. F/L Sooby and crew initially approached the target from the north at 15,000 feet but ran into intense searchlight and flak activity, which forced them to pull away and make further runs from the east and south until finally dropping their load from 13,000 feet after approaching from the west. Having bombed they dived to 8,000 feet and turned towards the north with flak shells following them out to sea and were fired upon again by the flak batteries on Heligoland. An engine cut as they turned onto finals, but F/L Sooby maintained control to carry out a safe landing at 00.20. It became clear at debriefings that only half of the force had attacked the Hamburg area and local sources confirmed seven large fires and hits on the Altona railway station but no significant damage.

Hamburg was "on" again twenty-four hours later, for which a force of ninety-six aircraft was assembled with a 5 Group contribution of twenty-seven Hampdens and ten Manchesters, three of the latter belonging to 61 Squadron. The crews of F/O Beard and P/Os Smith and Tofield were briefed to attack the city centre, and departed Woolfox Lodge between 17.20 and 17.30, arriving in the target area some three hours later to find two to eight-tenths cloud and the usual hostile defence. P/O Tofield and crew circled the city for some time before approaching from the north-west and dropping their incendiaries from 14,000 feet, evading the searchlight cones. F/O Beard glided down from 16,000 and the bomb-aimer released the incendiaries at 13,000 feet, and the Smith crew adopted a similar approach from the north-east and dropped their high explosives from 10,000 feet. Ten-tenth clouds over Lincolnshire with a base at 500 feet caused problems for returning crews, and after eight hours aloft, running short of fuel and failing to raise Bottesford on W/T, F/O Beard and crew abandoned L7495 at 01.00 some four miles east of Louth. This was one of eight crashes in England on top of the four failures to return. More than 50% of returning crews reported bombing in conditions of poor visibility, for which searchlight glare was probably to blame, and the raid proved to be another in the long line of disappointments since the start of the autumn. According to local sources, the emergency services dealt with thirty-six fires, only three of them classed as large, and there were no major incidents.

Having been selected as the third Lancaster unit after 44 and 97 Squadrons, 207 Squadron set up a Conversion Flight on the 16th in preparation for the arrival of its first example of the type. The flight would be equipped, initially, with two Manchesters, the type it had introduced into squadron service and had struggled with for more than a year. Once the first Lancaster arrived on the 25th, the conversion programme would begin with selected second pilots and crews from the squadron.

Attention remained on north-western Germany on the 17th, when Bremen was posted as the target for eighty-three aircraft, including twenty Hampdens and six Manchesters, 61 Squadron responsible for just one of the latter, containing the crew of F/O Parsons. They took off at 17.10 and had reached enemy territory when an undisclosed technical problem persuaded them to turn back. Bremen was found to be concealed beneath ten-tenths cloud at around 4,000 feet and only eight returning crews claimed to have attacked it, while Hamburg attracted others and reported eleven fires. Emden had been a regular destination for small forces since the 10th, sometimes with a contribution from 5 Group, and five Scampton Hampdens were detailed to join twenty Wellingtons to attack it on the 20th, after snow and severe frost had kept aircraft on the ground for two nights. Bremen and Emden shared the Command's attention on the night of the 21/22nd, when eleven Hampdens joined in a raid by fifty aircraft on the former, while twelve Hampdens and three Manchesters plied their trade at the latter in an overall force of thirty-eight aircraft. 61 Squadron supported the latter with two Manchesters containing the crews of P/O Searby and F/O Parsons, who departed Woolfox Lodge at 17.30 and 17.35 respectively. The former were tailed by an unidentified enemy aircraft for fifteen minutes from the Dutch coast, apparently guided by tracking lights on the ground, but no engagement took place, and they went on to bomb the target from 10,000 feet. F/O Parsons and crew released their load from the same altitude after gliding down from 15,000 feet and landed at North Luffenham with no hydraulics or brake pressure.

The seemingly interminable campaign against the enemy warships at Brest continued on the night of the 25/26th, for which a force of sixty-one aircraft was made ready, 5 Group contributing thirty-five Hampdens and fifteen Manchesters, 61 Squadron responsible for eight of the latter. They took off between 17.25 and 18.20, F/O Fraser last away, after being delayed by an engine issue, and the senior pilot on duty was S/L West, whose posting to the squadron is not recorded in the ORB. F/O McNaughton and crew were recalled after the dinghy broke out of its housing during the climb-out and Sgt Underwood and crew were defeated by low oil pressure and also returned early. The others made their way to the Cornish coast, where small amounts of cloud were encountered, but this increased during the Channel crossing to three to eight-tenths by the time that they arrived in the target area. The crews had a clear view of the coastline as they approached and those of S/L

West, F/L Page and P/Os Gilpin and Gunter circled out to sea at up to 17,000 feet for between twenty and forty-five minutes after arriving early. As they began their bombing runs they were guided to the aiming point by searchlights, flares and the heavy and accurate flak defence coming up at them through the ten-tenths cloud at around 8,000 feet. They delivered their attacks in one or two passes from between 7,000 and 15,000 feet, some after gliding down and P/O Gunter and crew crossed the French coast homebound at 2,000 feet having dived to evade the defences. S/L West and crew flew home at 3,000 feet, and all arrived safely to make their reports, F/L Page with a slightly wounded rear gunner and a little flak damage to repair. Despite a few claims of fires it was another in the series of inconclusive and frustrating raids, but unknown to the authorities, the Germans were planning and practicing this particular saga's endgame.

50 Squadron represented 5 Group at Hannover on the 26th in a force of seventy-one aircraft, fewer than half of which attacked the primary target. The next assault on Brest was posted on the 27th and required the services of thirty-two Hampdens and three Manchesters from Scampton, Syerston, North Luffenham and Bottesford. *(The Bomber Command War Diaries does not record any operations taking place on this night)*. It was reported that Prinz Eugen was also "still in town" as an added attraction for the force, which included the 61 Squadron crews of P/O Hubbard and F/O McNaughton, who took off at 00.55 and 01.15 respectively. They arrived in the target area under a bright half-moon and two to ten-tenths cloud with a base at 3,000 feet, but haze or a smoke-screen further obscured the docks area creating challenging conditions for target identification. P/O Hubbard and crew braved the flak and ran in to bomb at 9,000 feet, while F/O McNaughton and crew met no opposition as they glided down from 13,000 feet to release their bombs at 7,500 feet. Not all crews observed the fall of their bombs as they concentrated on weaving their way out of the searchlight and flak defence and no claims were made of direct hits.

The main event on the 28th was a raid on Münster, for which a force of fifty-five Wellingtons and twenty-nine Hampdens was prepared, while 83 Squadron joined the operational ranks of the Manchester brigade for an attack on the docks and shipping at Boulogne as part of a small force which included the 61 Squadron crews of P/O Gunter and F/Sgt Underwood. They took off at 19.45 and 19.50 respectively and arrived in the target area to be met by favourable conditions aided by moonlight. The Gunter crew reached Cap Gris Nez at 14,500 feet and carried out a long glide approach from the south to release the bombs from 10,000 feet and continued the glide out to sea with flak bursting in their wake. F/Sgt Underwood and crew went in low at 5,000 feet and observed hits in the docks area followed by fires.

On the last night of the month, a force of seventy-one aircraft took off for another tilt at the warships at Brest, and among them were forty-one Hampdens and eleven Manchesters representing 5 Group. 61 Squadron put up a record nine Manchesters, which departed Woolfox Lodge between 17.55 and 18.50 with F/L Page the senior pilot on duty and it is believed that all reached the target area. The crews of F/Sgt Noble and P/O Searby skirted the coast before carrying out glide attacks, the Searby crew releasing their bombs from 6,000 feet, while the Noble crew's failed to drop from 7,000 feet and had to be brought home. The target area was bathed in bright moonlight providing excellent visibility, but varying opinions as to the cloud conditions ranged from clear skies to eight-tenths. What was not in doubt, according to reports from other squadrons, was the smoke screen, which prevented many crews from establishing a pinpoint and carrying out an attack but was not mentioned in any 61 Squadron post-raid reports. F/O Archibald and crew ran in on an easterly course parallel with the docks and released their load in level flight from 5,500 feet, while P/O Smith and crew approached from the east before swinging to the north and attacking the western docks area from 7,000 feet, held for much of the time in a searchlight cone. F/O McNaughton's bomb-aimer was the only one to make a positive identification of part of one of the cleverly disguised enemy cruisers after they glided down from 13,500 to let their bombs go from 7,000 feet, and it was only after the engines were throttled up to extend the glide, that they attracted the attentions of flak batteries. P/O Gunter and crew approached at 14,000 feet on a south-westerly course before gliding down to the bomb release point at the northern end of the docks complex at 5,000 feet. At this point they were chased by searchlights and flak down to 1,000 feet and eventually crossed the Finistere coast heading west at 500 feet.

There was shock at North Luffenham and Woolfox Lodge when three 61 Squadron Manchesters and two 144 Squadron Hampdens failed to return, and they represented the entire losses from the operation. A distress signal was picked up from F/L Page and crew, which fixed them at a position some fifty miles south of Plymouth, and although two destroyers were detached from convoy escort duties to search the area, no trace of L7396 and its eight occupants was ever found. L7472 was coned by searchlights and set on fire by flak before clipping a balloon cable, which sealed its fate. Some crew members baled out when they were south of the target, leaving F/O Fraser and two others on board to carry out a ditching, which F/O Fraser survived, while the others became trapped and went down with the Manchester. All of the survivors were taken into captivity, where they were joined by two members of P/O Parson's crew from R5787, which had been fatally damaged by flak and crash landed some ten miles north-west of Brest. P/O Parsons and one other lost their lives, while two succumbed to their injuries, one within hours and the other on the 3rd of February and another retained his freedom thanks to the courage of local civilians and partisans.

During the course of the month, the squadron took part in ten operations and dispatched thirty-seven sorties for the loss of five Manchesters, three complete crews and two members of another.

February 1942

There were no operations for 5 Group during the first few days of the new month, and all available personnel were press-ganged into snow-clearing duties. Although the impending breakout from Brest by the three enemy warships would take the Royal Navy and the RAF by complete surprise in what would be a most humiliating episode for the government and the nation, there was clearly some advance warning, as three Manchesters were put on stand-by for daylight operations at Bottesford on the 4th in preparation for precisely that event, and six more on the 5th. 5 Group notified its stations on the 6th to prepare for daylight mining operations in the Nectarine I and II gardens off the southern and central Frisians, and between them they raised a force of thirty-three Hampdens and thirteen Manchesters. 61 Squadron dispatched ten Manchesters between 11.00 and 11.15 with W/C Weir and S/L Paape the senior pilots on duty, and apart from F/O Beard's windscreen icing over temporarily, all enjoyed uneventful outward flights and reached the target area to find generally favourable conditions. There was some flak fire from Terschelling, and a Dornier 215 was observed to be loitering in the distance, but there was sufficient cloud to mask their approach and timed runs to the briefed release points and all fulfilled their briefs without issue. That night, 3 Group sent fifty-seven Wellingtons and three Stirlings to continue the assault on Brest, but only a third of crews reported bombing through thick cloud.

The daylight gardening operation in the Frisians was repeated on the following day employing thirty-two Hampdens, when the target area on this occasion was further north in the Nectarine III garden off the island of Wangerooge in the Waddensee. 5 Group was not called into action again until the 10th, when the main railway station in Bremen was chosen as the aiming point for a force of fifty-five aircraft. The entire operation had descended into a shambles even before take-off, when the contributions from North Luffenham and Syerston were cancelled because of dangerous ice and water conditions on the aerodromes, and a similar situation at Scampton delayed the preparation of six of the original eighteen Hampdens and led to them also being scrubbed. The six-strong 61 Squadron element departed Woolfox Lodge between 01.55 and 02.25 with F/Os Archibald and McNaughton the senior pilots on duty and set course for the Lincolnshire coast, with P/O Smith and crew struggling to climb to a respectable height. Having reached 9,000 feet over the North Sea, they decided to end their outward journey at Terschelling, which they attacked in level flight from 8,000 feet before heading back home. F/Sgt Underwood and crew glided down to 9,000 feet to deliver their attack and R5834 sustained flak damage in the process, before climbing back up to 12,000 feet and reaching the enemy coast, where the starboard engine cut and the Manchester began rapidly to lose height. The propeller was feathered, which reduced the rate of descent, but with an airspeed hovering just above stall speed at one hundred mph, the Manchester twice entered a spin, on the second occasion the port engine cutting out also, only to restart after considerable height had been shed. Shortly after crossing the Norfolk coast the port engine failed again because of fuel starvation and a forced landing was carried out at 07.55 near Horsham St Faith without crew casualties but terminal damage to the Manchester. At debriefings, many crews reported reaching the target area but were unable to establish a position through cloud and haze, and any glimpses of the ground revealed a featureless blanket of snow. Most bombed the general area of the city, guided by searchlight and flak activity, or sought out alternative targets at Wilhelmshaven or Borkum.

Orders were received at Bottesford, Coningsby and Swinderby on the 11th to prepare a dozen Hampdens and six Manchesters between them for an operation that night against a railway station at Mannheim. They were part of an overall force of forty-nine aircraft, which enjoyed favourable conditions that enabled them to identify the target and release their bombs unopposed by flak in the vicinity of the briefed aiming point. Among other small-scale operations on this night was one against Brest by eighteen Wellingtons, the crews of which would have been unaware that they were the last to engage in this seemingly endless saga. As the sound of their engines receded into the eastern cloud-filled skies, Vice-Admiral Otto Cilliax, the Brest Group commander on board Scharnhorst put Operation Cerberus into action at 21.14, Scharnhorst, Gneisenau and Prinz Eugen slipping anchor, before heading into the English Channel under an escort of destroyers and E-Boats. It was an audacious bid for freedom, covered by bad weather, widespread jamming and meticulously planned support by the Kriegsmarine and the Luftwaffe, all of which had been rehearsed extensively during January. The planning, and a little good fortune, allowed the fleet to make undetected progress until spotted off Le Touquet by two Spitfires piloted by G/C Victor Beamish, the commanding officer of Kenley, and W/C Finlay Boyd, both of whom maintained radio silence and did not report their find until landing at 10.42 on the morning of the 12th.

The British authorities had prepared a plan in advance for precisely this eventuality, under the Codename, Operation Fuller, but so secret was it, that few, it seemed, either knew of its full requirements or even of its existence. Once the enemy fleet was spotted in the late morning, frantic efforts were made to get Coastal and Bomber Command aircraft away, but only 5 Group was standing by at four hours readiness. It was after 13.00 hours before the first sorties were launched, and the 5 Group stations worked frantically to get sixty-four Hampdens and fifteen Manchesters into the air. 61 Squadron briefed the crews of W/C Weir, S/Ls Paape and West, F/O Gilpin and P/O Hubbard, before launching them from Woolfox Lodge between 15.00 and 15.15 with orders to make for a search position off The Hague and the Hoek of Holland. They were part of the largest commitment of aircraft by daylight in the war to date, amounting to 242 sorties, and arrived to find rainstorms and squally conditions, a wedge of ten-tenths cloud between sea level and 1,000 feet and horizontal visibility of less than a mile. The conditions, as anticipated by the Germans, compounded the difficulties of locating a fleet at sea and most crews would fail in that regard, but W/C Weir and S/L Paape and their crews were able to make contact and attempt to fulfil their briefs.

On their way across the North Sea the Weir crew was stalked first by a Ju88 and them a BF110, both of which were evaded in cloud, and on arrival at the Dutch coast the first square search failed to locate the enemy fleet. They then flew south along the coast from Zandvoort to The Hague before heading west for fifteen miles and beginning a second search, which immediately revealed the enemy vessels at close range to the rear. They climbed into cloud and turned back to position themselves behind for an approach from the south, picking up the two main vessels to port and starboard but not directly underneath. Unable to position himself for an attack, W/C Weir climbed back into cloud for another go-around, but this time could not locate the targets and having been under heavy and accurate fire throughout, jettisoned the bombs and made for home, keeping a watchful eye on a severely damaged port mainplane. S/L Paape and crew pinpointed on the Dutch coast at 400 feet and carried out two runs along it ten miles out to sea, finding nothing, but when they began a second search thirty miles out, they came upon the fleet at 800 feet and were hit twice by flak as they positioned themselves for an attack on one of the cruisers. The bombs were released from 450 feet and undershot, straddling one of the escorting destroyers, and S/L Paape and crew were then chased out of the area at sea level by flak, which shredded the Manchester and left the bomb doors hanging down. After landing safely an inspection revealed that the hydraulics system had been shot away, leaving the aircraft without brakes, trim controls and working turrets, a petrol tank had been punctured and the tailplane riddled with holes. The remaining three crews searched in vain in impossible conditions and brought their bombs home.

What became known as "The Channel Dash" cost fifteen bomber Command aircraft, 5 Group alone posting missing nine Hampdens and crews, all lost in the North Sea, six of them without trace and they could be added to all of those others sacrificed to this endeavour over the past eleven months. Despite the heroic effort and sacrifice of the Bomber Command, Coastal Command and Fleet Air Arm crews, the enemy fleet made good its escape into open sea, and the entire affair was a huge embarrassment to the government and the nation. That said, at least this annoying itch would no longer be a distraction and claim Bomber Command lives or divert effort from targets to which the bomber force was better suited. As far as the enemy fleet was concerned, its own trials and tribulations were not yet over and after Scharnhorst struck a mine in the late afternoon, she began to fall back, while at 19.55, a magnetic mine detonated close enough to Gneisenau, when off Terschelling, to open a small hole in the starboard side and temporarily slow her progress also. Later still, at 21.34, when passing through the same stretch of water, Scharnhorst hit another mine which stopped both engines and damaged steering and fire control. The vessel got underway again at 22.23 using its starboard engines and making twelve knots, while carrying an additional one thousand tons of seawater.

The day's activities were not yet over for 5 Group, and the crews of fourteen Hampdens and nine Manchesters were briefed to lay mines in the Nectarine and Rosemary gardens, respectively off the Frisians and in the Heligoland Bight, through which the enemy fleet would have to pass to reach safety. 61 Squadron dispatched the crews of P/O Tofield and F/O Gunter to the latter at 23.35, the Tofield crew flying out at 8,000 feet and running into severe icing conditions and a snowstorm in which they lost height to 600 feet before abandoning their sortie. In contrast, the Gunter crew chose a low-level outward flight at 1,500 feet, which proved to be so turbulent and the visibility so limited that they, too, gave up and returned to base. Gneisenau and Prinz Eugen reached the Elbe Estuary at 07.00 on the 13th, and tied up at Brunsbüttel North Locks at 09.30, while Scharnhorst arrived at Wilhelmshaven at 10.00 with three months-worth of damage to repair. The mines had been laid almost certainly by 5 Group Hampdens over the preceding nights and demonstrated the remarkable effectiveness of this war-long campaign.

A new Air Ministry directive issued on the 14th was to change the emphasis of bomber operations from that point until the end of the war. Lengthy consideration having been given to the Butt Report and the future of an independent bomber force, the new policy authorised the blatant area bombing of Germany's industrial towns and cities in a direct assault on the morale of the civilian population, particularly its workers. This had, of course, been going on since the summer of 1940, but no longer would there be the pretence of claiming to be attacking industrial and military targets. Waiting in the wings, in fact, at this very moment, four days into his voyage from the United States in the armed merchantman, Alcantara, was a new leader, a man well-known to 5 Group, who not only would pursue this policy with a will, but also possessed the self-belief, arrogance and stubbornness to fight his corner against all-comers on behalf of his beleaguered Bomber Command.

That night, a force of ninety-eight aircraft took off to employ the main post office and railway station as the aiming points for an area attack on Mannheim, to which 5 Group contributed twenty-five Hampdens and nine Manchesters. 61 Squadron briefed the crews of F/O Beard, P/O Searby and F/Sgt Noble for the main event and the freshman crew of F/Sgt Williams for nickelling duties over Paris. They departed Woolfox Lodge together between 18.20 and 18.40 and F/O Beard and crew were initially led astray by a navigational error but were able to overcome the situation and cross the French and Belgian coasts like the others at 10,000 feet. The Williams crew dispensed their bundles of propaganda material thirty-five miles north of the French capital city in the expectation that the crosswind would carry it to its intended destination. The bombing trio reached the target area by homing in on the searchlight and flak activity and encountered four to ten-tenths cloud at between 2,000 and 12,000 feet, with fair visibility above and ground haze below. Such weather conditions proved to be unhelpful, and most crews abandoned their search for the briefed aiming points and bombed the general built-up area. P/O Searby and crew bombed in a glide from 7,500 feet and F/Sgt Noble and crew from a thousand feet higher while held in searchlights, and F/O Beard and crew believed that they had bombed the primary target from 10,000 feet only to discover later that the city of Karlsruhe had been beneath them at the time. Despite the claims of sixty-seven crews to have bombed the city, local reports spoke of two buildings destroyed and fifteen damaged.

5 Group detailed thirty-seven Hampdens and twelve Manchesters on the 16th to carry out mining duties in the Nectarine I garden off Terschelling and the Nectarine III garden, encompassing the eastern Frisian islands of Wangerooge, Juist and Borkum. The 61 Squadron crews of F/Sgt Underwood, P/O Smith and F/Sgt Webster departed Woolfox Lodge in that order between 18.35

and 19.10 and headed out over Skegness, while the crew of P/O Furby turned south for the Channel crossing on their way to the city of Rennes in north-western France. They were carrying bundles of reading matter, which the incoming commander-in-chief, who was notoriously opposed to the practice of nickelling, would refer to as "toilet paper". P/O Smith and crew adopted a low-level approach to avoid icing conditions and arrived in the target area to find ten-tenths cloud at between 1,000 and 5,000 feet and generally poor visibility. Even so, they were able to establish a pinpoint on Terschelling and planted their vegetable in the briefed location, while F/Sgt Underwood and crew, who had opted to fly higher, ran into severe icing conditions and were losing altitude so fast that they jettisoned the mine and turned back to land at Debden, the first aerodrome they came upon after crossing the coast. L7433 was shot down by flak and crashed into the sea off Terschelling, taking with it the crew of F/Sgt Webster. The remains of three crew members were washed ashore on the island in the summer and were buried locally. In all, fourteen Hampden and seven Manchester crews returned to report a successful conclusion to their sorties. The leafleteers passed the Channel Islands on their way to make landfall in the St-Malo area and dispensed their cargo in level flight from 8,000 feet before returning safely after four hours and forty minutes aloft.

The night of the 18/19th was devoted to mining and nickelling operations, the former undertaken by twenty-five Hampdens off the Frisians in all three Nectarine gardens, the Rosemary garden in the Heligoland Bight and the Yam garden in the Schillig Roads approaches to Jade Bay and the Weser estuary. 61 Squadron was not involved and was next called into action on the 21st to send the crews of F/O Archibald and P/O Searby off to the Yam garden at the mouth of the River Weser at 20.30 and 20.50, only for them to run into severe icing conditions and act on orders to turn back in such circumstances.

Air Chief Marshal Sir Arthur Harris took up his post as the new Commander-in-Chief of Bomber Command on the 22nd. He was a man well-known to 5 Group, having served as its A-O-C until November 1940, when he became second deputy to Sir Charles Portal, the Chief-of-the-Air-Staff. Harris arrived at the helm with firm ideas already in place on how to win the war by bombing alone, a pre-war theory, which no commander had yet had an opportunity to put into practice. It was obvious to him, that the small-scale raids on multiple targets favoured by his predecessor, served only to dilute the effort, and that such pin-prick attacks could not hurt Germany's war effort. He recognized the need to overwhelm the defences and emergency services, by pushing the maximum number of aircraft across the aiming point in the shortest possible time, and this would signal the birth of the bomber stream and an end to the former practice, whereby squadrons or even crews determined for themselves the details of their sorties. He knew also that urban areas are most efficiently destroyed by fire rather than blast, and it would not be long before the bomb loads carried in his aircraft reflected this thinking.

On the night of his appointment, 5 Group sent nineteen Hampdens to Wilhelmshaven and not one attacked the primary target in the prevailing weather conditions. The 61 Squadron crews of P/O Smith and F/Sgt Noble took off at 18.40 bound for the Rosemary garden in the Heligoland Bight, but the former's pitot head froze up in ice-bearing cloud and they abandoned their sortie. The latter continued on and when twenty minutes short of e.t.a. descended through cloud to 1,000 feet to find themselves to the west of Heligoland but decided to pinpoint on an island off the Danish coast, probably Rømø, and conducted a timed run from there to the release point.

On the night of the 23/24th, 5 Group detailed twenty-three Hampdens for mining duties in the Rosemary and Yam gardens in the Heligoland Bight and Schillig Roads respectively, and on the following night forty-two Hampdens and nine Manchesters for the same gardens plus Nectarine I and III. 61 Squadron contributed seven Manchesters to the Nectarine gardens and an eighth for nickelling duties in the Paris area and sent them on their way from Woolfox Lodge between 18.30 and 18.45 with F/L McNaughton the senior pilot on duty among the gardeners and the crew of P/O Clarke to deliver the mail. The main problem for the gardeners was a trigger-happy convoy off the Norfolk coast, which fired upon them and continued to do so even after the colours of the day had been fired. Flying over ten-tenths cloud, P/O Searby and crew set a course to the south on e.t.a. at Wangerooge and then turned to the east along a sandbank and passed over four vessels at anchor, one of which appeared to be a battleship or heavy cruiser. They unleashed a barrage of flak which required the Manchester to take evasive action, and the vegetables were eventually planted to the west of the warships. The crews of P/O Hubbard and F/Sgt Underwood pinpointed on Terschelling and undertook a timed run for around eight miles before planting their vegetables from 600 feet, the latter in a location alternative to that briefed. F/L McNaughton and crew released their mines from 700 feet after pinpointing on Wangerooge and the others were also successful and returned safely. Meanwhile, P/O Clarke and crew had dispensed their nickels into the slip-stream from 12,000 feet when north-east of Paris and landed after an uneventful sortie that lasted ten minutes short of five hours.

On the 25th, 5 Group detailed a dozen Manchesters to target the Gneisenau, now believed to be at Kiel, while eighteen Hampdens and a Manchester took care of gardening duties in the Nectarines I and II, Yam and Rosemary gardens. The Germans recorded this as a revenge raid for the "Channel Dash" embarrassment, and while Gneisenau was not hit, the accommodation ship, Monte Sarmiento, was and was burnt out with the loss of 120 lives. The main event on the 26th was a raid on the floating dock at Kiel for which 49 and 144 Squadrons detailed four and six Hampdens respectively to join Wellingtons and Halifaxes in an overall force of forty-nine aircraft. A further twenty-seven Hampdens were made ready for mining duties in the Yam, Hawthorn and Rosemary gardens, respectively in the Jade/Weser estuary, in the Waddensee off southern Jutland and in the Heligoland Bight. The Kiel operation threw up one of the war's great ironies, after a high explosive bomb struck the bows of Gneisenau, now supposedly in a safe haven after enduring eleven months of constant bombardment at Brest, and not only did it kill 116 of her crew, it also ended her sea-going career for good. Her main armament was removed for use in coastal defence, and she was towed to Gdynia, where she remained unrepaired for the remainder of the war.

The British authorities were unaware of the success, however, and sent another raid of sixty-eight aircraft on the 27th, which included a 5 Group contribution of eighteen Hampdens and seventeen Manchesters. 61 Squadron supported the operation with eight Manchesters, which departed Woolfox Lodge between 17.45 and 18.00 with F/Ls Gascoyne-Cecil and McNaughton the senior pilots on duty. P/O Searby and crew turned back from a position over the North Sea after the starboard engine began to overheat, and they brought their bombs home, while the crews of F/O Archibald and P/O Hubbard both jettisoned theirs off the Danish coast because of ice-accretion, the former having stalled twice. Those arriving in the target area encountered bright moonlight above the ten-tenths cloud, and this offered no chance of identifying the floating dock, most crews resorting to bombing on e.t.a. in the general area of the town, guided by the flashes of searchlights and flak. F/O Beard and crew reached the target on e.t.a., but dropped only nickels before turning for home, and F/O Gunter delivered their attack also on e.t.a., after gliding down from 17,000 to 12,000 feet. F/L McNaughton and crew attacked from 10,000 feet after gliding down, F/Sgt Noble and crew from a similar height in level flight and F/L Gascoyne-Cecil and crew jettisoned their load from 6,000 feet after unsuccessfully attempting to break cloud.

During the course of the month, the squadron carried out thirteen operations and dispatched forty-seven sorties for the loss of two Manchesters and one crew.

March 1942

Adverse weather conditions welcomed in the new month and kept the bomber force on the ground on the 1st and on the 2nd, and it was the 3rd before orders were received across the Command to prepare for an operation, which, in its bold conception, was a clear indication of what was to come. Bomber Command's evolution to war-winning capability was to be long, arduous and gradual, but the first signs of a new hand on the tiller came early on in Harris's reign with this meticulously planned attack on the Renault lorry factory, which was located in a loop of the Seine in the district of Billancourt to the south-west of central Paris. The plant was capable of producing 18,000 lorries per year, which was a massive boon to the German war effort, and the attempt to destroy it came in response to an Air Ministry request. The operation would be conducted in three waves, led by experienced crews, and would involve extensive use of flares to provide illumination. In the face of what was expected to be scant defence, crews were also encouraged to attack from as low a level as practicable, both for the sake of accuracy and in an attempt to avoid civilian casualties. In time, such operations would be led by Gee-equipped aircraft, but the 3 Group squadrons already employing the device were forbidden from taking part on this occasion, lest one be lost over enemy territory and its secrets revealed.

A force of 235 aircraft was assembled, a new record for a single target, and among them were forty-eight Hampdens and twenty-six Manchesters representing 5 Group, nine of the latter provided by 61 Squadron. They departed Woolfox Lodge between 19.10 and 19.35 with S/L Paape the senior pilot on duty and all reached the target area, where bright moonlight aided target location and most crews picked up the River Seine in good time to enable them to plan their bombing runs. Indeed, S/L Paape reported that he could see flares over Paris, more than ninety miles inland, even before crossing the French coast. The 61 Squadron crews delivered their bomb loads from between 3,500 and 8,000 feet and many bursts and explosions were observed, some watching debris being flung into the air. 223 crews reported successful sorties, many describing the factory buildings as well alight as they turned away, and post-raid reconnaissance confirmed the operation to have been an outstanding success for the loss of just one aircraft. 40% of the factory's buildings had been destroyed, and production was halted for four weeks, costing the Germans around 2,300 lorries, although, sadly, not all of the bombs had fallen precisely where intended. Inevitably, adjacent workers' housing had been hit by stray bombs, killing 367 French civilians, and severely injuring 341 others, some of whom would die. At the time, this was more than twice the heaviest death toll inflicted on a German target. It was somewhat paradoxical that, as a champion of area bombing, Harris should gain his first major victory against a precision target.

While the above was in progress, some 330 miles to the north, four Lancasters taxied to the runway under the approving eyes of the 5 Group A-O-C, AVM Slessor, each carrying four mines for delivery to the Yam and Rosemary gardens in the Schillig Roads and Heligoland Bight in what would be the type's maiden operation.

It rained all day on the 4th and snowed all day on the 5th, and it was the 7th before orders came through from 5 Group to make ready seventeen Hampdens for gardening duties in the Artichoke garden, on the approaches to the port of Lorient, an operation not recorded in the 5 Group ORB. Despite the fact that Essen, as home to the Krupp organisation, was the beating heart of the Ruhr Valley's war production, it had not been paid particular attention thus far in the war. This was about to change as Harris fixed his attention upon it, and like a dog with a bone, would not abandon his quest to destroy it until that aim had been achieved. It was a fight he would win, but the first twelve months would be frustrating, unrewarding and expensive, and began with the first of three raids on consecutive nights on the 8th. A force of 211 aircraft was assembled, of which thirty-seven Hampdens and twenty-two Manchesters were provided by 5 Group, while the leading aircraft, belonging to 3 Group, were equipped with the new Gee navigation device, which offered the great hope that it could solve the problem of blind target locating.

The eight 61 Squadron Manchesters departed Woolfox Lodge between 01.15 and 01.50 with S/L Paape the senior pilot on duty and each carrying a 4,000lb "cookie" blockbuster and SBCs of incendiaries. They were followed into the air at 02.20 and 02.25 respectively by the crews of Sgt Furby and P/O Clarke, who were bound for the Artichoke garden off the port of Lorient, and while they headed for the Dorset coast, those involved in the main event adopted a route that would take them via the Scheldt estuary to approach the Ruhr from the south. Contending with a starboard engine issue, P/O Searby and crew bombed Düsseldorf as an alternative target from 12,500 feet and managed to return to base without further incident, leaving the others to continue on to the target. On arrival they found clear skies and good visibility provided by a half-moon, but also the ever-present industrial haze, which obscured ground detail, including the assigned aiming point "B", the Krupp complex. On their way down in a glide from 11,500 to 6,000 feet, S/L Paape's bomb-aimer released the bomb load at 8,500 feet, after which they continued at low level to evade the searchlights and flak. F/O Beard and crew ended up twenty miles north of the target, perhaps having adopted a different route, and bombed from 12,000 feet, before turning east to skirt Dortmund and then race west across the Zuider Zee (Ijsselmeer) to gain the North Sea. The others attacked the built-up area from 9,900 to 11,500 feet, some observing bursts and others not and local sources reported a light raid with a little housing damage in southern districts. Meanwhile, more than five hundred miles to the south-west, P/O Clarke and crew pinpointed on the Ile-de-Groix, and under fire from shore-based heavy flak, planted their vegetables according to brief in two sticks from 600 and 900 feet. It took Sgt Furby and crew an hour to establish a pinpoint but once done, they, too, delivered their mines into the allotted locations.

The Krupp complex was back on twenty-four hours later as one of two aiming points at Essen, and a force of 187 aircraft made ready, which included a 5 Group contribution of fifteen Hampdens and ten Manchesters in the absence of a contribution from 61 Squadron. This figure had originally been higher, but adverse weather conditions, technical difficulties and a Manchester becoming bogged down on the way to take-off at Bottesford, reduced the numbers significantly. Some crews claimed to be able to see the flares over Essen even before reaching the Dutch coast, which confirmed that the horizontal visibility was reasonable, while vertical visibility at the target was again compromised by industrial haze. Major landmarks were identified through the five-tenths cloud with tops at around 8,000 feet, but not the Krupp districts in the western and north-western region of the city and the bombing was scattered over twenty-four other Ruhr towns and cities, with Hamborn and Duisburg the chief beneficiaries. The Essen authorities reported the destruction of two buildings, with seventy-two others damaged.

Essen was posted as the primary target again on the 10th, for which a force of 126 aircraft was made ready to attack two aiming points, the Krupp sector and the city centre. 5 Group provided almost half of the force in the form of forty-three Hampdens, thirteen Manchesters and, for the first time over Germany, two 44 (Rhodesia) Squadron Lancasters, which would be employing TR1335 (Gee) for the first time. 61 Squadron made ready eight Manchesters, seven of which took off between 20.00 and 20.15, leaving P/O Clarke and crew on the ground to clamber into the reserve aircraft after theirs became unserviceable. F/Ls Gascoyne-Cecil and McNaughton were the senior pilots on duty others as they headed out across the North Sea and reached the target area to find two to eight-tenths cloud at between 3,000 and 8,000 feet, extreme darkness and poor visibility, made worse by the glare from searchlights and flares and the attentions of intense and accurate flak. Unable to identify either the Krupp sector or the main square, most bombed the built-up area generally, those from 61 Squadron from between 7,500 and 14,000 feet, before turning for home to report some bursts and fires but no detail. An analysis revealed that fewer than half of the force had reached the primary target, while thirty-five aircraft had bombed alternatives, and according to local sources one house was destroyed and the nearest any bombs fell to the Krupp complex was on a railway line serving the area.

The Deutsche Werke, Germania Werft and Howaldtswerke U-Boot construction yards at Kiel were the targets for a force of sixty-eight Wellingtons on the night of the 12/13th, while forty Wellingtons and Whitleys, probably crewed by freshmen, attended to Emden and 5 Group committed twenty-six Hampdens and a lone Manchester to mining duties in the Yam, Hawthorn and Rosemary gardens off Germany's North Sea coast. Cologne was posted on the 13th as the target for a force of 135 aircraft of six different types, which included a contribution from 5 Group of a single Lancaster, twenty-two Hampdens and sixteen Manchesters, nine of which were made ready at Woolfox Lodge. They took off between 19.50 and 20.15 with S/L West the senior pilot on duty and soon lost the services of P/O Searby and crew to an undisclosed technical problem. They were not alone in contending with an issue, and for P/O Hubbard and crew it was a tendency to stall even at 150 mph, a situation that persuaded them to jettison the bomb load "safe" fifty miles out over the North Sea and try to make it home. After crossing the English coast, a coolant leak developed in the port engine, and when it appeared to be on the point of bursting into flames it was shut down and the propeller feathered. They reached a beacon at 4,000 feet and on receiving no response from base, the order was given to abandon ship, P/O Hubbard the last to jump from a lowly 2,200 feet, leaving L7395 to crash in flames near Wittering in Cambridgeshire.

Meanwhile, P/O Smith and crew had turned back because of an undisclosed serviceability problem after reaching enemy territory, and P/O Tofield and crew were over Charleroi in Belgium when they abandoned their sortie after struggling to maintain height at 10,500 feet. Those reaching the target found the visibility to be good through the partial cover of three to five-tenths cloud at between 8,000 and 12,000 feet and had to run the gauntlet of intense searchlight and flak to arrive at the aiming point. F/O Beard and crew became ensnared in a searchlight cone and dumped their bombs over the northern part of the city in order to aid their ultimately successful escape. Flares provided effective illumination for the other 61 Squadron participants, who bombed from 9,000 to 12,000 feet and contributed to an unusually effective raid that inflicted substantial damage on a number of war industry factories in the Nippes district located to the north of the city centre, west of the Rhine, where a major marshalling yard was also located. In addition to this, 1,500 houses were hit in what proved to be the first genuinely successful Gee-led raid.

5 Group spent the next six nights on the ground as the weather closed down operations and it was the 20th before thirteen Manchesters and six Lancasters were detailed for mining duties in the Nectarine gardens off the Frisians. 61 Squadron remained inactive until the 23rd, when a dozen Hampdens, two Manchesters and three 3 Group Stirlings were sent mining in the Artichoke garden off Lorient. The crews of Sgt Stewart and P/O Seibold took off at 19.45 and 19.50 respectively and both experienced difficulty in establishing a pinpoint despite clear conditions, the Seibold crew releasing their mines from 550 feet only to realise shortly afterwards that they had erred by five or six miles.

Harris resumed his campaign against Essen on the night of the 25/26th, when sending the largest force yet to a single target of 254 aircraft, 5 Group playing its part by contributing twenty Manchesters, nine Hampdens and seven Lancasters. A record ten 61 squadron Manchesters departed Woolfox Lodge between 20.05 and 21.10 with S/L West the senior pilot on duty. F/Sgt Williams and crew climbed to 9,000 feet over Holland but when a door blew off and communication was lost to the rear turret, they bombed a railway line between Emmerich and Wesel on the Rhine and almost came to grief in the Amsterdam flak on the way home. Despite predominantly clear skies and good visibility, thick industrial haze thwarted the attempts of all crews to identify ground features within Essen and those representing 61 Squadron delivered their cookie and incendiaries each into the built-up area from 6,500 to 14,000 feet. On return, crews commented that some of the Wellington-laid flares were burning at 18,000 feet, which was of no benefit, and the promise of Gee demonstrated in the recent attack on Cologne was not repeated, as much of the effort was wasted on a decoy site at Rheinberg some eighteen miles away. It was a bad night for 5 Group, which posted missing six aircraft, two-thirds of the overall casualty figure, and among them were five of the twenty Manchesters dispatched, a loss rate of 25%. 61 Squadron's L7497 was shot down by the night-fighter of Oblt Helmut Woltersdorf of NJG1 and crashed five miles west-south-west of Bocholt, north of the Ruhr with no survivors from the crew of Sgt Furby. L7518 was homebound when intercepted and shot down by the night-fighter of Oblt Helmut Lent of II./NJG2 to crash at 00.32 seven miles north-north-west of Alkmaar with the safety of the North Sea in sight. P/O Hubbard and the other four crew members forward of the main spar lost their lives, while both gunners survived to be taken into captivity. It will be recalled that the Hubbard crew had recently taken to their parachutes on return from Cologne, and it is uncanny how frequently such incidents occurred almost as a precursor to the loss of the same crew a short time hence.

On the 26th, instructions were received to withdraw Lancasters from operations and to restrict training flights to a fuel load not exceeding 580 gallons in inner tanks only. This resulted from an incident of wingtip rippling and loose rivets and brought an end to operations for 44 and 97 Squadrons for the remainder of the month. That night, a force of 115 Wellingtons and Stirlings returned to Essen, while 5 Group detailed thirty Hampdens and fifteen Manchesters to conduct mining operations in the Yam, Nectarines and Deodar gardens, respectively in Jade Bay/Weser estuary, off the Frisians and the Gironde estuary leading to the port of Bordeaux in south-western France. 61 Squadron supported the endeavour in Nectarine III with two Manchesters bearing aloft the crews of P/O Seibold and Sgt Stewart, which took off at 19.20 and were followed into the air thirty-five minutes later by the freshman crew of P/O Churchill, who's destination with a cargo of reading matter was Paris. The gardeners pinpointed on Spiekeroog before planting their vegetable according to brief from under 1,000 feet, watched by flak ships moored off the nearby islands of Borkum and Wangerooge, and all three Manchesters returned safely to base.

These operations preceded another foretaste of things to come, when Harris launched a major assault on the historic Hansastadt (ancient free-trade city of the Hanseatic League) city of Lübeck on the north German coast, believing, that if he could provide his crews with the means to locate a target, they would hit it. Coastlines offered the most distinctive features for the purpose of identification, hence, Lübeck, which not only lay on the Baltic coast to the east of Kiel, but the narrow streets and half-timbered buildings in its old town also represented the perfect target for destruction by fire. The operation, to be carried out on the night of the 28/29th, was to be conducted along the same lines as the highly successful attack on the Renault factory at the start of the month, and a force of 234 aircraft was assembled, 5 Group represented by forty-one Hampdens and twenty-one Manchesters, nine of the latter provided by 61 Squadron. They departed Woolfox Lodge between 21.15 and 21.55 with the deputy flight commanders, F/Ls Gascoyne-Cecil and McNaughton, the senior pilots on duty and set course via Mablethorpe for the North Sea crossing to make landfall on the islands off the western coast of Schleswig-Holstein. From there they made their way to the Baltic coast in excellent visibility under bright moonlight that allowed them to map-read all the way, easily following the coastline and identifying the River Trave leading to the island on which the city sits. The 61 Squadron crews attacked it from between 3,000 and 8,000 feet, some after a shallow glide approach and others in level flight, and many fires were seen to develop. After bombing, the crews of F/Ls Gascoyne-Cecil and McNaughton dived down to 100 feet and remained at that height as they raced back towards the west, strafing houses and an aerodrome on the way. Returning crews reported the burning city to be visible from seventy miles into the homeward flight and post-raid reconnaissance and local sources confirmed the operation to have been a major success. Some fifteen hundred houses had been destroyed and almost two thousand more seriously damaged in a 190-acre area of devastation representing an estimated 30% of the city's built-up area. It was the first major success for area bombing, and another sign of what was in store for the residents of Germany's towns and cities. There was an outcry following this unexpected attack on Lübeck, which was a city of culture and a vital port for the Red Cross. An agreement was struck that ensured its future protection from bombing, and, with a few exceptions, this was adhered to.

Eighteen Hampdens and eight Manchesters were made ready for gardening operations on the 29th, all but two assigned to the Nectarine gardens, while two of the 61 Squadron Manchesters were to venture as far as the Bottle garden off Haugesund on Norway's western coast. With a much greater distance to travel, the crews of F/O Archibold and S/L West took off from Woolfox Lodge first at 18.40 and 18.45, leaving the crews of Sgt Gregory and P/O Churchill on the ground until their departure for Nectarine I at 19.45 and 20.20. There was six-tenths cloud over the Bottle garden and good visibility as S/L West's bomb-aimer released the mines from 500 feet on the third run while an enemy light flak battery and the Manchester's rear gunner exchanged fire. F/O Archibald and crew flew up the fjord between green and white navigation lights to plant their vegetables in a gentle glide from 900 down to 500 feet. Sgt Gregory and crew were the first to land, at 23.40, after a round trip of five minutes under four hours. The return of L7454 was awaited in vain and no trace of the Manchester or the crew of P/O Churchill, who was operating as crew captain for only the second time, ever came to light.

During the course of the month the squadron undertook eleven operations and dispatched sixty-four sorties for the loss of three Manchesters and two crews.

April 1942

The new month began for 5 Group with operations on the 1st in company with Wellingtons, although not operating together. Twenty-two Hampden crews were briefed to take part in a raid on the docks and shipping at Le Havre, while fourteen others were to carry out low-level attacks on railway targets in north-western Germany in the Meppen and Lingen region just over the frontier with Holland. Elsewhere, 61 and 106 Squadrons provided eleven Manchesters between them for mining duties on the Deodar garden at the mouth of the Gironde on the approaches to Bordeaux, for which the Woolfox Lodge element of six took off between 19.30 and 19.40 with S/L West the senior pilot on duty. They were well into the long flight south when the crew of F/Sgt Turner took off at 20.55 to deliver "toilet paper" to the residents of Paris, a task which they completed according to brief, dispensing the bundles from 4,000 feet before returning safely after a trip lasting four-and-a-half hours. The gardeners benefitted from favourable conditions over France but lost the services of F/Sgt Williams and crew after straying from track and losing faith in their compass. The others were able to establish pinpoints from which to carry out a timed run and plant their vegetables from below 1,000 feet, and on the way home some descended to 50 feet to strafe targets of opportunity. The night turned into a disaster for 3 Group, whose railway targets were at Hanau and Lohr to the east of Frankfurt, from which five out of twelve 57 Squadron Wellingtons failed to return and seven of fourteen belonging to 214 Squadron. This caused a rethink by those responsible for planning operations, despite which, a similarly bad experience awaited 5 Group in December.

On the following night, twenty-three Hampdens were detailed for mining duties in the Gorse garden in Quiberon Bay, situated on the western coast of Brittany, north-west of St-Nazaire, while five Hampdens and three 61 Squadron Manchesters were assigned to attack the docks and shipping at Le Havre. The crews of P/O Seibold, F/Sgt Turner and Sgt Gregory departed Woolfox Lodge between 20.00 and 20.15 and flew out in moonlit conditions to carry out their attacks from between 8,000 and 9,500 feet, observing the bursts of their 500-pounders but no detail as they dodged the spirited defence from light and heavy flak. A daylight mining operation in one of the Nectarine gardens was planned for the late afternoon of the 4th, when crews would have to rely on cloud cover over the Frisians to provide protection, and when this failed to materialize, the operation was abandoned and all crews returned home with their stores.

The first major operation of the new month was directed at Cologne on the night of the 5/6th and involved a new record force of 263 aircraft, which included a 5 Group contribution of forty-four Hampdens and eleven Manchesters. The aiming point was the Klöckner-Humboldt engineering works in the Deutz district on the east bank of the Rhine in the city centre, which manufactured aero-engines and a wide range of military vehicles. 61 Squadron supported the operation with four Manchesters, which departed Woolfox Lodge between 01.00 and 02.00, the latter time that of F/Sgt Williams and crew, who were delayed by another aircraft becoming bogged down. The futility of continuing on was recognised by flying control and they were recalled almost immediately and returned their bombs to the station dump. The others arrived in the target area to encounter bright moonlight, which penetrated the up-to-nine-tenths cloud and glinted off an S-bend in the Rhine to the south of the city centre, thereby assisting some crews to establish a position for the bombing run. P/O Seibold and crew suffered a hydraulics failure over the target that prevented them from opening the bomb doors, and by the time that they were able to drop the bomb load, they found themselves over Bonn and then had to fly home with the bomb doors open and creating drag. F/Sgt Turner and crew attacked from 9,000 feet in a power dive and watched their bombs burst on the west bank of the Rhine, but Sgt Stewart and crew were unable to make a positive identification and dropped their load on a built-up area and started a fire that remained visible for thirty minutes into the return flight. Despite the advantageous conditions, many other crews failed to identify Cologne and those that did scattered their loads right across the built-up area, destroying or seriously damaging ninety houses but nothing of industrial significance.

On the following night, Harris turned his attention back upon Essen, with the first of three raids against it in six nights, to which 5 Group contributed eighteen Hampdens and ten Manchesters. The five-strong 61 Squadron element departed Woolfox Lodge between 00.30 and 00.40 with S/L Paape the senior pilot on duty and adopted the southerly route to the central Ruhr via Orford Ness, Blankenberg on the Belgian coast and Nivelles, before swinging south of Bonn on a northerly course for the target. S/L Paape and crew were airborne for only an hour after R5784 persistently stalled even at 160 mph and left them with no choice but to return to base, where they landed at 140 mph, well above the recommended velocity. F/O Gilpin and crew climbed to 7,000 feet after crossing the English coast, but an ailing starboard engine at the enemy coast persuaded them to turn back before finding a suitable last-resort target. The others encountered electrical storms and severe icing conditions over the North Sea that threatened to destroy lift and forced some crews to abandon their sortie before reaching the enemy coast. F/L Gascoyne-Cecil and crew dived from 9,000 down to 6,000 feet, where the bomb-aimer misheard the altitude as 2,000 feet, too low to drop the bombs "live" without risking damage to the aircraft, and he let them go "safe". In some kind of recompense, they flew home at low level and the front gunner strafed a train, while the mid-upper and rear gunners extinguished three searchlights. F/Sgt Williams and crew failed to identify the primary target and bombed an unidentified built-up area from 12,000 feet, before taking violent evasive action to thwart the flak defences. Only a third of crews reported bombing the primary target and Essen escaped with minor damage at a cost to the Command of five aircraft, three of them belonging to 5 Group and one of them to 61 Squadron. L7470 was shot down by the night-fighter of Oblt Eckart-Wilhelm von Bonin of II./NJG1 and crashed two miles east-north-east of Tongeren in Belgium with no survivors from the crew of F/Sgt Noble.

Hamburg was posted as the target on the 8th, and yet another record force, this time of 272 aircraft, was made ready. 5 Group stepped up with thirty-two Hampdens and thirteen Manchesters assigned to the Blohm & Voss shipyards located to the west of the city centre, while the seven Lancasters and nine further Hampdens were to attack aiming point C, the industrial centre of the city. 61 Squadron detailed the crews of F/Os Archibald and Beard and P/O Clark for the main event and dispatched them into clear skies from Woolfox Lodge between 22.10 and 22.35. They headed across the North Sea to encounter one of the towering electrical storms with icing conditions that frequently built up over it to bar the approaches to north-western Germany, and on this night, not all who set out would reach their intended destination. In fact, only 188 crews would report bombing the general area of Hamburg on estimated positions through ten-tenths cloud, among them the 61 Squadron trio from between 8,000 and 12,000 feet either side of midnight, guided largely by evidence of searchlights and flak. The result was another poor performance, which deposited no more than the equivalent of fourteen bomb loads in the city and caused eight fires.

There was a return to Essen for 254 aircraft on the 10th, an operation supported by 5 Group with forty-three Hampdens, ten Manchesters and eight Lancasters, 61 Squadron contributing the crews of F/O Tofield, P/O Searby and F/Sgt Underwood to the main event and those of F/Sgt Stewart and Sgt McSporran to a freshman raid on the docks and shipping at Le Havre. These would be the final operations launched by the squadron from Woolfox Lodge, the freshman pair departing first at 21.00 and 21.05 to be followed into the air between 21.20 and 21.30 by the bombing trio. They set course via Mablethorpe for Enkhuizen on the eastern shore of the Den Helder peninsula, before swinging round the eastern end of the Ruhr and running in on the target from east to west. F/Sgt Underwood and crew had to contend with an engine issue, which was too serious to allow them to continue and they jettisoned their bombs into the North Sea before landing at Colitishall on one engine. P/O Searby and crew lost their intercom and also turned back, leaving F/O Tofield to carry on as the squadron's sole representatives, and like the others, were expecting to find the clear skies forecast at briefing. Instead, they were confronted by a layer of eight-tenths cloud across the central Ruhr at between 5,000 and 8,000 feet, and the route in was described by F/L Sandford of 44 (Rhodesia) Squadron as "hot", with scores of searchlights from all sides working in conjunction with light and heavy flak. F/O Tofield and crew attacked in level flight from 12,000 feet, before being forced down to 4,000 feet to escape a searchlight cone, and only Sgt James and crew claimed to have bombed the primary from 15,000 feet at 00.15 and were among the returning crews to report bursts and the glow of fires beneath the cloud, but little else of use to the intelligence sections at debriefing. Meanwhile, F/Sgt Stewart and crew found the docks at Le Havre to be illuminated brilliantly by the flares from other aircraft and bombed from 9,000 feet after a glide approach. Sgt McSporran RCAF and crew were on their first operation together and were struggling back across the Channel with a flak-damaged starboard engine, which could not keep R5785 in the air and the inevitable ditching took place some twenty miles short of the coast. All managed to make it into the dinghy, where they would spend the next five days, but wireless operator, Sgt Meikle, attempted to swim ashore and drowned. They eventually landed on the Cherbourg peninsula, where they were taken into captivity suffering from exposure. Local sources in Essen confirmed the operation to have been another dismal failure, which destroyed only twelve houses and caused no industrial damage.

The first Lancasters arrived at Woolfox Lodge on the 12th and thus 61 Squadron became the fourth operational unit to receive the type, although it would be May before the conversion process was sufficiently advanced to allow a return to operations. In the meantime, the campaign against Essen continued that night at the hands of a force of 251 aircraft of which thirty-one Hampdens and nine Manchesters represented 5 Group, while the Lancaster element was busy training for an epic daylight raid five days hence. Other disappointing performances followed at Dortmund on the 14/15th and 15/16th and Hamburg on the 17/18th, all supported by 5 Group, and they demonstrated that the Command still had a long way to go before it became an effective force.

At noon on the 17th, six crews each from 44 (Rhodesia) and 97 (Straits Settlement) Squadrons filed into the briefing rooms at Waddington and Woodhall Spa to be enlightened as to their immediate future. They were incredulous to learn that they were soon to embark on Operation Margin, an epic low-level deep-penetration flight to Augsburg in Bavaria, to attack the diesel engine assembly shop in the middle of a large factory complex belonging to the Maschinen Fabrik Augsburg Nürnburg Aktien Gesellschaft, otherwise known as the M.A.N. works, situated on the outskirts of the beautiful and historic city. Strategically, this particular shop was the most important part of the factory and was believed to be the bottleneck in the entire U-Boot industry at a time when the Battle of the Atlantic was the main preoccupation of both Britain and the United States. Four of the 44 (Rhodesia) squadron Lancasters were shot down over France on the way out and a fifth crashed beyond the target and two 97 (Straits Settlement) Lancasters were also lost, but some useful damage was inflicted upon the target and S/L Nettleton of 44 (Rhodesia) Squadron was awarded the VC. Harris disliked low-level operations in heavy bombers, particularly in daylight, and the Augsburg losses cemented that opinion.

144 Squadron's association with Bomber Command ended on the 21st when it was transferred to Coastal Command, leaving behind a magnificent record of service to 5 Group. In an effort to repeat the success gained at Lübeck, Harris launched a series of four raids on consecutive nights against Rostock, also on the Baltic coast, beginning on the 23/24th. The presence of a Heinkel factory nearby was an added attraction, and a proportion of the 5 Group effort was directed specifically at this. The first raid was disappointing, but the following three inflicted widespread damage on the town, and the Heinkel factory was hit during the last two. By the end of the series on the 26/27th, 60% of the town's built-up area lay in ruins, with over seventeen hundred buildings destroyed.

Among examples of the Lancaster taken on 61 Squadron charge during the month were R5511, R5543, R5544, R5545, R5560, with R5562 and R5563 arriving on the 26th and R5561 on the 27th. During the course of the month the squadron took part in six operations and dispatched twenty-seven sorties for the loss of two Manchesters and crews.

May 1942

R5545 was promptly written off while trying to land at North Luffenham during training on the 1st of May, but Sgt Stewart RNZAF and the other occupant emerged from the wreckage unscathed. On the 5th of May the squadron completed its move from Woolfox Lodge/North Luffenham to Syerston, a station close to the A46 Leicester to Lincoln Road, a few miles to the south-west of Newark-on-Trent in Nottinghamshire. Opened on the 1st of December 1940, it originally belonged to 1 Group and was home to Polish Wellington squadrons until its transfer to 5 Group in July 1941, when 408 (Goose) Squadron moved in with its Hampdens. In preparation for the arrival of heavy bombers, the station had been shut down between December 1941 and May 1942 for the construction of a concrete runway and two T2 hangars, and for the next five months 61 Squadron would be its only resident unit. On the day of its arrival at Syerston 61 Squadron formed a Conversion Flight under the command of the newly promoted S/L Gascoyne-Cecil, taking on two Manchesters and a single Lancaster, which would be increased to three and two respectively. The intention was to convert four crews each month, all to be absorbed into the main squadron.

Later that day, the first two Lancaster sorties were briefed out to the crews of F/O Archibald and F/L McNaughton, who learned that ahead of them lay a round-trip of more than fifteen hundred miles to deliver propaganda leaflets to the residents of Marseilles and Toulon on France's Riviera coast. They departed Syerston at 19.45 and 19.50, delivered their nickels from 6,000 and 8,000 feet respectively and returned safely after more than eight hours in the air. The squadron focused on training for the ensuing two weeks and bade farewell temporarily to S/L Arthur Paape DFC and Bar on the 18th on his posting to 408 (Goose) Squadron Conversion Flight.

Eight crews were called to the briefing room on the 22nd and discovered that they also had a distant target area as their destination, the Geranium garden, which lay off the port of Swinemünde on the Baltic coast in what is now part of Poland. It represented a round-trip of some thirteen hundred miles, for which they departed Syerston between 21.35 and 21.55 with W/C Weir and S/L West the senior pilots on duty and lost the services of F/O Searby and crew to an oil leak during the climb-out. The others arrived in the target area to find clear skies, good visibility and the defences active, and pinpointed on a collection of lakes to the west of the target. The Schmollensee provided the start for the timed run for most, and apart from W/C Weir and crew, who encountered no opposition at all, the others ran the gauntlet of searchlights, flak and even night-fighters, all of which kept the Lancaster gunners busy. Flying home at low level across Germany, F/Sgt Underwood and crew ran into nests of light flak, and so low were they during evasive action that the tailwheel actually made contact with the ground. However, with all three turrets putting up a stout defence, they came through and claimed a number of searchlights as shot out. On landing in the hands of F/O Gunter, R5562's port undercarriage leg collapsed, suggesting that it had probably sustained damage at some point. Homebound with some 250 miles still to negotiate, Sgt Gregory had two engines cut suddenly at 3,000 feet, and control was only regained at 1,000 feet, after which they climbed slowly back to 10,000 feet, where the engines picked up and the panic subsided. When F/Sgt Stewart and crew sat down at debriefing, they reported that they had undertaken most of the flight on three engines.

The above operation took place during a lull in major operations, which came on the heels of another poor performance at Mannheim on the night of the 19/20th. At the time of his appointment as C-in-C, Harris had suggested that four thousand bombers were required to enable him to wrap up the war. Whilst there was not the slightest chance of procuring them, Harris, with a dark cloud still hanging over the existence of an independent bomber force, needed to ensure that those earmarked for him were not spirited away to what he considered to be less-deserving causes. The Command had not yet achieved sufficient success to silence the detractors, and the Admiralty was still calling for bomber aircraft to be diverted to the U-Boot campaign, while others demanded support for the North Africa campaign. Harris was in need of a major victory, and, perhaps, a dose of symbolism to make his point, and, out of this was born the Thousand Plan, Operation Millennium, the launching of a thousand aircraft in one night against a major German city, for which Hamburg had been pencilled in. Harris did not have a thousand front-line aircraft and required the support of other Commands to make up the numbers. This was forthcoming from Coastal and Flying Training Commands, and, in the case of the former, a letter to Harris on the 22nd promised 250 aircraft. However, following an intervention from the Admiralty, the offer was withdrawn, and most of the Flying Training Command aircraft were found to be not up to the task, leaving the Millennium force well short of the magic figure. Undaunted, Harris, or more probably his able deputy, AM Sir Robert Saundby, scraped together every airframe capable of controlled flight, or something resembling it, and pulled in the screened crews from their instructional duties. He also pressed into service aircraft and crews from within the Command's own training establishment, 91 Group. Come the night, not only would the thousand mark be achieved, but it would also be comfortably surpassed.

During the final week of the month, the arrival on bomber stations from Yorkshire to East Anglia of a motley collection of aircraft from training units gave rise to much speculation among crews and ground staff alike, but, as usual, only the NAAFI staff and the local civilians knew what was really afoot. The most pressing remaining question was the weather, and, as the days ticked by inexorably towards the end of May, this was showing no signs of complying. Harris was aware of the genuine danger, that the giant force might draw attention to itself, and thereby compromise security, and the point was fast approaching when the operation would have to take place or be abandoned for the time being. Harris released some of the pressure by sanctioning operations on the night of the 29/30th, for which the Gnome and Rhone aero-engine and Goodrich tyre factories at Gennevilliers in Paris were the main targets. A force of seventy-seven aircraft included a contribution from 5 Group of fourteen Lancasters and three Hampdens, two of the former provided by 61 Squadron, while two others were made available for mining duties in the Verbena garden off Copenhagen. The crews of F/O Tofield and P/O Clark took off at 22.05 and 22.10 bound for the Baltic, where they encountered unfavourable conditions, which prevented them from locating a suitable pinpoint and sent them heading back across Schleswig-Holstein to one of the Hawthorn gardens off Jutland's western coast. There, they found ideal conditions and pinpointed on Fanø Island before planting their vegetables effectively. F/Os Beard and Searby departed Syerston at 01.30 and 01.40 respectively and on approach to Paris found breaks in the cloud affording good vertical visibility that enabled them to pinpoint on the distinctive V-shaped dock and carry out an attack on the powerhouse from 6,500 and 6,000 feet. Both then had to hit the deck to evade the defences and vacate the target area, and when passing close to Rouen, F/O Searby's gunners strafed a moving train and caused it to stop. Most crews found it difficult to gain an accurate picture of the outcome and despite claims of a successful operation, the only damage caused was to eighty-seven houses, in which thirty-four people were killed and 167 injured.

It was in an atmosphere of frustration and hopeful expectation, that "morning prayers" began at Harris's High Wycombe HQ on the 30th, with all eyes turned upon the chief meteorological adviser, Magnus Spence. After careful deliberation, he was able to give a qualified assurance of clear skies over the Rhineland, while north-western Germany and Hamburg would be concealed under buckets of cloud. Thus, did the fickle fates decree that Cologne would bear the dubious honour of hosting the first one thousand bomber raid in history. At briefings, crews were told that the enormous force was to be pushed across the aiming point in just ninety minutes. This was unprecedented and gave rise to the question of collisions as hundreds of aircraft funnelled towards the aiming point. The answer, according to the experts, was to observe timings and flight levels, and they calculated also that just two aircraft would collide over the target. It is said that a wag in every briefing room asked, "do they know which two?"

At briefings on stations across the Command crews were assigned to three aiming points covering the central districts on the West Bank of the Rhine, most importantly A, located right at the commercial heart of the city from Nippes in the north to Zollstock in the south, an area containing the cathedral, main railway station and the Neumarkt. Aiming points X and Y adjoined A on its western side, the Hohenzollern Ring to the north of the centre line and the Hohenstauffen Ring to the south. Aiming point A was assigned to 1 and 3 Groups and all aircraft from the other groups and Commands operating from their stations, X to 4 Group and all aircraft from the other groups and Commands operating from its stations, plus Army Co-operation Command and 92 Group, and Y to 5 Group and all aircraft from the other groups and Commands operating from its stations plus 91 Group. The route for all aircraft was direct to the target, crossing the enemy coast over the Scheldt estuary, with a parallel return course a few miles to the south of the outward track.

5 Group had seventy-three Lancasters, forty-six Manchesters and thirty-four Hampdens bombed up and ready to go, and at Syerston, thirteen 61 Squadron Lancasters and three Manchesters awaited the arrival of their crews, who had been briefed to attack one of three areas spanning the city centre from north to south, in their case, aiming point Y, bordering the western and southern extremities on the West Bank. It had been intended to launch seven Flying Training Command Hampdens also from Syerston, but one crashed in transit on the 27th and the remainder had been declared unfit to take part. Late in the evening of the 30th, the first of an eventual 1,047 aircraft took off to deliver the now familiar three-wave-format attack on the Rhineland capital, the older

training hacks struggling somewhat reluctantly into the air, perhaps lifted more by the enthusiasm of their crews than by the power of their engines, and some of these, unable to climb to a respectable height, would fall easy prey to the defences or would simply drop from the sky through mechanical breakdown.

As part of the third wave the 61 Squadron element remained on the ground until after midnight, eventually departing Syerston between 00.10 and 01.15 with S/Ls Gascoyne-Cecil and West the senior pilots on duty and the now Flight Lieutenant Bill Deas back with the squadron for a second tour. F/O Tofield and crew had been last but one to take off, later than planned, and knowing that they would not reach the target in the allotted window, returned to base from the Suffolk coast with their bomb load intact. The others flew out over Southwold and soon lost the services of S/L Gascoyne-Cecil and crew to engine issues, which forced them to dump their cookie in the North Sea, and although it left the Lancaster "safe", it was seen to detonate on impact. The remainder pressed on across Belgium, drawn on for the last seventy miles by the glow of the already burning city, and were greeted at the target by precisely the weather conditions of clear skies and bright moonlight predicted by Magnus Spence. The Syerston crews carried out their attacks from between 7,000 and 17,000 feet employing a variety of tactics including power dives, throttled-back glides and level flight bombing runs, some while held in searchlight cones. After bombing the crews of F/Os Archibald and Smith descended to low level to strafe targets of opportunity, the former attacking factories and a gasometer, while the latter targeted a train in a siding. F/O Gilpin and crew landed on three engines after being attacked by a night-fighter during the bombing run and then sustaining damage to engines from flak bursts, which resulted in an engine fire when twenty miles from base. Returning crews described a city on fire from end to end, never-before-witnessed scenes and a red glow remaining on the horizon for a hundred miles and more into the return journey. Not among those at debriefing to express their views were P/O Underwood and crew, who had all lost their lives when R5561 crashed at Niederaussem, some fourteen miles west-north-west of Cologne city centre.

Post-raid reconnaissance confirmed that the operation had, by any standards, been an outstanding success, and had destroyed more than 3,300 buildings, while inflicting serious damage upon two thousand others. Although the loss of forty-one aircraft represented a new record high, the conditions had favoured both attackers and defenders alike, and in the context of the scale of success and the numbers dispatched, it could not be considered an inordinately high figure. 5 Group registered a loss of four Manchesters, one Lancaster and one Hampden, but it was the training units that sustained the greatest losses amounting to twenty-one aircraft.

During the course of the month, the squadron took part in five operations and dispatched twenty-seven Lancaster and three Manchester sorties for the loss of one Lancaster and crew.

June 1942

While the Millennium force remained assembled, Harris wanted to exploit its potential again immediately and was no doubt excited about the prospect of visiting upon the old enemy of Essen a similar ordeal to that just experienced by Cologne. A force of 956 aircraft was the best that could be achieved during the 1st, 5 Group managing seventy-three Lancasters, thirty-three Manchesters and twenty-six Hampdens. 61 Squadron's thirteen Lancasters and four Manchesters departed Syerston between 22.50 and 00.25, the latter time that of F/Sgt Stewart and crew in L7415, which had been scheduled to take-off with the other Manchesters in a slot between 23.00 and 23.25. However, an issue with the intercom system had kept it on the ground for a further hour and although a course was set for the target, it was clear within ninety minutes that Essen was out of reach within the allotted window and the bomb load was brought home. S/Ls Gascoyne-Cecil, McNaughton, West and Paape were the senior pilots on duty, the first and last mentioned in Manchesters R5491 and L7425 respectively, and flying as bomb-aimer in the eight-man crew of F/L Bill Deas, presumably as a guest, was a W/C McDonald. S/L Paape's L7425 developed excessive tail-shudder during the climb-out and was back on the ground just fifteen minutes after leaving it. P/O Seibold and crew crossed the North Sea and Den Helder peninsula, but at some point, lost the use of their wireless and turned back at Enkhuizen, unaware that all but two of them had only twenty-four hours of life ahead of them.

Crews had been briefed to employ the sprawl of the Krupp manufacturing sites in the Borbeck sector as the aiming point and were blessed with favourable weather conditions that promised the possibility of actually being able to identify ground detail. They ran into five to ten-tenths cloud at 4,000 to 6,000 feet over the target, which combined with industrial haze and smoke still drifting over from Cologne to muddy the vertical visibility, and bombing took place largely on TR (Gee) supported by occasional visual references on waterways. The 61 Squadron participants delivered their attacks from between 10,000 and 14,000 feet on a variety of headings ranging from north-east, through east to due west and most observed bursts and fires. An accurate assessment of the results was not possible, and crews returned with reports of many fires, some identified as dummies, but no detail and the authorities would have to wait for post-raid reconnaissance before they could assess what had happened on the ground. In the meantime, a counting of the cost revealed the loss of thirty-one aircraft, among them 61 Squadron's R5544, which crashed near Düsseldorf with fatal consequences for F/O Tofield and all but his bomb-aimer, who parachuted into the arms of his captors. Sadly, there would be no major success to mitigate the scale of the loss, local reports confirming that only eleven houses had been destroyed in Essen, and fewer than two hundred others damaged, mostly in southern districts. A greater number of bomb loads had actually fallen on the nearby locations of Oberhausen, Duisburg and Mülheim-an-der-Ruhr.

A follow-up raid was planned for twenty-four hours later, and a much-reduced force of 197 aircraft made ready, with 5 Group providing twenty-seven Lancasters and a dozen Hampdens, 61 Squadron contributing five of the former. They departed Syerston between 23.45 and 00.15 with no senior pilots on duty and found clear skies over the Ruhr with the usual industrial haze, but a low moon provided some illumination, and most crews would describe the visibility as good. The deployment of flares proved beneficial as they highlighted the Rhine over to the west, and those equipped with Gee confirmed their positions over what they believed to be the Krupp complex aiming point. The crews of F/Os Searby and Beard adopted glide approaches, the former from 18,000 down to 15,000 feet and the latter releasing at 12,000 feet, before continuing towards the east and running into searchlights and flak over Dortmund that forced them to make their escape at low level. Sgt Stewart and crew (not to be confused with F/Sgt Stewart) carried out their attack in level flight from 18,000 feet and particular mention was made at debriefing of the performance of navigator, W/O Brown. Missing from debriefing at Syerston were the crews of P/O Seibold RCAF and P/O Clark DFM in R5562 and R5613 respectively, the former having crashed at Rees to the north-west of the Ruhr with the Canadian navigator the sole survivor from the mixed RAF/RCAF crew. The latter was shot down by the night-fighter of Ofw Fritz Schelwat of 5./NJG1 and crashed at 02.26 some nine miles south-east of Brussels, killing all but the rear gunner, who, with the help of local partisans, evaded capture. Despite the apparent confidence of the crews that they had attacked Essen, local authorities reported just three high explosive bombs and three hundred incendiaries falling in the city to cause only minor damage. Such was the density of the Ruhr, with overlapping town and city boundaries, it was difficult not to hit something urban, but concentration was the key to success, and the scattering of bombs over a wide area was never going to achieve a knock-out blow. Harris was stubborn and would keep trying, but it would be a further nine months before the means were to hand to make a genuine impact.

For the next operation, on the 3rd, Harris turned his attention upon Bremen, which, along with Essen and Emden, would share the Command's attention for the remainder of the month. A force of 170 aircraft was made ready for the first major attack on the port-city since the previous October, for which a 5 Group force of fifteen Lancasters, nine Hampdens and six Manchesters was assembled with contributions from seven stations. At Syerston six crews attended briefing to learn of their part in the night's proceedings and took off between 23.15 and 23.25 with F/Ls Casement and Deas the senior pilots on duty, only for the latter to lose a port engine as he lifted off. Relying on his airmanship to keep the heavily-laden Lancaster flying, Deas gained sufficient speed and height to complete a circuit and return to base with the bomb load intact. The others reached the target under clear skies and in the light of flares F/L Casement and crew carried out their attack in a shallow dive and observed the burning remains of a gas works to the north, which had been the site of a massive explosion a little earlier. F/Sgt Williams and crew attacked from 12,000 feet, observing bursts in the southern part of the town area and afterwards taking quality photographs for the benefit of the intelligence section. F/O Smith and crew hit the docks area from 10,000 feet, while F/Sgt Stewart and crew watched their bombs fall into the general built-up area from 16,000 feet and on the way home witnessed a bomber being shot down in flames by a night-fighter over the Zuider Zee.

Returning crews lacked confidence in the effectiveness of the raid, but local reports told a story of heavy damage to residential property in six streets and to harbour installations, and there were also hits on U-Boot construction yards and the Focke-Wulf aircraft factory, although, any loss of production was slight. The operation cost eleven aircraft, two Lancasters and a Manchester belonging to 5 Group and the dispersal pan normally occupied by R5627 stood empty as dawn broke over Syerston. It would be learned eventually that the Lancaster had been shot down by the night-fighter of Lt Hans-Heinz König of NJG2 and had crashed on the southern perimeter of the aerodrome at Bad Zwischenahn. The second pilot, Sgt Holmes, was the only survivor from the crew of F/O Archibald and he was taken into captivity. Bomb-aimer, F/Sgt Lorimer had served previously with 44 Squadron and was the holder of a DFM.

The first of four attacks during the month on the naval port of Emden was posted on the 6th, and a force of 233 aircraft made ready, 5 Group contributing twenty Lancasters, fifteen Hampdens and seven Manchesters. Serving on the station staff at Syerston was W/C Richard Coad AFC, who was shortly to assume command of 61 Squadron on the departure of W/C Weir to HQ 5 Group on the 19th. W/C Coad's RAF career began in 1934 as an acting pilot officer on a short service commission, after which he rose through the ranks to be appointed temporary wing commander in 1940. Having no operational experience, he took the opportunity to fly to Emden as second pilot to F/L Deas in one of the five 61 Squadron Lancasters detailed. They departed Syerston between 23.20 and 23.50 and lost the services of F/Sgt Meyer and crew to the failure of their a.s.i. when over the North Sea, leaving the others to find the skies over the coast of north-western Germany to be clear of cloud and the visibility to be good, which enabled those dropping flares to illuminate the docks area for the bomb-aimers. F/L Deas and crew carried out a long and steady bombing run at 14,000 feet, taking advantage of the illumination, and observed bursts in the built-up area below. F/O Beard and crew also benefitted from the light from flares as they glided down from 18,000 to 15,000 feet to release their load and were somewhat surprised on return to Syerston to discover that they had landed with a full, fused bomb load, after it had hung-up. F/O Searby and crew bombed from 16,000 feet and were leaving the target area when the starboard-inner and port-outer engines began to show signs of stress, leading eventually to the latter catching fire. Both engines had to be shut down and the Lancaster limped home on the remaining two, special mention being made at debriefing of the performance of navigator, F/Sgt Mitchell. F/O Gunter and crew attacked from 14,000 feet and saw bursts in the built-up area, contributing according to photographic reconnaissance and local sources to the destruction of some three hundred houses and severe damage to a further two hundred in return for the loss of nine aircraft.

The Command entered a period of gardening and minor operations, thereafter, punctuated by two further attacks on Essen, and it was for the Nectarine I garden off the western Frisians that nine Lancasters and two Hampdens were detailed on the 7th, 61 Squadron providing four of the former. They departed Syerston between 01.10 and 01.20 with S/L West the senior pilot on duty and all reached the target area to find five to eight-tenths cloud at 3,000 feet and good visibility, in which pinpoints were easily established and mines released in sticks from between 1,000 and 2,000 feet. Eight or nine flame floats were observed in an area of a square half-mile and a flak ship was evident south of the target, but all returned safely from uneventful operations to spend the ensuing eight nights away from the operational scene, thus missing the next raid on Essen. This took place on the 8th at the hands of an initial force of 170 aircraft, including thirteen Lancasters and nine Hampdens belonging to 5 Group, but resulted in another disappointing and widely scattered raid, which caused only minor housing damage.

After spending four nights on the ground because of adverse weather conditions, the Command stirred itself on the 16th at Harris's behest to have another crack at Essen, for which 106 aircraft were made ready, 5 Group contributing fifteen Lancasters. 61 Squadron made ready eight Lancasters and sent them on their way from Syerston between 23.30 and 23.59 with S/L McNaughton the senior pilot on duty and all crews briefed to employ TR to locate the target and bomb blindly based on that, which, under the conditions of up to eight-tenths cloud on a moonless night with visibility down to three miles was the best that could be expected. If they failed to locate the primary target, the city of Bonn to the south or any other built-up area had been selected by the planners as alternative targets. F/Sgt Turner and crew were back on the ground within an hour after suffering an engine issue and dumping their cookie in The Wash. The others reached enemy territory and F/O Gunter and crew were closing on the target at 18,000 feet when the Gee and rear turret became unserviceable, at which point they bombed a built-up area north-east of the target. F/L Casement and crew assumed that Essen was beneath them as they bombed on Gee from 20,000 feet, and Sgt Stewart and crew were positive that they had found the primary target as they released their ordnance from the same altitude with heavy flak shells bursting two thousand feet above them and puncturing the Lancaster's skin. S/L McNaughton and crew were uncertain as to their position, and turning towards the south bombed a built-up area on e.t.a. from 16,000 feet, which they assumed to be Bonn. F/O Beard and crew also attacked Bonn from 15,000 feet and observed their bombs burst in the town area, while F/Sgt Gregory and crew released their cookie and incendiaries from 20,000 feet over Aachen and caused an immediate response from searchlight and flak batteries. F/Sgt Meyer and crew lost their Gee over Essen and in the face of unbroken cloud over

Germany, blind-bombed Haamstede from 17,000 feet on the way home. It emerged at debriefing that only sixteen crews claimed to have bombed the primary target, while fifty-six others had found alternatives, mostly the city of Bonn.

This concluded a series of five raids on Essen in sixteen nights, during which 1,607 sorties had been dispatched and eighty-four aircraft lost. The city had sustained no industrial damage, and a few wrecked houses was all that Bomber Command had to show for the massive effort expended.

5 Group devoted the 18th to mining duties off the Frisians and the Biscay coast, 61 Squadron detailing six Lancasters for the Nectarine II garden, for which they departed Syerston between 00.40 and 01.05 with an NCO pilot at the controls of each. They crossed the North Sea over eight to ten-tenths cloud at 2,000 feet and on arrival in the target area found ideal conditions in which to establish their positions by Gee-fix. F/Sgt Gregory's Gee failed during the sea crossing, but he was able to establish a visual pinpoint on Terschelling and Schiermonnikoog and timed his run from the latter to plant the vegetables, like the others, in the briefed locations.

Having hosted an effective attack earlier in the month, Emden became the focus for three raids in the space of four nights, beginning on the 19th, for which a force of 194 aircraft was assembled. 5 Group was represented by nine Lancasters and eleven Hampdens, whose crews had been briefed to switch to Osnabrück, eighty miles to the south, if the weather conditions over the coastal region became troublesome. Part of the flare force did, indeed, initiate an attack on Osnabrück by twenty-nine aircraft, leaving 131 others to claim that they had bombed the primary target. Despite the numbers, the Emden authorities reported only a handful of high-explosive bombs falling and a few hundred incendiaries. 185 aircraft were made ready to return to the port on the following night, among them twenty-four Lancaster and a dozen Hampdens provided by 5 Group. 61 Squadron contributed eight Lancasters, which departed Syerston between 23.30 and 23.45 with S/L McNaughton the senior pilot on duty and lost the services of F/L Deas and crew to intercom failure. F/O Beard's starboard-inner engine overheated and caught fire, terminating the sortie, while the others pressed on to make landfall over Dollart Bay and the Ems estuary, before seeking out the docks aiming point through the haze. Most employed Gee to establish their position, the 61 Squadron crews carrying out their attacks from between 14,000 and 19,000 feet and aiming at the general town area. However, local reports suggested that only a proportion of the force had located the target, and around a hundred houses had been damaged.

A force of 227 aircraft was assembled on the 22nd to deliver the third raid of the series on Emden, 5 Group contributing eleven Lancasters and eight Hampdens, five of the former representing 61 Squadron. They departed Syerston between 23.40 and 23.59 with S/L McNaughton the senior pilot on duty and all reached the target area to find moonlight and good visibility, which enabled them to identify the coastline and confirm their positions by a TR-fix backed up by flak and fires. One of F/O Beard's port engines began to overheat during the final approach to the target and when a fierce flame erupted from the exhaust stubs the propeller was feathered and the run continued on three engines. The bombs were dropped onto the marshalling yards from 15,000 feet and on the way home the starboard-inner engine caught fire and had to be shut down, prompting the crew to prepare for a possible ditching. In the event, Syerston was reached and circled until daylight provided more favourable conditions for a two-engine approach. Some returning crews had been able to distinguish between genuine and decoy fires, but the latter succeeded in drawing off many loads, and those finding the target destroyed a modest fifty houses and damaged a hundred more. The only Lancaster among the six missing aircraft was R5517, which crashed in the target area with no survivors from the crew of S/L McNaughton RCAF, a pre-war regular officer from a military family and the son of a general.

While the entire Command prepared for the final deployment of the "Thousand" force, twenty-one freshman crews were sent to St-Nazaire on the 24th to attack the docks and shipping. 5 Group offered four Lancasters and three Hampdens, the crews of Sgts Fenner and Joslin representing 61 Squadron and departing Syerston at 23.55 and 23.59 respectively. The latter bombed from 10,000 feet and counted ten of the 500-pounders bursting across the docks, while the former's bomb doors were opened too late on the first run and searchlights ruined the second run, causing the bombs to fall from 11,000 feet across the Loire some miles inland.

A force of 960 aircraft was assembled on the 25th to send to Bremen, 142 provided by 5 Group in the form of ninety-six Lancasters, twenty-six Hampdens and twenty Manchesters, the last-mentioned operating with Bomber Command for the final time. It was an indication of the failure of the Manchester, that the aircraft it had been intended to replace, the Hampden, would continue to serve 5 Group in small numbers until mid-September. To the above numbers were added five aircraft from Army Co-operation Command and 102 aircraft from Coastal Command, which had been ordered personally by Churchill to take part, although its contribution was to be deemed a separate operation. However, the 1,067 aircraft from all sources would represent a larger combined force than that sent to Cologne at the end of May. Fourteen Lancasters were made ready at Syerston along with a Conversion Flight Manchester, and it was the latter that took off first, at 23.05, bearing aloft the crew of F/Sgt Shriner, who had the Dutch coast in sight when the intercom system failed and left them with no option but to take their bombs home. The Lancaster element departed Syerston between 23.20 and 23.55 with S/L West the senior pilot on duty and W/C Coad accompanying him as second pilot, but the number soon became depleted by the early return first of Sgt Fenner and crew because of intercom failure, and then by F/Sgt Hobson and crew when they lost their oxygen system. Finally, F/Sgt Stewart and crew had reached enemy territory when a starboard engine had to be shut down and in order to maintain height the bombs were dumped safe near the Dutch coast.

The briefed aiming point for the 5 Group crews was the Focke-Wulf aircraft factory in the south-eastern district of Hemelingen on the eastern bank of the Weser, for which they set course after crossing the English coast between Mablethorpe and Skegness. They flew out above the ten-tenths cloud that persisted all the way from the English coast to the target area and occupied a sky that was extremely bright, courtesy of a full moon and the Northern Lights. A band of nine to ten-tenths cloud lay over Bremen at between 3,000 and 5,000 feet, completely obscuring ground detail, which precluded any chance of picking up the Focke-Wulf aircraft factory and positions were established by Gee-fix, the glow of fires on the ground and the volume of flak coming through the cloud. The 61 Squadron crews delivered their cookie and incendiaries each from between 10,300 and 16,000 feet and only F/Sgt Gregory and crew were involved in an incident of note after being hit by an incendiary from another aircraft as they vacated the target area. The elevator control was jammed slightly, but a safe return was accomplished along with the rest of the squadron, and at debriefing they could only estimate that they had hit the city, citing several areas of fire as evidence.

In truth, none of the 696 crews claiming to have attacked the primary target had any real clue as to the outcome. Local sources confirmed a number of hits on the Focke-Wulf aircraft factory and some shipyards, along with the destruction of 572 houses and damage to more than six thousand others, mostly in southern and eastern districts, but estimated the size of the bomber force to be around eighty. The level of success fell short of that achieved at Cologne, but surpassed by far the failure at Essen, albeit at a new record loss of forty-eight aircraft, which represented 5% of those dispatched. The O.T.Us of 91 Group suffered the highest casualty rate of 11.6%, largely because it was employing tired, old Whitleys, Wellingtons and Hampdens not up to the task, while 5 Group posted missing one Lancaster and a 50 Squadron Manchester, the very last of its type to be lost on operations.

The first of three follow-up raids on Bremen spanning the turn of the month was posted on the 27th and involved 144 aircraft including twenty-four Lancasters from 5 Group. 61 Squadron was called upon to provide five aircraft, which departed Syerston safely between 23.25 and 23.45 with F/Os Searby and Smith the senior pilots on duty and it is believed that all reached the target area. They found that the weather conditions were very much as those of two nights earlier, with ten-tenths cloud up to around 4,000 feet and decreasing amounts thereafter as high as 15,000 feet, and the sky above as bright as day under a large moon, even though the Northern Lights, on this occasion, were masked by high cloud. The bombing by the Syerston crews took place on the basis of a Gee-fix from 14,000 to 18,000 feet on the assumption that they were over the target, and local reports confirmed hits on the previously damaged Atlas Werke shipyard and the Korff refinery, while further details were scant and of little value. F/Sgt Gregory and crew failed to return in R5615, which crashed in the target area with no survivors.

After a night off, thirteen crews were called to briefing at Syerston on the 29th to learn of their part in that night's return to Bremen as part of an overall force of 253 aircraft. 5 Group contributed sixty-four Lancasters, which, together with the Stirling and Halifax elements, meant that, for the first time, four-engine bombers represented more than half of a major force. The 61 Squadron element took off between 23.39 and 00.05 with F/Ls Casement and Deas the senior pilots on duty, and it was not long before technical malfunctions began to take their toll. Sgt Meyer and crew were contending with a failing intercom system, which broke down completely as they approached the enemy coast and ended their interest in proceedings, and they dumped their cookie in the sea but retained the incendiaries. F/O Beard was wrestling with a starboard-inner engine problem, and when it burst into flames over the North Sea, he had to dive to extinguish the flames and also dump the bombs. On return to base on three engines the second pilot apparently collapsed, for which no cause was recorded, but he was revived. The rest of the squadron had flown out over six to ten-tenths cloud at between 3,000 and 5,000 feet, with excellent visibility above, and found around seven to eight-tenths cloud in layers up to 16,000 feet in the target area, with large gaps that afforded glimpses of the ground. Bombing was carried out on Gee from between 10,000 and 18,000 feet on a night when the northern horizon at no point became completely dark, and at least one pilot from another squadron reported such brightness that he was able to identify another Lancaster five miles away. Returning crews could provide only impressions of the raid, but local reports spoke of extensive damage to the Focke-Wulf factory, the A.G Weser U-Boot construction yard and three other important war-industry premises, along with the local gas works and some limited destruction of housing.

During the course of the month the squadron carried out thirteen bombing and mining operations, which generated ninety-four Lancaster sorties and one by a Manchester for the loss of six Lancasters and crews.

July 1942

A gentle start to the new month had 5 Group operating alone on the night of the 1/2nd, when sending two Lancasters each from 97 and 106 Squadrons to mine the waters of the Great Belt in the western Baltic. The campaign against Bremen continued on the 2nd, with the preparation of a force of 325 aircraft, more than half of which were Wellingtons, while 5 Group squadrons contributed fifty-three Lancasters and twenty-eight Hampdens. At Syerston each of eleven Lancasters had been loaded with a cookie and incendiaries before they were launched off the end of the runway between 23.35 and 00.05 with F/L Deas the senior pilot on duty. When Sgt Fenner became unwell shortly after taking off, the cookie was jettisoned over The Wash and four unsuccessful attempts were made to land, before the incendiaries were also dumped into The Wash and base was circled for a further three hours until a safe landing was carried out at dawn. F/Sgt Meyer and crew lost their intercom over the Ijsselmeer (Zuider Zee) and backtracked to Texel, where they bombed the aerodrome from 10,000 feet and observed the incendiaries set off fires. Those reaching the target found favourable weather conditions with excellent visibility, no low cloud, high cirrus at around 22,000 feet and only a little haze to spoil the view below. Positions were established by TR-fix confirmed by a visual check, but searchlight glare created great difficulty for the bomb-aimers trying to identify the Focke-Wulf aircraft factory aiming point, and most would settle for estimating the moment of bomb release. The 61 Squadron crews delivered their attacks from 11,000 to 16,000 feet hitting the town, the docks and the Focke-Wulf site, and on the way home F/O Smith and crew dropped down to 50 feet, from where they strafed a moving train and brought it to a halt amidst clouds of steam. Local reports spoke of a thousand houses damaged, along with four small industrial premises, while three cranes and seven ships were hit in the port, one of the vessels sinking and becoming a danger to navigation. The likelihood is, however, that much of the effort was wasted beyond the city's southern boundary.

While the rest of the Command remained at home on the 3rd, 61 and 207 Squadrons detailed three Lancasters each for mining duties in the Baltic, the crews of S/L West, F/L Casement and F/Sgt Williams assigned to the Nasturtium garden at the northern end of The Sound (Oresund) located in the channel between Demark's Zeeland Island (Copenhagen) and the Swedish mainland. They departed Syerston between 22.25 and 22.35 and only F/L Casement and crew returned seven hours later to report encountering ideal conditions of clear skies and bright moonlight and planting their vegetables according to brief. They also witnessed an aircraft come under fire and fall in flames into the sea, and this would soon be identified as R5663, which was a victim of flak from Helsingor and came down in shallow water close to the Swedish port of Hälsingborg. The Swedish authorities confirmed that F/Sgt Williams had been the sole survivor and that he was undergoing a term of internment. Having traversed Jutland homebound, the Casement crew then observed a glow in the sky in the area of Ringkøbing Fjord off western Jutland, and when five bodies washed ashore at various points on the Danish coast over the ensuing weeks, it was clear that they had come from R5488. Among them were the remains of S/L West DFC, a New Zealander serving in the RAF and someone who had served the squadron well as a flight commander. S/L Forsyth was posted in from 420 (Snowy Owl) Squadron RCAF to fill the breach, but he would need time to settle in and learn the ways of the Lancaster.

The remainder of the first half of the month would be low-key, with mining operations occupying much of the night-time activity, but it was the shipbuilding port of Wilhelmshaven for which 5

Group detailed fifty-two Lancasters and twenty-four Hampdens on the 8th as part of an overall force of 285 aircraft. The ten-strong 61 Squadron element departed Syerston between 23.45 and 00.15 with F/L Casement the senior pilot on duty, and all reached the target area to encounter around three-tenths thin cloud at 10,000 feet and haze below. This made it almost impossible for most to identify ground detail, including the docks and shipyards aiming points, and positions were established on e.t.a. and by TR (Gee)-fix, some backed up through a visual check assisted by the use of flares. The navigator and bomb-aimer in each crew worked together to provide accurate navigation, the navigator, unsighted in his closed-off cubicle, offering ground features to look out for and relying on the bomb-aimer to relay what he was observing from his excellent vantage point in the nose. On this night, Sgt Joslin's navigator and bomb-aimer were on their first sortie and an error in pinpointing led to them bombing the port of Emden in error from 13,000 feet. Those reaching the target carried out their attacks from between 13,000 and 17,000 feet, and on return most expressed confidence in the effectiveness of their work, and while local sources confirmed some damage in Wilhelmshaven, post-raid reconnaissance revealed that much of the bombing had missed the town to the west.

The first daylight foray deep into enemy territory by Lancasters, the previously mentioned raid on the M.A.N diesel engine factory at Augsburg in April, had cost seven of the twelve aircraft dispatched, and Harris, despite his antipathy towards such operations, sanctioned a similar plan by 5 Group for an attack on the 11th on the Danziger Werft U-Boot construction yards in the distant port of what is now Gdansk in Poland. The forty-four Lancasters of 61, 83, 97, 106 and 207 Squadrons were to fly out in formation at low level, before splitting up to cross Denmark and the Baltic independently and then climb to bombing altitude and make their own individual approaches to the target. The attack was to be carried out in the fading light, to allow a withdrawal to take place under the cover of darkness, and the 1,700-mile round-trip would be the longest yet attempted by the Command. The seven participating 61 Squadron Lancasters departed Syerston between 16.45 and 17.10 with F/L Deas the senior pilot on duty and RDX-filled 1,000-pounders in each bomb bay. An unanticipated band of ten-tenths ice-bearing cloud was encountered over the North Sea extending from 1,000 to 14,000 feet, and this ruined the plan as aircraft lost contact with each other, forcing the individual crews to break formation earlier than intended and make their way independently to the target. This would have a detrimental effect on the raid and cause some crews to abandon their sorties or arrive late, when darkness had already settled over the area to make identification a challenge.

As F/Sgt Stewart and crew reached the Baltic coast they ran into heavy and medium flak from Flensburg, which knocked out the rear turret and perforated the starboard mainplane with around twenty holes. They decided not to go on and instead headed north into the Kattegat, where they bombed Anholt Island from 11,000 feet before turning for home. F/Sgt Shriner and crew were unable to locate the target in darkness, and having failed also to relocate a convoy spotted earlier, jettisoned their bombs over the Baltic. F/Sgt Turner and crew went in at 600 feet in the face of a hail of light flak and sustained damage both from the defences and from the bursts of four of their own bombs in the Danziger Werft yard. As they raced away the gunners strafed the town and somehow, they all lived to tell the tale. The others from the squadron attacked from between 5,000 and 9,000 feet and observed bursts, some of which narrowly overshot the aiming point. A post-raid analysis revealed that twenty-six aircraft had bombed either the ship-building wharfs or the town, and two of them had been shot down by flak.

The first of a series of five operations over a four-week period against Duisburg was mounted on the night of the 13/14th and involved 194 aircraft, including thirteen Lancasters from the 5 Group stations of Bottesford and Coningsby. The operation failed to find the mark in adverse weather conditions consisting of electrical storms and heavy cloud and the bombing became widely scattered and ineffective.

On the 14th 61 Squadron was posted to St Eval in Cornwall to replace 44 (Rhodesia) Squadron and spend the next ten days conducting anti-U-Boot patrol duties under the orders of Coastal Command. The first patrol involved four aircraft and took place on the 17th, F/L Casement and crew enjoying instant success by sinking a U-Boot, U-751, with depth charges and anti-submarine bombs. There had been other claims of success by Bomber Command crews, but this one was confirmed by photographic evidence of the U-Boot crew swimming away from their sinking vessel. This would prove to be the high point of the detachment, as further patrols daily from the 18th to the 20th by four aircraft on each occasion were uneventful, as were those by six, six and four aircraft respectively on the 23rd, 25th and 26th. S/L Sheenan had been posted in from 19 O.T.U in mid-month and was sent within days to the Conversion Flight to learn the ways of the Lancaster. Also arriving at Syerston at this time from HQ Bomber Command was the legendary W/C Percy "Pick" Pickard, although the purpose of his three-week stay was not recorded, and one must assume his role was advisory. The last of the new arrivals was S/L Weston, who came in from SHQ Waddington during the last week of the month as flight commander elect.

While absent from Bomber Command the squadron missed a number of major operations, the first a raid on the 19th by ninety-nine four-engine types against the Vulkan U-Boot construction yards at Vegesack, situated on the River Weser a few miles to the north-west of Bremen city centre. 5 Group contributed twenty-eight Lancasters to the attack, and those arriving in the target area were met by up to ten-tenths cloud with tops at 10,000 to 12,000 feet and delivered their attacks on the basis of a Gee-fix (TR). They gained an impression that a lot was going on beneath the cloud, but in reality, the raid had completely missed the target, confirming the fact that Gee was useful as a guide to navigation, but was not precise enough to employ as a blind-bombing device.

A force of 291 aircraft was assembled on the 21st for the second raid of the series on Duisburg, and this number included twenty-nine Lancasters and seventeen Hampdens representing 5 Group. It was a moonless night, and despite the presence of clear skies over the target, extreme darkness and the usual industrial haze took their toll on vertical visibility, the effects of which, it was hoped, would be negated by flares dropped from the leading aircraft by TR. However, these proved to be not entirely accurate, and some illuminated an area of open country on the west bank of the Rhine. Returning crews could offer no useful information to the intelligence section at debriefing, but local reports confirmed extensive damage in residential districts, with ninety-four apartment buildings destroyed and 256 seriously damaged, and there was also mention of damage to the Thyssen steel works and to two other important war-industry factories.

A reduced force of 215 aircraft was made ready to continue the assault on Duisburg on the 23rd, and forty-five of these were Lancasters, those reaching the target encountering seven to ten-tenths cloud with tops as high as 12,000 feet in places but a large gap that afforded some crews a sight of the ground. Despite that, for many there was little chance of locating the briefed aiming point, which was probably the Thyssen steel works, and the Gee-based (TR) flares were again scattered and largely ineffective, leaving most crews to carry out their attacks on their own TR-fix. Returning crews were confident that they had hit the city's built-up area, many claiming to have identified specific ground features, and the outcome of the raid was similar to the previous one, with residential property sustaining the bulk of the damage.

The fourth raid on Duisburg was posted on the 25th, for which the largest force yet of the series was assembled amounting to 313 aircraft, among which were 177 Wellingtons and fourteen Hampdens, with the four-engine types, including thirty-three Lancasters, making up the numbers. They ran into around seven-tenths cloud over the target, with fair visibility, which enabled a visual confirmation of the TR-based approach, but not the briefed aiming point D, and the extensive and distinctive Ruhrort inland docks complex provided a solid reference point to bomb the built-up area generally for those unable to identify the briefed aiming point. It was left to local reports to confirm further damage to residential property, but less extensive than in the two previous attacks.

All but four 61 Squadron Lancasters returned to Syerston from Cornwall on the 26th in time for nine of them to participate that night in a maximum effort planned for the annual last-week-of-July attack on Germany's second city, Hamburg. A force of 404 aircraft was assembled, among them seventy-seven Lancasters and thirty-three Hampdens representing 5 Group, the Syerston element taking off between 22.50 and 23.10 with F/L Casement the senior pilot on duty and a cookie and incendiaries in each bomb bay. They flew out over the Lincolnshire coast and once over the North Sea, had to negotiate the frequently met conditions on this route of towering cloud, electrical storms and severe icing. The skies over the target were clear, however, and the visibility excellent, which allowed the crews to confirm their positions by visual reference, with the docks area standing out particularly clearly in the bright moonlight. They had been handed aiming point D, which was probably the shipbuilding yards to the west of the city centre but found smoke already drifting across the built-up area to obscure some ground detail. The 61 Squadron crews attacked from between 12,000 and 16,000 feet, contributing to thirty to forty fires, the glow from which remained visible on the horizon for around seventy miles into the homeward journey. At debriefings crews reported that the fires seemed to merge into one single conflagration, and the effectiveness of the raid was borne out by local reports, which spoke of eight hundred fires, more than five hundred of which were classed as large, and it seems that the residential and semi-commercial districts bore the brunt of the raid. When the flames had died down and the smoke cleared, 823 houses were found to have been reduced to ruins, with five thousand others damaged to some extent. It was a highly successful raid for the period, which the Command hoped to build upon forty-eight hours later until the weather took a hand to reduce the number of aircraft available.

The final four 61 Squadron Lancasters returned from St Eval on the 28th, but the squadron was not to be involved in another maximum effort raid on Hamburg called for that night, for which a force well in excess of four hundred aircraft had been assembled, 256 of them provided by 3 Group and the operational training units. It was to have been the debut in numbers of 49 Squadron Lancasters, but the weather conditions over the 1, 4 and 5 Group stations prompted the withdrawal of their contribution, and as conditions worsened over the North Sea, the O.T.U aircraft were recalled. Many of the 3 Group crews turned back also, and only sixty-eight would claim to have attacked the primary target, where fifteen large fires and forty smaller ones were reported. This modicum of success was gained at the high cost of twenty-five aircraft, 15% of those dispatched, and four O.T.U Wellingtons also failed to return, while a fifth, a Whitley, ditched, and its crew was picked up safely.

Saarbrücken was posted as the target on the 29th, and a force of 291 aircraft assembled, which would be the largest raid by far on this major industrial and coal-producing Saarland capital city, situated right on the frontier with France in south-western Germany. 5 Group contributed sixty-nine Lancasters and seventeen Hampdens, the crews of which had been briefed to attack aiming point C, and in the expected absence of a strong searchlight and flak defence, the intention was to attack from a lower level than customary for the period. 61 Squadron detailed thirteen Lancasters, which departed Syerston between 23.50 and 00.15 with F/Ls Casement and Deas the senior pilots on duty, and made landfall on the French coast, before following the frontier with Belgium and entering Germany south of Luxembourg. At the target, they encountered a layer of four to eight-tenths low cloud at between 2,000 and 9,000 feet, below which the visibility was good, and this enabled crews to confirm their TR positions by visual references on ground features like the River Saar. The Syerston crews delivered their cookies and SBCs of incendiaries from between 1,000 and 8,000 feet and observed numerous fires in the built-up area, marshalling yards and on a nearby aerodrome, and the confidence expressed on return that their bombs had found the mark was confirmed by local reports of severe damage in central and north-western districts, where almost four hundred buildings had been destroyed in return for the loss of nine aircraft. The were two pilots with the rank and name of F/Sgt Stewart recorded in the ORB as taking part in this operation, and it was the crew of J G Stewart RNZAF who failed to return in R5737, after it crashed at Vrizy on the western edge of the Ardennes in north-eastern France. Bomber Command Losses for 1942 shows the pilot as P/O Stewart and he lost his life alongside five of his crew with only the bomb-aimer surviving to fall into enemy hands.

The month ended with a major assault on the Ruhr city of Düsseldorf, for which a force of 630 aircraft was assembled, the numbers bolstered by a large contribution from the training units. 5 Group offered 113 Lancasters, the first time that the one hundred figure had been reached, and after a month on the sidelines converting to the Lancaster, 49 Squadron was finally able to make its presence felt. The heavy brigade would be accompanied by twenty-four Hampdens belonging to the two remaining operators of the type, the Canadian squadrons, 408 (Goose) and 420 (Snowy Owl). 61 Squadron contributed ten Lancasters, which departed Syerston between 00.15 and 01.15 with F/Ls Casement and Deas the senior pilots on duty and W/C Coad flying as second pilot to the former. Sgt Hobson lost the use of his artificial horizon and Sgt Joslin and crew their port-outer engine and both bomb loads ended up on the bed of the North Sea, leaving the others to press on to the target under bright moonlight from clear skies and visibility good enough to facilitate map-reading. Most crews pinpointed on the Rhine and confirmed their TR-fixed positions visually by an S-bend to the south, the Syerston crews then carrying out their attacks from between 12,000 and 16,000 feet in the face of an intense and accurate searchlight and flak defence. They observed a large number of explosions and fires and there was a general confidence at debriefing in the effectiveness of the attack, some commenting on a column of black smoke rising through 10,000 feet as they turned away. More than nine hundred tons of bombs were dropped, some wasted in open country, but the remainder had been scattered across all parts of the city and the neighbouring city of Neuss on the opposite bank of the Rhine. Local sources confirmed the destruction of 453 buildings, with varying degrees of damage to fifteen thousand more, and sixty-seven large fires had to be dealt with. The success came at the cost of twenty-nine aircraft, including five Hampdens and two Lancasters, and the O.T.U.s were again hit disproportionately hard, losing fifteen of their number.

During the course of the month the squadron took part in seven Bomber Command operations and dispatched sixty-three sorties for the loss of three Lancasters and crews. In addition, seven anti-U-Boot patrols generated thirty-two sorties without loss.

August 1942

A gentle start to the new month saw the heavy brigade remain at home because of unfavourable weather conditions on the first two nights, while 61 Squadron moved back to St Eval on the 2nd for a three-week spell of anti-U-Boot patrols. It would prove to be a frustrating and costly period, during which patrols by between one and seven aircraft on fifteen days generated sixty-three sorties, some lasting up to ten hours. Of greater concern, however, was the loss of four Lancasters and crews in attempting to sink the 12,000-ton Altmark class tanker, SS Corunna, a blockade runner, off the coast of northern Spain. The first action took place on the 19th, when S/L Weston led a patrol by seven aircraft, three of which failed to return, F/O Searby and crew in R5661, F/Sgt Shriner and crew in R5663, and F/Sgt Haynes and crew in R5605, all without survivors. S/L Weston attacked the ship but missed, as did F/Sgt Hobson and crew, while F/Sgt Dale and crew were driven off by ferocious defensive fire. F/Sgt Turner and crew claimed to have scored a number of hits, but they were unconfirmed, and on the following day, when a search was carried out to relocate the tanker, P/O Harrad and his crew failed to return in R5543. They had been shot down by a fighter from KG40 and none survived the crash at 15.40 near Cabanas in Portugal. On the 22nd, the detachment returned to Syerston.

During 61 Squadron's absence from the bombing war, 5 Group sent out orders to Swinderby and Woodhall Spa on the 3rd to prepare small numbers of Lancasters for mining duties in the Forget-me-not and Radish gardens, respectively Kiel Harbour and the Fehmarn Belt in the western Baltic. On the following night, 5 Group contributed a handful of Lancasters and Hampdens for further mining operations around the Frisians and off the Biscay coast and on the 5th, ten Lancasters from 44 (Rhodesia) and 97 (Straits Settlements) Squadrons joined twenty-eight other aircraft in a blind attack on Essen employing Gee. Once over enemy territory, they found in their path a towering, ice-bearing front with electrical storms, which topped out at 22,000 feet and extended over the Ruhr. Some crews opted not to press on to the primary target and dropped their bombs on alternatives, and just eighteen claimed to have attacked Essen based on TR readings. The authorities deemed it necessary to repeat the exercise twenty-four hours later, when eight Lancasters were among seventeen aircraft assigned to Essen along with eight for Bochum, the crews of which were to employ Gee to locate the target before bombing visually through gaps in the cloud. Only one Lancaster bombed the target and three Halifaxes, a Lancaster and a Wellington failed to return, 20% of those dispatched.

5 Group's contribution to the fifth and final operation of the three-week campaign against the Ruhr industrial city of Duisburg amounted to forty-seven Lancasters and ten Hampdens, which were part of an overall force of 216 aircraft assembled on the 6th. Those reaching the target area reported cloud conditions at zero to ten-tenths with tops at 10,000 feet and barrage balloons tethered as high as 12,000 feet. Positions had to be established by TR-fix confirmed by visual reference aided by fires, flak and flares, and the bombs were delivered from 14,000 to 21,000 feet, mostly without their fall being plotted. According to local reports, eighteen buildings were destroyed and sixty-six seriously damaged, giving a sum total over the five raids of 212 houses destroyed, 741 seriously damaged, and significant industrial damage resulting from just one raid. In return for this modest gain, Bomber Command had lost forty-three aircraft.

Earlier on the 6th, 420 (Snowy Owl) Squadron RCAF had vacated Waddington on transfer to 4 Group, where it would convert to Wellingtons, and on the 7th, 9 Squadron arrived from 3 Group to begin conversion to the Lancaster as the replacement for 83 Squadron, which was about to leave 5 Group for pastures new. Osnabrück was posted as the target on the 9th, and a force of 192 aircraft assembled accordingly, 5 Group contributing forty-two Lancasters to attack a specific "special" aiming point, which the 5 Group and squadron ORBs failed to identify. There were clear skies over the Münsterland region of Germany to the north of the Ruhr, but haze contributed to the poor visibility that awaited the approaching bombers, which all found that they were unable to establish their positions by TR after it was jammed by the enemy on crossing the Dutch coast. Flares were dropped to illuminate the area, and some crews picked out railway lines and the River Hase, but it was mainly the fires, searchlights and flak that pointed the way to the aiming point. The fires resulting from the ensuing attack remained visible for eighty to a hundred miles into the return flight, and TR functioned again once the Dutch coast had been crossed homebound. Local sources confirmed an effective raid, which destroyed 206 houses and a military building, and damaged a number of industrial premises along with four thousand other buildings, mostly lightly.

The first of two raids on consecutive nights against the city of Mainz, situated to the south-west of Frankfurt-am-Main in southern Germany, involved a force of 154 aircraft on the 11th, the number including a contribution from 5 Group of thirty-three Lancasters, for what would be the first large-scale operation against this target. The raid was highly successful, and caused major destruction in the central districts, where many historic and cultural buildings were damaged or destroyed at a cost to the Command of fourteen aircraft and four others in crashes at home. The ordeal was not yet over for Mainz, which was posted as the primary target again on the following day and a force of 138 aircraft made ready, to which 5 Group contributed thirty-three Lancasters and ten 408 (Goose) Squadron Hampdens. Further extensive damage was inflicted upon central and industrial districts for the loss this time of five aircraft, and a Bomber Command analysis assessed that 135 acres of the city had been destroyed in the two raids.

A new era for Bomber Command began on the 15th, with the formation of the Path Finder Force, and the arrival of the four founder heavy squadrons on their stations in Huntingdonshire and Cambridgeshire. 83 Squadron moved into Wyton, the Path Finder HQ, as the 5 Group representative operating Lancasters, and it would be the responsibility of 5 Group's front-line units to provide a steady supply of their most promising crews. The other founder members were 35 (Madras Presidency) Squadron, which took up residence at Graveley with Halifaxes to represent 4 Group, while 156 Squadron retained its Wellingtons for the time-being at Warboys, drawing fresh crews from 1 Group, and 3 Group would be represented by the Stirling-equipped 7 Squadron at Oakington. In addition to the above, 109 Squadron was posted to Wyton, where it would spend the next six months developing the Oboe blind-bombing device and marrying it to the Mosquito under the command of W/C Hal Bufton. The new force would occupy 3 Group stations, falling nominally under 3 Group administrative control and receiving its orders through that group, which was commanded by AVM Baldwin, whose tenure, which had lasted since just before the outbreak of war, was shortly to come to an end.

A "Path Finder Force" was the brainchild of the former 10 Squadron commanding officer, G/C Sid Bufton, Hal's brother, and now Director of Bomber Operations at the Air Ministry. He had used his best crews at 10 Squadron to find targets by the light of flares and attract other crews by firing off a coloured Verey light, and it could be said, that the concept of target-finding and marking had been born at 10 Squadron. Once at the Air Ministry, Bufton promoted his ideas with vigour and gained support among the other staff officers, culminating with the idea being put to Harris soon after his enthronement as Bomber Command C-in-C. Harris rejected the principle of establishing an elite target-finding and marking force, a view shared by the other group commanders with the exception of 4 Group's AVM Roddy Carr. However, once overruled by higher authority, Harris gave it his unstinting support, and his choice of the former 10 Squadron commanding officer, and still somewhat junior, G/C Don Bennett, as its commander was both controversial and inspired, and ruffled more than a few feathers among more senior officers. Australian, Bennett, was among the most experienced aviators in the RAF, a pilot and a Master Navigator of unparalleled experience, with many thousands of hours to his credit. He also had the recent and relevant experience as a bomber pilot through his commands of 77 and 10 Squadrons and had demonstrated his strong character when evading capture and returning from Norway after being shot down while attacking the Tirpitz in April. Despite his reserve, total lack of humour and his impatience with those whose brains operated on a lower plane than his, he would inspire in his men great affection and loyalty, along with enormous pride in being "Path Finders". He would forge the new force into a highly effective weapon, although this would not immediately be apparent.

There is some confusion surrounding 5 Group operations on the night of the 15/16th, the group ORB recording no operations because of the weather conditions, while at least five squadron ORBs revealed that their aircraft had contributed to an overall force of 131 aircraft bound for Düsseldorf. Those reaching the southern Ruhr encountered six to nine-tenths cloud at 10,000 feet with poor to modest visibility and not all were able to establish their position in relation to the briefed aiming point. Most employed a TR-fix confirmed by a visual confirmation on the River Rhine, while others simply relied on e.t.a. At debriefings, bomb bursts and flashes were reported, and the abiding impression was of a scattered attack, which was confirmed by local reports from Düsseldorf and its neighbour across the Rhine, Neuss, which described a light raid and no damage of note.

Orders were received at five 5 Group stations on the 17th to prepare for a return to Osnabrück that night as part of a 5 Group effort of thirty-two Lancasters and ten Hampdens in an overall force of 139 aircraft. It had been intended that the Path Finder Force would make its debut on this night, but the commanding officers decided that their squadrons were not yet ready, and the operation had to go ahead without them. Most 5 Group crews conducted a timed run from the Dümmer Sea, a large lake situated some twenty miles to the north-east and were greeted at the target by three to five-tenths cloud at between 11,000 and 14,000 feet with haze at 4,000 feet to compromise the vertical visibility. Some crews were able to identify the river and railway lines and bombs were aimed at either the briefed aiming point or the built-up area generally, and local sources confirmed a moderately destructive raid, which fell mainly into northern and north-western districts, and thereby, built on the damage inflicted eight nights earlier.

The Path Finders took to the air in anger for the first time on the 18th, when contributing thirty-one aircraft to an overall force of 118, of which twenty Lancasters and sixteen Hampdens were provided by 5 Group. They were bound for the naval and shipbuilding port of Flensburg, situated on the eastern coast of the Schleswig-Holstein peninsula close to the border with Denmark, where the U-Boot pens were the briefed aiming point. The bomber stream made landfall on the western coast of Jutland, before traversing the peninsula to what had been selected as a worthwhile and easy-to-locate target. Sadly, the planners had not factored in an incorrect wind forecast, which pushed the bomber stream north of the intended track and over southern Denmark, a situation that the Path Finders failed to notice. As a result, in conditions of haze and two-tenths cloud at 6,000 feet, they illuminated an area of similar coastal terrain north of where they believed themselves to be, which led to a scattering of bombs across Danish territory up to twenty-five miles north of the frontier and into the towns of Abenra and Sønderborg. It was an inauspicious operational debut for a force, which in time, would become a highly efficient, successful and vital component in Bomber Command's armoury.

Frankfurt was selected on the 24th to host the second Path Finder-led operation, for which a force of 226 aircraft was assembled, 5 Group contributing forty-seven Lancasters, six of them made ready at Syerston, which took off between 21.15 and 21.25 with S/L Forsyth the senior pilot on duty and S/L Sheenan flying as second pilot to F/Sgt Meyer. S/L Forsyth set course on readings from the DR compass, but when he found himself over Lincoln he backtracked to base and set a new course on the P4 compass, which took him over Boston. Convinced that both compasses were faulty, he jettisoned the bomb load in The Wash and returned home, leaving the others to head out across The Wash on course for the Belgian coast. Those reaching the target area found five to nine-tenths cloud at between 7,000 and 9,000 feet, with ground haze adding to the difficulties experienced by the Path Finders in locating the aiming point. The 61 Squadron crews positively identified the primary target, most by TR-fix after picking up glimpses of the Rivers Rhine and Main, which led them on e.t.a. to a built-up area, where they bombed from between 12,000 and 18,000 feet, and in some cases observed bursts and fires. Opinions at debriefing were mixed, some satisfied with the results and others not and no mention was made of the Path Finder contribution, which, at this early stage of its development, was restricted to identifying and then illuminating the target. Sixteen aircraft failed to return, 7.1% of those dispatched, and among them were five Path Finders. Absent from its dispersal pan at Syerston was R5662, which was now a smouldering wreck at Efferen, a Hamlet on the south-western outskirts of Cologne, where the remains of F/Sgt Meyer and his crew were being recovered for local burial.

The third Path Finder-led operation was directed at the city of Kassel, the home as previously mentioned to three Henschel aircraft and tank factories and other important war-industry contributors, as well as being the HQ for the military's Wehrkreis IX and the site of a subcamp of the Dachau concentration camp, which supplied slave labour to the factories. A force of 306 aircraft was assembled on the 27th, 5 Group detailing seventy-five Lancasters and a dozen Hampdens, ten of the former made ready at Syerston, before taking off between 20.40 and 21.30 with S/Ls Forsyth and Weston the senior pilots on duty. F/Sgt Turner and crew turned back early when the rear gunner reported his turret to be unserviceable, and they were followed home by F/L Deas and crew because of W/T failure. On approach to land the undercarriage refused to lock down, and it became necessary to head back out to sea to jettison the bombs in case of a collapse on touchdown, which, happily, did not occur. S/L Forsyth and crew arrived at the target ahead of schedule to be greeted by minimal cloud, bright moonlight and good visibility, and stooged around waiting for the Path Finders to open proceedings.

The Path Finder flares assisted greatly in enabling the crews to pick out ground detail, such as a bend in the River Fulda and lakes to the south-west, and the Syerston crews took advantage to deliver their cookies and incendiaries from 8,000 to 12,500 feet either side of midnight. On the way home and avoiding the defences at Münster, F/Sgt Dale and crew flew over the hotspot of Hamm, an important and well-defended railway hub on the northern rim of the Ruhr and were forced down to 800 feet in their bid to escape. They got away with it but were holed in a dozen places and had their hydraulics system shot to pieces, which left the bomb doors dangling in the slipstream for the remainder of the flight home. Local sources confirmed the effectiveness of the raid, which was spread across the city and destroyed 144 buildings, while causing serious damage to more than three hundred others. Among those afflicted to some extent were all three Henschel factories and a number of military establishments, and the fire services had to deal with seventy-three large blazes. However, the success was gained at the high cost of thirty-one aircraft, twenty-one of them Wellingtons.

A force of 159 aircraft was assembled on the 28th to send to the city of Nuremberg, deep in southern Germany, where the Path Finders were to employ target indicators (TIs) for the first time in adapted 250lb bomb casings. 5 Group detailed sixty-three Lancasters, while also contributing seventeen Hampdens to a simultaneous raid on Saarbrücken by a force of 113 "oddments", which included 4 Group Halifaxes and new crews from other groups, but no Path Finders. 61 Squadron made ready ten Lancasters and sent them on their way from Syerston between 20.45 and 21.10 with F/L Casement the senior pilot on duty. F/Sgt Dale and crew dropped out early on because of an engine issue, leaving the others to complete the six-hundred-mile outward leg across France and into the target area, which was found to be under clear skies. A four-fifths moon aided a visual identification of the city and enabled the Path Finder element to exploit the conditions to deliver their TIs with great accuracy. The Syerston crews pinpointed on waterways and autobahns leading into the city and delivered their cookie and incendiary bomb loads from between 8,500 and 12,000 feet and it was only later that F/Sgt Lever and crew realised that they had bombed Erlangen to the north of Nuremberg in error. F/Sgt Turner and crew also back-plotted their route from the navigator's log and discovered that they had bombed Munich, which accounted for the hostility of the flak response at one of Germany's most well-defended cities. There was no question in the minds of crews as they withdrew that they had hit the target, a belief confirmed by fires remaining visible for some seventy miles into the return flight. Twenty-three aircraft failed to return, 14.5% of the force, and the Wellingtons were hit particularly hard again, losing a third of their number. Missing from Syerston was R5742, which came down in southern Germany with no survivors from the freshman crew of Sgt Norgate, a mixed bunch including four members of the RCAF and an American in the RAF. Local sources suggested that about a third of the force had landed bombs within the city, causing damage to the Altstadt, but that others had wasted their effort on communities up to ten miles to the north.

On the 31st the crews of Sgt Davies, P/O Foster and F/Sgt Lever were detailed for mining duties in the Baltic, the first-mentioned in one of the Silverthorn gardens in the Kattegat region and the others in the Yewtree garden in the Læso Channel located between the Danish islands of Langeland and Lolland. They departed Syerston between 23.20 and 23.30, before heading north-eastwards over ten-tenths cloud, which in the target areas lay low over the sea with a base sometimes down to 600 feet. Sgt Davies and crew obtained a pinpoint from which to run in on the release point and planted their vegetables according to brief from 800 feet, while conditions in the Yewtree garden were more challenging and neither crew was able to establish a pinpoint. On return all three crews were diverted to Drem, a station situated east of Edinburgh.

During the course of the month the squadron took part in three bombing and one mining operation that generated twenty-nine sorties for the loss of two Lancasters and crews and carried out sixty-three anti-U-Boot sorties on fifteen days, losing in the process four Lancasters and crews.

September 1942

The first half of the new month would distinguish itself through an unprecedented series of effective operations, although, it would begin ignominiously for the Path Finder Force, when posting a "black" on the night of the 1/2nd by marking the wrong target. The city of Saarbrücken had been briefed out to 231 crews, of which sixty-nine represented 5 Group, sixty-two to fly Lancasters and seven in Hampdens, a type with just two more weeks of front-line service ahead of it. 61 Squadron made ready eight Lancasters and dispatched them from Syerston between 23.30 and 00.15 with S/L Weston the senior pilot on duty and W/C Coad flying as second pilot. All reached south-western Germany to find the target under clear skies with good visibility, and established their positions by TR, confirmed by visual identification of the River Saar and other ground features highlighted by Path Finder flares. They bombed from between 8,000 and 12,000 feet from around 02.00 onwards and most observed the burst of their cookie, while some crews from other squadrons reported the entire area of the North Bank of the Saar to be on fire and commented on a very large explosion occurring in the midst of the conflagration. There was no question in the minds of most crews as they retreated to the west, that this had been an outstandingly accurate attack, and some claimed to be able to see the glow of fires from up to 140 miles into the return flight. It was only later that the truth emerged, that the Path Finders had marked not Saarbrücken, but the non-industrial town of Saarlouis, situated thirteen miles to the north-west, which lay in a loop of the river similar to that at the intended target. Much to the chagrin of its inhabitants and those in surrounding communities, the main force bombing had been particularly accurate and concentrated, and heavy damage had been inflicted.

This could have been an ill-omen for the month's efforts but, in fact, the Command now embarked on the unprecedented run of effective operations mentioned above. It began at Karlsruhe on the night of the 2/3rd, a city that was home to a factory belonging to the Deutsche Waffen und Munitionsfabriken A.G, better known as DWM, which manufactured all types of firearms from pistols to automatic weapons for infantry and aircraft. A force of two hundred aircraft was made ready, the 4 Group Halifax brigade having now returned to operations following intensive training to restore confidence in the type after a period of above average losses and a series of design-flaw accidents. 5 Group put up sixty Lancasters and five Hampdens, of which eight of the former were provided by 61 Squadron and departed Syerston between 23.10 and 23.40 with S/L Forsyth the senior pilot on duty. The target lay some fifty miles beyond Saarbrücken, which enabled the force to adopt the same route as on the previous night, passing south of Liege in Belgium and entering Germany north of Luxembourg. It was a three-hour outward flight, at the end of which the force found the target area to be under clear skies, basking in moonlight and naked to the eyes of the bomb-aimers high above. The autobahn and the Rhine and its docks stood out clearly as a guide to the aiming point, and bombing was carried out by the Syerston crews between 7,000 and 16,000 feet. The city appeared to be swallowed by a sea of flames, before becoming obscured by smoke and returning crews reported as many as two hundred fires, a column of smoke rising through 10,000 feet and the glow remaining visible on the horizon for a hundred miles into the homeward journey. A message was received from S/L Forsyth DFC and his crew to the effect that they had been attacked by a night-fighter and were attempting to reach home on two engines, but W4136 and its crew were never seen again, and the conclusion must be that they were swallowed up by the Channel. Post-raid reconnaissance confirmed much residential and some industrial damage, and local reports mentioned seventy-three fatalities.

5 Group welcomed an addition to its ranks on the 4th on the transfer of 57 Squadron from 3 Group to join 49 Squadron at Scampton, where it would occupy the former 83 Squadron facilities. Having been an operator of the Wellington in its previous life, it would spend the next six weeks undergoing conversion to the Lancaster. Bremen was posted as the target for that night, and 5 Group responded with a contribution of forty-six Lancasters in an overall force of 251 aircraft. Crews were told at briefing that the Path Finders would be rolling out a new three-phase technique based on illumination, visual marking and backing-up, which, if successful, would form the basis of Path Finder operations for the remainder of the war. Nine 61 Squadron crews attended briefing, four to learn that their aiming point was the city, while five were assigned to the Focke-Wulf aircraft factory at Hemelingen. They departed Syerston between 23.59 and 00.25 with F/Ls Casement and Deas the senior pilots on duty and lost the services of P/O Foster and crew during the climb-out because of an unserviceable rear turret. Enemy night-fighters were operating over Holland and intercepted a number of bombers, while the others reached the target area to find cloudless skies and good visibility, although ground haze and smoke created challenging conditions for target identification. The first Path Finder flares and incendiaries went down at around 01.50, but not all of those assigned to the Focke-Wulf factory were able to identify it and attacked the general built-up area instead from between 8,000 and 14,000 feet. Generally, crews noticed a less-intense flak defence over the city than usual, but much increased hostility as they withdrew towards the Frisian island of Norderney. Twelve aircraft failed to return from this successful operation, and among them was 61 Squadron's R5682, which was hit by flak near the Dutch coast while outbound and finished off by a night-fighter. It crashed at 02.51 six miles south-east of the "Wespennest" or "Wasps Nest", the famed Luftwaffe aerodrome at Leeuwarden, birthplace of the ill-fated Great War spy, Mata Hari, and took the lives of F/Sgt Joslin and two of his crew, while the survivors were taken into captivity. Debriefing reports of fires in the central districts were confirmed by a local assessment, which listed 460 dwelling houses, six large/medium industrial premises and fifteen small ones destroyed, and a further fourteen hundred buildings seriously damaged.

The next operation was to be directed at the Ruhr city of Duisburg on the night of the 6/7th for which a force of 207 aircraft was assembled, fifty-four Lancasters and four Hampdens representing 5 Group. 61 Squadron's seven-strong element departed Syerston between 01.05 and 01.25 with F/L Deas the senior pilot on duty, and all reached the target area to find it partially concealed by cloud, below which, the usual industrial haze rendered ground detail indistinct. Positions were established by TR and confirmed as far as possible by visual reference in the light of flares, and the Syerston crews attacked from between 13,000 and 15,000 feet in the face of a searchlight and flak defence operating to its usual high standard. The crews of F/Sgt Dale and Sgt Meagher both reported being held in searchlights and coming under fire, and the former returned with a number of holes as evidence. The Duisburg authorities reported the heaviest raid to date, which destroyed 114 buildings and seriously damaged more than three hundred others, and, while this was only fairly modest, it still represented something of a victory at this notoriously elusive target.

There was no pattern to the choice of targets thus far in the month, southern and north-western Germany and the Ruhr all featuring during the busy first week, and Frankfurt in south-central Germany was posted as the latest target on the 8th, for which a force of 249 aircraft was assembled. 5 Group contributed sixty-two Lancasters and nine Hampdens, the eight participants from 61 Squadron departing Syerston between 20.40 and 21.15 with F/Ls Casement and Deas the senior pilots on duty. An electrical issue during the outward flight across France brought an early end to the sortie of F/Sgt Lever and crew, leaving the others to reach the target area, where, according to some, the skies were clear of cloud and the visibility good, while others reported up to eight-tenths cloud at 2,000 feet and poor to moderate visibility. Another factor was the intensity of the searchlight and flak activity, which should, perhaps, have helped to guide the Path Finders to the aiming point but, surprisingly, they failed to locate the city. Path Finder flares were in evidence but scattered over a wide area, and it was clear that they were by no means certain of their position in relation to Frankfurt.

Ultimately, crews established their own positions by what they could glimpse on the ground and the dozens of searchlights fingering the darkness, and all from 61 Squadron bombed from between 11,000 to 15,000 feet believing that the primary target lay beneath them. In fact, the crews of F/L Casement, F/Sgt Dale and Sgt Davies had attacked the town of Bauschheim, located a few miles east-south-east of Mainz and some fifteen miles from Frankfurt, while those of P/O Foster and Sgt Meagher had bombed at Rüsselsheim and F/Sgt Turner and crew at Königstädten. Five minutes before e.t.a., F/L Deas's bomb-aimer announced that they were over the primary target and let the bombs go without questioning the time discrepancy. Returning crews reported fires in built-up areas, but according to local sources, only a handful of bomb loads hit the intended target, and this halted the run of successes thus far in the month. The majority of bombs appeared to have fallen to the south-west of Frankfurt, and the authorities confirmed damage to the Opel tank works and a Michelin tyre factory at Rüsselsheim, which compensated in small measure for the failure to hit the primary target.

The night of the 9/10th was devoted to mining operations from the Biscay coast to the Baltic and involved the crew of Sgt Baker of 61 Squadron, who departed Syerston at 23.40 bound for one of the Silverthorn gardens in the Kattegat. On arrival in the target area, a night-fighter was observed taking off from a nearby aerodrome and making directly for the Lancaster with headlamps in the nose, and when a second twin-engine aircraft joined the first, the mines were jettisoned and successful evasive measures taken.

The Path Finder Force was constantly evolving in tactics and equipment and had a new weapon in its armoury for the next operation, which was to be against the Ruhr city of Düsseldorf on the 10th. "The Pink Pansy", which weighed in at 2,800lbs, was the latest attempt to produce a genuine target indicator and used converted 4,000lb cookie casings. A force of 479 aircraft included a contribution from the training units of 91, 92 and 93 Groups, and eighty-one Lancasters and eight Hampdens from 5 Group. 61 Squadron put up eleven Lancasters, which set off from Syerston between 20.00 and 20.40 with S/L Weston the senior pilot on duty and each carrying a cookie and twelve SBCs of incendiaries. F/Sgt Dale was contending with fluctuations in revolutions in his port-outer engine and on making landfall at the Scheldt the bombs were dropped somewhere near Ouddorp before he turned back. The others reached the target area to encounter clear skies with the usual industrial haze muddying the vertical visibility, but fires were already burning to help them identify the target visually and pick out major features like a bend in the Rhine and the docks complex. The red flares were reported by some to be a little north of the main city area with the greens over to the west, while the white illuminators highlighted the more central districts. F/Sgt Turner and crew were on a bombing run from south to north when an aircraft exploding directly ahead distracted them and the bombs went down some two miles short of the aiming point. P/O Foster's port-outer engine caught fire over the target, but the bombs were delivered from 13,000 feet and all went well on the homeward flight until the starboard-outer also caught fire at the English coast, despite which a safe landing was carried out. The other 61 Squadron crews bombed from between 12,200 and 14,500 feet, some observing bursts, and watched fires develop as they turned away from what they believed had been a successful operation.

Returning crews made complimentary comments about the performance of the Path Finders and reported the glow of the fires to be visible from the Scheldt on the way home. Post-raid reconnaissance and local reports confirmed this operation to have been probably the most successful since Operation Millennium at the end of May. Other than the northern districts, all parts of the city and its neighbour, Neuss, had been hit, and 911 houses had been destroyed with a further fifteen hundred seriously damaged. In addition to the destruction also of eight public buildings, fifty-two industrial firms in the two cities sustained damage sufficient to cause a total shutdown of production for varying periods. It had been an expensive victory for the Command, however, with thirty-three failures to return, of which sixteen were from the training units. It was a sad night for Syerston after the failure to return of R5888 and W4111 with the crews of F/Sgt Hobson and Sgt Davies respectively. Both Lancasters came down in the Ruhr region without survivors, the latter crew containing five members of the RCAF and a RAF pilot of just nineteen years of age.

Seven 61 Squadron crews attended briefing on the 13th to learn that Bremen was to be their target for that night and for the second time during the month and would face a force at take-off of 446 aircraft, the numbers again bolstered by aircraft and crews from the training groups, while 5 Group's contribution amounted to ninety-eight Lancasters and seven Hampdens. The Syerston element took off between 22.50 and 23.20 with F/Ls Casement and Deas the senior pilots on duty, and all reached the target area to find clear skies but considerable ground haze, which made pinpointing something of a challenge. Some major ground features, like the docks, could be identified visually, otherwise it was down to flares and fires to point the way, and the 61 Squadron participants mostly believed that they were over the built-up area as they carried out their attacks from between 9,000 and 14,000 feet. Sgt Elliott and crew arrived fifteen minutes early and had to wait for the Path Finder flares to signal the opening of the attack, after which they pinpointed on the docks area. A number of crews were convinced that some early arrivals had bombed at Delmenhorst, a few miles to the south-west of Bremen, and the 5 Group ORB described the Path Finder performance as unhelpful. However, the success of the operation suggested otherwise and by far exceeded the destruction resulting from June's Thousand Bomber raid. A total of 848 houses was destroyed and much damage was inflicted on the city's industry, including to the Lloyd Dynamo works, where two weeks production was lost and parts of the Focke-Wulf factory were put out of action for between two and eight days. Of the twenty-one aircraft lost, fifteen belonged to the training units.

The end of the Hampden era arrived on the following night, when the naval and shipbuilding port of Wilhelmshaven was posted as the target for 202 aircraft. Sixty-two Lancasters and four Hampdens were made ready as the 5 Group contribution, the latter from Balderton's 408 (Goose) Squadron RCAF. The four 61 Squadron aircraft were loaded with a cookie and either 4lb or 30lb incendiaries and departed Syerston between 20.15 and 20.20 with S/L Weston the senior pilot on duty. They arrived to find clear skies over the coastal region of Jade Bay, with extreme darkness and ground haze to impede vertical visibility, but the shoreline and the docks provided an adequate pinpoint for the Path Finders to establish their position and mark accurately. The Syerston crews carried out their attacks from between 10,500 and 15,500 feet with light flak bursting around them at between 15,000 and 17,000 feet, and while it was difficult to distinguish individual bomb bursts, the consensus was of a successful outcome. Some crews from other squadrons reported an enormous explosion, believed to be from an ammunition dump, which lit up the ground for five seconds and emitted flames a hundred feet into the air along with a cloud of smoke that rose to several thousand feet. Local sources confirmed that this had been the port's most destructive raid to date.

After such a run of successes, Harris had to have another go at Essen, and a force of 369 aircraft was assembled on the 16th, which again called upon the training units to supply aircraft and crews. Ninety-three Lancasters represented 5 Group, ten of them provided by 61 Squadron, and two 9 Squadron crews would be undertaking the unit's first Lancaster sorties in aircraft borrowed from 44 (Rhodesia) Squadron. The Syerston contingent took off between 19.55 and 20.20 with S/L Weston the senior pilot on duty and lost the services of Sgt Owen and crew to the failure of their intercom after crossing the Dutch coast. Rather than waste the effort already expended they found a flare-path some fifteen miles south-east of Amsterdam and announced themselves with a cookie. The others reached the target area to encounter between three and ten-tenths cloud, but generally good visibility despite the industrial haze, which could be penetrated sufficiently for some ground detail to be identified visually by the light of Path Finder flares. Even so, the overlapping boundaries of the Ruhr towns and cities made it difficult to establish positions with absolute certainty, and some of the crews dropping their bombs on e.t.a. would find from the evidence of their bombing photos that they had been over Bochum, Oberhausen or some other built-up expanse. Some of the Path Finder flares were estimated to be falling some twenty miles to the east of Essen, which would have put them over Dortmund and Hagen. The Syerston crews carried out their attacks from between 12,000 and 18,000 feet in the face of an intense searchlight and flak response and on return reported the glow of fires visible for a hundred miles into the return journey.

Local sources confirmed this to be Essen's worst night of the war to date and in addition to much housing damage and more than a hundred medium and large fires, fifteen high-explosive bombs had found their way onto the Krupp complex, as did a crashing bomber loaded with incendiaries. A post-raid analysis revealed that bombs had been scattered across a large part of the Ruhr, with Bochum, Wuppertal and Herne among the hardest hit, and until the advent of Oboe in the coming spring, such inaccuracies remained a fact of life. It was far from a one-sided affair, and cost the Command a massive thirty-nine aircraft, 10.6% of those dispatched, nineteen of them from the training units. 61 Squadron's W4174 crashed at Heiligenhaus-Hösel, some ten miles north-east of Düsseldorf, and there were no survivors from the crew of W/O Osman RNZAF. The squadron lost a second Lancaster from this operation, L7571 having been borrowed by a crew from 207 Squadron at Bottesford, who failed to bring it back. Happily, the crew all survived in enemy hands.

If any period in the Command's gradual evolution to war-winning capability could be seen as a turning point, then perhaps, the first half of September 1942 qualified. It can be no coincidence that the Path Finder Force was emerging from its hesitant start as the crews got to grips with the complexities of their demanding role, and new tactics and aids were being brought to bear against the enemy. It would be no overnight transformation, and failures would still outnumber victories for some time to come, but the encouraging signs were there that all of the elements of technical and tactical advance were coming together, and, with other technological wizardry in the pipeline, it boded ill for Germany's industrial towns and cities.

Extensive mining operations occupied 115 aircraft on the night of the 18/19th, 5 Group supporting the effort with forty-nine Lancasters assigned to three separate gardens in the Baltic including

Tangerine, the most distant of all gardens located off Pillau, now known as Baltiysk in Russia, on the eastern seaboard of Danzig Bay.

S/L Corr arrived on posting from 1654 Conversion Unit during w.e.f 19th, and as an experienced pilot, who had earned a DFC while serving with 50 Squadron on Hampdens, would be available for operations immediately. Munich was posted as one of two targets on the 19th, and would involve sixty-one 5 Group Lancasters, seven Lancasters from 83 Squadron of the Path Finders and twenty-one Stirlings from 3 Group and 7 Squadron of the Path Finders, while a simultaneous operation by 118 aircraft of 1, 3 and 4 Groups would target Saarbrücken, also with Path Finder support. The two forces followed a common route as far as Saarbrücken, leaving the 5 Group element a further 220 miles to travel to reach the Bavarian capital, the birthplace of Nazism and a city of cultural and industrial significance. 61 Squadron was called upon to contribute nine Lancasters, which departed Syerston between 19.40 and 20.10 with no senior pilots on duty and F/O Frow the highest ranking. Sgt Elliott and crew suffered a fuel-feed issue during the outward leg and jettisoned their bombs in the North Sea on the way home, and when they landed they found that F/Sgt Campbell and crew had beaten them home by ten minutes after losing their starboard-inner engine. The others flew out across France, entering southern Germany near Strasbourg to be greeted by clear skies and good visibility, which enabled them to identify the lakes to the south-west of the target city. Most crews adopted a time-and-distance run from Lake Constance to bring them to the aiming point, which had been well-illuminated by Path Finder flares, and the cookies and incendiaries were released from between 7,000 and 12,000 feet. Bomb bursts were observed in the city centre, along with a large explosion to the north and numerous fires, including an extensive one to the south-west, and 40% of returning crews would claim to have bombed within three miles of the city centre. Saarbrücken was reported to be well-alight by crews passing by 120 miles to the south on the way home, and the Path Finders were complimented on their performance at debriefings. Bombing photos revealed that the main weight of the attack had fallen into western, southern and eastern suburbs of Munich, but there was no confirmation from local sources, and Saarbrücken had largely escaped damage after the bombing became widely scattered.

The squadron was notified on the 23rd, that it would be operating that night against the Baltic coastal town of Wismar and the nearby Dornier aircraft factory as part of an all-5 Group affair involving eighty-three Lancasters. Two-thirds of the force was assigned to the town, situated some thirty miles east of Lübeck, and a third to the factory, and 61 Squadron made ready six Lancasters loaded, it is believed, with six 1,000-pounders with an eleven-second delay fuse for use against the factory. They departed Syerston between 22.50 and 23.10 with W/C Coad and the newly posted-in S/L Corr the senior pilots on duty and ran into a violent electrical storm when around a hundred miles short of Denmark's western coast. This caused many to turn back and added to a total of twenty-one early returns from all causes, while those reaching the target found ten-tenths cloud with tops in extreme cases at 20,000 feet but more generally at around 12,000 feet and a base just above the rooftops. There was also intense and accurate searchlight and flak activity awaiting any crews brave enough to venture low enough to break into clear air. Sgt Meagher and crew alone from Syerston located and bombed the target from a perilously low 50 feet and although sustaining flak damage, nothing vital was hit. W/C Coad and crew flew through violent thunderstorms before bombing a built-up area from 200 feet, while F/O Frow and crew dropped two 1,000-pounders on a railway bridge at Silkeborg in central Jutland. The others either jettisoned their bombs or returned them to the station dump and considered themselves fortunate to survive a night of such scary weather conditions. Some returning crews from other squadrons reported fires in the town and at the Dornier factory, while local sources listed thirty-two houses and eight industrial buildings seriously damaged, at a cost to the Command of four Lancasters.

On the following night, eleven 61 Squadron crews were briefed to join others from the group to conduct mining sorties in the Baltic. Three crews each were assigned to the Tangerine and Privet gardens, respectively off the ports of Pillau and Danzig, two to Geranium off Swinemünde and one each to Willow off Sassnitz, Sweetpea in the Bay of Mecklenburg and Radish in the Fehmarn Strait that links the Bay of Mecklenburg to Kiel Bay to the west. They departed Syerston between 19.25 and 20.20 with S/L Weston the senior pilot on duty and those bound for the most distant locations arrived to find up to six-tenths cloud but the light from a full moon to aid their search for a pinpoint. F/L Deas and crew ran out of time and headed instead for the Pollock garden off the Swedish Island of Bornholm, a target for some others from the group, and P/O Foster and crew selected that as an alternative location also after their intercom system failed. On a generally successful night for the squadron the others fulfilled their briefs during largely uneventful sorties, and it was while homebound that F/Sgt Campbell and crew found themselves fighting for their lives.

R5724 was passing over Viborg in central Jutland when flak set off a fire in the fuselage and blew all of the glass out of the cockpit and bomb-aimer's compartment. Two night-fighters, which had been stalking the Lancaster, chose this moment to close in for an attack and both gunners sustained wounds as they returned fire. The situation was resolved when the Lancaster stalled and plummeted to 4,000 feet, before F/Sgt Campbell and his second pilot, Sgt Gunnell, regained control and dived into cloud to successfully evade their assailants. Ahead lay a flight of some four hundred miles across the North Sea in extreme cold, blasted by the airflow in an aircraft devoid of Perspex and instruments and with two wounded crew members to make comfortable. Against the odds they reached Wittering near Peterborough, where they carried out a belly landing after eight hours and ten minutes aloft and each crew member received the immediate award of a DFM, while F/Sgt Campbell was further rewarded with an immediate commission. R5679 failed to return from the Sweetpea garden with the crew of Sgt Morrison, and it was established eventually that the Lancaster had crashed at 02.00 eleven miles south-west of Viborg, exploding on impact with fatal consequences for the occupants. Sadly, P/O Campbell and three members of his gallant crew would not survive to complete their tour and had just six weeks to live.

During the course of the month, the squadron carried out thirteen operations and dispatched ninety-nine sorties for the loss of nine Lancasters and seven crews.

October 1942

On the 1st, 106 Squadron completed its move from Coningsby to Syerston under the command of the soon to be famous W/C Guy Gibson, although his reputation within 5 Group was already waxing as he moulded his unit into one of the finest in 5 Group. The new month opened with a number of operations including a further attempt by 4 Group to hit the Flensburger-Schiffsbau Gesellschaft U-Boot construction yards at Flensburg, while elements of 3 and 5 Groups turned their attention upon other Baltic coast objectives at Lübeck and Wismar respectively. 5 Group detailed a force of seventy-eight Lancasters, eleven of them made ready by 61 Squadron, the crews of which learned at briefing that the plan called for three-quarters of the force to attack the town, with the main square as the aiming point, while the remainder targeted the Dornier aircraft factory. They took off between 17.45 and 18.25 with S/Ls Corr and Weston the senior pilots on duty, but as the latter cleared the runway the dinghy broke away from its stowage and fouled the tailplane, sending R5703 into a shallow dive, which terminated in a crash without survivors a mile north-east of Gunthorpe and four miles from Syerston.

The remainder climbed out safely at the start of what was a round-trip of some eleven hundred miles but lost the services of the crews of Sgt Meagher and Howarth to technical malfunctions and both jettisoned their loads in the North Sea. The others crossed Jutland seemingly without incident to arrive at the target area to encounter three to ten-tenths cloud with a base at between 1,500 and 7,000 feet. Poor visibility over the town was caused by heavy ground haze and an effective smoke screen, which combined with intense searchlight glare to blot out identifying features. Brief glimpses of the coastline provided a scant reference by which to establish position, and the 61 Squadron crews bombed the general town area on DR, the squadron scribe omitting further details from the record. Absent from debriefing was the crew of F/Sgt Dale RNZAF in R5759, which crashed at Sildemow, some three miles south of Rostock and only the bomb-aimer survived to fall into enemy hands. The unfavourable conditions led to the bombing of a number of locations along a 150-mile stretch of coastline from Wismar eastwards, and the entire undertaking proved to be a wasted effort at a cost of just two Lancasters.

The Ruhr city of Krefeld was posted as the target for a force of 188 aircraft on the 2nd, for which 5 Group contributed twenty-four Lancasters from Waddington, Coningsby and Syerston, while the rest of the group stood down. Located at the western edge of the Ruhr, a few miles to the south-west of Duisburg, Krefeld's industry had been based on silk and velvet textiles, but the presence of a Thyssen-Krupp steelworks was sufficient to attract the attention of Bomber Command. The force encountered dense industrial haze, which thwarted the Path Finders' best efforts to provide a reference for those following behind and most crews were reduced to bombing on estimated positions on DR and isolated Path Finder flares from 8,500 to 16,000 feet either side of 21.00. Returning crews reported some scattered fires, and local sources confirmed that three streets in the northern part of the city had sustained damage, but nothing commensurate with the size of the force and the effort expended.

All heavy groups were alerted on the 5th to an operation that night against the city of Aachen, for which a force of 257 aircraft was put together, 5 Group detailing sixty-nine Lancasters, seven of them from 61 Squadron. They departed Syerston between 19.00 and 19.40, each captained by a pilot of NCO rank and headed south on course for landfall on the French coast, passing through electrical storms and icing on the way. The stormy weather extended inland, which encouraged some of the force to descend for the rest of the journey to the target, Germany's most westerly city, nestling just inside the German borders with southern Holland and Belgium. On arrival in the target area flares were visible, but up to nine-tenths cloud at between 8,000 and 14,000 feet with haze below created poor visibility and challenging conditions. The 61 Squadron element arrived intact, mostly to search in vain for a reference on the ground and bombed the general built-up area from between 8,000 and 12,000 feet, few of them catching a glimpse of the ground, but some observed bursts and at least one large fire. Local sources reported that Aachen's southern district of Burtscheid had suffered quite extensive damage to housing and industry, and five large fires had required attention. Even so, they estimated the attack to have involved only around ten aircraft. Some bombs fell seventeen miles away onto the small Dutch town of Lutterade, and this would have minor consequences for the trials of the Oboe blind-bombing device in late December.

Osnabrück was posted as the target on the 6th, for which 237 aircraft were made ready, including fifty-nine Lancasters of 5 Group, 61 Squadron loading each of its eight aircraft with a cookie and twelve SBCs of incendiaries and dispatching them from Syerston between 19.10 and 19.55 with P/O Foster the senior pilot on duty. The Path Finders dropped flares over Makkum in Holland and the Dümmer See to the north-east of the target as route markers, and these proved to be very effective in guiding the main force in, although inevitably, some bomb loads were released early during the twenty-mile leg between the Dümmer See and the town. Four to eight-tenths cloud lay over the town at 8,000 feet and provided challenging conditions for accurate bombing, although opinions varied as to the quality of the visibility. The 61 Squadron scribe recorded scant detail but mentioned that Sgt Baker and crew ran in at 14,000 feet only to be forced down by flak to 10,000 feet and ultimately bombed from 7,000, believing that their bombs had overshot the aiming point. Returning crew described many fires and a glow visible by some from the Dutch coast homebound, and most had confidence in the effectiveness of the raid. According to local reports, 149 houses and six industrial buildings were destroyed, 530 houses seriously damaged and more than 2,700 others slightly damaged.

On the 7th, F/L Casement was posted to 5 Group HQ at the end of his tour, and the first of daily "Dixon" exercises was carried out in preparation for an as yet undisclosed operation to be conducted ten days hence. The weather conveniently precluded operational activity for 5 Group until the 12th, allowing squadrons to focus on the daylight formation flying that was going to be necessary.

5 Group notified its stations on the 12th that another shot at Wismar and the Dornier aircraft factory was to be launched that night, for which a force of fifty-nine Lancasters was assembled, ten of them provided by 61 Squadron and a dozen by 57 Squadron for its maiden Lancaster operation. They former departed Syerston between 17.29 and 17.56 with F/O Frow the senior pilot on duty, before setting course for the coast of Jutland and negotiating difficult weather conditions over the North Sea. This prevented many from establishing a pinpoint on their arrival at the enemy coast and forced them to navigate by DR, and it was at this point that F/O Frow and crew gave in to a troublesome port-outer engine and turned back with Jutland's western coast just ahead. Wismar lay under six to ten-tenths cloud in a band between 1,000 and 7,000 feet with extreme darkness adding to the challenges, and the lack of pinpoints forced some crews to search for up to thirty minutes before bombing on estimated positions, those representing 61 Squadron carrying out their attacks mostly on e.t.a. This inevitably led to a scattered and probably ineffective attack, despite which, some returning crews reported that the factory had been left burning furiously and the flames had remained visible for seventy miles into the homeward journey.

The naval and shipbuilding port of Kiel was posted as the target for a force of 288 aircraft that night, for which 5 Group weighed in with sixty-nine Lancasters, eight of them provided by 61 Squadron and loaded with a cookie and incendiaries. They departed Syerston between 18.35 and 19.15 with F/O Frow again the most senior pilot on duty and lost the services of W/O Lever and crew when their mid-upper turret malfunctioned, and they were followed home by Sgt Baker and crew, who had been some eighty miles short of the Jutland coast when the intercom connection to the rear turret was lost. The others reached the target area to find almost clear skies and good visibility and red and white flares marking out the Selenter Lake, some ten miles to the east. Illuminator flares were also deployed over the town to reveal a built-up area, which the 61 Squadron crews attacked from 10,000 to 18,000 feet at the end of timed runs, some observing the fall of their bombs close to the aiming point and others not. Probably 50% of crews were deceived by a decoy fire site, but the rest hit the town and caused an appropriate amount of damage. Returning crews reported a much-reduced searchlight and flak defence, and conscious that defensive measures attracted attention, this was a tactic employed occasionally and effectively by the Luftwaffe. It was believed initially that Sgt Game and crew had failed to return until news was received that W4233 had crashed at 01.30 into a hillside at Hagg House Moor in North Yorkshire and that the navigator and bomb-aimer had died at the scene. Sgt Game was seriously injured and lost his fight for life in hospital on the 15th.

A force of 289 aircraft was assembled on the 15th to send against Cologne, which had been left in peace for a considerable time, and the operation was supported by sixty-two Lancasters of 5 Group from Coningsby, Scampton, Syerston and Waddington. 61 Squadron made ready nine Lancasters and sent them on their way between 18.55 and 19.30 with S/L Corr the senior pilot on duty, setting a course for the Scheldt estuary and flying for a time through icing conditions. Some crews were eased off track by inaccurately forecast winds as they crossed northern Belgium, but the force arrived at the Rhineland capital to find it concealed beneath a layer of ten-tenths cloud. The Path Finder flares were scattered, and a large, effective decoy fire site combined with that to attract the main force crews away from the target. The 61 Squadron participants mostly caught a glimpse of the Rhine in the light of flares and carried out their attacks from 10,000 to 16,000 feet, some observing bursts and fires and others not. Few returning crews could offer any useful observations concerning the outcome, and it was left to local sources to mention that 224 houses had sustained slight damage from the single 4,000 pounder and three other high-explosive bombs and 210 incendiaries that had landed within the city, and this was out of a total of seventy-one 4,000 pounders, 231 other high explosive bombs and more than 68,000 incendiaries expended. It was a disappointment compounded by the loss to the Command of eighteen aircraft.

On the 17th, the purpose behind the "Dixon" formation-flying training that had been causing speculation for more than a week was revealed to crews in 5 Group briefing rooms. They learned that Operation Robinson was a daylight attack on the Schneider armaments works at Le Creusot, deep in eastern France, and the nearby Henri Paul transformer station at Montchanin, which provided its power. Often referred to as the French "Krupp", the company belonged to the Schneider family, which had donated the famous aviation trophy bearing its name. The Schneider Trophy was initially a prize to encourage technical advances in civil aviation but eventually became a speed contest for float and seaplanes competed for biannually by Britain, France, Italy and the USA. It was a massively prestigious and popular spectator event that drew crowds of up to 200,000 people and Britain claimed it outright after three consecutive wins culminating in 1931, when the revolutionary Supermarine S6B triumphed in the hands of the future first wartime commanding officer of 44 Squadron, W/C Boothman. Ninety-four Lancasters were to take part in the operation, which required an outward flight at low level by daylight, the attack at dusk, and a return under the cover of darkness. It was a bold plan to commit such a large force, which would be difficult to conceal, and it was only six months since the excessive losses from the Augsburg raid.

The plan called for eighty-eight aircraft to bomb the factory complex from as low as practicable, led by W/C Len Slee of 49 Squadron, while six others, two each from 106, 61 and 97 Squadrons went for the power station in a line-astern attack led by W/C Gibson. The 61 Squadron contribution of seven Lancasters departed Syerston between 12.00 and 12.05 with S/Ls Corr and Deas the senior pilots on duty and headed south to join up with the rest of the force over Upper Heyford, before setting course for Land's End at below 1,000 feet. Once over the sea, they were to aim for a point just south of the Ile d'Yeu to cross the French coast midway between St-Nazaire and La Rochelle at around 100 feet. Shortly before the sea crossing began, Coastal Command Whitleys carried out a sweep to force enemy U-Boots beneath the surface and prevent them from spotting the force and transmitting a warning. S/L Deas dropped out of the formation as they passed to the west of Brest after losing the port-outer engine and with it any chance of maintaining contact.

For most, the three-hundred-mile low-level dash across France would be relatively uneventful, but bird strikes became a constant threat, causing injury to a number of crewmen as they smashed Perspex, while others became ingested in engines. A pilot from 44 (Rhodesia) Squadron complained that the lead section was too low, which placed upon him an exhausting physical strain as he wrestled with slipstream turbulence, and others commented on bunching-up and occasional congestion, but there was also praise for 49 Squadron's leadership during the outward flight. Despite the challenges, this middle leg terminated successfully at the predetermined point some forty-five miles from the target, and it was at this juncture that the main force broke up to form into a fan and climb to a bombing height of between 4,500 and 7,000 feet. The target was reached at dusk under clear skies and in good visibility, and crews were able to follow a railway line directly to the heart of the factory complex, where the 61 Squadron crews bombed as briefed from between 5,000 and 7,000 feet. Some observed the fall of their bombs and commented on blue flashes as bombs hit the central power station on the south-eastern corner of the site, while others described explosions and smoke rising through 3,000 feet that eventually obscured the entire target area. S/L Burnett of 44 (Rhodesia) Squadron claimed that it was the most successful of the many operations that he had participated in. At Monchanin F/O Frow and crew attacked from 800 feet, but S/L Corr DFC and crew went in so low that W4774 flew into buildings inside the complex and crashed, killing all but the mid-upper gunner, who survived in enemy hands. All other aircraft returned safely home after a round-trip of ten hours, and at debriefing on all stations it was unanimously believed that the target had been utterly devastated. The apparent success prompted a message from the A-O-C 5 Group, AVM Coryton, who added to his own congratulations with similar sentiments from the Secretary of State for Air, Sir Archibald Sinclair and W/C Slee's leadership was rewarded with a DSO. Unfortunately, it would be discovered later that the damage had been less severe than first thought, and production had soon returned to normal. Another raid would be mounted against the plant eight months hence.

A new campaign, against Italian cities in support of land operations in North Africa under Operation Torch began on the night of the 22/23rd against the port-city of Genoa and the naval dockyard, where part of the Italian fleet was sheltering. It was the eve of the opening of the Battle of El Alamein, which, after twelve days' fighting, would see Montgomery push Rommel's forces all the way back to Tunisia and out of the war. Ten 5 Group squadrons mustered between them 101 Lancasters, while 83 Squadron of the Path Finders contributed eleven more to take care of target marking. 61 Squadron made ready nine Lancasters and sent them on their way from Syerston between 17.55 and 18.25 with W/C Coad and S/L Deas the senior pilots on duty and set course for the French coast. P/O Foster and crew were about to make landfall over what on D-Day would be the American landing grounds, Utah and Omaha, when both gunners reported that their guns had malfunctioned and that there was no point in pressing on. S/L Deas struggled all the way to maintain speed and altitude, and five minutes after the time that he and his crew should have arrived at the target they were still 180 miles short, at which point the bombs were jettisoned in the Alps region and the sortie terminated. Sgt Howarth and crew were forty-five minutes behind schedule after crossing the Alps and opted to follow the River Po to bomb the eastern part of Turin from 14,000 feet. The others had all passed south-west of Paris on the way to the wall of rock that was the Alps, which glistened under clear skies and an almost full moon.

Crews found the clear air and perfect visibility over Italy, a joy to behold after contending with the industrial haze at German targets and the Path Finder flares could be seen by approaching main force crews from sixty miles away. On arrival over the city, they found the flak defence to be wildly inaccurate, while a smoke screen proved ineffective as the wind blew it straight out to sea and they were able to establish their positions visually on the layout of the docks and the city. The 61 Squadron crews carried out their attacks from between 9,500 and 12,300 feet and observed many bursts, explosions and fires, which prompted some returning crews on other stations to describe the raid as a "miniature-Cologne". Local sources confirmed heavy damage in central and eastern districts, which, because of the need for fuel over bombs, had been achieved with just 180 tons of high-explosives and incendiaries, and remarkably, without loss.

Milan would host two raids on the 24th, the first in daylight by 5 Group, and while that was in progress, back home, seventy-one aircraft were being made ready by 1, 3 and 4 Groups and the Path Finders for a night attack. The city was home to many war factories, including the Isotta Fraschini luxury car works, which had been converted to military vehicle and aero engine manufacture, the Pirelli rubber works, Alfa Romeo, the Caproni aircraft plant, the Breda locomotive, armaments and aircraft works and the Innocenti machinery and vehicle factory. Eighty-eight 5 Group crews attended briefings on the morning of the 24th to learn that they would be undertaking the first daylight crossing of the Alps on their way to the target, and they would be required to spend an even longer flight over fighter-defended territory than during the Le Creusot operation a week earlier. That said, the meteorological bods assured them that cloud would protect them for most of the way across enemy territory, and this was in the minds of the nine 61 Squadron participants as they departed Syerston between 12.15 and 12.30 with S/L Deas the senior pilot on duty. The squadrons formed into a bomber stream as they headed for Selsey Bill to begin the Channel crossing at very low level under a Spitfire escort. Sgt Baker and crew were about to make landfall on the Normandy coast at Ouistreham when a number of instruments failed, and without them it was futile to press on. The meteorological briefing had included an expectation of cloud from a warm front awaiting them at the Normandy coast, however, to their discomfort, they saw that it had formed further inland, and they had to run the gauntlet of anti-aircraft fire as they raced over the clifftops with three hours to go to the Alps. A bank of cloud could be seen in the distance, to which the force climbed as rapidly as possible, and once reached, the crews had to plot their own individual course until rendezvousing over Lake Annecy, sixty miles short of the target. From there they formed a loose formation and lost height, until reaching the target to find eight to nine-tenths cloud with a base at 3,000 feet but sufficient gaps through which to establish their positions visually.

The marshalling yards, a seaplane base and an aerodrome were among ground features identified as the 61 Squadron crews delivered their high-explosive and incendiary payloads from between 4,500 and 10,000 feet, those at the lower altitudes having come beneath the cloud base to secure a better view of the ground. Knowing that a safe minimum height to escape the blast of a cookie was 4,000 feet, these crews demonstrated a disregard for their safety, and some even descended to a few hundred feet above the rooftops in order to strafe factories and other targets of opportunity. The sun was setting ahead of them as they crossed the Alps homebound, and France passed beneath them unseen in darkness, with enemy night-fighters waiting over the coastal region as the returning bombers passed through. At debriefings, crews were enthusiastic about the effectiveness of the raid, from which three Lancasters had failed to return, each of them shot down into the Channel on the way home. Post-raid reconnaissance revealed that the 135 tons of bombs had caused extensive damage to housing, public buildings and a number of war-industry factories, including the Caproni aircraft works, and had also seriously affected railway communications between Italy and Germany. Local reports confirmed a figure of 441 houses destroyed or seriously damaged along with nine public buildings.

Arriving at Syerston w.e.f 27th to begin a first tour was the crew of P/O Robert Norman George "Norm" Barlow RAAF, who in the coming March would find themselves posted as a founder member to Squadron X, shortly to be given the number 617. During the course of the month the squadron took part in nine operations and dispatched seventy-eight sorties for the loss of three Lancasters, two complete crews and three members of another.

It was at some time during October that 61 Squadron was selected to carry out operational trials on the Hercules-powered Mk II Lancasters, which were being built in Armstrong Whitworth factories in the Coventry area, and a C Flight was created for the purpose. An initial complement of six aircraft in the serial number range from DS603-610 was taken on charge, with a view to employing them on operations beginning in January.

November 1942

There would be no operations for the majority of the Command during the first week of the new month, largely as a result of the weather, and 5 Group crews were put on stand-by three times, only to be stood-down as the operations were cancelled. The first major operation to take place was a 5 and 8 Group effort against Genoa on the 6th, for which 5 Group detailed a main force of fifty-seven Lancasters, while fifteen belonging to 83 Squadron at Wyton were prepared for target-marking duties. The five-strong 61 Squadron element departed Syerston between 21.35 and 21.45 P/Os Campbell and Foster the commissioned pilots on duty only to lose the services of the former to an engine issue immediately after take-off. The others reached the target after an uneventful outward flight of four hours in favourable weather conditions, and were greeted by conditions affording excellent visibility, which together with accurately planted Path Finder flares enabled them to locate the aiming point visually after identifying ground features like the breakwater, harbour and town. They carried out their attacks from between 8,500 and 12,000 feet, observing that fires of increasing intensity were concentrated in the docks area and a number of ships appeared to be burning in the harbour. A pilot from another squadron counted a total of 116 fires across the city, while those arriving at the tail end of the raid found its effectiveness laid out before them and described a colossal fire on a hill near the city centre. The glow from the burning city remained visible from the Alps and Nice, some eighty miles away, but no local report emerged to reveal the full extent of the damage.

A follow-up raid on Genoa was posted on 3, 4 and 5 Group stations on the 7th and a force of 175 aircraft assembled, which included Halifaxes, Stirlings and a handful of Wellingtons to join eighty-one Lancasters of 5 Group. The six 61 Squadron participants departed Syerston between 17.31 and 17.41 with S/L Deas the senior pilot on duty and adopted the usual route across France without incident, until reaching the Dijon region with the foothills of the Alps beyond. At this point it became necessary to climb and pass through a patch of extreme icing conditions, after which they experienced the same ideal conditions as on the previous night, particularly on the far side of the Alps. It proved possible to make a visual identification of the coastline, harbour and aiming point in the light of the punctual and accurately delivered Path Finder flares and a smoke screen failed to provide the city with protection. The flak defence seemed to give up once the bombing began, although light flak from rooftops continued to fire, even if inaccurately as the 61 Squadron crews bombed from between 10,500 and 13,000 feet. At debriefings crews reported bombs exploding in the built-up area and causing numerous fires, and the many aiming point photographs added to those from reconnaissance flights, confirmed the operation to have been highly successful.

The campaigns against Italy and Germany would have to run side-by-side for the time being, and in a break from Italy, Hamburg was posted as the target on the 9th. No mention was made by the "met boys" during briefing of strong winds and ice-bearing cloud of the type that often lay in wait across the bombers' path to Germany's second city. The four heavy groups put together a force of 213 aircraft, of which, sixty-seven Lancasters were provided by 5 Group, just three of them belonging to 61 Squadron. Each received a standard city-busting bomb load of a cookie and incendiaries before departing Syerston between 17.40 and 17.55 bearing aloft the crews of F/Sgts Bird and Cockcroft and Sgt Howarth. They crossed the Lincolnshire coast on course for a point on the German coast to the north of the target and soon encountered the troublesome weather front of towering cumulonimbus cloud. It may have been at this point that Sgt Howarth and crew lost their intercom and oxygen systems and turned back, leaving the remaining two crews to negotiate the conditions and reach the target area, which they found to be completely hidden by ten-tenths cloud with tops at 16,000 feet. They flew past Hamburg and came upon the Ratzeburg Lake to the north-east of the city, employing it as the start of a timed run before bombing from 12.000 and 12,500 feet, largely on the evidence of the heavy naval flak shells detonating above the bombing height. It was impossible to assess what was happening beneath the cloud and a strong wind from the north almost certainly pushed the bombing south of the intended aiming point, a fact seemingly confirmed by local reports, that many bombs had fallen into the River Elbe or into open country, and only three large fires had required attention. Five of the fifteen failures to return were from 5 Group.

Mining operations occupied the ensuing two nights, 5 Group detailing a dozen Lancasters on the 10th to send that night to the Biscay coast to the Deodar, Elderberry and Furze gardens, located respectively in the Gironde estuary, off Bayonne further south and a dozen miles further south still at St-Jean-de-Luz, right down on the border between France and Spain. The destination for 61 Squadron's P/O Campbell DFM and crew, four of whom also wore the ribbon of the DFM, was the mouth of the Adour River, which lay within the Elderberry garden, for which they departed Syerston at 17.30 with a four-hour outward flight ahead of them. It is believed that they fulfilled their brief, but on return, while attempting to land at Exeter in extremely poor visibility, W4244 crashed at Dimonds Farm at Honiton killing all on board. It will be recalled that on the night of the 24/25th of September, the then F/Sgt Campbell and his crew had survived a four-hundred-mile return flight across the North Sea in a Lancaster devoid of Perspex and instruments and with two wounded crew members to make comfortable.

Orders were received at a number of 5 Group stations on the 13th to prepare for a 5 Group operation against Genoa that night involving sixty-one Lancasters, supported by a Path Finder element comprising six Lancasters of 83 Squadron and nine Stirlings of 7 Squadron at Oakington. Nineteen of the 5 Group element were to attack the Ansaldo engineering works, the Italian "Krupp", while the remainder had their own aiming point in the town. The nine-strong 61 Squadron element departed Syerston between 17.35 and 18.05 with the recently-arrived F/L Burns the senior pilot on duty and set course for Selsey Bill for the Channel crossing. Twenty-nine-year-old Kenneth Burns was a native of Portland, Oregon, and had been commissioned in the RAF in 1937 before spending the war to date as an instructor in Australia. After returning to the UK in 1942 he was posted to 19 O.T.U., where he picked up a crew, before joining 61 Squadron and undertaking this, their first operational sortie. They negotiated France without incident and traversed the Alps in good weather conditions that allowed the target to be identified visually from cloudless skies. The bombing by the 61 Squadron crews was carried out from between 6,800 and 11,000 feet in the face of a "beefed-up" searchlight and flak defence, and high explosive and incendiary bursts were observed right across the target area. Those that could be plotted were found to be at least a thousand yards from the aiming point, but there was no attempt to assess the outcome through reconnaissance. Some returning crews reported the glow of fires to be visible for 130 miles into the return flight, and confidence was high that the loss-free raid had been successful.

Two days later, a force of seventy-eight aircraft was made ready to continue the assault on Genoa, and twenty-one of twenty-seven Lancasters were provided by 5 Group in the absence of a contribution from 61 Squadron. The ten-tenths cloud to the south of the Alps stopped just short of the target to provide clear skies and moonlight, which the Path Finders exploited to illuminate the aiming point, allowing it to be identified visually for a force largely untroubled by the defences. Most of the bombing fell close to the aiming point and six large fires were counted in the built-up area, the glow from which remained visible on the horizon for up to a hundred miles into the return journey.

Mining operations off the Biscay coast, the Frisians and in the Baltic occupied sixty-five aircraft on the 16th, and involved the 61 Squadron crew of Sgt Dashper, who departed Syerston at 17.05 bound for the Silverthorn IV garden to the south of Anholt Island in the Kattegat. In favourable conditions they pinpointed on Anholt and planted their vegetables according to brief from 2,000 feet, before returning home after a round trip of seven hours and ten minutes. It was similar fare on the following night for the crews of F/Sgts Bird, Cockshott and Ferguson, only at a more distant Privet garden in the Bay of Danzig, for which they departed Syerston between 16.55 and 17.10. The Cockshott crew returned within three hours having sighted a distress signal, presumably in the North Sea, but no further details were recorded. The others reached the target area, where the Ferguson crew conducted a timed run of four-and-a-half minutes, before planting their vegetables from 700 feet, while the Bird crew released their mines, also in the briefed location, from 1,600 feet.

Attention turned upon the northern powerhouse of Turin on the 18th, which was home to Fiat's Lingotto and Mirafiori car plants, the Lancia motor works, the Arsenale army munitions factory, the Nebioli foundry, the R I V machine-gun factory and plants belonging to the American Westinghouse company. The force of seventy-seven aircraft made ready to attack the Fiat motor works had originally been significantly larger, but forty-two 5 Group Lancasters had been withdrawn because of doubts about the weather over their stations. The 61 Squadron element of eight departed Syerston between 18.20 and 18.40 with F/L Burns the senior pilot on duty and all arrived at the target some three-and-at-half hours later to find clear skies that left the city naked to the eyes of the bomb-aimers, who benefitted from another excellent performance by the Path Finders. The aiming point was squarely in their bomb-sights as the main force element ran in, the 61 Squadron crews at heights between 10,000 and 12,500 feet, and many fires were reported to have broken out in the city centre, the Fiat works sustaining an unspecified degree of damage, which was confirmed by bombing photographs.

Following the recent run of relatively small-scale operations to Italy, the 20th brought a return to the Fiat works at Turin with greater numbers, amounting this time to 232 aircraft, of which seventy-eight Lancasters were provided by 5 Group. 61 Squadron made ready eight of its own and dispatched them from Syerston between 18.05 and 18.40 with three pilots of pilot officer rank leading the way. It would take almost four hours to reach the target, which became academic for Sgt Howarth and crew when their rear turret was found to be unserviceable and forced them to turn back, leaving the rest to negotiate the seven-hundred-mile outward leg without incident. Those arriving at the front end of the attack were able to establish their position by following the autostrada and identifying ground features in the light of flares, and by the time that the majority of the Syerston crews reached the city, smoke was already drifting across it and ground features appeared only fleetingly, which created challenging conditions for target identification. Ground haze added to the difficulties, but even so, by running in at low to medium level, some crews were able to identify the factory visually and deliver the bombs with some degree of accuracy. The 61 Squadron participants attacked from between 9,000 and 12,000 feet and left behind them massive fires raging in the city centre, from which smoke was already rising through 6,000 feet. Returning crews were confident in the effectiveness of their work and a death toll of 117 would provide evidence of a damaging attack.

Sixty-four 5 Group crews attended briefings on the 22nd to learn that their destination that night was the southern industrial city of Stuttgart, home in particular to the motor, electronics and chemicals industries, for which a force of 222 aircraft was assembled. 61 Squadron made ready eight Lancasters, which departed Syerston between 18.25 and 18.47 with F/L Burns the senior pilot on duty, before flying out over Dungeness on the Kent coast and making landfall at Cayeux. P/O Foster and crew dropped out during the sea crossing because of a defective rear turret, while the remainder pressed on to the next pinpoint at Châtillon-sur-Seine, from where the bomber stream turned east to cross the German frontier near Strasbourg on course for Stuttgart, which, located in a series of valleys, was always a difficult city to identify. However, after an outward flight of three hours and fifteen minutes the first of the main force crews had Path Finder flares in their sights, illuminating the target area to apparently enable a visual identification of the aiming point. The bombs were dropped by the 61 Squadron crews from between 10,000 and 13,000 feet and their bursts observed, and on the way home at low level from what was described as a quiet trip, F/L Burns and crew strafed a freight train. A post-raid analysis discovered that a thin layer of cloud and ground haze had prevented the Path Finders from identifying the centre of the city, and that much of the bombing had fallen onto south-western and southern districts and outlying communities up to five miles from the city centre. Local sources confirmed that a modest eighty-eight houses had been destroyed and more than three hundred seriously damaged and reported two bombers attacking the city centre at low-level and causing extensive damage to the main railway station.

On the 23rd 5 Group detailed nine Lancasters for mining duties off the south-western reaches of the Biscay coast in the Deodar, Elderberry and Furze gardens. The 61 Squadron crews of P/Os Barlow and Lind and Sgt Champion departed Syerston between 17.45 and 18.00 bound for the Furze garden situated off St-Jean-de-Luz and pinpointed on Le Socoa and San Sebastian before planting their vegetables according to brief from 1,600 feet and below. Aircraft actually became airborne for operations on the 26th and 27th, only to be recalled immediately on receipt of cancellation orders.

Instructions came through to all heavy groups on the 28th to prepare its aircraft and crews for operations that night against Turin, and during the course of the day a force of 228 aircraft was assembled, ninety-one of the Lancasters on 5 Group stations. *(1 Group was in the process of converting from Wellingtons to Lancasters, and 101, 103 and 460 Squadrons had begun to operate the type in the past week).* 61 Squadron made ready nine aircraft, their bomb bays containing either a cookie and SBCs of incendiaries or all-incendiary loads and launched them from Syerston between 18.25 and 18.55 with F/L Burns the senior pilot on duty. The crews of P/O Lind and F/Sgt Bird turned back after around ninety minutes because of engine issues, leaving the others to continue on across France without incident to reach the target area under clear skies and just a little haze to mar the vertical visibility. Despite this, they were able to establish their positions by visual reference of the River Po assisted by Path Finder flares and the 61 Squadron crews bombed their briefed aiming point of the city centre from between 5,500 and 8,000 feet, observing bursts in the town and on the Fiat works under attack by other elements. One returning crew counted forty-seven fires when they were fifteen minutes into the homeward journey and others confirmed that the city was a mass of flames, commenting on a particularly large blaze in the centre and some others around the Royal Arsenal. W/C Gibson and F/L Whamond of 106 Squadron dropped the first two 8,000lb blockbusters to fall on Italy, and all indications were that the operation had been entirely successful.

During the course of the month, the squadron undertook a dozen operations and dispatched sixty-four sorties for the loss of a single Lancaster and crew.

December 1942

The weather at the start of the new month restricted operations, and an unsuccessful raid on Frankfurt involving 112 aircraft on the 2nd did not include a contribution from 5 Group. Squadrons were warned of operations daily between the 2nd and 5th, but each was cancelled, and it was the 6th before a bombing operation involving 5 Group actually took place, by which time S/L Ed Parker GC, DFC had arrived from 1654 Conversion Unit as a flight commander elect having served earlier in the war as a Hampden pilot with 49 Squadron. On the 6th, Mannheim was revealed as the target for seventy-four 5 Group Lancasters in an overall force of 272 aircraft, 61 Squadron contributing a dozen of its own, which departed Syerston between 17.05 and 17.55 with F/L Burns the senior pilot on duty. F/Sgt Cockshott and crew were back home within two hours after the failure of their port-inner engine, while the others reached the target to encounter eight to ten-tenths cloud at between 4,000 and 12,000 feet. This rendered ineffective the Path Finders' efforts to mark the city with flares and a decoy site was also operating some twenty miles to the south, which, inevitably, attracted a proportion of the bombing. Crews bombed only on DR and e.t.a., in the case of the 61 Squadron element from between 5,500 to 11,000 feet, F/L Burns and crew dropping below the cloud base at 3,500 to establish their position and then climbing back into the white stuff to bomb from 5,500 feet, aiming at the flashes from searchlight and flak batteries. On return, R5859 was written off in a crash-landing at 00.10 at Hopton Farm near Bodney aerodrome in Norfolk after clipping trees, but F/Sgt MacFarland and crew apparently walked away unscathed. At debriefings it became clear that most had no clue as to the fall of their bombs, but those venturing low enough to see the Rhine and built-up area observed scattered fires and at least one blazing factory complex.

On the following night, while 61 Squadron remained inactive, 5 Group called for nine crews to carry out gardening duties in the Elderberry and Furze gardens off the south-western coast of France.

Notification was received on 5 Group stations on the 8th that Turin was to be the target for that night, in an operation to be conducted by a 5 Group main force of ninety-eight Lancasters, supported by thirty-five Path Finder aircraft of all types. During bombing-up at Syerston, incendiaries fell out of the bomb bay of 61 Squadron's R5864 and ignited, an event witnessed from the control tower by the station commander, G/C "Gus" Walker, and the 106 Squadron commanding officer, W/C Guy Gibson. Walker, a man of short stature but giant character and former commanding officer of 50 Squadron, jumped into his car and raced across the airfield to warn everyone to get clear, and then ran towards the aircraft, hoping to be able to rake the burning incendiaries from underneath and prevent the detonation of the cookie. Sadly, it went off when he was yards away, and a piece of shrapnel took off his right arm below the elbow, despite which the irrepressible Walker insisted that medical personnel attend to others first. Following recovery from his injuries, he resumed his illustrious career, becoming a station and base commander in 4 Group, where he remained as one of the Command's legendary characters throughout the war.

The preparations for the night's operation continued and the 61 Squadron element of twelve Lancasters departed Syerston between 17.05 and 17.45 with W/C Coad the senior pilot on duty. Sgt Walters and crew lost their port-inner engine during the climb-out and headed directly to the jettison area off the Lincolnshire coast, while Sgt Dashper and crew turned back from the French coast because of issues with the mid-upper and rear turrets. The remainder all reached the eastern side of the Alps to find clear skies and good visibility, and the city visible to the south as they approached the final turning point. Swinging towards the start of their bombing run, over to port to the east of the city a large bend in the River Po provided a strong reference, which enabled the Path Finders to identify the aiming point and deliver their flares right on the mark. The 61 Squadron crews followed in their wake and registered that the aiming point was well-defined by two arcs of Path Finder flares and one massive explosion a mile-and-a-half to the south-west. The bombing was carried out from between 6,500 and 12,000 feet, and the city could be seen to be well-alight. Those arriving when the attack was already well underway reported smoke drifting across the aiming point and counted thirty to forty sizeable fires burning across the city. A huge pall of smoke was rising through 8,000 feet as the force retreated towards the Alps, and the fires would still be burning when the next bomber force arrived twenty-four hours later.

Orders came through on the 9th to prepare for another assault on Turin that night, and a dozen 61 Squadron crews attended the briefing at Syerston to learn that they would be part of a 5 Group effort of eighty-two Lancasters in an overall force of 227 aircraft. The briefed aiming point for the Syerston elements was the main railway station, for which those from 61 Squadron took off between 17.08 and 18.04 with F/L Burns the senior pilot on duty. They enjoyed an uneventful outward flight and were guided the final few miles to the target by the fires still burning from the previous night, which proved to be a double-edged sword as the smoke hanging over the city created challenging conditions for the Path Finders. They were unable to deliver as strong a performance this time and the raid was spread out over more than thirty minutes, during which the 61 Squadron crews attacked from between 6,000 and 10,000 feet. They contributed to the creation of many more fires that produced even larger volumes of smoke to obscure much of the ground from those arriving at the tail end of proceedings, and returning crews reported explosions and fires and a consensus of a less effective raid than that of the previous night. After bombing from 6,000 feet, F/L Burns carried out a reconnaissance run at 500 feet to ascertain that his incendiaries had fallen into a fire-gutted area between the cathedral and the railway station. On the way home, Sgt Howarth and crew were attacked by a BF109, and during the ensuing exchange of fire, rear gunner, Sgt Moore, with only two of his four Brownings serviceable, hit the enemy and watched it fall away in flames to crash. At 02.35, W4168 overshot the landing at Swinderby in the hands of Sgt Goodwin and crew and was written off without crew casualties.

For the third night in succession the torment of Turin continued, although at the hands of a reduced force of eighty-two aircraft drawn from 1 and 4 Groups and the Path Finders. They had to fight their way through severe icing conditions over France, and more than half of the force turned back before reaching the Alps. Those completing their sorties failed to inflict more than the slightest damage on the city, in what proved to be the final raid of this first Italian campaign. Sixty-eight aircraft were sent mining on the night of the 14/15th, but the twenty-three 5 Group Lancasters, including six from 61 Squadron assigned to the Nectarine II garden, were recalled after an hour because of concerns about the weather for their return.

The weather curtailed 5 Group operations from the 10th to the 16th inclusive and on the 17th, twenty-seven Lancasters were detailed to target eight small German towns for what was referred to in the 5 Group ORB as "Batter", against Soltau, some forty miles east of Bremen, and Neustadt-am-Rübenberge and Nienburg, located between Bremen to the north-west and Hannover to the south-east. A further ten Lancasters were assigned to "moling" sorties over five other towns in north-western Germany including, Cloppenburg, Diepholz and Quakenbrück, and one wonders if, in the cold light of dawn, anyone in raid planning recalled the disaster that had afflicted 57 and 214 Squadrons of 3 Group as a result of similar operations on the first night of April. Nine Lancasters failed to return, three belonging to 44 (Rhodesia) Squadron and two each to 9, 50 and 97 Squadrons. While the above was in progress, the 61 Squadron crews of F/O Foster and Sgts Elliott and Meagher departed Syerston between 16.33 and 16.35 bound for the Sweetpea garden in the Cadet Channel in the Bay of Mecklenburg. Battling severe icing conditions and unable to break cloud in the target area, all abandoned their sorties and brought their mines home.

Apart from isolated "moling" daylight operations, the Ruhr had been left in peace since Krefeld at the start of October, while attention had been focused on Italian targets. Now, on the 20th, Duisburg was posted as the target, and this would mask another operation of great significance for the Command that was taking place at the same time over Holland. Although, in the event, not all would proceed according to plan, it would be a mere blip in the development of the Oboe blind-bombing device. 61 Squadron's nine Lancasters each received a bomb load of a cookie and SBCs of incendiaries as part of the seventy-five-strong 5 Group contingent in an overall force of 232 aircraft assembled for the main event, and they departed Syerston between 17.35 and 18.15 with F/L Burns the senior pilot on duty. Some may have witnessed a tragic collision between two Waddington Lancasters over Lincoln, which resulted in the deaths of all fourteen occupants. It was not a night to remember for 61 Squadron as serviceability issues afflicted five aircraft and between 19.39 and 20.53 the crews of P/O Lind, F/O Foster, Sgt Walters, P/O Gillett and Sgt Champion returned in that order, none having progressed beyond the Dutch coast. The rest of the bomber stream had made landfall on the Den Helder peninsula, pinpointing first on Enkhuizen, before turning to the south-east for the run on the target. Favourable weather conditions prevailed in the target area, where bright moonlight provided the good visibility that enabled crews to identify the River Rhine and the Ruhrort docks complex through the industrial haze. Having established a firm visual reference, bombing was carried out by the four remaining 61 Squadron crews from between 10,500 and 14,500 feet, and at least fifteen fires were observed, many of them large.

Meanwhile, six 109 Squadron Oboe-equipped Mosquitos had targeted a power station at Lutterade in Holland, believing the target to be free of bomb craters so as not to impair the data gleaned from a calibration test to gauge the device's margin of error. Unfortunately, three of the Mosquitos suffered Oboe failure and went on to bomb Duisburg instead, leaving W/C Hal Bufton and two other crews to deliver the bombs. What they hadn't bargained for was a whole carpet of bomb craters left over from the attack on Aachen, seventeen miles away, in October, and it proved impossible to identify those aimed by Oboe. The calibration tests would continue, however, and come the spring, Oboe would be ready to unleash with devastating results against the Ruhr.

The 21st brought instructions to 1 and 5 Groups and the Path Finders to prepare a force of 137 aircraft for an operation that night against Munich, the Bavarian capital city located in the foothills of the Alps deep in southern Germany. As already mentioned, a few 1 Group squadrons had begun to receive Lancasters during the autumn, and would contribute in small numbers, but eighty-two of the 119 of the type made available for this operation were provided by 5 Group and some others by the 83 Squadron of the Path Finders. 61 Squadron briefed ten crews, who were in their aircraft and competing with their 106 Squadron counterparts for a place in the snake making its ungainly way to the runway threshold. They took off between 17.15 and 17.50 with the squadron navigation officer, F/L Giles, flying as captain in the crew of Sgt Oldham, who were operating together for the first time. The crews of P/Os Dierkes RCAF and Gillett returned early with communications problems, the former in R5699 crashing short of the runway at 20.30 after being hit by a severe down-draft, fortunately without serious consequences for the crew. The bomber stream, meanwhile, made its way across France to enter Germany north of Strasbourg with Munich 180 miles away a little to the south of due east. After a three-and-a-half-hour outward journey, crews arrived in the target area to find it concealed beneath ten-tenths cloud with tops at a lowly 2,000 feet. The Path Finders illuminated the Ammersee to the south-west of the city, and crews carried out a time-and-distance run from there to the aiming point, those representing 61 Squadron bombing from between 10,000 and 15,000 feet. There were plenty of flashes below the cloud, together with the glow of fires to convince the crews that they had found the mark, but it is likely that these came from a decoy site, as most bombing photos would reveal open country. Twelve aircraft failed to return, six of them belonging to 5 Group, but all from 61 Squadron made it back from what turned out to be their final operational activity of the year.

The fourth wartime Christmas was celebrated in traditional style across the Command, and operational activity ceased until the 29th, when fourteen 5 Group Lancasters were sent mining off France's Biscay coast. On New Year's Eve, eight Lancasters and two Mosquitos of the Path Finder Force carried out the first live trial of Oboe at Düsseldorf. During the course of the month, the squadron took part in seven operations and dispatched sixty-four sorties for the loss of three Lancasters in crashes at home, but no crew casualties.

As the New Year beckoned, a great responsibility lay on the nine operational Lancaster squadrons of 5 Group to carry the war to the enemy. There was no question that the Stirling and Mk II and V Halifaxes were inferior aircraft, and their limited availability and restricted bomb-carrying capacity meant that the Command still had to rely very much on the trusty but aging Wellington to make up the numbers if the defences were to be overwhelmed. That said, the advent of Oboe and the yet-to-be-introduced ground-mapping radar, H2S, would greatly enhance the Command's ability to deliver a telling blow, and 1943 would see the balance of power shift massively in the Command's favour.

January 1943

The year began with the official formation on New Year's Day of the Canadian 6 Group, and the handing over to it of the former 4 Group stations in North Yorkshire on which its squadrons had been lodging. Eventually, all Canadian squadrons would find a home in the group, which was financed by Canada and controlled by Harris, but initially, there were eight founder members, including 408 (Goose) and 420 (Snowy Owl) Squadrons, which had left 5 Group during the autumn. Further south, a continuation of the Oboe trials would occupy the first two weeks, during which 109 Squadron marked for small forces of 1 and 5 Group Lancasters at Essen on seven occasions and Duisburg once. For the first time, the cloud cover and ever-present blanket of industrial haze would have no bearing on the outcome of the raid as reliance on e.t.a., DR and Gee was cast aside in favour of Oboe, at least, that is, at targets within the device's range. Until the advent of mobile transmitter stations late in the war, Oboe would be restricted by the curvature of the earth and the altitude at which Mosquitos could fly, but this meant that the entire Ruhr lay within range of Harris's bombers. That said, the success of a raid would still rely on the ability of the Path Finders to back up the initial Oboe markers and maintain a supply of target indicators (TIs) on the aiming point.

Having spent the entire war to date at Scampton, 49 Squadron took up residence at Fiskerton on the 2nd, leaving 57 Squadron alone and awaiting the arrival of another unit to occupy the spare accommodation. The Oboe trials programme got under way on the night of the 3/4th, when three Oboe Mosquitos were to provide the marking for nineteen Lancasters, of which ten were made ready at Syerston, their crews briefed to attack the Krupp complex in the Borbeck segment. The five-strong 61 Squadron element took off between 17.15 and 17.20 with F/L Burns the senior pilot on duty and lost the services of P/O Barlow and crew to the failure of the rear gunner's heated flying suit, while Sgt Cockshott and crew turned back because of an engine issue that restricted their ability to climb to operational altitude. The others arrived over the target two hours twenty-five minutes later, in conditions of little cloud and good visibility and watched the Mosquito-delivered parachute marker flares ignite over the target as they fell. The bomb-aimers in the crews of F/L Burns and Sgt Meagher aimed their bombs at them from 20,000 and 21,000 feet respectively, and although unable to plot their fall, observed a number of fires develop. Returning crews commented on the abundance of searchlights and some flak, but unable to add their own testimony was the crew of F/Sgt Bird, whose remains were found in the wreckage of W4769 near Middenmeer on the eastern side of the Den Helder peninsula, where the Lancaster had crashed at 21.00. This total loss of life was the start of a trend, and it would be June before the first crewman survived from one of the squadron's missing aircraft. Post-raid reconnaissance revealed that the centre of the city rather than the Krupp-dominated Borbeck districts had sustained some damage, which had not happened too frequently in the past, and this suggested that Oboe might perhaps, indeed, provide the answer to hitting Ruhr targets.

1 Group provided the main force Lancaster element for the second Essen raid twenty-four hours later, but Syerston was called into action to support the third on the night of the 7/8th, with five 61 Squadron Lancasters and one representing 106 Squadron. The crews of F/Ls Barlow, Burns and Lind, F/Sgt Cockshott and Sgt Champion took off between 03.05 and 03.35 and lost the services of F/L Barlow and crew after the rear gunner suffered from oxygen starvation. The others encountered ten-tenths cloud with tops at 12,000 feet but identified the target by Path Finder flares and delivered their cookie and ten SBCs each from between 19,500 feet and 22,000 feet shortly after 06.00 in the face of heavy opposition. The attack was less effective than the previous two and only incendiaries were recorded by local authorities, who reported nine buildings destroyed and more than thirty seriously damaged.

The 8th was a momentous day for the Path Finder Force, which was awarded group status as 8 Group, and the 3 Group stations at Wyton, Graveley, Oakington and Warboys, upon which its squadrons had been lodging since mid-August, were duly transferred over. 61 Squadron called the crew of Sgt Dashper to briefing during the afternoon of the 8th and told them that they were to represent the squadron for the next Oboe raid against Duisburg, which involved three Mosquitos marking for a 5 Group main force of thirty-eight Lancasters. They departed Syerston at 16.55 among six others belonging to 106 Squadron and returned two hours and twenty minutes later on three engines having jettisoned their bomb load in the North Sea. It became a bad night generally for Syerston, when four of the 106 Squadron element also turned back, and this from the squadron with the best rate of serviceability in the group. Those reaching the target found good visibility above the eight to ten-tenths cloud tops at 14,000 feet, and, unable to see the ground, identified the target by the Path Finder parachute flares. This was precisely what Oboe was all about, the ability to bomb blind, secure in the knowledge that the genius of electronic warfare had guided a crew to within a few hundred yards of an aiming point.

Syerston had further business to attend to on that evening and dispatched the crews of Sgt Oldham, F/Sgt Woodward and Sgt Goodwin in that order between 19.20 and 19.50 bound for either the Nectarine III or Sweetpea gardens respectively off the eastern Frisians and in the Mecklenburg Bay region of the Baltic. It is believed that the Woodward crew had been assigned to the more distant target area, but after reporting that their port-outer flame trap was flapping, they were recalled by base. The Goodwin crew was unable to establish a pinpoint in low cloud and abandoned their search after twenty-five minutes, jettisoning their mines in the North Sea, which left just Sgt Oldham and crew to fulfil their brief after finding a pinpoint on Baltrum Island and planting their vegetables from 2,000 feet.

The size of the main force element for the Oboe trials series gradually increased raid by raid, and a main force of fifty 1 and 5 Group Lancasters was assembled for Essen on the night of the 9th, of which six represented 61 Squadron. They departed Syerston between 16.40 and 17.35 with F/Ls Burns the senior pilot on duty among four of flight lieutenant rank and two NCO-captained crews, only for the serviceability gremlins to strike and reduce the numbers by half. Sgt Champion's take-off was delayed, and a navigational equipment failure sealed their early return, while the crews of F/L Dierkes and F/Sgt Cockshott were defeated also by Gee failure. The others reached the central Ruhr to find it clear of cloud, but blanketed by considerable haze, through which some ground detail was discernible. For most it was the accuracy of the Path Finder flares that provided the best reference, and they attracted the bombs of the 61 Squadron trio from 20,000 and 21,000 feet in the face of a hostile flak defence. Bursts and fires were observed, and local sources confirmed that 127 buildings had been destroyed or seriously damaged in central districts. However, when a 106

Squadron bombing photo revealed roads, a railway and open country, it was plotted to be thirteen miles from the Krupp complex, suggesting that there was still much work to do to perfect the system.

On the 10th Syerston welcomed to its bosom Major Richard Dimbleby, the acclaimed BBC war correspondent, who was to stay for a number of days embedded in 106 Squadron to fulfil a "special" assignment. Seventy-two Lancasters of 1 and 5 Groups were detailed for the next round of Oboe series against Essen on the 11th, and among them were nine from 61 Squadron, including the first two Mk II variants, DS607 and DS610, containing the crews of Sgt Meagher and F/L Gilpin respectively. This would prove to be the largest raid of the series for which the 61 Squadron element departed Syerston between 16.40 and 17.00 with F/Ls Dierkes and Gillett the other senior pilots on duty. On another night of poor serviceability for Syerston, eight aircraft returned early, five from 61 Squadron landing between 19.10 and 20.25, four of them, including both Mk IIs, having failed to attain sufficient altitude. The remaining 61 Squadron participants focused on the Path Finder skymarker flares, which tended to drift across the target at the behest of the wind, and on this night, there were red and green warning flares and white flares as aiming point indicators. They bombed from between 19,000 and 21,400 feet in the face of heavy flak, at debriefings expressing doubt as to the effectiveness of the attack, and unusually for Essen, no local report was forthcoming to shed light on the outcome.

The operation on the night of the 12/13th involved fifty-five Lancasters of 1 and 5 Groups, of which eight were provided by 61 Squadron and departed Syerston between 03.20 and 03.40 with F/L Burns the senior pilot on duty. For once there were no early returns and all reached the Ruhr to find ten-tenths cloud with tops at 15,000 feet and release point flares drifting towards them and heavy flak shells bursting through them to detonate at bombing height. The 61 Squadron crews delivered their bomb loads from between 19,000 and 22,000 feet but were unable to assess the results of their efforts. A post-raid analysis concluded that the operation failed largely because the Oboe equipment in the lead Mosquito became unserviceable, and the three other Mosquitos arrived late, resulting in sparse and inadequate marking. The only missing Lancaster was 61 Squadron's W4192, which crashed ten miles east-north-east of Düsseldorf with fatal consequences for F/L Gillett and crew.

The final operation of the series was mounted on the night of the 13/14th, when 61 Squadron put up five Lancasters as part of a main force of sixty-six and sent them on their way from Syerston between 16.40 and 17.05 each with an NCO pilot at the controls. Alarm bells must have been sounding at 5 Group HQ at the squadron's poor rate of serviceability, which was the worst in the group and contrasted starkly with that of fellow Syerston residents, 106 Squadron, which was top of the group's serviceability ladder. On this night the crews of F/Sgt Woodward and Sgts Champion and Oldham turned back because of engine and performance issues, leaving the crews of F/Sgt Macfarlane and Sgt Meagher to press on to the target and encounter eight-tenths cloud at 10,000 feet. They dropped their cookie and twelve SBCs of 4lb incendiaries each on Path Finder release point flares from 20,000 feet, and although they were unable to comment on the outcome, they did describe heavy flak and searchlight activity. A post-raid analysis concluded that problems afflicting the Oboe element, two Mosquitos returning early and the flares from a third failing to ignite above the clouds, had compromised the effectiveness of the raid, despite which, many bombs did fall within the city, where fifty-two buildings were destroyed.

A new Air Ministry directive was issued on the 14th, which authorised the area bombing of the French ports with concrete bunkers and support facilities providing a home for U-Boots. A list was drawn up accordingly, headed by Lorient and included St-Nazaire, Brest and La Pallice. As mentioned earlier, between February 1941 and January 1942, the Germans had built three giant concrete structures K1, K2 and K3 on the southernmost point of Lorient's Keroman Peninsula. They were capable of housing and servicing thirty U-Boots and providing accommodation for their crews and were impregnable to the bombs available to Bomber Command at the time. The purpose of this new campaign, therefore, was to render the town and port uninhabitable and block or sever all road and rail communications to them. The first of the series of nine attacks on the port over the ensuing four weeks took place that very night at the hands of a force of 122 aircraft in the absence of 5 Group, and, despite accurate marking by the Path Finder element, the main force bombing was scattered and destroyed a modest 120 buildings.

5 Group's involvement with Lorient would come in February, and in the meantime, Harris planned two operations against the "Big City", Berlin, beginning on the 16th, for which a force of 201 aircraft was made ready, the crews briefed to aim for the Alexander Platz railway station in the heart of the city to the north of the River Spree. This would be the first raid on Germany's capital for fourteen months and brought with it the first use of custom-designed target indicators (TIs). The main force would be made up predominantly of 5 Group Lancasters, with others from 1 Group, while eleven Halifaxes of 35 (Madras Presidency) Squadron were included in the Path Finder element. Those reaching the target would share the airspace over it with the broadcaster, Richard Dimbleby, who was in a 106 Squadron Lancaster captained by W/C Guy Gibson. *(In some of my previous books, I have fallen into the trap of repeating the errors of others by recording Dimbleby's participation during the second Berlin raid that took place on the following night. This could not be the case, as, according to the 106 Squadron ORB, Gibson was not involved in the second Berlin raid.)*

61 Squadron detailed a record seventeen Lancasters, including five Mk IIs from C Flight containing the crews of W/C Coad, F/L Gilpin, F/Sgt Cockshott and Sgts Champion and Meagher, while S/L Parker was the senior pilot among the Mk I/III Merlin-powered element. They departed Syerston between 16.16 and 16.51, before heading for Mandø Island off Denmark's western coast, and it was during the North Sea crossing that an escape hatch blew off F/L Lind's W4270 and smashed the mid-upper turret Perspex. The occupant, Sgt Brown, steadfastly remained at his post to enable the sortie to continue and they reached the target, following the briefed route across southern Jutland to the western Baltic and then along the coastline eastwards to Swinemünde, where they swung to the south for the run on the target. Engine trouble forced W/C Coad and crew to terminate their sortie over the Island of Rügen and bomb a last-resort target on the mainland at Greifswald, leaving the others to press on and reach the target under moonlight, with good visibility above six-tenths cloud at 10,000 feet.

The main force element picked up the lakes to the west of the city and followed autobahns, before being guided to the mark first by red warning flares and then cascading red and green TIs over what was assumed to be the aiming point. The 61 Squadron crews carried out their attacks from between 11,000 and 19,200 feet, not all with a clear view of the ground, although some recognised that they were over the southern outskirts of the city, where the Tempelhof district could be identified. At debriefing, some crews reported black smoke rising through 5,000 feet as they turned away, but many were unconvinced of the effectiveness of the raid, and this was borne out by local sources. One notable scalp was the ten-thousand-seater Deutschlandhalle, the largest covered venue in Europe, which was hosting the annual circus as the bombers approached and was efficiently emptied of people and animals with only a few minor injuries. Shortly afterwards, incendiaries set fire to the building and reduced it to ruins. Remarkably, only a single Lancaster failed to return from this operation, and that was 61 Squadron's ED332, which was brought down in the target area, killing S/L Edward Parker GC, DFC and his crew, three of whom were members of the RCAF. S/L Parker had earned the George Cross for saving the life of his wireless operator after crash-landing his 49 Squadron Hampden in June 1940 when a pilot officer.

170 Lancasters and seventeen Halifaxes were made ready on 1, 4, 5 and 8 Group stations on the 17th for the return to Berlin that night, when they would follow the same route as for twenty-four hours earlier with a three-and-a-half-hour outward flight ahead of them, stalked constantly by night-fighters once they reached western Denmark. There was a mix of Mk I and II Lancasters in the dozen belonging to 61 Squadron that departed Syerston between 16.39 and 17.32 with F/L Burns the senior pilot on duty, and those containing the crews of F/Sgts Baker and Woodward turned back early, the former because of oxygen system failure with the Danish coast in sight. The others continued on across southern Jutland and bypassed the searchlights and flak in the Kiel defence zone as they gained the Baltic to follow the coast as far as the turning point at Swinemünde. Those reaching the target area were greeted by eight to ten-tenths cloud with tops at between 10,000 and 14,000 feet, through which it was possible for most to pick out the Müggelsee to the south-east of the capital, from where a timed run was carried out to the aiming point. Some crews failed to see any flares, which was understandable as the Path Finders arrived thirty-seven minutes late, and so bombed on e.t.a. or DR, while others did benefit from target marking, which was once more concentrated over the southern fringes of the city rather than over the centre. The 61 Squadron crews carried out their attacks from between 15,000 and 19,000 feet, those arriving towards the tail end of the raid guided by some Path Finder flares. Little was seen of the results of the bombing, and local reports confirmed that the operation had not been successful, and no significant damage had occurred. The disappointment was compounded by the loss of twenty-two bombers, 11.8% of those dispatched, and many of these disappeared without trace in the Baltic or North Sea. 61 Squadron posted missing the crew of P/O Woolford RCAF in W4767, which was brought down by flak on the way home over Kiel and crashed in the town at 22.06 with no survivors.

A force of seventy-nine Lancasters and three Mosquitos was assembled to resume the Oboe trials programme at Essen on the 21st, for which 61 Squadron briefed five crews, that of F/Sgt Elliott in a Mk II, before dispatching them from Syerston between 17.01 and 17.16 with F/L Lind the senior pilot on duty. The crews of F/L Lind and F/Sgt Walters returned early, the latter with a frost-bitten rear gunner, and both dumped their cookie in the North Sea and brought their incendiaries home. The others reached the target area, noting that condensation trails were forming at 18,000 feet to advertise their presence to the German defences, and there was the usual range of opinions concerning the amount of cloud, some reporting clear skies and others ten-tenths cloud, neither of which would have mattered if the Oboe marking had worked and been visible to all. In the event, the entire Ruhr was concealed beneath thick industrial haze, which proved to be impenetrable, and the 61 Squadron crews could only estimate that they were over Essen when they let their bombs go from between 15,000 and 18,000 feet in the face of an intense flak barrage. As far as many returning crews were concerned, there had been no Path Finder markers to point the way and the outcome of the raid remained undetermined at a cost to the Command of four Lancasters.

The Oboe trials programme moved to Düsseldorf on the 23rd, the huge industrial city situated some fifteen miles south-south-east of Essen, for which 1, 5 and 8 Groups assembled a force of eighty Lancasters and three Mosquitos. At Syerston, 61 Squadron loaded each of four Mk II and three Mk I Lancasters with a cookie and a dozen SBCs of 4lb incendiaries and launched them into the air between 16.49 and 17.22 with F/L Gilpin the senior pilot on duty. F/Sgt Macfarlane and crew were climbing-out when an escape hatch broke loose and smashed the mid-upper turret, and they were joined on the ground at 20.47 by F/L Gilpin and crew and at 21.31 by F/Sgt Goodwin and crew because of engine and oxygen supply issues. Those reaching the target area found ten-tenths cloud at 12,000 feet, heavy, accurate flak and Path Finder release point flares drifting towards the cloud tops. The 61 Squadron element bombed on these from between 19,500 and 20,000 feet but saw nothing of the outcome through the cloud. While this operation was in progress, Lorient had faced another assault by a force of 121 aircraft with a token Lancaster presence, which inflicted further heavy damage. The fourth raid took place on the night of the 26/27th at the hands of an initial force of 157 aircraft, which attacked in poor weather conditions.

Düsseldorf was selected again as the primary target on the 27th, when the Path Finders were to use ground marking for the first time rather than skymarking. Ground markers, which were TIs fused to burst and cascade just above the ground, could be seen through thin or partial cloud and industrial haze and were much more reliable than the previously-employed parachute flares, that drifted in the wind. However, skymarkers would remain an indispensable part of target marking techniques on nights of heavy cloud or to use in combination with ground markers. From this night onwards, Path Finder heavy aircraft would back-up the Mosquito-laid Oboe markers to ensure that the aiming point remained marked throughout the operation. A heavy force of 124 Lancasters and thirty-three Halifaxes was made ready on 1, 4, 5 and 8 Group stations, 61 Squadron providing nine of the Lancasters, including a single Mk II, which departed Syerston between 17.36 and 18.01 with F/L Barlow the senior pilot on duty. Sgt Oldham and crew turned back because of engine trouble over the North Sea, while the remainder pressed on to the target to be greeted by a thin layer of five to ten-tenths cloud at 10,000 feet, through which the red and green TIs could be seen burning on the aiming point. They carried out their part in the proceedings from between 14,000 and 20,000 feet, and returned safely, impressed by the potential of ground marking and confident that they had hit the aiming point. The effectiveness of the attack was confirmed by local sources, which spoke of widespread destruction in southern districts amounting to 456 houses, ten industrial premises and nine public buildings destroyed or seriously damaged, and many others afflicted to a lesser extent.

Seventy-five Wellingtons and Halifaxes of 1, 4 and 6 Groups carried out the fifth attack of the series on Lorient on the night of the 29/30th, and in the absence of a Path Finder element produced scattered bombing. Another new blind-bombing device, the ground-mapping H2S radar, was to be employed operationally for the first time at Hamburg on the 30th, for which a force of 135 Lancasters of 1, 5 and 8 Groups would be joined by thirteen H2S-equipped Path Finder Stirlings and Halifaxes of 7 and 35 (Madras Presidency) Squadrons respectively. The H2S equipment was housed in a cupola aft of the bomb bay and projected an image of the terrain onto a cathode-ray tube in the navigator's compartment. It was the job of the operator to interpret what he was seeing and guide the pilot to the aiming point, but this was no easy task, particularly with the Mk I set, and it proved difficult to distinguish particular ground features in the jumble of images presented to him. It would take much practice and experience to master the device, but, in time, and once the Mk III set became available, H2S would become an indispensable tool. Initially employed only by Path Finder aircraft, it would eventually become standard equipment in main force squadrons also.

61 Squadron made ready nine Lancasters for Hamburg, loading each with a cookie and incendiaries before sending them on their way from Syerston between 23.30 and 23.54 with W/C Coad the senior pilot on duty. As mentioned frequently before, north-western Germany had a "gatekeeper" in the form of weather fronts, which on this night, contained severe icing conditions and electrical storms for the bombers to negotiate as they made their way across the North Sea. A few aircraft dropped out of the bomber stream at this stage because of the conditions, among them W/C Coad in a Mk II, while it was rear turret failure than ended the sortie of F/Sgt Goodwin and crew. Those making it through the conditions encountered cloud over the target ranging between zero and ten-tenths with tops at between 6,000 and 15,000 feet. The 61 Squadron element bombed on flares or cascading TIs from between 18,000 and 21,000 feet and observed the reflections of explosions in the cloud. A consensus that the operation had been effective was partially confirmed by local reports that mentioned seventy-one large fires, but much of the bombing had fallen either into the Elbe or into marshland outside of the city. This would have been disappointing to the raid planners, as Hamburg, with the nearby coastline and wide River Elbe, was an ideal target for H2S and should have been easy to identify on the cathode-ray tubes.

During the course of the month, the squadron took part in fourteen operations and dispatched 101 sorties for the loss of four Lancasters and crews.

February 1943

S/L Peter Ward-Hunt was posted to the squadron from 1661 Conversion Unit at the end of January and would remain for just a month before moving across the tarmac to join 106 Squadron as a flight commander under W/C Gibson. Born on Gibraltar in 1916, he was a man of small stature but enormous drive and personality who liked to lead from the front and had gained his spurs by being in at the start of strategic bombing in May 1940 when serving with 49 Squadron at Scampton. At the end of a tour of thirty-two operations he had been awarded a DFC and after a period of screening, joined 207 Squadron to fly Manchesters, taking part in the attack on the Renault lorry factory in Paris, and later, while an instructor, flying a training unit Manchester hack on the first thousand bomber raid on Cologne. His arrival at Syerston coincided with the departure to 1661 Conversion Unit of acting S/L Bill Deas DFC at the conclusion of his second tour with 61 Squadron. A year hence, with fifty-five sorties under his belt, the highly popular South African, who had added a Bar to his DFC, would be appointed commanding officer of 57 Squadron at East Kirkby and lose his life on his sixty-ninth sortie in July 1944. A second new arrival at 61 Squadron at the start of the month was that of S/L Hall, who was posted in from 1654 Conversion Unit.

This was a time of honing and refining for Bomber Command in preparation for the launching of a major campaign a month hence and February would bring an increase in operations. It opened with the posting of Cologne as the target for an experimental operation on the 2nd, in which two marking methods were to be employed. Situated just to the south of the Ruhr, the Rhineland capital city was within range of Oboe Mosquitos, and these were to be supplemented by Path Finder aircraft relying on H2S. A force of 159 heavies included seventy-four 5 Group Lancasters, while two Path Finder Mosquitos of 109 Squadron carried the Oboe markers. The seven-strong 61 Squadron contingent, which included two Mk IIs, departed Syerston between 17.54 and 18.25 with

F/L Dierkes the senior pilot on duty, and all made it through a cold front, which caused many guns to freeze solid. They reached the target to find a layer of two to five tenths thin cloud up to 8,000 feet and patches above, which afforded good vertical visibility and a clear sight of the red and green skymarkers even from some distance on approach to the bombing run. There was some debate as to the accuracy and concentration of the markers, which a few crews from other squadrons would report as five to ten miles to the north-west of the city, while others described them as scattered. Most of the 61 Squadron crews picked up the red flares with green stars and cascading TIs above the ground and had them in the bomb sight as they delivered their cookie and incendiaries from between 17,500 and 22,000 feet. Although few were able to observe their own bombs bursting, many scattered fires were evident, the glow from which could be seen from a hundred miles into the return journey. Local reports confirmed bombs falling all over the city, but nowhere with concentration, and damage, consequently, was not commensurate with the size of the force, the effort expended and the loss of five aircraft.

Hamburg was posted as the target on the 3rd, for which a force of 263 aircraft was made ready, unusually, with Halifaxes representing the most populous type followed by Stirlings. 5 Group contributed forty of the sixty-two Lancasters, four of them, including three Mk IIs, belonging to 61 Squadron, and they departed Syerston between 17.55 and 18.30 with F/Ls Dierkes and Gilpin the senior pilots on duty. Fifteen 5 Group crews turned back on encountering the towering cloud and severe icing conditions common to this route over the North Sea, and most of them cited frozen guns. The crews of F/L Dierkes and Sgt Cockshott were in Mk IIs and turned back early, the former because of oxygen system failure and the latter for an undisclosed reason. This left the crews of F/L Gilpin and Sgt Oldham to arrive in the target area and find nine to ten-tenths cloud, which they estimated topped out at 12,000 feet, while 207 Squadron crews reported the cloud to be at 17,000 to 20,000 feet. Scattered red and green Path Finder H2S-laid skymarker flares were in the bomb sight as Sgt Oldham and crew let their bomb load go from 22,000 feet and F/L Gilpin's bomb-aimer attempted to follow suit, only to be thwarted by the failure of the release system. He finally persuaded them to fall away over Lüneburg as they headed south out of the target area. No results were observed, and the impression was of an ineffective attack, which was confirmed by local reports of forty-five large fires but no concentration or significant damage, and this disappointing outcome cost the Command sixteen aircraft. The losses by type made interesting reading and would reflect the trend for the remainder of the year, with the Stirlings suffering the highest numerical and percentage casualties, followed by the Halifaxes and Wellingtons, with the Lancasters clearly at the top of the food chain.

A return to Italy was posted on the 4th with Turin the target for a force of 188 aircraft, while 128 others, mostly Wellingtons, were prepared to continue the assault on Lorient. 5 Group contributed forty-eight Lancasters to the former and eight with freshman crews to the latter, 61 Squadron putting up three Lancasters for Italy including a Mk II. The crews of F/Sgts Baker, Cockshott and Woodward departed Syerston between 18.08 and 18.24, and were followed into the air at 19.08 by the debutant crew of Sgt Leigh, who had been briefed for Lorient and were accompanied by the squadron navigation leader, F/L Giles, acting as crew captain and mentor. The Italy-bound bomber stream followed the usual route across France, and after crossing the Alps in cloud at 21,000 feet found conditions on the Italian side much improved with clear skies and excellent visibility, which facilitated a visual confirmation of the accuracy of the Path Finder TIs. An estimated one hundred searchlights were active, and the flak defence had also been "beefed-up" but was still inaccurate and in keeping with expectations at an Italian target. *(Following a raid on a German target, a bomb symbol was painted on the forward fuselage below the glasshouse, but after a raid on an*

Italian target, the symbol would be an ice-cream cone.) Red TIs were much in evidence in the city centre as the 61 Squadron trio carried out their attacks from 12,000 and 12,500 feet and were enthusiastic about the effectiveness of their work. Local sources confirmed later that serious and widespread damage had resulted. Meanwhile the rookie crew bombed Lorient from 14,000 feet and brought back an aiming point photograph.

The seventh raid in the series on Lorient was scheduled for the 7th and was by far the largest to date, employing 323 aircraft, of which forty-three of eighty Lancasters were provided by 5 Group. It was to be conducted in two waves, an hour apart, and it was for the second wave that 61 Squadron made ready five Lancasters, including two Mk IIs, and sent them on their way from Syerston between 19.10 and 19.44 with S/L Hall the senior pilot on duty. The first wave had arrived in the target area to find clear skies and ideal bombing conditions, which they exploited after making a visual identification of the aiming point confirmed by Path Finder TIs. As they were returning home to report an outstandingly destructive raid, they left behind them a glow in the sky visible from the English coast, which acted as a beacon for the second-phase element to home in on. They encountered heavy smoke and haze over the target, through which the 61 Squadron crews bombed from between 10,000 and 12,000 feet, before four of them headed home to confirm a devastating raid. Absent from debriefing was the freshman crew of Sgt Lewis RCAF, who had lost their lives when ED359 was brought down in the target area.

Before the penultimate raid on Lorient took place, W/C Coad was posted to Bomber Command HQ and was succeeded by W/C Bill Penman AFC, a London-born Scotsman who was posted in from 1660 Conversion Unit, where he had learned to fly the Lancaster. He had represented his country in a Rugby football international match in 1939 and had spent the war to date involved in training both in the UK and in Canada.

On the 11th, attention switched to the important naval and shipbuilding port of Wilhelmshaven, situated on the north-western coast of Jade Bay, some sixty miles to the west of Hamburg. A force of 177 aircraft was put together, of which 129 were Lancasters, sixty-eight of them representing 5 Group. Seven Merlin-powered Lancasters were made ready by 61 Squadron at Syerston and took off between 17.30 and 17.53 with S/L Hall the senior pilot on duty, and over a period of ninety minutes the crew of Sgt Walters returned with a dead starboard-outer engine, F/Sgt Goodwin and crew because of severe icing conditions and Sgt Dashper and crew with a faulty compass. The others reached the target area to find ten-tenths cloud with tops at around 10,000 feet, and the least reliable marking method, H2S skymarking, in progress. On the credit side, at a smaller, more compact urban target, like Wilhelmshaven, it was easier to interpret the images on the cathode-ray screens, and on this night, great accuracy was achieved. The red and green flares were right over the aiming point as the remaining 61 Squadron crews delivered their cookies and incendiaries from between 13,000 and 17,000 feet, but it was impossible to assess what was happening beneath the cloud until an enormous explosion took place, the glow from which lingered for ten minutes. Many crews commented on this at debriefings across the Command, and there must have been much speculation about the source, which turned out to be the naval ammunition depot at Mariensiel, situated to the south of the town. It blew itself into oblivion, devastating 120 acres and causing widespread damage in the dockyard and town.

There followed a return to Lorient for seven 61 Squadron crews on the 13th, who learned at briefing that they were to be part of the largest force yet sent to the port of 466 aircraft, 103 of them 5 Group Lancasters. The six Merlin-powered and single Hercules-powered Lancasters departed

Syerston between 19.10 and 19.23 as part of the second wave with S/L Ward-Hunt the senior pilot on duty and as they began the Channel crossing in the Exmouth area, some crews reported observing flares going down over the target as the first wave attacked. Sgt Dundas and crew lost the use of their rear turret to a hydraulics leak when around two hours out and had to turn back. It had been planned to station a number of Path Finder aircraft over the Ile-de-Groix, an island situated some five miles off the mouth of the estuary leading to the port and illuminate it continuously as a navigation point. The other Path Finder crews followed up over Lorient itself with flares, green TIs and 1,000-pounders in a number of passes from 11,000 to 14,000 feet between 20.35 and 20.56, paving the way for the main force element to carry out their attacks. The target was located with ease in excellent visibility under clear skies, which allowed them to make a visual identification of both aiming points, the U-Boot pens on the Keroman peninsula and the town, before smoke began to drift across the area. The 61 Squadron crews bombed from between 11,000 and 13,500 feet and all returned safely to report massive fires right across the town and the port area.

Orders came through from 5 Group on the 14th to make ready for a return to Italy that night for a crack this time at Milan. A force of 142 Lancasters of 1, 5 and 8 Groups was assembled to carry out the attack, while 243 Halifaxes, Stirlings and Wellingtons were made ready to try their hand at Cologne. Among the eighty-nine 5 Group Lancasters were a dozen representing 61 Squadron, seven of them Mk IIs, and they departed Syerston between 18.28 and 18.50 with S/Ls Hall and Ward-Hunt the senior pilots on duty. The latter's outward progress lasted no more than an hour after issues with a trimming tab control and a fuel feed problem forced him to turn back, to be followed home within twenty minutes by Sgt Dashper and crew because of an unserviceable rear turret. The others continued on across France and reached the target area after a trouble-free outward flight to be guided to the aiming point by green and red Path Finder route-marker flares. Crews were able to identify the aiming point visually before carrying out their bombing-runs, those from 61 Squadron at altitudes between 8,000 and 14,000 feet. Most loads were observed to hit the city, and many fires were reported, the glow from which remained visible for at least a hundred miles into the return journey. The operation was hailed as a success, although no local report was forthcoming to confirm or deny.

The final raid of the series on Lorient was posted on the 16th, for which another large force was made ready, this time of 377 aircraft. Of seventy-five Lancasters offered by 5 Group, ten were made ready by 61 Squadron at Syerston, five of each mark, and took off between 18.26 and 18.49 with W/C Penman the senior pilot on duty. They were among the earlier arrivals at the target and found clear conditions aided by an almost full moon, which enabled them to deliver their cookies and SBCs of incendiaries on red TIs onto the Keroman peninsula from between 10,000 and 13,200 feet. The majority of the force dropped incendiaries into the town, which, after nine attacks, 1,926 sorties and four thousand tons of bombs, was now a desolate and deserted ruin. This was the last operation in which 61 Squadron operated Mk II Lancasters, and with 3 Group beginning a slow conversion to Lancasters, they found their way to 115 Squadron and later, 514 Squadron of 3 Group, and a number of 6 Group squadrons would operate the type with great success. The 61 Squadron ORB does not record when the C Flight was disbanded.

Preparations were put in hand on the 18th to make ready 195 aircraft for the second of four raids on Wilhelmshaven during the month, 5 Group contributing seventy-nine Lancasters, including five belonging to 61 Squadron. They departed Syerston between 18.12 and 18.44 with S/L Hall the senior pilot on duty and all reached the target area to identify it visually in excellent conditions.

Red TIs were in the bomb sights as the 61 Squadron bomb bays were emptied from between 12,000 and 17,000 feet and bursts were observed followed by fires springing up, and returning crews were confident that an accurate and concentrated attack had taken place. However, bombing photos revealed that the operation had been a failure, after the main weight of bombs had fallen into open country to the west of the town, and this demonstrated how easy it was to be misled by what the eye saw. Local reports admitted to a number of bombs hitting the town, causing no serious damage or casualties. While the above crews were on their way home, Sgt Warne and crew took W4270 for a training flight, and all died when an engine fire led to a crash at 22.56 in the Bottesford circuit.

Twenty-four hours later a force of 338 aircraft set off to return to Wilhelmshaven, with Wellingtons and Halifaxes accounting for 230 of the number and Stirlings and Lancasters the rest. 5 Group dispatched thirty-three Lancasters, seven of them containing 61 Squadron crews, who departed Syerston between 17.36 and 18.13 with F/L Cooper the senior pilot on duty. Once again, they found the conditions to be excellent with visibility that enabled them to identify the coastline and line themselves up on the target, before bombing on green TIs from between 12,000 and 16,000 feet. The bomb-bursts and fires observed in the docks area and the town left the crews with the impression that another successful raid had taken place, only for bombing photos to tell a different story and reveal that the Path Finder marking had fallen to the north of the built-up area, partly through reliance upon outdated maps, which would now be replaced. Of the twelve missing aircraft, five were Stirlings and represented 8.9% of those dispatched, thus confirming the type's vulnerability compared with the Lancaster and Halifax. The four missing Lancasters represented a 7.7% loss rate, while no Halifaxes failed to return, but this would prove to be a blip, as during the course of the year, the food chain would become established with Lancasters firmly at the top, Halifaxes in the middle and Stirlings at the bottom, when all four-engine types operated together.

On the 21st, an all-Lancaster main force from 1 and 5 Groups was made ready to attack the U-Boot construction yards at Vegesack, situated on the east bank of the Weser to the north-west of Bremen. Path Finder Lancasters, Halifaxes and Stirlings were to provide the marking in an overall force of 143 aircraft of which seventy-four of the Lancasters were put up by 5 Group. Eight of these departed Syerston between 18.12 and 18.39 to represent 61 Squadron with S/L Hall the senior pilot on duty but lost the services of F/L Gilpin and crew to a serious fuel leak and turret issues when closing on Germany's north-western coast. The others reached the target area after attempting to follow scattered route-marker flares and were greeted by ten-tenths cloud at 3,000 feet, above which, red and green skymarker flares drifted down, also in a somewhat scattered manner and up to nine minutes late to join the dimly visible TIs burning on the ground. The 61 Squadron crews carried out their attacks from between 16,000 and 19,000 feet, and a considerable glow from beneath the clouds suggested a successful outcome. Bombing photos depicted only cloud, and no local report was available to provide details of any damage.

The current series of raids on Wilhelmshaven was concluded on the 24th by 6 and 8 Groups, which put together a force of 115 aircraft that produced indeterminate results, and the port would now be left in peace until October 1944. A major operation against Nuremberg was posted on stations across the Command on the 25th, and 5 Group responded with a maximum effort of 101 Lancasters, fourteen of them belonging to 61 Squadron and loaded with a cookie and SBCs of 4lb and 30lb incendiaries. They departed Syerston between 19.05 and 19.40, led by the familiar figure of S/L Gascoyne-Cecil, who, just days earlier, had been posted in from 1660 Conversion Unit to begin a second tour, this time as a flight commander from the start. The target area lay under clear skies with good all-round visibility, but the main force had to wait for the Path Finder element to turn up some sixteen to twenty minutes after the raid was due to begin. Once on the scene, they dropped marker flares on the approach, from which the 5 Group crews carried out a time-and-distance run to the aiming point marked by red and green TIs. The 61 Squadron element bombed from between 13,000 and 18,000 feet, and all of the indications, including what looked like an oil-depot exploding, suggested a concentrated attack falling predominantly in northern and western districts. This was confirmed by local reports, which mentioned damage to three hundred buildings but also revealed that bombs had fallen onto other communities and open country up to seven miles to the north.

When Cologne was posted as the target on the 26th, 5 Group responded with ninety Lancasters, fourteen of which were made ready by 61 Squadron at Syerston as part of an overall force of 427 aircraft. They took off between 18.50 and 19.31 with W/C Penman and S/L Hall the senior pilots on duty and all reached the Cologne area on a night of almost perfect serviceability for the group and good vertical visibility for the bomb-aimers, some of whom were able to identify the bridges over the Rhine. It seems from some comments from other squadrons that a proportion of the force bombed before the Path Finders had a chance to mark, but once the red and green TIs appeared on the ground, the 61 Squadron crews aimed their cookies and incendiaries at them from between 14,000 and 18,500 feet. Fires were reported in the city centre, as were decoys to the west of the city, and bombing photos showed fire tracks and smoke that suggested an effective raid. In fact, a large proportion of the effort had fallen to the south-west of the city, and perhaps only a quarter had landed in the built-up area, causing much damage to housing, minor industry and public buildings.

On the following night, 5 Group detailed thirteen Lancasters for mining duties in one of the Nectarine gardens off the Frisians, which provided an opportunity for the freshman crews of F/O Chivers and Sgt Parsons to gain some useful experience. They took off at 18.46 and arrived in the target area under clear skies with a little sea mist to contend with and planted their vegetables according to brief after pinpointing on Juist.

Having dealt with Lorient under the January Directive, attention now turned upon St-Nazaire, situated further south along the Biscay coast. The force of 437 aircraft assembled on the 28th included a contribution from 5 Group of eighty-nine Lancasters, of which thirteen represented 61 Squadron. They departed Syerston between 18.08 and 18.52 with W/C Penman and S/L Gascoyne-Cecil the senior pilots on duty, and all reached the target area to find clear skies and good visibility with only a little ground haze to contend with. They bombed on red TIs from between 12,500 and 15,000, and it was clear from the many explosions and at least forty fires burning in the docks that the port was undergoing an ordeal of destruction. Post-raid reconnaissance revealed that the marking had been concentrated and the bombing accurate, and local reports confirmed that 60% of the town had been destroyed.

This concluded the month's activity, during the course of which the squadron had taken part in sixteen operations and had dispatched 119 sorties for the loss of two Lancasters and crews. At some point late in the month, S/L Peter Ward-Hunt crossed the tarmac to join 106 Squadron as a flight commander and would be immediately in action.

March 1943

March would bring with it the opening rounds of the Ruhr campaign, the first for which the Command was adequately equipped and genuinely prepared, with a predominantly four-engine bomber force at its disposal to carry an increasing weight of bombs and Oboe to provide accuracy. First, however, the crews had to negotiate operations to Germany's capital and second cities, and it was the "Big City" itself, Berlin, that opened the month's account on the 1st. The crews learned at briefing that six Path Finder Halifaxes and ten Stirlings equipped with H2S were to drop a "landmark" yellow TI each at Butzow, situated some eighty miles north of Berlin, which were to be backed up by seven Halifaxes and sixteen Lancasters. The "special" (H2S-equipped) aircraft were then to release red warning flares twelve miles short of the target followed by red TIs on the aiming-point at the time-on-target of 22.00, which the seven Halifaxes and sixteen Lancasters would back-up with green TIs. As always, the plan was based on a forecast of favourable conditions, in the absence of which, skymarkers would substitute for TIs. A force of 302 aircraft was assembled, made up of 156 Lancasters, eighty-six Halifaxes and sixty Stirlings, 5 Group putting up a maximum effort of ninety-eight Lancasters, of which ten represented 61 Squadron.

They departed Syerston between 18.31 and 19.12 with S/Ls Gascoyne-Cecil and Hall the senior pilots on duty and lost the services of F/O Eyre and crew after they were coned by searchlights and bombarded with flak at Kiel and had to jettison their bombs in order to escape. Eleven 5 Group Lancasters turned back early, no others from among the 61 Squadron contingent, and those reaching the target found it to be under clear skies with only haze to impair the vertical visibility. However, reliant upon H2S, the Path Finder navigators experienced great difficulty in establishing their positions based on the images on their cathode-ray tubes over such a massive urban sprawl, and this led to scattered marking. As a result, the main weight of the attack fell into south-western districts, where the 61 Squadron crews bombed on red and green TIs from between 15,000 and 18,000 feet. Some returning crews reported the glow of fires to be visible from two hundred miles into the return flight, but seventeen crews failed to make it to debriefing, and among them was that of 61 Squadron's Sgt Champion RCAF and crew, who disappeared without trace in W4920. A post-raid analysis based on bombing photos revealed the attack to have been spread over an area of a hundred square miles, but because of the increasing bomb tonnage now carried, more damage was inflicted on the city than on any previous raid. 875 buildings, mostly houses, were destroyed and twenty factories seriously damaged, along with railway workshops in the Tempelhof district. It is interesting to analyse the percentage loss rate of each type on this night, as it would be an accurate indicator of their future fortunes. The statistics revealed the loss rate of Lancasters to be 4.5%, and those of the Halifaxes and Stirlings to be 7%.

A force of 417 aircraft was assembled to send against Hamburg on the 3rd, and eighty-nine of 149 Lancasters were provided by 5 Group, nine of them by 61 Squadron at Syerston, where each had a cookie and twelve SBCs of incendiaries winched into its cavernous thirty-three-foot-long bomb bay. They took off between 18.38 and 18.55 with F/Ls Barlow, Cooper and Dierkes the senior pilots on duty and all negotiated the North Sea crossing to find the target basking under clear skies and in good visibility. Some Path Finder and main force crews identified the Hamburg-America landing stage, the Blohm & Voss shipyards, the Binnen-Alster Lake and the main railway station and those from 61 Squadron carried out their attacks from between 14,000 and 18,500 feet, aided by the H2S-laid Path Finder TIs. On return, crews reported numerous fires in the docks area along with black smoke rising to meet them as they turned away. What was not appreciated, was the fact that a proportion of the markers had fallen onto the town of Wedel, situated some thirteen miles downstream of the Elbe, and had attracted perhaps the bulk of the bombs, while those hitting the primary target had caused a hundred fires that needed to be dealt with before the fire services could go to the aid of their neighbour. Ten aircraft failed to return, but there were no empty 61 Squadron dispersal pans at Syerston.

On the following night, 5 Group sent six Lancasters to mine the waters of Danzig Bay and two from 61 Squadron for similar duties in one of the Silverthorn gardens in the Kattegat region of the Baltic. The crews of Sgt Parsons and F/O Chivers took off at 17.39 and 18.32 respectively and arrived safely to find favourable conditions, in which they were able to establish pinpoints and plant their vegetables according to brief.

The night off for most of the Command provided the opportunity for maximum serviceability as the decks were now cleared for the opening of the Ruhr offensive, which over the ensuing months, would change the face of bombing and provide for the enemy an indication of the burgeoning power of the Command. This was a culmination of all that had gone before during three and a half years of Bomber Command operations, the backs-to-the-wall desperation of 1940, the tentative almost token offensives of 1941, the treading water and gradual metamorphosis under Harris in 1942, when failures still far outnumbered successes. It had all been leading to this night, from which point would begin the calculated and systematic dismantling of Germany's industrial and population centres. The only shining light during these dark years had been the quality and spirit of the aircrew, and this had never faltered. The new era began on the 5th at Essen, Harris's nemesis thus far and the home of the giant armaments-producing Krupp complex occupying the Borbeck districts, and for the first time since the war began, the Command would have at its disposal a device which would negate the industrial haze protecting this city and its neighbours. The magnificent pioneering work on Oboe by W/C Hal Bufton and his crews at 109 Squadron was about to bear fruit in spectacular fashion, and the towns and cities of Germany's arsenal would suffer destruction on an unprecedented scale.

A force of 442 aircraft included ninety-seven Lancasters representing 5 Group, 61 Squadron contributing a dozen Lancasters on this momentous occasion, the crews learning at briefing that the main force element was to bomb in three waves, Halifaxes first, followed by Wellingtons and Stirlings with Lancasters bringing up the rear. Six Path Finder Halifax and fifteen Lancaster crews had been briefed to drop a warning yellow TI each fifteen miles from the target, before backing up the Mosquitos' red TIs on the aiming-point with greens. The bomber stream was to adopt the southern route to the central Ruhr, making landfall over the Scheldt estuary, and the 61 Squadron element departed Syerston between 18.36 and 19.03 with S/L Gascoyne-Cecil the senior pilot on duty. An unusually high number of early returns included a modest seven from 5 Group, but three of these were from 61 Squadron's ranks, the crews of F/Sgts Goodwin and Woodward because of engine and oxygen supply failures respectively, while F/O Chivers was unable to attain operational altitude. Together with those bombing alternative targets, this reduced the size of the force reaching Essen and bombing as briefed to 362 aircraft. 5 Group favoured a time-and-distance approach to the aiming point, and its crews employed the Path Finders' yellow route markers as the initial reference point, before exploiting the good visibility to bomb through the industrial haze onto red and green TIs, those from 61 Squadron from between 15,000 and 19,000 feet. The overwhelming impression was of a concentrated attack, which left many fires burning and a glow in the sky reported by some to be visible from the North Sea homebound. At debriefings, crews across the

Command reported terrific explosions and fires, which lit up the sky and illuminated the pall of smoke hanging above the dull, red centre of the conflagration. The operation cost the Command an acceptable fourteen aircraft, just two of them belonging to 5 Group, while post-raid reconnaissance revealed 160 acres of devastation and damage to fifty-three buildings within the Krupp district. The success of the operation was confirmed by local sources, who reported the destruction of 3,018 houses and serious damage to more than two thousand others in what was a most encouraging start to the offensive.

It would be a further week before round two of the Ruhr offensive was mounted, and in the meantime, Harris turned his attention upon southern Germany, beginning with Nuremberg on the 8th. A force of 338 aircraft included 105 Lancasters of 5 Group, the crews of which learned at briefing that zero hour was to be 23.15 and that three Path Finder Stirlings and two Halifaxes were to drop illumination flares across the target in two sticks by H2S, to be followed by six Stirlings and three Halifaxes dropping green TIs on the aiming-point, also by H2S, and employing additional flares if necessary. The remaining Path Finder marker aircraft were to back up with green TIs, unless cloud negated the illuminator flares, in which case, red TIs were to be dropped by the H2S-equipped aircraft and backed up by the others with greens, and all Path Finder aircraft were to deliver yellow route markers on the way in and out. The fifteen-strong 61 Squadron element departed Syerston between 19.13 and 19.38 with F/Ls Barlow, Cooper, Dierkes and Giles the senior pilots on duty, and a cookie and assorted incendiaries in each bomb bay.

Sgt Dundas and crew lost their port-outer engine during the sea crossing and turned back, while F/Sgt Woodward and crew were over France when the failure of their starboard-inner engine ended their interest in proceedings also. The others reached the target area by following yellow route markers and encountered clear skies with ground haze and extreme darkness. This seemed to impede the Path Finders' ability to locate the city centre blind by H2S, and the main force crews experienced the same difficulty in identifying ground detail, allowing themselves to be guided to the aiming point by a few red and green TIs, which appeared to lack concentration and soon burned out. The 61 Squadron crews had predominantly red TIs in the bomb sights but also a few scattered greens and carried out their attacks from between 15,000 and 18,500 feet. The initial impression was of a scattered raid, but a greater concentration of fires developed and the glow from these was reported by some to be visible for two hundred miles into the return journey. At debriefing, 83 Squadron's S/L Cooke reported that a cookie and yellow TIs had been jettisoned east of Heilbronn, some forty miles short of the target and accurately backed-up by other Path Finders. Inevitably, this would have drawn off other bomb loads, and local sources confirmed the marking and bombing of Nuremberg to have been spread along a ten-mile stretch, half of it falling short of the city boundaries. The rest, however, destroyed six hundred buildings and damaged fourteen hundred others, including a number of important war-industry factories, at a cost to the Command of eight aircraft. W4903 failed to return with the crew of F/L Giles DFC RAAF, having crashed at Fürth, probably at the start of the bombing run, and in time the Red Cross would confirm that none had survived.

On the following day, preparations were put in hand to return to southern Germany to attack the city of Munich, situated deep in the Bavarian mountains of south-eastern Germany, a round-trip of more than 1,200 miles. A force of 264 aircraft included a 5 Group contribution of eighty-one Lancasters, eleven of them made ready at Syerston and loaded with a cookie each and SBCs of incendiaries. At briefings, the crews learned the details of the plan of attack, which called for white TIs to be dropped by the Path Finders as route markers to aid the main force crews, and then white and green flares over the northern tip of the Ammersee, a large lake situated some twenty miles to the west-south-west of the city centre, which the 5 Group crews, in particular, would use as the starting point for their time-and-distance runs. Nine Stirlings and four Halifaxes were to ground mark by H2S with red TIs at the same time as releasing white illuminating flares, and four Lancasters were to drop flares also, if required, and then join with eleven Lancasters and four Halifaxes to back up the aiming point with green TIs.

The 61 Squadron element took off between 20.20 and 20.35 with S/L Gascoyne-Cecil the senior pilot on duty and all reached the target area, where clear skies and good visibility prevailed, and the Path Finder green and white TIs could be seen to have fallen within the built-up area. An enormous orange explosion occurred in a south-western district as crews were carrying out their timed runs to the aiming point from the Ammersee, and those from 61 Squadron had the TIs in the bomb sights as they released their loads from between 14,500 and 18,000 feet. Another huge explosion at 00.25 lit up the sky for twenty seconds and illuminated an area of ground with a ten-mile radius, described by some as the largest they had experienced, and another particularly large one occurred at 00.43. Fires were taking hold and sending a large pall of smoke rising above the city as the bomber force withdrew to the west, and one 5 Group crew counted eighteen blazes in or close to the city centre. A relatively modest eight aircraft failed to return, and only two from 5 Group, but one of them was 61 Squadron's ED703, which crashed at Fürstenfeldbruck, to the north-west of Munich, probably after bombing, and there were no survivors from the crew of Sgt Walters. A post-raid analysis concluded that a strong wind had pushed the attack into the western half of the city, where 291 buildings had been destroyed and 660 severely damaged. The aero-engine assembly shop at the B.M.W factory was put out of action for six weeks, and many other industrial concerns also lost vital production.

On the following night, 5 Group ordered four mining sorties, according to the ORB, in one of the Silverthorn gardens in the Kattegat, while the 61 Squadron ORB recorded the destination as the Tangerine garden, located off the port of Pillau, now Baltiysk in Russia, the most distant of all of the Command's mining areas. The crews of F/L Gilpin, the recently commissioned P/O Cockshott and Sgt Rawes departed Syerston in that order between 18.20 and 18.34 and planted their vegetables according to brief from 2,500 and 3,000 feet. On the way home the Gilpin crew was intercepted three times by four night-fighters and their Lancaster badly shot up, but they made it home to land after more than nine hours aloft, which confirmed that they had, indeed, been to Tangerine. The Cockshott crew had spent more than ten hours in the air by the time they landed at 04.46.

The trio of operations to destinations in southern Germany concluded at the highly industrial city of Stuttgart, for which a force of 314 aircraft was assembled on the 11th, 5 Group contributing ninety-six of 152 Lancasters, nine of them belonging to 61 Squadron. Briefings revealed that the Path Finders were to deliver flares and red TIs by H2S across the aiming point, and that these were to be backed up visually with green TIs. At Syerston, take-off was accomplished safely between 19.56 and 20.35 with F/Ls Barlow and Cooper the senior pilots on duty, but F/O Chivers and crew fell behind schedule at the coast and Sgt Rawes and crew had to contend with a fire in their starboard-outer engine. The others crossed the English coast over Eastbourne, heading for the French coast near Dieppe, before pushing on across France to enter Germany in the Strasbourg area with Stuttgart fifty miles straight ahead on an easterly track. The main force element arrived late because of inaccurately forecast winds and although finding excellent visibility, the Path Finder TIs were already burning out on the ground. This left the way clear for dummy TIs to lure the bombing away from the city centre, and in this endeavour, they were largely successful, although to the bomb-aimers high above, the green TIs appeared to be legitimate and were bombed by the 61 Squadron crews from between 14,000 and 18,000 feet. Most of the effort was wasted in open country but the south-western suburbs of Vaihingen and Kaltental were hit and 118 buildings, mostly houses, were destroyed. It was a disappointing outcome, which cost eleven aircraft, only one of which was from 5 Group.

Round two of the Ruhr campaign was posted on the 12th, when 457 crews learned at briefing that Essen was once more to be their destination with a time-on-target for the Path Finders of 21.15. They were to adopt the northern route to the Ruhr, and sixteen Path Finders were to ground mark the town of Dorsten with white TIs as a track guide, before backing up the Mosquito-borne Oboe red TIs with greens to provide the main force crews with a solid aiming point. 5 Group detailed ninety-five Lancasters, of which nine were made ready by 61 Squadron and departed Syerston between 18.57 and 19.12 with S/Ls Gascoyne-Cecil and Hall the senior pilots on duty. They all reached the target, where fierce fires were already burning beneath clear skies, the smoke from which combined with industrial haze to blot out ground detail. Oboe rendered this of little consequence as the red and green Path Finder TIs marked out the aiming point for the main force crews, those from 61 Squadron attacking from between 17,000 and 19,000 feet. It was clear that the bombing was accurate and mostly concentrated around the Oboe-laid TIs, and this time, the Krupp complex found itself in the centre of the area of destruction. The defences fought back to claim twenty-three bombers, in return for which, according to post-raid reconnaissance, another highly successful assault on this centre of war production had been achieved. In fact, substantially fewer buildings had been destroyed, but a greater concentration of bombs had inflicted 30% more damage on Krupp than the raid of a week earlier.

On the following night 5 Group sent seventeen Lancasters on mining sorties in the Baltic, the 61 Squadron crews of P/O Cockshott and F/Sgt Macfarlane departing Syerston at 19.27 and 19.55 respectively bound for the Privet garden off the port of Danzig, now Gdansk in Poland, with Silverthorn 8 having been briefed as the alternative target area. After finding ten-tenths cloud with a base at sea level, both crews backtracked to the alternative garden located in the Kattegat, and in clear conditions, pinpointed on Anholt Island before planting their vegetables.

5 Group stood down for a week after Essen, as a spell of adverse weather prevailed, and it was the 22nd before orders came through to prepare for the next assault on St-Nazaire, for which a force of 357 aircraft was assembled, including a contribution from 5 Group of 120 Lancasters. 61 Squadron's thirteen Lancasters departed Syerston between 19.20 and 20.03 with S/Ls Gascoyne-Cecil and Hall the senior pilots on duty. They flew out over Portland Bill, and all reached the target area, where they attacked from between 9,600 and 14,000 feet under clear skies and moonlight that had enabled the target to be identified visually and by the abundance of red and green TIs. Despite the recall of the 3 Group Stirlings, to which fifty-five crews responded, the main force bombed with accuracy and concentration, leaving the town and port areas in flames and massively damaged. Ninety of the 5 Group participants were diverted on return to airfields from Scotland to Cornwall and it took time to collate all of the debriefing reports.

Duisburg was selected as the host for the third operation of the Ruhr offensive, for which a force of 455 aircraft was assembled, ninety-four of them Lancasters provided by 5 Group. Crews learned at briefing that the Oboe Mosquitos were to drop warning flares five and two-and-a-half minutes before reaching the aiming-point and then employ the "Musical Wanganui" marking method, the code for Oboe skymarking, releasing red flares with green stars at regular intervals thereafter. 61 Squadron contributed eleven Lancasters, which departed Syerston between 18.29 and 18.43 with S/Ls Gascoyne-Cecil and Hall the senior pilots on duty and lost the services of Sgt Dashper and crew to navigational problems after around ninety minutes. The others pressed on to the target area to find ten-tenths cloud with tops at 10,000 feet and good visibility above and were greeted by the Oboe release-point parachute flares, which were in the bomb sights as they dropped their cookies and incendiaries from between 18,000 and 20,000 feet. A large explosion was witnessed at 21.53, suggesting some level of success, but what the crews could not know, was that five of the Oboe Mosquitos had returned early with equipment failure and a sixth had been shot down. This left just three to deliver what could only be sparse marking, which was insufficient and led to a scattered and ineffective attack, and to some crews, including two from 61 Squadron, attacking Essen as the briefed alternative target. According to local sources, Duisburg sustained only minor damage at the relatively low cost to the Command of six aircraft, none belonging to 5 Group.

Orders were received on stations across the Command on the 27th to prepare for a trip to the "Big City" that night, and a force of 396 aircraft was duly assembled. At briefings, the Path Finder crews were told of their part in the plan, which required eleven Stirlings and eight Halifaxes to drop green route marker flares and yellow warning flares by H2S, before marking the aiming-point with red TIs for two Stirlings, five Halifaxes and twenty-one Lancasters to back up with green TIs. In the event of cloud blotting out the ground, skymarking would be employed. 5 Group contributed 111 Lancasters, eleven of them belonging to 61 Squadron, which departed Syerston between 19.59 and 20.34 with four pilots of flight lieutenant rank leading the way and station commander, G/C Odbert, flying as second pilot to F/L Barlow. F/Sgt Macfarlane and crew returned early for an undisclosed reason, while the rest of the bomber stream adopted a route that took them into enemy territory between the Frisian Islands of Texel and Vlieland and then on a course a little north of Hannover to a point to the south-west of the capital for the run-in to the intended city-centre aiming-point. The Path Finders were reliant upon H2S and established two areas of marking, both well short, and the main force crews had little choice but to aim for them. There was the usual discrepancy in the reported cloud state of zero to nine-tenths as the Syerston crews tracked in across yellow TIs and carried out their attacks from between 14,000 and 20,000 feet, and from bombing altitude, the attack appeared to be effective. However, local reports confirmed that the main weight of bombs had fallen between seven and seventeen miles short of the target, and 25% of those hitting the city had failed to detonate.

There would be a chance to rectify the failure two nights hence, but in the meantime, St-Nazaire faced its third heavy assault under the January Directive, for which a force of 323 aircraft was made ready on the 28th. 5 Group detailed twenty-one freshman crews, while 61 Squadron remained on the ground, and those reaching the target area encountered good visibility and red and green Oboe-laid TIs marking out the aiming point. Returning crews reported concentrated fires, and post-raid reconnaissance confirmed the accuracy and effectiveness of the raid.

The month's final operation was posted on the 29th, when the red tape on the briefing-room wall maps ended again at Berlin. A force of 329 aircraft was made ready for the main event, while 149 Wellingtons were prepared for an attack on Bochum in the central Ruhr. 5 Group contributed 106 Lancasters, a dozen of them representing 61 Squadron, and their crews attended briefings to learn that the plan for the main event required all Path Finder aircraft to drop yellow route markers at predetermined points, and the marker crews to illuminate the Müggelsee to the south-east of Berlin with sticks of white flares and bundles of green flares with red stars by H2S. They were then to join the backer-up marker crews to carry out a DR run to the aiming-point to deliver red TIs. The 61 Squadron contingent departed Syerston between 21.30 and 22.00 with S/L Hall the senior pilot on duty and F/L Barlow and crew undertaking their final sortie with the squadron and crossed the English coast over Mablethorpe on course for Mandø Island off Jutland's western coast. They met bad weather in the form of heavy ice-bearing cloud and static electricity extending from the North Sea to the Baltic, which forced many crews to turn for home, among them eighteen belonging to 5 Group and a massive twenty-four from 4 Group. The 61 Squadron crews of Sgt Shipway, F/Sgt Rawes and W/O Frost abandoned their sorties because of severe icing, while Sgt Dashper and crew had to abort theirs after losing their port-inner engine.

The others continued on across Jutland and traversed Kiel Bight and Mecklenburg Bay, before crossing the German coast between Wismar and Rostock on track for the "Big City", where good visibility enabled them to identify the Müggelsee to the south-east of the city as a reference point from which to run in on the aiming-point. The Path Finders were again short with their marking, and the main force arrived late after some of the markers had already burned themselves out. The 61 Squadron crews bombed from between 17,000 and 20,600 feet in the face of a heavy searchlight and flak defence and set off home in the belief that the fires they had left behind, the glow from which was still visible from 150 miles away, indicated that an effective attack had been delivered. An analysis of the operation revealed that most of the bombing had been wasted in open country to the south-east of the city, and an accurate figure for damage was not forthcoming.

The Stuttgart operation on the 11th had been the final one for W/C Guy Gibson as commanding officer of 106 Squadron, and on the 15th he was called to a meeting with the recently installed Air-Officer-Commanding 5 Group, The Hon. Sir Ralph Cochrane, at 5 Group HQ at St Vincents in Grantham, when he was invited to form a new squadron for a special operation to be mounted two months hence. Squadron X was formed on the 21st at Scampton, taking over the accommodation vacated by 49 Squadron in January, and on the 24th the first seven crews arrived on posting to be followed on the 25th by a further seven, with other personnel arriving, as individuals or part crews, before the end of the month. The nucleus of what would soon be numbered 617 Squadron was provided by C Flight of 57 Squadron, the other resident unit at Scampton, and all 5 Group squadrons with the exception of 9 Squadron contributed at least one crew. 61 Squadron gave up F/L Robert "Norm" Barlow RAAF, who had just completed a tour, had been recommended for a DFC, and apparently preferred to throw himself immediately into a second tour rather than be screened at a training establishment. He took with him his flight engineer, Sgt Sam Whillis, and his bomb aimer Sgt Alan Gillespie, a veteran of thirty-three operations, and also joining him from 61 Squadron were F/O Philip Burgess as navigator, F/O Charlie Williams DFC RAAF as wireless operator, F/O Harvey Glinz RCAF as front gunner, and Sgt Jack Liddell as rear gunner. Together they formed an experienced if unusual bunch, three of them, Barlow, Whillis and Williams, already in their thirties, and at thirty-five years-of-age, Williams would be the oldest to take part in Operation Chastise. He was courting a local girl, whom he hoped to marry and take back to Australia when it was all over. In contrast, rear gunner, Sgt Jack Liddell, who had a full tour of operations behind him, was only eighteen and must have withheld his true age when enlisting in 1941.

During the course of the month, the squadron took part in fourteen operations and dispatched 129 sorties for the loss of three Lancasters and crews.

April 1943

April would be the least rewarding month during the Ruhr offensive, principally, because of the number of operations directed at targets in regions of Germany beyond the range of Oboe. On the 2nd, orders were received to prepare for the final raids on St-Nazaire and Lorient that night, which would bring down the curtain on the January directive, and forces of fifty-five and forty-seven aircraft were made ready with eight 5 Group Lancasters included in the former. 61 Squadron was represented by the freshman crew of Sgt Alderton, who departed Syerston at 20.55 and returned five hours later to report bombing in favourable conditions in the face of heavy and accurate flak and watching from 13,000 feet as the bombs detonated half-a-mile north of the TIs, which had fallen into the sea. Meanwhile, Sgt Phillips and crew, who had taken off at 20.12, planted vegetables in the Deodar garden in the Gironde estuary on the approaches to Bordeaux and also returned safely after more than eight hours in the air. No reports came out of Lorient and St-Nazaire, which had long since been abandoned by the civilian populations.

At this time P/O Cockshott was posted to Syerston station HQ, and like F/L Barlow, would eventually join 617 Squadron, serving as a flight commander in 1944 and 1945. In one of those coincidences thrown up by war, the day on which he arrived at Woodhall Spa from 1660 Conversion Unit, the 31st of July, a celebrated former 61 Squadron pilot, F/L Bill Reid VC, failed to return from a daylight operation and would spend the rest of the in enemy hands. That was all in the future and will be dealt with at the appropriate juncture.

The next round of the Ruhr campaign was announced across the Command on the 3rd, when Essen was posted as the target for the third time and a force of 348 aircraft made ready. The heavy brigade consisted of 225 Lancasters and 113 Halifaxes, 123 of the former representing 5 Group, and this would be the first occasion on which more than two hundred Lancasters had operated against a single target. The Path Finder contribution amounted to ten Oboe Mosquitos and twenty Lancasters from 83 and 156 Squadrons, the crews of which were to identify the Krupp complex as the aiming-point, and in the event of cloud, sky-mark it with coloured flares, or if clear skies prevailed, ground-mark with red TIs. The fourteen-strong 61 Squadron element departed Syerston between 19.18 and 19.35 with S/Ls Gascoyne-Cecil and Hall the senior pilots on duty and joined the bomber stream over the North Sea on their way to making landfall on the Dutch coast near Haarlem and uncomfortably close to the Amsterdam defences. F/L Cooper and crew turned back from near the Dutch coast because of an engine issue, leaving the others to arrive over the Ruhr from the north under almost clear skies. F/O Chivers and crew came under attack from a single-engine fighter in the target area and when the port-outer engine began to fail, the bombs were jettisoned, while the rest of the main force found the anticipated industrial haze negated by the accuracy of the Oboe markers falling around the aiming-point.

The attack began slowly, some crews apparently confused by the employment of both sky and ground markers on a clear night, but it built to a crescendo, during which a massive explosion was observed by many crews in the centre of the bombing area. The 61 Squadron crews attacked from between 16,000 and 19,000 feet, aiming mostly at the TIs burning on the ground and many explosions were witnessed, with fires emitting large volumes of smoke. Returning crews reported the glow from the burning city to be visible from the Dutch coast homebound and the consensus was of a successful raid, which was confirmed by bombing photographs and local reports of widespread destruction in central and western districts, where 635 buildings had been reduced to rubble and many more seriously damaged. The searchlight and flak defence had been intense, and it became an expensive night for the Command, which registered the loss of a dozen Halifaxes and nine Lancasters. This represented 6% of those dispatched, but most revealing were the respective loss rates, with the Halifaxes suffering 10.62% compared with 4% for the Lancasters.

The largest non-1,000 force to date of 577 aircraft was made ready on the 4th for an attack that night on the naval and shipbuilding port of Kiel, for which 5 Group detailed 112 Lancasters, eleven belonging to 61 Squadron. Crews learned at briefings that the plan of attack called for a time-on-target of 23.00 and for yellow TIs to be dropped by the Path Finders as route markers, before the H2S marker crews in ten Stirlings and six Halifaxes illuminated the aiming-point with flares and marked it with red TIs. Two Stirlings, five Halifaxes and fifteen Lancasters were then to back up with green TIs, leaving two of each type to bomb with the main force. The 61 Squadron contingent departed Syerston between 20.50 and 20.59 and all reached the target area, where they were guided towards the aiming point by yellow route marker flares, released by the Path Finder heavy brigade either side of 23.00. Kiel was found to be concealed beneath ten-tenths cloud with good visibility above, and the cookies and incendiaries were released by the 61 Squadron participants from estimated positions onto the glow of fires below the cloud from between 18,000 and 19,000 feet. It was not possible to assess the outcome, and as bombing photos revealed only cloud, it was left to a post-raid analysis to conclude that decoy fires had been operating and had probably lured away a proportion of the effort, while the strong wind had caused the markers to drift, leading the remainder astray and resulting in most of the bombs missing the target altogether. According to local reports, only eleven houses were destroyed, and this was a major disappointment in view of the size of the force involved.

The Ruhr offensive was to continue at Duisburg on the 8th, for which a mixed force of 379 Lancasters, Wellingtons, Halifaxes and Stirlings was assembled as the heavy element, while ten Oboe Mosquitos were to provide the initial marking, backed up by the Path Finder heavy brigade consisting of four Stirlings, twenty Lancasters and eight Halifaxes. 5 Group contributed eighty-four of the Lancasters, nine of them belonging to 61 Squadron, which departed Syerston between 20.40 and 21.01 with F/Ls Cooper and Dierkes the senior pilots on duty, the former accompanied by S/L Storey, whose arrival on the squadron was not recorded. However, his appearance as a flight commander at 49 Squadron later in the month suggests that he was gaining operational experience after a spell on the sidelines. They headed out over Sheringham on the Norfolk coast and had to climb through ten-tenths ice-bearing cloud over the North Sea before breaking into clear air at 12,000 feet and making landfall at Egmond with a time-on-target set for 23.15. Ahead of them, the ten Oboe Mosquitos were to drop red warning flares and then greens with red stars and green TIs over the aiming-point, and if the weather conditions permitted, one Stirling, seven Halifaxes and fourteen Lancasters were to back up with red TIs, while the remaining 8 Group aircraft supported the main force. The bomber stream reached the western Ruhr to encounter ten-tenths cloud with tops in places as high as 20,500 feet, such conditions completely nullifying the Path Finders' attempts to mark either the route or the target, and the bombing had to be carried out on e.t.a., some crews embarking on a time-and-distance run from as far away as the Dutch coast as the last visual reference. The 61 Squadron crews attacked from between 17,500 and 20,000 feet and had nothing of value to pass on to the intelligence section at debriefing. There were three missing 5 Group crews in an overall loss of nineteen aircraft, in return for which, local sources confirmed a widely scattered raid that hit at least fifteen other Ruhr locations and destroyed just forty buildings in Duisburg.

While the above operation was in progress, five Syerston Lancasters were sent to the south-western extremity of the Biscay coast for mining duties in the Elderberry and Furze gardens, respectively off Bayonne and St-Jean-de-Luz. The 61 Squadron freshman crews of Sgts Alderton and Allcroft took off at 20.39 and 20.51 respectively bound for the latter and the Alderton crew pinpointed on Cap Higuer, before map-reading their way to the drop zone and planting their vegetables from 1,000 feet. The Allcroft crew, in contrast, searched the area at 800 feet, but failed to locate a suitable pinpoint and brought their mines home.

Not content with the outcome, Harris ordered another raid twenty-four hours later, only this time employing a much-reduced force of 104 Lancasters and five Mosquitos. 5 Group detailed seventy Lancasters, of which seven represented 61 Squadron and departed Syerston between 20.24 and 20.46 with F/L Dierkes the senior pilot on duty and each Lancaster carrying a cookie and twelve SBCs of incendiaries. F/O Chivers and crew turned back at Sheringham after the oxygen system failed and Sgt Shipway and crew lost the use of their rear turret and also had to abandon their sortie, while the others were guided to the target by red route-marker flares and then red and green skymarkers over the aiming point, which was hidden by ten-tenths cloud with tops at 5,000 to 15,000 feet. The remaining 61 Squadron crews delivered their bomb loads from between 19,000 and 21,000 feet, some observing a large red glow reflected in the clouds. F/L Dierkes and crew were attacked by a night-fighter at 16,000 feet near The Hague on the way home, but the encounter was inconclusive, and no damage was reported. Local sources confirmed that this was another highly scattered raid, which spread bombs over a wide area of the Ruhr and destroyed only fifty houses in Duisburg.

Frankfurt was posted as the destination on the 10th for 502 aircraft, of which the 144 Wellingtons would represent the most populous type, demonstrating that this trusty old warhorse still had an important role to play in Bomber Command operations. 5 Group provided sixty-six of 136 Lancasters, seven of them belonging to 61 Squadron, which departed Syerston between 23.58 and 00.34 with S/L Hall the senior pilot on duty. The plan was standard for a target beyond the range of Oboe and required eleven Stirlings and six Halifaxes to drop yellow TIs as route markers by H2S, followed by preliminary warning flares, all of which were to be backed up by two Stirlings, ten Halifaxes and seventeen Lancasters. Cloud conditions permitting, the aiming-point was then to be marked by red TIs on H2S, and if not, by green flares with red stars and a white flare, with appropriate backing up with green TIs or coloured flares. They adopted the usual course to this region of Germany, following the line of the Franco/Belgian frontier to cross into Germany on an east-north-easterly heading north of Saarbrücken. The H2S marker crews arrived in the target area to be confronted by ten-tenths cloud with tops at between 8,000 and 12,000 feet but found that their red TIs were visible and opted not to sky mark. This was fine in the early stages, until it became impossible to distinguish the genuine TIs from decoys, incendiaries and searchlights, and the backer-up crews experienced great difficulty in establishing an aiming-point. The 61 Squadron crews went in at between 14,000 and 19,000 feet, having been guided by preliminary warning flares, and some bombed at whatever was glowing beneath the cloud or on e.t.a., without being able to assess the outcome. Bombing photos revealed nothing but cloud, and local sources confirmed that only a few bombs had fallen into the southern suburbs.

On the 11th, 5 Group sent six Lancasters back to the Elderberry and Furze gardens, 61 Squadron providing the crews of Sgts Phillips, Shipway and Parsons, who departed Syerston in that order between 20.35 and 20.45. Arriving in the target area in favourable conditions, each pinpointed on

Pointe-St-Martin, before planting their vegetables according to brief from between 1,000 and 3,500 feet and returning safely after eight-hour round-trips.

On the 13th, 208 Lancaster crews were notified of a change of scenery for their next operation, which was to be against the docks at La Spezia on Italy's northern coast some forty miles south-east of Genoa, where elements of the Italian fleet were believed to be at berth. 5 Group detailed 124 of the Lancasters, with the remainder provided by 1 and 8 Groups, the latter also sending three Halifaxes as part of the marker force. 61 Squadron loaded its fifteen aircraft with 1,000 pounders and SBCs of incendiaries and departed Syerston between 20.28 and 20.40 with S/L Hall the senior pilot on duty. F/L Cooper and crew had reached the midpoint of the Channel when the Oxygen system failed, while F/L Benjamin and crew were defeated by an electrical fault in the bomb-release circuitry. As they turned back, the rest of the force made landfall over the Normandy coast, traversed France and arrived on the Italian side of the Alps to find almost cloudless skies and only haze and smoke to mar the vertical visibility. They established their positions by visual reference of ground detail, such as rivers and the docks, confirmed by Path Finder flares and bombing by the 61 Squadron element took place from between 6,000 and 10,000 feet. Three large vessels observed tied together east of the outer harbour were seen to be on fire, and the naval oil stores were targeted by some crews, but none positively identified the main objectives, the battleships.

By the later stages of the raid, many fires had added to the smoke obscuring the town, and a number of large explosions encouraged the crews' belief that a successful operation had taken place, which, ultimately, would be confirmed. Sgt Pullan and crew had pinpointed on Lakes Bourget and Savona but failed to identify the target area despite conducting a square search, and when the Lancaster began to struggle to maintain height the bombs were jettisoned and a southerly course set for North Africa. In the absence of a functioning W/T they landed in a ploughed field, scrounged petrol from an American unit and took off on three engines for Maison Blanche, one of the captured former enemy airfields in Algeria. They found two other Lancasters undergoing repair in what was the first unofficial "shuttle" raid and returned to England sometime later via Gibraltar. Meanwhile, ED717 had ditched at 07.45 off the Isles of Scilly and fortunately was spotted by a Coastal Command Whitley, which directed a high-speed ASR launch to pick up F/O Chivers and crew after they had spent sixty-three hours in a dinghy.

The busy round of non-Ruhr operations continued with the posting of Stuttgart as the target on the 14th, for which a force of 462 aircraft was made ready, 5 Group providing fifty-seven Lancasters, nine of them made ready by 61 Squadron and loaded with a cookie and twelve SBCs of incendiaries. At briefing, crews took in the details of the plan, which involved Path Finder aircraft dropping yellow TIs as route markers at two locations, while, at the target, nine Stirlings and eight Halifaxes were to ground-mark the aiming-point with red TIs on H2S, at the same time as releasing a short stick of flares. One Stirling and four Lancasters were then to identify the aiming-point visually, and mark it with green TIs, for three Stirlings, six Halifaxes and eleven Lancasters to back up also with greens. This would leave three Stirlings, three Halifaxes and five Lancasters to bolster the efforts of the main force. The 61 Squadron contingent departed Syerston between 22.06 and 22.14 with F/Ls Benjamin and Cooper the senior pilots on duty, with F/L Adams for the second time appointed captain of the Benjamin crew, presumably as a mentor. F/Sgt Rawes and crew lost an engine and turned back from a position west of Etaples, and Sgt Dashper and crew were about to cross the French coast near Dieppe when they, too, lost and engine and had to abandon their sortie.

The others followed the Franco/Belgian frontier and passed beyond Luxembourg to enter Germany in the Strasbourg area before approaching the city from the north-east to find an absence of cloud. The Path Finder ground marker crews established their positions by H2S confirmed by visual reference, but as evidence of the shortcomings of H2S in its early form, they were actually short of the city centre when they delivered bundles of white flares, red TIs and 1,000 pounders between 00.47 and 00.56. The backers carried four green TIs, one of them of the long-burning variety, four 1,000 pounders and a single 500 pounder each, which they dropped between 00.50 and 01.14, also to the north-east of the planned aiming-point. The main force crews were greeted by plentiful red and green TIs concentrated in a built-up area, and some would claim later to have picked out ground details such as marshalling yards, the railway station, the river and the Bosch factory through the copious volumes of smoke rising through 8,000 feet. This reinforced their belief that they were over the briefed aiming-point, where the TIs had mostly burned out by the time that the 61 Squadron crews delivered their attacks on concentrations of fire from between 11,000 and 17,000 feet, and there was little information to glean and pass on at debriefing.

Bombing photos and post-raid reconnaissance confirmed that the Path Finders had not marked the centre of the city, and that a "creep-back" had developed, which had spread along the line of approach. Creep-back was a feature of many large raids and was caused by crews bombing the first fires they came upon, rather than pushing through to the planned aiming-point. It could work for or against the effectiveness of an attack, and on this night, worked in the Command's favour by falling across the industrial district of Bad-Canstatt, situated to the north-east of the city centre on the east bank of the River Neckar. The bombing continued to spread further back along the line of approach onto the residential suburbs of Münster and Mühlhausen, and it was here that the majority of the 393 buildings were destroyed and more than nine hundred others severely damaged.

Two major operations were planned for the 16th, the main one employing 327 Lancasters and Halifaxes to target the Skoda armaments factory at distant Pilsen in Czechoslovakia, while a force of 271 aircraft, consisting predominantly of Wellingtons and Stirlings, created a large-scale diversion at Mannheim some 240 miles to the west. A force of 197 Lancasters and 130 Halifaxes was detailed for Pilsen, of which 102 of the former were provided by 5 Group, thirteen of them made ready by 61 Squadron at Syerston. In an unnecessarily complicated plan, the Path Finders were to drop yellow route markers at the final turning point, seven miles from the target, which the main force crews were then to locate visually in the anticipated bright moonlight and bomb from as low a level as practicable. The plan briefed out to the Path Finder crews was more detailed and seemed to contain elements that were not part of the main force briefings. It called for six 35 (Madras Presidency) Squadron crews to employ H2S to drop long sticks of flares from south-west to north-east across the city and green TIs on the south-western edge of the Skoda works as a rough guide. These were to be backed up by green TIs delivered by two Halifaxes and twenty Lancasters, unless cloud conditions rendered this impossible, in which case, red TIs were to be employed by both the markers and backers-up. Two further Halifaxes and five Lancasters were to attack with the main force. It was a plan of attack that invited confusion and failure, and the outcome would question the quality of some of the briefings.

The 61 Squadron element took off between 21.11 and 21.23 with S/L Gascoyne-Cecil the senior pilot on duty and a round-trip of some 1,500 miles to negotiate. They headed for Dungeness on the Kent coast to make landfall on the French coast in the area of Cayeux-sur-Mer, before swinging round Amiens and tracking eastwards towards the German frontier near Saarbrücken. Defective trimming tabs caused P/O Frost and crew to turn back, but the rest of the squadron participants reached the target area to find the forecast favourable weather conditions, with a layer of eight-tenths cloud at around 9,000 feet, below which, visibility was good and ground features could be made out clearly in bright moonlight. They delivered their bomb loads from between 6,000 and 9,000 feet and were genuine in their belief, expressed at debriefing, that they had identified and attacked the Skoda factory complex creating copious amounts of smoke and dust.

The briefings should have made clear that the bombing was to be carried out visually from below the cloud base after making a timed run from the turning-point, which had been marked by yellow TIs. Many 5 Group crews reported bombing on TIs, proving that they had failed to understand and comply with the instructions at briefing and had bombed the turning point and not the target. Some made reference to yellow and green TIs and white illuminator flares, but all described difficulty in locating and identifying the factory buildings, some after spending time searching while having to dodge searchlights and flak. The details of the crew reports across the groups demonstrated that they could not have related to the Skoda works and post-raid reconnaissance revealed the truth, that, despite the claims of returning crews, no bombs had fallen within miles of the factory and had been concentrated instead around an asylum at Dobrany, some seven miles to the south-west. This failure was compounded by the loss of thirty-six aircraft, split equally between the two types, and this represented a massive 11% of the force. 61 Squadron's W4317 was shot down by the night-fighter of Hptm Rudolf Altendorf of I./NJG4 and crashed at 04.30 seven miles south-east of Mons in Belgium, killing P/O Macfarlane and the other seven occupants. The losses from Pilsen had to be added to the eighteen aircraft also missing from the Mannheim contingent, which had, at least, achieved the destruction of 130 buildings and damage to some degree to three thousand others. The combined casualty figure of fifty-four aircraft represented a new record for a single night.

On the 18th, 97 (Straits Settlements) Squadron left 5 Group for a new role as a Path Finder Unit, although a year to the day hence it would find itself back on 5 Group territory on permanent loan. A return to the docks at La Spezia was notified to the Lancaster squadrons of 1, 5 and 8 Groups on the 18th, and 8 Group would also contribute five Halifaxes to the overall force of 178 aircraft. The eighty-nine 5 Group Lancasters included thirteen representing 61 Squadron, which departed Syerston between 20.51 and 21.09 with S/Ls Gascoyne-Cecil and Hall the senior pilots on duty. They all negotiated the outward flight across France and the Alps and found the weather to be ideal and visibility good in the target area, although an effective smoke screen partially obscured the town, docks and any warships at berth until it drifted to the south to hang over the gulf. The aiming point was identified visually after a timed run from Palmaria Island to the south, and confirmed by red Path Finder TIs, on which the 61 Squadron crews bombed from between 6,500 and 10,000 feet. The fires were becoming concentrated as they turned away and set course for home, completely satisfied with their night's work, and six brought back aiming point photos. Photographic reconnaissance revealed that the marking and bombing had fallen to the north-west of the dockyards but had caused extensive damage to the railway station and public buildings in the town centre.

On the 20th, the port-city of Stettin was posted as the target for a force of 339 aircraft, including ninety-one Lancasters representing 5 Group, thirteen of them belonging to 61 Squadron. The target was situated 640 miles from the Lincolnshire bomber stations as the crow flies but lay almost thirty miles south of the port of Swinemünde, beyond the Stettiner Haff and Stettin Lagoon inland seas and on the western bank of the River Oder. As the Lancasters were being prepared for battle, their crews were devouring the details of the route that would take the bomber stream across the North

Sea to a point north of Esbjerg on the Danish coast, before traversing Jutland, then to head southeast towards the target. The distance, which was similar to that for Pilsen, would keep some crews in the air for more than nine hours, and would require a small reduction in bombs among the main force element in favour of fuel. Navigation by coastline was expected to be simple in the prevailing conditions, which negated the need for route markers, and once illuminating flares had laid bare the aiming point, the marking would be by H2S-based TIs backed up by greens.

The 61 Squadron element departed Syerston between 21.24 and 21.50 with F/Ls Benjamin and Cooper the senior pilots on duty, before heading out over Mablethorpe to rendezvous with the rest of the bomber stream and completed the outward flight under clear skies. The favourable conditions persisted all the way to the target, where they benefitted from bright moonlight and horizontal visibility estimated to be fifty miles. They were able to identify ground features as they bore down on the aiming point and the 61 Squadron crews bombed on green TIs from between 12,000 and 14,500 feet and observed black smoke rising through 10,000 feet. There were targets, like Duisburg and, later, Braunschweig, that, for a period at least, seemed to enjoy something of a charmed life and managed to dodge the worst ravages of a Bomber Command attack, but Stettin was not among them, perhaps because of its location near an easily identifiable coastline. On this night, the perfect conditions paved the way for the Path Finders to deliver a flawless marking performance, which was exploited by the main force crews to devastating effect. Returning crews reported fires raging across the built-up area and the glow from the burning port-city visible for ninety miles into the return journey. The success cost the Command twenty-one aircraft, four of which belonged to 5 Group, and among these was 61 Squadron's W4795, which crashed at 02.30 somewhere in the Berlin defence zone on the way home and there were no survivors from the crew of P/O Rossignol RCAF, an American from Daytona Beach, Florida. It was thirty-six hours before a reconnaissance aircraft captured photographs of the still-burning city, and these revealed an area of one hundred acres of devastation across the centre. Local reports confirmed that thirteen industrial premises and 380 houses had been destroyed.

Orders on the 26th signalled a return to the Ruhr and Duisburg, for which a large force of 561 aircraft was assembled, the numbers bolstered by the inclusion of 135 Wellingtons, while 215 Lancasters represented the largest contribution by type. 8 Group was boosted by the operational debut of 97 (Straits Settlements) Squadron and 405 (Vancouver) Squadron RCAF in a plan that called for eight Oboe Mosquitos to drop yellow route markers and red TIs on the aiming-point. The yellows were to be backed up by others of the same colour delivered by a dozen Lancasters, while three Stirlings, five 35 (Madras Presidency) Squadron Halifaxes and seven Lancasters backed up at the aiming-point with green TIs. 5 Group was responsible for 105 of the Lancasters and 61 Squadron fourteen, which departed Syerston between 23.31 and 00.40 with W/C Penman the senior pilot on duty. After climbing out, they set course for the Dutch coast near The Hague for the northern approach to the Ruhr and reached the target area after approaching from the northeast. They found largely clear skies and good visibility and were guided to the aiming point by red and green TIs, upon which the bombing by the 61 Squadron crews was carried out from between 18,000 and 20,000 feet. F/O Thomas and crew were coned by searchlights at 19,000 feet and during violent evasive action jettisoned the bomb load north-east of the target from 16,000 feet. A large orange explosion was witnessed by many crews to the east of the aiming point at 02.34, but fires had not fully gained a hold by the time that the force withdrew, although black smoke was rising through 7,000 feet. Opinions were divided as to the degree of concentration achieved, but what was not in doubt was the failure to return of seventeen aircraft, just one of which belonged to 5 Group. Post-raid reconnaissance revealed that the attack had fallen short of the city centre and had been focused on the north-eastern districts under the line of approach, thus sparing Duisburg yet again from the full weight of a Bomber Command heavy raid. Even so, local reports confirmed the destruction of more than three hundred buildings, which represented something of a telling blow at this target.

The 27th was devoted to the largest mining operation of the war to date, which involved 160 aircraft targeting the waters off the Brittany and Biscay coasts and the Frisians. Twenty-eight 5 Group Lancasters were detailed, four of them representing 61 Squadron, which departed Syerston between 01.23 and 02.09 bound for the Nectarine I garden off the western Frisians and bearing aloft the crews of P/Os Dundas and Frost and Sgts Alderton and Phillips. Low cloud and poor visibility hampered attempts to locate a pinpoint for a timed run, but vegetables were planted from between 1,000 and 1,500 feet after establishing positions on Ameland by Gee-fix.

The following night brought an even larger gardening effort involving 207 aircraft, of which forty-one Lancasters were provided by 5 Group, 61 Squadron's six crews assigned to five separate gardens. The crews of Sgt Madgett, Sgt Lowe, Sgt Allcroft, P/O Dashper, W/O Collenette and Sgt Ellis departed Syerston between 20.26 and 20.51 bound for the Silverthorne 1 and V gardens in the Kattegat, the Hollyhock garden off Travemünde in the Bay of Mecklenburg, the Daffodil II garden at the southern end of The Sound (Oresund), and the Verbena garden off Copenhagen, where they planted their vegetables from between 1,000 and 2,000 feet. W/O Collenette DFM and crew failed to return from Verbena after W4898 disappeared in the target area, and the sea eventually gave up the remains of the pilot, flight engineer and navigator for burial at a number of cemeteries. The 5 Group crews operating over the Baltic had experienced favourable conditions, while elsewhere, low cloud was encountered and flak proved to be troublesome, contributing to the loss of twenty-one other aircraft. This would be the largest-ever loss to result in a single night from mining, but, on the credit side, the number of mines delivered, 593, was also a record for one night and would not be surpassed.

Essen was posted as the target on the 30th, as attention swung once more towards the Ruhr and would remain upon it almost exclusively now until well into July. A force of 305 aircraft included 101 Lancasters of 5 Group, the dozen representing 61 Squadron each receiving a bomb load of a cookie and twelve SBCs before departing Syerston between 23.54 and 00.28 with F/O Chivers the senior pilot on duty. Sgt Phillips and crew were back on the ground after an hour having dealt with an engine fire, while the rest encountered a layer of ice-bearing cloud that lay across the bomber stream's path over the North Sea. Most crews negotiated it and were greeted at the target by ten-tenths cloud with tops in places as high as 21,000 feet and red and green Oboe-laid Wanganui flares (skymarkers) identifying the aiming point. Some crews carried out a time-and-distance run from green tracking markers, and all had some kind of flare in the bomb sight, or at least the glow of one, as the 61 Squadron crews released their loads from between 16,000 and 21,700 feet. Returning crews reported the glow of fires beneath the cloud and a number of large explosions, but it was impossible to determine whether or not concentration had been achieved, particularly as bombing photos showed only cloud. Post-raid reconnaissance and local reports confirmed a lack of concentration and the liberal distribution of bombs onto ten other Ruhr locations, particularly Bottrop to the north, but 189 buildings were destroyed and 237 severely damaged in Essen, and importantly, Krupp manufacturing sites sustained further damage.

During the course of the month, the squadron took part in eighteen operations and dispatched 154 sorties for the loss of three Lancasters and crews.

P/O Bill MacFarlane crew. Lancaster W4317 QR-R

All crew killed 17th April 1943 on a Plzen operation when they were shot down by a night-fighter, exploded in mid-air and crashed in Belgium. Crew: P/O William MacFarlane (Pilot), Sgt Peter John Keay RAAF (2nd Pilot), F/Sgt William Dawson (Obs), F/O Cyril Williams (Nav), Sgt Edward Davidson (2nd Nav), P/O John Edwards DFM (W.Op/AG), Sgt Jack Rees (MUG), P/O Donald Holdsworth (RG).

Remains of Lancaster W4317   *(Aircrew Remembered)*

S/L Reginald Ayles DFC DFM Completed 22 operations with 61 Squadron and had four different crews.

P/O R N Ayles was awarded the DFC on the 13th July 1943.

P/O R N Ayles with Crew and Groundcrew.
Following his tour with 103 Squadron, W/O Ayles instructed at 27 OTU. He was called up for participation in the thousand bomber raid on Cologne on 30th May 1942, then joined 61 Squadron on the 7th December 1942.

Lancaster EE190 QR-M
Wrecked while trying to land at Blida Airfield, Algiers 16th July 1943. No injuries reported.

Lancaster MkII with Bristol Hercules radial engines, taken by F/L Dr John S Cook (pilot) in 1943.

*F/L Alfred Mullins DFM
Flight Engineer in P/O Parsons' Crew*

P/O Parsons' navigator Bob Dyson at his desk. P/O Dyson was killed when a piece of flak penetrated the fuselage.

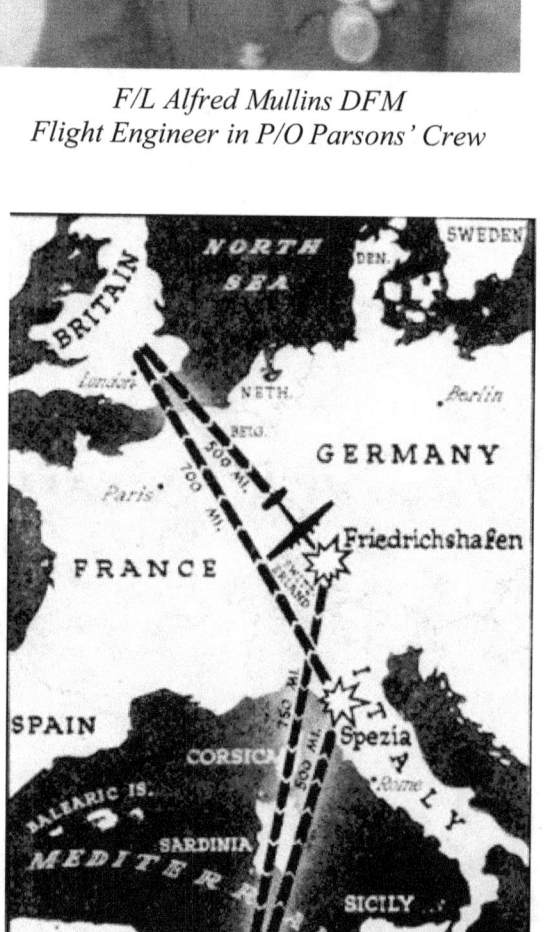

Operation Bellicose

After take-off from Britain, the Avro Lancasters bombed from 15,000ft rather than the planned 10,000 ft. due to heavy flak. First the Pathfinder Force (PFF) dropped offset markers at a distance from the target for the main bombing force to use unobscured by smoke. the second stage was to use 'time-and-distance bombing runs' from a location on the Lake Constance shore along a measured distance to the target.

The attack hit the V-2 rocket facility of the Zeppelin Works, which made Operation Bellicose the first mission that bombed a long-range weapon facility.

From Friedrichshafen the planes refuelled at Blida, Algeria in North Africa.

P/O Ward Parsons DFC
Pilot

Sgt A (Nobby) Clark. DFM
Wireless Operator/Air Gunner

Sgt. George Issacs. DFM.
Gunner

Sgt C D Towse DFM
Rear Gunner

F/Sgt Frank J. Poole. DFM
Bomb Aimer

*Maison Blanche Airfield, Algiers. June 1943.
61 Squadron. Lancaster W5002 QR-L.*

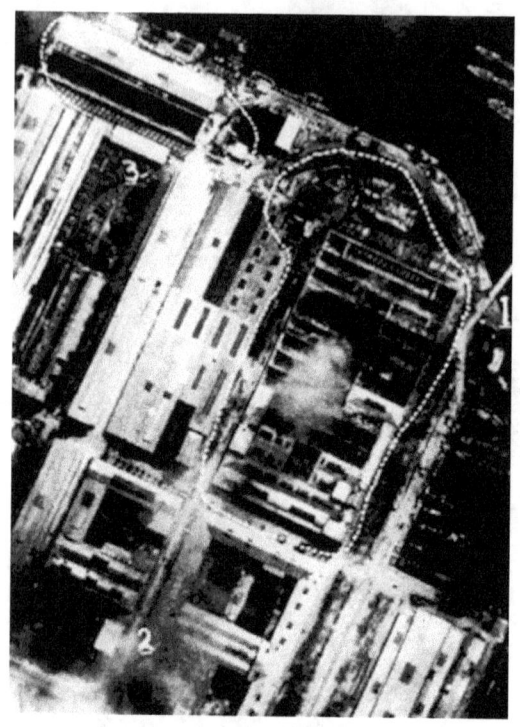

Left: *The Italian naval base at La Spezia, Liguria, Italy*

*The Parsons' Crew
Back row: Nobby Clark (W/Op), Danny Towse (R/G), George Isaccs (MUG), Bob Dyson (Nav). Sitting:
Frank Poole (BA) Fred Mullins (Eng) Ward Parsons (Pilot)*

61 Squadron Lancaster EE176 QR-M Mickey the Moocher with crew

*S/L John De Lacy Wooldridge,
DSO, DFC and Bar, DFM*

*F/O Phil Martin RAAF joined
617 Squadron after completing
a tour with 61 Squadron.*

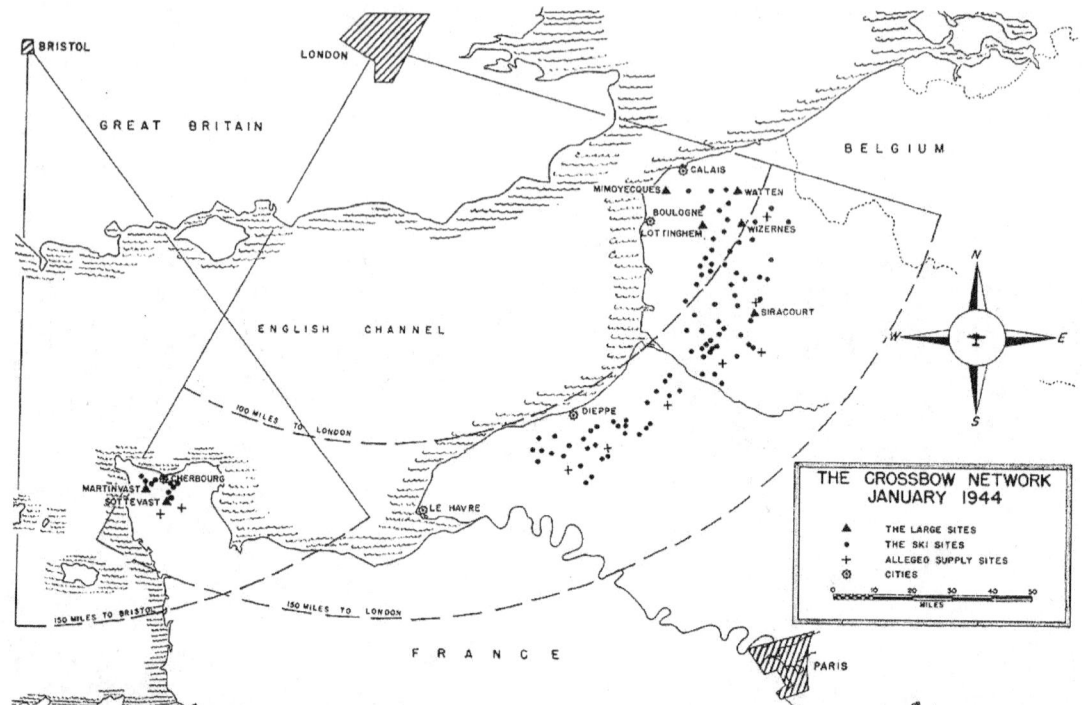

A World War II map shows the two areas where the Germans were setting up their secret "V" weapons to bombard England (right, centre). These are the areas in which the Royal Air Force and 8th Air Force heavy bombers concentrated their bombs to destroy the weapons -- part of the pre-invasion plan. This event was given the operational code name Crossbow during World War II.

Attack on Rilly la Montagne V-1 site, France

The map reveals the extent of destruction in the centre of Berlin (darkened area) wrought by RAF Bomber Command up to February 1944.

Low-level oblique aerial photograph showing the heavily bombed flying-bomb assembly and launch bunker at Siracourt, France 1944.

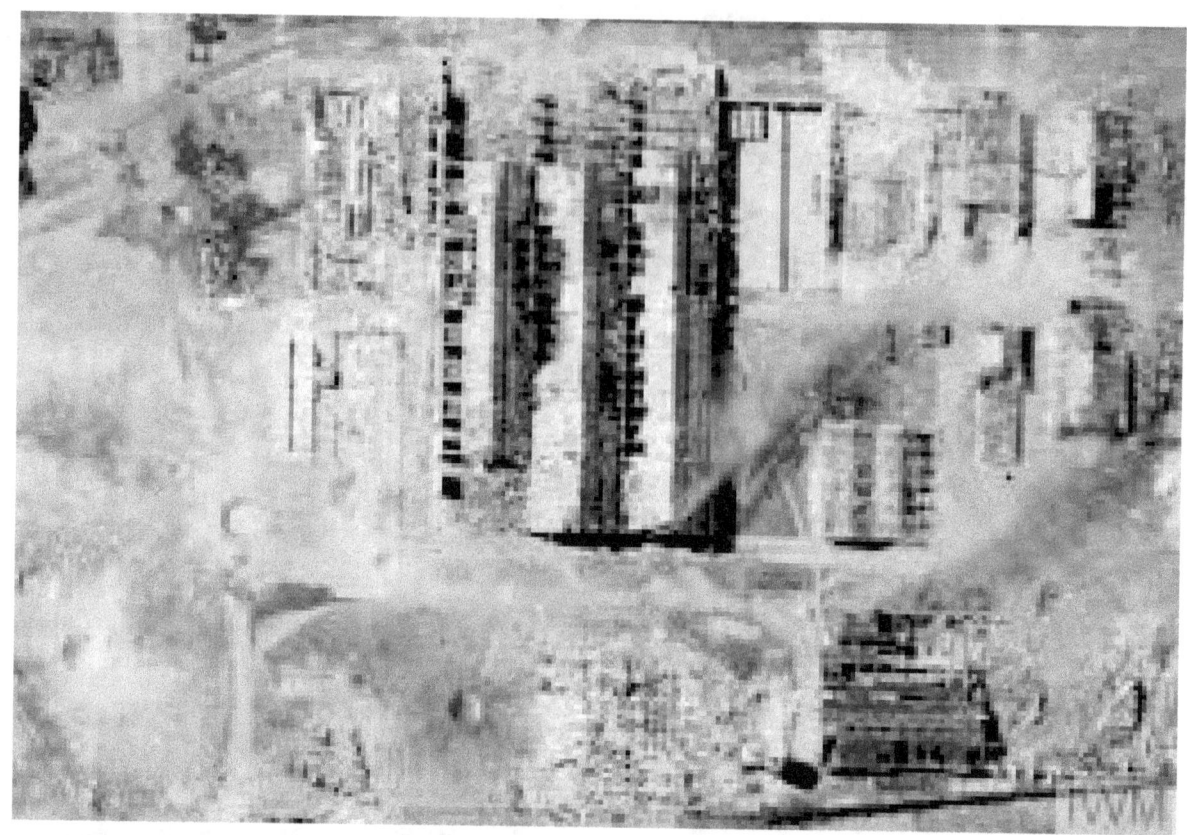
Toulouse Aircraft Plant attacked by Bomber Command including 61 Squadron April 1944

This post-raid reconnaissance photograph shows the destruction at the German barracks and battle-tank depot at Mailly-Le-Camp after the raid on 3/4th May 1944.

Raid on the V1 storage and assembly areas in the caves at St Leu d'Esserent, near Criel, north of Paris, on the 4/5th July 1944.

F/L J Gray DFM *F/L N F Turner DFM* *F/L T S Cook*

F/L W E Grantham *P/O F Mouritz* *W/O A E Perry*
(KIA 8th July 1944) *(F/O Pearse's Crew)*

F/L Bill North *Sgt Denis Bartlett and Sgt Les Morton.*

The Grantham Crew

L – R: F/L William 'Ted' Grantham (Pilot), Sgt Geoffrey Berry (FE), F/Sgt Thomas 'Cliff' Young (BA), F/Sgt William Hobbs (Nav), F/Sgt Ronald Towndrow (W.Op/AG), Sgt Peter Baigent (RG), Sgt Charles Balser (MUG). Except Sgt Berry who was captured and F/Sgt Young who evaded, all were killed on the 8th July 1944 on a St. Leu raid.

The Mouritz Crew

L – R: Jim Leith (FE), Dennis Cluett (RG), Peter Smith (BA), Frank Mouritz (Pilot), Arthur Bass (MUG), Laurie Cooper (Nav), Dave Blomfield (W.Op). October 1944

F/O John Condon was killed flying Lancaster LD470 over Germany on 23rd September 1944.

F/Sgt Keith Finch RAAF died on flying operations over Germany on 25th March 1944, aged 19.

Warrant Officer John Manning. Gunner who left 61 Squadron to join 617 Squadron in 1944.

F/O Laurie Pearse RAAF was the pilot of the ill fated QR-N Nan which crashed on take-off on what should have been its 131st operation.

Centurian Lancaster ED860 QR-N receiving her 100th bomb symbol in late 1944. This is one of the earliest dated photos of a Lancaster fitted with 'Z' equipment in the bomb aimer's blister.

Lancaster ED860 QR-N Nan's mounted bomb panel.

QR-N NAN's 131st operation 28th October 1944.
At 22.35 hours F/O Pearse lined his Lancaster at the end of Skellingthorpe runway and opened the throttle against the brakes to see if all Merlin engines responded evenly. He then throttled back, released the brakes and began to reopen the throttles again. The heavily loaded aircraft slowly built-up speed until it was thundering down the runway, but before the young Aussie pilot had full control a dangerous swing developed, and the aircraft swung violently to port hitting a runway glim lamp which burst a tyre, and the undercarriage collapsed. The resulting ground loop tore off part of the port wing spilling fuel from ruptured fuel tanks and by the time the aircraft finally came to a halt the heavy fuel and bomb load had crushed the bomb bay doors and lower fuselage. Before emergency services arrived on the scene all the crew had managed to scramble out of the aircraft and distance themselves from the very dangerous situation. They were all feeling very shaken after such a devastating experience, but otherwise unhurt. The C/O at that time was furious at the loss of the squadron's record-breaking aircraft and made Pearse go to all sections to apologise. The crew were also given the silent treatment by other aircrews!

P/O Laurie Pearse and Crew
Despite the setback to his career regarding the loss of QR-N, F/O Pearse went on to prove his courage and skill by completing 26 difficult and dangerous operations. The end of the WWII coming too soon for him to complete his tour. Crew: F/Sgt R Pettigrew (Nav), F/Sgt J Murray (FE), Sgt R Gillander (RG), F/O L Pearse (Pilot), Sgt D Baker (BA), Sgt A Barker (MUG), F/Sgt A Perry (W.Op)

Official war art by W. Krogman
The painting imagines a bombing raid on the German city of Cologne. The city's cathedral is clearly visible. It survived the war, despite being hit dozens of times by Allied bombs.

May 1943

May would bring a return to winning ways, with a number of outstanding successes and new records as the Ruhr offensive expanded its horizons to include targets other than Essen and Duisburg. It was, in fact, Duisburg that was posted as the target for each of the first three nights of the new month, before the operations were cancelled. The first of the "new" targets was Dortmund, which had been attacked many times before, but not on the scale that it was about to face on the 4th, when the force of 596 aircraft represented the largest non-1,000 effort to date. 5 Group made available 125 Lancasters, of which fourteen were prepared by 61 Squadron at Syerston, each receiving a bomb load of a cookie and twelve SBCs of incendiaries, while their crews were being informed of the plan at briefing. Oboe Mosquitos were to drop yellow track markers, before eight of them ground-marked the aiming-point with green TIs, leaving two in reserve to bomb with the main force if not required for marking duties. Twenty-two Lancasters and two Halifaxes were to back up with red TIs, and all remaining Path Finder aircraft were to bomb with the main force. The 61 Squadron contingent took off between 21.59 and 22.20 with W/C Penman and S/L Hall the senior pilots on duty and F/Sgt Lancaster and crew undertaking their first sortie since joining the squadron in the final week of April.

They had been serving with 57 Squadron at Scampton and were involved in the posting of C Flight to form the nucleus of 617 Squadron in late March, performing well during training to the extent that their average bombing error was among the best in the squadron. This probably irked W/C Gibson, who could not disguise his contempt for NCOs and would certainly not want one to outshine his officer-captained crews. Gibson picked a fight with George Lancaster and crew and issued an ultimatum to either replace the navigator or leave the squadron and return to 57 Squadron. Crew loyalty was the glue that held squadrons together and to his credit, Lancaster opted to leave 617 Squadron, one suspects after such a heated exchange between him and Gibson, that he and his crew were banished from Scampton altogether and could not, therefore, resume their tour with 57 Squadron, which was 61 Squadron's gain.

They crossed the Lincolnshire coast with the rest of the squadron on their way to rendezvous with the bomber stream over the North Sea but were unable to maintain height and had to turn back. They were followed home from the midpoint of the North Sea by the crew of Sgt Phillips after an engine fire ended their interest in proceedings. The others pushed on across Holland to enter Germany to the north of the Ruhr and make their way to the eastern end, where they found clear skies, good visibility and only industrial and smoke haze to spoil the vertical view. Yellow Path Finder tracking skymarkers were used as the starting point for a timed run to the target, while the defences responded with many searchlight cones and intense heavy flak, and much evasive action would be required after bombing to vacate the target area intact. The initial Path Finder marking was accurately placed around the city centre, but some of the backing-up fell short and a decoy site was also successful in luring away a proportion of the bombing. P/O Dundas lost one of his engines to an oil leak over the target, and the bomb-aimer then reported a fault in the bomb-release system, and by the time that the bombs fell away, they were eight miles north of the aiming point.

The other 61 Squadron crews aimed at red or green TIs from between 18,000 and 22,000 feet, some leaving a gap of up to ten seconds between the release of the cookie and incendiaries. On return, they reported many sizeable explosions, including a particularly large on at 01.12, which may have been the one reported by a 50 Squadron crew that threw flame to a height of 2,000 feet and burned for ten seconds. They also described developing fires, the glow from which could be seen, according to some, from 150 miles into the return flight. Post-raid reconnaissance revealed that approximately half of the force had bombed within three miles of the aiming point and had destroyed 1,218 buildings and seriously damaged more than two thousand others. Local reports confirmed a death toll of 693 people, which was a record from a Bomber Command attack. It was not a one-sided affair, however, and the loss of thirty-one aircraft was a foretaste of what was in store for the bomber crews operating over "Happy Valley".

There would be no major operations during the ensuing week, and when the Command as a whole was next called into action, on the 12th, it was for a major assault on Duisburg, for which a heavy force of 562 aircraft was assembled. Nine Oboe Mosquitos were to drop yellow TIs on track as a preliminary warning and red TIs on the aiming-point, which would be backed up with green TIs by five Stirlings, five Halifaxes and twenty Lancasters. 5 Group detailed 119 of the 238 Lancasters, and they would be accompanied by 142 Halifaxes, 112 Wellingtons and seventy Stirlings. The fourteen 61 Squadron Lancasters departed Syerston between 23.48 and 00.21 with S/Ls Gascoyne-Cecil and Hall the senior pilots on duty, and after climbing out over the station, they headed for the North Sea to rendezvous with the bomber stream and make landfall on the Dutch coast in the area of Castricum-aan-Zee. They reached the target area guided by the yellow tracking flares and found ideal bombing conditions with no cloud and good visibility, which helped the Oboe and H2S crews to mark with great accuracy and focus. The main force crews were able to identify ground features and exploit the opportunity to produce a display of unusually concentrated bombing, those from 61 Squadron delivering their attacks mostly onto red TIs from between 16,500 and 21,000 feet.

Perhaps, for the first time at this target, the attack proceeded according to plan, and Duisburg finally succumbed to a devastating assault, returning crews describing a large explosion at 02.30 and streets outlined by fire. For many crews, it was the best they had yet witnessed, and their impressions were confirmed by photo-reconnaissance, which revealed extensive damage in the city centre and the Ruhrort Rhine docks, the largest inland port in Germany. It was assessed that 1,596 buildings had been totally destroyed and the Thyssen steelworks hit, while dozens of barges and ships were sunk or damaged. However, many crews were absent from debriefing at stations across the Command, and it soon became clear that the success had been gained at the high cost of thirty-four aircraft. 61 Squadron's W4269 was still outbound with the crew of Sgt Alderton when brought down by flak to crash without survivors at 02.06 in the outskirts of Amsterdam. The loss rates by type again made interesting reading and confirmed the established food chain, the Lancasters sustaining a 4.2% loss, compared with 8.9% for Wellingtons, 7.1% for Stirlings and 6.3% for Halifaxes. Such was the level of destruction that Duisburg would now be left in peace for a year.

On the following night, the squadron contributed fourteen aircraft to a 5 Group force of 124 Lancasters, which, with thirty-two other Lancasters and twelve Halifaxes of 8 Group, would attempt to rectify the recent failure at the Skoda armaments works at Pilsen. A simultaneous raid was planned against the Ruhr city of Bochum, another new target for the campaign, and would involve 442 aircraft from the other groups. The 61 Squadron element departed Syerston between 21.28 and 21.51 with W/C Penman and S/L Hall the senior pilots on duty and lost the services of the crews of Sgts Allcroft and Ellis to engine and intercom failures respectively at the midpoint of the North Sea crossing. The others completed the 650-mile outward leg across France and southern

Germany and reached the target to find clear skies and good visibility, but with ground haze and a smokescreen to impair the vertical visibility. The Path Finders dropped yellow and white track markers and red TIs with a fairly good concentration that would have been perfectly adequate over a built-up area, while at a precision target like the Skoda works, they were too scattered to be effective. Bombing by the 61 Squadron crews was carried out from between 8,800 and 10,500 feet, and the impression was that most of the hardware fell among the TIs and the opinion was voiced that if the TIs had been on the target, the operation had been successful. Sadly, they were found to have missed the factory complex, and most of the bombs had fallen into open country to the north. Some compensation was gained at Bochum, where almost four hundred buildings were destroyed and seven hundred seriously damaged at a cost of twenty-four aircraft, and these were added to the nine Lancasters missing from Pilsen.

The above operations proved to be the last major outings for the Path Finders and main force squadrons for nine days, and it was during this lull, that 617 Squadron entered bomber folklore with its epic attack on the Ruhr Dams under Operation Chastise on the night of the 16/17th. Among those taking part were the former sons of 61 Squadron, F/L "Norm" Barlow and his crew. The nineteen Lancasters were assigned to three waves, nine in wave 1 to attack the Möhne and Eder Dams, five in wave 2 with the Sorpe Dam as their objective and five in wave 3 to act as a mobile reserve. Waves 1 and 3 were to enter enemy territory over the Scheldt estuary, while, in order to provide a diversion, wave 2 was to make landfall over the western Frisians a hundred miles to the north. With a greater distance to fly, wave 2 was scheduled to take off first and after F/L Joe McCarthy and crew were temporarily delayed, the Barlow crew found themselves at 21.28 the first to take off on this momentous operation. At 23.50, having crossed the Rhine and set a new course for the target, ED927 AJ-E flew into high-tension cables and crashed on farmland at Heeren-Herken without survivors. The Upkeep weapon failed to detonate, was recovered intact and taken to the research and development centre at Rechlin, and, within ten days, technical drawings had been produced of the bomb, its workings and the modifications to the Lancaster.

By the time that the next major operation was posted on the 23rd, the main force squadrons had undergone an expansion with the addition to many units of a third or C Flight, which, in most cases, would eventually be hived off to form the nucleus of a brand-new squadron. The giant force of 826 aircraft was the largest non-1,000 force to date and surpassed the previous record set three weeks earlier by a clear 230 aircraft. The number of available Lancasters had leapt by eighty-eight, Halifaxes by forty-eight, Stirlings by forty and Wellingtons by forty-one, and their destination for the second time in the month was Dortmund. The Command had been restored to full health and vigour and activity on all participating stations was hectic as preparations were put in hand to resume the Ruhr offensive. The ground crews and armourers worked tirelessly, while the crews attended briefings to learn of their part in the night's grand plan, which called for eleven Mosquitos to drop yellow preliminary warning TIs on track, before marking the aiming-point with Oboe-laid red TIs, which eight Stirlings, eleven Halifaxes and fourteen Lancasters were to back up with green TIs. 5 Group detailed a record 154 Lancasters, and having re-established the C Flight that had been disbanded when the Mk II Lancasters departed, 61 Squadron made ready seventeen at Syerston, where they were loaded with the standard Ruhr load of a cookie and twelve SBCs of incendiaries. They took off between 22.58 and 23.52 with W/C Penman and S/L Hall the senior pilots on duty and headed out over Skegness to join up with the bomber stream, losing the services F/O Chivers and crew to an engine issue on the way.

Having made landfall near Castricum-aan-Zee, the bombers adopted a south-easterly course to the eastern Ruhr, where they were greeted by clear skies but considerable industrial haze. Before the advent of Oboe, this would have rendered the attack a lottery, but now the thirteen Path Finder Mosquitos marked the centre of the city accurately and the Path Finder heavy brigade backed-up to maintain the aiming point with red and green TIs. These could be seen from twenty miles away on approach, as could the yellow track markers assisting the early 5 Group arrivals for their time-and-distance runs. The 61 Squadron crews bombed largely on the clusters of red and green TIs from between 15,000 and 22,500 feet, the lower height that of W/C Penman and crew, who had lost an engine and were unable to claw any extra feet. Returning crews reported many explosions and fires, which were merging into a large area of conflagration with thick columns of black smoke rising up through 18,000 feet as the bombers turned away. They also commented on fierce night-fighter activity over the target and on the way home, and this was reflected in the high casualty rate of thirty-eight aircraft, the largest loss of the campaign to date, almost half of which were Halifaxes and eight Lancasters, four belonging to 5 Group.

The Ruhr offensive continued with the posting of Düsseldorf as the target on the 25th, for which a force of 759 aircraft was assembled, 5 Group contributing 139 Lancasters, a record eighteen of them representing 61 Squadron. Briefings revealed the standard procedure of Mosquito-laid yellow preliminary warning TIs on track and red TIs delivered by Oboe onto the aiming-point, after which eight Stirlings, twelve Halifaxes and twenty-three Lancasters were to back these up with green TIs, leaving five Stirlings, fourteen Halifaxes and twenty-five Lancasters to bomb with the main force. The 61 Squadron contingent departed Syerston between 23.05 and 23.40 with W/C Penman and S/L Gascoyne-Cecil the senior pilots on duty, station commander, G/C Odbert, flying as second pilot with the latter and each Lancaster carrying a cookie and twelve SBCs of incendiaries. F/L Talbot's port wing dropped almost to ground level on take-off, but he dragged the Lancaster into the air and continued on towards Southwold in the hope of being able to correct the problem with trimming controls. When this proved to be ineffective, he headed directly to the jettison area off the coast and dumped the cookie before returning to base.

The others continued on to the Dutch coast, where some crews claimed that they were able to observe feverish activity at the target some one hundred miles and thirty minutes flying time away. Düsseldorf lay beneath two layers of thin cloud, and the generally poor visibility impacted the Path Finders' ability to back up the Mosquito-laid TIs to the extent that two red TIs were seen to be thirty miles apart. There were also decoy markers and dummy fire sites operating, which succeeded in causing confusion and prevented a concentration of bombing. The 5 Group crews carried out time-and-distant runs from yellow track markers, before identifying the target visually and by red and green TIs and the 61 Squadron participants bombed from between 16,500 and 23,000 feet. Post-raid reconnaissance and local reports confirmed that the raid had failed to achieve concentration and had developed into an "old-style" scattering of bombs across a wide area, leading to the destruction in Düsseldorf of fewer than a hundred buildings. Twenty-seven aircraft failed to return, five of them belonging to 5 Group and among them was the one containing 207 Squadron's commanding officer.

Harris was not yet done with Essen and the fifth visitation by the bomber force during the campaign was notified to stations on the 27th, for which a force of 518 aircraft was assembled, 5 Group putting up 133 Lancasters, a new record of nineteen representing 61 Squadron. 8 Group prepared two plans of attack, one for ground marking and an alternative for skymarking in the event of cloud cover. As matters turned out, the latter would be employed, which called for a dozen Oboe

Mosquitos to drop red flares nineteen miles short of the target and green ones ten-and-a-half miles short as a preliminary warning. Continuing on to the target, they were then to skymark the aiming-point with red flares with green stars and two white flares, allowing the rest of the 8 Group participants to bomb with the main force. The 61 Squadron element became safely airborne between 21.46 and 22.51 with five pilots of flight lieutenant rank leading the way, among them F/L Cooper, who was on the final sortie of his tour. For the second operation running, F/L Talbot and crew had to turn back early, this time because of starboard-outer engine failure. The others reached the target area to be greeted by six to eight-tenths cloud with tops at 12,000 feet, and were led in by tracking flares, ahead of which Wanganui skymarkers were gently descending into the cloud tops over the aiming point. The 5 Group crews carried out time-and-distance runs and bombed on white flares and red parachute markers with green stars, those from 61 Squadron from between 18,500 and 22,000 feet. Post-raid reconnaissance revealed that much of the bombing had fallen short, but 488 buildings had been destroyed, mostly in central and northern districts, and ten nearby towns reported themselves to be victims of collateral damage. Twenty-three aircraft failed to return, and the Halifaxes again represented almost half of the casualties.

A force of 719 aircraft was assembled on the 29th to pitch against another new Ruhr target, the conurbation known as Wuppertal, perched on the southern rim of the Ruhr Valley east of Düsseldorf. It consisted of the towns of Barmen and Elberfeld, which had grown wealthy on the proceeds of rich coal deposits. The aiming-point for this night's attack was to be the Barmen half at the eastern end, for which 5 Group detailed 129 Lancasters, seventeen of them representing 61 Squadron and departing Syerston between 22.17 and 22.51, again with pilots of flight lieutenant rank leading the way. On a night of poor serviceability for the squadron, the crews of Sgts Eager and Phillips and F/Sgt Docker aborted their sorties respectively because of rear turret failure, an inability to climb above 13,000 feet and an engine issue. On this occasion, the route markers were to be dropped by two 8 Group Stirlings and two Halifaxes, while ahead, the Oboe Mosquitos took care of ground marking with red TIs. These would be backed up by four Stirlings, eleven Halifaxes and twenty-three Lancasters with greens, at the same time as thirteen Stirlings, twenty Halifaxes and twenty-one Lancasters acted as fire raisers by dropping incendiaries, leaving two Stirlings, five Halifaxes and seven Lancasters to bomb with the main force.

Having negotiated the southern approach to the Ruhr, running the gauntlet of searchlights and flak in the Cologne and Düsseldorf corridor, crews were greeted by clear skies in the target area, with the usual industrial haze extending up to 10,000 feet. The yellow tracking flares clearly identified the final turning-point, and the backers-up went in at 16,000 to 18,000 feet between 01.03 and 01.51 to reinforce the red TIs with greens. Meanwhile, the thirteen fire-raisers had attacked with a 2,000 pounder and 1,164 x 4lb incendiaries each, leaving the way clear for the main force to exploit the opportunity to deliver a massive blow. The depleted 61 Squadron element delivered cookies and 4lb and 30lb incendiaries from between 15,000 and 22,000 feet and it was clear to all that something extraordinary was taking place as the built-up area beneath them became a sea of explosions and flames with smoke rising very rapidly through 15,000 feet. On return, Sgt Ellis and crew reported that they had been coned as they passed over Solingen at 22,000 feet just a few miles short of the aiming point, and having sustain damage to the bomb doors, fuselage and tailplane, jettisoned their load "live" onto the town below and turned for home. Post-raid reconnaissance revealed this to be the most awesomely destructive raid of the campaign thus far, which devastated by fire a thousand acres, or around 80% of the built-up area, and destroyed almost four thousand houses, five of the six largest factories and more than two hundred other industrial buildings. It would be some time before the human cost could be established, but it is now accepted that 3,400 people lost their lives during this savage Saturday night. The defenders had their say also, and fought back to claim thirty-three bombers, including seven Lancasters, of which three were from 5 Group.

During the course of the month, the squadron carried out seven operations and dispatched 113 sorties for the loss of a single Lancaster and crew.

June 1943

There were no major operations at the start of June because of the moon period, and, although 5 Group stations were alerted on most of the first ten days, no operations actually took place. This kept the Path Finder and main force crews kicking their heels on the ground until the 11th, when Düsseldorf was briefed out to 783 crews. The plan would follow the standard pattern, in which Mosquito yellow preliminary warning flares were to be backed up by the other 8 Group aircraft and the Oboe-laid red TIs on the aiming-point backed up with greens. However, uncertainty concerning the weather conditions resulted in the Mosquitos also carrying target-marking red flares with green stars. 5 Group was responsible for 162 of the 326 Lancasters, and eighteen of them belonging to 61 Squadron were loaded with a cookie and SBCs of incendiaries each at Syerston and dispatched in two waves between 22.24 and 22.48 and 23.05 and 23.38 with W/C Penman the senior pilot on duty. The bomber stream adopted the southern approach to the Ruhr via the Scheldt estuary and had to contend with static and lightning conditions in towering ten-tenths cloud as they made their way across the North Sea, some reporting the tops to be at 23,500 feet. This had largely dissipated to leave just small amounts at 2,000, 5,000 and 10,000 feet over the southern Ruhr, depending upon the time of arrival on final approach.

Those in the vanguard of the main force were drawn on by yellow tracking flares from 01.05, and red skymarkers with green stars at 01.16, while those a little further back in the bomber stream were guided to the mark by red and green skymarkers. The Paramatta marking (ground-marking TIs) did not seem to appear until these crews were turning away, but they were clearly visible to those in the rear-guard, by which time a sea of flames had spread over a massive area with columns of smoke rising through 21,000 feet. The 61 Squadron crews delivered their attacks on red TIs from between 16,500 and 21,500 feet, before returning safely to report a successful night's work. When all aircraft had been accounted for, thirty-eight were found to be missing, a figure that equalled the heaviest loss of the offensive to date. Post-raid reconnaissance revealed an area of fire across central districts measuring eight by five kilometres, and local reports confirmed 8,882 individual fire incidents. More than seventy war-industry factories suffered a complete or partial loss of production, 140,000 people were bombed out of their homes and 1,292 lost their lives. Had it not been for an errant Oboe marker attracting a proportion of the bombing onto open country some fourteen miles to the north-east, the destruction would have been greater.

Bochum faced its second heavy visitation of the campaign on the 12th, and a force of 503 aircraft was made ready for the purpose, 5 Group contributing 165 Lancasters, eighteen of them provided by 61 Squadron. Briefings revealed that two Mosquitos were to drop yellow preliminary warning TIs, before joining seven others to mark the aiming-point with red TIs, which twenty-five Lancasters were to back up with greens. The 61 Squadron crews departed Syerston between 22.10

and 22.56 with F/Ls Benjamin, Stewart, Thomas and Wellburn the senior pilots on duty and set course via Texel to pass over central Holland. The entry point into Germany was to the west of Münster, before the course turned to the south for a direct run on Bochum, situated between Essen to the west and Dortmund to the east. F/Sgt Lancaster turned back when the rear gunner became unwell, which usually signified oxygen starvation, but that was the only 61 Squadron "boomerang", while the rest had to pass through night-fighters waiting in Dutch airspace and over the frontier region. A number of bombers fell victim at this stage of the operation, but the majority slipped through the net and on arrival at the target, the leading Path Finder crews encountered clear skies but eight to ten-tenths stratocumulus drifting across the city with tops at 14,000 feet that obscured ground detail. The 61 Squadron crews attacked from between 19,000 and 21,500 feet with red and green TIs in their bomb sights, and on return reported concentrated fires, the glow from which was visible for up to a hundred miles into the homeward journey. Twenty-four aircraft failed to return, at least nine of them having fallen victim to night-fighters, and there were six empty dispersal pans on 5 Group stations. Photo-reconnaissance revealed 130 acres of devastation, backed up by local reports that 449 buildings had been destroyed and more than nine hundred severely damaged.

Following a night's rest, the Ruhr offensive continued at Oberhausen, situated between Duisburg to the west and Essen to the east and home of the Ruhr Chemie synthetic oil plant at Sterkrade-Holten on the northern outskirts. Although the town itself had not been targeted in numbers before, it had been hit by many bombs intended for its near-neighbours, and on this night would face an all-Lancaster heavy force numbering 197 aircraft, 108 of them provided by 5 Group. A dozen belonging to 61 Squadron departed Syerston between 22.17 and 22.50 with F/Ls Stewart, Thomas and Wellburn the senior pilots on duty and each crew sitting on a cookie, four 500-pounders and a mix of 4lb and 30lb incendiaries. They set course for the Scheldt estuary to bypass Antwerp on their way to the Belgian/German frontier and soon lost the services of F/O Millar and crew to a defective compass. They were among fifteen 5 Group crews to turn back on what turned into a bad night for the squadron and the group. F/L Stewart and crew evaded an enemy night-fighter at the Dutch coast but observed five bombers falling in flames before the target was reached, the main force element arriving to find three to ten-tenths cloud with tops in places at 18,000 feet, which were bathed in very bright moonlight. Tracking flares were drifting down to provide a reference for the start of the time-and-distance runs, and over the aiming point main force crews aimed at reds with green stars and white skymarkers dropped by the six Oboe Mosquitos and backed-up by 8 Group heavies. F/Sgt Madgett and crew were contending with an oxygen supply issue, which caused the bomb-aimer to pass out, but fortunately an under-training bomb-aimer was on board to gain experience and he let the bombs go. The 61 Squadron crews delivered their loads from between 17,500 and 22,000 feet in the face of intense heavy flak, which continued to chase them out of the target area into the guns of night-fighters. Between them, the defences accounted for seventeen Lancasters, 8.4% of the force, ten of which belonged to 5 Group, but the two empty dispersal pans at Syerston belonged to 106 Squadron aircraft. Local sources confirmed that the Wanganui flares had been right over the city centre, where 267 buildings had been destroyed and 584 seriously damaged.

On the 16th, 1, 5 and 8 Group stations were notified that Cologne was to be the target for that night, for which a force of 202 Lancasters and ten Halifaxes was made ready, while their crews learned at briefings that there would be no Oboe Mosquitos on hand to mark the target, as that role was to be undertaken by the Path Finder Halifax element and six Lancasters employing H2S. 5 Group detailed eighty Lancasters, of which a dozen belonging to 61 Squadron were loaded with a cookie, four 500-pounders and ten SBCs of incendiaries and dispatched from Syerston between 22.15 and 22.33 with F/Ls Chivers, Stewart, Thomas and Wellburn the senior pilots on duty. Heading for the Scheldt estuary, F/L Chivers and crew had to abandon their sortie after the failure of the superchargers in all engines, and Sgt Ellis and crew must have crossed the enemy coast when having to turn back because of at least one indisposed crew member. Sgt Lowe and crew were engaged by a night-fighter as they made landfall near Flushing, the Lancaster sustaining damage and the rear gunner wounds, which required his removal from the turret at the same time as the enemy aircraft was seen to spiral down emitting smoke and sparks. The rear gunner was made comfortable as they continued on to the target with the rest of the squadron to be confronted by six to ten-tenths cloud and green tracking flares from which to make a time-and-distance run to the aiming point.

The Path Finders were late on target, and problems with some of the H2S sets led to sparse and scattered marking with solid white flares and reds with green stars. The 61 Squadron crews bombed from between 19,000 and 22,500 feet, and a number witnessed a large orange explosion at 01.08, although generally, they were unable to assess the outcome. Of five missing 5 Group Lancasters, one belonged to 61 Squadron, W4789 containing the crew of P/O Pullan and an under-training navigator. The mid-upper gunner was the only survivor and was taken into captivity, and the fact that only one body was recovered for burial suggests that the Lancaster was obliterated when the bomb load received a direct hit. The post-raid impression was that a proportion of the bombing had been concentrated where intended, but that some crews had been lured away by dummy markers, and local reports suggesting that only around a hundred aircraft had been involved, tended to support this view. Residential districts bore the brunt of the raid, and 401 houses were destroyed with 13,000 others sustaining damage to some extent, mostly lightly, while sixteen industrial premises and nine railway stations were hit, along with public and utility buildings.

The recent successes in the Ruhr had been aided by the sheer size of the urban areas below, which all but guaranteed that the bombs would hit something useful, even after smoke had obscured the aiming point TIs. It was a different matter at a small or precision target, however, which would rapidly be enveloped in smoke from the first bombs before the rest of the attacking force had a chance to draw a bead on the aiming point. When, on the 20th, therefore, an attack was mounted under the codename Operation Bellicose against the production site of the Würzburg radar sets, which the enemy was employing very successfully to warn of and intercept Bomber Command raids, a plan was already in place to combat the problem by adopting the oft-used and still-under-development 5 Group time-and-distance method. Briefings actually took place on the day before, when crews learned that the factory was housed in the old Zeppelin sheds at Friedrichshafen, situated on the shore of Lake Constance (Bodensee) on the frontier with Switzerland, and represented a very small target. The plan was to use a designated "Master of Ceremonies" to direct the bombing, much in the manner of Gibson at the Dams, and the officer chosen was the highly experienced G/C Len Slee, the former 49 Squadron commanding officer, with the popular W/C Gomm, commanding officer of 467 Squadron RAAF, as his deputy. 5 Group was to provide the main force element of fifty-six Lancasters, five of them from 61 Squadron, with four others from 8 Group's 97 (Straits Settlements) Squadron to provide the marking for the selected crews at the head of the stream. The plan called for the Channel to be crossed at a standard altitude, before descending gradually to 10,000 feet by the time that Orleans was reached, and thereafter, to fly at between 2,500 and 3,000 feet all the way to the Rhine. After crossing the Rhine, they were to climb to their briefed bombing height of between 5,000 and 10,000 feet for the rendezvous over the north-western shore of Lake Constance and then circle until receiving the start signal.

The 61 Squadron quintet departed Syerston between 21.44 and 21.52 with F/L Ed Benjamin the senior pilot on duty, and all would make it to the target on a rare night when not a single aircraft from the entire force turned back, despite encountering electrical storms and having to adjust the briefed course. That said, G/C Slee lost an engine to flak over France and was forced to drop back into the formation and hand over the lead to W/C Gomm, who, on arrival at the target under clear skies and in bright moonlight, became concerned about the hostility of the searchlight and light flak defences. In order to reduce the very real risk of heavy casualties, he decided to add five thousand feet to the bombing height, where, unknown to him, the wind was stronger and would push the bombing towards the north-east. The Path Finder element also had little time to climb to the new height, and this caused a slight delay in the opening of the attack. The first TI fell wide of the aiming point, but the second one was assessed by W/C Gomm to be accurate, upon which he called in the first crews, whose high explosives and incendiaries created the expected smoke and obscured the target. He decided that another TI on the aiming point might still provide a reference for some crews, but the Path Finders were driven off by the searchlights and light flak and abandoned the attempt. They were then ordered to drop flares along the shore of Lake Constance, to enable the remaining crews to begin their runs from a pre-determined landmark, fly across the lake to the opposite shore, pick up another landmark 2,000 yards from the target and continue at a constant speed for the requisite number of seconds to cover the distance to bomb release. The 61 Squadron crews carried out their attacks on cascading green TIs from between 11,750 and 14,700 feet either side of 02.50 and observed explosions and fires, some of which remained visible for eighty miles into the onward flight to landing grounds in North Africa, in what was the first official shuttle operation of the war. Post-raid reconnaissance revealed that a proportion of the bombs had hit the target, causing extensive damage, and there had been no losses among the attacking force.

While these crews were absent from England, a hectic round of four major operations to the Ruhr in the space of five nights began at Krefeld on the 21st, for which a force of 705 aircraft was assembled. 5 Group contributed ninety-two Lancasters, of which eleven represented 61 Squadron, and they departed Syerston between 23.03 and 23.34 with S/L Gascoyne-Cecil the senior pilot on duty. There were no early returns, and all reached the target, situated a short distance to the southwest of Duisburg and on the opposite side of the Rhine. Conditions in the target area were ideal, with small amounts of thin cloud at between 6,000 and 10,000 feet and bright moonlight, which would benefit attacker and defender alike. The Path Finders delivered a near-perfect marking performance, red TIs falling in concentrated fashion to clearly identify the city centre aiming point for the main force crews, among which those representing 61 Squadron carried out their attacks from between 17,200 and 20,500 feet and described a sea of red fire giving off masses of smoke, with one particular jet-black column rising through 18,000 feet as they turned away. All were convinced of the success of the operation, and one crew likened it to the Wuppertal-Barmen raid. There was no hint of troublesome flak or night-fighters, and yet forty-four aircraft failed to return, the heaviest casualties of the campaign to date. Many of these were lost to the Nachtjagd but 5 Group escaped relatively lightly with the loss of three Lancasters.

The medium-sized town of Mülheim-an-der-Ruhr, a close neighbour of Duisburg, Oberhausen and Essen, lies around a dozen miles to the north-east of Krefeld, and it was here that the red ribbon terminated on the target maps at briefings across the Command on the 22nd. A force of 557 aircraft was prepared, of which ninety of the Lancasters were provided by 5 Group, eleven of them representing 61 Squadron. The plan of attack called for eight Oboe Mosquitos plus two in reserve to drop yellow preliminary warning TIs on track, before marking the aiming-point with red TIs for twenty-nine Path Finder Lancasters to back up with greens. The 61 Squadron element departed Syerston between 22.22 and 23.01 with F/Ls Chivers, Stewart, Talbot and Thomas the senior pilots on duty and made their way via the Scheldt through the Cologne corridor, arriving at the target to find small amounts of cumulostratus cloud at between 5,000 and 10,000 feet, with red and green TIs clearly visible and defining the aiming point. They bombed from between 18,000 and 20,500 feet and witnessed the development of a concentrated area of fire, which was visible from the Dutch coast homebound. Returning crews commented on the intense searchlight and flak response and the number of night-fighters and reported that Krefeld was still burning from the night before. Local reports confirmed that the town had suffered severe damage, particularly in the northern districts, where 1,135 houses had been destroyed and more than 12,000 others damaged to some extent. The road and telephone communications to Oberhausen had been cut, preventing any passage out of the town other than on foot. In fact, some of the bombing had spilled into the eastern districts of Oberhausen, which was linked to Mülheim for air-raid purposes. It was another expensive night for the Command, however, which registered the loss of thirty-five aircraft, with the Halifaxes and Stirlings representing two-thirds of them and suffering a respective loss rate of 7.7% and 11.8%.

While the Path Finder and main force units were enjoying a night off and girding their loins for the next round of the Ruhr offensive, fifty of the 5 Group Lancasters that had landed in North Africa following the Friedrichshafen raid took off with two 97 (Straits Settlements) Squadron Path Finder aircraft to bomb the docks at La Spezia on the way home to England. The 61 Squadron crews of F/L Benjamin and P/Os Phillips, Dundas and Parsons departed Maison Blanche in that order between 19.51 and 20.02, leaving behind P/O Allcroft and crew, whose aircraft was unserviceable, and arrived in the target area to find clear skies but hazy conditions made worse by a smoke-screen. There appeared to be a degree of confusion in getting the raid started, but a lucky hit on an oil storage facility resulted in a large explosion at 23.41 just as the main force was running-in, and most crews were able to identify the target visually, thereafter, and by red, green and white Path Finder flares. Bombing was carried out by the 61 Squadron quartet in accordance with instructions from a Master Bomber from 9,750 to 12,700 feet between 21.33 and 21.36, and all returned safely home to moan about the length of time it had taken for the raid to develop and the poor communications with the raid controller. The authorities seemed happy to claim the destruction of the oil depot and an armaments store and declared the operation to be a success. *(The timing of the attack provided by the 49 Squadron ORB is two hours later than above, while the departure from Blida is concurrent.)*

Having destroyed the Barmen half of Wuppertal at the end of May in one of the most devastating attacks to date, it was time to visit the same catastrophe on the western half, Elberfeld, for which a force of 630 aircraft was made ready on the 24th. 5 Group supported the operation with 103 Lancasters, a dozen of which were provided by 61 Squadron, and on this occasion, six Lancasters, three Stirlings and three Halifaxes of 8 Group were to deliver the yellow route markers on H2S, while seven Oboe Mosquitos marked the aiming-point with red TIs and eighteen Lancasters, seven Halifaxes and three Stirlings backed them up with greens. The 61 squadron participants departed Syerston between 22.17 and 22.58 with F/Ls Chivers, Stewart and Thomas the senior pilots on duty, and lost the services of F/L Chivers and crew to wireless failure at Southwold. The others made landfall over the Scheldt estuary and ran the usual gauntlet of searchlights and flak from the Cologne and Düsseldorf defence zones, the crews of which were aided by the formation of condensation trails at between 18,000 and 21,000 feet to advertise the presence of the bomber stream. There seemed to be fewer guns firing at them over the target, where small amounts of cloud with tops at 17,000 feet were insufficient to obscure the ground and the 5 Group crews carried out time-and-distant runs from yellow tracking flares until observing cascading red and green TIs. The 61 Squadron element bombed from between 12,500 and 21,000 feet, and those arriving at the tail end of the attack, when the built-up area was well-alight, described thick columns of smoke already passing through 19,000 feet and the glow of fires visible from the Dutch coast. Post-raid reconnaissance revealed another massively concentrated and accurate attack, which had reduced to rubble an estimated 90% of Elberfeld's built-up area, including three thousand houses and 171 industrial premises. It had also severely damaged 2,500 houses and dozens of important factory buildings, and the fact that more buildings were destroyed than damaged, provided a telling commentary on the conditions on the ground. The number of fatalities stood at around eighteen hundred, and some of the survivors might have been cheered to know that thirty-four bombers, containing 240 of their tormentors, would not be returning to England that night. Remarkably, only two of these belonged to 5 Group.

Instructions were received across the Command on the 25th to prepare for the first major attack on the Ruhr city of Gelsenkirchen since 1941, when it had been a regular destination under the Oil Directive. A force of 473 aircraft was assembled, and the crews briefed to focus on the Nordstern synthetic oil plant (Gelsenberg A.G.), which was a Bergius-process manufacturer of high-grade petroleum products, particularly aviation fuel. 8 Group was to provide seven Oboe Mosquitos plus two in reserve to drop route markers and sky mark the aiming-point, and two others to bomb after the main force had finished, but none of its heavy aircraft was to be involved. 5 Group stations bombed up 114 Lancasters, sixteen on the 61 squadron dispersals at Syerston with a cookie, four 500-pounders and thirteen SBCs of 4lb and 30lb incendiaries each, and they were dispatched between 22.29 and 23.06 with W/C Penman the senior pilot on duty. They reached the target area to find ten-tenths stratus lying over the region with tops at 10,000 to 15,000 feet, which would not have been a problem for Oboe, had five of the twelve participating Mosquitos not suffered equipment failures. This caused tracking flares to be late and to drop in the wrong sequence in a somewhat scattered manner at a time when the crews were contending with an intense flak barrage.

Searchlights illuminated the cloud as those from 61 Squadron bombed either on red flares with green stars or evidence of fires and flak from between 17,500 and 21,000 feet. A large explosion was witnessed at 01.43, and the glow from the target was visible from the Dutch coast, to which the returning bombers were chased by a large deployment of enemy night-fighters. Post-raid reconnaissance and local reports confirmed that the operation had failed to achieve accuracy and concentration, and in an echo of the past, bombs had been sprayed all over the Ruhr, leaving Gelsenkirchen largely untouched. Thirty aircraft were missing, and this time eight of them were from 5 Group, four alone from 106 Squadron on a bad night for Syerston. 61 Squadron's W4830 had been damaged by flak over the target, and as Sgt Pearce and crew crossed the coast at Sheringham, the port-outer engine burst into flames. At 3,000 feet, the crew was ordered to abandon the Lancaster, Sgt Pearce the last to leave at 1,000 feet, and he watched it crash two hundred yards away at 04.30 with the mid-upper gunner still aboard. When these events were recorded in the ORB on the 28th, the navigator was still missing, even though his parachute and harness had been found near the crash site at Baston, near Spalding. No further mention of Sgt Beasley appeared in the ORB and Bill Chorley's Bomber Command Losses records him as failing to survive.

A series of three operations against Cologne spanned the turn of the month and began on the night of the 28/29th, when 608 aircraft took off in the late evening to deliver what would be the Rhineland capital's greatest ordeal of the war to date. At briefings, crews took in the details, which, for those of 8 Group, involved nine Mosquitos dropping green flares as route markers sixteen miles short of the target, and then red TIs and red flares with green stars on the aiming-point, which four Stirlings, ten Halifaxes and eighteen Lancasters were to back up with green TIs. 5 Group contributed 131 Lancasters, the 61 Squadron element of fifteen departing Syerston between 22.45 and 23.26 with F/L Chivers the senior pilot on duty, and at 01.30 at a location short of the target, (*the ORB entry too corrupted to decipher*) P/O Phillips's Lancaster was illuminated by flares from a Ju88 and engaged, resulting in a hole in the starboard-inner fuel tank and the destruction of the recuperator in the mid-upper turret. The bombs were dropped from 18,000 feet at 01.43, while the rest of the bomber stream continued on and encountered ten-tenths cloud below them at 8,000 to 10,000 feet and good visibility above. The main force crews were unaware that five of the Oboe Mosquitos had turned back and a sixth was unable to drop its skymarkers, leaving just six to do so, and these were behind schedule by seven minutes and could manage only intermittent flares. The omens for a successful attack were not good, particularly as skymarking was the least reliable method because of drift, but by the time that the 61 Squadron crews arrived, they were greeted by red and white flares, upon which they carried out their attacks from between 15,500 and 21,500 feet and deduced from the glow beneath the clouds and the presence of smoke rising through them that they had contributed to a successful operation. This was confirmed by post-raid reconnaissance and local reports, which provided details of forty-three industrial buildings and 6,374 others completely destroyed, and a further fifteen thousand sustaining damage to some extent. The death toll was put at 4,377, the greatest by far from a Bomber Command attack, and 230,000 others had lost their homes for varying periods. By recent standards, the figure of twenty-five missing aircraft could be considered moderate, but that was no consolation to the individual stations with an empty dispersal pan.

During the course of the month the squadron participated in eleven operations and dispatched 134 sorties for the loss of two Lancasters, one complete crew and two members of another.

July 1943

The first two days of the new month were beset by poor weather conditions, which kept all but a few gardeners and Mosquitos on the ground, but among those in action were the 61 Squadron freshman crews of Sgts Roberts, Mathews and Miller, who departed Syerston in that order between 22.26 and 22.31 bound for the Nectarine I garden off the western Frisians. They returned from uneventful sorties three to three-and-a-half hours later to report planting their vegetables from 4,000 feet, their positions based on Gee-fixes. It was at this time that S/L Gascoyne-Cecil concluded his second tour and was posted to Scampton for administrative duties.

The second attack of the current campaign against Cologne was scheduled for the night of the 3/4th, and crews were called to briefings on all operational stations during the late afternoon as a force of 653 aircraft was assembled. The Path Finder crews listened with interest as they were told that ten Mosquitos would drop green flares four-and-a-half miles from the target as a preliminary warning, and red, green and white flares and red TIs on the aiming-point. On this night, the aiming-point was on the east bank of the Rhine in the industrial Deutz district, where the Klöckner-Humboldt-Deutz works manufactured aero-engines and heavy and tracked vehicles for the

Wehrmacht, served by the nearby Kalk and Gremberg marshalling yards. Nine Halifaxes and twenty-four Lancasters were to back up the red TIs with greens, but in the event that cloud concealed the TIs, they were to bomb on H2S with the main force, along with the remaining nine Halifaxes and seventeen Lancasters. 5 Group contributed 141 Lancasters, the sixteen made ready by 61 Squadron departing Syerston in two elements of eight, the first between 22.20 and 22.35 and 23.00 and 23.20 with W/C Penman the senior pilot on duty.

The meteorological experts had forecast nine-tenths cloud from the English coast all the way to the target, but what the leading Path Finder heavy crews actually encountered was a clear sky and red Oboe-laid TIs in the bomb sights, which they backed up with greens. There was a certain amount of haze or perhaps, two to three-tenths cloud at 8,000 feet, but this did not interfere with the accuracy of the attack, which developed in concentrated form. At the start of the raid an intense flak defence fired shells that burst at 25,000 feet aided by around two hundred searchlights operating in cones of thirty to forty beams. The crews in the first phase were drawn on by green tracking flares and bombed from between 18,000 and 21,500 feet and by the time the raid reached its crescendo, Cologne was visible to approaching crews from a hundred miles away. On their arrival, it was nine-tenths smoke rather than cloud that greeted them and through which the second phase 61 Squadron participants delivered their bombs on red and green TIs from between 18,200 and 21,000 feet. F/L Chivers and crew were coned and as they took violent evasive action the bombs were released two miles south-west of Cologne. Returning crews described a highly successful raid, which left the city a mass of flames visible from 170 miles into the homeward flight, with smoke rising to 10,000 feet and blotting out ground detail. Some reported a large explosion to the west of the Rhine and a mile from the planned aiming point at 01.18 and noted that the early bombing had been falling short. Some other crews also noticed a creep-back, while the overall impression was of another operation more successful than the "Thousand" raid against this city at the end of May 1942. Post-raid reconnaissance and local reports confirmed another stunningly accurate and concentrated attack, in which twenty industrial premises and 2,200 houses had been destroyed and 72,000 people bombed out of their homes at a cost to the Command of thirty aircraft.

Some crews commented on the presence of day fighters over the target, and this was clear evidence of a new tactic being employed by the Luftwaffe. The newly formed JG300 was operating for the first time, employing the Wilde Sau (Wild Boar) tactics, which was the brainchild of former bomber pilot, Major Hans-Joachim (Hajo) Herrmann. The unit had been formed in June with borrowed standard BF109 and FW190 single-engine day fighters to operate directly over a target, seeking out bombers silhouetted against the fires and TIs. On this night, the unit would claim twelve victories but would have to share them with the flak batteries, which claimed them also. Unaccustomed to being pursued by fighters over a target, it would take time for the bomber crews to work out what was happening, and until they did, friendly fire would often be blamed for damage incurred by unseen causes.

The third and final raid of the mini-series against Cologne was posted on the 8th and an all-Lancaster heavy force of 282 aircraft was drawn from 1, 5 and 8 Groups, with six Oboe Mosquitos to carry out the initial marking. 5 Group provided 151 Lancasters, of which sixteen belonged to 61 Squadron and they departed Syerston between 22.10 and 22.49 with F/L Thomas the senior pilot on duty. Sgt Strange lost his flying instruments, while Sgt Lowe's gunners complained that their heated flying suits were not working and they were among an alarming fourteen 5 Group crews to turn back, leaving the others to fly through the tops of towering cumulonimbus as they made their way to the target. On arrival they were greeted by ten-tenths cloud at around 10,000 to 15,000 feet, and followed tracking flares to the aiming point, only to find that the release-point flares were late, prompting some crews to bomb on e.t.a. before they were deployed. The 61 Squadron crews mostly carried out their attacks on red flares with green stars from 18,500 to 23,000 feet between 01.11 and 01.25 in the face of an intense flak barrage. A large explosion at 01.17 lit up the clouds for eight seconds and another very large one was observed at 01.23, which contributed to the impression that another devastating blow had been dealt to the Rhineland capital. Post-raid reconnaissance and local reports confirmed a highly successful operation, which had caused extensive damage in north-western and south-western districts, where nineteen industrial premises and 2,381 houses had been destroyed. The success cost a modest seven Lancasters, five of them from 5 Group, but it was a bad night for Syerston and 106 Squadron, which registered two failures to return and one crash in which only two crew members survived. When the dust had settled over Cologne, the local authorities catalogued the destruction over the three raids of more than eleven thousand buildings and a death toll of almost 5,500 people, with a further 350,000 rendered homeless.

The Ruhr campaign was winding down by the time that Gelsenkirchen was posted across Lancaster and Halifax stations on the 9th as the target for that night, for which a heavy force of 408 aircraft was made ready. At briefings, the crews learned of the plan, which required seven Oboe Mosquitos to drop red flares twenty miles short of the target and green flares nine miles further on, before marking the aiming-point with white flares and reds with green stars. Fifteen 61 Squadron Lancasters were among 112 representing 5 Group, and they departed Syerston between 22.21 and 22.53 with F/Ls Chivers and Thomas the senior pilots on duty. Sgt Roberts and crew were compromised by an engine coolant issue and attacked a heavy flak battery on Terschelling as a last resort target after conducting a timed run. The others made their way to the target above ten-tenths cloud, which stretched over the Ruhr at around 16,000 feet and topped out in places at 20,000 feet. The Oboe skymarkers were several minutes late, partly as a result of a 50% failure rate of the Oboe equipment, while a sixth Mosquito dropped its markers ten miles to the north. The 61 Squadron crews carried out their attacks mostly on red and green skymarkers or on e.t.a. from between 18,000 and 23,000 feet and reported large explosions at 01.22, 01.38 and 01.41, the last one lighting up the sky like day for ten seconds. A red glow beneath the cloud suggested that an extensive fire was developing, but returning crews could offer only impressions at debriefing and none was certain as to the outcome. Absent from debriefing was the crew of Sgt Parsons, who, on their way out of the target area, had run into flak five to ten miles south of Bonn, and the only fragment of shrapnel to penetrate the fuselage mortally wounded the navigator, F/Sgt Dyson. Other members of the crew took over the navigation and the Lancaster landed safely at Manston. Also absent was the crew of F/O Ingram, whose W4763 had been hit by flak at the German/Dutch frontier near Gronau and had caught fire before crashing at 01.22 six miles north-east of Enschede in Holland. F/O Ingram lost his life, while his crew, some badly injured, fell into enemy hands. According to local sources in Gelsenkirchen, it appeared that the attack had been meant for Bochum and Wattenscheid, which received more bombs than Gelsenkirchen, where limited damage occurred in southern districts.

Although two more operations to the region would be launched late in the month, Harris was already planning his next attempt to shorten the war by bombing and was buoyed by the success of the spring offensive. He could look back on the past four and a half months with genuine satisfaction at the performance of his squadrons, and as a champion of technological innovation, take particular pride in the performance of Oboe, which had been the decisive factor. Although losses had been grievously high and the Ruhr's reputation as "Happy Valley" well earned, its most important towns and cities had suffered catastrophic destruction. In Britain, the aircraft factories had more than kept pace with the rate of attrition, while the training units both at home and overseas were pouring eager new crews into the fray to fill the gaps. With confidence high in the ability of his Command to destroy almost any target at will, Harris prepared for his next major campaign, the erasure from the map of a prominent German city in a short, sharp series of maximum effort raids to be launched during the final week of the month.

In the meantime, 1, 5 and 8 Groups were alerted to prepare for a trip to Italy to attack the city of Turin, for which 295 Lancasters were made ready on the 12th, 130 of them provided by 5 Group. The fourteen-strong 61 Squadron element departed Syerston between 22.15 and 22.43 with W/C Penman the senior pilot on duty and set course for Dungeness on the Kent coast with the intention of making landfall on the other side of the Channel at Cayeux-sur-Mer. S/L Gilpin and crew turned back when their rear turret became unserviceable, leaving the others to negotiate poor weather conditions, including icing over France. They pinpointed on Lake Annecy in the foothills of the Alps before arriving in the target area to be greeted by clear skies, good visibility and defences up to their usual poor standard, characterised by ineffective searchlights and inaccurate light flak rising to 15,000 feet. The marking was punctual, accurate and concentrated, inviting the bombing by the 61 Squadron crews to be carried out from between 16,200 and 19,000 feet, and a column of black smoke was observed rising through 12,000 feet as they withdrew. The return route involved a low-level circumnavigation of the Brest peninsula, and many of the thirteen missing Lancasters disappeared without trace into the sea after running into enemy night-fighters in this area. This was certainly the fate of W/C Nettleton VC, the veteran of the Augsburg raid and commanding officer of 44 (Rhodesia) Squadron. Reconnaissance showed the main weight of the attack to have fallen just north of the city centre, and a local report stated that 792 people had lost their lives, the largest number of fatalities from a Bomber Command attack on Italy.

Aachen, Germany's most westerly city and an important railway hub between Germany and the occupied countries, was posted as the target on the 13th and a force of 374 aircraft made ready. This consisted largely of Halifaxes, Wellingtons and Stirlings and in the absence of a 5 Group presence, just eighteen Lancasters among the 8 Group contribution. It was left to local sources to confirm the severity of the damage inflicted upon the city, which amounted to 2,927 buildings completely destroyed, with many industrial, public and cultural buildings seriously damaged.

On the 15th, a dozen 617 Squadron crews carried out the squadron's first operation since the Dams in company with twelve others from 5 Group, when targeting two electrical transformer stations near Bologna and at Reggio Nell Emilia near Genoa to disrupt railway movements of enemy reinforcements to Sicily. Syerston provided three crews each from 61 and 106 Squadrons to attack the former, while a similar number from 9 and 50 Squadrons attended to the latter. The 61 Squadron crews of F/Ls Stewart and Thomas and P/O Frost departed Syerston in that order between 22.15 and 22.19 and all reached the target, where after making a visual identification and carrying out multiple passes, they dropped 500-pounders from between 1,500 and 2,000 feet and observed blue flashes and white smoke. They remained at low level, strafing targets of opportunity as they made their way south to land at Blida in Algeria after almost ten hours in the air. The operations were only modestly effective, and it was decided to attack two similar targets on the following night, one at Cislago and the identity of the other was unrecorded for which eighteen crews from 44 (Rhodesia), 49 and 57 Squadrons were detailed. Again, all reached the target area and found a full moon, clear skies and excellent visibility in which to carry out their attacks, after which they also made for Blida. Back home, F/Sgt Lancaster and crew had finished their tour and George Lancaster himself was posted to 27 O.T.U to pass on his skills and experience. Had he not fallen out with Gibson, his name might have been celebrated along with the others who took part in Operation Chastise. His consolation was a clear conscience, having remained loyal to his crew, and he could rightly claim to have been a founder member of the most famous squadron in the RAF.

Hamburg had been a regular target for the Command throughout the war to date, and had been attacked, amongst other occasions, during the final week of July in 1940, 1941 and 1942. It had been spared by the weather from hosting the first "One Thousand" bomber raid at the end of May 1942, but Harris now identified it as the ideal candidate for destruction under Operation Gomorrah, the intention of which was to cause the maximum impact to the enemy's morale in a short, sharp campaign employing ten thousand tons of bombs. Hamburg's political status was second only to Berlin's, and its value to the war effort in terms of ship and U-Boot construction and other war production was undeniable, but it suited Harris's criteria also in other respects. Its location close to a coastline aided navigation and made it accessible from the North Sea without the need to spend time over hostile territory, and its relatively short distance from the bomber stations enabled a force to approach and retreat during the few hours of darkness afforded by mid-summer. Finally, lying beyond the range of Oboe, which had proved so decisive at the Ruhr, Hamburg had the wide River Elbe to provide a solid H2S signature for the navigators high above.

There had been no operations for most squadrons for nine days, despite a number being posted, and by the time that 791 crews trooped into their respective briefing rooms on the 24th, they probably expected the day to end with yet another scrub. Instead, they were read a special message from the commander-in-chief, to announce the beginning of the Battle of Hamburg. They listened intently to the revelation that they would be aided by the first operational use of "window", aluminium-backed strips of paper of precise length, which, when released in bundles into the airstream at a predetermined point, would drift down slowly in vast clouds to swamp the enemy night-fighter, searchlight and gun-laying radar with false returns and render it blind. The device had actually been available for a year, but its use had been vetoed in case the enemy copied it for use against Britain. It was not realized that Germany had, in fact, already developed its own version called Düppel, which it had withheld for the same reason.

The plan of attack called for eleven Lancasters and nine Halifaxes to drop yellow TIs as route markers, before continuing on to mark the aiming-point with yellow TIs, and if conditions permitted, illuminator flares. The route markers were to be backed up by six Stirlings, thirteen Lancasters and nine Halifaxes, and six Lancasters and two Halifaxes were to use the yellow TIs as a guide, and with the aid of flares, mark the aiming-point with red TIs, which would be backed up with green TIs by the remaining marker crews. 5 Group supported the operation with 143 Lancasters, fourteen of them belonging to 61 Squadron, after the newly-promoted S/L Ed Benjamin had been withdrawn at the last minute, leaving the newly promoted S/L Wellburn as the senior pilot on duty. As they departed Syerston between 22.21 and 23.05, almost twelve hundred miles to the south, their colleagues at Blida were already on their way to bomb the docks at Leghorn before returning to Syerston. They would arrive home safely in a twenty-four-minute window from 04.47 and report that they had attacked the target in generally poor visibility from between 14,700 and 15,200 feet and observed a fire in an oil refinery north of the town, which was emitting flames to 200 feet following an explosion.

There were no early returns to deplete the squadron's contribution to the main event, and at a predetermined point over the North Sea, wireless operators began to dispense "window" through the flare chute, beginning shortly after 00.30, and the effects appeared to be immediate as few fighters rose to meet the approaching bombers. A number of aircraft were shot down over the sea during the outward flight, two of them 103 Squadron Lancasters, but these were off course and outside of the protection of the bomber stream and may well have been among those returning early with technical difficulties. The efficacy of "window" was made more apparent in the target area, where the crews noticed an absence of the usually efficient co-ordination between the searchlights and flak batteries and defence appeared random and sporadic. This offered the Path Finders the opportunity to mark the target by visual reference and H2S virtually unmolested, and although the red and green TIs were a little misplaced and scattered, they landed in sufficient numbers close to the city centre to provide the main force crews with ample opportunity to deliver a massive blow. It rarely happened that aircraft arrived in strict bands according to their task, and some main force crews were already over the target from the opening of the raid at 01.00. The 61 Squadron crews carried out their attacks from between 16,500 and 21,000 feet and on return reported a successful operation that had left part of the city ablaze with a column of smoke rising through 20,000 feet. Post-raid reconnaissance revealed that a six-mile-long creep-back had developed, which cut a swathe of destruction from the city centre along the line of approach, out across the north-western districts and into open country, where a proportion of the bombing had been wasted. In fact, less than half of the force had bombed within three miles of the city centre during the fifty-minute-long raid, in which 2,284 tons of bombs had been delivered, despite which the city had suffered a telling blow, and fifteen hundred of its inhabitants lay dead. For the Command it was an encouraging start to the campaign, particularly in the light of just twelve missing aircraft, for which "window" was largely responsible.

On the 25th, and in the expectation that Hamburg would be covered by smoke, Harris switched his force to Essen, where he could take advantage of the body blow dealt to the enemy defensive system by Window. A force of 705 aircraft was made ready and a plan prepared, which called for Halifaxes and Lancasters of 35 (Madras Presidency) and 156 Squadrons to drop preliminary yellow warning TIs on track by H2S, which would be backed up by elements of 7 and 156 Squadrons. Ahead, fourteen Oboe Mosquitos would mark the aiming-point with red TIs, which nineteen Lancasters, nine Halifaxes and five Stirlings were to back up with greens. 5 Group detailed 136 Lancasters, the sixteen representing 61 Squadron departing Syerston between 21.54 and 22.35 with S/Ls Benjamin and Wellburn the senior pilots on duty and lost the services first of F/L Stewart and crew to the failure of flying instruments, then P/O Phillips and crew to an engine fire and finally F/Sgt Wilson and crew also to an engine issue. They were among seventeen early returns from the 5 Group contingent, the remainder arriving in the target area to find four to five-tenths cloud to the west but clear skies over the aiming-point, with just the usual ground haze to spoil the vertical visibility. They carried out their bombing runs at between 16,700 and 21,000 feet and watched a highly concentrated attack develop, which left the ground enveloped in smoke from the many fires and explosions. Returning crews reported concentrated fires around the aiming-point in a one-and-a-half-square-mile area of the city, two large, red explosions at 00.36 and 00.39 and a column of smoke rising through 20,000 feet as they withdrew to the west, the glow remaining visible from as far away as the Dutch coast.

Post-raid reconnaissance confirmed the raid to be another outstanding success against this important war materials producing city, with more than 2,800 houses destroyed, while the complex of Krupp manufacturing sites suffered its heaviest damage of the war to date. Twenty-six aircraft failed to return, only two of which belonged to 5 Group, but among them was 61 Squadron's ED613, which crashed at Karnap, a town beyond the northern rim of the city. There were no survivors from the crew of F/O Alderdice, most of whom were highly experienced and on the first operation of their second tour. In contrast, it was the very first operation for nineteen-year-old flight engineer, F/Sgt Peter Gore, who had joined the crew at Winthorpe six weeks earlier and had written home about his good fortune to be joining such an experienced bunch.

During the course of the 27th, a force of 787 aircraft was assembled for round two of Operation Gomorrah, for which 5 Group detailed 155 Lancasters, sixteen of them made ready by 61 Squadron. They attended briefing to learn that yellow route markers would be dropped by H2S on the enemy coast and backed up, and that "Y" aircraft (H2S blind markers) were to deliver red TIs and a stick of flares over the aiming-point for visual markers to confirm and back up with green TIs. They departed Syerston between 22.10 and 22.51 with F/Ls Laing and Thomas the senior pilots on duty and all reached the Schleswig-Holstein coast to the north of Hansastadt Hamburg, none of them having any concept of the events that were to follow their arrival. A previously unknown and terrible phenomenon was about to present itself to the world and introduce a new word "firestorm" into the English language. A number of factors would conspire on this night to seal the fate of this great city and its hapless inhabitants in an orgy of destruction that was quite unprecedented in air warfare. An uncharacteristically hot and dry spell of weather had left the city a tinderbox, and the spark to ignite it came with the Path Finders' H2S-laid yellow and green TIs, which fell with almost total concentration some two miles to the east of the intended city-centre aiming-point and into the densely populated working-class residential districts of Hamm, Hammerbrook and Borgfeld. To compound this, the main force, which had been drawn on to the target by yellow release-point flares, bombed with rare precision and almost no creep-back and deposited much of its 2,300 tons of bombs into this relatively compact area. The 61 Squadron crews delivered their bomb loads from between 15,600 and 22,500 feet and observed many explosions and a sea of flames developing below. Those bombing towards the later stages of the raid observed a pall of smoke rising through 20,000 feet, and the glow of fires was reported to remain visible for up to two hundred miles into the return journey.

On the ground, individual fires began to join together to form one giant conflagration, which sucked in oxygen from surrounding areas at hurricane speeds to feed its voracious appetite. Trees were uprooted and flung bodily into the inferno, along with debris and people and temperatures at the seat of the flames exceeded one thousand degrees Celcius. The defences were overwhelmed and the fire service unable to pass through the rubble-strewn streets to gain access to the worst-affected areas. Even had they done so, they could not have entered the firestorm area, and only after all of the combustible material had been consumed did the flames subside. By this time, there was no-one alive to rescue and an estimated forty thousand people died on this one night alone. A mass exodus from the city, which would ultimately exceed one million people, began on the following morning and this undoubtedly saved many from the ravages of the next raid, which would come two nights hence. Seventeen aircraft failed to return, reflecting the enemy's developing response to the advantage gained by the Command through Window. No gain was ever permanent, however, and the balance of power would continue to shift from one side to the other for the next year. For a change, it was the Lancaster brigade that sustained the highest numerical casualties on this night, accounting for eleven of the failures to return.

Bomber Command's heavy brigade stayed at home on the following night, while four Mosquitos carried out a nuisance raid on Hamburg to ensure that the residents' sleep was disturbed. A force of 777 aircraft was put together to continue Hamburg's torment on the 29th, while the crews attended briefings to learn of their part in the proceedings. They were told that red TIs and flares were to be employed as route markers, before seventeen Lancasters and eight Halifaxes marked the aiming-point with yellow TIs by H2S to be backed up by thirty-four Lancasters, six Stirlings and nine Halifaxes. 5 Group contributed 148 Lancasters, of which seventeen were made ready by 61 Squadron before departing Syerston between 22.13 and 23.04 with F/Ls Laing and Thomas the senior pilots on duty. F/Sgt Wilson and crew lost their starboard-inner engine and had to turn back, while the remainder pressed on across the North Sea and reached the target area to find clear skies and the city protected only by slight ground haze. The plan involved approaching from due north to hit the northern and north-eastern districts, which, thus far, had escaped serious damage, but the Path Finders strayed two miles to the east of the intended track and dropped their markers just to the south of the already devastated firestorm area. A four-mile creep-back rescued the situation for the Command, by spreading along the line of approach into the residential districts of Wandsbek and Barmbek and parts of Uhlenhorst and Winterhude. F/O Webb and crew were contending with engine trouble as they began their bombing run at 15,000 feet and were unable to climb when caught in a searchlight cone. The only option was to jettison the bombs "live" some two minutes short of e.t.a., and make their escape, presumably at low level. The other 61 Squadron crews carried out their attacks from between 17,500 and 20,500 feet on yellow and green TIs, before returning home to report smoke rising through 17,000 feet and fires visible for two hundred miles into the homeward journey. It was another massive blow against this proud city, but as the defenders began to recover from the effects of "window", so the bomber losses began to creep up, and twenty-eight aircraft failed to return home on this night, five of them from 5 Group. ED782 was shot down by a night-fighter and crashed into the North Sea east-north-east of Heligoland with no survivors from the experienced crew of F/O Phillips. The sea gave up the remains of four for local burials and they were removed postwar and reinterred in cemeteries in Hamburg and Kiel.

Before the final round of Operation Gomorrah took place, the curtain on the Ruhr offensive was brought down finally with a raid on the town of Remscheid, situated on the southern edge of the region some six miles south of Wuppertal, where the main industries were mechanical engineering and tool-making. Up until this point, only twenty-six people had lost their lives in this town as a result of stray bombs, but it was now to face a modest force of 273 aircraft consisting of roughly equal numbers of Lancasters, Halifaxes and Stirlings with six Oboe Mosquitos to mark out the aiming-point with red TIs. 5 Group put up thirty-nine Lancasters, four of which belonged to 61 Squadron and loaded with a cookie and up to seventeen SBCs of various incendiaries before departing Syerston between 21.59 and 22.04 bearing aloft the crews of P/O Eager, F/Sgt Wilson and Sgts Halkier and Strange. They all reached the target area to find clear skies and good visibility and bombed on red TIs from between 17,000 and 20,000 feet, observing the burst of many cookies and a pall of smoke rising through 5,000 feet. They returned home with a red glow in the sky behind them that remained visible as they crossed the enemy coast homebound and gave promise of another Ruhr town in ruins. It would be left to a post-war bombing survey to establish that a mere 871 tons of bombs had laid waste to around 83% of Remscheid's built-up area, destroying 107 industrial buildings and 3,117 houses. Three months war production was lost, and the town's industry never recovered fully, and this was in exchange for the failure to return of fifteen aircraft, the Stirling brigade suffering 10% casualties.

During the course of the month, the squadron took part in twelve operations and dispatched 137 sorties for the loss of three Lancasters and crews and one other crew member.

August 1943

Briefings for the final act of Operation Gomorrah took place on the 2nd, and a force of 740 aircraft assembled, 128 of them Lancasters belonging to 5 Group. 61 Squadron briefed sixteen crews, setting out the intention for the Path Finders to mark the aiming-point with red TIs by H2S and for the visual markers to follow up with yellow TIs for the backers-up to reinforce with greens. They lifted off from Syerston between 23.16 and 23.59 with F/L Laing the senior pilot on duty and the first off the ground, before heading for the Lincolnshire coast to begin the North Sea crossing and rendezvous with the bomber stream. The weather conditions, initially, were favourable, until coming into contact with a towering bank of ice-bearing cumulonimbus cloud at 7 degrees east, a not unusual feature of this regular route into north-western Germany, but on this occasion, a particularly imposing one, which could not be circumnavigated and stretched upwards to 20,000 feet and beyond. Upon entering it, aircraft were thrown around by violent electrical storms and it was a hugely terrifying experience beyond anything that most crews had ever experienced, with enormous flashes of lightning, thunder, electrical discharges that sent instruments haywire. The level of discomfort experienced by many crews told them that to continue on would be futile and persuaded them to turn back, among them the 61 Squadron crews of F/Os Webb and Woods and Sgts Strange and Willsher. F/O Webb was assisted in his decision to turn back by an overheating port-outer engine, while the Woods and Strange crews were within thirty-five miles of Hamburg when dumping their bombs in the Rotenburg and Sandbostel areas respectively and could see evidence of fires in the target area. Sgt Lowe had been contending with engine issues since crossing the enemy coast, both inner engines cutting out intermittently, and when the starboar-inner failed completely at the start of the bombing run, the bombs were jettisoned ten miles short of the aiming point.

Those battling through the conditions to reach the target area found seven to ten-tenths cloud, and while some caught a glimpse of the Elbe and isolated yellow and green Path Finder flares, which might have been jettisoned rather than placed, the majority bombed on e.t.a., the 61 Squadron element attacking from between 13,000 and 17,800 feet. Bombs were spread over a hundred square miles of Schleswig-Holstein, the town of Elmshorn, some fifteen miles to the north-west of Hamburg, seeming to attract the most attention and 254 houses were destroyed. Few crews had any idea of their precise location and bombed on the glow of fires beneath the cloud and the smoke rising through it. On return, they expressed themselves to be shaken by their experience and were unanimous in their conviction that the operation had been a total failure. The outcome was of little consequence in view of what had gone before, but the Command suffered the relatively heavy loss of thirty aircraft, some of them having fallen victim to the weather conditions. W5000 disappeared without trace with the crew of F/O Lyon, who were on their fourth operation, while JA873 was shot down by a night-fighter to crash in the vicinity of Lüneburg with fatal consequences for F/L Laing and his crew on their thirteenth sortie together. During the course of the four raids of Operation Gomorrah, the squadron dispatched sixty-three sorties, fifty-five of which fulfilled their brief and suffered the loss of three Lancasters and crews. (The Battle of Hamburg. Martin Middlebrook).

Italy was now teetering on the brink of capitulation and Bomber Command was invited to help nudge it over the edge with a short offensive against its major cities, beginning with the preparation of an all-Lancaster force drawn from 1, 5 and 8 Groups for an attack on Genoa, Milan and Turin on the 7th. With preparations already in hand for, perhaps, the most important operation of the war to date to be launched in ten days' time, the Turin raid was to be used to test the merits of employing a raid controller, or Master of Ceremonies, in the manner of W/C Gibson during Operation Chastise. The man selected for the job was Group Captain John Searby, currently serving as commanding officer of 83 Squadron of the Path Finder Force, and before that, Gibson's successor as commanding officer of 106 Squadron. At Syerston nine 61 Squadron Lancasters joined ten from 106 Squadron snaking their way to the runway threshold and took off between 21.01 and 21.22 with W/C Penman and S/L Wellburn the senior pilots on duty. The target was located without difficulty in good weather conditions, and the 61 Squadron crews carried out their attacks predominantly on green TIs from between 16,000 and 18,500 feet, before all but one returned safely, some with plottable bombing photographs, to report a successful operation, a large explosion and the fact that, many miles to the south, Genoa was observed to be ablaze. Absent from debriefing was the crew of Sgt Halkier, who all lost their lives when LM339 was brought down in the target area. It is believed that all 197 aircraft reached their respective targets after flying out in excellent weather conditions, and although the Master Bomber experiment at Turin was not entirely successful, experience was gained which would prove useful for the forthcoming Operation Hydra.

Fifteen 61 Squadron crews were called to briefing on the 9th to learn of their part in a raid on Mannheim that night as part of a 5 Group contribution of 143 Lancasters in an overall force of 457 aircraft. They departed Syerston between 22.47 and 23.25 with F/Ls Chivers and Stewart the senior pilots on duty and after climbing out, headed for the rendezvous point over Reading, before embarking on the Channel crossing at Beachy Head on course for the French coast at Boulogne. There were no early returns to deplete the squadron's impact as they arrived in the target area to be greeted by a five-tenths layer of broken cloud at 4,000 feet and eight-tenths at 10,000 feet, despite which, the visibility was fair and the conditions irrelevant as far as the H2S-equipped Path Finder marker crews were concerned anyway. The 61 Squadron crews attacked from between 17,000 and 19,500 feet aiming at yellow and green TIs and set off home to report a number of very large fires but what appeared to be a generally scattered raid. According to local sources and against expectations, 1,316 buildings had been destroyed in Mannheim, forty-two industrial concerns had lost production, and more than fifteen hundred fires of varying sizes had required attention. Six Halifaxes and three Lancasters failed to return, two of the latter belonging to 5 Group and for the third operation in a row 61 Squadron was represented. Sgt Whitley and crew had been outbound over Belgium when intercepted and shot down by the night-fighter of Lt Norbert Pietrek of II./NJG4. W4236, a veteran Lancaster that had served the squadron since September 1942, crashed at 01.20 at Marbehan in Luxembourg, killing the flight engineer and both gunners, while the four survivors were spirited away by local partisans and managed to retain their freedom.

The following night brought a return to southern Germany, this time to Nuremberg, for which a force of 653 aircraft was made ready, and the presence of Stirlings, the type usually at the bottom of the food chain, probably served as a boost to the Halifax crews, which in a Lancaster/Halifax force, invariably came off second best. 5 Group contributed 128 of the Lancasters and 61 Squadron briefed thirteen crews while their Lancasters were being loaded with a cookie and up to twelve SBCs of incendiaries and sufficient fuel and reserves for the 1,300-mile round-trip. They departed Syerston between 21.44 and 22.20 with W/C Penman the senior pilot on duty, and after climbing-out set course for Beachy Head to follow a route similar to that of the previous night. Again, there had been no early returns by the time that the 61 Squadron contingent arrived in the target area, where the conditions reflected those of twenty-four hours earlier with eight to ten-tenths cloud at

12,000 feet. Despite this, the Path Finders elected to ground-mark, which meant that there were no release-point flares to draw the main force on, but the green TIs were visible to most, and the 61 Squadron crews delivered their bomb loads onto them from between 16,700 and 20,000 feet. At debriefing, crews reported a good concentration of fires, the glow from which remained visible for 150 miles into the return journey. The operation was moderately successful and caused substantial housing damage in central and southern districts, while a death toll of 577 people was evidence of the intensity of the bombing. It was achieved for the relatively modest loss of sixteen aircraft, seven Halifaxes, six Lancasters and three Stirlings, which, in percentage terms, was respectively 3.2, 1.9 and 2.5.

The Italian campaign continued on the 12th, when Milan and Turin were the targets, the former for a force of 504 aircraft including 130 Lancasters provided by 5 Group, while 152 aircraft from 3 and 8 Groups attended to the latter. 61 Squadron made ready fourteen Lancasters, which departed Syerston between 21.29 and 21.46 with W/C Penman and S/L Wellburn the senior pilots on duty and set course for the south coast at Selsey Bill to begin the Channel crossing that would terminate on the Normandy coast at Cabourg. Thereafter, they headed south-east in a straight leg across central France to the northern tip of Lake Bourget, before traversing the Alps and skirting southern Switzerland. The final run-in on the target was conducted under clear skies with just ground mist to spoil the vertical view, and on arrival, the 61 Squadron crews bombed visually or on yellow flares and green TIs from between 16,000 and 19,000 feet in accordance with the instructions of the "Master of Ceremonies". They observed large fires in the city centre, which could be seen for a hundred miles and more into the return flight, and local reports, though short on detail, confirmed that four important war-industry factories had sustained serious damage during August and most of it probably occurred on this night.

Milan would face two further attacks before the Command's interest in Italy ceased for good, and the first of these was posted on the 14th, for which 1, 5 and 8 Groups put together a force of 140 Lancasters, fifty-nine of them representing 5 Group. 61 Squadron made ready six of its own and sent them on their way from Syerston between 21.20 and 21.25 with F/Os Hughes and Mortimer the senior pilots on duty. They all reached the target area under clear skies and in good visibility aided by a brilliant moon and Path Finder route markers and ahead observed the Path Finder green TIs falling accurately and in concentrated fashion on the city centre aiming point. The 61 Squadron crews exploited the opportunity from between 16,000 and 19,000 feet and watched as many fires took hold, one in particular at the Breda aircraft and armaments factory, and the glow from the burning city remained visible on the horizon for a considerable distance into the return flight.

There was to be no respite for Milan as a force of 199 Lancasters was made ready later on the 15th for a return that night for what would be the last time over Italy for main force Lancasters. 61 Squadron provided eight of the eighty-five 5 Group Lancasters, which took off from Syerston between 20.18 and 20.37 with F/L Chivers the senior pilot on duty and joined up with the bomber stream as it passed over Reading on their way south to begin the Channel crossing at Selsey Bill. After making landfall at Cabourg on the French side of the Channel, the bombers set course to traverse France and make for the northern tip of Lake Bourget, but the 61 Squadron Lancasters were still over northern France when, it is believed, two of them were intercepted and shot down by night-fighters and one by flak. DV186 crashed near Lisieux, some fifteen miles inland from the Normandy coast, and there were no survivors from the crew of F/O Steer, while W5002 was some thirty-five miles to the south-east when coming down near Rugles. A 49 Squadron Lancaster is known to have crashed close by after being hit by flak and it seems likely that the 61 Squadron

Lancaster suffered a similar fate. The fact that the pilot, Sgt Matthews, was the sole survivor suggests that the Lancaster was torn asunder when the bomb load detonated, and he was flung clear already attached to his seat parachute. ED722 had reached a point some forty miles further along the briefed track when crashing near Chartres, killing Sgt Miller and five of the eight occupants. The flight engineer and second navigator fell into enemy hands, but the bomb-aimer evaded a similar fate thanks to the local partisan organisation and would eventually return home.

Those reaching the target area found clear skies and the Path Finder green flares to guide them over lake Bourget, and on arrival at the target encountered haze and smoke hanging over the city from the previous night. This spoiled to an extent the vertical visibility, but the Path Finders marked the city-centre aiming point with green TIs, and these were bombed to good effect, by the 61 Squadron crews from between 16,000 and 19,000 feet. Seven Lancasters failed to return, among them the one containing 467 Squadron's popular commanding officer, W/C Cosme Gomm DSO, DFC, who died with all but one of his crew. The consensus of returning crews was of a concentrated attack, but no local report was forthcoming to confirm or deny.

The final raid of the war on an Italian city was carried out by 154 aircraft of 3 and 8 Groups against Turin on the following night. A successful raid was claimed at the modest cost of four aircraft, but many of the participating Stirlings were diverted on return and did not reach their home stations in time to be made ready for the night's highly important operation, for which a maximum effort had been planned. This would deplete the available number of Stirlings by sixty and heap an even greater responsibility upon the rest of the force to destroy the Peenemünde site, ideally, at the first attempt, otherwise, crews were told at briefing, they would have to go back. A force of 596 aircraft was assembled made up of 324 Lancasters, 218 Halifaxes and fifty-four Stirlings, 117 of the Lancasters provided by 5 Group.

Since the very beginning of the war, intelligence had suggested that Germany was researching into and developing rocket technology, and although scant regard was given to the reports by some of the leading scientific experts, photographic reconnaissance had confirmed the existence of an establishment at Peenemünde at the northern tip of the island of Usedom on the Baltic coast. The activities there were monitored through Ultra intercepts and surreptitious reconnaissance flights, and the V-1, known to the photographic interpreters at Medmenham because of its wingspan as the "Peenemünde 20", was captured on a photograph. The brilliant scientist, Dr R V Jones, had been able to gain vital information concerning the V-1's range, which would ultimately be used to feed disinformation to the enemy, largely through the double agent "Zigzag", otherwise known as Eddie Chapman. Unfortunately, Churchill's chief scientific adviser, Professor Lindemann, or Lord Cherwell as he became, steadfastly refused to give credence to the existence and feasibility of rocket weapons and held stubbornly to his viewpoint even when presented with a photograph of a V-2 on a trailer, taken by a PRU Mosquito in June 1943. It required the combined urgings of Duncan Sandys and Dr Jones to persuade Churchill of the urgency to act, and Operation Hydra was planned for the first available opportunity, which occurred on the night of the 17/18th. Earlier in the day, the USAAF 8th Air Force had carried out its first deep-penetration raids into Germany to attack ball-bearing production at Schweinfurt and the Messerschmidt aircraft plant at Regensburg, and to the shock of its leaders, had learned the harsh lesson that unescorted daylight raids in 1943 were not viable. The folks at home would not be told that sixty B17s had failed to return. A force of 596 aircraft and crews answered the call to arms for Peenemünde, 5 Group contributing 117 of the 324 Lancasters, with Fiskerton making ready twelve, and the rest of the force was comprised of 218 Halifaxes and fifty-four Stirlings.

The operation had been meticulously planned to account for the three vital components of Peenemünde, the housing estate, where the scientific and technical staff lived, the factory buildings in which the weapons were assembled and the experimental site, where testing took place. Each was assigned to a specific wave of aircraft, which would attack from medium level, with the Path Finders bearing the huge responsibility of re-directing the point of aim accordingly, for which each squadron was to provide one crew as a "shifter". That apart, once route markers had been dropped on Rügen island, the Path Finder markers and backers-up were to follow the standard routine of red, yellow and green TIs. After last minute alterations, 3 and 4 Groups were given the first mentioned, 1 Group the second, and 5 and 6 Groups the third. The whole operation was to be overseen by a Master of Ceremonies (referred to hereafter as Master Bomber), and the officer selected for this hazardous and demanding role was G/C Searby of 83 Squadron, who, as already mentioned, had stepped into Gibson's shoes at 106 Squadron after Gibson was posted out to form 617 Squadron. Searby's role was to direct the marking and bombing by VHF and to encourage the crews to press on to the aiming-point, a task requiring him to remain in the target area and within range of the defences throughout the attack. In an attempt to protect the bombers from the attentions of enemy night-fighters for as long as possible, eight Mosquitos of 139 Squadron were to carry out a spoof raid on Berlin beginning at 23.00, seventy-five minutes before the opening of the main event, and would be led by the highly experienced and former 49 Squadron commander, G/C Len Slee. In the expectation of encountering drifting smoke as the last wave on target, the 5 Group crews were instructed to employ their oft-used time-and-distance approach to the aiming-point and had practiced this over a stretch of coast near the Wainfleet bombing range at the mouth of the Wash in Lincolnshire, progressively cutting the margin of error from one thousand to three hundred yards.

The 61 Squadron element of thirteen comprised the crews of W/C Penman in ED718, F/Ls Stewart and Thomas in W4766 and DV228, F/Os Hughes and Webb in W4934 and JA874, P/Os Eager and Madgett in DV232 and ED661, F/Sgts Docker and Wilson in JA900 and W4198, and Sgts Lowe, Roberts, Strange and Willsher in ED630, ED314, W4729 and W4900, the last named shortly to volunteer for a posting to 617 Squadron. They departed Syerston between 21.11 and 22.03 on a night when many squadron commanders elected to fly, in some cases, with fatal consequences. Accompanying W/C Penman as second pilot was W/C John Balmer, an Australian who had served in the Far East earlier in the war, and had commanded 100 Squadron RAAF, a Beaufort unit carrying out bombing and torpedo operations against Japanese targets during the New Guinea campaign. Posted to England in 1943, he had been earmarked to take command of 467 Squadron RAAF, currently stationed at Bottesford, which was currently under the temporary command of S/L Raphael after the loss two nights earlier of W/C Gomm. Sgt Willsher and crew returned early after their port-outer engine caught fire, but the overall early-return rate was lower than normal, just three from 5 Group, suggesting that crews had taken to heart the importance of the operation. The various groups made their way individually to a rendezvous point some ninety minutes flying time or three hundred miles from the English coast and sixty miles from Denmark's western coast, where they formed into a stream. Darkness had fallen as they crossed the North Sea, and twenty miles short of landfall over the southern tip of Fanø island, south of Esbjerg, windowing began in order to simulate a standard raid on a northern or north-eastern city. Southern Denmark was traversed by the Lancaster brigade at 18,000 feet, twice the altitude required for the attack, but worryingly, in a band of cloudless sky under a bright moon. They adopted an east-south-easterly course and began to shed altitude gradually during the 240-mile run to the target a little over an hour away, and at the rear of the stream, the 5 Group crews focused on the island of Rügen, the ideal starting point for their timed run to Peenemünde, which lay some fifteen miles beyond to the south-east.

The initial marking of the housing estate went awry, and some target indicators fell onto the forced workers camp at Trassenheide, more than a mile south of the intended aiming point. Many of the 3 and 4 Group bombs fell here, inflicting grievous casualties on friendly foreign nationals, who were trapped inside their wooden barracks. Once rectified, however, the attack proceeded according to plan and a number of important members of the technical staff were killed. The 1 Group second-wave crews encountered strong crosswinds over the narrow section of the island where the construction sheds were located, but this phase of the operation largely achieved its aims and they were on their way home before the night-fighters arrived from Berlin, having been attracted by the glow of fires well to the north. On arrival at Rügen in three waves, the 5 Group crews began their timed run, reaching the experimental site to encounter the expected smoke and bombed on green TIs, in the case of the 61 Squadron element, from 7,000 feet. They and the 6 Group Halifaxes and Lancasters then ran into the night-fighters, which proceeded to take a heavy toll of bombers both in the skies over the target and on the route home towards Denmark.

Twenty-nine of the forty missing aircraft came from this third wave, seventeen of them belonging to 5 Group and twelve to 6 Group, which represented a loss rate for the Canadians of 19.7%. The first of the 61 Squadron Lancasters to go down was W4766, which was attacked by a night-fighter and exploded over the target, throwing clear F/L Stewart DFM RNZAF and his bomb-aimer, who fell into enemy hands as the sole survivors of the eight occupants. Most were on the eighteenth sortie of their second tour. P/O Madgett DFM was on the final sortie of his tour and died with the other seven men on board ED661, when it crashed near Greifswald on the way out of the target area. In the sequence of the operation's losses, they were the tenth and eleventh respectively, and the twelfth was JA900, which was another to crash in the Greifswald area with no survivors from the eight-man crew of F/Sgt Docker, who were undertaking their sixteenth sortie. Seventeenth down was W4934, which went into the Baltic with the crew of F/O Hughes and gave up the remains of just two crew members. As if in compensation, all nine of the 106 Squadron participants bombed the target and returned to Syerston. Many crews brought home aiming point photographs, despite the fact that the time-and-distance method was found to have been not entirely effective. Returning crews praised the work of the Path Finders and the Master Bomber, and post-raid reconnaissance revealed the raid to have been sufficiently effective to delay the V-2 development programme by a number of months and ultimately to force the manufacture of secret weapons underground. The flight testing of the V-2 was eventually withdrawn eastwards into Poland, beyond the range of Harris's bombers, and thus Peenemünde had been nullified as a threat.

Before the next campaign began, Leverkusen was posted on the 22nd as the target for a heavy force of 449 Lancasters and Halifaxes with 8 Group Oboe-Mosquito to provide the initial marking. Situated on the Rhine just a stone's throw north of Cologne, the city was home to a factory belonging to the infamous I G Farben chemicals company. A 5 Group contribution of 108 Lancasters included ten belonging to 61 Squadron, which departed Syerston between 20.52 and 21.23 and after climbing out, headed for the Belgian coast at Knokke. Sgt Roberts and crew lost their port-outer engine and turned back, leaving the rest to follow a well-worn route to the southern Ruhr, which would require them to pass through the searchlight and flak belt near Cologne that was guaranteed to provide a hot welcome. They all made it safely through the narrow searchlight and flak corridor to reach the target, where ten-tenths cloud with tops at 18,000 feet blanketed the area.

Oboe-equipment failures forced most crews to bomb on e.t.a. in the absence of markers, until the glow of fires came to their aid as the raid developed, although a small number of crews spotted green TIs on the ground and aimed for them. Bombing was carried out by the 61 Squadron crews in the face of intense flak, but from what heights was a detail that the squadron scribe failed to record in the ORB. The average bombing height according to the records of other units was between 18,000 and 20,000 feet, and the glow of fires and the flash of explosions were initially the only confirmation of something happening under the cloud until a column of smoke was observed to be rising through 12,000 feet. Local reports revealed that up to a dozen neighbouring towns and cities had been hit, Düsseldorf alone suffering the destruction of 132 buildings. The operation cost three Lancasters and two Halifaxes and 61 Squadron's disastrous run of casualties continued with the failure to return of DV228 and the crew of Sgt Spencer. The Lancaster had been shot down by the night-fighter of Lt Heinz Bock of III./NJG1 and had crashed at 01.49 at Heicop, north-west of the Dutch city of Utrecht with just one survivor, who was taken into captivity.

Harris had long believed that the key to ultimate victory lay in the destruction of Berlin, the seat of the Nazi government and the symbol of its power. On the 23rd, orders were received on stations across the Command to prepare for a maximum effort that night against Germany's capital city, which had not been visited by the heavy brigade since the end of March. The crews, of course, could not know that this was to be the first of an eventual nineteen raids on the "Big City", in an offensive which, with an autumn break, would drag on until the following spring. It was a campaign that would test the resolve of the crews to the absolute limit, whilst also sealing the fate of the Stirlings and the Mk II and V Halifaxes as front-line bombers. There are varying opinions concerning the true start date of what became known as the Berlin offensive or the Battle of Berlin, some commentators believing these first three operations in August and September to be the start, while others point to the sixteen raids from mid-November. However, there was little doubt in Bomber Command circles that this was it, a fact demonstrated by the comments in numerous squadron ORBs, which spoke of the "long-awaited Berlin campaign" and similar sentiments. There would be a Master Bomber on hand for this operation and the officer chosen was Canadian W/C "Johnny" Fauquier, the tough, grizzled and one-time bush pilot and frequent brawler, who was enjoying his second spell as the commanding officer of 405 (Vancouver) Squadron, once of 4 Group, but since April, proud to be the only Canadian Path Finder unit.

The route had been planned to take the bomber stream to a rendezvous point over the North Sea, before crossing the Dutch coast near Haarlem and entering Germany between Meppen to the north and Osnabrück to the south. It would then pass between Bremen and Hannover to bypass the southern rim of Berlin, before turning back sharply on a north-westerly course across the city centre. After bombing, aircraft were to pass out over the Baltic coast in the direction of the Schleswig-Holstein peninsula. Finally, seventeen Mosquitos were to precede the Path Finder and main force elements to drop route markers at key points in an attempt to keep the bomber stream on track.

A force of 727 aircraft was assembled, of which 124 Lancasters represented 5 Group, a dozen of them belonging to 61 Squadron, and they departed Syerston between 20.05 and 20.31 with W/C Penman and S/L Benjamin the senior pilots on duty. Among seven 5 Group Lancasters to turn back early was the one containing F/L Thomas and crew after they lost an engine when an hour out over the North Sea. In their absence the bomber stream pressed on to the target area and found clear skies and moonlight, conditions which the Path Finders were unable to exploit after failing to identify the aiming point in the centre of the city, a result of the inherent difficulties of interpreting the H2S images over such a massive urban sprawl. The TIs fell into the southern outskirts instead, and to compound the error, many main force crews then cut the corner and approached the city from the south-west rather than south-east. This resulted in the wastage of many bomb loads in open country and on outlying communities, something which would become a feature of the campaign. The 61 Squadron participants delivered their cookie and incendiaries visually and on red and green TIs from between 15,000 and 20,600 feet either side of midnight in the face of intense searchlight activity and moderate flak. Returning crews reported large explosions and many fires, the glow from which was visible for at least 140 miles, and a pall of smoke had already risen to meet them as they turned towards the north-west.

Curiously, only a few crews commented on hearing the Master Bomber and finding his instructions helpful. A new record of fifty-six aircraft failed to return, twenty-three Halifaxes, seventeen Lancasters and sixteen Stirlings, representing a percentage loss rate respectively of 9.1, 5.1 and 12.9, which perfectly reflected the food chain when all three types operated together. Berlin experienced a scattered raid, but because of the number of aircraft involved, extensive damage was caused, a little in or near the centre but mostly in south-western residential districts and industrialised areas a little further east. Local sources reported that 2,611 buildings had been destroyed or seriously damaged, and the death toll of 854 people was surprisingly high, caused largely, perhaps, by a failure to heed the alarms and go to the assigned shelters.

Orders were received on the 27th to prepare for an operation that night against Nuremberg, the plan for which included an additional ten 139 Squadron Mosquitos to provide a "window" screen in advance of the bomber stream. The Oboe Mosquitos were to mark the route with red and green TIs, backed up by H2S Lancasters, but as Berlin was beyond the range of Oboe, the aiming-point was to be marked with red TIs by H2S, backed up by greens. A force of 674 aircraft lined up for take-off in mid-evening, 5 Group contributing 140 Lancasters, the sixteen provided by 61 Squadron taking to the air from Syerston between 20.36 and 21.21 with S/Ls Benjamin and Wellburn the senior pilots on duty. After climbing out, they headed for the French coast and lost the services of P/O Todd and crew to technical malfunctions on the way. After making landfall the bomber stream followed the line of the frontier with Belgium until crossing into Germany south of Luxembourg on a direct course for the target, where clear skies and intense darkness prevailed. The Path Finders had been briefed to check their H2S equipment by dropping a 1,000-pounder on Heilbronn, and some crews complied, while others, it seems, experienced technical difficulties. The initial marking was accurate, but a creep-back developed, which the backers-up and the Master Bomber could not correct, and this resulted in many bomb loads falling into open country, while others hit Nuremberg's south-eastern and eastern districts. The 61 Squadron crews aimed at green TIs from between 18,000 and 22,900 feet and generally gained an impression of a fairly concentrated and accurate attack, which produced many fires. They reported searchlights and night-fighters to be numerous and evidence of this came with the failure to return of thirty-three aircraft, eleven of each type, which again confirmed the vulnerability of the Stirlings and Halifaxes when operating alongside Lancasters. The loss rate on this night was 3.1% for the Lancaster, 5% for the Halifax and 10.6% for the Stirlings.

The main event on the night of the 30/31st was a two-phase attack on the twin towns of Mönchengladbach and Rheydt, the first time that either faced a major Bomber Command assault. Situated some ten miles west of the centre of Düsseldorf in the south-western Ruhr, they would face an initial force of 660 aircraft of four types, in what for the crews, was a short-penetration trip across the Dutch frontier and a welcome change from the recent long slogs to eastern and southern Germany. The plan called for the first wave to hit Mönchengladbach, before a two-minute pause in the bombing allowed the Path Finders to head south to mark Rheydt. 61 Squadron put up seventeen Lancasters as part of a 5 Group contribution of 138 and took off in two phases between 23.21 and 00.09 with no pilots on duty above flying officer rank. There were no early returns to Fiskerton, and they reached the target area to find good visibility above the seven to ten-tenths cloud at 8,000 feet, and a near-perfect display of target-marking by Oboe delivered red and green flares to draw on the main force to bomb with scarcely any creep-back. The 61 Squadron element carried out their bombing runs from between 16,500 and 20,000 feet and on return reported many fires, the glow from which could be seen from the Dutch coast homebound. Photo-reconnaissance confirmed a highly accurate and concentrated attack, which destroyed more than 2,300 buildings in the two towns, 171 of them of an industrial nature, along with 869 residential properties. Twenty-five aircraft failed to return, and Halifaxes narrowly sustained the highest numerical casualties.

The month ended with the second of the Berlin operations on the night of the 31st, for which 622 aircraft were made ready, more than half of them Lancasters, 129 of them provided by 5 Group. 61 Squadron loaded sixteen of its own with a cookie and nine SBCs of incendiaries each and dispatched them from Syerston between 20.04 and 20.50 with S/L Wellburn the senior pilot on duty. The route on this night took the bomber stream on an east-south-easterly heading across Texel to a position between Hannover and Leipzig, before turning to pass to the south-east of Berlin and approach the city-centre aiming point on a north-westerly track. The return leg would involve a south-westerly course to a position south of Cologne for an exit over the French coast, but despite the attempts to outwit the enemy night-fighter controller, he would be able to predict to some extent where to concentrate his fighters. The crews of F/Sgt McAlpine and P/O Truscott and crew turned back after an hour because of engine trouble, and they were followed home by F/O Woods and crew with a defective rear turret. Sgt Buckley and crew had been struggling to maintain height and speed after the starboard-outer engine failed, and having also lost the use of the mid-upper turret, dropped their load south of Nordhorn the moment they crossed the Dutch/German frontier.

The remainder pressed on, and for the first time reported the use by the Germans of "fighter flares" to mark out the path of the bombers to and from the target. The Path Finders encountered five to six-tenths cloud in the target area and this combined with H2S equipment failure and a spirited night-fighter response to cause the markers to be dropped well to the south of the planned aiming point. F/Sgt Wilson and crew came under attack from night-fighters during the bombing run and were forced to jettison the bombs to aid their escape, but not before the Lancaster sustained damage to the tailplane and rear turret, and rear gunner unspecified wounds. The other 61 Squadron crews reported up to eight-tenths thin cloud and bombed on red and green TIs from between 18,000 and 22,000 feet, observing many fires over a wide area. On the way home, P/O Moss became disorientated by lack of oxygen and strayed over Frankfurt, where the local flak batteries took chunks out of the Lancaster and slightly wounded the bomb-aimer, despite which they made it back to England to land at Wittering. As Canadian S/L Wellburn DFC and his crew entered the Syerston circuit, JB132 collided with R5698 of 1654 Conversion Unit and crashed some six miles south-west of Newark in Nottinghamshire, killing all eight occupants.

It was noted by some at debriefing that two groups of green TIs had been dropped ten miles apart and woefully short of the planned aiming point and both had attracted attention from the main force element. The outcome of the raid was a major disappointment, brought about by the wayward marking and a pronounced creep-back stretching back some thirty miles into open country and outlying communities. Local sources reported the destruction of just eighty-five houses, a figure in no way commensurate with the effort expended and the loss of forty-seven heavy bombers. The percentage loss rates made alarming reading at Bomber Command HQ, the Lancasters with an acceptable and sustainable 3%, the Halifaxes with 11.3% and the Stirlings with 16%.

F/L Chilvers had now completed his tour and was posted to 28 O.T.U. during w.e.f 26th to pass on his skills. During the course of the month the squadron participated in thirteen operations and dispatched 165 sorties for the loss of thirteen Lancasters and their crews.

September 1943

The new month began operationally for fifteen 5 Group freshman crews on the 2nd with a mining operation in the Nectarine I garden, situated a fraction north of due east on the other side of the North Sea. The five-strong 61 Squadron element departed Syerston between 20.17 and 20.26 and all reached the target area to find four to eight-tenths cloud with tops at around 3,000 feet and good visibility despite the absence of a moon. They homed-in on the drop zone by Gee-fix to plant their vegetables on e.t.a. into the briefed locations from 5,000 and 6,000 feet, P/O Scott and crew on three engines after having to shut down the starboard-outer.

Probably as a result of the heavy losses recently incurred by the Halifaxes and Stirlings, an all-Lancaster force of 316 aircraft was assembled on the 3rd to conclude the current series of operations against the "Big City". 5 Group contributed 121 aircraft, including thirteen representing 61 Squadron, which departed Syerston between 19.54 and 20.17 with S/L Benjamin the senior pilot on duty. P/O Eager and crew turned back with a frozen rear gunner, whose electrically heated suit had let him down, while the rest of the force rendezvoused over the North Sea as a complete bomber stream crossed the Dutch coast over the Den Helder peninsula. After making landfall they adopted a direct course of 350 miles, which took them north of Hannover to Brandenburg, some thirty-five miles short of the target. Long, straight legs were rarely employed because of the risk of interception by the Luftwaffe, but the forecast heavy cloud with tops at 18,000 feet accompanied the stream all the way from the Dutch coast to the target area and helped to keep the enemy at bay. The Path Finders had been briefed to use H2S to navigate their way via the region's lakes to the city centre aiming point, but the cloud miraculously dispersed in time to leave clear skies and allow them to drop ground-marking TIs rather than the less reliable skymarkers.

The first TIs fell right over the aiming point, before others crept back for between two and five miles along the line of approach from the west. Fortunately, the backers up maintained the marking as the main force Lancasters came in in a single wave, and, although much of the bombing fell short of the city centre, most of it landed within the city boundaries, falling principally into the largely residential districts of Tiergarten, Wedding, Moabit and Charlottenburg and the industrial Siemensstadt, where much useful damage occurred that resulted in a loss of war production. The 61 Squadron crews carried out a time-and-distance run from yellow track markers and bombed on red and green TIs from between 16,000 and 21,000 feet. Many fires were observed, which appeared to be merging as the bombers turned towards the north for a return route that would intentionally violate Swedish airspace. Four Mosquitos laid spoof route marker flares well away from the actual track to mislead the night-fighters, but in the absence of the poorer performing Halifaxes and Stirlings, twenty-two Lancasters failed to return, almost 7% of those dispatched.

Whether by design, or as a result of the losses sustained, Berlin was now shelved for the next ten weeks, while Harris sought other suitable targets, of which there were many. He would shortly begin a four-raid series against Hannover stretching over a four-week period but first he focused on southern Germany, beginning on the 5th with the twin cities of Mannheim and Ludwigshafen, which face each other from the east and west banks respectively of the Rhine. The plan was to exploit the creep-back phenomenon that attended most large operations, by approaching the target from the west and marking the eastern half of Mannheim, with the expectation that the bombing would spread back along the line of approach across western Mannheim and into Ludwigshafen. A force of 605 aircraft was assembled, which included 108 Lancasters of 5 Group, fourteen of them belonging to 61 Squadron, each of which received a bomb load of a cookie and variety of incendiaries packed in up to eighteen SBCs. They departed Syerston between 19.53 and 20.36 with no pilots on duty above the rank of flying officer, and after climbing out set course for Beachy Head and the Channel crossing. On a night of poor serviceability for 5 Group ten returned early, four of them from the ranks of 61 Squadron, beginning with F/O Moss at the English coast when the navigator became unwell. The crews of Sgt Wallis and F/O Fitch were unable to maintain height and the latter were on their way home when an engine caught fire, and the pilot ordered his crew to bale out. He landed safely at Winthorpe and was reunited with his crew on return to Syerston. The others tracked across France to a point five miles south of Luxembourg, where route markers established the final turning point for a direct run on the target, and it was shortly after crossing the Franco/German frontier that P/O Todd and crew experienced engine trouble that forced them to jettison their load from 15,000 feet at a point between Saarbrücken and the target. Undisclosed difficulties were experienced during attempts to land at base and DV232 ended up in the River Trent a few miles from Newark at 03.45, happily without crew casualties.

The Path Finders were routed in over Kaiserslautern some thirty miles due west of Mannheim, from where they were to carry out a timed run to the aiming-point. The main force crews arrived to find clear skies and the Path Finders performing at their absolute best, and after first observing red and yellow markers, the 61 Squadron crews had green TIs in their bomb sights as they let their loads go from between 18,700 and 21,000 feet. Those arriving towards the later stages of the raid were drawn on by the burgeoning fires fifty miles ahead, and a number of large, red explosions were observed at 23.12, 23.23 and 23.27, the last of which was followed by a purplish-red mushroom of fire. Searchlights were numerous but the flak negligible, and it was the abundance of night-fighters that posed the greatest risk to life and limb, although the 61 Squadron crews appeared to avoid any contact. Black smoke was rising through 15,000 feet as the bombers withdrew to the west, and the glow from the burning cities was visible for 150 miles and more into the return journey, which thirty-four aircraft would fail to complete. Thirteen Lancasters, an equal number of Halifaxes and eight Stirlings were missing, and the percentage loss rates continued to tell the same story. Local reports confirmed that both Mannheim and Ludwigshafen had suffered catastrophic destruction, with almost two thousand fires in the latter alone, 986 of them classed as large. Mannheim's reporting system broke down completely and little detail emerged of this raid, although it would recover in time for the next assault in fewer than three weeks' time. What is known, is that the main railway station in Mannheim and three suburban stations were destroyed and the tank and military tractor factories belonging to Heinrich Lanz and Josef Vogele respectively sustained serious damage, as did the Rashig & Sulzer chemicals plant.

Munich was posted as the target on the 6th, for which the squadron made ready a dozen Lancasters as part of the ninety-two-strong 5 Group element in an overall force of 257 Lancasters and 147 Halifaxes, the Stirling brigade made conspicuous by its absence. The 61 Squadron element took to the air at Syerston between 19.46 and 20.08 with no senior pilots on duty, and each Lancaster carrying a similar bomb load and adopting the same route as for the previous night. P/O Walker and crew turned back just short of the French coast near Dieppe because of the persistent illness of the rear gunner. The others accompanied the bomber stream all the way to the Bavarian capital city and arrived under conditions that were not ideal. The cloud varied between five and nine-tenths, although some ground features, like the River Isar, could be identified and the red, yellow and green TIs observed. The 61 Squadron crews were among those carrying out a timed run from the Ammersee, located twenty-one miles away to the south-west, and bombed from between 18,000 and 22,000 feet. A large number of fires was observed to be grouped around the markers, but an accurate assessment was not possible. On the way home P/O Scott passed out through oxygen starvation but came to in time to regain control of the Lancaster only to discover that the bomb-aimer had baled out. Despite the disappearance of all navigational material, a safe return was completed with a landing at Ford on the south coast. At debriefings crews commented on the ineffectiveness of the searchlights because of the cloud but reported large numbers of night-fighters and the consensus was that the main weight of the attack had been scattered across southern and western districts. F/O Williams and crew mentioned the mythical "scarecrow", which, for reasons of morale, Bomber Command encouraged crews to believe was a special shell designed by the Germans to simulate a bomber blowing up with a full bomb load on board. No such shells existed, and what was called a scarecrow was, indeed, a bomber blowing up. Sixteen aircraft failed to return, thirteen of them Halifaxes, a percentage loss rate of 8.8, compared with 1.2 for the Lancasters.

While 5 Group left the war to the other groups for the ensuing two weeks, a series of operations against French targets began on the night of the 8/9th with the bombing of heavy gun emplacements near the small coastal resort town of Le Portel. This was the final phase of Operation Starkey, a rehearsal for invasion, which began on the 16th of August, and which was intended to deceive the enemy into believing that the invasion was imminent. Harris was less than enthusiastic about allowing his squadrons to participate in what he considered to be "play-acting" and managed to restrict Bomber Command's involvement to token gestures as on this night. The batteries, codenamed Religion and Andante, were to be attacked forty minutes apart, but much confusion surrounded the marking, and the subsequent inaccurate bombing caused massive destruction to the town of Le Portel and many casualties. (For a detailed analysis of this operation, see the excellent book, The Starkey Sacrifice, by Michael Cumming, published by Sutton).

It was not until the commencement of the series of raids on Hannover that 5 Group, as a whole, was roused from its slumber. The irony of such long layoffs was that airmen, despite occupying the most dangerous jobs in the fighting services, grew listless and bored when left to kick their heels, attend lectures and take part in PT, and no doubt cheered when the tannoys called them to briefing on the 22nd. They learned that they were to be part of a force of 711 aircraft to attack the ancient city of Hannover, situated in northern Germany midway between the Dutch frontier and Berlin. They were told that it was home to much war industry, and it was also the location of seven Nazi concentration camps, although, this was not known at the time among the Allies. According to Martin Middlebrook and Chris Everitt in Bomber Command War Diaries, the first two operations produced concentrated bombing but mostly outside of the target, while only the third one succeeded in causing extensive damage, which, if the figures are to be believed, seem to be massively out of proportion. The author contends that the reports of the crews after the first two operations suggest strongly that the damage to Hannover was accumulative over the first three raids and did not result from just one, as will be explained in the following narrative. The telling feature is, perhaps, that no reports came out of Hannover to corroborate the testimony of the crews on the first two raids, although post-raid reconnaissance by the RAF after the second one did show that some of the bombing had fallen into open country, and the Path Finders did admit to at least one poor performance.

Sixteen 61 Squadron Lancasters were prepared at Syerston and took off between 18.38 and 19.10 with W/C Penman the senior pilot on duty, before climbing out and joining up with the other 135 participants from 5 Group for the 430-mile outward leg. P/O Buckley and crew turned back with a dead port-outer engine, but the rest reached the target area, where good visibility prevailed but stronger-than-forecast winds played their part in pushing the marking and bombing towards the south-east. The attack was scheduled to begin at 21.30 and the first red TIs were observed three minutes later, before another was seen to cascade after overshooting the aiming point by an estimated four miles. This was followed by other red TIs overshooting by one to four miles with many greens falling among them, while the yellows seemed to be undershooting the reds by two miles and were closer to the city centre aiming-point. The 61 Squadron crews aimed at red and green TIs from between 16,000 and 22,000 feet while dodging the intense searchlights and heavy flak, which was bursting at around 18,000 feet. The low height was that of P/O Bird and crew, who were coned for five minutes on their way to the target and attacked by three night-fighters, which set the port-outer engine on fire and caused sufficient damage to flying controls to send the Lancaster out of control. When control was regained, it was discovered that the navigator, bomb-aimer and mid-upper gunner had baled out, despite which, P/O Bird continued on to the target with his remaining three crew members in support and the bombs were jettisoned "live" into the city. Some returning crews reported a line of fires developing from west to east, with smoke rising through 14,000 feet, while others claimed that fires ran from the aiming point in a north-north-westerly direction across the city. All were unanimous, however, that the raid had been highly successful and that the glow of fires was still visible from the Dutch coast, a distance of two hundred miles. Twenty-six aircraft failed to return, twelve of them Halifaxes, which again sustained the highest numerical losses, and this time, at 5.3%, even exceeded the Stirling's loss rate.

Let us now examine the claim that the main weight of bombs fell two to five miles south-south-east from the city centre and that the operation largely failed. Firstly, two to five miles in any city means that the bombing fell within the boundaries and, therefore, within the built-up area. Secondly, the majority of crews, if not all, reported a highly successful raid with fires right across the city, smoke rising to 14,000 feet as they left the scene and the glow visible from the Dutch coast. It is true that crews were very frequently mistaken in their belief that an attack had been successful, but the evidence on this occasion would seem to confirm their testimony. Decoy fire-sites do not produce a glow visible from a distance of two hundred miles or sufficient volumes of smoke to reach bombing height during the short duration of a raid and be dense enough to be visible at night.

On the 23rd, and for the second time in the month, Mannheim was posted as the target and faced a force numbering 628 aircraft, 139 of them 5 Group Lancasters, sixteen belonging to 61 Squadron at Syerston. The crews learned at briefing that Mosquitos were to drop red and green route markers, before the Path Finder blind marker crews delivered flares and red TIs over the target by H2S to guide the visual markers to the precise aiming-point. This had been placed in the less-severely afflicted northern districts, which they would mark with yellow TIs, followed by the backers-up with greens. The 61 Squadron element took off between 18.53 and 19.22 led for the first time by S/L Cousens, who had been posted in from 1660 Conversion Unit during w.e.f 8th, and for the fifth operation running one crew turned back early, on this occasion that of F/O Williams because of an unserviceable rear turret. The bomber stream traversed France and entered southern Germany south of Luxembourg to encounter largely clear skies and good visibility.

At the head of the stream, the Path Finders carried out accurate and concentrated marking of the northern districts, which had not been hit so severely during the previous operation, allowing the 61 Squadron crews to attack on red, green and yellow TIs from between 15,000 and 22,000 feet. Later bombing spilled over into the northern fringe of Ludwigshafen and out into the nearby towns of Oppau and Frankenthal, where much damage resulted. Returning crews reported smoke rising through 15,000 feet as they turned away and that the glow of fires remained visible for 150 miles into the return journey. Thirty-two crews were absent from debriefing, and this time eighteen of them were in Lancasters, compared with seven each for the Halifaxes and Stirlings. This provided a somewhat topsy-turvy and unusual loss-rate of 5.7%, 3.6% and 6% respectively. Post-raid reconnaissance and local reports revealed that 927 houses and twenty industrial premises had been destroyed in Mannheim and that the I G Farben factory in Ludwigshafen had sustained serious damage.

Hannover was posted again as the target on the 27th and a force of 678 aircraft made ready, which included a 5 Group contribution of 141 Lancasters, fifteen of them belonging to 61 Squadron. The crews learned at briefing that the Steinhude Lake to the north-west of the city was to be employed again by the Path Finder blind marker crews as the starting point for a timed run to the aiming point, which would be marked with yellow TIs on H2S and identified visually by the backers-up and marked with reds and greens. They departed Syerston between 19.12 and 19.56 with S/L Cousens the senior pilot on duty, only for him to abandon the sortie when the rear gunner's heated flying suit suffered some kind of damage and stopped working. The others joined up with the bomber stream, at the head of which the leading Path Finder crews were unaware that the weather forecasts on which their performance would be based were incorrect. The result of that would be to push the marking some five miles from the city centre towards the north, but at least the weather improved markedly over Germany to present the crews with clear skies at the target. The 61 Squadron crews delivered their cookie and 4lb and 30lb incendiaries each mostly on green TIs from between 18,000 and 22,000 feet and observed many fires with smoke rising through 15,000 feet.

Returning crews again reported the glow of fires visible from the Dutch coast, and confidence in the success of the operation was unanimous across the Command, giving lie to the claim that little damage resulted. Post-raid photos did reveal many bomb craters in open country, but the fire and smoke evidence did not support decoy fire-sites, and no local report was forthcoming to shed further light. The loss of thirty-eight aircraft was probably something of a shock, but at least common sense returned to the statistics to re-establish the status-quo after the topsy-turvy outcome of the Mannheim raid. Seventeen Halifaxes, ten Lancasters, ten Stirlings and one Wellington failed to return, giving loss-rates for the four-engine types of 9% for the Stirling, 7.3% for the Halifax and 3.2% for the Lancaster. 61 Squadron's ED314 was shot down while outbound and P/O Buckley and five of his crew found themselves in enemy hands, while the mid-upper gunner failed to survive.

The month ended with an operation to Bochum in the central Ruhr on the 29th, for which 61 Squadron made ready eleven Lancasters in a 5 Group effort of 111, and they were part of an overall heavy force of 343 aircraft. The plan of attack required the Mosquito element to drop green warning flares, before Oboe-marking the aiming-point with red TIs, and in case they could not be seen through cloud, with red flares with green stars. The 61 Squadron element departed Syerston between 18.20 and 18.50 with S/L Cousens the senior pilot on duty and lost the services of P/O Wallis and crew because of an inability to drag their Lancaster above 12,000 feet. The others proceeded to the target, kept on track by two route-marker flares at 20,000 feet, and after a two-and-a-half-hour outward flight, established their positions visually in good visibility. The Path Finders marked the aiming point with green TIs and the bombing was carried out from between 19,000 and 21,500 feet in the face of a strong searchlight and moderate flak defence. Some returning crews described the target as a mass of flames with smoke rising rapidly to meet them, while local reports confirmed the destruction of 527 houses, with 742 others seriously damaged.

While this operation was in progress, fourteen 5 Group Lancasters were sent to the Baltic to mine the waters of the Privet I and II gardens off distant Danzig (Gdansk). 61 Squadron donated the crews of P/O Strange and F/Sgt Wilson, whose take-off times as recorded in the ORB are unreliable, but were probably around 18.00, and arrived at their destination under clear skies and in extreme darkness to deliver their mines into the briefed location in the Gulf of Pucka from 5,000 feet.

During the course of the month, the squadron carried out nine operations and dispatched 104 sorties for the loss of a single Lancaster and its crew and three members of another.

October 1943

The start of October was a busy time for the Lancaster squadrons, which would be called upon to participate in six major operations in the first eight nights. P/O Dickie Willsher and crew had responded to the request from 617 Squadron for volunteers to attend interviews to assess their suitability to join the now famous squadron, which, having suffered heavy casualties during the Dams and recent Dortmund-Ems Canal operations, had acquired a reputation as a "chop" unit. The Willshire crew was accepted, and they would go on to complete a tour that included operations with Tallboy earthquake bombs against U-Boot pens and other precision targets. In September 1944 they were posted to 5 Lancaster Finishing School and would survive the war.

The month's account was opened at Hagen at the eastern end of the Ruhr on the 1st, for which a moderately sized heavy force of 243 Lancasters was drawn from 1, 5 and 8 Groups. 5 Group contributed 125 aircraft, a dozen of them representing 61 Squadron, and they were loaded with a cookie and up to sixteen SBCs of incendiaries each, before departing Syerston between 18.11 and 18.53 with W/C Penman the senior pilot on duty. They flew out over Skegness aiming for Egmond on the Dutch coast, to then skirt the northern edge of the Ruhr as far as Werl, a town to the north of the now famous Möhne reservoir, from where they would turn sharply to the south-west to run in on the target. F/O Story and crew were contending with an undisclosed technical issue, which according to their position suggested a faulty compass, and jettisoned their bombs from 16,000 feet onto a searchlight and flak position to the north-east of Cologne, some thirty miles from their intended target. The others arrived in the target area to find ten-tenths cloud with tops at 8,000 feet and red and green Oboe-laid skymarkers to aim at and carried out their attacks from between 16,000 and 20,400 feet. Returning crews reported a column of black smoke rising through the clouds and some described a large bluish-green explosion at 21.03, the glow of fires beneath the cloud and an effective Path Finder performance. In addition to the usual housing damage, local reports confirmed the destruction of forty-six industrial firms, among them a manufacturer of accumulator batteries for U-Boots, and this would have an impact on U-Boot production. Also misled by a faulty compass was 49 Squadron's commanding officer, W/C Adams, and in an unusual decision by higher authority, he and his navigator had the sortie disallowed, the former for not having a drill in place for checking the accuracy of the compass and the navigator for complacency.

On the following day 294 crews from 1, 5 and 8 Groups were called to briefings to learn that Munich was to be their destination that night, for which 5 Group detailed 113 Lancasters, among them ten representing 61 Squadron, whose crews, like the others of 5 Group, were to adopt the time-and-distance method of bombing. Their Lancasters were loaded at Syerston with a cookie and ten SBCs each before taking off between 18.25 and 19.05 with S/Ls Benjamin and Cousens the senior pilots on duty. They set a course to the south coast to begin the Channel crossing for landfall on the other side in the Dunkerque region, before traversing France to enter Germany south of Strasbourg. They reached the target area after an outward flight of some three-and-a-half hours and encountered cloud over the Wörthsee, situated some fifteen miles west-south-west of the centre of Munich, which had been selected as the starting point for the time-and-distance run. The skies over the city were clear of cloud, but the marking was scattered and led to most of the early bombing falling into southern and south-eastern districts. The 5 Group crews were unable to establish a firm fix on the Wörthsee, and this would lead to a creep-back of up to fifteen miles along the line of approach. The 61 Squadron crews bombed on red and green TIs from between 19,000 and 21,000 feet, but it was not all plain-sailing in the face of a hostile defence that included night-fighters that had been awaiting their arrival in the target area, and eight Lancasters were lost. ED718 was homebound when intercepted by a night-fighter and subjected to a sustained attack, which S/L Cousens countered by diving. However, a fire broke out and at 6,000 feet the Lancaster exploded, throwing clear S/L Cousens and his mid-upper gunner, Sgt Dunn, as the only survivors. Both fell into enemy hands, S/L Cousens being held initially in a local village jail. Returning crews suggested that the raid appeared to be concentrated on the eastern side of the city, and local authorities reported that 339 buildings had been destroyed.

Kassel, the industrial city located some eighty miles to the east of the Ruhr, would receive two visits from the Command during the month, the first on the 3rd, for which a force of 547 aircraft was assembled consisting of 223 Halifaxes, 204 Lancasters and 113 Stirlings. 5 Group supported the operation with ninety-two Lancasters, of which ten were made ready by 61 Squadron at Syerston. At briefings the crews learned of the plan of attack, which called for the Mosquitos to provide route markers and for the Path Finder H2S crews to mark the target blind with yellow TIs and flares. The visual markers were then to identify the aiming-point and mark it with red TIs for the backers-up to maintain with greens. The 61 Squadron element took off between 18.45 and

18.56 with W/C Penman the senior pilot on duty and for the third operation running there were no early returns. Arriving in the target area, they found largely clear skies but thick ground haze, which may have been responsible for the Path Finder H2S "blind" markers overshooting the planned aiming point, and because of the haze and, possibly, decoy markers, the backers-up, whose job was to confirm their accuracy by visual means, were unable to correct the error. The 61 Squadron crews identified the target visually and by green TIs and bombed from between 19,000 and 21,000 feet, reporting on their return what appeared to be a good concentration of fires and a pall of smoke rising to meet them.

In fact, the main weight of the attack had fallen onto the western suburbs, where the Henschel aircraft and tank factories and the Fieseler aircraft plant were hit, but a stray bomb load had also detonated an ammunition dump at Ihringshausen, situated close to the north-eastern suburb of Wolfsanger, which was left devastated by the blast. Twenty-four aircraft failed to return, fourteen Halifaxes, six Stirlings and four Lancasters, which gave a loss-rate of 6.3%, 3.2% and 2.9% respectively. W4279 crashed at Rothwesten, some six miles north-north-west of the centre of Kassel with no survivors from the crew of W/C Penman DFC, AFC, MiD, and when a squadron commander went missing, he usually took with him a bunch of highly experienced crew members including trade leaders, and apart from the mid-upper gunner, whose rank was warrant officer, the others were all commissioned, three of them of flight lieutenant rank.

W/C Penman was succeeded as 61 Squadron commanding officer by the twenty-eight-year-old W/C Reg Stidolph, a Rhodesian serving in the RAF and an officer with extensive operational experience behind him, all of it gained overseas. He had served against Rommel's forces in North Africa leading up to El Alamein in 1941 and 1942 and against Japanese targets in the Far East in 1942. He had flown an unusually large number of aircraft types, from bi-plane torpedo bombers and float planes to twin engine bombers, and had commanded 113 Squadron, a Blenheim unit. On his posting to England in 1943 he was sent to 1654 Conversion Unit at Wigsley in Nottinghamshire to learn to fly the Lancaster and arrived at Syerston on the 4th.

He presided over his first briefing that afternoon as the busy schedule of operations continued with the posting of Frankfurt as the target, for which a force of 406 aircraft was made ready. The American confidence in the ability of its forces to deliver daylight attacks on military and war production targets in Germany had been shaken by the high loss rates, which were not sustainable. Since the first Hannover raid, a small number of 8th Air Force B17s had been flirting with night raids alongside their RAF colleagues and this night would bring their final involvement. 5 Group detailed ninety-five Lancasters, of which nine represented 61 Squadron, and they departed Syerston between 18.24 and 18.50 with F/Ls Moss, Vowels and Williams the senior pilots on duty. They had to follow a somewhat circuitous route, which departed England over the Sussex coast and tracked across Belgium as if heading for southern Germany, before swinging to the north-east and passing to the west of Frankfurt for the final run-in of around eighty miles. This added significantly to the mileage but avoided the flak hotspots from the Dutch coast and north of the Ruhr. P/O Wallis and crew turned back after an hour when the navigator became unwell and the mid-upper turret failed, while the others reached the target reached after a four-hour outward flight, although an hour of that was generally accounted for in climbing-out and gaining height before setting course. Frankfurt was found to be clear of cloud, and the Path Finders produced a masterful marking performance to leave the city at the mercy of the main force element, among which, the 61 Squadron crews bombed on red and green TIs from between 18,000 and 21,500 feet. They witnessed a highly-concentrated attack that left the eastern half of the city and the docks area a sea of flames and noted a large red explosion at 21.37, which threw flames up to 3,000 feet, while a column of smoke was rising through 8,000 feet. Some crews reported the glow from the burning city to be visible for 120 miles into the homeward leg and the successful outcome was gained for the modest cost of ten aircraft.

The busy first week of the month concluded with an operation against Stuttgart, for which a force of 343 Lancasters was drawn from 1, 3, 5, 6 and 8 Groups on the 7th. A new weapon in the Command's armoury was introduced for the first time in numbers on this night with the participation of a night-fighter-communications-jamming device called "Jostle" fitted in Lancasters of 1 Group's 101 Squadron. It required a specialist operator in addition to the standard crew of seven, who, though not necessarily a German speaker, could recognise the language and on hearing it, jam the signals on up to three frequencies by broadcasting engine noise over them. At 101 Squadron the device was referred to as ABC or Airborne Cigar, and once proved to be effective, ABC Lancasters would be spread through the bomber stream for all major operations, whether or not 1 Group was otherwise involved. The Lancaster would also carry a full bomb load reduced by 1,000lbs to compensate for the weight of the equipment and its operator.

5 Group put up 128 Lancasters for this operation, of which a dozen were made ready by 61 Squadron at Syerston and took off between 20.14 and 21.00 with no fewer than six pilots of flight lieutenant rank leading the way. P/O Coulson and crew lost their port-inner engine and turned back, leaving the others to reach the target area, where ten-tenths cloud at 10,000 feet concealed the ground from view. The Path Finders employed H2S and established two areas of marking, which led to bombs falling in many parts of the city from the centre to the south-west. The 61 Squadron crews bombed from between 19,000 and 21,000 feet, before returning safely to report their impressions of a scattered attack, which, on the credit side, cost a remarkably modest four aircraft. Whether or not the presence of the radio-countermeasures Lancasters was responsible for the low casualty rate could not be determined absolutely, but it was a promising start and would lead, ultimately, to the formation of the dedicated RCM 100 Group in November.

The third raid of the series on Hannover was posted to take place that night, and a force of 504 aircraft duly assembled, 5 Group contributing eighty-four Lancasters, just six of them made ready by 61 Squadron at Syerston. A large diversionary raid was planned for Bremen to begin at 01.15, five minutes ahead of zero-hour at the main event and would involve seventeen 8 Group Halifaxes and seven Lancasters marking for a main force of ninety-five Stirlings. The 61 Squadron element took off between 22.47 and 23.08 with F/Ls Moss and Williams the senior pilots on duty and after climbing out, set course for the northern tip of Texel to traverse northern Holland and enter Germany north of Meppen. F/L Moss and crew dropped out when the gunners tested their equipment over the sea and none of the guns worked. The others reached the target area to find largely clear skies and red and green TIs marking out the city-centre aiming point, inviting the bombs of the main force crews, those from 61 Squadron delivering theirs from between 19,500 and 20,500 feet. Having arrived in the early stages of the attack, they saw fires just beginning to take hold and it became clear as they retreated westwards that the fires were developing into a serious conflagration. Curiously, despite the claim by some commentators that this was the one unquestionably successful raid of the series, there was no mention of the glow of fire remaining visible on the horizon from a considerable distance, as had been the case with the first two operations. This time a local report did emerge, which described heavy damage in all districts except for those in the west, with a large area of fire engulfing the central districts. A total of 3,932 buildings was destroyed, while thirty thousand others were damaged to some extent and the death toll amounted to 1,200 people. These statistics seem somewhat excessive for a single operation by fewer than five hundred aircraft, particularly in the absence of the kind of crew reports common to the first two raids, and this adds weight to the author's contention, that the damage was accumulative over the three operations. Twenty-seven aircraft failed to return, and there were three empty dispersals at Syerston, one of them formerly belonging to DV239, which was now a smouldering wreck on the ground at Hainholz, a northern suburb of Hannover, where it had crashed at 01.24 with no survivors from the crew of P/O Coulson.

There followed what was effectively a stand-down for the Path Finder and main force squadrons that would last for a period of ten days, and in the meantime, it was left to the Mosquitos of 8 Group to take the war to Germany. It was the 18th when the Lancaster groups were called upon to provide aircraft and crews for that night's operation, the call to briefings no doubt a relief to the crews, who had become bored with filling their days with routine non-operational tasks. They learned that Hannover was the target for this all-Lancaster affair involving 360 aircraft, 143 of them provided by 5 Group and thirteen by 61 Squadron, which departed Syerston between 17.10 and 17.49 with S/L Benjamin and the newly promoted S/L Moss the senior pilots on duty. They made landfall over Texel and continued on an easterly track across Holland aiming for Cloppenburg and thence Nienburg and Celle, before turning to the south-west to run in on the target close to the Misburg oil refinery. They remained unmolested by the defences until encountering a nest of night-fighters on crossing the frontier into Germany, and at least thirteen aircraft were brought down during the ensuing forty-five minutes encompassing the approach and withdrawal phases. A layer of eight to ten-tenths cloud hung over Hannover with tops at 12,000 to 15,000 feet, and these conditions made it difficult for the Path Finders to establish the aiming point. It resulted in them dropping both sky and ground markers that lacked concentration, which would lead to a scattering of the effort. The 61 Squadron crews bombed mostly on red and green TIs or on release-point flares from between 20,000 and 21,500 feet, and a colossal explosion was observed at around 20.19. The strong night-fighter presence dissuaded crews from hanging around to assess the outcome further, and the impression of those returning was of a scattered attack. It was established later that most of the bombs had fallen into open country, a disappointment compounded by the loss of eighteen Lancasters. The four raids on Hannover had cost the Command 110 aircraft from 2,253 sorties, a loss rate of 4.9%, but much of the city now lay in ruins and would receive no further attention for a year, when the oil offensive and the close proximity of the Misburg synthetic oil plant to the east would return the region to prominence.

The first major attack of the war on the eastern city of Leipzig was planned for the 20th, for which an all-Lancaster force of 358 aircraft was assembled from 1, 5, 6 and 8 Groups. 5 Group was responsible for 140 Lancasters and 61 Squadron fourteen, which took off from Syerston between 17.00 and 17.38 with S/L Moss the senior pilot on duty. The crews of F/Sgt Whitecross and F/L Woods were back in the circuit within four hours reporting compass and intercom failure respectively, and as a result avoided the atrocious weather conditions encountered by the others outbound, with a towering front of ice-bearing cumulonimbus east of Hannover extending beyond 20,000 feet. Many crews were persuaded to turn back as engines began to falter and ice-accretion destroyed lift, while those pushing on through the front reached the target after a three-and-a-half-hour outward flight to encounter seven to ten-tenths cloud with tops as high as 14,000 feet. The Path Finders had been unable in the conditions to establish and mark the aiming point, leaving crews to bomb on e.t.a., on fires glimpsed through the cloud or on scattered skymarkers, the 61 Squadron participants from between 18,000 and 22,000 feet. S/L Moss and crew believed that they had bombed Leipzig, but on return plotted their position and discovered that they had actually attacked Dessau, some forty miles to the north. Sixteen Lancasters failed to return, and those crews that did make it home were unable to offer any useful details at debriefing.

The final major operation of the month was the second one against Kassel, for which preparations were put in hand on the 22nd and a force of 569 aircraft assembled, 133 of them 5 Group Lancasters. 61 Squadron's fifteen-strong element departed Syerston between 17.47 and 18.26 with W/C Stidolph leading the squadron for the first time, although this first sortie ended in disappointment as a fire in his starboard-outer engine forced him to turn back. Some ran into an electrical storm over the North Sea, and it was at this stage of the operation that F/L Turner and crew abandoned their sortie on the failure of the a.s.i., and they were followed home within minutes by P/O Farmiloe and crew because of a navigational issue. Those emerging on the other side of the front traversed Belgium, still in continuing unfavourable weather conditions, which miraculously improved in the target area to leave clear skies between the bombers and the target but ten-tenths cloud above them at 24,000 feet. At the opening of the raid, the H2S "blind" markers overshot the city-centre aiming point, leaving the success of the operation reliant upon the backing-up skills of the visual marker crews, and they did not disappoint. The red and green TIs were concentrated right on the aiming point and the main force crews followed up with accurate and concentrated bombing with scarcely any creep-back. The 61 Squadron crews carried out their attacks from between 18,400 and 21,000 feet and observed the fires just beginning to take hold as they turned away. It was after the sound of their engines had receded that the fires joined together to engulf the city in what, in some areas, developed into a firestorm, though not one as fierce as that experienced in Hamburg.

The massively successful operation was achieved at a high cost of forty-three bombers, twenty-five of them Halifaxes, but among the nine missing 5 Group Lancasters were two belonging to 61 Squadron. W4357, QR-A "Annie" came down some sixty miles north-east of Kassel after the crew of P/O Truscott and taken to their parachutes to drift down into the arms of their captors. ED630 crashed at 21.30 near Uslar, some thirty miles north of the target, and only the bomb-aimer escaped with his life from the crew of F/Sgt Whitecross, and he joined his squadron colleagues in captivity. On the way home F/O Ames and crew were attacked by three night-fighters and their Lancaster severely damaged, despite which they made it home to claim the destruction of one of their assailants. In Kassel, the shell-shocked inhabitants emerged from their shelters to find their city devastated and unrecognizable. After 3,600 fires had been dealt with, it would be established eventually that more than 4,300 apartment blocks containing 53,000 dwelling units had been destroyed or damaged, leaving up to 120,000 people without homes and in excess of six thousand others killed. 155 industrial buildings had also been destroyed or severely damaged, along with numerous schools, hospitals, churches and public buildings.

During the course of the month, the squadron participated in nine operations and dispatched 101 sorties for the loss of five Lancasters and crews.

November 1943

November brought with it the long, dark, cloudy nights which enabled Harris to return to his main theme, the destruction of Germany's capital city. The next four months would bring the bloodiest, hardest-fought air battles between Bomber Command and the Luftwaffe Nachtjagd and test the hard-pressed crews to the limit of their endurance. In a minute to Churchill on the 3rd, Harris stated, that with the participation of the American 8th Air Force, he could "wreck Berlin from end to end". He estimated that the campaign would cost the two forces between four and five hundred aircraft, but that it would cost Germany the war. This would remove the need for the kind of bloody, expensive and protracted land campaign, which he had personally witnessed during the Great War and had prompted him to "get into the air" at the earliest opportunity. It should be remembered that this was the first time in the history of air warfare, that the means had existed to prove the theory, that an enemy could be defeated by bombing alone. It is only in the light of more recent experiences that we have learned of the need, in a conventional conflict at least, to occupy the enemy's territory to secure submission. The Americans, however, were committed to victory on land, where film cameras could capture the glory and would not accompany Harris to Berlin.

When crews were called to briefings on the 3rd they learned that Düsseldorf had been selected to open the month's operational account, and no doubt, while the Prime Minister was digesting Harris's epistle, a force of 589 Lancasters and Halifaxes was being prepared for action. 5 Group's contribution amounted to 147 Lancasters, of which eleven represented 61 Squadron, and they were each loaded with a cookie and SBCs of various incendiaries before departing Syerston between 16.58 and 17.20 with W/C Stidolph the senior pilots on duty. There were no early returns among the 61 Squadron contingent, which joined the bomber stream over the North Sea and approached the south-western Ruhr after flying out over Belgium and through the concentration of fifty to sixty searchlights in the Mönchengladbach-Cologne corridor, some fifteen miles from the target. Shortly after crossing the enemy coast, LM630 was attacked by a BF110, the fire from which shattered the windscreen and damaged the rear turret. Reid sustained wounds, despite which he pressed on towards the target, only to be attacked again, this time by a FW190, which inflicted further wounds on Reid and his flight engineer, killed the navigator and mortally wounded the wireless operator. Still, with four healthy engines, he refused to turn back, recognising the danger of collision in turning across the stream, and reached the target, where small patches of cloud below at 12,000 feet drifted across it along with smoke from the early fires. The visibility remained generally good and the Path Finders employed both sky and ground markers to good effect to identify the aiming point in the city centre and bombing by the 61 Squadron crews took place on red and green TIs and skymarkers from between 18,500 and 21,600 feet. Fires were observed to be developing on both sides of the Rhine with black smoke rising through 6,000 feet as the bombers turned away, the Reid crew without the assistance of a navigator finding their way to Shipdham in Norfolk, a USAAF base, which guided them in with searchlights. On touchdown the undercarriage collapsed, and the Lancaster slid to a halt, severely damaged but repairable. The wireless operator succumbed to his wounds within hours and Reid and his flight engineer required hospital treatment before they, too, returned to operations, Reid having been awarded a Victoria Cross. Eighteen aircraft failed to return, and, unusually, eleven were Lancasters and only seven Halifaxes. Post-raid reconnaissance revealed that central and southern districts had sustained widespread damage to industry and housing, but no report came out of Düsseldorf to provide detail.

The only serious activity for 5 Group squadrons, thereafter, until the resumption of the Berlin campaign, was an operation on the night of the 10/11th in company with 8 Group against railway yards at Modane, situated in the foothills of the Alps in south-eastern France. A force of 313 Lancasters included a contribution from 5 Group of 136, fourteen of them representing 61 Squadron, which departed Syerston between 20.25 and 21.12 with F/Ls Mortimer and Woods the senior pilots on duty and an outward flight ahead of them of more than 650 miles. There were no early returns among the 61 Squadron contingent and they arrived at the target in around four-and-a-quarter hours to be rewarded by the presence of a full moon shining brightly from a cloudless sky. The initial pinpoint was Lake Bissorte, from where they carried out a time-and-distance run to the aiming point, identified visually and by red and green TIs, before most bombed from a uniform 15,000 feet, with a spread by three others between 14,000 and 19,700 feet. The attack seemed to be concentrated around the markers and fires appeared to be taking hold, while a large explosion was observed at 01.13. Returning crews were fairly confident in the quality of their night's efforts and brought back two hundred bombing photos that revealed extensive damage to track and installations within one mile of the aiming point, a success gained at no cost in aircraft and crews.

On the following day 106 squadron moved out of Syerston to take up residence at a newly constructed airfield at Metheringham, located in the Lincolnshire dales a few miles to the west of Woodhall Spa and Coningsby. On the 15th, 61 Squadron followed 106 Squadron out of Syerston and moved to Skellingthorpe, situated to the west of Lincoln, where it joined 50 Squadron. On the same day, 630 Squadron was formed around a nucleus of experienced crews from 57 Squadron at East Kirkby, situated to the east of Woodhall Spa and Coningsby.

Undaunted by the American response to his invitation to join the Berlin party, Harris would return alone, and the rocky road to the Germany's capital was re-joined by an all-Lancaster heavy force on the night of the 18/19th, while a predominantly Halifax and Stirling contingent of 395 aircraft acted as a diversion by raiding Mannheim and Ludwigshafen three hundred miles to the south-west. The Berlin-bound crews would benefit from four Mosquitos dropping dummy fighter flares, while other Mosquitos carried out a spoof raid on Frankfurt to protect the Mannheim force. The two formations would cross the enemy coast simultaneously some 250 miles apart to confuse the enemy night-fighter controllers, the route chosen for the Berlin brigade taking it via the Frisian Island of Texel to a point north of Hannover, and thence to the target to pass over its centre on an east-north-easterly heading. The return route would pass south of Berlin and Cologne, before crossing central Belgium to gain the English Channel via the French coast. An innovation for this operation was a shortening of the bomber stream to reduce the time over the target to sixteen minutes. When the first Thousand Bomber raid had taken place in May 1942, with an unprecedented twelve aircraft per minute crossing the aiming point, there was considered to be a high risk of collisions. The number had since increased to sixteen per minute, with large raids lasting up to forty-five minutes, but on this night, twenty-seven aircraft per minute were to pass over the aiming point.

61 Squadron made ready thirteen Lancasters as part of a 5 Group force of 182, and take-off from Skellingthorpe was accomplished without incident between 17.03 and 17.50 with W/C Stidolph and S/L Moss the senior pilots on duty. A blanket of cloud with tops at between 6,000 and 12,000 feet covered the whole of northern Germany and crews were grateful for the red spotfire route marker dropped by the Path Finders north-east of Hannover, which confirmed that they were on track. They benefitted from good horizontal visibility despite the absence of a moon, and once at

the target searchlights illuminated the cloud as the 61 Squadron crews carried out their attacks on H2S-laid red and green skymarkers from between 20,000 and 22,000 feet. Condensation trails formed above 22,000 feet to advertise the bombers' presence and on the way home at 25,000 feet the crews of F/L Mortimer and P/O McConnell passed through a flak belt between Cologne and Bonn and sustained flak damage. There was little that crews could pass on to the intelligence bods at debriefings, and most suspected that the bombing had been scattered and probably ineffective. Local sources confirmed that there had been no concentration of bombing and catalogued the destruction of 169 houses and a number of industrial units, with many more damaged to some extent. The diversion at Mannheim was deemed to have been successful in its purpose and caused some useful industrial damage, most seriously to the Daimler-Benz motor factory, which suffered a 90% loss of production for an unknown period. In addition to this, more than three hundred buildings were destroyed at a cost of twenty-three aircraft, while the losses from Berlin were encouragingly low at just nine.

Later on the afternoon of the 19th the crews of F/L Vowels and Sgt Gray conducted a sea search for a dinghy, but returned after two hours with nothing to report. The Lancasters stayed at home that night, while 3, 4, 6 and 8 Groups combined to put 170 Halifaxes, eighty-six Stirlings and 10 Mosquitos into the air for a raid on the Ruhr city of Leverkusen, home to a major I G Farben manufacturing plant. They were greeted in the target area by ten-tenths cloud and an absence of marking, which was caused by equipment failure among the Oboe Mosquitos. A few green TIs were spotted some five to ten miles to the north-west of the target during the approach, but the crews were left to establish their positions on the basis of their own H2S, which, over a region as densely built-up as the Ruhr, was a challenge. As a result, the operation was a complete failure, which sprayed bombs over twenty-seven towns in the region, mostly to the north of Leverkusen. Fiskerton's FIDO system was fired up in earnest for the first time on the 21st for night flying training and proved to be effective, and the station could now expect to be a welcome haven for crews across the Command seeking somewhere to land on foggy nights.

Harris called for a maximum effort on Berlin on the 22nd, and 764 aircraft were made available, of which fourteen of 5 Group's 166 Lancasters were provided by 61 Squadron, which departed Skellingthorpe between 16.36 and 17.17 with S/L Benjamin the senior pilot on duty and after climbing out, adopted an outward route similar to that employed by the all-Lancaster force four nights earlier. This took them from Texel to a point north-west of Hannover, where a slight dogleg to port put them on a due-easterly heading directly to the target. Unlike the previous raid, however, rather than the circuitous return south of Cologne and out over the French coast, they would come home via a reciprocal route. This was based on a forecast of low cloud and fog over Germany, which would inhibit the night-fighter effort, while broken, medium-level cloud over Berlin would facilitate ground marking. An additional bonus was the availability to the Path Finders of five new H2S Mk III sets, while a new record of thirty-four aircraft per minute passing over the aiming point would be achieved by abandoning the long-standing practice of allocating aircraft types to specific waves. On this night, aircraft of all types would be spread through the bomber stream, and this was bad news for the Stirlings, which, by the very nature of their design, would be below the Lancaster and Halifax elements and in danger of being hit by friendly bombs.

P/O Eaves and crew were on their way home within ninety minutes because of an inoperable rear turret, leaving the others to discover that the meteorological forecast had been inaccurate, and that Berlin was hidden under a blanket of ten-tenths cloud with tops at around 12,000 feet. This meant that ground marking would be largely ineffective, and that the least reliable Wanganui (skymarking) method would have to be employed. Crews ran into intense predicted flak and a mass of searchlights as they began their bombing runs, and those from 61 Squadron, which were allotted to various waves within the bomber stream, aimed at red and green TIs and release-point flares from between 20,000 and 21,500 feet. The glow of fires was observed beneath the clouds and numerous explosions witnessed, one of very large proportions lighting up the sky at 20.10. The impression was of a successful operation, but an assessment through the clouds was impossible and it was only once post-raid reconnaissance had taken place, and local reports had filtered out that the scale of success would be realised. In the meantime, the families of twenty-six crews had to be informed that their son, husband or brother was missing as a result of air operations and for the purpose of morale, all trace of them had to be eradicated from the billets. This sad task fell on each station to a team from the Committee of Adjustment, who bagged up personal belongings to be returned to families and prepared the bed space for the next occupant. Eleven Lancasters, ten Halifaxes and five Stirlings had failed to return, which amounted to a loss-rate among the types respectively of 2.3%, 4.2% and 10.0%.

The Stirling losses proved to be the final straw for Harris because of its short wing design, which restricted it to a low service ceiling, and the configuration of its bomb bay to small calibre bombs up to 2,000lbs. Unlike the Lancaster and Halifax, it lacked development potential and was immediately withdrawn from future operations over Germany. It would still have an important role to play on secondary duties, however, bombing over occupied territory, mining, and in 1944, it would replace the Halifax to become the aircraft of choice for the two SOE squadrons, 138 and 161, at Tempsford. Many of those released from Bomber Command service would find their way to 38 Group, where they would give valuable service as transports and glider-tugs for airborne landings. At a stroke, and with the exception of the Mk II Lancaster-equipped 115 and 514 Squadrons, 3 Group had effectively been withdrawn from front-line operations,

Reconnaissance photos revealed this last raid on Berlin to have been the most effective against it of the war to date and had caused a swathe of destruction from the city centre through the western residential districts of Tiergarten and Charlottenburg as far as the suburb town of Spandau. A number of firestorm areas were reported, and the catalogue of destruction included three thousand houses and twenty-three industrial premises. Many thousands more sustained varying degrees of damage, costing 175,000 people their homes and an estimated two thousand their lives, and by daylight on the 23rd, the smoke had risen to almost 19,000 feet.

A heavy force of 365 Lancasters and ten Halifaxes was made ready with some difficulty on the 23rd for a return to Berlin, back-to-back long-range operations placing a strain on those charged with the responsibility of getting the aircraft off the ground. On this night the Ludford Magna armourers were unable to load all nineteen 101 Squadron Lancasters with the intended weight of bombs and sent them off 2,000lb short. 5 Group detailed 141 Lancasters, of which the twelve belonging to 61 Squadron each received a bomb load of a cookie, and some had a 1,000-pounder along with their SBCs of incendiaries. They departed Skellingthorpe between 17.08 and 17.33 with S/L Moss the senior pilot on duty, and lost P/O Strange and crew to an unserviceable rear turret after around an hour, one of eighteen 5 Group early returns among forty-six from the force as a whole, which was a further indication of the strain of back-to-back long-range operations. Another was the dumping of bombs over the North Sea by crews intending to push on to the target but wanting to gain more height. It involved largely those from 1 Group, who were shedding their cookies in protest at their A-O-C's policy of loading each Lancaster to its maximum all-up weight at the expense of altitude. The slogan "H-E-I-G-H-T spells safety" could be found on the walls of most bomber station briefing rooms at the time.

The target was reached by way of the same route adopted on the previous night and was found to be covered by ten-tenths cloud with tops at between 10,000 and 15,000 feet, through which the glow of fires still burning from the night before provided a reference, and the presence of red and green TIs, the 61 Squadron crews bombed on the red Wanganui parachute flares and green TIs from between 19,000 and 20,000 feet, contributing to another stunning blow. Returning crews described a column of smoke reaching 20,000 feet and the glow of fires visible again from the Hannover area some 150 miles from the target. It was on this night that fake broadcasts from England caused annoyance to the night-fighter force by ordering them to land because of fog over their bases, despite which, they still had a major hand in the bringing-down of twenty Lancasters. Post-raid reconnaissance and local reports confirmed that this operation had destroyed a further two thousand buildings and killed around fifteen hundred people.

While 1, 3 and 5 Groups enjoyed a night off on the 25th, 216 Halifaxes of 4 and 6 Groups and forty-six 8 Group Halifaxes and Lancasters carried out an operation against Frankfurt, where the blind markers established a firm H2S fix and delivered yellow TIs and red flares with green stars to coincide with the e.t.a. of the main force crews. Local reports described a modest amount of housing damage and 3,500 people bombed out of their homes, in return for which, eleven Halifaxes and a single Lancaster failed to return.

After a three-night rest for most of the Lancaster crews, 443 of them were briefed on the 26th for a return to the "Big City" for the fourth attack since the resumption of the campaign, 5 Group detailing 161 Lancasters, fifteen of them made ready by 61 Squadron. They departed Skellingthorpe between 17.11 and 17.51 with F/Ls Harvey, Turner, Vowels and Williams the senior pilots on duty. A diversionary raid on Stuttgart by a predominantly Halifax force followed the same route as those bound for Berlin, which involved an outward leg across the French coast and Belgium to a point north of Frankfurt, where they diverged. An indication of the beneficial effects of the three-day lay-off was a 44% reduction in early returns by 5 Group crews compared with the previous Berlin raid. The 61 Squadron crews were spread among the waves in the bomber stream and found Berlin under clear skies, but despite the favourable conditions, the Path Finders overshot the city centre aiming point by six or seven miles and marked an area well to the north-west, which happened to contain many war-industry factories. The 61 Squadron crews bombed on red and green TIs from between 19,000 and 22,000 feet and on return spoke of a mass of fires and thick smoke rising to 15,000 feet.

There was shock at Skellingthorpe when seven Lancasters failed to return, but a message was received from the 4 Group station at Melbourne that two of the 50 Squadron Lancasters had landed there and been involved in a collision on the ground, happily without casualties, and another had crashed into a farmhouse while trying to land at Pocklington. There was no good news concerning the three absent 61 Squadron Lancasters, and when information eventually filtered through from the Red Cross it would confirm that there had been no survivors from the crews of P/O Eaves, P/O Strange and P/O McAlpine in W4198, DV297 and DV339 respectively. The first mentioned crashed within sight of the Dutch frontier north of Meppen and the last mentioned was lost without trace, while only one crew member from DV297 was recovered for burial in the Berlin War Cemetery. Night-fighters were largely responsible for bringing down the heavy toll of bombers during the return flight and there were twenty-eight empty dispersal pans to contemplate in the cold light of dawn. It was learned later that thirty-eight war-industry factories had been destroyed in Berlin and many others damaged.

These last three operations against Berlin undoubtedly represented the best phase of the entire campaign, and according to local reports, the total death toll on the ground resulting from them amounted to 4,330 people, while the destruction of 8,700 apartment buildings containing more than 104,500 flats and damage to several times that number, robbed 450,000 residents of their homes for varying lengths of time. However, Berlin was not Hamburg, where narrow streets had aided the spread of fire. Berlin was a modern city of concrete and steel with wide thoroughfares and open spaces to create natural firebreaks, and each building destroyed added to these, so that the campaign would become a bitter struggle of ever decreasing returns.

During the course of the month the squadron took part in six operations and dispatched seventy-nine sorties for the loss of three Lancasters and crews.

December 1943

Berlin would continue to be the dominant theme during December, and, as November had ended, so December began with the assembly on the 2nd of a heavy force of 443 aircraft, all but fifteen of them Lancasters, after the main Halifax element had been withdrawn because of fog over their Yorkshire stations. 5 Group contributed 145 Lancasters, of which ten represented 61 Squadron and departed Skellingthorpe between 16.46 and 17.15 with F/Ls Turner and Williams the senior pilots on duty. After climbing out, they headed for the Lincolnshire coast to rendezvous over the North Sea with the rest of the force for a straight-in-straight-out route across Holland and northern Germany with no feints or diversions. First, however, the crews had to negotiate a towering front of ice-bearing cloud over the North Sea, which would contribute to a 10% rate of early returns, although it was engine issues that persuaded P/O Paul and crew to return to Skellingthorpe. The others pushed through the challenging conditions and made it to the target area, mostly south of track after variable winds had thrown them off course and dispersed the bomber stream. They also had to contend with large numbers of enemy night-fighters that would harass the bombers all the way to the target, after the controller had been able correctly to predict it.

The Path Finders employed H2S to establish their position at Stendal, but had strayed some fifteen miles south of track and mistakenly used the town of Genthin as their reference for the run-in. The 61 Squadron crews were spread among the three waves and found good visibility as they were guided by release-point flares to the aiming point. During the bombing run they encountered a thin layer of two to three-tenths cloud at around 5,000 feet but up to nine-tenths between 10,000 and 12,000 feet, which the searchlights were able to pierce. They bombed on skymarkers and red and green TIs and, where possible, ground detail like burning streets, from a uniform 20,000 feet and reported scattered fires and a number of large explosions, some claiming the glow to be visible from 120 miles into the homeward leg. It was a bad night for the bomber force, which lost forty aircraft, mostly in the target area and on the way home and bombing photographs suggested that the raid had been only partially successful, causing useful damage in industrial districts in the west and east, but scattering the main weight of bombs over the southern districts and outlying communities to the south.

Having been spared by the weather from experiencing an effective attack in October and exploiting the enemy's expectation that Berlin would be the target again, Leipzig found itself at the end of the red tape on briefing-room wall-maps from County Durham to Cambridgeshire on the 3rd. A force of 527 aircraft was made ready, which included 103 Lancasters of 5 Group, eight of them belonging to 61 Squadron, which departed Skellingthorpe between 00.05 and 00.38 with F/Ls Harvey and Webb the senior pilots on duty. The bomber stream headed for Berlin as a feint, passing north of Hannover and Braunschweig with ten-tenths cloud beneath them and an hour's journey to Leipzig still ahead, and then, as they turned towards the south-east, the Mosquito element continued on to carry out a diversion at the capital. Night-fighters had already infiltrated the stream at the Dutch coast, but the feint had the desired effect, and few night-fighters were encountered in the target area, where two layers of ten-tenths cloud prevailed with tops at around 7,000 and 15,000 feet. The Path Finders marked by H2S with green skymarkers and the 61 Squadron crews bombed on these from between 20,000 and 23,000 feet, observing explosions and a strong glow beneath the clouds. The emergence through the cloud tops of black smoke suggested that an accurate and concentrated attack had taken place, and the smoke and glow remained visible for 150 miles into the return journey south-east towards the French frontier. Had many aircraft not then strayed into the Frankfurt defence zone, the losses may have been fewer, but twenty-four aircraft failed to return, fifteen of them Halifaxes. Local reports confirmed this as a highly successful operation, which had hit residential and industrial areas and was the most destructive raid visited upon this eastern city during the war. Sadly, for the Command, it would take its revenge in time.

Thereafter, minor operations carried the Command through to mid-month, and during this period S/L Ed Benjamin was posted to the 5 Group Aircrew School to be trained as a Master Bomber and operate out of 54 Base at Coningsby. He was replaced at 61 Squadron by S/L beard, who was posted in from 1660 Conversion Unit w.e.f 12th. While operating in a Mosquito as the Master Bomber for an operation against an oil refinery at Böhlen near Leipzig on the 19th of February 1945, W/C Benjamin DFC and Bar was shot down by flak and he and his navigator lost their lives.

It was the 16th when the Lancaster stations were next roused and instructed to prepare 483 of the type for that night's operation to Berlin for the sixth time since the resumption of the campaign. 5 Group put up 165 aircraft, fourteen of them representing 61 Squadron, which departed Skellingthorpe between 16.17 and 16.47 with F/Ls Harvey, Turner and Webb the senior pilots on duty. P/O Wallis and crew abandoned their sortie after losing their W/T, leaving the bomber stream to cross the Dutch coast in the region of Castricum-aan-Zee and then head due east all the way to the target with no deviations. However, it was hoped that the very early take-off and the expectation of fog over enemy night-fighter stations would reduce the risk of interception. As events turned out, night-fighters were sent to meet the bomber stream at the Dutch coast and claimed a goodly number of Lancasters, while the others pressed on to find Berlin obscured by ten-tenths cloud with tops at around 5,000 feet, but still identifiable by red and green skymarkers. The 61 Squadron crews bombed from between 17,500 and 21,000 feet, the lower height that of the crews of F/Sgt Burgess and F/L Harvey having jettisoned two 1,000-pounders and a cookie respectively to compensate for the loss of an engine. A three-quarter moon rose during the long return leg over the Baltic and Denmark to aid night-fighters, but most avoided contact and the return journey passed largely without major incident.

The greatest difficulties awaited the 1, 6 and 8 Group crews as they arrived home to find their airfields covered by a blanket of dense fog, and with little reserves of fuel, they began a frantic search for somewhere to land, stumbling blindly through the murk to catch a glimpse of the ground. For many, this proved fatal, while others gave up any hope of landing and abandoned their aircraft. Twenty-nine Lancasters and a mine-laying Stirling were thus lost and more than 150 airmen killed in these most tragic of circumstances, and to this number was added the twenty-five Lancasters failing to return from the raid. At debriefings crews reported the glow of fires, while others saw nothing through the cloud and it was a local report that confirmed a moderately effective raid, which had fallen principally onto central and eastern districts, where housing suffered most.

A three-day stand-down allowed the crews to recover from the Berlin operation and it was the 20th when all stations were notified of an operation that night to Frankfurt, for which a force of 390 Lancasters and 257 Halifaxes was assembled. 5 Group made ready 168 Lancasters and at Skellingthorpe, fourteen 61 Squadron Lancasters were loaded with the requisite amount of fuel and a cookie and sixteen SBCs of incendiaries each and dispatched between 16.56 and 17.25 with S/Ls Beard and Moss the senior pilots on duty. While the main operation was in progress, forty-four Lancasters and ten Mosquitos of 1 and 8 Groups were to carry out a diversion at Mannheim, some forty miles to the south. After climbing out, the crews bound for the main event set course for Southwold and the North Sea-crossing to the Scheldt estuary, before passing north of Antwerp and flying the length of Belgium to the German frontier north of Luxembourg. However, S/L Beard's first sortie with the squadron ended in disappointment during the sea crossing when his starboard-inner engine failed and forced him to turn back, while it was the loss of the port-inner engine that ended the sortie of F/O West and crew shortly afterwards. The German night-fighter controller had picked up transmissions from the bomber stream as soon as it left the English coast and was able to track it all the way to the target and vector his fighters into position. Many combats took place during the outward flight and the diversion failed to draw fighters away from the main action. The problems continued at the primary target, where the forecast clear skies failed to materialise, and the crews were greeted by four to nine-tenths cloud at between 5,000 and 10,000 feet. This allowed some of them to pick out ground features, while others fixed their positions by H2S, if so equipped, and the main force Lancaster crews simply waited for TIs on e.t.a.

The Path Finders had prepared a ground-marking plan in expectation of good vertical visibility, and dropped red, green and yellow TIs, while the Germans lit a decoy fire-site five miles to the south-east of the city. Some crews described the marking as late and erratic, and those from 61 Squadron bombed on red and green TIs from between 19,000 and 20,600 feet. Most thought the attack to be scattered in the early stages, becoming more concentrated as it progressed, and many commented on the fact that the new cookies detonated with a brighter flash than the old ones. In fact, they had contributed to a moderately successful raid, and at least one crew reported the glow of fires remaining visible for 150 miles into the return journey. Any success was achieved largely as the result of the creep-back from the decoy site, which fell across the suburbs of Offenbach and Sachsenhausen, situated on the southern bank of the River Main. 466 houses were destroyed and more than nineteen hundred seriously damaged, despite which, the operation fell well short of its aims and the loss of forty-one aircraft was a high price to pay. The Halifaxes suffered heavily, losing twenty-seven of their number, a loss-rate of 10.5% compared with 3.6% for the Lancasters.

Just two more operations remained before the year ended and both were to be directed against Germany's capital city, the first, posted on the 23rd, to involve an all-Lancaster heavy force with seven Halifaxes among the Path Finder element and eight Mosquitos to provide a diversion. The

130 Lancasters of 5 Group included fifteen representing 61 Squadron, which were loaded with a cookie and eleven SBCs each and launched into the cold night air between 23.33 and 00.18 with S/L Beard the senior pilot on duty. F/O Einarson were thwarted by a faulty compass and had to abandon their sortie, leaving the rest to adopt the somewhat circuitous route to the target that took the bomber stream in a south-easterly direction to the Scheldt estuary, before hugging the Belgian/Dutch frontier to cross into Germany south of Aachen, as if threatening Frankfurt. When a point was reached south of Leipzig, the route turned sharply towards the north and Berlin, while the Mosquito feint threatened Leipzig. P/O Ewens and crew were thwarted by the failure of navigation equipment and turned back, while the vanguard of the bomber stream reached the target to find it enveloped in up to eight-tenths cloud at between 5,000 and 10,000 feet. This might not have been critical had the Path Finders not suffered an unusually high failure rate of their H2S equipment, which resulted in scattered and sparse sky-marking. The 61 Squadron crews found red and green skymarker flares at which to aim their bombs from between 20,000 and 24,000 feet and observed well-concentrated fires and at least four large explosions, one described as orange and red and lasting for thirty seconds. A relatively modest sixteen Lancasters failed to return, and after attending debriefing, those making it back home spent the better part of Christmas Eve in bed and looking forward, hopefully, to a fifth wartime Christmas uninterrupted by operations. Local sources in Berlin identified the south-eastern suburbs of Köpenick and Treptow as the ones to sustain the most damage, with 287 houses and other buildings suffering complete destruction.

The festivities over, the "Big City" was posted again as the target when operations resumed on the 29th, for what, for the Lancaster operators, would be the first of three raids on it in five nights spanning the turn of the year. A force of 712 aircraft included 163 Lancasters of 5 Group, of which seventeen represented 61 Squadron and departed Skellingthorpe between 16.22 and 17.16 with six pilots of flight lieutenant rank leading the way. It was from this juncture that the intolerable strain on the crews of successive long-range flights in difficult weather conditions would begin to become manifest in some squadrons through the rate of early returns, which on this night reached forty-five or 6.3%. The bomber stream was routed out over the Dutch Frisian islands pointing directly for Leipzig and having reached a point just to the north of that city, was to turn to the north towards Berlin, while Mosquitos carried out spoof raids on Leipzig and Magdeburg. 61 Squadron lost the services of P/O Burgess and crew to an engine fire, but the remainder of its crews reached the target area to find ten-tenths cloud with tops at anywhere between 7,000 and 18,000 feet. Red and green Path Finder release-point flares could be seen hanging over the city, at which they aimed their bombs from between 20,000 and 23,000 feet and at debriefing reported a considerable red glow beneath the clouds, which remained visible for a hundred miles into the return flight.

However, the impression of a concentrated and successful assault was not entirely borne out by reports from local sources, which revealed that the main weight of the raid had fallen onto southern and south-eastern districts and also into outlying communities to the east. 388 buildings were destroyed, although none of significance, and ten thousand people were bombed out of their homes. Eleven Lancasters and nine Halifaxes failed to return, a loss-rate of 2.4% for the former and 3.5% for the latter. 61 Squadron suffered its final casualty of the year with the failure to return of the experienced F/L Harvey RAAF and crew in DV399, which was hit by flak. According to the sole survivor, mid-upper gunner, P/O Thomas RCAF, a fierce fire erupted in the bomb bay and central fuselage, which he attempted to quell, but a small explosion sent him racing for the rear exit, and as he drifted down into the arms of his captors, the Lancaster was blown apart.

During the course of the month the squadron participated in six operations and dispatched seventy-eight sorties for the loss of a single Lancaster and crew. It had been a testing end to a year which had brought major successes and advances in tactics, but it had also been a year of high losses, particularly among the Stirling and Halifax squadrons. While "window" had been an instant success, it had also caused the Luftwaffe to rethink and reorganise, and the night-fighter force which emerged from the ruins of the old system was a leaner, more efficient and altogether more lethal beast than that of before. As far as the crews of Bomber Command were concerned, the New Year offered the same fare as the old one, which few would view with relish and the next three months would see morale at its lowest ebb as the winter campaign ground on.

January 1944

The change of year was not destined to effect a change in the emphasis of operations, and this was, no doubt, a disappointment not only to the hard-pressed crews of Bomber Command but also to the beleaguered residents of Germany's capital city. Proud of their status as Berliners first and Germans second, they were a hardy breed and just like their counterparts in London during the Blitz of 1940, would bear their trials with fortitude and humour and would not buckle under the constant assault from above. "You may break our walls", proclaimed banners in the streets, "but not out hearts", and the most popular song of the day, "Nach jedem Dezember kommt immer ein Mai", "After every December there's always a May", was played endlessly over the airwaves, its sentiments hinting at a change in fortunes with the onset of spring. Harris allowed the Berliners little time to enjoy New Year, and as New Year's Day dawned, plans were already in hand to continue the onslaught. Before it ended, the first of 421 Lancasters, 161 representing 5 Group, would be taking off and heading eastwards to arrive over the city as the clock showed 03.00 hours on the 2nd.

Take-off had actually been delayed because of doubts over the weather, and this meant that insufficient hours of daylight remained to allow the planned outward route over Denmark and the Baltic. Instead, the bomber stream would adopt the previously used almost direct route across Holland and northern Germany, but return as originally planned more circuitously, passing east of Leipzig, before racing across Germany between the Ruhr and Frankfurt and traversing Belgium to reach the Channel near the French port of Boulogne. 61 Squadron's sixteen participants departed Skellingthorpe between 23.31 and 00.08 with F/Ls Einarson, Scott and Williams the senior pilots on duty and each Lancaster carrying a mix of high explosives and 4lb and 30lb incendiaries. The force was gradually depleted by twenty-nine early returns, the 61 Squadron crews of P/O Paul, F/L Williams and P/O Nixon landing back at base between 02.20 and 03.03 with engine issues, the last-mentioned having hit trees on take-off and damaging the tailplane also. The bomber stream had covered the four-hundred-mile leg from the Dutch coast to Berlin in under two hours without once catching a glimpse of the ground through the dense cloud, and it was no different at the target, which was completely obscured by a layer of ten-tenths cloud with tops in places as high as 19,000 feet.

The Path Finders had to employ skymarking (Wanganui), which was somewhat scattered, and the 61 Squadron crews aimed for these parachute flares from between 20,000 and 23,000 feet, observing the glow of fires and smoke rising through the cloud tops. A huge explosion was witnessed at 03.07, which lit up the clouds for three seconds, but it was impossible to assess what was happening on the ground. It was established, ultimately, that the operation had been a failure, which had scattered bombs across the southern fringes of the city causing only minor damage, while the main weight of the attack had fallen beyond the city boundaries into wooded and open country. The disappointment was compounded by the loss of twenty-eight Lancasters, a dozen of them belonging to 5 Group, among which were 61 Squadron's LM377 and DV344. The former was outbound and had reached a point north-west of Hannover when intercepted and shot down by a night-fighter to crash six miles north-north-east of Neustadt an Rübenberge with no survivors from the crew of F/O Sharpe RCAF. The latter was leaving the target area and was some twenty miles south of the centre of Berlin when the end came for F/O Cunningham and his crew.

During the course of the 2nd, a heavy force of 362 Lancasters and nine new Mk III Hercules-powered Halifaxes was made ready for a return to Berlin that night, and many of the crews trudging through the snow to briefings were still tired from being late to bed following the almost-eight-hour round trip the night before. 5 Group cancelled twenty-five of its intended contribution, probably the less experienced crews, leaving 119 to take part, and some of these were in a mutinous frame of mind at being on the order of battle for back-to-back exhausting long-range trips. The ten-strong 61 Squadron element departed Skellingthorpe between 23.15 and 23.44 with S/L Beard the senior pilot on duty and lost the services of P/O Moroney and crew when a three-foot-long sheet of flame began to issue from the starboard-inner engine exhaust, suggesting a coolant leak. They were among a massive sixty early returns, 15.7% of those dispatched, many defeated by severe icing conditions, while others abandoned their sorties because of minor problems that might have seen them carry on had they been fully rested. The outward route crossed the Dutch coast near Castricum and took the bomber stream to a point south-east of Bremen, followed by a dogleg to the north-west and, finally, a ninety degree change of course to the south-east in the Parchim area to leave a ninety-mile run to the target. The route changes worked well to throw off the night-fighters, but they would congregate in the target area after the controller correctly identified Berlin as the target forty minutes before zero-hour.

The presence of ten-tenths cloud with tops at 16,000 feet forced the bombing to take place on red skymarkers with green stars or on the glow of fires, the 61 Squadron crews carrying out their attacks from between 18,000 and 23,000 feet and reporting smoke rising to 20,000 feet as they turned away. It was not possible to make an accurate assessment of the outcome, and the impression was of an effective attack, when, in fact, it had been another failure. Bombs had been scattered across the city and destroyed just eighty-two houses for the loss of twenty-seven Lancasters, most of which had fallen victim to night-fighters in the target area. 61 Squadron's DV401 was outbound and had just crossed the Ijsselmeer (Zuider Zee) when crashing at 01.30 at Bakhuizen on the eastern shore with fatal consequences for F/O Tull and crew.

After three trips to the "Big City" in five nights, it would now be left to the Mosquitos of 8 Group's Mosquito squadrons to disrupt the resident's sleep with cookies until the final third of the month, allowing Harris to turn his attention on the 5th upon the Baltic port-city of Stettin, which had not been attacked in numbers since the previous April. It was to be another predominantly Lancaster affair involving 348 of the type accompanied by ten Halifaxes, 5 Group putting up 120 aircraft and 61 Squadron eight, which departed Skellingthorpe between 23.50 and 00.11 with W/C Stidolph the senior pilot on duty. In contrast to the seventeen early returns by 5 Group crews during the last Berlin operation, only one came home early on this night, and those continuing on found themselves in thick cloud at cruising altitude. Some struggled to find a clear lane even when as high as 23,000 feet, but on the plus side, they all benefitted from a Mosquito diversion at Berlin, which kept the night-fighters off the scent. Stettin was found to be partially visible through five-tenths thin cloud with tops at around 10,000 feet, and crews were able to identify some ground features before focusing on H2S-laid flares and green TIs, which the 61 Squadron crews bombed from between 21,000 and 22,500 feet.

On their way out of the target area at 22,000 feet, W/C Stidolph and crew were intercepted by a ME210 at 03.58 and an engagement took place in which the Lancaster sustained damage to the port fin, rudder, aileron, tailplane and mainplane, the port-outer engine was set on fire and successfully feathered, the mid-upper turret was holed and the rear turret knocked out of action. However, by this time each turret had poured four hundred rounds into the fighter's starboard engine and cockpit, and it was claimed as probably destroyed, and attention now turned to bringing the Lancaster home. It became unstable on three engines at normal power, and the return flight was undertaken with both inboard engines on maximum boost and revolutions and the starboard outer throttled back. Shortly after crossing the Norfolk coast near Sheringham, they landed at Matlaske with just eight-and-a-half gallons of petrol in the tanks. At debriefings the intelligence section interviewers were regaled with accounts of a highly accurate and concentrated attack, which seemed to leave the entire city on fire. Fourteen Lancasters and two Halifaxes failed to return, in exchange for which, post-raid reconnaissance and local reports confirmed heavy damage in central and western districts, where 504 houses and twenty industrial buildings had been destroyed, a further 1,148 houses and twenty-nine industrial buildings seriously damaged and eight ships sunk in the harbour.

Following this operation, the crews of the heavy squadrons were rested until mid-month, while the Halifax units would spend three weeks in virtual hibernation apart from isolated mining forays. When briefings finally took place on the 14th, there was doubtless a degree of relief that the red tape on the wall maps terminated some way short of Berlin. It led, in fact, to Braunschweig (Brunswick), the historic and culturally significant city situated some thirty-five miles to the east of Hannover, which had not yet faced a heavy attack by the Command and on this night would face a force numbering 496 Lancasters and two Halifaxes. 5 Group supported the operation with 153 Lancasters, of which eleven represented 61 Squadron and departed Skellingthorpe between 16.41 and 16.55 with S/L Moss the senior pilot on duty. After climbing out they headed towards Germany's north-western coast, where they were met by part of the enemy night-fighter response, which would harass the bomber stream all the way to the target and back. Complete cloud cover at the target, in places up to around 15,000 feet, dictated the use of red skymarkers with green stars, at which the 61 Squadron crews aimed their cookies and incendiaries from between 18,500 and 23,000 feet. The enemy fighters scored consistently and accounted for the majority of the thirty-eight missing Lancasters, many of which came down around Hannover, but the 61 Squadron contingent seemed to avoid contact and made no mention of night-fighters. An analysis revealed that the attack had almost entirely missed the city, falling mostly onto outlying communities to the south and was reported locally as a light raid. This would be a continuing theme in future attacks up to the autumn, as Braunschweig enjoyed something of a charmed life, leading to a belief among the populace of the surrounding villages that they were being targeted intentionally in an attempt to drive them into the city, before a major operation destroyed it with them in it!

The Path Finders, in particular, had been taking a beating since the turn of the year, with 156 Squadron alone losing fourteen Lancasters and crews in just three operations, four and five on Berlin, and five again on Braunschweig. This was creating something of a crisis in Path Finder manpower, particularly with regard to experienced crews, and a number of sideways postings took place between the squadrons to ensure a leavening of experience in each one. One of the solutions was to take the cream from among the crews emerging from the training units, rather than wait for them to gain experience at a main force squadron.

Another lull in operations kept the bomber force on the ground until the 20th, when orders were received to prepare for a maximum effort for the next round of the Berlin offensive. The Halifax squadrons, which had largely remained dormant since late December, were roused from their slumber and 264 of them joined 495 Lancasters to constitute the Path Finder and main force elements, while two small Mosquito sections carried out spoof raids on Kiel and Hannover. 5 Group weighed in with 155 Lancasters, thirteen of them made ready by 61 Squadron and assigned to various main force waves, before departing Skellingthorpe between 16.07 and 16.45 with S/L Moss the senior pilot on duty. It was still light and as they circled for height it was a rare pleasure for them to observe dozens of other Lancasters rising up into the dusk to join them from the neighbouring stations. After crossing the Lincolnshire coast, they turned their snouts towards the west coast of Schleswig-Holstein at a point opposite Kiel, rendezvousing with the other groups over the North Sea and all the time shedding individual aircraft as a hefty seventy-five crews abandoned their sorties and turned back. P/O Burgess and crew were the 61 Squadron "boomerang" after the port-outer engine caught fire.

The others made landfall over the Nordfriesland coast, before turning to the south-east on a more-or-less direct course for Berlin and soon found themselves being hounded by night-fighters. The enemy controller had fed a proportion of his resources into the bomber stream east of Hamburg, and they would remain in contact until a point between Leipzig and Hannover on the way home, although, curiously, the 5 Group brigade saw nothing of this and would lose just a single 57 Squadron Lancaster. The two Mosquito diversions had been completely ignored by the Luftwaffe controller, who knew well in advance that Berlin was to be the target. The Path Finders arrived over the Müritzsee to the north of Berlin with a sixty-mile run-in to the aiming point, and they found this to be concealed beneath the same ten-tenths cloud that had accompanied them for the entire outward leg. The tops of the cloud lay beneath the bombers at up to 15,000 feet as the main force crews carried out their attacks on red skymarkers with green stars, those from 61 Squadron from between 21,000 and 23,000 feet. On return, the crews commented on the lack of flak activity over Berlin and reported the glow of large fires under the cloud and smoke rising through the tops. Thirty-five aircraft failed to return, twenty-two of them Halifaxes, which represented an 8.3% casualty rate compared with 2.6% for the Lancasters. It took a little time for an assessment of the operation to be made because of continuing cloud over north-eastern Germany, by which time four further raids had been carried out. It seems from local reports that the eastern districts had received the heaviest weight of bombs in an eight-mile stretch from Weissensee in the north to Neukölln in the south, although no details of destruction emerged.

On the following day, the city of Magdeburg was posted to receive its first major attack of the war, having been a regular destination for small forces as far back as the summer of 1940. At that time, the Command had targeted a ship lift at the eastern end of the Mittelland Canal at its junction with the River Elbe and the important Bergius-process Braunkohle A.G synthetic oil refinery (hydrogenation plant), both located in the same Rothensee district to the north of Magdeburg city centre. Situated some fifty miles from Braunschweig and slightly to the south of east, it was on an increasingly familiar route as far as the enemy night-fighter controllers were concerned, and within easy striking distance of the night-fighter assembly beacons. In an attempt to deceive the enemy, a small-scale diversion was planned at Berlin involving twenty-two Lancaster of 5 Group and twelve Mosquitos of 8 Group. 5 Group contributed 122 Lancasters to the main event, eleven of them made ready by 61 Squadron, which were loaded with a cookie and SBCs of incendiaries each. The Lancaster of F/L Einarson and crew had a cookie and 1,000 and 500-pounders winched into its bomb bay to drop on Berlin as part of the diversionary force and took off ahead of the main element at 19.36. The others followed on between 19.53 and 20.39 with F/Ls Scott and Woods the senior pilots on duty and flew out over the North Sea to a point some one hundred miles off the west coast of Schleswig-Holstein, before turning to the south-east to pass between Hamburg and Hannover. Enemy radar was able to detect H2S transmissions during night-flying tests and equipment checks, and the night-fighter controller was, thereby, always aware of an imminent heavy raid. On this night, the night-fighters were able to infiltrate the bomber stream even before the German coast was crossed and the recently introduced "Tame Boar" night-fighter system provided a running commentary on the bomber stream's progress, enabling the fighters to latch onto it and remain in contact. P/O Todd and crew were between Bremen to the south-west and Hamburg to the north-east when the port-outer engine had to be shut down and the cookie was jettisoned to enable them to maintain height and continue on to the target. The final turning-point was twenty-five miles north-east of the target, and this was identified both by Path Finder markers and the bombing of twenty-seven main force aircraft. These had been driven by stronger-than-forecast winds to arrive ahead of schedule and contained crews anxious to get the job done and get out of the target area as soon as possible. They bombed using their own H2S without waiting for the TIs to go down, and together with dummy fires, would be blamed by the Path Finders as the reason for their failure to produce concentrated marking.

The conditions over Magdeburg varied according to the time of arrival, the early birds encountering seven to nine-tenths thin cloud at around 6,000 feet, while those turning up towards the end of the raid found the northern half of the city completely clear with cloud over the southern half only. The 61 Squadron crews experienced a mixture of eight-tenths cloud and relatively clear skies, and in the face of fairly modest opposition, bombed on green TIs from between 19,500 and 23,000 feet, the lower height that of the Todd crew, all gaining the impression that the attack was concentrated around the markers. Returning crews from other groups reported explosions and fires or their glow, and smoke rising as they turned away, while others reported a flash some twelve minutes after bombing that lit up the clouds for seven seconds, and two large explosions at 23.15. Fires that initially seemed to be scattered, appeared to become more concentrated as the crews headed for home and the impression was of a successful operation. While all of this was in progress, the diversionary force arrived at Berlin, some seventy miles away to the north-east, where F/L Einarson and crew found a layer of eight to ten-tenths cloud at 10,000 feet, through which they bombed on red TIs from 22,000 shortly before 23.00. The 5 Group ORB expressed the opinion that the diversion had succeeded in the early stages in reducing the impact of the Nachtjagd, although this was not borne out by the figures. In the absence of post-raid reconnaissance and a local report, the outcome at Magdeburg was not confirmed and it is generally believed now that most of the bombing fell outside of the city boundaries. A record fifty-seven aircraft failed to return, thirty-five of them Halifaxes, and this provided another alarming statistic of a 15.6% loss-rate compared with 5.2% for the Lancasters. 61 Squadron posted missing the all-NCO crew of Sgt Martin in the veteran Lancaster R5565, which came down within the Berlin defence zone with no survivors.

The end of the month would bring the final concerted effort to destroy Berlin and involve three trips in the space of an unprecedented four nights, this hectic round of operations beginning on the

27th, after five nights of rest since the bruising experience of Magdeburg. An all-Lancaster heavy force of 515 aircraft was assembled, 5 Group putting up a record 172, fourteen of them belonging to 61 Squadron, which departed Skellingthorpe between 17.05 and 17.42 with S/L Moss the senior pilot on duty. After climbing out and rendezvousing with the rest of the group, they set course on a complex route that would take the bomber stream towards the north German coast, before swinging to the south-east to enter enemy territory over the Frisians and northern Holland. Having then feinted towards central Germany, suggesting Leipzig as the target, the force was to turn north-east to a point west of Berlin, from where the final run-in would commence. The long return route passed to the west of Leipzig before turning due east to miss Frankfurt on its northern side and traverse Belgium to gain the Channel south of Boulogne. As the main eventers pressed on towards the target, a mining diversion off Heligoland and the dispensing of dummy fighter flares and route-markers partially succeeded in reducing the numbers of enemy night-fighters making contact. It was, therefore, a relatively intact bomber force that approached the target over ten-tenths cloud with tops at 15,000 feet, conditions that required the Path Finders to use sky-marking, and it was the red Wanganui flares with green stars that led the main force crews to the aiming point.

The 61 Squadron participants bombed from between 18,500 and 23,000 feet, and at debriefing reported the glow of fires and the appearance of a successful raid, but no detailed assessment. Of course, not all would make it back to tell their stories at debriefing, and thirty-three Lancaster dispersal pans stood empty in dawn's early light, among them that of 61 Squadron's W4315. Damaged by flak south of Hannover, P/O Williams and crew had struggled on beyond the Brittany coast to a point north of the Channel Island of Guernsey, where a ditching became inevitable. The flight engineer was washed away, and both gunners went down with the Lancaster, while the pilot and three others were rescued at 18.00. There was no news initially of F/O West and crew in DV400 until information was received from the Red Cross that none had survived the crash in the Hannover area. Reports from Berlin described bombs falling over a wide area, more so in the south than the north, and damage to fifty industrial premises, a number of them engaged in important war work, while twenty thousand people were bombed out of their homes. A feature of the campaign was the number of outlying communities suffering collateral damage, and on this night sixty-one such hamlets recorded bombs falling.

The early time-on-target had allowed crews to get a full night in bed and they were, hopefully, fully rested, when news came through on the 28th that many of them would be returning to the "Big City" that night. A heavy force of 673 aircraft was assembled, of which 432 were Lancasters and 241 Halifaxes, 155 of the former provided by 5 Group. 61 Squadron made ready fourteen Lancasters, which departed Skellingthorpe between 23.45 and 00.43 with S/L Beard the senior pilot on duty. They were routed out over southern Denmark before turning south-east on a direct course for the target, with an almost reciprocal return and various diversionary measures to distract the night-fighter controller. Sixty-six crews turned back early, suggesting some adverse reaction to the back-to-back operations, and among them was that of F/O Todd, whose starboard-inner engine caught fire. Those reaching the target area encountered ten-tenths cloud and a mixture of sky and ground-marking to aim at, the 61 Squadron crews delivering their bombs on red and green release-point flares from between 21,000 and 23,500 feet. Some crews reported huge explosions at 03.15, 03.18 and 03.25, the second-mentioned one described by a 10 Squadron crew as lighting up the sky over a radius of fifty miles. Forty-six aircraft failed to return, twenty-six of them Halifaxes as the defenders fought back to exact another heavy toll of bombers, and the impression gained from those that did make it back was of a concentrated and effective attack. This was partly borne-out by local reports of heavy damage in western and southern districts, where 180,000 people were bombed out of their homes. However, as had been the pattern throughout the campaign against Berlin, seventy-seven outlying communities had also been afflicted.

After a night's rest a force of 534 aircraft was made ready on the 30th for the final operation of this concerted effort against Berlin, 5 Group offering 156 Lancasters, of which fourteen were made ready by 61 Squadron before departing Skellingthorpe between 16.46 and 17.43 with F/Ls Einarson, Fitch, Scott and Webb the senior pilots on duty. After climbing out, they joined with the rest of the group to follow a route similar to that adopted two nights earlier, the bomber stream remaining relatively free of harassment all the way to the target. On arrival crews were greeted by ten-tenths cloud at around 8,000 feet and the sight of Path Finder skymarking in progress. The 61 Squadron crews bombed on these from between 20,000 and 22,500 feet, and all commented on the smoke rising through 12,000 feet and the glow of fires beneath the cloud, which, according to some, was still visible from a hundred miles into the return flight. Thirty-two Lancasters and a single Halifax failed to make it home, among them eleven belonging to 5 Group, and in return for these significant losses, according to local sources, central and south-western districts suffered heavy damage and serious areas of fire. Other parts of the city were also hit, while many bomb loads were again scattered liberally onto outlying communities, and at least a thousand people lost their lives. These three attacks on Berlin at the end of the month had resulted in the loss of 112 heavy bombers and their crews, and with the introduction of the enemy's highly efficient Tame Boar night-fighter system based on running commentaries, the advantage had swung back in the defenders' favour.

Two further heavy raids would be directed at Berlin before the end of the winter offensive, one in February and the other in March, but they would be almost in isolation. There is no question that Germany's capital city had been sorely afflicted by the campaign thus far, but it remained a functioning city and showed no signs of imminent collapse. During the course of the month the squadron participated in ten operations and dispatched 112 sorties for the loss of six Lancasters, five complete crews and three members of another.

February 1944

On the 1st the squadron moved eastwards across Lincolnshire to Coningsby, where it would share the facilities with 619 Squadron and enjoy a relatively short stay. Harris had intended to maintain the pressure on Berlin, and would have launched a further attack had he not been thwarted by the conditions, which kept all but the Mosquitos and 617 Squadron on the ground for two whole weeks and to the horror of the crews condemned them to fill their time with training, lectures, snow-clearing and P.T. When the Path Finder and main force squadrons next took to the air, it would be for a record-breaking effort to Berlin on the 15th and would also be the penultimate operation of the campaign, and indeed of the war by Bomber Command's heavy brigade against Germany's capital city. The force of 891 aircraft represented the largest non-1,000 force to date, and, therefore, the greatest-ever to be sent against the Capital, and it would be the first time that more than five hundred Lancasters and three hundred Halifaxes had operated together. 5 Group surpassed its previous best effort by fifty Lancasters when putting 226 of them into the air, eighteen of them representing 61 Squadron. The bomb bays of this huge armada would convey to Berlin the greatest-ever tonnage of bombs to any target to date, in the case of the 5 Group contingent mostly in the form of cookies and 30lb and 4lb incendiaries, but also some 500-pounders. The 61 Squadron participants departed Coningsby between 16.33 and 17.32 with W/C Stidolph and S/Ls Beard and Moss the senior pilots on duty, and after joining up with the rest of the 5 Group squadrons, set course for the western coast of Denmark. Having traversed southern Jutland the route entered Germany via the Baltic coast between Rostock and Stralsund on a direct heading for the target and after bombing it required returning crews to pass south of Hannover and Bremen and cross Holland to the North Sea via Castricum. Extensive diversionary measures included a mining operation in Kiel Bay ahead of the arrival of the bombers, a raid on Frankfurt-an-Oder to the east of Berlin by a small force of 8 Group Lancasters and Oboe Mosquitos attacking five night-fighter airfields in Holland.

The bomber stream shed aircraft at regular intervals and had been depleted by seventy-five early returns by the time the remainder homed in on the target, the 61 Squadron crews of P/O Wallis, F/L Fitch and P/O Stone dropping out at 18.56, 19.25 and 20.03 respectively when at various positions over the North Sea, two because of oxygen supply issues and one with an unserviceable rear turret. When closing on the target P/O Nixon's rear gunner became unresponsive through oxygen starvation, and although he was eventually revived, his turret remained unmanned for the remainder of the sortie. Berlin was found to be concealed beneath ten-tenths cloud at around 10,000 feet, but those with H2S were able to confirm their positions, while the others relied on the Path Finders' red release-point flares with green stars and red and green TIs on the ground. The 61 Squadron crews bombed on these from 21,000 to 24,000 feet between 21.14 and 21.46, and on return reported the markers to be highly effective and well-concentrated. The burgeoning glow beneath the clouds convinced them that they had taken part in a successful operation, and this was borne out by local reports, which confirmed that the 2,642 tons of bombs had caused extensive damage in central and south-western districts but had also spilled out into surrounding communities. A thousand houses and more than five hundred temporary wooden barracks were destroyed and important war-industry factories in the Siemensstadt district were damaged in return for the loss to the Command of forty-three aircraft, twenty-six Lancasters, (4.6%) and seventeen Halifaxes, (5.4%). Perhaps slightly disturbing was the fact that eight of the missing Halifaxes were Mk IIIs, only one fewer than the nine now obsolete Mk II/Vs.

Despite the recent heavy losses, when orders were received on the 19th to prepare for another major assault that night, this time on Leipzig, where four Messerschmitt aircraft factories were the principal targets, the heavy squadrons were able offer 816 aircraft, 561 Lancasters and 255 Halifaxes. 5 Group managed to put up 209 Lancasters, fifteen of them belonging to 61 Squadron, which departed Coningsby between 23.24 and 00.23 with S/Ls Beard and Moss the senior pilots on duty. After climbing out over the station, they joined up with the others heading for the Dutch coast near Groningen, losing the services of P/O Stone and crew early on because of W/T failure. A proportion of the Luftwaffe Nachtjagd was waiting for the approaching bombers at the Dutch coast, while others had been drawn away by a mining diversion off Kiel. The bomber stream continued on to pass south of Bremen and north of Hannover on a south-easterly course, parts of it to become embroiled in a running battle with night-fighters all the way into eastern Germany. Inaccurately forecast winds caused some aircraft to reach the target early, forcing them to orbit while they waited for the Path Finders to arrive, and the local flak batteries accounted for around twenty of these, while four others were lost through collisions.

The 61 Squadron crews arrived to find ten-tenths cloud with tops at around 10,000 feet and bombed on green Wanganui flares and red and green TIs from 20,000 to 23,000 feet between 03.59 and

04.15. It seems that there was a brief period during the attack when skymarking stopped and led to some scattering of bombs, but the marker-flares were soon replenished with the arrival of more backers-up and a considerable glow beneath the cloud remained visible for some fifty minutes into the return journey, giving the impression of a successful assault. When all of those aircraft returning home had been accounted for, there was a massive shortfall of seventy-eight, a record loss by a clear twenty-one aircraft. Forty-four Lancasters and thirty-four Halifaxes had failed to return, with a loss-rate of 7.8% and 13.3% respectively, prompting Harris to immediately withdraw the less efficient Mk II and V Merlin-powered Halifaxes from further operations over Germany, which at a stroke, removed a proportion of 4 and 6 Groups' fire-power from the front line until they could re-equip with the Mk III. In the meantime, the Mk II and V operators would focus their energies for the remainder of the month on gardening duties. 61 Squadron posted missing the crews of P/Os Wallis and Golightly in HK538 and ME591 respectively, the former crashing near Gifhorn, in the Hannover defence zone and the latter possibly in the same area. The only survivors were the flight engineer and navigator in the Wallis crew, and they were taken into captivity, one after hospital treatment.

Notwithstanding this depletion of available numbers, a force of 598 aircraft was made ready on the 20th for an operation that night against Stuttgart, which would be the first of three against the city over a three-week period. 61 Squadron detailed fifteen Lancasters and loaded each with a cookie and eleven SBCs of incendiaries before sending them on their way from Coningsby between 23.29 and 00.16 with W/C Stidolph the senior pilot on duty. After climbing out over the station they headed south to join the rest of the force and begin the Channel crossing at Worthing. With the coast in sight, W/C Stidolph and his navigator and wireless operator exhibited signs of oxygen starvation and were revived in time to save the aircraft from disaster, but the sortie had to be abandoned. The bomber stream made landfall over the French coast near Dieppe, from where the cloud remained at ten-tenths with tops at 8,000 feet all the way into southern Germany. A North Sea sweep and a diversionary raid on Munich two hours ahead of the main activity had caused the Luftwaffe to deploy its forces early, and this allowed the bomber stream to push on unmolested to the target. By the time it hove into view, the cloud had thinned to five to eight-tenths at around 6,000 feet and the excellent visibility enabled the crews to draw a bead on the Path Finder red and green sky-markers and similar-coloured TIs on the ground. The 61 Squadron crews bombed from 22,000 to 25,000 feet between 04.00 and 04.15, observing many large fires, and on return there were reports that the glow from the burning city was still visible on the horizon from 250 miles into the return flight. Despite some scattering of bombs, local reports described central districts and those in a quadrant from north-west to north-east suffering extensive damage, and a Bosch factory was one of the important war industry concerns to be hard-hit. In contrast to twenty-four hours earlier, a modest nine aircraft failed to return.

In an attempt to reduce the prohibitive losses of recent weeks, a new tactic was introduced for the next two operations. A force of 734 aircraft was assembled on the 24th for an operation to the centre of Germany's ball-bearing production, Schweinfurt, situated some sixty miles to the east of Frankfurt in south-central Germany. The city contained four companies, Kugelfischer-Georg-Schäfer, Fichtel & Sachs, Vereinigte Kugellagerfabriken A.G and Deutsche Star GmbH, which together were responsible for 50% of Germany's output. The plan of attack called for 392 aircraft to depart their stations between 18.00 and 19.00 and to be followed into the air two hours later by 342 others in the hope of catching the night-fighters on the ground refuelling and re-arming as the second wave passed through. While this operation was in progress, extensive diversionary measures would be put in hand that involved more than three hundred other aircraft, including 179 from the training units conducting a North Sea sweep and 110 Halifaxes and Stirlings mining in northern waters. 5 Group contributed 204 Lancasters, of which seventeen were made ready by 61 Squadron, five assigned to the first phase and the remainder to the second, the former departing Coningsby between 18.29 and 18.37 with F/Ls Webb and Woods the senior pilots on duty to be followed by the second wave element between 20.00 and 20.45 led by S/L Beard. Some 5 Group crews had been assigned to Path Finder support duties, which required them to accompany the target-marking force across the target to beef up the numbers and prevent searchlights and flak from latching onto individual aircraft but retain their bombs and release them during a second pass.

P/O Auckland and crew were at 20,000 feet as they approached Douai in north-eastern France and were suddenly confronted by a fire in the cockpit caused by a transformer in the Gee-box, which filled the front of the aircraft with smoke. The captain ordered the crew to bale out, and the bomb-aimer and mid-upper gunner complied, before the smoke was sucked out of the open hatches and the bale-out order was rescinded. The first phase bombers reached the target to find three-tenths cloud at 3,000 to 4,000 feet, with haze spoiling the vertical visibility, but the aiming point marked out by red and green TIs and already established fires towards the south-western edge of the town. The 61 Squadron crews bombed from 22,000 and 23,000 feet between 23.15 and 23.25 and two columns of black smoke were observed to be rising through 5,000 feet as they turned away. The consensus was of an effective, if, somewhat scattered attack, but not present to offer an opinion was the crew of F/L Webb RNZAF, who were very close to the end of their tour and had been shot down in the target area. All but the flight engineer survived the demise of LM310 and drifted down into the arms of their captors.

Meanwhile, P/O Cannon and crew in the second phase element were forced to abandon their sortie over the Surrey/Sussex county line when the oxygen supply system failed. Those reaching the target area picked up the glow of fires from the earlier raid at a distance of two hundred miles, and the visibility in the target area remained good, despite the rising smoke. The 61 Squadron crews delivered their bomb loads from almost cloudless skies onto red and green TIs from 21,000 to 23,000 feet between 01.05 and 01.18, and all indications suggested an effective raid. A post-raid analysis revealed that both phases of the operation had suffered from undershooting after some Path Finder backers-up failed to press on to the aiming point. In that regard, it was a disappointing night, but an interesting feature was the loss of 50% fewer aircraft from the second wave in comparison with the first in an overall casualty figure of thirty-three, and this suggested some merit in the tactic. Since the turn of the year, a wind-finder system had been in use, which employed selected crews to monitor wind speed and direction and pass their findings back to HQ, where the figures were collated and any changes from the briefed conditions re-broadcast to the bomber stream. This had been found to be extremely useful, but as would be discovered in the ensuing weeks, the system had its limitations.

The main operation on the following night was directed at the beautiful and culturally significant southern city of Augsburg, situated around thirty miles north-west of Munich. It was home to a major Maschinenfabrik Augsburg Nuremberg (M.A.N) diesel engine factory, which had been the target for the previously mentioned epic low-level daylight raid by 44 and 97 Squadrons in April 1942. On this night, 594 aircraft were divided into two waves, and among them were 164 Lancasters of 5 Group, including a dozen representing 61 Squadron, which were all assigned to the first phase, and departed Coningsby between 18.08 and 18.38 with W/C Stidolph the senior pilot on duty. The first wave bomber stream flew out over Belgium with ten-tenths cloud beneath them, and W/C Stidolph and crew were approaching Reims when the oxygen system let them down, forcing them to turn back and deposit their bombs on a searchlight position twenty-five miles south of Dieppe as they headed for the Channel. The cloud had dissipated by the time that the target drew near, and on arrival, it was possible for crews to gain a visual reference. The Path Finders' red and green TIs were in the bomb sights as the 61 Squadron crews carried out their attacks from 19,000 to 23,000 feet between 22.45 and 22.59, and fires were beginning to take hold as they turned away.

The second wave crews were drawn on by the glow in the sky from a hundred miles away and arrived to find visibility still good despite copious amounts of smoke rising through 10,000 feet. The main force element bombed on existing fires and red and green Wanganui flares and TIs from an average of 21,000 feet either side of 01.15, the loss of twenty-one aircraft seeming to confirm the benefits of splitting the forces, and the tactic would remain an important part of Bomber Command planning for the remainder of the war. Two dispersal pans stood empty at Coningsby, those belonging to DV294 and LL775, the former having crashed at Menil-Annelles on the edge of the Ardennes in north-eastern France with no survivors from the crew of F/O Nixon. The latter came down further south at Lagarde in the Moselle region some twenty miles east of Nancy, killing F/L Einarson DFC, DFM RCAF, who was close to the end of his second tour and would be sorely missed by the squadron. He died alongside all but one of his crew, the bomb-aimer, one of three members of the RAAF on board, the only survivor, and he was spirited away by the local partisans to evade capture. It had been a devastatingly destructive operation, in which all facets of the plan had come together in near perfect harmony, spelling disaster for this lightly defended historical treasure trove. Its heart was torn out by blast and fire that destroyed almost three thousand houses along with buildings of outstanding historical significance, and centuries of irreplaceable culture was lost forever. There was also some industrial damage, and around ninety-thousand people were bombed out of their homes.

During the course of the month the squadron carried out five operations and dispatched seventy-seven sorties for the loss of five Lancasters and crews and two other airmen.

March 1944

March would bring an end to the winter campaign, but a long and bitter month would have to be endured first before any respite came from long-range forays into Germany. The crews had enjoyed a few nights off when the second raid of the series on Stuttgart was posted on the 1st, for which a force of 557 aircraft was made ready. This number included 178 Lancasters representing 5 Group, fourteen belonging to 61 Squadron, which departed Coningsby without incident between 23.00 and 23.56 with W/C Stidolph and S/Ls Beard and Moss the senior pilots on duty. They flew out over ten-tenths cloud with tops at between 12,000 and 17,000 feet and lost the services of the crew of P/O Cannon and crew to intercom and oxygen supply issues and F/L Fitch and crew because someone had forgotten to remove the pitot head cover, denying the pilot and flight engineer vital information on speed. encountered similar conditions in the target area, where the Path Finders employed a combination of sky and ground-marking. This, unfortunately, became scattered, and the bombing was directed between two main concentrations, the 61 Squadron crews carrying out their attacks on Wanganui red markers with green stars from 19,500 and 23,000 feet between 03.02 and 03.14. It was not possible to assess the accuracy of the attack, although a column of smoke had reached 25,000 feet by the end of the raid and large fires were evident from the glow in the sky visible from up to 150 miles away. The presence of thick cloud all the way there and back made conditions difficult for enemy night-fighters and a remarkably modest four aircraft failed to return. It was eventually established that the raid had been an outstanding success, which had caused extensive damage in central, western and northern districts, where a number of important war-industry factories, including those belonging to Bosch and Daimler-Benz, had sustained damage.

At the end of the first week, the Halifax brigade, particularly those withdrawn from operations over Germany, fired the opening salvoes of the pre-invasion campaign, the purpose of which was to dismantle by bombing thirty-seven railway centres in France, Belgium and western Germany. It began on the night of the 6/7th at Trappes marshalling yards, situated some ten miles west-south-west of Paris and continued at Le Mans in north-western France on the following night. For most of the heavy crews, however, there was no employment following Stuttgart, until a return there in mid-month, but in the meantime, matters were afoot at 5 Group, and had been ever since a frustrating series of operations against flying bomb launching sites conducted by 617 Squadron since December had failed to achieve the desired results. The problem had been an inability to put markers right on the aiming point, which was vital to destroy small, precision targets, and Oboe was just not precise enough. Effective though Oboe undoubtedly was at an urban target, where a margin of error of 400 to 600 yards represented pinpoint accuracy, precision targets required more. 617 Squadron had obliterated the Oboe markers, only for bombing photos to show that the targets, situated only a matter of yards away, had remained intact. W/C Cheshire and S/L Martin experimented with a dive-bombing technique, which had proved to be successful but impracticable in a Lancaster and Cheshire had borrowed a Mosquito for further trials. These were so promising, that the 5 Group A-O-C, AVM Cochrane, authorized a number of operations by the squadron against factory targets in France, before taking the idea to Harris. Harris approved, paving the way for 5 Group to become effectively independent of the main bomber force and begin larger-scale trials.

Orders were received at Bardney, Skellingthorpe and Waddington on the 9th to prepare eleven Lancasters each for a 5 Group attack that night against the Lioré et Olivier aircraft factory at Marignane, situated a few miles to the north of Marseilles in southern France. The area had been the main pre-war hub for commercial flying boat operations, particularly for the Pan American Clipper Class flights, and the factory had been engaged in the manufacture of the LeO 45 twin-engine medium bomber for the French Air Force. They took off in mid-evening with a round-trip ahead of them of some 1,350 miles if they flew direct and arrived in the target area under clear skies and bright moonlight, which facilitated an easy identification of the factory buildings marked by red spotfires. The bombing was carried out from medium level either side of 01.30, and the high-explosives were seen to fall among the buildings, while the incendiaries appeared to be a little scattered. A large explosion was witnessed at 01.24 and a huge pall of smoke was rising through 6,000 feet as the force turned away. All arrived home safely, most having spent more than nine hours aloft.

5 Group received orders on the 10th to prepare 102 Lancasters to form four small forces, each to attack a specific factory in France that night. The targets were the Michelin tyre factory at Clermont-Ferrand, the Bloch aircraft factory at Châteauroux, which was the first to be set up by the famed designer, Marcel Dassault, in 1935, the Morane Saulnier aircraft plant at Ossun, just

north of the Pyrenese and the Ricamerie needle-bearing works at St-Etienne, the last-mentioned, the objective for sixteen Lancasters from 617 Squadron. 54 Base, comprising the stations at Coningsby, Woodhall Spa and Metheringham, was assigned to the Bloch factory, for which ten 61 Squadron crews were briefed at Coningsby before taking off between 19.53 and 20.21 with W/C Stidolph and S/L Beard the senior pilots on duty. F/L Berry and crew were heading south across the Cambridgeshire fens when the starboard-outer engine caught fire and forced them to turn back. They arrived in the target area to find clear skies and bright moonlight in which they were able to identify the factory visually and by three red spotfires and delivered their attacks from 6,900 to 9,600 feet between 22.44 and 22.54. The factory buildings were observed to be engulfed in bomb bursts and explosions and six aiming point photographs were captured. There was no opposition, and all four operations were concluded successfully for the loss of a single Lancaster occupied by the crew of a 207 Squadron flight commander.

Now that the Mk III Halifax was becoming available in larger numbers, the Command was quickly returning to full strength, and it was a force of 863 aircraft that set out for Stuttgart in the early-evening of the 15th. This number included 206 Lancasters provided by 5 Group, the seventeen belonging to 61 Squadron departing Coningsby between 18.41 and 19.19 with S/L Moss the senior pilot on duty. They rendezvoused with the rest of the force as they passed over Reading on their way to the south coast, and shortly afterwards P/O Williams and crew gave up on a failing engine and turned back, while P/O Auckland and crew had reached a point some twenty miles south of Worthing when the oxygen supply to the rear turret failed through icing. It was an elongated bomber stream that crossed the French coast at 20,000 feet over broken cloud with clear conditions above, maintaining a course, thereafter, parallel with the frontiers of Belgium, Luxembourg and Germany as if heading for Switzerland, before crossing the German border between Strasbourg and Freiburg and turning towards the north-east for the run-in to the target. It was during this final leg that the night-fighters managed to infiltrate a section of the stream and score heavily, while ahead, adverse winds were responsible for the Path Finders arriving up to six minutes late to open the attack. They employed both sky and ground-markers in the face of seven to ten-tenths cloud at between 8,000 and 15,000 feet, but the Wanganui flares drifted in the wind, marking an area to the north-east of the River Neckar, while the TIs landed far apart in the north and south of the city. The 61 Squadron crews bombed on whatever markers presented themselves, mostly red TIs, from 20,000 to 23,000 feet between 23.15 and 23.39 and observed a spread of fires, including two large ones ten miles apart and smoke rising to bombing altitude. It would be established later that some of the early bombing had been accurate, but that most of it had undershot and fallen into open country, a disappointment compounded by the loss, mostly to night-fighters, of thirty-seven aircraft.

Many operations had been mounted against Frankfurt during the preceding two years, only a small number of which had been really effective, but this state of affairs was about to be rectified, and the first of two raids against this south-central powerhouse of industry was posted on the 18th, for which a force of 846 aircraft was made ready. 5 Group supported the operation with 212 Lancasters, the sixteen made ready by 61 Squadron each receiving a bomb load of a cookie and a variety of incendiaries, before departing Coningsby between 18.48 and 19.26 with F/L Berry the senior pilot on duty. P/O Hallett and crew became the latest to have their sortie curtailed by an oxygen supply issue, and they were followed home minutes later by P/O Farmiloe and crew, who had lost their port-outer engine shortly after crossing the French coast and dropped their load on a flak position to the east of Dunkerque. The bomber stream benefitted from favourable weather conditions as it pressed on across France and entered Germany to encounter a layer of haze 20,000 feet thick over the target, and according to most, no more than three-tenths cloud. This allowed the Path Finders to employ the Newhaven ground marking technique (blind marking by H2S, followed by visual backing-up), which the 61 Squadron crews exploited when carrying out their attacks on red and green TIs from 20,000 to 23,000 feet between 22.00 and 22.09. A large explosion was witnessed at 22.05, and the participants in the raid flew home confident that their efforts had been worthwhile. They had, indeed, contributed to an outstandingly successful raid, during which, 5 Group alone dropped more than one thousand tons of bombs for the first time at a single target. Local reports calculated that six thousand buildings had been destroyed or seriously damaged in predominantly eastern, central and western districts, and this was in return for the loss of twenty-two aircraft, five of which were from 5 Group. ND727 came down somewhere in southern Germany, and there were no survivors from the crew of P/O Cannon.

Frankfurt was named again on the 22nd as the target for that night, and 217 crews of 5 Group learned that they were to be part of another huge force of 816 aircraft, the nineteen participants from 61 Squadron departing Coningsby between 18.32 to 19.10 with W/C Stidolph and S/L Moss the senior pilots on duty. F/L Turner and crew abandoned their sortie during the climb-out after losing their intercom, while the remainder formed up as they made their way out over the Lincolnshire coast and adopted an unusual route for a target south of the Ruhr. Making landfall on the enemy coast over the Frisian Islands of Vlieland and Terschelling, they were to pass to the east of Osnabrück on a direct southerly course across the Ruhr. The head of the main force element arrived at the target to find five to six-tenths thin, low cloud at around 4,000 feet and Paramatta marking (blind marking by H2S) in progress. The 61 Squadron crews focused their attention on the release-point flares and red and green TIs marking out the aiming point, before bombing from 20,000 to 23,000 feet between 21.54 and 22.04. A massive rectangular area of unbroken fire was observed across the centre of the city, the glow from which could be seen for at least a hundred miles into the return flight.

Returning crews reported numerous searchlights lighting up the cloud, and moderate to intense flak that reached up to the bombers' flight level. Local reports confirmed the enormity of the devastation, which was particularly severe in western districts and left this half of the city without electricity, gas and water for an extended period. More than nine hundred people lost their lives and a further 120,000 were bombed out of their homes at a cost to the Command of twenty-six Lancasters and seven Halifaxes, a loss-rate of 4.2% and 3.8% respectively. It was a bad night for senior officers, 207 and 7 Squadrons losing their commanding officers, while Bardney's station commander, G/C Norman Pleasance, failed to return in a 9 Squadron Lancaster. What was about to happen over the next week and a half, however, would overshadow anything that had gone before and would certainly not fall within what might be considered acceptable.

It was more than five weeks since the main force had last visited the "Big City", and 811 aircraft were made ready on the 24th for what would be the final raid of the war upon it by RAF heavy bombers. 5 Group put up 193 Lancasters, of which sixteen were made ready by 61 Squadron and departed Coningsby between 18.21 and 18.57 with S/Ls Beard and Moss the senior pilots on duty. They had a long flight ahead of them, which would take them across the North Sea to the Danish coast near Ringkøbing and then to a point on the German Baltic coast near Rostock. When northeast of Berlin, they were to adopt a south-westerly course for the bombing run, and once clear of the defence zone homebound, dogleg to the west and then north-west to pass around Hannover on its southern and western sides, before heading for Holland and an exit via the Castricum coast. The extended outward leg provided a time-on-target of around 22.30, but an unexpected difficulty would be encountered, which would render void all of the meticulous planning. The existence of what we now know as "Jetstream" winds was unknown at the time, and the one blowing from the north with unprecedented strength on this night pushed the bomber stream south of its intended track. Navigators, who were expecting to see the northern tip of Sylt on their H2S screens, were horrified to find the southern end, which meant that they were thirty miles south of track and about to fly over Germany rather than Denmark. The previously mentioned "wind-finder" system had been set up for precisely this eventuality, but the problem on this night was that the wind-finders refused to believe what their instruments were telling them. Winds in excess of one hundred m.p.h had never been encountered before, and fearing that they would be disbelieved, many modified the figures downward. The same thing happened at raid control, where the figures were modified again, so that the information rebroadcast to the bomber stream bore no resemblance to the reality of the situation.

By the time that the head of the bomber stream reached Westerhever on the west coast of Schleswig-Holstein, most crews realised that they were some distance south of track and set course for the north to try to regain the planned route and avoid the defences that would be met if they turned east over Germany rather than Jutland. Many commented on the inaccurate wind information received during the outward journey, and having arrived in the target area, some were convinced that the Path Finders were up to ten minutes late in opening the raid. This was confirmed to some by the voice of the Master Bomber exhorting them to hurry up. Crews reported a variety of cloud conditions from three to ten-tenths at between 6,000 and 15,000 feet, but most were able to pick out the red and green TIs on the ground, and if not, found red Wanganui flares with green stars to guide them to the aiming point. The 61 Squadron crews delivered their attacks from 18,500 to 23,500 feet between 22.27 and 22.47, the low height that of P/O Farmiloe and crew, who were kept in the air by two good engines with a third on fire throughout the bombing run and for part of the return journey, and it was only by dumping every removable object that they made it home.

The consensus at debriefings was of a scattered attack in the early stages, until fires began to become more concentrated in three distinct areas and large explosions were witnessed at 22.42 and 22.54. The defences were very active with moderate flak bursting at up to 24,000 feet and light flak attempting to shoot out the skymarkers, but night-fighter activity was described by the 5 Group ORB as unusually quiet. There was a shock awaiting the Command as the returning aircraft landed to leave a shortfall of seventy-two, and it would be established later that two-thirds of them had fallen victim to the Ruhr flak batteries after being driven into that region's defence zone by the wind on the way home. 5 Group posted missing eleven Lancasters, the crews of P/O Carbutt and F/O Cox RNZAF in DV397 and JB129 respectively, belonging to 61 Squadron, the former crashing at Gehrden, south-west of Hannover, after the bomb-aimer had escaped with his life to fall into enemy hands. The latter was shot down by a night-fighter and crashed near Warburg, some fifty miles to the east of the Ruhr with fatal consequences for all on board. Post-raid analysis revealed that the wind had also played havoc with the marking and bombing and had pushed the attack towards the south-western districts of the capital, where most of the damage occurred, while 126 outlying communities also received bombs. 61 Squadron had been present on each of the nineteen main raids to Berlin from August onwards, and the diversion there on the night of the Magdeburg debacle in January and had dispatched 267 sorties for the loss of eleven of its Lancasters in which seventy-one crewmen lost their lives and just two survived as PoWs. (The Berlin Raids. Martin Middlebrook).

Twenty 5 Group Lancasters were invited to take part in an attack on the extensive railway yards at Aulnoye in north-eastern France to be carried out on the evening of the 25th, while twenty-two 617 Squadron Lancasters returned to the Sigma aero-engine factory at Lyons. Although Berlin had now been consigned to the past, the winter campaign still had a week to run, and two more major operations for the crews to negotiate. The first of these was posted on the 26th and would bring a return to the old enemy of Essen that night, for which a force of 705 aircraft was made ready. 5 Group contributed 172 of the 476 Lancasters, a dozen of them provided by 61 Squadron, which departed Coningsby between 19.36 and 20.06 with F/Ls Berry and Fitch the senior pilots on duty. They climbed out over the station and set course for the Dutch coast to pass north of Haarlem and Amsterdam, before swinging to the south-east on a direct run to the target. P/O Hallett and crew turned back from a point forty miles off Skegness because of an issue with hydraulics pressure, leaving the rest to reach the target and find it covered by eight to ten-tenths cloud with tops in places as high as 14,000 feet. Oboe performed well and enabled the Path Finders to mark the city with red and green TIs and Wanganui flares, which the 61 Squadron crews bombed from 19,000 to 22,200 feet between 22.00 and 22.09, before returning safely, having been unable to assess the results of their efforts. The impression was of a successful raid, and this was based on a considerable glow beneath the clouds as they withdrew. Post-raid reconnaissance soon confirmed another outstandingly destructive operation against this once elusive target, thus continuing the remarkable run of successes here since the introduction of Oboe to main force operations a year earlier. Over seventeen hundred houses were destroyed in the attack, with dozens of war industry factories sustaining serious damage, and on a night when the night-fighter controllers were caught off guard by the switch to the Ruhr, the success was gained for the modest loss of nine aircraft.

The period known as the Battle of Berlin, but which was better referred to as the winter campaign, was to be brought to an end on the night of the 30/31st with a standard maximum-effort raid on Nuremberg. The plan of operation departed from normal practice in only one important respect, and this was to prove critical. It had become standard practice for 8 Group to plan operations and to employ diversions and feints to confuse the enemy night-fighter controllers. Sometimes they were successful and sometimes not, but with the night-fighter force having clearly gained the upper hand with its "Tame Boar" running commentary system, all possible means had to be adopted to protect the bomber stream. During a conference held early on the 30th, the Lancaster Group A-O-Cs expressed a preference for a 5 Group-inspired route, which would require the bomber stream to fly a long straight leg across Belgium and Germany to a point about fifty miles north of Nuremberg, from where the final run-in would commence. The Halifax A-O-Cs were less convinced of the benefits, and AVM Bennett, the Path Finder chief, was positively overcome by the potential dangers and predicted a disaster, only to be overruled. A force of 795 aircraft was made ready, of which 201 Lancasters were to be provided by 5 Group, sixteen of them representing 49 Squadron, and the crews attended briefings to be told of the route, wind conditions and the belief that a layer of cloud would conceal them from enemy night-fighters. Before take-off, a Meteorological Flight Mosquito crew radioed in to cast doubts upon the weather conditions, which they could see differed markedly from those that had been forecast. This also went unheeded, and from around 21.45 for the next hour or so, the crews took off for the rendezvous area, and headed into a conspiracy of circumstances, which would inflict upon Bomber Command its heaviest defeat of the war.

At Coningsby fourteen 61 Squadron crew attended briefing and were given positions within the five waves of the main force element before taking off between 21.50 and 22.25 with S/L Moss and F/L Fitch the senior pilots on duty and all other crews captained by pilots of pilot officer rank.

P/O Hallett and crew were in trouble immediately after the flaps crept up during take-off, reducing lift, which caused the Lancaster to hit a beam installation damaging the mainplane and tailplane on the port side and puncturing a petrol tank. They flew out over Mablethorpe, presumably to dump the bombs, before returning to base. It was not long into the flight before crews began to notice some unusual features in the conditions, which included uncommonly bright moonlight and a crystal clarity of visibility that allowed them the rare sight of other aircraft in the stream. On most nights, crews would feel themselves to be completely alone in the sky all the way to the target, until bang on schedule, TIs would be seen to fall, and other aircraft would make their presence felt by the turbulence of their slipstreams as they funnelled towards the aiming point. Once at cruising altitude on this night, however, they were alarmed to note that the forecast cloud was conspicuous by its absence, and instead lay beneath them as a white tablecloth, against which they were silhouetted like flies. Condensation trails began to form in the cold, clear air to further advertise their presence to the enemy and the Jetstream winds, which had so adversely affected the Berlin raid a week earlier, were also present, only this time blowing from the south. As then, the wind-finder system failed to cope, and this would have a serious impact on the outcome of the operation. The final insult on this sad night was the route's close proximity to two night-fighter beacons, which the enemy aircraft were orbiting while they awaited their instructions, unaware initially that they were about to have the cream of Bomber Command handed to them on a plate.

The carnage began over Charleroi in Belgium, and from there to the target, the route was sign-posted by the burning wreckage on the ground of eighty Bomber Command aircraft. P/O Paul and crew were some thirty miles into Germany west of Coblenz when attacked in succession by three Ju88s, which between them knocked out both starboard engines but also sustained damage themselves from return fire and one would be claimed as probably destroyed after being observed to go down with its port engine on fire. All movable equipment was jettisoned and against all odds, they arrived back at base to land safely at 02.05. P/O Freeman and crew were deeper inside Germany, north-east of Frankfurt, when they too came under attack from a BF110 and two Ju88s, which left veteran Lancaster R5856 shredded from stem to stern with Perspex blown out, navigational equipment destroyed, and four crew members wounded. They turned back with more than 220 miles of enemy territory to negotiate before reaching the sanctuary of the North Sea, but they made it home to describe the return flight as "uneventful". The wind-finder system broke down again, and those crews who either failed to detect the strength of the wind, or simply refused to believe the evidence, were driven up to fifty miles north of their intended track, and as a result turned towards Nuremberg from a false position. This led to more than a hundred aircraft bombing at Schweinfurt in error, P/O Gray and crew among them, which combined with the massive losses sustained before the target was reached to reduce considerably the numbers arriving at the primary target.

The remaining 61 Squadron crews arrived over Nuremberg to encounter eight to nine-tenths cloud with tops as high as 16,000 feet and bombed from 19,000 to 22,000 feet between 01.20 and 01.28, aiming at red and green TIs and sky-markers. Many fires were observed, the glow from which, according to some reports, remained visible for 120 miles into the return journey. On the way home and approaching the Norfolk coast, P/O Forrest and crew ran into a violent electrical storm with hail and sleet, and some kind of electrical explosion caused the pilot to lose control and order his crew to bale out. Whether or not he knew they were still over the sea is unclear, but fortunately only the wireless operator and mid-upper gunner had time to comply before control was regained at 1,000 feet and a safe landing carried out on an unidentified aerodrome in the county. The fate of the two crewmen is not recorded in the ORB, but their inclusion in the Roll of Honour confirms that they probably drowned. Ninety-five aircraft failed to return home, twenty-one of them from 5 Group, and many others were written off in landing crashes or with battle damage too severe to repair. At Coningsby the return of the crews of S/L Moss DFC and P/O Haste RAAF in DV311 and R5734 respectively was awaited in vain, both Lancasters now smouldering wrecks on enemy soil. The former was the fifty-first to go down and crashed at Rimbach, to the north-east of Mannheim, with no survivors from the crew, who were on their twentieth operation. The latter was among the last to fall, the ninety-first, and crashed at Monin some thirty miles to the east of Charleroi in Belgium. possibly the victim of a Ju88 flown by Major Rudolf Schoenert of NJG10. The crew were on their eighth operation and again there were no survivors. The shock of the losses was compounded when it became clear that the strong wind had driven the marking beyond the city to the east, and Nuremberg had, consequently, escaped serious damage.

During the course of the month, the squadron participated in eight operations and dispatched 118 sorties for the loss of five Lancasters and crews and two additional crew members.

April 1944

The winter campaign had brought the Command to its low point of the war and was the only time when the morale of the crews was in question, but what now lay before the hard-pressed men of Bomber Command was in marked contrast to that which had been endured over the seemingly interminable winter months. In place of the long slog to Germany on dark, often dirty nights, shorter range hops to France and Belgium in improving weather conditions would become the order of the day. However, these operations would be equally demanding in their way and require of the crews a greater commitment to accuracy to avoid casualties among friendly civilians. Despite this, a decree from on high insisted that such operations were worthy of counting as just one third of a sortie towards the completion of a tour, and until this flawed policy was grudgingly rescinded late in the war, a sense of injustice pervaded the crew rooms. In fact, the number of sorties to complete a tour would fluctuate up and down between this point and the end of hostilities. Despite the horrendous losses of the winter campaign, the Command was in remarkably fine fettle to face its new challenge, with 3 Group gradually changing to Lancasters and the much-improved Hercules powered Halifaxes equipping 4 Group and most of 6 Group. Harris was now in the enviable position of being able to achieve what had eluded his predecessor, namely, to attack multiple targets simultaneously with enough strength to be effective. Such was the hitting-power now at his disposal, that he could assign targets to individual groups, to groups in tandem or to the Command as a whole, as dictated by operational requirements. Although invasion considerations would come first, while Harris was at the helm his favoured policy of city-busting would never be entirely shelved.

5 Group returned to operations on the 5th, with an undertaking involving 144 Lancasters and a Mosquito flown by W/C Cheshire of 617 Squadron. The target was the former Dewoitine aircraft factory at Toulouse in south-western France, which, under a nationalisation plan in 1936 involving six aircraft companies, including Lioré et Olivier and Potez, was now operating under the name SNCASE, or Sud Est for short. Cheshire was to mark it with spotfires from low level, using the system that he was instrumental in developing, and one which would become an integral part of 5 Group operations, with refinements, from this point on. This would be Cheshire's first operational

flight in a Mosquito and the first time that he marked a target for 5 Group rather than just 617 Squadron and much depended upon its success if Harris were to become sold on the idea of the low-level visual marking technique and give it his backing. S/L Woodroffe had arrived at Coningsby from 49 Squadron to succeed S/L Moss as a flight commander, but he was not involved in this night's operation, for which 61 Squadron bombed up a dozen of its Lancasters and sent them on their way between 20.18 and 20.37 with S/L Beard the senior pilot on duty. W/C Adams, S/L Miller and F/L Adams of 49 Squadron had been appointed as Master Bomber and Deputies, and they positioned themselves close to the head of the bomber stream for outward flight of more than four hours.

The main force element arrived in time to watch W/C Cheshire lob two red spotfires onto the roof of the factory at 00.17 during his third pass, and so accurate were they, that the two 617 Squadron Lancaster backers-up were not required. The main force bombed in bright moonlight, those representing 61 Squadron delivering their loads from 12,250 to 14,750 feet between 00.20 and 00.29 and observing large fires with smoke rising through 7,000 feet. F/Sgt Woolnough and crew were approaching the target when a pipe burst in the wireless operator's cabin and caused the loss of all hydraulic pressure except in the turrets. The bomb doors had to be opened by means of the emergency bottle and this was accomplished in time to drop the bombs, but the wheels and bomb doors hung down all the way home to an emergency landing. The squadron brought back seven aiming point photos from this highly successful operation, which cost just one 207 Squadron Lancaster to flak over the target. Within hours, Harris gave the go ahead for 5 Group to take on its own target marking force, and become, in effect, an independent entity.

It would be almost two weeks before the necessary moves took place, and in the meantime, the pre-invasion campaign got into full swing with the posting of two operations on the 9th. The Lille-Delivrance goods station in north-eastern France was assigned to 239 aircraft from 3, 4, 6 and 8 Groups, while the marshalling yards at Villeneuve-St-Georges, on the southern outskirts of Paris, were to be targeted by 225 aircraft drawn from all groups. The weather conditions were excellent, and clear skies greeted the latter force as it crossed the French coast at around 14,000 feet. The target could be identified visually, but crews aimed for the red and green TIs that had been accurately placed by the Path Finders, delivering their hardware from between 13,000 and 14,500 feet in the face of little opposition. Many bomb bursts were observed along with orange explosions, and to those high above, the raid appeared to be highly successful. In fact, many bomb loads had fallen into adjacent residential districts, where four hundred houses had been destroyed or seriously damaged, and ninety-three people killed. This was far fewer than had died in the simultaneous operation at Lille, many miles to the north-east, where over two thousand items of rolling stock had been destroyed and buildings and installations seriously damaged, but at a collateral cost of 456 French civilian lives. Civilian casualties would prove to be an unavoidable by-product of the campaign.

On the following day, Monday the 10th, a further five railway yards, four in France and one in Belgium, were posted as the targets for that night and assigned to individual groups, 5 Group handed those at Tours in the Loire region of western France, for which 180 Lancasters were made ready, fifteen of them by 61 Squadron. They departed Coningsby between 22.09 and 22.42 with W/C Stidolph and S/Ls Beard and Woodroffe the senior pilots on duty and the station commander, G/C "Tiny" Evans-Evans, commandeering P/O Newman and his crew. They set course for the south coast and the Channel crossing, and there had been no early returns by the time that they arrived at the target to find bright moonlight and red spotfires marking the aiming point. Master

Bombers were on hand to direct the two phases of the attack, the first against the western side of the yards and the second its eastern counterpart, but comments from returning crews revealed a somewhat chaotic raid, in which a good plan was hampered by poor communication. Congestion at the datum point apparently reached suicidal proportions, and then the delay in receiving W/T instructions had crews orbiting for an extended period. The 61 Squadron crews attacked aiming point "A" mostly from 5,500 to 7,500 feet between 01.29 and 01.55, S/L Beard, acting as 1st Deputy Master Bomber carrying out seven runs including three dummies between 01.04 and 01.50 and dropping successively red spotfires, a cookie and finally incendiaries. The attack on aiming point "B" was hampered by smoke drifting across from the earlier attack and rising through 7,000 feet, and this eventually persuaded the Master Bomber to call a halt to proceedings at 02.48 and any crews with bombs still on board were sent home. There were mixed opinions as to the effectiveness of the operation, some gaining the impression that the eastern half of the yards had not been touched, but others claimed the attack to have been accurate and concentrated within the yards, and two large fires were observed. Post-raid reconnaissance confirmed the success of the attack, but the Germans would round up local civilians and force them into repairing the damage to get the yards working again before long.

Aachen was a major railway centre with marshalling yards at both the western and eastern ends, but the attack planned for the night of the 11/12th was clearly designed as a city-busting exercise for which a force of 341 heavy aircraft was drawn from 1, 3, 5 and 8 Groups. 61 Squadron detailed fourteen Lancasters, which departed Coningsby between 20.22 and 20.50 with F/Ls Berry and Fitch the senior pilots on duty. The bomber stream climbed to between 18,000 and 20,000 feet by the time it reached the Belgian coast at 3° east and maintained that altitude all the way to the target, where six to ten-tenths thin cloud was encountered at 7,000 to 8,000 feet. Red and green TIs identified the aiming point and the 61 Squadron crews attacked it from 18,250 and 19,000 feet between 22.42 and 22.51, observing many bomb bursts and fires, which suggested that the attack was accurate. The crews maintained height on the way home until fifty miles from the coast, at which position they began a gentle descent to exit enemy territory at 15,000 feet or above. Nine Lancasters failed to return, and among them was 61 Squadron's JA695, which came down somewhere in the Antwerp region of Belgium with fatal consequences for F/O Williams DFC and all but the bomb-aimer, who was taken into captivity. Reports coming out of Aachen revealed this to be the city's worst experience of the war to date, with extensive damage in central and southern districts, disruption of its transport infrastructure and a death toll of 1,525 people. However, post-raid reconnaissance revealed that the railway yards had not been destroyed and would require further attention.

On the 14th, the Command became officially subject to the orders coming from the Supreme Headquarters of the Allied Expeditionary Force (SHAEF), under General Dwight D Eisenhower, and would remain thus shackled until the Allied armies were sweeping towards the German frontier at the end of the summer. On the 15th, 61 and 619 Squadrons moved out of Coningsby, the former to return to Skellingthorpe and the latter to Dunholme Lodge to allow 83 and 97 Squadrons to take up residence. They had been loaned to 5 Group from the Path Finder Force, on what amounted to a permanent detachment, along with the Mosquito unit, 627 Squadron, which made its home alongside 617 Squadron at Woodhall Spa. The Lancaster units were to become the 5 Group heavy markers, while the Mosquitos would eventually take over the low-level marking role currently performed by 617 Squadron. This was a major coup for AVM Cochrane and 5 Group and a bitter blow to AVM Bennett, the Path Finder Force chief.

Relations between Cochrane and Bennett had never been cordial, but this plunged them to new depths. Both were brilliant men, Bennett, an Australian, in particular, a man of the greatest intellect, who, despite his total lack of humour, commanded the deepest respect and loyalty from his men. He and Cochrane possessed vastly different opinions on the subject of target marking, Bennett believing that a low-level method exposed the crews to unnecessary danger, while Cochrane insisted that the risks in a fast-flying Mosquito were negligible and would produce greater accuracy. Though 83 and 97 Squadrons were formerly of 5 Group, and, at that time, had undoubtedly considered themselves part of the elite, most of the current crop of crews, despite beginning their operational careers in 5 Group, had come to see 8 Group as the pinnacle and were upset at being removed from what they considered to be an elevated status. They were fiercely proud, once qualified, to wear the Path Finder badge and enjoyed the enhanced benefits of their status, although, happily for them, as the squadrons were only officially on loan to 5 Group, they would retain these privileges.

5 Group, of course, had always considered itself to be the elite of the Command, and probably felt that the newcomers should see the move as a promotion. Any resentment might have been smoothed over had their reception at Coningsby been handled better, but as the newly arrived crews tumbled out of their transports, they were summoned immediately to the briefing room to be lectured by the 54 Base commander, Air Commodore "Bobby" Sharp. Rather than welcoming them as brothers-in-arms, he harangued them over their bad 8 Group habits and ordered them to buckle down to learning 5 Group ways. This was an insult to experienced airmen, for whom the task of illuminating targets for 5 Group would be a piece of cake compared with the complexities of their 8 Group duties. The fact that the insult was being delivered by a pompous, self-important man with no relevant operational experience made it doubly unpalatable. From this point on, 5 Group would be known in 8 Group circles somewhat disparagingly as the "Independent Air Force", or "The Lincolnshire Poachers".

The 5 Group target on the 18th was the marshalling yards at Juvisy, situated on the west bank of the Seine south of Paris, which was one of four similar targets for the night. The intention had been for the new arrivals to participate, but the disgruntled commanding officers, G/C Lawrence Deane of 83 Squadron and W/C Jimmy Carter of 97 (Straits Settlements) Squadrons, announced that they were not yet ready, and the operation would have to go ahead without them. 202 Lancasters and four Mosquitos were made ready, the latter belonging to 617 Squadron, while 8 Group provided three Oboe Mosquitos to deliver the initial marking. 61 Squadron made ready sixteen Lancasters, which departed Skellingthorpe between 20.37 and 21.15 with W/C Stidolph the senior pilot on duty and reached their target to find clear skies and ideal bombing conditions, in which they observed W/C Cheshire's red spotfires in the process of being backed up by green TIs. Despite black smoke drifting across the aiming point and upwards from the destruction of a fuel dump at 23.32, the 61 Squadron crews were able to hit the markers from 7,000 to 10,500 between 23.29 and 23.44, and returning crews were enthusiastic about the success of the operation. This was confirmed by post-raid reconnaissance and prompted the crews to make the valid comment that, to count this operation as just one-third of a sortie was undervaluing it, a sentiment shared by all whose job involved putting their lives on the line.

Briefings on 5 Group stations on the 20th informed crews of their part in the first operation to include the three newly transferred squadrons, which was a two-phase attack on railway yards at La Chapelle, situated just to the north of Paris, while the night's main event was to be conducted by a force of 357 Lancasters and twenty-two Mosquitos drawn from 1, 3, 6 and 8 Groups against

Cologne. A meticulous plan had been prepared for 5 Group, in which the phases were to be separated by an hour, each with its own specific aiming point, and 83 Squadron's W/C Deane was to be the Master Bomber with S/L Sparks his deputy. The plan called for 8 Group Mosquitos to drop cascading flares by Oboe to provide an initial reference and for a Mosquito element from 627 Squadron to lay a "window" screen ahead of the main force Lancasters. Once the target had been identified, the first members of the 83 Squadron flare force were to provide illumination for the low-level marker Mosquitos of 617 Squadron, which would mark the first aiming point with red spot fires for the main force element to aim at. The whole procedure would then be repeated at the second aiming point. At Coningsby, W/C Deane conducted the briefing, and at its conclusion, wished the assembled throng good luck, before dismissing them, whereupon a voice from the back declared that the briefing wasn't over and that the base and station commanders wanted their say. This had not been standard practice in 8 Group, and it left Deane mystified and a little humiliated. The senior officers had only waffle to offer, but it made them feel important, while confirming the first impressions of the crews, that A/C Sharp was a self-important and irrelevant link in the chain of command.

61 Squadron made ready fifteen Lancasters as part of the overall force of 247 representing 5 Group and twenty-two Mosquitos of 5 and 8 Groups, and they departed Skellingthorpe between 22.47 and 23.16 with W/C Stidolph and S/L Beard the senior pilots on duty, the former for the last time. They were assigned to various waves attacking the first aiming point with a mix of 1,000 and 500 pounders and arrived at the target to find largely clear skies, good visibility and some ground haze to mar the view. Zero hour for the opening phase was set for 00.05, but the Oboe Mosquitos were two minutes late and some communications problems had to be ironed out before matters began to run smoothly. The 61 Squadron crews bombed from 7,750 to 11,000 feet between 00.21 and 00.35, and a large, orange explosion at 00.28 sent a column of black smoke skyward, impairing visibility to some extent. Even so, those attacking afterwards were able to identify a red spotfire and bomb it, observing large explosions and fires that were visible to the second phase crews as they approached. Following the second phase attack, the fires remained visible for a hundred miles into the return flight and at debriefing, crews expressed confidence that they had contributed to a successful operation. Post-raid reconnaissance confirmed the success of both phases of the raid, which had left the yards severely damaged for the loss of six Lancasters. A congratulatory message from A-O-C Cochrane was received on all participating stations.

At the end of a highly successful tour as commanding officer, W/C Stidolph was posted to 55 Base, comprising at the time the stations at East Kirkby and Spilsby, to which Strubby would be added later in the year. He was succeeded by W/C Arthur Doubleday, who had been a farmer back in New South Wales and was about to celebrate his thirty-second birthday. He had completed a tour on Wellingtons with 460 Squadron RAAF in 1942 and spent the next period of his service as an instructor at 27 O.T.U, at Lichfield, where Australians were trained. He was posted to Skellingthorpe from 467 Squadron RAAF at Waddington, with which he had been serving as a flight commander since December and presided over his first briefing on the evening of his arrival.

The real test for the 5 Group low-level marking system would come at a heavily defended German target, for which Braunschweig was selected on the 22nd, while the rest of the Command targeted the Ruhr city of Düsseldorf. 5 Group put together a force of 238 Lancasters and seventeen Mosquitos, with ten ABC Lancasters of 1 Group's 101 Squadron to provide radio countermeasures (RCM) cover. 61 Squadron contributed sixteen Lancasters, which departed Skellingthorpe between 22.56 and 23.43 with S/L Beard the senior pilot on duty and reached the target area after being kept on track by route-markers. They found six to eight-tenths thin cloud at between 8,000 and 10,000 feet and accurate marking by the 617 Squadron Mosquito element, despite which, the main force crews were unable to properly identify the target. The situation was again compounded by communications problems between various controllers, caused by the failure of VHF and the consequent need to pass on instructions instead by W/T. This led to confusion, and many crews were forced to orbit for up to fifteen minutes before bombing. The 61 Squadron crews carried out their attacks on green TIs and red spotfires from 12,500 to 19,000 feet between 01.54 and 02.08 and most returned safely to report what appeared to be a successful operation, while also complaining about the dangers of orbiting a target with aircraft heading in a variety of directions. Four Lancasters failed to return, and among them was 61 Squadron's LM476, which exploded, presumably as a result of the bomb load being hit and spread its wreckage over an area to the south-west of the town of Hamelin. F/L Bird DFC and his navigator were catapulted into space and survived in enemy hands, while the other six occupants lost their lives. A post-raid analysis revealed that some bombs had fallen in the city centre, but most were directed at reserve H2S-laid TIs to the south of the city, and damage was less severe than might otherwise have been.

When Munich was posted across 5 Group as the target on the 24th for another live test of the low-level visual marking method, it might have been seen as somewhat ambitious to select such a major city, that was protected by two hundred flak guns. The main operation on this night was to be conducted by a force of 637 aircraft against Karlsruhe, 150 miles to the north-west, which would help to distract the night-fighters. 234 Lancasters were made ready by 5 Group and supplemented by ten of the ABC variety from 101 Squadron, while four Mosquitos of 617 Squadron were loaded with spotfires to carry out the marking and twelve of 627 Squadron with "window" to dispense during the final approach to the target. 61 Squadron's thirteen Lancasters took to the air from Skellingthorpe between 20.44 and 21.16 with F/Os Acott, Jeavons and Paul the senior pilots on duty and headed for the south coast before setting course across France towards the south-east and feinting towards Italy. The 617 and 627 Squadron Mosquitos took off three hours after the heavy brigade and adopted a direct route, the latter laying a "window" screen from high level six minutes from the target to mask the arrival of the flare force that was to provide seven minutes of illumination for the 617 marker Mosquitos.

The main force element reached the target area to encounter clear skies and good visibility, while ahead and thousands of feet below, W/C Cheshire dived onto the aiming point in the face of murderous light flak, before racing away across the rooftops to safety. The main force element was called in to attack, and those of 61 Squadron bombed on the red spotfires and green TIs from 15,250 to 21,250 feet between 01.45 and 01.54 in the face of intense searchlight and flak activity. Many fires were seen to take hold, and as the bombers pointed their snouts back towards France to eventually pass to the north of Paris, Karlsruhe could be seen burning over to starboard. Among ten missing Lancasters was 61 Squadron's LM359, which crashed in east-central France some fifty miles from the Swiss frontier, killing P/O Newman and all but the navigator, who was helped by partisans to retain his freedom. Post-raid reconnaissance and local reports confirmed the success of the raid, which left 1,104 buildings in ruins and a further thirteen hundred severely damaged. It was probably this operation that sealed the award to Cheshire of the Victoria Cross at the conclusion of his operational career six weeks hence after one hundred sorties.

At briefing on the 26th, thirteen 61 Squadron crews were told that Schweinfurt was to be their target that night, after the failure of the RAF to destroy it in February and the American 8th Air Force just two weeks ago. The tone was very much, "leave it to RAF Bomber Command", and with the satisfaction of Munich still fresh in the mind and the natural rivalry between the two Allied bomber organisations keen, such attitudes were to be expected. They learned that, for this operation, 627 Squadron would act as the low-level marker force for the first time and for a main force of 215 Lancasters, including nine from 101 Squadron to provide RCM protection. This was just one of three major operations taking place, the main event at Essen involving 493 aircraft from all but 5 Group, while the railway yards at Villeneuve-St-Georges was the objective for a predominantly Halifax main force. The 61 Squadron element departed Skellingthorpe between 21.16 and 21.48 with S/L Beard the senior pilot on duty and joined up with the bomber stream as they headed south. P/O Freeman and crew had been contending with a lack of power and a consequent inability to climb as they crossed the Channel, and shortly after making landfall on the Normandy coast, gave up and turned for home.

Stronger-than-forecast head winds delayed the arrival in the target area of the heavy brigade, but once there they found generally clear skies and good visibility, which the 627 Squadron crews failed to exploit as their debut marking effort proved to be inaccurate. The 83 Squadron crews remarked on the lack of illumination and those carrying hooded flares were called in a number of times to back-up. The 61 Squadron crews bombed from 14,500 to 21,000 feet between 02.27 and 02.41 aiming at red spotfires and green TIs, some following the instructions of the Master Bomber to overshoot by a thousand yards. A large white explosion was witnessed at 02.29, and many fires were reported, but once again at this target, most of the hardware fell outside of the target area, leaving ball-bearing production more or less unscathed. Night-fighters got amongst the heavy force on both sides of the Franco-German frontier and twenty-one Lancasters failed to return, a hefty 9.3%, among them five representing 106 at Metheringham.

5 Group made preparations on the 28th to send a force of eighty-eight Lancasters and four Mosquitos to attack the Alfred Nobel Dynamit A.G explosives works at St-Médard-en-Jalles, situated in a wood on the north-western outskirts of Bordeaux in south-western France. A further fifty-one Lancasters and four Mosquitos would head in the opposite direction to target an aircraft maintenance facility at the Kjeller Flyfabrikk, some ten miles north-east of Oslo, which had been occupied by the Germans since April 1940 and was used by Junkers, Daimler-Benz and BMW. The former was the target for fifteen 61 Squadron crews, which departed Skellingthorpe between 22.45 and 23.22 with W/C Doubleday leading the squadron into battle for the first time. Each Lancaster was carrying eleven 1,000 and two 500-pounders, some of the former of American manufacture, and all of this hardware found its way to the target area, where clear skies prevailed. Bombing began at around 02.45 and between then and 03.28, twenty-five bomb loads went down, including five from 61 Squadron aircraft from 4,500 to 6,000 feet between 02.46 and 03.29. The others responded to a signal from the Master Bomber to orbit after some flares landed in a nearby wood, causing volumes of smoke to drift across the factory and obscure it from view. Some spent up to sixty-six minutes circling the target while the Master Bomber assessed the situation, eventually calling a halt to proceedings at 03.30 and ordering the remaining crews to take their bombs home.

Meanwhile, more than eleven hundred miles to the north over southern Norway, the crews had found clear skies and excellent visibility, and had identified the target by H2S, confirmed by yellow TIs at the start of the bombing run and flares and red spotfires supposedly on the aiming-point. In the event, a two-thousand-yard correction was broadcast to compensate for a poor marking performance, which resulted in explosions on the airfield and runway, and among barrack buildings and some of the sheds, and an ammunition dump went up at 01.40.

The operation against the explosives works was rescheduled for the following night, when the Michelin tyre factory at Clermont-Ferrand was added to the target list and forces of sixty-eight and fifty-four Lancasters were assigned respectively with five 627 Squadron Mosquitos at each to provide the low-level marking. The 61 Squadron element of ten departed Skellingthorpe between 22.14 and 22.51 with S/Ls Beard and Woodroffe the senior pilots on duty, and all reached the target area to be met by clear skies and haze. The aiming-point was identified both visually and by red spotfires and red and green TIs, which could be seen burning between factory buildings, and the 61 Squadron crews bombed them from 4,250 to 6,000 feet between 02.24 and 02.33, in accordance with instructions from the Master Bomber. All returned safely to Skellingthorpe, filled with enthusiasm at the explosions that had ripped the site apart, and some crews commented that it was the most destructive attack they had taken part in. Post-raid reconnaissance confirmed that both targets had been severely damaged with a massive loss of production.

During the course of the month the squadron participated in ten operations and dispatched 139 sorties for the loss of three Lancasters and crews.

May 1944

Now that the invasion was just five weeks away, the new month would be devoted to attacks on railway targets and coastal defences, in the case of the latter with the focus on the Pas-de-Calais region of north-eastern France, to try to reinforce the enemy's belief that the landings would take place there. Ten 61 Squadron crews were called to briefing at Skellingthorpe on the 1st to learn that they would be going to Toulouse in southern France that night as part of a 5 Group force of 131 Lancasters and eight Mosquitos to attack two targets, the Proudrerie explosives works and a SNCASE aircraft assembly factory in the western suburb of Saint-Martin-du-Touch. At the same time, a third 5 Group force of forty-six Lancasters and four Mosquitos would be sent against an aircraft repair workshop at Tours in western France. The 61 Squadron element took off between 21.26 and 21.47 with S/L Woodroffe the senior pilot on duty and employed Gee for the first part of the outward flight until it was jammed, relying, thereafter, on good navigation, green track markers provided by the Path Finders, and H2S. They all reached the target to find moonlight, clear skies and excellent visibility, with flares and red spotfires marking out the aiming point and carried out their attacks from 5,000 to 7,000 feet between 01.46 and 01.57 in accordance with the instructions of the Master Bomber. The attack was clearly focused on the aiming point, where many bomb bursts and large explosions were observed and the glow of the burning site remained visible for a hundred miles into the return journey. All crews returned to their respective stations confident of a successful outcome, and post-raid reconnaissance revealed all three factories to have been heavily damaged. P/O Hallett and crew brought their bombs home after failing to identify the target in the absence of markers or illumination.

Briefings took place on 1 and 5 Group stations on the 3rd, for what would become a highly contentious operation that night against a Panzer training camp and transport depot at Mailly-le-Camp, situated some seventy-five miles east of Paris in north-eastern France. The units based there posed a potential threat to Allied forces as the invasion unfolded and needed to be eliminated. The events of the operation proved to be so controversial that recriminations abound to this day concerning the 5 Group leadership provided by W/Cs Cheshire and Deane. Although the grudges by 1 Group aircrew against them can be understood in the light of what happened, they are unjust and based on emotion and incorrect information and it is worthwhile to examine the conduct of the operation in some detail. W/C Cheshire was appointed as marker leader, and was piloting one of four 617 Squadron Mosquitos, while 83 Squadron's commanding officer, W/C Deane, was overall raid controller with S/L Sparks his Deputy. Deane and Cheshire attended separate briefings, and neither seemed aware of the complete plan, particularly the role of the newly-formed 1 Group Special Duties Flight from Binbrook, which was assigned to its own specific aiming point to mark for an element of the 1 Group force.

The fourteen 61 Squadron participants became airborne from Skellingthorpe between 21.50 and 22.10 with S/L Woodroffe the senior pilot on duty and all reached the target area to find clear skies, moonlight and excellent bombing conditions, but confusion already beginning to influence events. 617 Squadron's W/C Cheshire and S/L Shannon were in position before midnight, and as the first flares from the 83 and 97 Squadron Lancasters illuminated the target below, Cheshire released his two red spot fires onto the first aiming point at 00.00½ from 1,500 feet. Shannon backed them up from 400 feet five and a half minutes later, and as far as Cheshire was concerned, the operation was bang on schedule at this stage. A 97 Squadron Lancaster also laid markers accurately to ensure a constant focal point, and Cheshire passed instructions to Deane to call the bombers in. It was at this stage of the operation that matters began to go awry, when a commercial radio station, believed to be an American forces network, jammed the VHF frequencies in use. Deane called in the 5 Group element, elated that everything was proceeding according to plan, but nothing happened. He checked with his wireless operator that the instructions had been transmitted and called up S/L Sparks, who was also mystified by the lack of bombing.

Post raid reports are contradictory, and it is impossible to establish an accurate course of events, particularly when Deane and Cheshire's understanding of the exact time of zero hour differed by five minutes. Remarkably, it also seems, that Deane was unaware that there were two marking points, or three, if one includes 1 Group's Special Duties Flight. Cheshire, initially at least, appeared happy with the early stages of the attack and described the bombing as concentrated and accurate. It seems certain, however, that many minutes had passed between the dropping of Cheshire's markers and the first main force bombs falling, during which period, Deane was coming to terms with the fact that his instructions were not getting through. A plausible scenario is, that in the absence of instructions, and with red spot fires clearly visible in the target, some crews from 9, 207 and 467 Squadrons opted to bomb, and others followed suit. The 61 Squadron crews of P/Os Auckland, Eastwood, Gray, Stone and Street attacked from 5,200 to 8,000 feet between 00.08 and 00.12, finding the target to be well-marked and the air above it ridiculously congested. It was at this point that W/C Deane attempted to control the operation by W/T, which also failed.

Now a new problem was arising as smoke from these first salvoes threatened to obliterate the entire camp, and Cheshire had to decide whether or not to send in Fawke and Kearns to mark the second aiming point. His feeling and that of Deane, as it later transpired, was that it was unnecessary as the volume of bombs still to fall into the relatively compact area of the target would ensure destruction of the entire site. By 00.16, the first phase of bombing should have been completed, leaving a clear run for Fawke and Kearns across the target, however, the majority of 5 Group crews were still on their bombing run, a fact unknown to Cheshire, who asked Deane for a pause in the bombing while the two Mosquitos went in. As far as Cheshire was concerned, there was no response from Deane, who would anyway have been confused by mention of a second aiming point. In the event, Deane's deputy, S/L Sparks, eventually found a channel free of interference, and did, in fact, transmit an instruction to halt the bombing both by W/T and R/T, and some crews reported hearing something. While utter chaos reigned, Kearns and Fawke dived in among the falling cookies at 00.23 and 00.25 respectively to mark the second aiming point on the western edge of the camp. At 2,000 feet, they were lucky to survive the turbulence created by the exploding 4,000 pounders, when 4,000 feet was considered to be a minimum safe height. They were not entirely happy with their work, but F/O Edwards of 97 Squadron dropped a stick of markers precisely on the mark, and S/L Sparks was then able to call the 1 Group main force in along with any from 5 Group with bombs still on board.

Among the latter were the remaining nine 61 Squadron crews who attacked from 5,000 to 8,000 feet between 00.25 and 00.33, some having been sent to orbit a yellow marker fifteen miles away and spending an uncomfortable thirty minutes watching Lancasters fall from the sky in flames. Meanwhile, the night-fighters continued to create havoc among the 1 Group Lancasters milling around in the target area, and as burning aircraft were seen to fall all around, some Australian crews succumbed to their anxiety and frustration and in a rare breakdown of R/T discipline, let fly with comments of an uncomplimentary nature, many of which were intended for, and, indeed, heard by Deane.

Despite the problems, the operation was a major success, which destroyed 80% of the camp's buildings and 102 vehicles, of which thirty-seven were tanks, while over two hundred men were killed. Forty-two Lancasters failed to return, however, two thirds of them from 1 Group, and 50 Squadron was 5 Group's most afflicted unit with four Lancasters and crews unaccounted for, while, miraculously, 61 Squadron came through unscathed. At debriefing, S/L Blome-Jones of 207 Squadron described the situation as a complete shambles and chaos, the controller as inefficient and the discipline of some crews as bad, while others voiced the opinion that this was a trip worthy of more than one-third of a sortie. On the following day, an inquest into the conduct of the raid revealed that the wireless transmitter in Deane's Lancaster had been sufficiently off frequency to allow the interference from the American network to mask the transmission of instructions and prevent the call to bomb from reaching the main force crews. The 1 Group A-O-C, AVM Rice, decided he would not participate in further operations organized by 5 Group, which was probably not a blow to Cochrane, who was confident that his group did not need back-up.

On the 6th, 1 and 5 Groups were invited to send a modest force each to attack ammunition dumps in France, 5 Group detailing sixty-four Lancasters and four Mosquitos for a site at Louailles, situated some four miles south-east of the town of Sable-sur-Sarthe, south-west of Le-Mans in north-western France. 61 Squadron put up eleven Lancasters, each loaded with eleven 1,000 and four 500-pounders, which had to wait until the start of the 7th before departing Skellingthorpe between 00.34 and 00.57 with no senior pilot on duty. All reached the target to find clear skies and excellent visibility, and a Master Bomber on hand to direct the attack once the red spotfires had been delivered by the low-level Mosquitos. His assessment was that the markers had fallen fifty yards north of the aiming-point, and his instruction was to bomb fifty yards to the south on a northerly heading. The 61 Squadron crews complied from 5,000 to 7,000 feet between 02.47 and 03.03 and observed numerous bomb flashes that lit up long sheds, and two enormous explosions that each resulted in a large mushroom of smoke rising through 3,000 feet as the force withdrew.

53 Base (Waddington, Skellingthorpe and Bardney) sat out the night of the 7/8th, while five small-scale operations were mounted against airfields, ammunition dumps and a coastal battery in

support of the coming invasion. 5 Group was involved in two raids, the airfield at Tours and an ammunition dump at Salbris, some sixty miles to the east, and post-raid reconnaissance confirmed that both targets had been attacked accurately and effectively in perfect bombing conditions to leave them severely damaged. Another small-scale operation was mounted by the group on the 8th against the airfield and seaplane base at Lanveoc-Poulmic, located on the northern side of the peninsula forming the southern boundary of the L'Elorn estuary opposite Brest. A force of fifty-eight Lancasters and six Mosquitos included eleven of the former provided by 61 Squadron, and they departed Skellingthorpe between 21.20 and 21.39 with F/L Farmiloe the senior pilot on duty and a cookie and sixteen 500-pounders in each bomb bay. All reached the destination, where the target was easily identified by the coastline and hangars but communication with the Master Bomber were poor and no wind information was passed on until the raid was effectively over. Red spotfires provided a reference for some crews but not all saw them, and for some it was the illumination from explosions that identified the aiming point. The 61 Squadron crews bombed from 7,250 to 9,500 feet between 23.58 and 00.05 and observed hangars and other buildings to be on fire and enveloped in smoke at the conclusion of the attack.

The night of the 9/10th brought attacks on seven coastal batteries in the Pas-de-Calais by four hundred aircraft. The purpose of these operations was to confirm in the mind of the enemy the belief that the Allied invasion forces would land at Calais, and right up to D-Day itself, the coastal region between Gravelines to the east of the port and Berck-sur-Mer to the south-west, would be subjected to constant bombardment. 5 Group, meanwhile, prepared fifty-six Lancasters and eight Mosquitos to attack two factories, the Gnome and Rhône aero-engine works and another unspecified one at Gennevilliers in northern Paris, while a second force of thirty-nine Lancasters and four Mosquitos targeted a small ball-bearing factory at Annecy, situated in south-eastern France close to the frontiers with Switzerland and Italy. Skellingthorpe was not called into action on this night, but those entrusted with the responsibility claimed to have produced accurate bombing at both sites, and post-raid reconnaissance confirmed the Annecy site to have been severely damaged.

Five railway targets were selected for attention on the 10th, among them the marshalling yards at Lille for 5 Group, for which 61 Squadron dispatched fifteen Lancasters from Skellingthorpe between 21.54 and 22.15 with W/C Doubleday the senior pilot on duty. They found the target area to be under clear skies, with the aiming-point slightly obscured by ground haze, but this was a situation easily negated by red spotfires and green TIs, and bombing by the 61 Squadron crews took place in the light of flares from 8,000 to 10,000 feet between 23.36 and midnight. Bomb bursts were seen across the tracks, and two large explosions were observed to confirm a successful assault on this important hub linking north-eastern France with Belgium. Night-fighters were out in force, and most of the night's casualties resulted from the attack at Lille, from which a dozen Lancasters failed to return.

5 Group put together a force of 190 Lancasters and eight Mosquitos on the 11th to target a military camp at Bourg-Leopold in north-eastern Belgium, for which 61 Squadron made ready eleven Lancasters. They departed Skellingthorpe between 22.16 and 22.35 with F/Ls Berry and Farmiloe the senior pilots on duty and lost the services of P/O North and crew to a faulty compass. The others reached the target to find hazy conditions and a little thin cloud at around 10,000 feet, despite which, they were able to identify ground detail in the form of buildings and huts in the light of illuminating flares. Three Oboe Mosquitos were on hand to deliver the initial marking, but inaccurately forecast winds caused the 83 Squadron element to arrive late, by which time the main

force crews had begun to orbit to await instructions. A communications problem prevented some crews from hearing the Master Bomber's broadcasts, but the aiming point could be seen to be marked by red spotfires and green TIs. From the Master Bomber's perspective, the initial Oboe marker had been visible only to a few crews and quickly burned out, and so he called for another Mosquito to drop a red spot fire onto the aiming point.

Before this was accomplished, however, the main force began to bomb, and among ninety-four crews to do so were nine from 61 Squadron, who attacked from 14,500 to 16,000 feet between 00.22 and 00.27. As smoke began to obscure the ground, the Master Bomber, S/L Mitchell, quickly became uncomfortable about the close proximity of civilian residential property and called a halt to the bombing at 00.35, before sending the rest of the force home, some of them after circling for more than twenty minutes. On return to base, LM478 ran off the end of the runway and ended up in a ditch, never to fly again, but F/Sgt Woolnough RAAF and crew emerged unscathed to resume their tour. P/O Eastwood and crew were absent from debriefing, and it was learned eventually that LM454 had been shot down by a night-fighter while outbound and crashed seven miles north-east of Sint-Niklaas in Belgium shortly after crossing the Scheldt estuary. Only the mid-upper gunner survived to fall into enemy hands.

Minor operations occupied elements of the Command, thereafter, until the 19th, when the station teleprinters worked overtime dispensing the details of five operations for that night against marshalling yards, two on coastal batteries and one against a radar station. 5 Group detailed 225 Lancasters, 112 to be sent to Amiens with eight Mosquitos and 113 for Tours with four Mosquitos, 53 Base assigned to the latter. A previous attack by 5 Group had targeted the installations on the outskirts of the town, while this night's effort was directed at those in the central district between the rivers Loire to the north and La Cher to the south. The eighteen-strong 61 squadron element departed Skellingthorpe between 21.58 and 22.43 with S/L Woodroffe the senior pilot on duty and eleven US-supplied 1,000-pounders and four of 500lbs in each bomb bay. They set course for north-eastern France via Hastings and Dieppe and lost the services of P/O Street and crew at the midpoint of the Channel crossing on discovering that the bomb-sight was unserviceable. The target was found under clear skies and visibility good enough to identify ground detail, and the aiming-point was marked by red spotfires, and, in view of the close proximity of civilian housing, the Master Bomber took great care and much time before issuing the order to bomb. This would extend the time on target, but, fortunately, the Luftwaffe was absent, and the bombing by the 61 Squadron element was carried out from 5,500 to 12,000 feet between 00.49 and 00.57. P/O North and crew alone received a signal at 01.05 to cease bombing and return to base and jettisoned three 1,000-pounders in the Channel on the way home. The accuracy of the bombing was sufficient to cause massive damage to the target, with only a little collateral damage and there were no losses from Skellingthorpe.

At Amiens, the target was found to be shrouded in a layer of eight to ten-tenths cloud between 6,000 and 11,000 feet, and the red spotfires dropped on what was believed to be the aiming point, when checked on H2S, were found to be up to five miles off, which prompted the Master Bomber to issue instructions via W/T at 01.25 to terminate the attack and return home. That was too late for thirty-seven crews who had already bombed.

For the first time in a year, Duisburg was posted as the target for a heavy raid on the 21st, for which a force of 510 Lancasters and twenty-two Mosquitos was drawn from 1, 3, 5 and 8 Groups. While this operation was in progress, seventy Lancasters, including some from 5 Group, and thirty-seven

Halifaxes undertook gardening duties in the Nectarines and Rosemary gardens around the Frisians and off Heligoland, and in the Silverthorn and Quince gardens in the Kattegat and Kiel Bay regions of the Baltic. 61 Squadron supported only the main event, for which eighteen Lancasters were made ready and dispatched from Skellingthorpe between 22.21 and 23.13 with F/Ls Acott, Berry, Farmiloe and Jeavons the senior pilots on duty. Crews had been told at briefing to adhere to the plan for the outward route, which involved a few aircraft from 3 Group gaining height as they adopted a north-westerly course as far as Sleaford, so as not to cross into enemy radar cover earlier than necessary. The groups would rendezvous at 18,000 feet over the North Sea at 3° east to cross the enemy coast at 20,000 feet and climb to 22,000 or 23,000 feet, before increasing speed for the run across the target.

All of the 61 Squadron participants reached the Ruhr, which they found to be concealed beneath ten-tenths cloud with tops at between 11,000 and 20,000 feet, into which the red-with-yellow-stars Wanganui parachute marker flares fell almost before they could be seen. A number of crews commented on the data provided by the windfinder system to be inaccurate, and this made it a challenge to establish positions. The 61 Squadron crews used the explosion of cookies, the glow of fires and the evidence of intense flak as references and bombed from 18,250 to 22,000 feet between 01.10 and 01.27, before returning home with little useful information to report. The loss of twenty-nine Lancasters was a reminder to the Command that the Ruhr remained a dangerous destination, although most of the missing had come down onto Dutch and Belgian soil or into the sea homebound after falling victim to night-fighters. Martin Drewes of III./NJG1 alone accounted for at least three Lancasters. Returning crews were not enthusiastic about the outcome, and post-raid reconnaissance confirmed that a modest 350 buildings had been destroyed in the southern half of Duisburg, and 665 others had been seriously damaged.

Just like Duisburg, Dortmund was posted on the 22nd to host its first large-scale visit from the Command for a year and would face an all-Lancaster heavy force of 361 aircraft drawn from 1, 3, 6 and 8 Groups. While this operation was in progress, 220 Lancasters of 5 Group and five from 101 Squadron were to target Braunschweig, which, thus far, had evaded severe damage at the hands of the Command. 61 Squadron made ready seventeen Lancasters, which departed Skellingthorpe between 22.18 and 22.48 led by the same four pilots of flight lieutenant rank as for the previous operation. They joined up with the bomber stream as it made its way across the North Sea and through the clearly evident night-fighter activity from the Dutch coast all the way to the target. They negotiated the patches of ten-tenths cloud over northern Germany and intense searchlight activity as they passed between Bremen and Osnabrück and expected to find the forecast clear skies over Braunschweig, but in fact, the marker force encountered four to seven-tenths drifting cloud with tops up to 7,000 feet. Although highly effective in the right weather conditions, the 5 Group low-level visual marking method could easily be rendered ineffective by cloud cover.

The "Y" aircraft, the H2S heavy marker Lancasters, dropped skymarkers, while the 627 Squadron Mosquito element went in at low level to release red spotfires in the light of illuminator flares, which if absent, rendered the Mosquito crews blind. Some crews described "hopeless confusion" with flares and incendiaries spread over a distance and many had to rely on their own H2S to establish their position. Some found a complete absence of marking and orbited for up to fifteen minutes until a few green TIs appeared, after which, the bombing by the 61 Squadron element took place on these or on incendiary fires from 19,250 to 22,000 feet between 00.56 and 01.34. Considerable interference over R/T communications added to the problems, and although the

Master Bomber could be heard in discussions with his Deputies, no instructions were received from him and the attack lacked cohesion. Post-raid reconnaissance confirmed that most of the bombing had fallen onto outlying communities, confirming in the minds of the residents that this was an intentional ploy by the Command, and it was a relatively expensive failure that cost thirteen Lancasters.

The main operation on the 24th involved 442 aircraft in an attack on two marshalling yards at Aachen, Aachen-West and Rothe-Erde in the east. As the most westerly city in Germany, sitting on the frontiers of both Holland and Belgium, it was a major link in the railway network that would provide a route for reinforcements to the Normandy battle front. Other operations on this night were to be directed at coastal batteries in the Pas-de-Calais and war-industry factories in Holland and Belgium. 5 Group detailed forty-four Lancasters to attack the Ford Motor works in Antwerp, and fifty-nine for the Philips electronics factory at Eindhoven in southern Holland, and it was for the latter that 61 Squadron made ready nine Lancasters and dispatched them from Skellingthorpe between 22.58 and 23.10 with the four "usual suspects" the senior pilots on duty. P/O Norton and crew turned back early with port-inner engine failure, while the others were more than an hour into the outward journey when the Master Bomber sent them home by W/T, presumably after a Met Flight Mosquito crew had found poor visibility in the target area. There were no such difficulties at Antwerp, where the target was identified by illuminating flares, a yellow TI and red spotfires, despite which, post-raid reconnaissance revealed the factory to be intact.

The night of the 27/28th was to be one of feverish activity, which would generate more than eleven hundred sorties, reflecting the close proximity of the invasion, now just ten days away. The largest operation would bring a return to the military camp at Bourg Leopold in Belgium, the previous attack on which, two weeks earlier, had been abandoned part-way through. There was also a repeat of the Aachen attack of the 24th, which had failed to destroy the Rothe-Erde marshalling yards at the eastern end of the city and needed further attention. 5 Group was not involved in either of the above, and instead prepared forces of one hundred Lancasters and four Mosquitos and seventy-eight Lancasters and five Mosquitos respectively to target marshalling yards and workshops at Nantes and the aerodrome at Rennes, situated some fifty miles apart in north-western France. The group would also support operations against coastal batteries, of which there were five on this night, including one at Morsalines, situated on the eastern seaboard of the Cherbourg peninsula, some ten miles north of what, during the forthcoming Operation Overlord, would be the Americans' Utah landing ground.

53 Base was assigned to Nantes, and the sixteen 61 Squadron Lancasters departed Skellingthorpe between 22.28 and 23.10 with F/Ls Acott and Berry the senior pilots on duty, fourteen 1,000-pounders in each bomb bay and Australian F/Sgt Phil Martin and crew undertaking their first sortie since joining the squadron a few days earlier from 51 Base. The Martin crew would join 617 Squadron later in the year and an iconic cine-film of a Grand Slam dropping from the belly of their Lancaster towards the Arnsberg viaduct in March 1945 regularly appears in documentaries. They all reached the target area to find clear skies and good visibility, and the aiming-point marked by red spotfires, and the first fifty aircraft bombed so accurately, that the Master Bomber was satisfied and called a halt to proceedings. Eleven of the 61 Squadron element were among those delivering their bombs from 8,000 to 10,000 feet between 01.37 and 01.53, while the others jettisoned part of their load to facilitate a safe landing weight and brought the rest home.

On the 28th, 181 Lancasters and twenty Mosquitos were made ready to attack three coastal batteries overlooking the Normandy beaches, which, a week hence, would be the scene of Operation Overlord. The target for the eleven Lancasters each of 50 and 61 squadrons was at Sainte-Martin-de-Varrevilles, situated close to what would be Utah Beach, the landing ground for the American 1st Division. The 61 Squadron element departed Skellingthorpe between 22.29 and 22.53 with F/O Turner the senior pilot on duty, and each crew sitting on fifteen semi-armour-piercing (SAP) and general purpose (GP) 1,000-pounders of American manufacture, all of which reached the target under clear skies and in excellent visibility. The aiming-point was marked by red spotfires backed up by green TIs, and bombing took place from 6,400 to 9,000 feet between 00.26 and 00.40 in accordance with the instructions of a Master Bomber. Bomb bursts were observed close to the markers, and a large explosion occurred at 00.29, which suggested a successful conclusion to the operation, as far as that was possible at such difficult-to-eliminate targets.

On the 31st, 5 Group assembled a force of eighty-two Lancasters and four Mosquitos to attack a railway junction at Saumur in the Loire Valley, and another of sixty-eight Lancasters to target a coastal battery at Maisy, overlooking Omaha Beach. It was for the former that 61 Squadron prepared sixteen Lancasters, which departed Skellingthorpe between 22.58 and 23.49 with W/C Doubleday and S/L Beard the senior pilots on duty. They had to fly through a belt of storm-bearing clouds as they passed over Norfolk, heading south, during which JB138 was hit by lightning and entered a partial spin after the port wing dropped. Control was regained at 1,100 feet and cloud broken at 900 feet, but the Lancaster remained unstable, and P/O Freeman, having fallen twenty minutes behind schedule, opted to return to base. The others managed to negotiate the violent thunderstorm and reached the target to find clear skies and good visibility and orbited to await the instructions of the Master Bomber. Twelve 61 Squadron crews had carried out their attacks from 6,250 and 8,000 between 02.31 and 02.35, before a "stand-by" order was received, followed a few minutes later by "return to base", leaving W/C Doubleday and two others with their bomb loads intact. This operation was deemed to be a success, but cloud over the Maisy site caused the abandonment of the attack after just six crews had bombed.

During the course of the month the squadron carried out thirteen operations and dispatched 175 sorties for the loss of two Lancasters and one crew.

June 1944

June was to be a hectic month, which would make great demands on the crews for whom the bombing of coastal batteries was to be the priority during the first few days leading up to D-Day. However, 5 Group opened its account by returning to Saumur to attack a second railway junction on the 1st, a day which dawned cloudy and cold, and such conditions would persist throughout the first week of the month, causing concern among the invasion planners. The 53 Base squadrons remained at home, while fifty-eight Lancasters took off in the late evening to find ten-tenths cloud covering the route out to within twenty miles of the town, where it dispersed completely to leave clear skies and good visibility under a three-quarter moon. The flare force was almost superfluous in the conditions, but the first wave was called in by the Master Bomber, W/C Jeudwine, to release from 15,000 feet at 01.08, and the first red spot fire from an Oboe Mosquito fell bang on the aiming-point two minutes later. Smoke became a problem as it drifted across the area to obscure the spotfire that was still burning, and a green TI was dropped to maintain the aiming-point. Apart from a few scattered sticks to the north, and on an island in the Loire to the south, the attack seemed to be accurate. Returning crews reported little opposition, fires in the yards and a large explosion at 01.35, and the success of the raid was confirmed by photo-reconnaissance, which showed severe damage to the track.

Sixty-one 5 Group crews were called to briefings on the 2nd to be told that they would be attacking a heavy gun battery mounted on a rail platform at Wimereux, situated south-west of Calais. On their arrival the Master Bomber was uncomfortable with the conditions and called a halt to proceedings at 01.45, by which time some crews had already bombed. They had not been told the date of the invasion or where the landings would take place, and were not, therefore, aware that the operation was a smoke screen as part of the deception plan.

Seventeen 61 Squadron crews joined fifteen from 50 Squadron in the briefing room at Skellingthorpe on the 3rd to learn that they were to be part of a force of ninety-six Lancasters to attack a listening station at Ferme-d'Urville, situated on the Cherbourg peninsular to the west of the port, which had escaped damage when attacked by Halifaxes two nights earlier. They took off between 22.41 and 23.21 with S/Ls Beard and Woodroffe the senior pilots on duty, and all reached the target area to find clear skies and good visibility apart from ground haze. The first of three Oboe Mosquitos dropped a red TI at 00.50, and this was followed by a second one seven minutes later, and these were supplemented shortly afterwards by green TIs from the heavy marker aircraft. The 61 Squadron crews carried out their bombing from 5,500 to 10,000 feet between 01.01 and 01.07 and returned to report a successful attack that had been focused in a five-hundred-yard radius of the aiming-point. Photographic reconnaissance confirmed that the listening station had ceased to exist.

Orders came through on the 4th to prepare for attacks that night on coastal batteries, three in the Pas-de-Calais to maintain the deception, and the one at Maisy, overlooking the Utah and Omaha beaches. 259 aircraft of 1, 4, 5, 6 and 8 Groups were made ready, the majority for the deception targets, while fifty-two of the Lancasters, all representing 5 Group, were assigned to Maisy. 53 Base squadrons were not involved in these pre-dawn attacks, which took place through ten-tenths cloud with a base at around 4,000 feet. This necessitated the use of Oboe skymarkers, and positions were confirmed by Gee-fix and a faint red glow, before the bombing was carried out from just above the cloud tops. It was impossible to assess the outcome, and similar cloudy conditions had thwarted two of the three attempts in the Pas-de-Calais.

The night of the 5/6th was D-Day Eve, and during the course of the night, a record number of 1,211 sorties would be flown against coastal defences and in support and diversionary operations. Nineteen 61 Squadron crews attended briefing at Skellingthorpe, where no direct reference was made to the invasion, but unusually, they were given strict altitudes at which to fly and were told not to jettison bombs over the sea. They also learned that they would be among more than a thousand aircraft targeting ten heavy gun batteries along the Normandy coast, and that their specific objective was at Sainte-Pierre-du-Mont, which, although not disclosed to them, was the closest to Omaha Beach. The plan called for 5 Group to provide 115 Lancasters and four Mosquitos, among which would be a 97 (Straits Settlements) Squadron presence of seventeen Lancasters led by W/C Carter to provide the illumination and marking. 61 Squadron loaded its Lancasters with a mixture of 1,000 and 500-pounders and launched them from Skellingthorpe between 02.26 and 03.05 with W/C Doubleday and S/Ls Beard and Woodroffe the senior pilots on duty. They all arrived in the target area to find a layer of ten-tenths cloud with a base at around 7,000 feet and tops at 12,000 feet, with broken cloud below. The first Oboe marker was late and landed just off the shore, but others were accurate and were backed up by red and green TIs, before the 61 Squadron crews bombed from 6,250 to 12,500 feet between 04.41 and 05.02. Any homeward-bound crews looking down through the occasional gaps in the clouds were rewarded by the incredible sight of the greatest armada in history ploughing its way sedately southwards towards the French coast. A total of five thousand tons of bombs was dropped during the night, a new record and most of those returning to Skellingthorpe reported that the bombing appeared to be concentrated around the markers. However, S/L Woodroffe was scathing about the performance of the Master Bomber, who, he claimed, should have called the force down to below the cloud base rather than call for a general reduction in height of two thousand feet, which left half of the force in or above cloud and wasted 50% of the bombing. Only seven aircraft failed to return from these operations, three of them from Sainte-Pierre, two from 97 Squadron, including the one containing W/C "Jimmy" Carter and seven highly experienced others, all but one of whom held either a DFC or DFM.

As the beachheads were being established during the course of the 6th, preparations were put in hand to support the ground forces by attacking nine road and railway communications centres through which the enemy could bring reinforcements. 5 Group was assigned to two targets, Argentan supply depot and railway centre located some thirty miles south-east of Caen, and a road bridge in Caen itself, for which forces of 112 Lancasters and six Mosquitos and 120 Lancasters and four Mosquitos respectively were assembled. 61 Squadron made ready eighteen Lancasters for the former, and they departed Skellingthorpe between 23.16 and 23.58 with W/C Doubleday and S/Ls Beard and Woodroffe the senior pilots on duty. All reached the target area to find ten-tenths cloud with a base at 5,000 to 6,000 feet, below which, red spotfires and red TIs could be seen marking out the aiming-point. The 61 Squadron crews bombed from 3,000 to 6,100 feet between 01.27 and 01.40, in accordance with the Master Bomber's instructions, and observed a large explosion at 01.33, other bomb bursts and a number of fires. P/O Cooper and crew were attacked by two FW190s, the fire from which wounded the rear gunner, who, despite bleeding profusely, remained at his post until the attack was over. The port-outer engine had to be shut down and a landing was made at the first available airfield, the location of which was not recorded. At debriefing, at least three crews reported that a Lancaster had been shot down in flames over the Channel by Royal Navy flak, despite firing off colours of the day. Six Lancasters failed to return from the Caen raid, and this resulted largely from the need for the force to orbit while the markers were assessed. Post-raid reconnaissance confirmed severe damage to the railway installations and the town at Argentan.

Four railway targets were earmarked for attention by a force of 337 aircraft on the 7th, while elements of 5 Group were being prepared to join forces with 1 and 8 Groups to attack a six-way road junction at Balleroy, situated fifteen miles west of Caen on the approach to the Foret-de-Cerisy, where it was believed the enemy was concealing a fuel dump and tank units. The Skellingthorpe squadrons were not involved in the operation, which took place in conditions of ten-tenths cloud with a base at 8,000 to 10,000 feet and haze below. The initial Oboe markers appeared to be accurate and on time, but another marker fell simultaneously some five miles to the south-west and attracted some bomb loads. The Master Bomber quickly gained control of the situation and directed the bombing to the correct marker, which was pounded by concentrated bombing. Dense clouds of black smoke and one particularly large explosion were evidence of a successful outcome, during which the gunners in the crew of the 207 Squadron commanding officer shot down three enemy fighters in a twenty-minute period.

The night of the 8/9th was devoted to the disruption of railway communications, for which 483 aircraft were detailed and assigned to five centres, Skellingthorpe receiving orders to prepare seventeen Lancasters from each of its squadrons as part of a 5 Group force of ninety-seven Lancasters and four Mosquitos to attack railway installations at Rennes in Brittany. A second force of fifty-four Lancasters and four Mosquitos was assigned to a similar target at Pontabault, thirty miles to the north-east. 617 Squadron would also operate on this night to deliver the very first Barnes Wallis-designed 12,000lb Tallboy earthquake bombs against the railway tunnel at Saumur. The 61 Squadron element took off between 22.44 and 23.20 with S/L Woodroffe the senior pilot on duty, and all reached the target area to encounter ten-tenths thin cloud with a base at 6,000 to 7,000 feet. The aiming-point was marked by red spotfires and red and green TIs and bombed by the squadron from 4,000 to 9,000 feet between 01.36 and 01.55. Returning crews reported concentrated bombing on or near the markers, and the target area becoming obscured by smoke and dust as they withdrew.

401 aircraft from 1, 4, 6 and 8 Groups were detailed on the 9th to target airfields in the battle area, while 5 Group concentrated on a railway junction at Etampes, south of Paris. 108 Lancasters and four Mosquitos took part, while the Skellingthorpe squadrons stayed at home. Those reaching the target found eight to ten-tenths cloud with a base at 8,000 feet, and patches of two to three-tenths lower down at 4,000 feet, but this had had no effect on the marking with red spotfires, backed up with green and yellow TIs and illumination flares. Some crews thought that they had picked up a recall signal, and others a message at around midnight to orbit, until being called in to bomb. The Master Bomber called an end to bombing at 00.17, after what appeared to be a successful operation for the loss of six Lancasters. Photo-reconnaissance confirmed that all tracks had been cut for a distance of four hundred yards to the north-east of the junction, but it revealed also that the town had sustained collateral damage, which caused many civilian casualties.

5 Group detailed 108 Lancasters and four Mosquitos on the 10th and briefed the crews for an attack on marshalling yards in the city of Orleans, situated some thirty miles south-west of Paris. 61 Squadron made ready eighteen Lancasters, which departed Skellingthorpe between 22.10 and 22.47 with F/L Forrest the senior pilot on duty, and all reached northern France to find clear skies and good visibility, and the aiming-point marked by red spotfires and green TIs, which they bombed from 2,000 to 7,750 feet between 00.40 and 00.53. P/O White and crew were unable to identify the aiming point and brought their full bomb load home and a few crews at the tail end of the raid had not bombed when the Master Bomber called a halt to proceedings and told them to return their bombs to store. The consensus was that the success of the operation depended on the accuracy of the markers, which had attracted the bulk of the bombing, but there were no post-raid reports to confirm the outcome.

The campaign against communications targets continued on the 12th at six locations, including Caen and Poitiers, for which 5 Group detailed forces of 109 Lancasters and four Mosquitos and 112 Lancasters and four Mosquitos respectively. 61 Squadron made ready eighteen Lancasters to take part at the latter, situated in west-central France, and they departed Skellingthorpe between 22.15 and 22.49 with F/Ls Forrest, Jeavons, Norton and Turner the senior pilots on duty. All reached the target area, where they encountered clear skies with good visibility, conditions which they exploited to deliver their four 1,000 and twelve 500-pounders each onto the red spotfires and red and green TIs from 6,700 to 10,000 feet between 01.45 and 02.00. A number of large explosions were witnessed, and the fires remained visible for fifty miles into the return journey, but it was photo-reconnaissance that revealed the Paris to Bordeaux line to have been cut in seven places.

A new oil campaign began on this night, prosecuted by 286 Lancasters and seventeen Mosquitos of 1, 3 and 8 Groups, whose target was the Nordstern (Gelsenberg A.G.) plant at Gelsenkirchen. Such was the accuracy of the attack, that all production of vital aviation fuel was halted for a number of weeks at a cost to the Germans of a thousand tons per day.

The 14th brought the Command's first daylight operation since the departure of 2 Group twelve months earlier. The target was the port of Le Havre, from where the enemy's fast, light marine craft were posing a threat to Allied shipping supplying the Normandy beachheads. The two-phase operation was conducted by predominantly 1 and 3 Groups with 617 Squadron representing 5 Group and took place in the evening under the umbrella of a fighter escort. The attack was highly successful, and few craft survived the onslaught. Other operations on this night were directed against railway installations at three locations in France, while elements of 4, 5 and 8 Groups attended to enemy troop and vehicle concentrations at Aunay-sur-Odon and Évrecy near Caen. 5 Group assembled a force of 214 Lancasters and five Mosquitos for the former, of which the nineteen provided by 61 Squadron departed Skellingthorpe between 22.12 and 22.50 with F/Ls Jeavons, Norton and Turner the senior pilots on duty. The weather was generally clear with some low cloud, but this did not hamper the marking process, which proceeded punctually and accurately. W/C Jeudwine was the Master Bomber, with 83 Squadron's W/C "Joe" Northrop as Deputy, and the latter made four passes over the target, at 00.30 at 8,000 feet, 00.41 at 10,000 feet, and at 00.54 and 01.00 at 11,000 feet, dropping clusters of flares on the first two, green TIs on the third and red TIs on the fourth. The 61 Squadron crews bombed the TIs from 6,000 to 10,000 feet between 00.32 and 01.07, observing what appeared to be a concentrated attack that produced explosions, numerous fires and much black smoke.

A force of 297 aircraft from 1, 4, 5, 6 and 8 Groups was assembled on that day to try to do to Boulogne what had been done to Le Havre twenty-four hours earlier. It was again left to 617 Squadron to represent 5 Group, and the operation was concluded with equal success. While this was in progress, 5 Group dispatched 110 Lancasters and four Mosquitos to deal with a fuel dump at Châtellerault, situated between Tours and Poitiers in western France. 61 Squadron loaded seventeen Lancasters with two 1,000 and fourteen-500 pounders each and dispatched them from Skellingthorpe between 21.07 and 21.42 with F/Ls Forrest, Jeavons and Turner the senior pilots on duty. Clear skies and good visibility greeted their arrival in the target area, and red spotfires and green TIs marked out the aiming-point for the 61 Squadron crews to bomb from 7,000 to 10,000 feet between 00.53 and 01.04. On the way home over London, the local flak opened up and continued to fire despite the firing of the colours of the day, and two 61 Squadron Lancasters arrived home damaged. Absent from debriefing was the crew of P/O Goodyer RNZAF, the first to go missing for more than a month, and all had lost their lives when ME783 crashed on French soil. Post-raid reconnaissance confirmed that eight out of thirty-five individual fuel storage sites within the target had been destroyed.

The Skellingthorpe squadrons remained at home on the 16th, when plans were put in hand to launch 829 sorties that night against a number of targets in what was the second new campaign to begin during the month. The first V-1 flying bombs had landed on London three days earlier, prompting a response by Bomber Command to target the revolutionary weapon's launching and storage sites in the Pas-de-Calais. Four targets were earmarked for attention, the one handed to 5 Group a storage site at Beauvoir, located some twenty miles inland from Berck-sur-Mer. The large storage sites, many in various stages of construction, were referred to in Bomber Command parlance as "constructional works", while others, called "ski sites", were small buildings in the shape of a hockey stick and were attached to launching ramps. 112 Lancasters were detailed, and those reaching the target area found nine to ten-tenths cloud with tops at 6,000 to 8,000 feet and bombed on the faint glow of red Oboe markers. It was impossible to assess the outcome, which left crews with little to pass on to the intelligence section at debriefing. The oil campaign continued on this night in the hands of 1, 4, 6 and 8 Groups at Sterkrade-Holten, a district of Oberhausen in the Ruhr and home to the Ruhr-Chemie synthetic oil plant, but cloudy conditions caused the bombing to be scattered, and there was little impact on production.

The 5 Group ORB records that eighteen Lancasters and two Mosquitos were sent to attack the constructional works at Watten on the 19th, and that all but one had bombed and one direct hit was scored. The 61 Squadron ORB, on the other hand, records that twenty-two Lancasters departed Skellingthorpe between 22.14 and 22.55 with S/L Beard the senior pilot on duty and eleven 1,000 and four 500-pounders in each bomb bay, but all were recalled before reaching the target and the delayed-action 1,000 and 500-pounders jettisoned into the sea.

5 Group had to wait until Mid-Summer's Night, the 21st, before becoming involved in the oil offensive, and was handed two targets to attack simultaneously. A force of 120 Lancasters from 52 and 55 Bases and 83 Squadron Lancasters and six Mosquitos of 54 Base was assigned to the Union Rheinische Braunkohlen-Treibstoff refinery at Wesseling, south of Cologne, and 120 Lancasters and four Mosquitos from 53 and 54 Bases to the Hydrierwerke Scholven plant in the Buer district of Gelsenkirchen, both with a sprinkling of ABC Lancasters of 101 Squadron for RCM duties and the latter including a number of Oboe Mosquitos to carry out the initial marking. 61 Squadron made ready twenty-one Lancasters for Scholven-Buer, and they departed Skellingthorpe between 22.54 and 23.33 with F/Ls Acott, Forrest, Jeavons, Norton and Turner the senior pilots on duty. F/L Norton and crew were at the midpoint of the North Sea crossing when the starboard-inner engine caught fire and ended their interest in proceedings, while P/O Passant and crew were some five miles north of Eindhoven when damaged by a night-fighter, which left the bomb doors inoperable and forced them also to abandon their sortie.

Those arriving in the target area expected to find clear skies, instead of which they encountered ten-tenths cloud with a very low base, which, at a stroke, rendered the 5 Group low-level marking method ineffective. Instead of marking by 627 Squadron Mosquitos, the preliminary 8 Group Mosquito Oboe markers had to be backed up by Lancaster-delivered red and green TIs, the glow from which could be observed only dimly through the cloud. The 61 Squadron element aimed for these from 17,000 to 20,000 feet between 01.38 and 01.47 and found it impossible to assess the outcome, but at least all returned to base, while eight from the group failed to do so. Night-fighters had been waiting to greet them as they crossed Holland outbound, and the Lancaster containing the crew of a 50 Squadron flight commander was one of at least six to fall victim in this way. Although most considered the operation to have been a failure, a secret German report would suggest a 20% loss of production for a limited period.

While this operation was in progress, matters were going seriously awry for the Wesseling force, and a catastrophic ordeal was befalling it, that would make the above casualty figure seem like a slight flesh wound. The Luftwaffe Nachtjagd got amongst the Lancasters during the approach to the target and were responsible for the majority of the casualties resulting from this operation. Those reaching Wesseling had also expected to find clear skies, and conditions ideal for the 5 Group low-level marking method, but were met instead by ten-tenths low cloud and accurate predicted heavy flak. This meant, that low-level marking was not an option, and, faced with this situation, the Master Bomber, W/C James "Willie" Tait, had ordered a blind attack, forcing the Lancaster crews to bomb on H2S or the feint glow of red TIs. After the war, a secret German report would suggest a 40% loss of production at the site, but this was probably of very short duration, as the limited number of casualties on the ground pointed to a scattered and largely ineffective raid. Whatever the level of success, it was gained at the high cost of thirty-seven Lancasters, a massive 28%, and all but two of them belonged to 5 Group Squadrons. 44, 49, 57 and 619 Squadrons each lost six Lancasters, although one from 57 ditched off the English coast and the crew was rescued, while 207 and 630 Squadrons each had five empty dispersals to contemplate in the cold light of dawn.

While more than four hundred aircraft of 3, 4, 6 and 8 Groups targeted four flying-bomb sites on the 23rd, elements of 1 and 5 Groups were sent respectively against marshalling yards at Saintes and Limoges in western France. Ninety-seven Lancasters and four Mosquitos were detailed for the latter, with 53 Base squadrons among those in action, including twenty-one representing 61 Squadron, which departed Skellingthorpe between 22.22 and 23.02 with F/Ls Acott, Berry, Norton and Turner the senior pilots on duty, and all reached the target area to find clear skies and good visibility, in which ground features like the River Vienne and the railway sidings stood out prominently. Red spotfires and green TIs marked out the aiming-point, which the 61 Squadron crews bombed from 5,000 to 8,000 feet between 02.00 and 02.09, observing a number of large explosions, fires and much smoke. Returning crews were confident in the quality of their work and post-raid reconnaissance confirmed a highly accurate and concentrated attack.

617 Squadron had attempted to continue the Tallboy assault on the constructional works at Wizernes in daylight on the 22nd, but the attack had been abandoned in the face of ten-tenths low cloud. The squadron returned the bombs to store and brought them back to France on the 24th to score a number of direct hits.

Thirty-seven crews were called to briefing at Skellingthorpe later on the 24th to learn of their part in a busy night of operations involving more than seven hundred aircraft targeting seven flying-bomb sites. 5 Group was assigned to Pommeréval and Prouville, situated respectively some fifteen miles south-east of Dieppe, and east of Abbeville, and detailed 103 Lancasters and four Mosquitos for each. The 53 Base squadrons were among those assigned to the latter, and 61 Squadron's twenty participants took off between 22.31 and 23.15 with F/Ls Berry, Forrest, Jeavons and Turner the senior pilots on duty. P/O Watkins and crew were approaching the French coast when the starboard-outer engine began to leak oil and persuaded them to turn back. It is believed that the others reached the target area, where clear skies prevailed, and only slight ground haze lay between the Lancasters and the aiming-point. The preliminary Oboe Mosquito was punctual, but the subsequent marking was hampered by intense searchlight activity working in co-operation with flak and night-fighters, and bombing was delayed while the aiming-point was positively identified and marked. It took until all of the illuminator flares had been expended before the low-level Mosquitos dropped red spotfires and the heavy brigade from 97 Squadron backed up with red and green TIs. The 61 Squadron crews delivered their attacks from 9,000 to 13,000 feet between 00.21 and 00.40 in accordance with the instructions of the Master Bomber, and the impression was of a somewhat haphazard attack that lacked concentration. Thirteen Lancasters failed to return, possibly as a result of the delay in opening the attack, and among them were four from Skellingthorpe. 61 Squadron's LM518 was shot down by a night-fighter and crashed near Bienfay, west-south-west of Abbeville, and only the flight engineer survived from the experienced crew of F/L Forrest RAAF. ND987 came down in the same general area and P/O Kramer RCAF perished with all but the rear gunner who was helped by local partisans to evade capture.

More than seven hundred aircraft were detailed for operations against six flying-bomb sites on the 27th, while two railway yards would occupy the attention of other elements. There were two targets for 5 Group, a flying-bomb site at Marquise, situated some five miles inland from Cap Gris-Nez, and railway yards at Vitry-le-Francois south-east of Reims. 103 Lancasters and four Mosquitos were assigned to the latter, 53 Base squadrons providing the main force element, of which the nineteen belonging to 61 Squadron departed Skellingthorpe between 21.29 and 22.09 with F/Ls Acott, Norton and Turner the senior pilots on duty. P/O Passant and crew lost their port inner engine soon after take-off, leaving the others to continue on to the target, which they reached to find varying amounts of cloud between zero and seven-tenths at around 7,000 feet, but good visibility and the aiming-point clearly marked by red spotfires and green TIs. Bombing took place from 5,000 to 7,500 feet between 01.46 and 01.56, at which point the Master Bomber called a halt and ordered crews with bombs still aboard to take them home. The 61 Squadron crews of F/O Church and P/O Bates were among these, as was 50 Squadron's newly appointed commanding officer, W/C Frogley, who was critical of the decision to abandon the attack, suggesting that, if the first spotfire had not been accurate, the bombing should never even have started in the first place. In fact, it had been smoke obscuring the aiming-point that prompted the Master Bomber to send the final wave home with their bombs. P/O Dear and crew reported a fault in the bomb door mechanism which prevented the bombs from being released on the target, and they were let go the moment the bomb doors opened.

Although the month's operational activity was over for some elements of 5 Group, 53 and 54 Bases were alerted on the 29th to provide eighty-five Lancasters and four Mosquitos as part of an overall force of 286 Lancasters and nineteen Mosquitos of 1, 5 and 8 Groups for a daylight attack on two flying-bomb launching sites and one storage site. Eighteen 61 Squadron Lancasters departed Skellingthorpe between 11.53 and 12.15 bound for the previously-attacked Beauvoir storage site, located twenty miles inland from the Pas-de-Calais coast with S/L Woodroffe the senior pilot on duty. They reached the target to find clear conditions beneath the 15,000-foot cloud level and bombed either visually or on red TIs from 14,000 to 19,000 feet between 13.45 and 14.09, observing large volumes of smoke, which partially obscured the site. The attack was believed to have been concentrated around the aiming-point, and losses amounted to a single Lancaster and Mosquito.

During the course of the month, the squadron operated on fourteen occasions and dispatched a record 264 sorties for the loss of three Lancasters and crews.

July 1944

The new month began as June had ended, with flying-bomb sites providing employment for over three hundred aircraft on both the 1st and 2nd, but it was the 4th before the Independent Air Force was invited to re-enter the fray, when called upon to attack a V-Weapon storage site in caves at St-Leu-d'Esserent, some thirty miles north of Paris. The caves had originally been used for growing mushrooms, and they were protected by some twenty-five feet of clay and soft limestone, to say nothing of the anti-aircraft defences brought in by the Germans. There were actually two aiming points, the first of which was the road and railway communications to the area dump for the main force of 211 Lancasters and eleven Mosquitos of 5 Group, plus three 101 Squadron ABC Lancasters to provide RCM cover, and three 8 Group Oboe Mosquitos to carry out the marking of an initial reference-point. The second aiming point was the tunnel complex at Creil, a settlement located three miles north-east of St Leu, for which a force was detailed comprising seventeen Lancasters, a Mosquito and Cheshire's Mustang from 617 Squadron and forty-nine Lancasters from 52 Base. The twenty 61 Squadron Lancasters departed Skellingthorpe between 22.55 and 23.35 with five pilots of flight lieutenant rank leading the way. P/O Parker and crew were among a number to misinterpret a signal from the Master Bomber as they passed to the east of Rouen at 01.13 and turned back, leaving the rest to complete the forty miles to reach the target area under clear skies and in good visibility, which was of equal assistance to the enemy's night-fighter force.

Despite the absence of searchlights, the expected volume of flak was thrown up as the two elements ran across their respective aiming points, the 61 Squadron crews carrying out their attacks with 1,000 and 500-pounders from 12,000 to 18,000 feet between 01.35 and 01.45. Night-fighters pounced on the bombers over the target and on the route home and thirteen Lancasters were missing from their stations, one of them belonging to 61 Squadron. EE186 was a veteran with thirteen months of service with 49, 106 and 61 Squadrons behind it and crashed at around 02.00 at Harquency, a town located to the east of the Seine and some twenty miles south-east of Rouen. P/O North and crew were able to save themselves five to fall into enemy hands, while the flight engineer and navigator were spirited away by local partisans to evade a similar fate. Post-raid reconnaissance revealed that a large area of subsidence had blocked the side entrance to the caves at St-Leu and that the road and railway links had been cut over a distance of four hundred yards.

On the 6th, over five hundred aircraft were engaged on operations against V-Weapons targets, and 617 Squadron was assigned to a V-3 super-gun site at Mimoyecques. Originally planned as one of two sites near Cap Gris Nez containing twenty-five barrels each, test failures and delays meant that a single three-barrel shaft stretching a hundred metres into the limestone hill, five miles from the coast and 103 miles from its target, was all that existed at the time. Each fifteen-metre-long smooth-bore barrel, which was angled at 50 degrees and aimed at London, was designed on the multiple-charge principle to progressively boost the acceleration of the one-ton projectile as it travelled towards the muzzle. Once completed, the site would be capable of pounding London at the rate of hundreds of rounds per day without let-up. It was protected by a concrete slab thirty meters wide and five-and-a-half meters thick, which was correctly believed by the designers to be impregnable to conventional bombs. It had been attacked on a number of occasions without success, but 617 Squadron scored direct hits with Tallboys, and provisional reconnaissance revealed four deep craters in the immediate target area, one causing a large corner of the concrete slab to collapse. The extent of the damage underground would not be apparent to the planners at Bomber Command, but the shafts and tunnels had collapsed, and the site had been abandoned. Although Cheshire did not know it, this was to be his final operation, not only with 617 Squadron, but also of the war in Europe.

At around this time, S/L Woodroffe was posted to 54 Base, where he would join 5 Group's Master Bomber fraternity, a vacancy having been opened up after the departure of W/C James Tait to succeed Cheshire as commanding officer of 617 Squadron. The authorities were not convinced that the site at St-Leu-d'Esserent had received terminal damage and scheduled another attack on it for the late evening of the 7th. Before the operation got under way, more than 450 aircraft from 1, 4, 6 and 8 Groups had carried out the first major operation in support of the Canadian 1st and British 2nd Armies, which were trying to break out of Caen. The target had been changed from German-fortified villages to an area of open ground north of Caen, where almost 2,300 tons of bombs were dropped somewhat ineffectively, and ultimately, that decision proved to be counter-productive by causing damage to the northern suburbs of the city rather than to German forces.

5 Group detailed 208 Lancasters and fifteen Mosquitos for St-Leu, the 61 Squadron element of seventeen departing Skellingthorpe between 22.06 and 22.43 with F/Ls Grantham, Jeavons, Norton and Stone the senior pilots on duty. F/L Norton and crew were over the Channel some twenty miles south of Worthing when the failure of their port-inner engine ended their interest in proceedings. The others arrived in the target area to find medium-level cloud, which prevented the moonlight from providing illumination, although the visibility was good below the cloud level. The Master Bomber was the former 207 Squadron pilot, W/C Ed Porter, and he oversaw the delivery of the Oboe yellow TI at 01.06, which was followed by the first stick of flares four minutes later. The first red spot fire went down at 01.08, a hundred yards south of the aiming point but in line with the direction of the bombing run and backing-up by red and green TIs continued until 01.13. The marking was assessed as sufficiently accurate to call in the main force at 01.15, and the 61 Squadron crews dropped their loads of eleven 1,000 and four-500 pounders each from 11,250 to 15,000 feet between 01.13 and 01.29. The Master Bomber's VHF was indistinct, so 83 Squadron's S/L Eggins assumed control and sent the force home at 01.25.

Twenty-nine Lancasters and two Mosquitos failed to return after night-fighters got amongst them, and this represented 14% of the force and another sobering night for 5 Group at a time when the losses from Mid-Summer's Night was still an open wound. There was particular dismay at Skellingthorpe at the failure to return of three 50 Squadron Lancasters and two from 61 Squadron, the veteran R5856 and the more recently acquired ND867. The former was some nine miles north-west of Creil and closing on the aiming point at St-Leu when rent by the explosion of the bomb load, which distributed wreckage over a wide area and took the lives of P/O Passant RAAF and his crew. The latter crashed at around 01.30 at Moliens, some twenty miles south of Abbeville, killing F/L Grantham and four of his crew and leaving the flight engineer in enemy hands and the bomb-aimer under the protection of local partisans. Photo-reconnaissance revealed that both ends of the tunnel complex had collapsed, as had a section in the middle, and the approach road and rail links had been heavily cratered and blocked. There was no immediate opportunity for the afflicted squadrons, particularly 106 and 207, which had lost five crews each, to "get back on the horse", and there must have been a sombre air, while the populations of RAF Metheringham and Spilsby joined with those at Skellingthorpe to come to terms with the loss of thirty-five familiar faces in one night. A special congratulatory message arrived on the participating stations from A-O-C, AVM Sir Ralph Cochrane, who considered it the finest effort by the group to successfully press home the attack in the face of the fiercest opposition.

Operations were posted on 5 Group stations on the 10th and 11th, and then cancelled, before the 12th, when a dozen 61 Squadron crews were called to briefing to be given the details of that night's operation against railway installations at Culmont-Chalindrey in eastern France. Two aiming points were planned, at the western and eastern ends, for which a force of 157 Lancasters and four Mosquitos was made ready, and while this operation was in progress, another by elements of 1 Group would take place further south at a railway junction at Revigny. The 61 Squadron element departed Skellingthorpe between 21.45 and 22.12 with F/Ls Acott, Jeavons and Norton the senior pilots on duty and headed for Bridport to begin the Channel crossing. At the Channel Islands, the bomber stream turned east-south-east to traverse the Cherbourg peninsula and pass south of Paris to reach the target. Eight-tenths low cloud prevailed until shortly before the target area, where the conditions improved to provide clear skies, and promisingly, no sign of defensive activity from the ground. The controller at the eastern aiming point experienced VHF communications problems, which delayed that part of the attack, and eventually the entire force was directed to the western aiming point. The 61 Squadron crews delivered their eight 1,000 and three 500-pounders each onto two red spotfires from 5,000 to 8,000 feet between 01.54 and 02.12, and explosions were observed, followed by fires that remained visible for fifty miles into the return flight. The high proportion of delayed action fuses in use prevented an immediate assessment of results, but post-raid reconnaissance would confirm an effective operation.

Eight Lancasters were provided by each of the Skellingthorpe squadrons on the 14th for an attack on the huge marshalling yards at Villeneuve-St-Georges, situated on the southern rim of Paris. They were part of a force of 111 Lancasters, six Mosquitos and an American twin-engine P38 Lightning containing the Master Bomber, W/C Jeudwine and those from 61 Squadron took off between 22.04 and 22.19 with F/Ls Simmons, Stone and Turner the senior pilots on duty and a mix of 1,000 and 500-pounders in each bomb bay. All reached the target area to find a large amount of cloud with a base at 5,000 feet and clear conditions below, but W/C Jeudwine was having compass trouble and would arrive on target twelve minutes late, so contacted his Deputy, 83 Squadron's W/C Joe Northrop, to take matters in hand. Joe could clearly see the target and judging the Oboe marker to be within fifty yards of the planned aiming-point, called in the 5 Group marker force, which lobbed the TIs within the confines of the yards, and the operation appeared to be proceeding smoothly and precisely according to plan. The 61 Squadron crews bombed on red and green TIs from 6,000 to 8,000 feet between 01.35 and 01.55, and most of the hardware hit the yards, while a proportion also fell outside to the east. Meanwhile, 1 Group had returned to Revigny, but had been thwarted by ground haze, which forced the Master Bomber to abandon the attack before any bombing could take place. Seven Lancasters were lost for no gain, and it would fall to 5 Group to finish the job a few nights hence at great expense.

Flying-bomb sites and railways dominated the target list on the 15th, and 5 Group was handed a railway junction at Nevers, a city on the northern bank of the Loire in central France, for which 61 Squadron made ready eight Lancasters as part of the force of 104 with four Mosquitos to carry out the low-level marking. They departed Skellingthorpe between 22.19 and 22.30 with five pilots of flight lieutenant rank leading the way and all reached the target after an outward flight of more than three-and-a-half hours. They found clear skies with a little haze and favourable conditions, which the marker force exploited to mark promptly and accurately. The 61 Squadron crews delivered their nine 1,000 and four-500 pounders each onto a red spotfire and green TIs from 4,000 to 5,500 feet between 02.01 and 02.08, but as the entire force was carrying delayed-action ordnance, no immediate assessment could be made. A large explosion suggested, perhaps, that an ammunition train or dump had been hit and photographic reconnaissance later in the day revealed that the Nevers site had been all but obliterated and much rolling stock damaged.

Eighteen 61 Squadron crews were called to briefing at midnight on the 17/18th to learn of their part in a tactical support operation to be carried out at dawn by a force of 942 aircraft, of which 201 of the Lancasters were to be provided by 5 Group. It was the start of the ground forces' Operation Goodwood, which was Montgomery's plan for a decisive breakout into wider France as a prelude to the march towards the German frontier. The aiming points were five enemy-held villages to the east of Caen, Colombelles, Mondeville, Sannerville, Cagny and Manneville, all of which stood in the path of the advancing British 2nd Army. The 61 Squadron contingent departed Skellingthorpe between 03.29 and 04.24 with S/Ls Beard and Richard Pexton the senior pilots on duty, the latter, a former fighter pilot, having arrived from 51 Base early in the month. All reached the target area to find their aiming point, the Mondeville steel works, which the Germans had converted into a strongly defended fortress, already marked by red and yellow TIs but about to be swallowed up and obscured by drifting smoke. Bombing by the 61 Squadron crews took place from 6,000 to 10,000 feet between 05.42 and 06.11, either overshooting the yellow TIs or undershooting the reds in accordance with instructions from the Master Bomber, and as far as could be determined, most of the hardware fell accurately where intended. The RAF dropped five thousand tons of bombs to good effect onto the two German divisions in just half an hour, and the Americans followed up with a further two thousand tons.

Operations were not done for the day, and eight 61 Squadron crews joined eight from 50 squadron at briefing at teatime to learn of their part in what promised to be an unspectacular and routine operation, six of them, those of F/L Stone and F/Os Bates, Cooper, Gilmore, Inness and Martin, about to undertake their second sortie of the day. Following two failed attempts by 1 Group to cut a railway junction at Revigny at a combined cost of seventeen Lancasters, the job was handed to a 5 Group element of 109 Lancasters, four Mosquitos and a P38 Lightning containing the Master Bomber, W/C Jeudwine. It was to be a busy night of operations, which included another railway and two oil targets, along with support and diversionary activities involving a total of 972 sorties. 61 Squadron launched eight Lancasters from Skellingthorpe between 23.03 and 23.19 with F/Ls Parker and Stone the senior pilots on duty and they crossed the French coast near Dieppe, passing through an intense searchlight belt some twenty miles inland. The other Bomber Command operations had come and gone and the attention of the Luftwaffe night-fighters was now fixed on the Revigny-bound force, making contact with it shortly after it entered enemy airspace and harrying it all the way into eastern France. One of the early casualties was 61 Squadron's DV304, which was shot down by a night-fighter to crash at Marcilly, north-north-east of Paris with no survivors from among the eight occupants captained by P/O Cooper. It was one of sixteen Lancasters to fall victim to night-fighters and one to flak within forty-five minutes, the first eleven falling during the long, straight leg to the final turning point at Aube. The surviving crews reached the target to find clear skies, but haze obscuring ground detail, and this elusive target continued to present problems, beginning with the first wave of flares, delivered at about 01.30, which were too far to the east. More flares were ordered, and the bombing was put back by five minutes, while Wanganui markers were dropped by Mosquito, and the situation was assessed.

F/O Bates and crew were at 8,000 feet a few miles south-west of the target when a Ju88 was spotted by the gunners at 150 yards range on the starboard beam and slightly below. They opened fire and hit the enemy's port engine, mainplane and fuselage and watched a fire develop, but failing to observe it crash, claimed it only as damaged. Eleven minutes later, while bearing down on the aiming point, an unidentified enemy aircraft attacked with rocket projectiles from 350 yards range and missed, and this time Sgt Hancock and P/O Fletcher had the satisfaction of shooting it down and watching it impact the ground. Unfortunately, the engagement had occurred at a critical time in the bombing run, and as the target could not be picked up again, the bombs were eventually jettisoned on the way home. Meanwhile, the whole attack seemed chaotic, and the use of many delayed-action bombs meant that it was difficult to see what was happening on the ground until F/O Inness and crew scored a direct hit from 7,600 feet at 01.43. Three of the supposedly delayed-action 1,000-pounders detonated on impact and produced a blinding flash, which many crews reported at debriefing appeared to be an ammunition truck exploding, and this belief was backed up by photographic evidence. The other 61 Squadron crews were over the target at 7,000 to 10,000 feet between 01.43 and 01.47 and released their eleven 1,000 and four 500-pounders each onto a red spotfire, in accordance with instructions from the Master Bomber. Photo-reconnaissance revealed that the operation had been successful in cutting the railway link to the battle front, but had cost twenty-four Lancasters, almost 22% of those dispatched. *(For a full and highly detailed account of the three Revigny raids, read the amazing book, Massacre over the Marne, by Oliver Clutton-Brock.*

5 Group crews stood-by on the 19th for a possible daylight operation, and it was evening before orders came through to prepare for an attack on a flying-bomb storage site at Thiverny, situated just to the north of St-Leu-d'Esserent. A force of 103 Lancasters and two Mosquitos was made ready, eight of the former provided by 61 Squadron, which departed Skellingthorpe between 19.15 and 19.27 with S/L Pexton the senior pilot on duty. The attack was to take place in daylight under the protection of a Spitfire escort, which was picked up at the south coast and all from the squadron reached the target in fine weather conditions, but with ground haze making it difficult to identify the aiming-point. Late preliminary marking by the Path Finder element and communications problems between the Master Bomber and his Deputy added to the frustrations and led to most crews having to bomb visually in the face of moderate to intense heavy flak bursting as high as 18,000 feet. They were over the target between 21.30 and 21.37 at altitudes ranging from 15,000 to 18,000 feet, and the operation was concluded without loss. Reconnaissance revealed some loose bombing, but sufficient aiming-point photographs were brought back to suggest a successful outcome.

Railway yards and a triangle junction at Courtrai (Kortrijk) in Belgium provided the targets for a joint effort by 1, 5 and 8 Groups on the 20th, for which 61 Squadron contributed seventeen Lancasters to the 5 Group force of 190 Lancasters and five Mosquitos. They departed Skellingthorpe between 22.58 and 23.36 with S/L Pexton the senior pilot on duty, and all reached the target area to find it free of cloud and slightly obscured by ground haze. The Oboe marking was well-placed in the marshalling yards and backed up by green TIs, onto which the squadron participants delivered their eleven 1,000 and four 500-pounders each from 10,400 to 13,750 feet between 00.56 and 01.05. They returned home safely to report a large orange explosion at 00.57 and a successful outcome, which was confirmed by post-raid reconnaissance that revealed both aiming-points to have been obliterated in return for the loss of nine Lancasters.

Following two nights at home for 5 Group and a two-month break from city-busting, Harris sanctioned a major raid on the naval and shipbuilding port of Kiel on the 23rd, for which a force of 629 aircraft was made ready. S/L Pexton was the senior pilot on duty as the nine 61 Squadron Lancasters departed Skellingthorpe between 22.46 and 23.05 as part of a 5 Group force of ninety-nine Lancasters. They headed for the rendezvous point to form up behind an elaborate "Mandrel" jamming screen laid on by 100 Group, before setting course for Denmark's western coast. *(In November 1943, 100 Group had been formed to take over the Radio Countermeasures (RCM) role, which had been the preserve of 101 Squadron since its introduction a number of months earlier. 101 Squadron, however, would remain in 1 Group and continue to provide RCM for the remainder of the war.)* When they arrived unexpectedly and with complete surprise in Kiel airspace, they rendered the enemy night-fighter controller confused and unable to bring his night-fighter resources to bear. Kiel was covered by a nine to ten-tenths veil of thin cloud with tops at 4,000 feet and a skymarking plan was put into action, which enabled the main force crews to bomb on the glow, first of the flares, and then of fires. The 61 Squadron contingent carried out their attacks from 16,000 to 19,000 feet between 01.24 and 01.30, and although the glow of fires remained visible for a hundred miles into the return journey to suggest an effective raid, it was not possible to determine the outcome. However, local sources conceded that this had been the town's most destructive raid of the war and had inflicted heavy damage on the port and shipyards, cutting off water supplies for three days and gas for three weeks. Many delayed-action bombs had been dropped, and these continued to cause problems for some time.

5 Group divided its forces on the 24th to enable it to support the first of a three-raid series in five nights on the southern city of Stuttgart and an oil refinery and fuel dump at Donges, situated on the north bank of the River Loire to the east of St-Nazaire. The latter target had been attacked successfully by elements of 6 and 8 Groups on the previous night but clearly required further attention, and 5 Group detailed 104 Lancasters and four Mosquitos, ten of the former belonging to 61 Squadron, to take matters in hand, supported by five 8 Group Oboe Mosquitos. A further ninety-nine Lancasters were provided by 5 Group for southern Germany in an overall force of 614, the 61 Squadron contingent of nine departing Skellingthorpe between 21.35 and 21.50 with F/Ls Acott, Jeavons, Norton and Parker the senior pilots on duty, to be followed into the air between 22.16 and 22.36 by Donges-bound force led by S/Ls Beard and Pexton. They arrived in the target area to find clear skies and excellent visibility, which the marker element exploited to leave the aiming point accurately marked with green TIs. The 61 Squadron crews carried out their attacks from 8,250 to 11,000 feet between 01.43 and 01.51 in accordance with the instructions of the Master Bomber and large explosions were observed at 01.46 and 01.49, the former followed by a column of thick, black smoke. They set course for home fairly satisfied with the outcome, although it was impossible to make an accurate assessment after smoke drifted across the site to obscure detail. On return, P/O Bates and reported that a Lancaster had fired upon them and bullets had hit a tail fin and fuselage, and ND902 had been further damaged in the fuselage by heavy flak.

Meanwhile, some five hundred miles to the east, clear skies and good visibility greeted the main force crews and enable them to pick out ground detail in the light of the illuminator flares. The raid progressed more or less according to plan and returning crews reported a glow of fires covering an area of perhaps five square miles, which remained visible for eighty miles into the return journey. The 61 squadron crews had lost the services of F/L Jeavons and crew to an engine issue early on, while F/L Norton and crew had been attacked by a night-fighter at Karlsruhe and continued on to the target on three engines shedding height to 14,000 feet. Sadly, their determination and press-on spirit was not rewarded as the bomb doors refused to open and the bombs could not be released. They were eventually jettisoned manually but once opened the bomb doors could not be shut, and they were still deployed when a landing was carried out on the emergency strip at Woodbridge in Suffolk. The others from the squadron played their part from 18,500 to 22,000 feet between 01.49 and 02.04, but no local report came out of Stuttgart to confirm the degree of damage. However, it had been a successful and destructive raid, although gained at a cost of seventeen Lancasters and four Halifaxes.

5 Group split its forces again on the 25th to support the second of the raids on Stuttgart with eighty-three Lancasters and a daylight attack on an aerodrome and signals depot at Saint-Cyr involving ninety-four Lancasters and six Mosquitos. *(There are at least four locations called Saint-Cyr, and it is believed that the one targeted on this night was in the Ile-de-France to the west of Paris.)* 61 Squadron briefed eighteen crews for the latter operation, while loading their Lancasters with a cookie, a single 1,000 pounder and fourteen 500-pounders each and dispatching them from Skellingthorpe between 17.11 and 18.01 with W/C Doubleday and S/L Pexton the senior pilots on duty. They all enjoyed an incident-free outward flight and arrived at the target to find good visibility below the 12,000-foot cloud base and Oboe preliminary marking in progress. Each of the three aiming-points was marked by a red spotfire and bombed from 8,500 to 12,500 feet between 19.56 and 19.57 in the face of a hostile flak defence that caused varying amounts of damage to the Lancasters of F/L Parker, F/O Martin, F/O King, F/O Taylor, F/O Gilmore, F/O Bates and F/Sgt Harrison. A huge pall of smoke rose through the cloud as they turned away and post-raid reconnaissance confirmed a successful attack, which had left all of the buildings in a state of ruin. When F/O Watkins and crew landed in LM481 it was noticed that the rear turret was missing, having been sliced off by a bomb from above, and it had to be concluded that its occupant had perished.

Meanwhile, the aircraft for the main event were crossing France and entering Germany, accompanied by layers of cloud, which, over the target, was at five to ten-tenths with tops in places as high as 20,000 feet. There was haze below the cloud level to create further challenges for the marker force, and the red and green TIs appeared to the main force crews to be somewhat scattered. Bombing took place from around 17,000 to 21,000 feet either side of 02.00, but it was impossible to assess the outcome and there was little optimism at debriefings that a successful operation had taken place. In fact, this was probably the most destructive of the three raids in this current series, at a cost of eight Lancasters and four Halifaxes, but it would be only after the third one that cumulative reports came out of the city to confirm much destruction and heavy casualties.

The hectic round of operations continued for 5 Group on the 26th with preparations for an attack on two aiming-points in the marshalling yards at Givors, situated on the west bank of the River Rhône in south-east-central France. 178 Lancasters and nine Mosquitos were made ready, eighteen of the former by 61 Squadron, which departed Skellingthorpe between 21.03 and 21.43 with W/C Doubleday the senior pilot on duty. Ahead of them lay a round-trip of eleven hundred miles, and while the "Met" men had predicted bad weather, the conditions during the outward leg over France were even worse than forecast. Severe icing and electrical storms were complicit in the early return of up to fourteen aircraft, but it was a coolant leak in the starboard-inner engine that persuaded F/O Gilmore and crew to turn back. The bomber stream covered the almost five-hour outward flight to reach the target to be greeted by severe weather conditions in the form of rain, thunderstorms and lightning. The cloud was down to around 7,000 feet with poor visibility below, and the flare force made a number of runs across the target between 01.42 and 02.07, orbiting in between to await instructions. There were occasional glimpses of the ground, but the Master Bomber was experiencing great difficulty in getting Mosquito TIs onto the two aiming points. Eventually, one of the Deputies managed to put a green TI onto the southern aiming-point and the main force began to bomb at around 02.00. The 61 Squadron crews carried out their attacks from 4,000 to 8,500 feet between 02.11 and 02.22, using the light from flares and aiming at green TIs, all in accordance with instructions. F/Sgt Scholes and crew waited for thirty minutes for the appearance of the briefed yellow TIs, but when they failed to materialise, they headed for home and dumped the bombs on the way. Crews could offer little to the intelligence section at debriefing, and it was left to post-raid reconnaissance to reveal that the attack at Givors had fulfilled its aims in closing the tracks to the north of the junction and damaging the locomotive depot in the yards.

The night of the 28/29th would prove to be busy, eventful and expensive as the Command prepared for major operations against Stuttgart and Hamburg and a number of smaller undertakings involving a total of 1,126 aircraft. The final raid of the series on Stuttgart was to be an all-Lancaster affair of 494 aircraft drawn from 1, 3, 5 and 8 Groups, while 307 Lancasters and Halifaxes of 1, 6 and 8 Groups carried out the annual last-week-of-July attack on Hamburg, a year and a day after the devastating firestorm of Operation Gomorrah. 5 Group put up 176 Lancasters, sixteen of them made ready by 61 Squadron and departing Skellingthorpe between 21.55 and 22.21 with F/Ls Jeavons, Simmons and Stone the senior pilots on duty. They joined other elements of the force over Reading and during the Channel crossing lost the services of F/O Heath and crew to W/T failure. The others made landfall on the French coast south of Fécamp, before flying on across France in bright moonlight above the cloud layer. However, the forecast medium cloud at 18,000 feet was absent, which left them exposed to the night-fighter hordes that had infiltrated the bomber stream as it closed on the target. It was the Luftwaffe's Nachtjagd that would gain the upper hand on this night, and 61 Squadron's LM452 was probably one of its victims outbound when crashing somewhere in France with fatal consequences for F/Sgt MacPherson and all but his bomb-aimer, who was taken into captivity. There was a layer of up to ten-tenths thin cloud over the city, with tops in places at around 10,000 feet, and the Path Finders initially employed skymarker flares (Wanganui) and then green TIs, at which the 61 Squadron crews aimed their bombs from 16,500 to 18,000 feet between 01.503and 02.04. Thirty-nine Lancasters failed to return, fourteen of them from 5 Group, and night-fighters also caught the Hamburg force on its way home, bringing down a further twenty-two aircraft to raise the night's casualty figure to sixty-one aircraft. Although it was difficult to make an accurate assessment of this final Stuttgart raid, the series had severely damaged the city, leaving its central districts devastated with most of its public and cultural buildings in ruins and 1,171 of its inhabitants dead.

Fifteen 61 Squadron crews were briefed and put on stand-by at Skellingthorpe late on the 29th in anticipation of an early-morning tactical support operation in the Villers Bocage-Caumont region of the Normandy battle area south-west of Caen. They were to be part of an overall force of 692 aircraft to attack six enemy positions facing predominantly American forces and departed Skellingthorpe for their aiming-point at Cahagnes between 05.45 and 06.28 with W/C Doubleday the senior pilot on duty. They approached the target over ten-tenths cloud with tops at 5,000 feet and a base at 3,500 feet and were five minutes from the bombing run at 07.59, when the Master Bomber called off the attack and sent them home.

5 Group prepared for two daylight operations on the 31st, one of them an evening attack on a flying bomb storage tunnel at Rilly-la-Montagne, some five miles south of Reims, in which a 5 Group force of ninety-seven Lancasters and three Mosquitos included sixteen Lancasters of 617 Squadron, led by its recently appointed successor to Cheshire, W/C James "Willie" Tait. Tait was well-known to 5 Group crews as a member of the Master Bomber fraternity at Coningsby but had spent most of his long operational career in 4 Group and was among the most experienced pilots in the entire Command. A second operation was to be directed at locomotive facilities and marshalling yards at Joigny-la-Roche, situated north of Auxerre and some ninety miles south-east

of Paris, and would involve 127 Lancasters and four Mosquitos of 1 and 5 Groups. 61 Squadron supported both operations, assigning seven Lancasters to the former and eight to the latter, which departed Skellingthorpe respectively between 17.20 and 17.25 and 17.28 and 17.41 with F/Ls Parker and Turner and F/Ls Simmons and Stone the senior pilots on duty. They made their way south to rendezvous with the rest of the two forces, 83 Squadron forming into two vics, one at 15,000 and the other at 18,000 feet, to lead the Rilly force to the target and seven from 97 (Straits Settlements) Squadron performing a similar function for the Joigny force, both under a fighter escort.

Weather conditions at Rilly were clear, and the aiming point could be identified visually until the tallboys went down to create a blanket of dust and smoke that made it difficult to assess the outcome, a problem compounded by the use of delayed-action fuses. The 61 Squadron element identified the target visually and bombed from 15,000 to 18,000 feet between 20.18 and 20.20, while some ninety miles to the south-south-west the Joigny-la-Roche force closing on the target area to find no more than three-tenths cloud with tops at 7,000 feet, and good enough visibility to enable a visual identification of the aiming-point. The marking was concentrated, as was the bombing onto the red TIs, and the 61 Squadron crews delivered their standard bomb loads from 12,000 to 14,750 feet between 20.26 and 20.28. Post-raid reconnaissance confirmed both operations to have been successful for the loss of a single Lancaster from Joigny and two from Rilly, one of the latter one of the latter a 617 Squadron aircraft containing the former 61 Squadron crew of F/L Bill Reid VC, who survived with one of his crew after their Lancaster was hit by bombs from above.

During the course of the month, the squadron carried out eighteen operations and dispatched 226 sorties for the loss of five Lancasters and crews and a rear gunner.

The Alexanderplatz Berlin C.1930's. Target of many of Bomber Command's Berlin operations.

Lancaster ME732 QR-P named 'Ali Oop! I go - I come back!'

Before and after photographs of Bochum, attacked by Bomber Command 1944

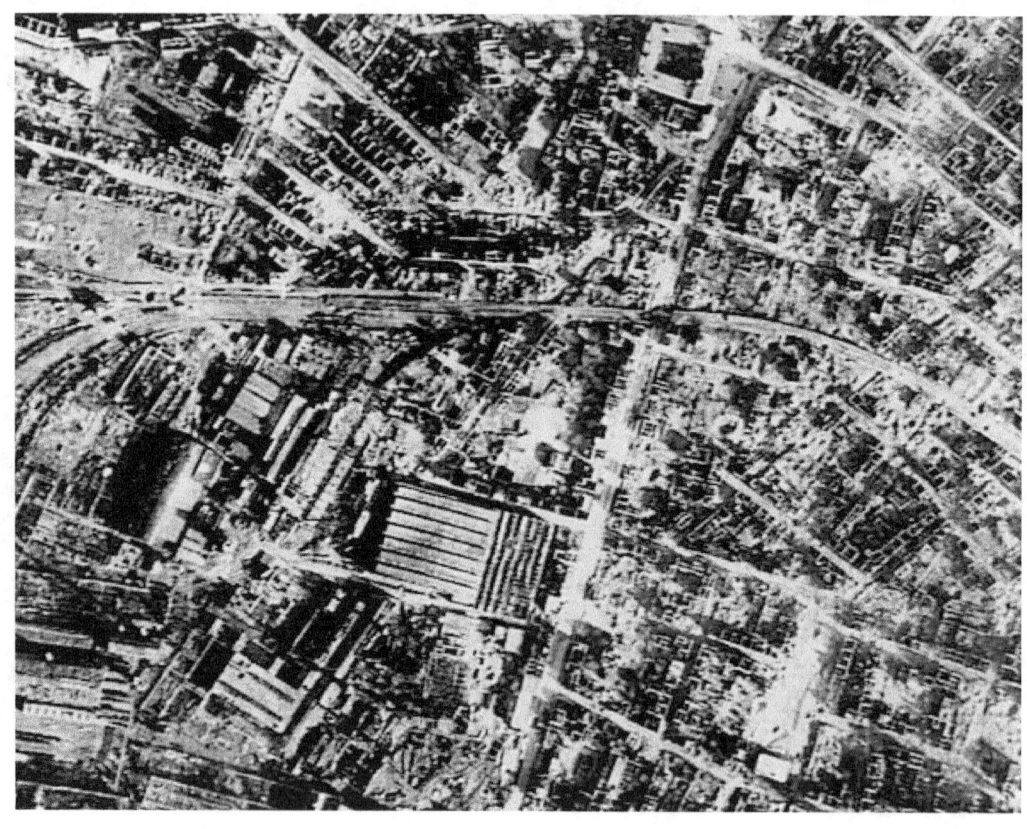

The Scholes Crew
Bill Jackman, Geoff Allen, Ron Myall, Ron Foreman, Dave Scholes, Jock Gardner (Des Murray missing from photo).

Lancasters ED860 QR-N and ED588 VN-G (50 Squadron)
Over the previous 18 months, Lancaster ED860 QR-N had successfully carried out 130 operations and survived fighter attacks and the heavy flak thrown up over the Ruhr Valley and during the Battle of Berlin. 1944.

Sgt Herbert Jennings (Gunner) Killed 23rd September 1944 on a Ladbergen raid together with F/Sgt G Twyneham. Both in S/L Horsley's crew, the remainder of which were either captured or evaded.

This young Dutch boy found Sgt Jennings body, buried it in a shallow grave to hide it from the Germans. Later he returned, recovered it and took it to the local cemetery.

F/L Bill North and crew in front of a Stirling bomber March 1944. RAF Winthorpe, Heavy Conversion Unit.

DFM Citation – "Flight Sergeant Gilbert has operated with skill, determination and enthusiasm as a gunner over a period when strong fighter opposition was encountered and has completed a tour of operation. In July 1944, when detailed to attack St. Leu d'Esserent, the aircraft in which Flight Sergeant Gilbert was a rear gunner was attacked by an enemy fighter. At a range of three hundred yards, he opened fire. Soon after hits were observed on the enemy fighter and it caught fire and crashed to the ground where it exploded. A considerable measure of the successes achieved is attributable to Flight Sergeant Gilbert's ceaseless, untiring and skilful watch, while his keen and unflagging spirit has set an example to other gunners of the squadron."

Warrant Officer Geoff Gilbert DFM

The Acott Crew
L to R: F/Sgt T Bowyer (later DFC recipient), Sgt May, Sgt Rudd, Sgt Harraway, F/O Bob Acott, Sgt Atkinson, Sgt Bryant.

Lancaster W4236 QR-K P/O W Eager's Air and ground crew

F/O George Sharpe and crew. Lancaster LM377 QR-F
All killed on a Berlin raid on the 2nd January 1944 when they were shot down. Crew: F/O George Sharpe RCAF, (Pilot), Sgt Basil Imber (FE), F/O Ernest Willard (Nav), F/O Alfred Shirley (BA), Sgt Alexander Ross (W.Op/AG), Sgt William Churcher (MUG), Sgt Henry Patrick (RG).

F/O W G Corewyn and crew
All crew killed when their Lancaster LM720 flew into a radar mast in Norfolk 15th January 1945 when returning from an operation to attack Leuna oil refinery. Crew: F/O William Corewyn (Pilot), F/Sgt Ronald Battersby (Nav), F/Sgt Edward Boakes (BA), Sgt John Douglas (MUG), Sgt Peter Earl (FE) F/Sgt Sidney James (W.Op), Sgt Richard Richardson (RG). Below: Leuna Oil Refinery

F/O Don Street DFC *F/L Don Paul DFC* *F/L Bernard Fitch DFC*

The Cook Crew
L – R: F/O J Cook, F/O R Jack, F/O R Hall, W/C J Gray DSO DFC, F/O L Sutherland DFC and Bar, F/O W McIntosh DFC and Bar, DFM.

S/L Jack Lawrence *P/O Joseph Spencer KIA 23rd August 1943.* *P/O Alan Potter*

Above: John Williams's Crew with P/O Potter as gunner. They moved together to join 617 Squadron in 1944. Below: Lancaster EE176 Mickey the Moocher, Alan Potter's regular aircraft.

F/L Arthur Edward Stone DFC AFC

*W/C A W Doubleday DSO DFC
CO 61 Squadron 1944*

Gee! 61 Squadron nose art

A 61 Squadron Lancaster, possibly DV401 QR-W, at RAF Coningsby

Lancaster DV401 QR-Z lost on the 3rd January 1944.

Lancaster DV401 QR-Z crash site in Holland, January 1944.
Crew lost: F/O George Tull (Pilot), Sgt Gordon Edward Heasman (FE), Sgt Joseph Holden (Nav), Sgt John Baldwin (BA), Sgt James Stock (W.Op), Sgt Charles Crosby (MUG), Sgt Charles Ablett (RG).

Lancaster EE186 QR-D crash site in France 4/5th July 1944
Two of the crew evaded and the remaining five became PoWs. The Lancaster had survived thirteen months and three squadrons before its crash, chalking up 434.35 flying hours.

Houffalize, Belgium

Gutted and bomb-blasted buildings and installation of the synthetic oil plant of Braunkohle Benzin A. G. at Bohlen.

S/L H W Horsley
Evaded after the crash of Lancaster LM7188 but killed 1st February 1945 when engines failed immediately after take off.

Three van Hock girls on the fuselage of LM718 QR-K. The stricken bomber missed the top of their family farmhouse crashing 1000 yards away in one of their fields.

F/Sgt Donald Easton RAAF
Along with the crew, he was lost on operations on 21st March 1945 over Germany. The other crew members were F/O John Swales RAAF, F/O Charles Saunders, F/Sgt Ralph Taylor, Sgt William Lane, Sgt Thomas Torney and Sgt John Davies.

F/O Hugh Spencer. Carried out nine operations with 61 Squadron before moving to 44 Squadron.

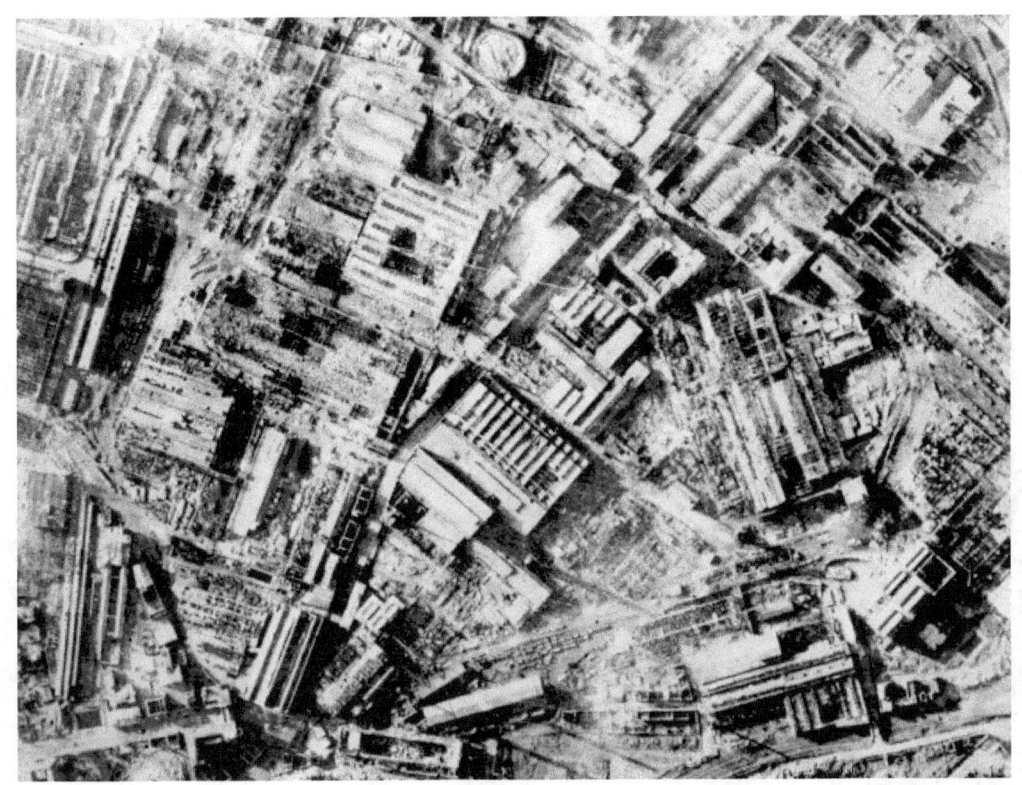

A large area of the great Krupp armaments works at Essen as it appeared after attack by RAF Bomber Command in which aircraft of 61 Squadron took part in December 1944.

Royal Air Force Bomber Command, 1942-1945. RAF officers inspect an unfinished siege gun in a wrecked building of the Krupps armaments works at Essen, Germany, a principal target for Bomber Command throughout the war.

Remains of the Alexanderplatz railway station Berlin 1945 and below, its modern rebuild.

One of the last major bombing operations of the war – the oil refinery at Tonsberg, Norway.

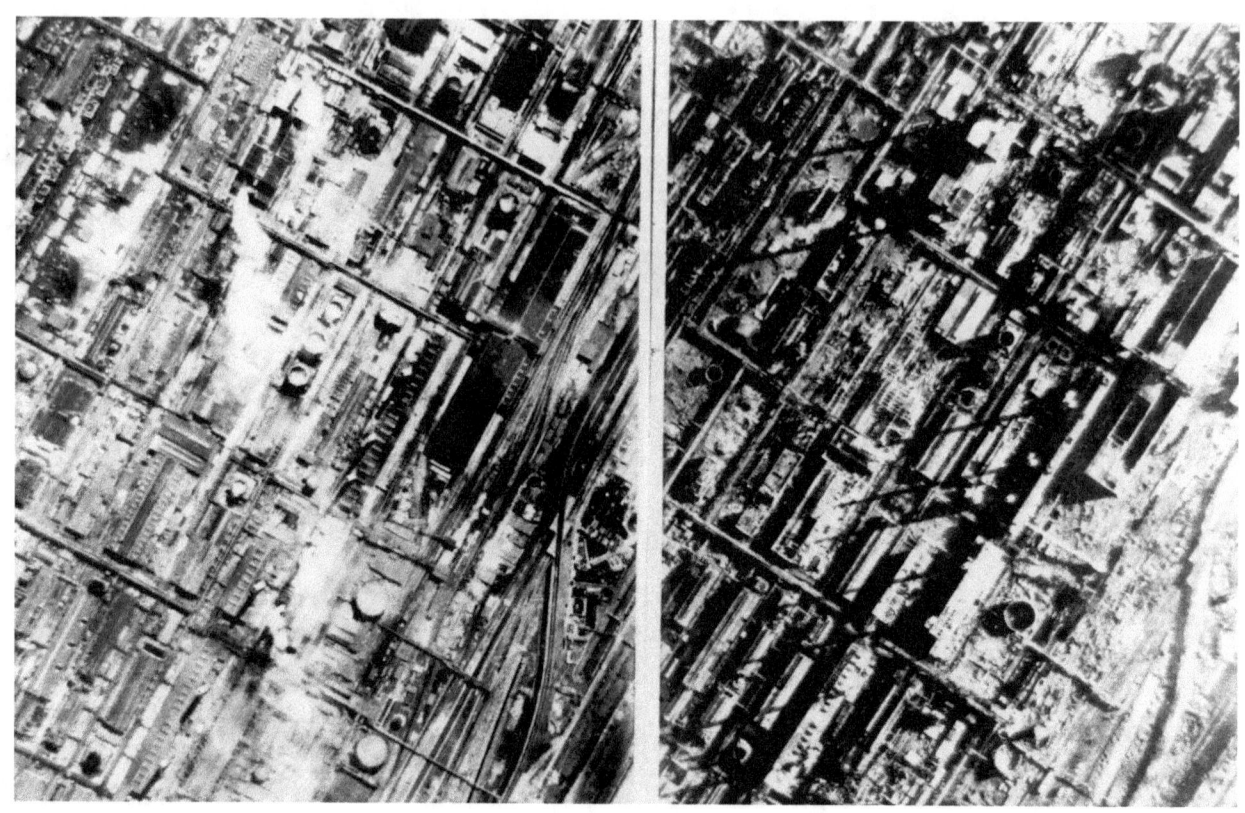
Before and after the 14/15th January 1945 bombing of the Leuna works.

An unidentified 61 Squadron crew walking out to their Lancaster.

August 1944

August would bring an end to the flying bomb offensive and also see a return to major night operations against industrial Germany, but the eradication of the flying bomb menace would dominate the first half of the month with daylight attacks on its storage and launching sites on each of the first six days. It began with the commitment of 777 aircraft to operations against numerous flying bomb-related sites on the afternoon of the 1st, although there were serious doubts about the weather conditions, which were poor all over England. 5 Group's targets were at La Breteque, situated in Normandy some ten miles east-south-east of Rouen, Mont Candon, a mile or two south-west of Dieppe, and Siracourt, located some thirty miles east of the coastal town of Berck-sur-Mer. Forces of fifty-three Lancasters, fifty-nine Lancasters and a Lightning and Mosquito and sixty-seven Lancasters and four Mosquitos respectively were made ready, the two last-mentioned supported by 61 Squadron with a total of eighteen Lancasters. An element of five departed Skellingthorpe between 15.00 and 15.15 bound for Siracourt with F/Ls Simmons and Turner in the lead, and they were followed into the air by thirteen others between 16.30 and 17.01 with F/Ls Parker and Stone the senior pilots on duty. The headed towards the south to join forces with the others of their respective formations and lost the cloud as they began the Channel crossing, only for it to build again to nine to ten-tenths stratocumulus with tops at between 2,000 and 5,000 feet over the Pas-de-Calais region. One Lancaster bombed at La Breteque, before the Master Bomber called a halt to proceedings at 18.35, and the other two attacks were abandoned before any bombing took place. It was a similar story for the other groups, and in total, only seventy-nine aircraft bombed.

On the following afternoon, 5 Group contributed 194 Lancasters, two Mosquitos and a P38 Lightning to operations by 394 aircraft against one flying bomb launching and three supply sites. Ninety-four Lancasters and two Mosquitos were assigned to a storage site at Trossy-St-Maximin, situated north of Paris and close to St-Leu d'Esserent, and a hundred Lancasters and the P38 to the Bois-de-Cassan facility. 61 Squadron loaded eighteen Lancasters with a mix of 1,000 and 500-pounders destined for the latter, some with a delay fuse of up to thirty-six hours and dispatched them from Skellingthorpe between 14.20 and 14.55 with F/L Parker, Simmons, Stone and Turner the senior pilots on duty. F/O Harrison and crew lost their starboard-inner engine at Basingstoke, while F/L Parker was unable to keep up with the formation and jettisoned the bombs in order to catch up, and, it seems, continued to the target. They found three to five-tenths patchy cloud over the target, but few saw the Oboe proximity markers go down, and most bombed on visual reference, the 61 Squadron crews from 15,000 to 18,000 feet between 17.10 and 17.21. The lead aircraft turned suddenly at the last moment and caused a number of those following to overshoot the aiming-point, and their bombs were seen to fall wide of the mark. A patch of cloud obscured the target from F/O Church and crew, and they withheld their bombs. The consensus at debriefings was of generally scattered bombing towards the north-east of the aiming-point, but post-raid reconnaissance revealed fresh damage to both sites, with many new craters, and at Trossy, a large rectangular building stripped of its roof and sides, and the southern end of two road-over-rail bridges demolished.

Despite the effectiveness of the operation, the Trossy-St-Maximin site was included among targets for more than eleven hundred aircraft on the following day. The 1 and 5 Group crews were told at briefing that the importance of the site to the Third Reich demanded that no building be left intact, and one or two may have escaped damage during the previous day's attack. 187 Lancasters, one Mosquito and the P38 Lightning were made ready as 5 Group's contribution to the operation, the fourteen 61 Squadron participants departing Skellingthorpe between 11.40 and 12.08 with S/L Beard the senior pilot on duty. Each Lancaster was loaded with a dozen 1,000 pounders and four of 500lbs, all of which reached the target area, where the 5 Group element was scheduled to attack about fifteen minutes after 1 Group. As they reached the start of the bombing run, smoke could be seen rising to 8,000 feet, and this combined with a fierce flak defence to present the crews with challenging conditions. The 61 Squadron element bombed on a visual reference from 16,000 to 18,000 feet between 14.32 and 14.34 in accordance with instruction from the Master Bomber, having been prevented by the smoke from seeing the markers. PA162 is believed to have been brought down by flak from the Creil/St-Leu defence area and F/L Gilmore RCAF perished alongside all but one of his predominantly RCAF crew, the navigator alone surviving and retaining his freedom after landing close to Allied-held territory. Many aircraft returned to their respective stations bearing flak damage, although the 52 Base crews were more concerned about the dense concentration of aircraft over the aiming-point, which put them in danger of being hit from above and caused them to spread out with a consequent scattering of bombs. Photo-reconnaissance was unable to confirm that the site had been obliterated, and it would need to be attacked again on the following day, a job that would be handed to 6 Group, while most of 5 Group stayed at home.

The 5th dawned bright and clear and brilliant sunshine glinted off the Perspex of fourteen 61 Squadron Lancasters as they took off from Skellingthorpe between 10.30 and 11.08 bound for familiar airspace over St-Leu-d'Esserent with W/C Doubleday the senior pilot on duty. They were part of a 5 Group force of 189 Lancasters and one Mosquito, which in turn, represented about 25% of the effort by 4, 5, 6 and 8 Groups against two flying-bomb sites, the other in the Forét-de-Nieppe, close to the Belgian frontier. It was an almost intact force that homed in on the target to find it partially protected by up to six-tenths patchy cloud with tops at about 12,000 feet. This prevented the Master Bomber from picking up the aiming-point until thirty seconds from it, which meant a very late course change to bring the bombers into position. This was achieved, although smoke and cloud hid the markers from view and most crews picked up the aiming-point by means of ground features as they ran through a spirited flak defence to the point of bomb release. With the exception of W/C Doubleday and crew, who were unable to identify the aiming point, the 61 Squadron element bombed from 15,000 to 18,000 feet between 13.33 and 13.35 and returning crews reported a fairly concentrated attack with smoke rising through 6,000 feet as they turned away. PRU photos seemed to confirm the effectiveness of the bombing, with views of fresh damage and heavily cratered approaches.

50 and 61 Squadrons detailed nine crews each for operations on the morning of the 6th, and they were in their Lancasters before 09.00 to carry out the checks before departing for another swipe at the flying-bomb launching site at Bois-de-Cassan in the L'Isle-Adam, a few miles to the south-west of St-Leu. They were part of a 5 Group force of ninety-nine Lancasters and the P38 Lightning and departed Skellingthorpe together between 09.30 and 09.50 to join up with the rest of the formation as they made their way south. The heavy element was led by 83 Squadron's G/C Deane with F/L Drinkall acting as his deputy, but Deane began to experience problems with his navigation homing equipment as he crossed the English coast outbound and decided to hand over to F/L Drinkall. When about forty miles inland of the French coast, a large cumulus cloud stretch upwards of 20,000 feet barred the way, and F/L Drinkall communicated his intention to take the force below it, descending to 16,000 feet. G/C Deane warned him not to go below 15,000, and advised him not to enter the cloud, but to turn to starboard. However, they were immediately enveloped in cloud,

and G/C Deane did his best to hang on to F/L Drinkall's tail as he continued to descend, and the two eventually became separated. Emerging on the other side of the cloud, Deane saw a large formation in the distance and followed it, but it had become widely scattered and could not be reformed. Only thirty-eight aircraft bombed after picking up the aiming-point visually, four and three respectively from 61 Squadron carrying out their attacks from 13,000 to 16,000 feet between 12.16 and 12.21. Fifty-eight crews were unable to bomb but still had to contend with a fierce flak and fighter defence and three Lancasters failed to return, among them that of F/L Drinkall and crew, who failed to survive. Photo-reconnaissance revealed some fresh damage to the eastern side of the target, but two large buildings on the main roadway immediately south of the aiming point remained intact, and further operations would be required.

Other than night flying tests (NFTs), there was little activity during the day on the 7th, the first time during the month that no daylight operations had been mounted. It was from teatime onwards that the feverish activity began with the preparation of 1,019 aircraft for attacks on five enemy positions facing Allied ground forces in the Normandy battle area. The aiming-point for 179 Lancasters and one Mosquito from 5 Group was the fortified village of Secqueville, situated some fifteen miles east of Le Havre. Fifteen 61 Squadron Lancasters departed Skellingthorpe between 21.05 and 21.42 with W/C Doubleday the senior pilot and included in the list of participating crews was one captained by a W/C Rayner Baker, whose name appears regularly in August during a period of detachment from 51 Base at Swinderby. He had earned a DFC while serving with 44 Squadron in 1940/41 and was now gaining operational experience before securing a posting as a flight commander to 97 (Straits Settlements) Squadron. They joined up with the others as they travelled south towards the target, which could be seen by the approaching bombers to be under clear skies, although haze shrouded ground detail to an extent, and star shells were fired from the ground to illuminate the aiming-point. This enabled the Path Finder aircraft to drop red TIs onto it for the main force crews to aim at, and the first phase of bombing proceeded according to plan in concentrated fashion, lasting fifteen minutes. However, smoke began to obscure the markers, persuading the Master Bomber to call a halt to proceedings at 23.24, by which time W/C Doubleday and three others from 61 Squadron had bombed red TIs from 6,800 to 7,750 feet between 23.23 and 23.25, leaving the remaining eleven to jettison part of their load and take the rest home.

A rare day off for 5 Group crews on the 8th led to another for them on the 9th until late afternoon, when briefings took place for that night's operation against an oil storage dump in the Forét-de-Châtellerault, situated south of Tours in western France. It was to be predominantly a 5 Group show involving 171 Lancasters and fourteen Mosquitos, but with five 101 Squadron Lancasters to provide RCM cover. 61 Squadron dispatched seventeen Lancasters from Skellingthorpe between 20.27 and 21.04 with W/C Baker and S/L Pexton the senior pilots on duty and all arrived in the target area under clear skies. However, the presence of considerable ground haze created poor visibility for the marker crews attempting to identify the two aiming-points. The flares dropped by the first two waves of the marker force were scattered, and this prompted the Mosquito marker leader to drop a Wanganui flare as a guide to the third flare-force crews. This meant that some crews had to orbit for up to twenty minutes before the Master Bomber was satisfied that the green TIs were in the right spot and called in the main force. They produced accurate bombing, resulting in three large explosions and volumes of black smoke, which, within five minutes, completely obscured the aiming-point. A pause in the bombing was called, before it recommenced, until the lack of a verifiable marker compelled the Master Bomber to call a halt. Only F/Sgt Harrison and crew of the 61 Squadron participants had not bombed by this point, the others having carried out their attacks from 5,000 to 8,000 feet between 00.03 and 00.18.

The mighty Gironde estuary, situated on France's Biscay coast, narrows as it leads inland towards the south-east, before dividing to become the Garonne River to the west and the Dordogne to the east. Its banks and islands were home to a number of important oil production and storage sites at Pauillac, Blaye, Bec-d'Ambe and Bassens, and the region was a frequent destination for gardening activities. Bordeaux itself was a vitally important port to the enemy as a gateway to the Atlantic and contained U-Boot pens, which required it to be heavily defended along the entire length of the waterway. Orders were received on 52, 54 and 55 Base stations at teatime on the 10th to prepare sixty-two Lancasters and five Mosquitos to bomb oil storage facilities at Bassens, situated just to the north of the city of Bordeaux. Nine Lancasters from 83 Squadron were to act as the flare and marker force and the outward flight in daylight enabled the Deputy Master Bomber to recognise that the formation had become somewhat disorganised. There were about twenty main force aircraft ahead of the flare force, and the remainder behind it to starboard, but they were catching up and veering further and further to starboard until they were some ten to twenty miles off track. Fortunately, the situation rectified itself and the force arrived in the target area to find clear skies with a little ground haze. As they ran in on the aiming-point, a limited amount of heavy flak began to burst at 16,000 to 18,000 feet, while the considerable light flak fell short, and neither proved to be troublesome. Within thirty seconds of the flares illuminating the ground, the TIs were burning close to the aiming-point and returning crews were confident of a successful attack, despite the difficulty of accurately assessing the outcome.

On the 11th, while 617 Squadron took care of the U-Boot pens in the deep-water port at la Pallice, 5 Group detailed thirty-nine Lancasters from 53 Base and two Mosquitos for an attack on a similar target at Bordeaux under the protection for most of the trip of six "Serrate"-equipped night-fighter Mosquitos of 100 Group. *(Serrate was a highly effective and successful radar device that enabled 100 Group Mosquito night-fighters to home in on enemy night-fighters and turn the hunters into the hunted).* 61 Squadron dispatched nine Lancasters from Skellingthorpe between 11.57 and 12.30 with W/C Baker and F/L Simmons the senior pilots on duty and each crew sitting on six 2,000lb armour-piercing bombs. P/O Brooker and crew returned early because of an engine issue, but the others reached the target area to find good bombing conditions, which enabled them to make a visual identification of the T-shaped basin and U-Boot pens. The 61 Squadron crews attacked largely unopposed from 16,200 to 18,750 feet between 16.32 and 16.34 and were satisfied that the bombing was concentrated on the aiming-point. An escort of Spitfires was waiting off the Finistere coast to take over the escort duties from the Mosquitos and the operation was concluded without loss.

That evening, 5 Group was switched to communications targets at Givors, located about twenty miles to the south of Lyon in south-east-central France, where there were two aiming-points, the town's marshalling yards to the north and a railway junction to the south. 61 Squadron's seven participants were assigned to the latter in an overall force of 175 Lancasters and ten Mosquitos and departed Skellingthorpe between 20.40 and 20.58 with S/L Pexton the senior pilot on duty and eight 1,000 and four-500 pounders in each bomb bay. All reached the target area to find clear skies and a little haze, and while confusion reigned over the marshalling yards, matters proceeded smoothly at the junction, which was marked by green TIs and bombed by the 61 Squadron crews from 6,000 to 9,000 feet between 01.01 and 01.05. All returned to home airspace, many of those involved in the attack on the marshalling yards critical of some aspects of the raid, but confident that it had been concluded successfully. Photo-reconnaissance revealed heavy damage to both aiming-points, with the ground badly-cratered and many tracks severed, and the middle span of the railway bridge over the River Rhône was seen to have received a direct hit.

The main operation on the 12th was an experiment to gauge the ability of main force crews to locate and attack an urban target on the strength of their own H2S equipment in the absence of a Path Finder element. This resulted from the huge volume of operations generated by the four concurrent campaigns, each of which called upon the finite resources of 8 Group, compelling it, in the short term at least, to spread itself more and more thinly. The conclusion of the flying-bomb campaign at the end of the month together with the end of tactical support for the ground forces would remove the pressure and the planned independence of 3 Group through the G-H bombing system from the autumn would solve the problem altogether. In the meantime, however, no one knew what demands might be made of the Command, and it would be useful to see what main force crews could do when left to their own devices. The target was to be the northern city of Braunschweig, for which a force of 379 aircraft was assembled, seventy-two of the Lancasters provided by 5 Group's 52 and 54 Bases. It was a night of heavy Bomber Command activity at numerous locations involving more than eleven hundred sorties, of which 297, including sixty by 5 Group Lancasters, were assigned to a second large operation over Germany against the Opel tank works at Rüsselsheim, two hundred miles to the south. This would not weaken the enemy night-fighter defences, and powerful elements of the Nachtjagd were waiting for the Braunschweig force as it crossed the German coast at around 18,000 feet. Night-fighter flares were in evidence from then until the coast was crossed again on the way home, and it would prove to be an expensive operation that cost the Command seventeen Lancasters and ten Halifaxes. Some of the bombing did hit Braunschweig, but there was no concentration, and, typically at this target, many outlying communities also reported bombs falling.

53 Base contributed twenty-six Lancasters to the Rüsselsheim operation, fifteen of them belonging to 61 Squadron, which departed Skellingthorpe between 21.20 and 21.46 with W/C Baker and S/L Pexton the senior pilots on duty with a single 2,000 pounder and twelve 500lb J-Type cluster bombs in each bomb bay. In the target area they found up to three-tenths cloud with tops as high as 20,000 feet and ground haze, despite which the conditions for an attack were favourable, and the red and green TIs marking out the aiming-point were clearly visible, if a little scattered. Bombing by the 61 Squadron element took place from 18,800 to 21,000 feet between 00.15 and 00.24, but they found it difficult to assess what was happening on the ground, and bombing photos would provide little detail. It was left to post-raid reconnaissance to ascertain that a number of buildings had been damaged within the Opel factory complex, but nothing vital to production, and fires had spread through a wood three miles away and adjacent housing estates to the south-east. There were also many bomb craters in open country, confirming that this target would need further attention. Twenty aircraft failed to return from this disappointing effort, and among them was 61 Squadron's ME596, which crashed somewhere in Germany killing P/O Taylor RCAF and all but his bomb-aimer, who was taken into captivity. The rear gunner, Sgt Scrimshaw, was thirty-nine years-old, and flight engineer, F/Sgt Burnside DFM, was probably on his second tour.

While the above was in progress, a "rush job" called upon the services of 144 crews to attack German troop concentrations and a road junction north of Falaise. 5 Group supported the attack with twenty-five Lancasters, the crews of which found a blanket of ten-tenths stratus cloud with tops at 2,000 feet, through which the green TIs were clearly visible and bombed. Post-raid reconnaissance confirmed that the area around the junction had been heavily cratered and the roads leading from it were mostly blocked.

Later, on the 13th, 5 Group notified 617 Squadron to prepare aircraft for an attack on the U-Boot pens and a cruiser at Brest, and fifteen Lancasters from 53 Base to target an oil storage depot at Bordeaux. 61 Squadron's six participants departed Skellingthorpe between 16.19 and 16.35 with W/C Baker and F/L Parker the senior pilots on duty and six 2,000-pounders in each bomb bay and all reached the target, where conditions were sufficiently favourable for the aiming-point to be identified visually. Bombing by the 61 Squadron crews took place from 15,000 to 17,500 feet between 20.03 and 20.04. F/L Parker and crew suffered the frustration of an unserviceable bomb sight and brought their bombs home, complaining at debriefing that the Master Bomber had vacated the target area too fast and left a straggling bomber stream in his wake. The bombs had been seen to straddle the aiming point and U-Boot pens, but it was not possible to assess damage, particularly as reinforced concrete structures were largely impervious to the available bombs, other than the Tallboys carried by 617 and 9 Squadrons.

The main activity during the afternoon of the 14th was an operation in support of Canadian divisions in the Falaise area, which involved 805 aircraft targeting seven enemy troop positions. 5 Group took part, by sending sixty-one Lancasters from 52 and 54 Bases to the village of Quesnay, where accurate bombing left the village in ruins. Master Bombers were on hand to control the bombing at each aiming-point because of the close proximity of the opposing armies, but, despite the most stringent efforts to avoid friendly fire incidents, some bombs did fall into a quarry occupied by Canadian troops, killing thirteen men, injuring fifty-three others and destroying a large number of vehicles.

5 Group had actually begun the day with an attack by elements of 617 and 9 Squadrons on the derelict French cruiser Gueydon at berth at Brest, which, it was believed, the enemy might sink strategically along with other ships in the harbour to render it unusable if liberated. In the evening, 128 Lancasters and two Mosquitos were made ready to send back to Brest for another go at the Gueydon, a tanker and a hulk, and among those taking part were fourteen crews representing 61 Squadron, who departed Skellingthorpe between 17.32 and 17.53 with F/L Simmons the senior pilot on duty. They arrived over the port to find clear skies and excellent visibility, but also a fierce flak defence, and a number of aircraft would return bearing the scars of battle. The 61 Squadron crews bombed from 15,500 to 17,000 feet between 20.24 and 20.28, and a number of direct hits were observed on both vessels, with smoke issuing out of the tanker. Photo-reconnaissance revealed that the tanker had settled on the bottom, and the cruiser had suffered a similar fate and its decks were awash.

In preparation for his new night offensive against Germany, Harris called for operations against enemy night-fighter airfields in Holland and Belgium, in response to which, a list of eight such targets was prepared for attention. Those at Eindhoven, Soesterberg, Volkel, Melsbroek, St-Trond, Tirlemont-Gossancourt and Le Culot were to be targeted in daylight during the course of the morning and early afternoon of the 15th, and Venlo that night, involving, in all, 1004 aircraft. 5 Group was handed Deelen in central Holland and Gilze-Rijen in the south and prepared forces of ninety-four Lancasters and five Mosquitos for the former and 103 Lancasters, four Mosquitos and the P38 Lightning for the latter. The P38 must have been a two-seat variant as it allegedly contained S/L "Count" Ciano and W/C Guy Gibson, the latter desperate to get back onto operations. 53 Base was assigned to Gilze-Rijen, and 61 Squadron dispatched its fourteen Lancasters from Skellingthorpe between 09.36 and 10.17 with S/L Pexton the senior pilot on duty, each carrying eleven 1,000-pounders and up to five of 500lbs. They found the target to be under clear skies in excellent visibility and were able to identify the aiming point visually to deliver their payloads from 15,500 to 17,000 feet between 12.10 and 12.20 in accordance with instructions from the Master Bomber. Bombs were observed to fall on runway intersections, and buildings could be seen burning as the force withdrew to leave a column of smoke rising through 5,000 feet, post-raid reconnaissance confirming almost eight hundred craters on the landing ground and a hundred on the runways.

The new offensive began with simultaneous attacks on Stettin and Kiel on the night of the 16/17th, 5 Group contributing 145 aircraft to the overall all-Lancaster force of 461 assigned to the former. 61 Squadron made ready fourteen Lancasters, which departed Skellingthorpe between 21.00 and 21.25 with W/C Baker and F/Ls Parker and Simmons the senior pilots on duty but lost the services first of F/Sgt Loneon and crew when some forty miles north-east of Skegness and F/O Church and crew seventy miles off the western coast of Jutland, both because of an unserviceable rear turret. The others completed the three-and-a-half-hour outward flight and were greeted at the target by up to nine-tenths high cloud with a base at 18,000 to 20,000 feet and sufficient breaks to register clear visibility below. Concentrated red and green TIs could be seen marking out the aiming-point, and the 61 Squadron crews bombed these from 17,000 to 21,500 feet between 01.05 and 01.12 and reported fires taking hold. Smoke had reached 20,000 feet by the end of the raid but not all returning crews were confident about the outcome, some suggesting it to have been scattered, when, in fact, it had been highly successful, destroying fifteen hundred houses, numerous industrial premises and sinking five ships in the harbour, while seriously damaging eight more. The attack on Kiel had been less effective but had caused extensive damage in the docks area and among the shipbuilding yards, while wasting much of the effort outside of the town to the north-west.

Fourteen 61 Squadron crews were called to briefing early on the 18th to be told of that morning's operation against two flying-bomb dumps in the Forét-de-L'Isle Adam, north of Paris. 158 Lancasters, six Mosquitos and the P38 Lightning were to be involved, with 83 Squadron leading and providing the back-up marking on the heels of the low-level Mosquitos at the two aiming-points in the east and west. The 61 Squadron contingent departed Skellingthorpe between 11.20 and 11.55 with F/L Parker the senior pilot on duty and each Lancaster carrying ten 1,000 and four 500-pounders. They headed south in squadron formation to rendezvous with the rest of the force and pick up the fighter escort, and when over the mid-point of the Channel at 13.15, sixty or seventy American Liberators passed across the bows of the gaggle, heading east a thousand feet higher, prompting the lead Lancaster to change course. This may have been the cause of comments by some crews on return, that not all had observed station keeping as set out at briefing, a situation that would result in aircraft bombing out of the planned sequence and on incorrect headings. On arrival in the target area, they encountered five to seven-tenths cloud with tops at around 8,000 feet, which hampered identification of both aiming-points and instructions were issued by the Master Bomber to not bomb unless a clear view of the target had been established. Some were able to pick out the aiming-points assisted by smoke markers, and the 61 Squadron crews bombed from 11,000 to 14,000 feet between 14.09 and 14.11, observing a number of bursts. Some aircraft returned with flak damage picked up either over the target or to the north of Rouen and the suggestion at debriefing was that the bombing had been a little scattered. Bombing photos offered a similar conclusion, that the attack had overshot to the north and this was confirmed later by PRU photos.

Later in the day, twenty-six 5 Group crews attended briefings for an operation against oil storage facilities at Bassens/Bordeaux, F/O Heath and crew alone representing 61 Squadron and departing

Skellingthorpe at 16.07. Those arriving at the target found haze the only impediment to target identification but established the aiming point on the eastern bank of the Garonne visually and the Heath crew bombed from 17,000 feet at 20.09, observing a good concentration of bombs around the aiming point.

53 Base was called into action on the 19th to provide fifty-two Lancasters for an attack on a jetty at La Pallice on the Biscay coast, 61 Squadron responsible for thirteen of them, each of which received a bomb load of eleven 1,000 and four 500-pounders. They departed Skellingthorpe between 05.09 and 05.38 with S/L Pexton the senior pilot on duty, and all reached the target area, where six to nine-tenths cloud hung over the western aiming-point, and seven to eight-tenths over the eastern one with tops at 15,000 feet. This created challenging conditions in which to identify the targets, made more so by intense light flak, but the 61 Squadron crews claimed to have done so visually before bombing from 10,000 to 12,200 feet between 09.08 and 09.16. This was the first day of a spell of wet, cloudy and, sometimes, windy weather, which would last for the next week, and although crews at Skellingthorpe were detailed for operations daily, nothing came of it.

Major operations resumed on the 25th, when preparations were put in hand to make ready more than nine hundred aircraft to launch against three main targets, the Opel tank works at Rüsselsheim and the nearby city of Darmstadt in southern Germany, and the port of Brest, while a further four hundred would be engaged in a variety of smaller endeavours. The largest operation was to be the all-Lancaster affair involving 461 aircraft from 1, 3, 6 and 8 Groups in a return to the Opel works, while 334 others attended to eight coastal batteries around Brest. 5 Group was assigned to Darmstadt, a university city and centre of scientific research and development and one of a few almost virgin targets considered to be worthy of attention. 5 Group assembled a force of 191 Lancasters and six Mosquitos, eighteen of the former made ready by 61 Squadron, before departing Skellingthorpe between 20.21 and 21.04 with S/L Pexton the senior pilot. The Master Bomber was one of five crews to return early, leaving his two Deputies from 83 Squadron, F/L Meggeson DFC and S/L Williams DFC to step into the breach and find the target area to be free of cloud. Some ground haze was present, but this was not responsible for matters going awry early on as a result of VHF communication proving to be weak, which made it difficult for the Deputy Master Bombers to pass on instructions.

When five aircraft dropped flares at 01.05, they turned out to be too far to the west and the low-level Mosquitos reported at 01.07 that they were unable to find the aiming point. H-hour was pushed back to 01.22, although bombing actually began at 01.19, and soon afterwards, someone left their VHF on transmit, creating a noise that drowned out all voice communications at the same time that W/T became jammed. One of the Deputies was heard indistinctly instructing the crews to "bomb on the box" (H2S), and then he and the other Deputy were shot down. The main force crews did their best to comply, among them the 61 Squadron element, which was over the target at 8,000 to 10,500 feet between 01.19 and 01.39 and described a widely scattered attack. The lack of marking persuaded some of the force to seek alternative targets and they joined in at Rüsselsheim, while other chose targets of opportunity. Among seven missing Lancasters was 61 Squadron's PA998, which crashed near the town of Gross-Gerau, a few miles to the south-east of Rüsselsheim, killing F/L Church RCAF and three others of his predominantly RCAF crew and delivering the survivors into enemy hands.

The German port of Königsberg, now Kaliningrad in Lithuania, is located on the eastern side of the Bay of Danzig and was being used by the enemy to supply its eastern front. It lay some 860 miles in a straight line from the bomber stations surrounding Lincoln, which increased to a round trip of 1,900 miles when the routing across Denmark was taken into account. This made it the most distant location ever targeted by the Command and was exceeded only by SOE flights to Poland. Such a distance required sacrificing bombs for fuel, and it was a reduced load of a single 2,000 pounder and twelve 500lb J-Type cluster bombs that was loaded into each of 61 Squadron's seventeen Lancasters, which were part of an overall heavy force of 174. Having been briefed for this target twice before without going, there was some doubt as to whether or not this one would take place, but it did, and the 61 Squadron contingent departed Skellingthorpe between 19.55 and 20.32 with S/L Pexton the senior pilot on duty. Ahead of them lay a ten-hour marathon, the outward flight providing the challenges of electrical storms and icing conditions over Denmark which all from 61 Squadron negotiated successfully to arrive at the target under skies and good visibility. The head of the bomber stream was greeted by around a hundred searchlights and an intense flak defence, through which the flare force went in at 14,000 to 15,000 feet between 01.05 and 01.12, to be followed minutes later by the heavy markers at a lower level. The 61 Squadron crews identified the aiming-point by red TIs and bombed them from 8,000 to 10,000 feet between 01.18 and 01.25, the latter time a minute after the Master Bomber had issued the order to cease bombing. Returning crews were fairly enthusiastic about the outcome, reporting punctual marking, concentrated bombing and fires that could be seen, according to some, from 250 miles into the return journey. Photo-reconnaissance revealed that the main weight of the attack had fallen into the town's north-eastern districts, where fire had ripped through many building blocks in return for the modest loss of four Lancasters. However, an analysis suggested that the job had not been done, and a second operation would have to be mounted.

The final operations in the long-running flying-bomb campaign were conducted by small Oboe-led forces against twelve sites on the 28th, and Allied ground forces took control of the Pas-de-Calais a few days later. It was clear, that a decisive blow had not been delivered on Königsberg, and at 17.30 on the 29th, briefings took place on the participating 5 Group stations for the return. Sixteen 61 Squadron crews learned that they were to be part of a 5 Group force of 189 Lancasters, and they departed Skellingthorpe between 19.59 and 20.38 with F/L King, Parker, Simmons and Stone the senior pilots on duty, and because of the extreme range, they again carried between them only 480 tons of bombs to deliver onto four aiming-points. The bomber stream made its way across the North Sea and Denmark and reached the target to encounter eight to ten-tenths cloud with a base at around 10,000 feet, the Master Bomber, W/C Woodroffe, formerly of 61 and 49 Squadrons, and one of 5 Group's most experienced raid controllers, having decided upon a visual attack.

He instructed the first flare force wave to drop below the cloud, while keeping the spearhead of the main force circling for twenty minutes before the marking began. The later arrivals could see the markers going down as they approached for what was a complex plan of attack that proceeded with the first flares going down at around 01.05 and continuing at regular intervals thereafter. At 01.24, the third flare force wave was instructed to illuminate the red spot fire, and a minute later an instruction was given to overshoot by 400 yards to the east of the aiming-point. At 01.26, a marker aircraft was told to run over the red marker and overshoot by 300 yards, while, at 01.27, another was ordered to overshoot by 600 yards east of the aiming-point, before the visual backers-up were sent to track over the reds and greens and overshoot by 300 yards. The flare force was invited to go home at 01.30, and, at 01.34, the visual marker crews were instructed first to back up the greens by 600 yards on a westerly heading, and, two minutes later, the concentrations of reds and greens.

The 61 Squadron crews identified the target by the red and green TIs and searchlight concentrations and confirmed their positions by H2S before bombing from 4,000 to 10,000 feet between 01.33 and 01.49. The Master Bomber called a halt to bombing at 01.52 and sent the crews home, which meant that those of F/Os Brooker, Cookey and Scholes were too late and retained their ordnance. The absence of four 50 Squadron Lancasters and PB436 of 61 Squadron at Skellingthorpe prompted a scathing review of W/C Woodroffe's performance, blaming his stubbornness for the high casualty rate of fifteen Lancasters, 7.9% of those dispatched. They maintained that the backers-up had confirmed the marking to be on the aiming point, despite which, he kept some crews orbiting for up to forty minutes. There was at least good news concerning the crew of F/Sgt Loneon RAAF, who were on the fourth or fifth sortie together, and all survived, the pilot and navigator to evade capture. Post-raid reconnaissance confirmed that the operation had been an outstanding success, which destroyed over 40% of the town's residential and 20% of its industrial buildings.

The flying-bomb campaign may now have ended, but a new one against V-2 rocket storage and launching sites began on the 31st with raids on nine suspected locations in northern France. 5 Group sent three forces of forty-nine, forty-six and fifty-two Lancasters with two Mosquitos each to respectively target sites at Auchy-les-Hesdin, Rollancourt and Bergueneuse, all situated some twenty miles inland from the coast at Berck-sur-Mer. Fifteen 61 Squadron crews were briefed for Rollancourt and departed Skellingthorpe between 16.00 and 16.22 with S/L Pexton the senior pilot on duty, and all reached the target to be greeted by five to seven-tenths cloud with a base at 3,000 feet dispensing occasional heavy showers. The main force orbited until a bank of cloud had partially cleared, at which point the Master Bomber directed the bombing to be carried out visually on smoke-puff markers, all but two of the 61 Squadron participants complying from a uniform 14,000 feet, while one bombed from 10,000 feet and another from 15,000 between 18.10 and 18.30.

This concluded a month of feverish and record activity for most heavy squadrons, during which 61 Squadron carried out twenty-two operations and dispatched 278 sorties for the loss of four Lancasters and crews.

September 1944

The destructive power of the Command was now almost beyond belief, each of its heavy bomber groups now capable of laying waste to a German town and city at one go, and from this point until the end of the war, this would be demonstrated in awesome and horrific fashion. Much of the Command's effort during the new month would be directed towards the liberation of the three French ports remaining in enemy hands, but operations began for 5 Group with an attack on shipping at Brest on the 2nd, for which sixty-seven Lancasters were detailed from 52 and 55 Bases. In fact, there would be a gentle start to the new month for the group as crews were stood-down to allow them the opportunity to get to grips with the new Village Inn night-fighter defence system, otherwise known as Automatic Gun Laying Turret (AGLT). It was at around this time that the talents of F/O Phil Martin and crew were recognised and they were offered the chance to join 617 Squadron at Woodhall Spa, an opportunity that they grasped with both hands. Skellingthorpe sat out the following morning's attacks on six Luftwaffe-occupied aerodromes in southern Holland involving a total of 675 aircraft, including 103 Lancasters and two Mosquitos of 5 Group. They were assigned to Deelen, on the way to which they met challenging conditions for formation-keeping in the form of varying amounts of cloud up to nine-tenths with tops at 7,000 feet. Once at the target they were instructed to orbit to await gaps through which to identify the aiming-point visually, and the bombing took place in the face of a spirited flak defence from the airfield only to be halted by the Master Bomber before all aircraft had attacked. There were no losses, but almost every Lancaster from Dunholme Lodge returned with flak damage to some degree. It was the 6th before photo-reconnaissance provided a partial cover of the target area and revealed at least sixty craters around runway intersections and taxiways.

Most of 5 Group remained at home over the ensuing five days, while enemy strong-points in and around Le Havre received daylight visitations from other elements of the Command on the 5th, 6th, 8th and 9th. These operations took place during a spell of unhelpful weather conditions, and the attacks of the 8th and 9th were not fully pressed home. As this campaign began, 53 Base was roused from its inactivity on the 5th to provide aircraft for a two-phase evening daylight attack on a coastal battery holding out at Brest. The force of sixty Lancasters and seven Mosquitos included a marking element from 54 Base, and seventeen Lancasters representing 61 Squadron, which departed Skellingthorpe as part of the first phase between 15.56 and 16.25, with S/L Pexton the senior pilot on duty. Cloud conditions at the target varied from zero to five-tenths in a layer between 2,500 and 6,800 feet, and the aiming-point was identified by smoke markers backed up by green TIs, upon which the 61 Squadron crews emptied the contents of their bomb bays from 5,000 to 9,000 feet between 18.51 and 19.10. There were mixed opinions as to the accuracy of the bombing, ranging from accurate and concentrated around the TIs, to undershooting, but smoke was rising as the bombers turned away and no post-raid report was forthcoming.

Mönchengladbach was posted as the target for 113 Lancasters and fourteen Mosquitos of 5 Group on the 9th, in the absence of a contribution from 53 Base. The aiming-point was the centre, which, with Operation Market Garden looming, was expected soon to be within striking distance of the advancing Allied forces. The crews would have to wait until the early hours of the 10th before departing their stations, eventually to set course for the target by way of Ostend. They found clear skies and good visibility as they followed on the heels of the flare forces, and bombed on red TIs, observing a number of large explosions and the glow of fires from the Dutch coast up to eighty miles away. There were no losses, and photo-reconnaissance confirmed the town centre to be in ruins.

A further attack on German positions around Le Havre was carried out on the 10th and involved almost a thousand aircraft, 5 Group supporting the effort with 108 Lancasters and two Mosquitos. 61 Squadron contributed twenty Lancasters, which departed Skellingthorpe between 15.00 and 15.35 with F/Ls Kilgour, King and Watkins the senior pilots on duty, and they were greeted at the French coast by clear skies and just a little ground haze, which enabled them to identify the target visually. They released their bombs almost as one and entirely unopposed onto red TIs from 11,000 to 14,000 feet between 17.22 and 17.29, and by the time that they turned for home, the area had become enveloped in smoke. The 11th brought the final attacks on the environs of the port, and involved 218 aircraft drawn from 4, 5, 6 and 8 Groups. 5 Group contributed ninety-three Lancasters from 53, 54 and 55 Bases, ten representing 61 Squadron, which departed Skellingthorpe between 03.58 and 04.45 with S/L Pexton the senior pilot on duty and arrived in the target area just after dawn under clear skies with slight haze. They located their respective aiming points to the north and south of the outer defences, each named after a car manufacturer, like Cadillac and Alvis, but finding no markers on the northern aiming-point and receiving no instructions from the Master Bomber, crews were left to their own devices. At the southern aiming point the 61 Squadron participants carried out their attacks on red and green TIs from 10,000 to 13,000 feet between 07.21 and 07.51 and photo-reconnaissance confirmed accurate and concentrated bombing. Within hours of this operation, the German garrison surrendered to British forces and the port of Le Havre was liberated.

Many of the crews involved in the morning activity found themselves on the order of battle and back in the briefing room later in the day to learn of their part in 5 Group's return to Darmstadt, which had escaped serious damage at its hands during the last week of August. A force of 221 Lancasters and fourteen Mosquitos was made ready, the 61 Squadron element of twenty departing Skellingthorpe between 20.30 and 21.06 with F/Ls Kilgour, King, Parker and Watkins the senior pilots on duty. They began the Channel crossing at Beachy Head, aiming for the French coast near Berck-sur-Mer, before traversing France to enter Germany in the Strasbourg area and turning north towards the target. They arrived to find the skies over southern Germany clear of cloud, and despite some ground haze, good visibility prevailing as the flare force went in at 17,000 feet at 23.52, homing in on a green TI delivered by a Mosquito. The Master bomber seemed satisfied with the illumination and required no further flares, leaving the backers-up to drop their TIs over the ensuing four minutes, before sending them home at 23.59. The main force crews followed up with extreme accuracy and concentration, those from 61 Squadron bombing on red and green TIs from 13,000 to 16,000 feet between 23.57 and 00.07. The city centre became engulfed in flames, which spread outwards to consume large parts of the built-up area and the glow, according to some, could be seen from the French coast 250 miles away.

The conditions had been ideal for the 5 Group marking method, and photo-reconnaissance confirmed the main weight of the attack to have fallen in the central and surrounding districts to the south and east. It was learned after the war that the attack had resulted in a genuine firestorm, only the third to be recorded after Hamburg and Kassel in 1943, although a number of local ones may have occurred in other cities like Berlin and Stuttgart. More than twelve thousand people died in the inferno, and a further seventy thousand, 60% of a total population of 120,000, were made homeless, in return for which, 5 Group posted missing a dozen Lancasters and crews.

Orders were received on 5 Group stations on the 12th to prepare for a return to southern Germany that night, this time to target the industrial city of Stuttgart, and eighteen 61 Squadron crews attended the briefing at Skellingthorpe to learn that they were to be part of a force of 195 Lancasters and fourteen Mosquitos. They would benefit from RCM cover provided by nine ABC Lancasters from 1 Group's 101 Squadron, while a simultaneous operation by 378 Lancasters and nine Mosquitos of 1, 3 and 8 Groups a hundred miles to the north at Frankfurt would help to divide the enemy night-fighter force. The 61 Squadron element took off between 18.20 and 19.12 with F/L Kilgour the senior pilot on duty and the recently posted-in S/L Horsley flying as second pilot to F/O Inness. PB434 crashed almost immediately upon the failure of its port-outer engine but F/O Cooksey and crew emerged from the wreckage apparently unscathed. They joined the bomber stream as they headed south to adopt a course similar to that of twenty-four hours earlier and mostly enjoyed an uneventful flight across France to Stuttgart, which was found to be under clear skies with moderate visibility and ground haze, and therefore, ideal conditions for the low-level Mosquito marker crews. The marking and backing up were very accurate, and the main force bombing concentrated upon the city centre with a slight tendency to creep back towards the north-eastern district of Bad Canstatt and beyond into Feuerbach. The 61 Squadron crews bombed on red TIs from 14,000 to 16,100 feet between 23.10 and 23.22, and all returned safely to report a successful operation and a huge explosion at 23.25, which lasted for about five seconds. When a PRU aircraft photographed the city on the following morning, the entire centre was obscured by the smoke from numerous and widespread fires, and the effectiveness of the raid was confirmed by local sources, which described the central districts as "erased". It seems that a firestorm had erupted in northern and west-central districts, wiping them from the map and almost twelve hundred people lost their lives, the highest death toll ever in this much-bombed city, in exchange for which, only four Lancasters were missing.

Other than the first of 617 Squadron's three attacks on Tirpitz on the 15th, launched from Yagodnik in Russia, 5 Group undertook no further operations until the morning of the 17th, when contributing to a total of 762 aircraft assembled to attack troop positions at seven locations around the port of Boulogne. The raids would be staggered over a four-hour period and benefit from a 5 Group effort of 195 Lancasters and four Mosquitos, twenty-one of the former representing 61 Squadron and departing Skellingthorpe between 07.30 and 08.10 with S/Ls Horsley and Pexton the senior pilots on duty. They were part of the second wave of aircraft to attack one of two aiming-points assigned to 5 Group and, an hour behind the first wave, found clear skies with good visibility and a little flak from a coastal position to the north, which did not impede their progress. The delivered their eleven 1,000 and four 500-pounders each onto red TIs from 7,000 to 9,000 feet between 09.42 and 09.45 and observed a concentration of bomb bursts on the aiming point with few stray bomb loads. A total of three thousand tons of bombs was sufficient to pave the way for Allied ground forces to move in shortly afterwards to accept the surrender of the German garrison. This left only Calais of the major French ports still under enemy occupation.

Operation Market Garden, Montgomery's brilliant but ill-fated plan to speed up the advance into Germany by capturing nine bridges spanning the Lower Rhine in Holland, was launched on the 17th, Bomber Command's first involvement provided by elements of 1 and 8 Groups against German flak positions. During the night a further 241 aircraft conducted diversionary sweeps in a vain attempt to bring the Holland-based Luftwaffe into battle.

5 Group stations received orders on the 18th to prepare for an operation that night against the port of Bremerhaven, located on the east bank at the mouth of the River Weser, some thirty miles north of Bremen. It was to be a classic 5 Group-style attack, employing the low-level visual marking method and involved 206 Lancasters and seven Mosquitos. At Skellingthorpe 61 Squadron loaded twenty Lancasters with a mix of 2,000-pounders and 500lb J-Type cluster bombs plus incendiaries and sent them on their way between 17.54 and 18.44 with S/L Horsley the senior pilot on duty. There were no early returns among the 61 Squadron contingent, which arrived at the target to find favourable weather conditions and good visibility as they ran in on the aiming-point at medium level. The bombs were released onto red TIs from 12,000 to 17,000 feet between 21.01 and 21.09, mostly in accordance with the Master Bomber's instructions and a number of huge explosions were witnessed at 21.02 and 21.07. As they headed out of the target area, they could see many large fires spreading throughout the built-up area, the glow from which remained visible on the horizon for at least 150 miles. Post-raid reconnaissance revealed that this first major attack on the port, carried out by what, at the time, could be considered to be a modest force, had devasted the built-up areas north and south of the harbour entrance, wiping out installations and warehousing, and only the most northerly and southerly suburbs had escaped complete destruction. Local reports produced a figure of 2,670 buildings reduced to rubble and thirty-thousand people bombed out of their homes, all at the modest cost to 5 Group of a single Lancaster and a Mosquito.

Twenty 61 Squadron crews assembled for the briefing at Skellingthorpe on the 19th and learned that they were to be part of a predominantly 5 Group attack on the twin towns of Mönchengladbach and Rheydt. This represented a shallow penetration into Germany, just ten minutes from the Dutch border, and therefore, a short round trip of four-and-a-half to five hours followed by a night in bed. 217 Lancasters and ten Mosquitos were made ready, along with ten ABC Lancasters from 101 Squadron, and the 61 Squadron participants took off between 18.31 and 19.12 with S/L Horsley the senior pilot on duty and each Lancaster carrying a 2,000-pounder and eleven 500lb J-Type cluster bombs. The Master Bomber for the operation was W/C Guy Gibson VC, DSO, DFC, who had been agitating to get back into the war before it was over and didn't want his service to end in a backwater, while others gained the glory by being in at the death. Gibson was a warrior, and the war had brought out of him qualities, which in peacetime may have lain dormant and it had also given him a direction and an opportunity to revel in the company of fellow operational types, particularly those of the officer class. Having been torn away from the operational scene following the success of Operation Chastise, his purpose had gone and he had become listless, frustrated and discontented. His time in the operational wilderness had not, however, deprived him of his arrogance and self-belief, and when the opportunity to fly as Master Bomber on the coming raid presented itself, he grabbed it.

He was driven the three miles from Coningsby to Woodhall Spa to collect his 627 Squadron Mosquito, which, for whatever reason, he rejected and swapped with F/L Mallender, causing a degree of resentment. Gibson had already set the tone for the evening by rejecting the advice of W/C Charles Owen, who had been Master Bomber at this target ten nights earlier, to leave the target by a south-westerly route and cross north-eastern France to the coast, and also to observe orders to remain above 10,000 feet. Gibson insisted that he would fly home via a direct route across Holland at low level and took off ahead of the 627 Squadron element at 19.51 to meet up with the main force over the target, where two aiming-points were to be marked. F/L Lockhart and crew were at the midpoint of the sea crossing when the pilot became unwell, and F/O Greenfield and crew turned back from a position some fifteen miles south of Charleroi when the rear turret became unserviceable. Some crews reported icing clouds at around 9,000 feet as they made their way to the target over Belgium and chose to keep below, before climbing fast to 15,000 feet as the cloud dispersed.

The marking was complex, with a green marker to be dropped on a factory in a western district of Mönchengladbach and a yellow marker on railway yards in the north, while a red marker was to be placed on railway yards in Rheydt, two miles to the south. It would have been a demanding plan even for an experienced Master Bomber, which Gibson was not, but even so, his instructions were heard clearly. All seemed to be going to plan, with accurate and punctual marking for the green and yellow forces, but late, though accurate marking for the red force, and some of the red force crews were diverted to the green aiming-point. The 61 Squadron crews were assigned to the green force and identified it by flares and TIs before bombing from 10,000 to 13,000 feet between 21.49 and 21.58, observing the target to be well ablaze with the glow visible for at least a hundred miles into the return flight. Four Lancasters and a Mosquito failed to return from what post-raid reconnaissance confirmed to have been a highly destructive attack on both towns. Gibson had returned low over Holland, just as he said he would, and crashed on the outskirts of Steenbergen in south-western Holland, with fatal consequences for him and Coningsby's recently appointed station navigation officer, S/L James Warwick. The cause of the crash is unresolved, but the general belief is that Gibson's lack of familiarity with the Mosquito led to his failure to locate fuel transfer taps, and the engines became starved of petrol.

It was now time to turn attention upon Calais as the final port still under enemy occupation, but only one 5 Group Lancaster was involved in the first round of attacks on enemy positions on the 20th, after which, the group remained inactive until the 23rd. Orders came through on that morning to prepare 136 Lancasters and five Mosquitos for an attack that night on the aqueduct section of the Dortmund-Ems Canal south of Ladbergen, which had been the scene of a disaster for 617 Squadron in September 1943, when five of eight crews had failed to return. An element from 617 Squadron would be on scene also on this night to open the attack with Tallboys, to which the raised banks containing the waterway were particularly vulnerable. Germany's canal system was a vital component in the transport network and facilitated the import of raw materials and the export of finished goods to support the war effort. Its wide thoroughfares allowed the passage of large barges, and as the slack in Germany's war production was taken up during 1944, traffic was being pushed through at increasing levels. While this operation was in progress, a second 5 Group force of 108 Lancasters, four Mosquitos and the P38 Lightning would hit the Handorf night-fighter airfield some ten miles to the south to prevent it from interfering. The main operation on this night, however, would be conducted by 549 aircraft from 1, 3, 4 and 8 Groups seventy miles to the southwest at Neuss, situated across the Rhine opposite Düsseldorf, and this, hopefully, might help to split the enemy defences.

The 61 Squadron ORB is confusing concerning the targets for its nineteen Lancasters, stating Münster as the destination, but as the Ladbergen section of the Dortmund-Ems Canal and Handorf aerodrome are close by to the north and north-east, it would seem to be a general reference to the target area. According to the 50 Squadron ORB, nineteen of its Lancasters were assigned to the Dortmund-Ems Canal, and they and their 61 Squadron counterparts departed Skellingthorpe together between 18.39 and 19.48 with S/L Horsley the senior 61 Squadron pilot on duty, presumably bound for the same destination. F/O Boon and crew turned back from a point west of Antwerp because of damage sustained, probably flak in the well-defended Antwerp area, while the remainder reached the target area to encounter a layer of ten-tenths cloud at between 8,000 and 9,500 feet, but with good visibility beneath. The Master Bomber found himself unable to direct the attack, and experienced great difficulty in communicating the fact to his Deputy because of intense interference on VHF. Identification and marking of the aiming-point proved to be difficult, and only two green TIs could be seen by a few crews. There would be complaints later that there was no control, and some crews orbited and remained in the target area for up to thirty-five minutes before bombing either on green TIs at Handorf or on yellows at Münster, which was selected as the last-resort target.

In Bomber Command Losses for 1944, Bill Chorley records F/O Hornibrook RAAF and crew failing to return from Münster in veteran Lancaster ED470, which crashed into the River Waal, leaving only the rear gunner to survive in enemy hands. The three other failures to return on this sombre night for 61 Squadron are recorded by Chorley as missing from Ladbergen, which confirms that the Dortmund-Ems Canal was the squadron's primary target and that the Hornibrook crew had probably attacked Münster as a last resort target. Bombing by the 61 Squadron contingent was carried out on the glow of red TIs from 7,000 to 15,000 feet between 21.49 and 22.05. Six Lancasters failed to return to Skellingthorpe after the Canal-Busters were badly mauled by night-fighters on the way home, one already mentioned, two belonging to 50 Squadron and the 61 Squadron crews of S/L Horsley, F/L Stone and F/O Campbell RNZAF. LM718 crashed on farmland near Deurne to the east of Antwerp, killing two members of the crew, while two were taken into captivity and S/L Horsley and two others evaded a similar fate. S/L Horsley and his rear gunner would rejoin the squadron but not survive the war. ME732 crashed at 23.13 at Almelo, a town just inside Holland's frontier with Germany, and F/L Stone and five others lost their lives, while one was captured, and another was spirited away by local partisans. ND988 came down at around 23.30 on the outskirts of the town of Tecklenburg, south-west of Osnabrück and only the rear gunner survived to fall into enemy hands.

The second of the series of raids on enemy positions around Calais was mounted by 188 aircraft on the 24th, for which 5 Group detailed thirty Lancasters from the 53 Base stations of Skellingthorpe and Waddington. 61 Squadron contributed seven aircraft, which took off between 17.20 and 17.35 with F/L King the senior pilot on duty. F/O Brian and crew turned back at Dover because of port-inner engine failure, and shortly afterwards, at around 18.20 to 18.26, signals were received from the Master Bomber to "cease bombing", by which time most crews were still over the sea or on their bombing run. He had found the target to be obscured beneath ten-tenths cloud with a base at 2,000 feet, and recognised the futility of carrying on, however, some red TIs had been delivered, and the crews of F/Os Abbott and Miller bombed them from 2,000 feet at 18.31 without observing any results. In the event, only 126 aircraft bombed, eight of them from 5 Group, and they attacked either on a reference provided by Oboe skymarkers or came below the cloud base to bomb visually. At such a height, they were sitting ducks for the heavy and light flak batteries, which accounted for seven Lancasters and a Halifax. 61 Squadron's NF914 crashed into the sea off Calais, killing F/O Freeman DFC and four of his crew, while the flight engineer and mid-upper gunner survived and managed to make it to the Allied lines.

On the 25th, W/C Pexton was promoted to wing commander rank to succeed W/C Doubleday as squadron commander, the latter having completed his wartime service with fifty-three sorties to his credit. On his return to Australia, he famously described disembarking from the liner in anonymity and walking into a hotel for a lamb chop lunch. On the afternoon of the 26th, fifteen 61 Squadron crews attended briefing and learned that the night's operation was to be against the city of Karlsruhe in southern Germany, for which 216 Lancasters of 5 Group were made ready along with ten of the ABC variety from 101 Squadron and eleven Mosquitos. It was to be a two-phase attack with a two-hour gap between and the 52, 53 and 55 Base elements assigned to the second phase. This meant a late take-off and it was between 00.29 and 00.15 when the 61 Squadron element departed Skellingthorpe with F/Ls Crampton, Grynkiewicz, King and Watkins the senior pilots on duty. F/O Cooksey and crew turned back when over Surrey because of an engine issue, leaving the rest to fly out over France with ten-tenths cloud beneath them and persisting all the way to the target, where it thinned to a narrow band with the base estimated to be at between 6,000 and 7,000 feet. The plan was to bomb through the cloud on H2S, guided by Wanganui flares, and some approaching crews observed a red TI cascade above the cloud at 03.54. The 61 Squadron crews focused on the glow of red and green TIs and bombed them from 7,000 to 12,500 feet between 04.01 and 04.08 in accordance with the instructions of the Master Bomber. F/O Abbott and crew were unable to identify either red or green TIs and brought part of their bomb load home. All returned safely to report what appeared to be a city in flames and the glow of fires visible for up to 150 miles into the return journey. There were no plottable bombing photos, but reconnaissance confirmed that the attack had been spread throughout the city and had left a large part of it devastated at a cost to the Command of two Lancasters.

As the crews returned to their stations after 07.00, elements of 1, 3, 4 and 8 Groups were preparing to leave theirs for a further attack on the Calais area. On arrival, the Master Bomber ordered the

340-strong force to come below the cloud base to bomb visually and another successful operation ensued. Later that day, an advance party from 619 Squadron headed east by road to establish a squadron presence at Strubby, a station located three miles north of Alford, west of Sutton-on-Sea, which had opened in April as a sub-station of 55 Base at East Kirkby. It had been occupied first by Coastal Command as a base for its Warwick air-sea rescue operations, and then elements of the 2nd Tactical Air Force, but was now to be home for the remainder of the war to 619 Squadron.

Meanwhile, at Skellingthorpe, fifteen 61 Squadron crews attended briefing for an operation that night against Kaiserslautern, an historic city on the edge of the Palatinate Forest, some thirty miles west of Mannheim. It would be the first major attack of the war on this location, for which a heavy force of 217 Lancasters was assembled, including ten from of the ABC variety provided by 101 Squadron, while ten Mosquitos were prepared for the low-level marking role. The 61 Squadron Lancasters were loaded with 2,000-pounders, 500lb J-Type cluster bombs and 4lb incendiaries, which they lifted into the air between 21.42 and 22.33 with W/C Pexton the senior pilot on duty. Clear skies over England gave way to a build-up of cloud over the Channel, and from the French coast to near the target they encountered ten-tenths cumulus with a base at 2,800 feet. The target was partially covered by a thin layer of five to eight-tenths cloud with tops at 3,000 feet, with a further layer at 6,000 to 7,000 feet. The marking with red and green TIs was punctual and accurate, and a green TI visible in the centre of the town became the objective for the main force crews in accordance with the Master Bomber's instructions at 00.58. The 61 Squadron crews attacked from 3,500 to 5,500 feet between 01.05 and 01.12, observing concentrated bombing, two yellow explosions at 01.02 and fires beginning to take hold as the force retreated towards the west. Reconnaissance revealed massive damage within the city, caused by more than nine hundred tons of bombs, which left an estimated 36% of the built-up area in ruins.

The final raids on German positions around Calais were carried out by 490 aircraft of 1, 3, 6 and 8 Groups on the 28th and the garrison surrendered to Canadian forces shortly thereafter. 619 Squadron completed its move to Strubby on this day, while 44 (Rhodesia) Squadron joined 207 Squadron at Spilsby, and together with East Kirkby, this constituted the new 55 Base, while 52 Base was about to be disbanded. Dunholme Lodge, like nearby Scampton, was transferred to 1 Group and welcomed the recently reformed 170 Squadron with its Lancasters. However, because of its close proximity to Scampton, Faldingworth, Wickenby and Fiskerton with overlapping circuits, it was decided to take Dunholme Lodge out of the front line and 170 Squadron would move out at the end of November.

During the course of the month the squadron participated in a dozen operations and dispatched 202 sorties for the loss of six Lancasters and five crews.

October 1944

Having now discharged his primary obligation to SHAEF, Harris turned his attention once more fully towards industrial Germany with a particular emphasis on oil production. A theme running throughout October was a campaign against the island of Walcheren in the Scheldt estuary, where heavy gun emplacements were barring the approaches to the much-needed port of Antwerp some forty miles upstream. Attempts to bomb these positions in September had proved unsuccessful, and it was decided to flood the land to inundate the batteries and render the terrain difficult to defend when the ground forces moved in. 252 Lancasters were drawn from 1, 5 and 8 Groups and made ready on the 3rd to attack the seawalls at Westkapelle, the most westerly point of the island. 5 Group contributed 128 Lancasters, allotted to four of eight waves of thirty aircraft each, with the Tallboy-carrying 617 Squadron Lancasters standing off to be called in only if required. A breach was opened by the fifth wave, which was extended by those following behind and the flood waters had reached the town by the time the last Lancasters turned for home.

The Skellingthorpe squadrons had not been invited to take part, and had to wait until 5 Group's first major outing of the month, which was posted on the 5th, as a daylight attempt to bomb the port of Wilhelmshaven through ten-tenths cloud on H2S. A force of 227 Lancasters, one Mosquito and the P38 Lightning was assembled with 61 Squadron providing nineteen aircraft, and they set out from Skellingthorpe between 07.20 and 08.43 with W/C Pexton and the newly posted-in S/L Fadden the senior pilots on duty. Whether or not it was part of the plan, the controller led the force around the northern side of Heligoland, before heading for Jade Bay, where they found the target, as forecast, concealed under a layer of ten-tenths cloud at between 3,000 and 5,000 feet with good visibility above. The 61 Squadron crews established their positions by H2S-fix or by observing others and delivered their ten 1,000-pounders and four 500lb J-Type cluster bombs each from 17,000 to 18,000 feet between 11.03 and 11.09. No results were observed, and there was no possibility of making an assessment, but the impression of a scattered attack was confirmed later when the cloud conditions allowed photo-reconnaissance to take place.

From this point until the end of the war, German towns and cities were to be subjected to a new and terrible bomber offensive, beginning with a second Ruhr campaign, which was posted to open at Dortmund on the 6th. A force of 523 aircraft was assembled from 3, 6 and 8 Groups, while 5 Group prepared 237 Lancasters and seven Mosquitos for what would prove to be the thirty-second and final raid of the war on the city of port-city of Bremen. 61 Squadron loaded nineteen Lancasters with a mixture of high explosives and incendiaries and dispatched them from Skellingthorpe between 17.25 and 17.56 with S/L Fadden the senior pilot on duty. Having climbed out and set course, they left the cloud behind and headed into crystal clear skies over the North Sea with a three-quarter moon to light the way. F/O Scholes and crew were approaching the midpoint of the sea crossing when the rear gunner reported his turret to be unserviceable and they had to turn back. The others found the target area to be free of cloud, which was ideal for the 5 Group low-level marking method and the conditions handed the hapless city on a plate to the bombers.

The 61 Squadron crews carried out their attacks in the face of many searchlights and the usual flak response, aiming for the red and green TIs from 15,750 to 17,000 feet between 20.28 and 20.43 with a twenty-six-second overshoot in accordance with instructions from the Master Bomber. When they turned for home, crews observed a city in flames, the glow from which remained visible on the horizon for a hundred miles and more. The success of the operation was confirmed by post-raid reconnaissance and local reports, which described a huge area of fire and catalogued the destruction of more than 4,800 houses and apartment blocks, along with severe damage to war industry factories, all achieved at the modest cost of five aircraft. Now that the focus of operations had moved from France to Germany, the number of sorties to complete a tour had been reduced from thirty-five to thirty-three, and this represented an unexpected bonus to some.

A new addition to 5 Group's strength came with the reformation of 227 Squadron from 9 Squadron's A Flight and 619 Squadron's B Flight on the 7th. After bedding in at Bardney for two weeks, the new unit would move on to Balderton on the outskirts of Newark and in April 1945 to Strubby. Following the failure of Operation Market Garden, the German frontier towns of Cleves (Kleve) and Emmerich, five miles apart and separated by the Rhine, were earmarked for attention by daylight on the 7th and both would suffer massive damage at the hands of large forces from 1, 3, 4 and 8 Groups. 5 Group, meanwhile, detailed 121 Lancasters and three Mosquitos for a return to Walcheren to target the seawalls near Flushing, 61 Squadron contributing a dozen Lancasters and sending them on their way from Skellingthorpe between 12.10 and 12.31 with W/C Pexton and S/L Fadden the senior pilots on duty. They all reached the target area to identify the two aiming-points visually and by red TIs, before attacking both in separate passes, delivering seven 1,000-pounders on each from 5,500 to 6,800 feet between 13.57 and 14.10. Many of the bomb carried by other squadrons contained a thirty-minute delay fuse, but some were primed to detonate on impact, and the dyke was already beginning to crumble as the bombers headed home, where confirmation of a successful outcome would catch up with them.

Focus remained on the Scheldt defences, and the gun battery at Fort Frederik Hendrik near Breskens on the East Scheldt was targeted by elements of 1 and 8 Groups on the 11th, while 115 Lancasters from 5 Group were assigned to others near Flushing on the north bank of the West Scheldt. At the same time sixty-one Lancasters and two Mosquitos from the group were to attempt to breach the seawalls at Veere, situated on the eastern side of Walcheren opposite Westkapelle. 61 Squadron contributed eighteen Lancasters to Flushing, and they departed Skellingthorpe between 13.12 and 13.37 with W/C Pexton and S/L Fadden the senior pilots on duty. On arrival in the target area shortly before 15.00, the crews encountered varying amounts of cloud between two and seven-tenths with tops at 4,000 to 5,000 feet, and only ten of the 61 Squadron crews were able to carry out an attack from 2,900 to 7,000 feet between 14.55 and 15.45, some having orbited for fifty minutes. The Master Bomber's signal to abandon the attack was received either side of 15.30, but clearly some crews either failed to pick it up or ignored it. Post-raid reconnaissance revealed an area of flooding of 800 x 250 yards at Veere, but no new damage to the gun positions.

The 14th was the day on which were fired the opening salvoes of Operation Hurricane, a terrifying demonstration to the enemy of the overwhelming superiority of the Allied air forces ranged against it. Bomber Command ordered a maximum effort from all but 5 Group to attack Duisburg, for which 1,013 Lancasters, Halifaxes and Mosquitos answered the call. The American 8th Air Force would also be in business on this day, targeting the Cologne area further south with 1,250 bombers escorted by 749 fighters. The RAF force took off at first light, picked up its own fighter escort, and delivered 4,500 tons of high-explosives and incendiaries into Duisburg shortly after breakfast time, causing unimaginable destruction. That night, similar numbers returned to press home the point about superiority, bringing the total weight of bombs over the two raids to 9,000 tons from 2,018 sorties in fewer than twenty-four hours. The only involvement by 5 Group were single sorties by a Lancaster and a Mosquito to conduct a photo-reconnaissance of the operation.

However, 5 Group took advantage of the evening activity over the Ruhr to return to Braunschweig, the scene of quite a number of unsatisfactory previous attempts to land a really telling blow. A force of 232 Lancasters and eight Mosquitos was made ready, of which eighteen of the former were provided by 61 Squadron and departed Skellingthorpe between 22.19 and 23.05 with S/L Fadden the senior pilot on duty. F/O Greenfield and crew were a little over an hour out when the pilot became unwell, and they had to turn back. The rest reached the target area to find conditions ideal for low-level marking but had to approach the aiming-point at 18,000 feet from the south-west, passing over Hallendorf and Salzgitter, the latter the home to the Reichswerke Hermann

Göring steelworks. This forced them to run the gauntlet of searchlight cones and heavy flak for the three minutes it took to pass through, but once on the other side they were greeted by clear skies and good visibility, which facilitated accurate marking with red and green TIs. Although the early stages of bombing tended to undershoot, the Master Bomber quickly brought the attack back on track, calling for crews to overshoot by up to nineteen seconds. The 61 Squadron contingent passed over the aiming-point at 16,000 to 17,000 feet between 02.30 and 02.37 and delivered their loads accurately to contribute to a highly effective raid. 83 Squadron's F/O Price complained that main force crews were jettisoning incendiaries all the way back as far as the Rhine and thereby illuminating the track for any stalking night-fighters. In the event, only a single Lancaster failed to return, 61 Squadron's ME595, from which F/O Hoad and five of his crew escaped with their lives to fall into enemy hands, while the flight engineer and wireless operator lost their lives. Post-raid reconnaissance and local sources confirmed the outstanding success of the operation, which had wiped out the entire centre of this historic city, and visited damage on almost every district.

Earlier in the day, an advance party from 49 Squadron had arrived at Fulbeck to prepare the way for the main party's move on the 16th. Located some six miles to the east of Newark, the station opened in 1940 and had been home to both RAF and USAAF units engaged predominantly in troop-carrying activities. Along with Syerston and Balderton, it would now form 56 Base under the command of G/C Pope, and in time would include 49, 189 and 227 Squadrons.

The main operation on the 15th was the fourteenth and final major raid on the important shipbuilding and naval port of Wilhelmshaven, for which a force of 506 aircraft was drawn from all but 5 Group. What may have been spoof green TIs were reported some five miles to the west and north-west of the target, and these attracted a number of bomb loads, while the rest of the bombing appeared to be scattered, a fact largely confirmed by local sources, which named only the Rathaus (Town Council HQ) as completely destroyed. Stubborn resistance by the occupiers on Walcheren demanded further operations against the seawalls at Westkapelle, which came with an afternoon attack by forty-seven Lancasters and three Mosquitos from 55 and 54 Bases on the 17th. They found favourable conditions in which to deliver their delay-fused bombs, and most brought back an aiming-point photo, despite which, those taken by a reconnaissance aircraft, which had remained over the target from 14.55 to 15.10 to record the bomb blasts, revealed no extension to the breach in the dyke.

An operation of significance on the morning of the 18th represented a major step forward in Bomber Command's evolution and brought with it for 3 Group the same level of independence enjoyed by 5 Group. The G-H bombing system had been under development for around two years and mirrored to an extent the American method of releasing bombs on observing the leader's fall away. While the American system was exclusively for daylight operations, the RAF system was equally effective at night and in 3 Group hands would prove to be particularly effective against precision targets like oil refineries and railways. As one of a few relatively intact German cities, Bonn, situated some twenty miles to the south-east of Cologne, was selected as the target for the first massed live trial on the assumption that fresh damage would be easily identified to assess the performance of G-H. The operation was not entirely successful, but time and practice would iron out the wrinkles.

Following a break of four nights, eighteen 61 Squadron crews reported to the Skellingthorpe briefing room on the 19th, to receive details of the operation that night against Nuremberg, which was to be a 5 Group affair involving a new record for the group of 263 Lancasters and seven

Mosquitos. Meanwhile, 560 aircraft from the other groups would be plying their trade at Stuttgart, some ninety miles to the south-west. The 61 Squadron crews took off between 17.10 and 17.44 with W/C Pexton the senior pilot on duty and lost the services of F/O Corewyn and crew to the failure of their port-inner engine when north of Amiens. For the others, the outward flight across France was uneventful, but the target was found to be covered by a wedge of eight to ten-tenths cloud at between 3,000 and 10,000 feet, with poor visibility below. The marker force laid down flares and backed them up with others along with red and green TIs, which were observed to be somewhat scattered, and bombing had to take place on their glow observed through the cloud. The 61 Squadron crews carried out their attacks from 14,100 to 16,300 feet between 20.59 and 21.05 in accordance with the Master Bomber's instructions, before returning home uncertain as to the outcome. The impression given by the glow of fires was of an effective attack, but post-raid reconnaissance revealed the bombing to have fallen not on the intended city centre aiming-point, but predominantly into the more industrial southern districts, where almost four hundred houses were destroyed, along with forty-one industrial buildings.

A return to Walcheren on the 23rd involved 112 Lancasters of 5 Group, this time to target the coastal battery at Flushing, for which 61 Squadron loaded twenty Lancasters with eleven 1,000-pounders each and dispatched them from Skellingthorpe between 14.30 and 14.49 with S/Ls Fadden and Horsley the senior pilots on duty. They were greeted at the target by eight to ten-tenths cloud with a base at between 3,000 and 5,000 feet, and poor visibility below caused by haze and rain. The force was led in on what appeared to be a decent approach but was ordered to "orbit port" as the lead crews experienced great difficulty in identifying their respective aiming-points. A second run was no more revealing, even for those crews who ventured down as low as 2,000 feet, and twenty would still have their bombs on board when ordered to go home. All but one of the 61 Squadron crews carried out a visual attack from 3,900 to 5,000 feet between 16.12 and 16.40 and observed their bombs to fall within the target area, and only F/O Scholes and crew withheld their ordnance after failing to identify the aiming point. Post-raid reconnaissance revealed evidence of seventy bomb bursts, including four near-misses, and the destruction of a number of buildings on the site.

That evening, a new record force of 1,055 aircraft was sent against Essen as part of the Hurricane "message" and dropped 4,538 tons of bombs, more than 90% of which was high explosive. This number was achieved without 5 Group, which took the night off and committed only twenty-five Lancasters to gardening duties in northern waters on the following night. Essen was pounded again by more than seven hundred aircraft in daylight on the 25th, by which time it had ceased to be an important source of war production. Operation Hurricane moved on to Cologne on the 28th, when two districts east of the centre were totally devastated by more than seven hundred aircraft.

5 Group occupied the 28th with the preparation of a force of 237 Lancasters and seven Mosquitos for an operation that night against the U-Boot pens at Bergen in Norway, for which 61 Squadron made ready seventeen Lancasters and sent them on their way from Skellingthorpe between 22.07 and 23.09 with F/Ls Greenfield and Grynkiewicz the senior pilots on duty. Veteran Lancaster ED860 swung out of control on take-off and crashed, ending its flying career after 130 sorties, but the crew of F/O Pearse escaped without serious injury. The bomber stream had to battle its way through electrical storms and lost only two of its number to early returns during the three-and-a-half-hour outward flight, at the end of which the crews were expecting to find the forecast clear conditions. It is true that some doubts had been expressed about the forecast, and these were confirmed when the force was met by eight-to ten-tenths cloud at between 4,000 and 14,000 feet,

which obscured the aiming-point. This would not have been a problem over Germany, but the risk to Norwegian civilians was uppermost in the mind of the Master Bomber as he pondered his options, before calling for the main force to descend. Even then, most were unable to pick out any markers and the situation was exacerbated by intermittent VHF reception, which persuaded 83 Squadron's F/L Cornish to fly up and down the coast acting as a communications link between the Master Bomber and the main force. The flare force element did what it could to illuminate the area from between 12,500 and 15,000 feet and some main force crews flew as low as 4,500 feet without being able to identify the target. Forty-seven crews found some kind of reference, before the Master Bomber called a halt to proceedings, among them those of F/O Hutchins and F/L Greenfield, who bombed on a red TI from 6,000 and 4,400 feet at 02.03 and 02.16 respectively. ND902 came under sustained attack in the target area and although nursed home by F/O Miller and crew, was found to have sustained sufficient damage to be declared beyond economical repair.

The final operations against Walcheren were undertaken by 5 Group on the 30th, when two forces of fifty-one Lancasters and four Mosquitos each were sent against coastal batteries at Westkapelle and Flushing two hours apart. Ground forces went in on the following day, and a week of heavy fighting preceded the island's capture. Even then, the clearing of mines from the approaches to Antwerp kept the port out of commission for a further three weeks. On the evening of the 30th, nine hundred aircraft returned to Cologne, and almost five hundred went back again twenty-four hours later to complete the destruction of the Rhineland capital.

During the course of the month, the squadron operated on eight occasions and dispatched 141 sorties for the loss of three Lancasters and one crew.

November 1944

The new month began with a daylight operation on the afternoon of the 1st, against the Meerbeck synthetic oil refinery at Moers/Homberg, or, to give it its full title, the Gewerkschaft Rheinpreussen A.G plant, located on the west bank of the Rhine opposite Duisburg on the western edge of the Ruhr. The name of this target would strike fear into the hearts of 3 Group crews, who had suffered heavy casualties while attacking the plant during the summer, but it meant nothing to 5 Group crews, who were less familiar with it and would have found the name of Wesseling far more unsettling. 61 Squadron briefed sixteen crews as part of an overall 5 Group force of 226 Lancasters and two Mosquitos, which were to be joined by fourteen 8 Group Mosquitos to provide the Oboe marking. They departed Skellingthorpe between 13.34 and 14.10 with S/L Horsley the senior pilot on duty, he having returned to the squadron after evading capture in September and reached the target to find it completely obscured by cloud with tops at between 6,000 and 9,000 feet. Wanganui flares from earlier arrivals were well-scattered over a circle with a ten-mile radius, prompting a backer-up from 83 Squadron to drop a yellow TI over the built-up area in the hope of attracting some bombing. The problem seemed to be, that crews at the head of the stream had seen no markers or were past them by the time that they became evident and had taken their bombs home. Ten 61 Squadron crews caught a glimpse of the target area through a chink in the cloud, while others carried out a time-and-distance run from the last visual pinpoint, before aiming at red skymarkers with green stars to deliver their fourteen 1,000-pounders each from 15,500 to 19,600 feet between 16.08 and 16.12. Five others withheld their bombs and one attacked an alternative target at Moers and all faced an intense flak response, which inflicted damage on a number of aircraft. At debriefings, many crews reported difficulty in hearing the Master Bomber, after his VHF transmissions became jammed by a transmit button left on in another aircraft. Ultimately, the conditions rendered the whole attack ineffective, and although 159 crews released their bombs, it is unlikely that any hit the intended target.

Düsseldorf's turn to face a massive force came on the 2nd, when 992 aircraft were made ready for what would prove to be the final major raid of the war on this much-bombed city. The "Lincolnshire Poachers" put up 187 Lancasters for this rare experience to operate with the rest of the Command and 61 Squadron pitched in with sixteen, which departed Skellingthorpe between 16.17 and 17.10 with S/L Fadden the senior pilot on duty and joined up with the rest of the bomber stream as it passed over Reading on its way to beachy head for a southern approach to the Ruhr. W/O Souter and crew lost their port-outer engine and turned back with the French coast some twenty miles ahead, while the others found the target to be basking in moonlight streaming from clear skies, with only ground haze to slightly mar the vertical visibility. The moonlight nullified the glare of searchlights ringing the city, but of greater concern was the heavy flak bursting at 17,000 to 20,000 feet, which the main force crews had to negotiate on their way to the well-illuminated aiming-point marked out with red and green TIs. The 61 Squadron participants dropped a cookie, six 1,000-pounders and six-500 pounders each from 17,000 to 21,100 feet between 19.15 and 19.30 and on return reported fires beginning to take hold and smoke rising though 2,000 feet as they turned away. Eleven Lancasters and eight Halifaxes failed to return, although four of them came down in Allied-held territory, among the latter 61 Squadron's PD199. F/O McGillivray and his mid-upper gunner failed to survive, which suggests that a forced-landing was attempted, but the other members of the crew were apparently unharmed. The effectiveness of the operation was confirmed by post-raid reconnaissance, which revealed that the northern half of the city had received the main weight of bombs and that five thousand houses had been destroyed or seriously damaged.

The new campaign against Ruhr cities continued on the 4th with the assembling of a force of 749 aircraft to attack Bochum, while 5 Group renewed its acquaintance with the Dortmund-Ems Canal at Ladbergen, which had been repaired following the successful breaching of its banks in September. Now that Germany's railways were being pounded to destruction, the Dortmund-Ems and the nearby Mittelland Canal took on a greater significance as vital components in the transportation system, particularly with regard to the movement of raw materials to and from the Ruhr region. A force of 168 Lancasters and two Mosquitos contained a dozen 61 Squadron aircraft, which departed Skellingthorpe between 17.35 and 17.58 with no senior pilot on duty. They were heading for the familiar aqueduct section of the canal south of Ladbergen and hoped to sneak in under cover of the main operation sixty miles to the south, hopefully, thereby, to avoid the attentions of night-fighters. The first marker aircraft of 83 Squadron arrived at the target at 19.19 after making a GPI run (ground position indicated) by means of H2S from Münster and encountered clear skies with ground haze. A blind-dropped green TI burst on the canal bank four hundred yards short of the aiming-point, and the flare force went in to illuminate the area between 19.20 and 19.28. Red TIs were observed to fall between the two aqueducts, after which, the Master Bomber cancelled the third wave of flare-carriers and sent them all home to leave the way clear for the main force crews. The first bombs tended to overshoot, but, thereafter, the crews produced an accurate and concentrated attack, those from 61 Squadron bombing from 10,250 to 13,000 feet between 19.31 and 19.37. Photo-reconnaissance confirmed that both branches of the canal had been breached and drained, leaving barges stranded and the waterway unnavigable, a success achieved for the loss of just three Lancasters.

To capitalize on the success, an attack was planned for the 6th against the Mittelland Canal at Gravenhorst, a point about a mile north of Das Nasse Dreieck, the "Wet Triangle" at Bergeshövede. As previously mentioned, this is a triangular basin into which the Dortmund-Ems and Mittelland Canals flow about ten miles north of Ladbergen, before the Dortmund-Ems continues on to the west and the Mittelland to the north and then east. It was a 5 Group show involving 239 Lancasters and seven Mosquitos, twenty of the former representing 61 Squadron. They departed Skellingthorpe between 16.18 and 16.55 with S/L Horsley the senior pilot on duty and all reached the target area to find clear skies but haze up to around 4,000 feet that affected the visibility. The Master Bomber called in the flare force, despite which, the low-level Mosquito markers experienced great difficulty in identifying the aiming-point. A single Mosquito eventually did deliver its target indicator accurately onto the aiming-point, where it fell into the water and was extinguished. The Master Bomber called a halt to proceedings at 19.38 after thirty-one aircraft had bombed, including the one containing the 61 Squadron crew of F/O Donnelly, who attacked a section of the canal a mile-and-a-half from the TIs from 10,000 feet at 19.39. The others jettisoned the delayed-action 1,000-pounders before setting course for home and encountering not only night-fighter activity, but also very challenging weather conditions of electrical storms and low cloud. F/O MacFarlane and crew were attacked first by a jet fighter and then by a Ju88, both of which were shot out of the sky by the Lancaster's gunners and were seen to impact the ground. Ten Lancasters failed to return, and among them was PB725 of 61 Squadron, from which F/O Goodbrand and three of his crew escaped with their lives to be taken into captivity, while two others were killed and one succumbed to his injuries.

Earlier on the 6th, a series of raids on Ruhr oil refineries had begun with a heavy area attack at Gelsenkirchen, and this was followed by smaller-scale operations at Homberg on the 8th, the Krupp Treibstoffwerke at Wanne-Eickel on the 9th and the Klöckner Werke A.G refinery at Castrop-Rauxel on the morning of the 11th. Seventeen 61 Squadron crews attended briefing at Skellingthorpe later that afternoon to learn that they would shortly be attacking the Rhenania-Ossag synthetic oil refinery at Harburg, situated on the south bank of the Elbe opposite Hamburg. 237 Lancasters and eight Mosquitos were to take part in this all-5 Group show, while elements of 1 and 8 Groups targeted the Hoesch-Benzin plant 170 miles to the south in the Wambel district of Dortmund. Most of the Lancasters were loaded with a cookie, six 1,000 and five 500-pounders, while a few would carry fourteen N°14 J-Type cluster bombs with their cookie. Another early evening take-off had the 61 Squadron element airborne between 16.11 and 16.41 with W/C Pexton the senior pilot on duty and all reached the target area to find largely clear conditions, with only a thin layer of stratus at 8,000 feet and another at 17,000 to 18,000 feet between them and the aiming-point. This they identified either by H2S or red and green TIs, before all but two delivered their loads from 16,000 to 19,000 feet between 19.19 and 19.25. The crews of F/O Amatt and Cooksey each suffered the frustration of a total hang-up and jettisoned their cookie on the way home. At debriefing, crews reported a large explosion at 19.28 followed by an oil fire, and local reports would confirm that heavy damage had been inflicted upon the town's residential and industrial districts.

The 16th was devoted to the destruction of the three small towns of Heinsberg, Jülich and Düren, located respectively in an arc from north to east of Aachen and close to the German lines upon which American ground forces were advancing. An overall force of 1,188 aircraft was involved, and 1, 5 and 8 Groups provided the heavy bombing and marking force of 485 Lancasters for the last-mentioned. 61 Squadron contributed nineteen aircraft to the 5 Group effort of 214, and they departed Skellingthorpe between 12.15 and 12.55 with W/C Pexton the senior pilot on duty and each carrying eleven 1,000 and four-500 pounders. They flew to the target over ten-tenths cloud, which cleared to three-tenths stratus above 6,000 feet as they approached the aiming-point in the final wave of the attack. They bombed in accordance with the instructions of the Master Bomber from 9,800 to 13,000 feet between 15.35 and 15.40 and observed smoke rising through 9,000 feet as they turned for home, confident in the success of the attack. All of the Skellingthorpe crews believed that they had hit the target, but most of the photos were unplottable because of the smoke covering the area. Post-raid reconnaissance confirmed that the operation had been a complete success at a cost of just three aircraft and revealed that the town had been all-but erased from the map, local sources claiming a death toll in excess of three thousand inhabitants. In the event, unfavourable ground conditions prevented the American advance from succeeding.

Nineteen 61 Squadron crews attended briefing at Skellingthorpe on the 21st to be told that they were going back to the Dortmund-Ems Canal on a night of multiple operations involving 1,345 sorties. Three operations, each by 270 aircraft, were to be directed at railway yards at Aschaffenburg, situated about twenty miles south-east of Frankfurt, and oil plants at Castrop-Rauxel and Sterkrade in the Ruhr. 5 Group prepared two forces of 137 and 123 Lancasters respectively, with Mosquito support, for the Mittelland and Dortmund-Ems Canals, while a whole host of minor operations would complete the order of battle. 53 Base was one of those assigned to the latter at Ladbergen, for which the 61 Squadron element took off between 17.16 and 17.51 with F/Ls Burns, Crampton, Greenfield and Hill the senior pilots on duty. They encountered a layer of six to ten-tenths cloud in the target area between 4,000 and 8,000 feet, which did not inhibit the accuracy of the marking, and the canal could be identified visually during the run-up but could not be seen from above. That mattered little as red TIs clearly marked out the aiming-point, and clear instructions from the Master Bomber kept the attack on track. The 61 Squadron crews bombed from 3,000 to 10,500 feet between 21.03 and 21.09, and all involved in the operation returned safely to report a successful attack, many also praising the performance of the Master Bomber.

In contrast, his opposite number at Gravenhorst was accused of causing confusion by issuing contradictory instructions, despite which, post-raid reconnaissance revealed that the canal had been breached over a distance of fifty feet on the western bank, south of the road bridge, and had been drained over a thirty-mile stretch to leave fifty-nine vessels stranded and damaged by direct hits. Just two Lancasters were lost, both from Fulbeck, one of them containing the station commander, G/C Weir, who was the sole survivor after his Lancaster exploded over the target and catapulted him into space attached to his seat parachute. He regained consciousness in the drained and muddy canal with no memory of his miraculous deliverance and was taken into captivity. Among those losing their lives was the navigator, S/L "Pat" Kelly DFC and Bar, who had a long and distinguished career behind him, including a spell with 617 Squadron as a member of Cheshire's crew. Like some of the others on board the Lancaster, he did not need to put his life at risk but found it hard to resist the lure of operations.

Reconnaissance at Ladbergen revealed success also, showing the left-hand channel, the one repaired since the last attack, to have been breached again where it crossed the River Glane, which had been unable to cope with the volume of water released, and this resulted in extensive flooding on both sides of the canal. The Germans recognised that repairing the canals was an open invitation to Bomber Command to return, but so vital were they to the transportation system, that they could not be abandoned. The answer was to complete repairs, but to leave the sections drained and apparently still under repair, until sufficient traffic had built up to push through in one night. They would then be flooded and re-emptied to dupe RAF reconnaissance flights and maintain the deception.

On the following night the group dispatched 171 Lancasters and seven Mosquitos to attack the U-Boot pens at Trondheim in Norway, a straight-line distance from Skellingthorpe of some eight hundred miles. 61 Squadron launched seventeen Lancasters into the air between 15.38 and 16.16 with S/L Fadden the senior pilot on duty, and all arrived in the target area some five-and-a-half hours later to find clear skies and excellent visibility. However, an effective smoke screen prevented the marker force from finding the aiming-point, and the Master Bomber had no option but to send the force home, where all but one arrived in a state of exhaustion between 01.17 and 03.19 flying on nothing but fumes after more than eleven hours aloft. NG179 disappeared without trace into the sea at some point during the operation and took with it the crew of F/O James. 5 Group mounted a rare daylight mining operation on the 23rd, for which fourteen Lancasters were detailed, while 53 Base remained at home.

The weather was mainly responsible for curtailing operations over the next few days until the 26th, when briefings took place on 5 Group stations at 20.00 to inform 270 Lancaster and ten Mosquito crews that Munich was to be the target for an all-5 Group maximum effort operation. The eighteen-strong 61 Squadron contingent departed Skellingthorpe between 23.09 and 00.06 with F/Ls Boon and Davies the senior pilots on duty and each crew sitting on a 1,000-pounder and thirteen N°14 J-Type cluster bombs. Forming up and climbing to operational altitude was a time-consuming business and it would be five hours before the target was reached. In the meantime, the crews of F/Os Amatt and Heath reached the midpoint of the Channel crossing with some sixty miles between them, before turning back because of engine and hydraulics issues respectively, while F/O Bain and crew made it as far as the city of Orleans only to be defeated by the failure of the Gee-box, the a.s.i, and Loran, a new American navigation device based on Gee with a longer range. Those arriving in the target area found it to be under clear skies with good visibility, and confirmed their positions by means of H2S, while the low-level marking was being carried out. Aside from one errant red TI, it was accurate, and the Master Bomber ensured that the crews focused upon the reds and greens on and close to the planned aiming-point. The 61 Squadron crews bombed from 16,000 to 20,000 feet between 05.01 and 05.19 with a twenty-two-second overshoot as directed by the Master Bomber and returned safely to praise the quality of the route and target marking and the concentration of the attack. The last-mentioned was confirmed by post-raid reconnaissance and a local report that singled out railway installations as being particularly hard-hit.

This was the final operation of the month for 5 Group, but among others taking place before the end was an attack by 1 and 8 Groups on Freiburg in southern Germany. It was a minor railway centre within thirty-five miles of advancing American and French ground forces and was thought to be harbouring large numbers of enemy soldiers. The force of over 330 Lancasters delivered 1,900 tons of bombs, missing the railway yards, but destroying two thousand houses and killing over two thousand inhabitants.

During the course of the month, the squadron took part in nine operations and dispatched 154 sorties for the loss of three Lancasters and crews.

December 1944

There were no operations for 5 Group for the first three nights of the new month, largely because of the weather, and in the meantime, 1, 4, 6 and 8 Groups pounded the Ruhr town of Hagen on the night of the 2/3rd. Worthwhile targets were becoming more and more scarce at a time when the Command was at its most powerful, and this final period of the war would bring the most devastating attacks to date upon the German homeland. When the 53 Base squadrons returned to action in the early evening of the 4th, it was to contribute to a 5 Group force of 282 Lancasters and ten Mosquitos, the target for which was the city of Heilbronn. Situated thirty miles due north of Stuttgart, it sat astride the River Neckar and a north-south railway link but otherwise had no genuine strategic importance and its populace would not have been expecting to be attacked. The main operation on this night was actually by 535 aircraft of 1, 6 and 8 Groups at Karlsruhe, some fifty-six miles west-south-west of Heilbronn, and the concentration of aircraft in this area would be certain to bring out the night-fighters. The 61 Squadron element of twenty Lancasters departed Skellingthorpe between 16.09 and 16.44 with S/L Fadden the senior pilot on duty and each Lancaster carrying a cookie and either five 1,000-pounders or twelve SBCs of 4lb incendiaries. They flew out across France in good conditions to find three to five-tenths thin stratus over the target at around 12,000 feet, through which some crews were able to pick out the Neckar and the aiming-points.

The marshalling yards and the built-up area were illuminated by the flare force ahead of the low-level Mosquitos' run to drop red TIs for the visual marker crews to back up. The marshalling yards were marked with yellows, which the main force element was unable to distinguish in the burgeoning fires, and this persuaded them to focus on the red and green TIs in the city itself instead. All but one of the 61 Squadron crews added to the general destruction as they delivered their attacks from 13,200 to 15,000 feet between 19.30 and 19.40 with overshoots of between three and seventeen seconds as directed by the Master Bomber. F/O Collins and crew suffered a hang-up and made a second pass over the aiming point without being able to release the bombs and eventually dumped the cookie on the way home. As the force retreated westwards into electrical storms, leaving a pall of smoke rising to bombing height, 82% of the city's built-up area was in the process of being destroyed by what probably amounted to a firestorm. The post-war British Bombing Survey estimated 351 acres of destruction and a death toll of at least seven thousand people, in return for which 5 Group suffered the relatively high cost for the period of twelve aircraft. The operation against Karlsruhe had also been an outstanding success, which left southern and western districts, in particular, severely damaged.

On a night of heavy Bomber Command activity on the 6th, 475 Lancasters of 1, 3 and 8 Groups were to target the I G Farbenindustrie A.G Merseburg-Leuna oil refinery near Liepzig in the east, the second largest oil plant in Germany and the one responsible for developing the Bergius refining process. Elsewhere, 450 aircraft from predominantly 4 and 6 Groups were assigned to attack railway installations at Osnabrück in the north, while 5 Group's target was the town of Giessen, situated some eighty-five miles south-east of Cologne in west-central Germany and thirty-five miles north of Frankfurt. A force of 255 Lancasters was assembled, twenty of them belonging to 61 Squadron at Skellingthorpe, where the armourers loaded each with a cookie and thirteen SBCs of 4lb incendiaries. The main force crews had been briefed for two aiming-points, two-thirds of them to the town and the remainder to the marshalling yards, and it was for the former that the 61

Squadron element took off between 16.31 and 17.17 with S/L Horsley the senior pilot on duty. Those arriving in the target area found up to eight-tenths thin cloud and good visibility, by which time the flare force had begun illuminating, three minutes early, and to the west of the target as events were to prove. However, the Mosquito-laid red TIs fell close to the aiming-point and the Master Bomber ensured that they were backed up by greens, which the 61 Squadron crews bombed from 8,500 to 11,000 feet between 20.10 and 20.24.

As the bombs fell away from LL777, it was attacked by enemy fighters, whose fire killed the mid-upper gunner and added to damage caused by flak and incendiaries from another aircraft. When some twenty miles south-west of Giessen the flight engineer, bomb-aimer, navigator and rear gunner complied with the pilot's order to bale out, but the wireless operator failed to hear the order and remained on board as the Lancaster's flying career ended in a forced-landing on an Allied-held aerodrome. The fact that the mid-upper gunner was laid to rest in Brussels town cemetery suggests that the aerodrome was Melsbroek. The ORB records that a second 61 Squadron aircraft was damaged by a night-fighter and the navigator mortally wounded but does not identify the crew. The Lancaster landed at the emergency strip at Woodbridge and as F/O Bain and crew were the only ones to report being attacked, it must be concluded that NG182 was the Lancaster involved and F/Sgt Harding the fatality. ME725 failed to return with the crew of F/O Donnelly RAAF, who survived with four others in enemy hands after coming down in the Hannover defence zone. In the absence of a report by local sources, reconnaissance photographs revealed the operation to have been another outstanding success.

The Urft Dam was one of a number of similar structures in the beautiful Eifel region of western Germany, close to the Belgian frontier, and its presence generated a fear that the enemy might strategically release flood water to hamper the American advance into Germany. It was decided to attempt to breach the dam to allow any excess water to drain away, and the first of a number of attacks on the region took place on the 3rd at Heimbach, the small town nestling against the northern reaches of the reservoir. The 1 and 8 Group force failed to identify it and no bombs fell, prompting a second attack on the following day by a small 8 Group force on the dam itself, which was unsuccessful, as was a 3 Group attack on the nearby Schwammenauel Dam on the 5th. The job was handed to 5 Group on the 8th, for which a force of 205 Lancasters was made ready, fourteen of them by 61 Squadron, while nineteen from 617 Squadron would carry Tallboys. They departed Skellingthorpe between 08.13 and 08.47 with S/L Horsley the senior pilot on duty and arrived at the target to be greeted by six to nine-tenths cloud at between 6,000 and 8,000 feet and moderate visibility. Most crews made multiple runs across the target area seeking out the dam and all but two of the 61 Squadron crews carried out their attacks from 2,400 to 10,000 feet between 10.48 and 11.00. They were among 129 to bomb before the Master Bomber called a halt and sent the force home, while the crews of F/Os Amatt and Smith withheld their bombs after failing to identify the aiming point.

The conditions had prevented any assessment of results, which meant that another attempt on the dam would be necessary, and preparations were put in hand on the 9th to return with a force of 217 Lancasters early on the morning of the 10th. 61 Squadron remained at home while 50 Squadron represented Skellingthorpe took to the air on a cold and frosty morning only to be recalled with the rest of the force before it reached the English coast. The operation was rescheduled for early on the following morning, when 233 Lancasters and a Mosquito were to join five 8 Group Mosquitos at the target, but take-off was postponed until midday. The fifteen 61 Squadron participants departed Skellingthorpe between 11.52 and 12.18 with W/C Pexton the senior pilot on duty and encountered icing conditions at the French coast, before discovering that the weather in the target area was hardly an improvement on that of the previous day. Up to nine-tenths cloud with tops at 8,000 feet made life difficult for the Master Bomber, who tried to bring the crews down below the cloud base, some complying, while others were able to identify the aiming-point through a four-mile-long gap. All but one of the 61 Squadron crews attacked from 7,000 to 10,800 feet between 14.30 and 14.49 before the Master Bomber's "Dewdrop" instruction to cease bombing and go home. F/L Davies and crew had been unable to identify the aiming point and jettisoned four 1,000-pounders on the way home to achieve a safe landing weight. Post-raid reconnaissance revealed a number of hits on the stepped apron of the dam and cratering all around, but no actual breach had occurred. *(The cratering in the surrounding woodland remains visible to this day.)*

The main operation on the night of the 15/16th was directed at Ludwigshafen in southern Germany, home to a number of I G Farben factories, which were among the most blatant exploiters of slave workers in the production of synthetic oil. The attack by 327 Lancasters and fourteen Mosquitos of 1, 6 and 8 Groups landed 450 high explosive bombs and incendiaries in the plant, causing massive damage and fires and was the greatest setback to production during the war. Further north, the Oppau factory ceased production completely for an extended period and five other industrial concerns also sustained severe damage, as did some residential areas. It was on the 16th that German ground forces began a new offensive in the Ardennes, in an attempt to break through the American lines and reach the port of Antwerp in what would become known as the Battle of the Bulge.

Munich had become something of a 5 Group preserve during the year, and a further operation against it was planned for the night of the 17/18th, which would turn out to be another night of heavy Bomber Command activity. The main raid was to be by more than five hundred aircraft, predominantly of 4 and 6 Groups on Duisburg, while 1 Group targeted Ulm with over three hundred Lancasters, leaving 5 Group to send 280 Lancasters some seventy miles beyond to the Bavarian capital city. 61 Squadron briefed twenty crews, who departed Skellingthorpe between 16.08 and 16.46 with S/L Fadden the senior pilot on duty and lost the services of F/L Bartlett and crew to an indisposed navigator at the French coast at Le Havre, some distance south-west of where they were supposed to cross the French coast near Berck-sur-Mer. The others reached the target to find generally clear skies and good visibility and bombed on red and green TIs with an overshoot of up to twenty-three seconds from 11,000 to 13,100 feet between 22.02 and 22.11 in accordance with the instructions of the Master Bomber, who declared himself satisfied with the results. The crew of F/O Friend still had a full bomb load beneath their feet and were twenty miles short of the target when the Master Bomber called a halt to proceedings at 22.12, and they returned with their bomb load still intact. They confirmed that the attack appeared to be effective with smoke rising through 7,000 feet and the resultant fires visible from a hundred miles into the return journey. As usual at this target, however, no local report emerged but Bomber Command claimed severe and widespread damage to the city at a cost of seven Lancasters. LM729 failed to return to Skellingthorpe having fallen victim to flak south of Munich and only the rear gunner from the crew of F/O Newland RCAF survived to fall into enemy hands.

The 1 Group raid on the virgin target of Ulm, situated on the Danube to the south-east of Stuttgart and west of Augsburg in southern Germany, is worthy of mention. It was similar in nature to the recently-bombed Heilbronn, and as a result of the catastrophic raid there, the local Gauleiter had urged the women and children to evacuate the inner city urgently. Plans were put in place to begin evacuation on Monday the 18th, so that Advent could be observed on the Sunday, but something caused a change of plan and loudspeaker vans toured the city on Sunday urging the population to leave at once in what proved to be a fortuitous move. Unlike Heilbronn, Ulm contained industry, including the important Magirus-Deutz and Kässbohrer lorry factories, and there were also military barracks and depots. An accurate and concentrated raid resulted in fierce fires that consumed a square kilometre of the built-up area, and it would be established later that almost 82% of the city's buildings had sustained damage to some extent, including both lorry factories. There is no question that the evacuation saved many thousands of lives and restricted the civilian death toll to six hundred, while Bomber Command lost just two Lancasters.

On the following night, it was the turn of the distant Baltic port of Gdynia to play host to 5 Group, for which 61 Squadron put up seventeen Lancasters in an overall force of 236 of the type. The intention was to catch elements of the German fleet at anchor, in particular, the Lützow, and also to destroy harbour installations, as well as cause damage within the town. *(The original Lützow was actually never completed and had been sold to the Russian navy in 1940 as a hull minus superstructure. The pocket battleship, Deutschland, was renamed Lützow, to avoid humiliation for the nation should she be lost in battle.)* While this operation was in progress, fourteen other Lancasters of the group were to sneak in under cover of the main activity to deliver mines to the Privet and Spinach gardens in Danzig (Gdansk) Bay. The 61 Squadron element departed Skellingthorpe between 16.52 and 17.26 with S/L Horsley the senior pilot on duty and lost the services of the crews of F/O Shaw and F/L Boon to technical malfunctions when over the North Sea. F/O Tasker and crew were led astray by faulty Loran fixes and when fifteen minutes from the target complied with the Master Bomber's order to cease bombing and go home The others had reached the target area after an outward flight of almost five hours and found clear skies and good visibility in which the harbour and town could be picked out visually until the activation of a smoke screen. In keeping with standard practice, the initial identification was by H2S before the illumination and marking proceeded according to plan and the 61 Squadron crews delivered their eight 1,000-pounders each on red and green TIs from 11,000 to 14,000 feet between 21.56 and 22.08 in accordance with the Master Bomber's instructions and in the face of intense light flak. The smoke screen eventually obscured the Lützow, and crews with bombs still to deliver turned their attention upon the port area and town. It was not possible to make an accurate assessment of results, but bomb bursts were seen across the docks and quaysides. Reconnaissance photos confirmed that damage had been inflicted upon shipping, port installations and residential property in the waterfront districts, at the modest cost to the Command of four Lancasters.

Thick fog kept the Command on the ground on the 20th, and threatened to do so also on the 21st, but an operation was called on the basis that the weather over Scotland after midnight would be clear for returning aircraft, even if Lincolnshire remained fogbound. Sixteen 61 Squadron Lancasters were detailed for the 5 Group operation that night, and briefings took place while the ground crews did their best to get the aircraft ready in time. In briefing rooms across southern and south-eastern Lincolnshire, crews learned that their target would require them to retrace their recent steps to Germany's eastern Baltic region, although the I G Farben-owned Wintershall oil refinery at Politz, situated less than ten miles north of the port of Stettin, was some two hundred miles short of their trip to Gdynia. *(This location is often wrongly spelled Pölitz, which is a town in Germany's Schleswig-Holstein region at the western end of the Baltic. Politz is now Police in Poland.)* A force of 207 Lancasters and a single Mosquito was assembled, and unusually, it included an element from 617 Squadron carrying Tallboys. The 61 Squadron element departed Skellingthorpe between 16.21 and 17.12 with F/Ls Bartlett, Boon, Miller and Rawle the senior pilots on duty and each Lancaster carrying a cookie and twelve 500-pounders. Many crews cut corners to keep up with the bomber stream and found clear skies with ground haze over the refinery, which may have been a smoke screen. This important war-industry asset was protected by around fifty searchlights, and heavy flak accompanied the Lancasters as they ran in on the aiming-point. The markers fell some two thousand yards north-north-west of the plant, a situation recognized by the Master Bomber, but he was unable to persuade the backers-up to shift the point of aim accordingly and most of the bombing would miss the mark. The 61 Squadron element bombed on red and green TIs from 15,500 to 19,000 feet between 22.00 and 22.15 and observed most of the bomb bursts to be around the markers. Fires remained visible for almost a hundred miles into the return journey, but photo-reconnaissance revealed that the plant had not been destroyed, and it would be necessary to mount further raids.

The final wartime Christmas period was celebrated on 5 Group stations in traditional style and undisturbed by operational activity between the 22nd and Boxing Day, which was not the case for some other groups. The peace came to an end on the 26th, when crews from all groups were roused from any resulting stupor to attend briefings for operations against enemy troop positions at St Vith in Belgium. The German advance towards Antwerp had been protected from air attack by a blanket of low cloud, but the push had now run out of steam after its earlier successes, and starved of fuel and ammunition, it was now attempting to withdraw back into Germany. 5 Group contributed twenty-six Lancasters to the force of 296 aircraft for the first joint operation since October, and the target, situated within five miles of the German frontier, was found to be under clear skies with good visibility, which enabled crews to identify the aiming-point visually and by a red TI. When this became obscured by smoke, the Master Bomber ordered the crews to descend to 10,000 feet and bomb the upwind edge of the smoke.

53 Base was called into action on the 27th to provide aircraft for an attack on marshalling yards at Rheydt, for a which a force of two hundred Lancasters and eleven Mosquitos was drawn from 1, 3, 5 and 8 Groups. 61 Squadron provided nine of the forty-four 5 Group Lancasters, and they departed Skellingthorpe between 12.14 and 12.29 with S/L Horsley the senior pilot on duty. They all reached the target, where the skies were clear and the aiming-point could be identified visually, although red and green TIs marked it out to provide a more solid reference. The 61 Squadron element bombed from 16,000 to 19,000 feet between 15.01 and 15.05 in accordance with the instructions of the Master Bomber, and dust and smoke was obscuring the area as they turned away. The attack was well concentrated, but no explosions or fires were reported, and, it seems, there was no post-raid reconnaissance.

On the 28th, five crews each from 50 and 61 Squadrons were told that they would be part of a 5 Group force of sixty-seven Lancasters targeting shipping, specifically the cruiser Köln, at Horten and Moss, located respectively on the western and eastern coasts of Oslo Fjord, thirty miles south of Norway's capital city. The 50 and 61 Squadron ORBs specified Moss as the target, for which the 61 Squadron element departed Skellingthorpe between 19.29 and 19.45 with W/C Pexton the senior pilot on duty. They all reached the target area after an outward flight of four-and-a-half hours and found the skies to be relatively clear and the visibility good, but a thin layer of alto-cumulus cloud at between 15,000 and 20,000 feet reduced the brightness of the moonlight and cast deceptive shadows on the water to prevent a clear identification of the target. The aiming-points at Horten were marked by Wanganui flares, but most crews followed the Master Bomber's instructions after establishing their own reference point. A patch of light flak to the north-east of the harbour mole was thought to be concealing a large naval unit, and this area was marked and bombed. Some crews would claim to have attacked a large vessel moving from this area in a southerly direction, and other shipping in the harbour, all in the face of intense shipboard and shore-based light flak. Meanwhile to the east, the 61 Squadron crews identified a number of vessels at the northern end of the narrow strait between Moss and Jeløya island, about a mile south of Kambo, and marked them with flame floats, before making two runs and bombing from 6,500 to 8,000 feet between 23.35 and 23.49. It was difficult to assess the outcome, and no direct hits were claimed, but a crew attacking Horten believed that they could see smoke issuing from one vessel.

1, 6 and 8 Groups combined on the afternoon of the 29th to dispatch 324 Lancasters to attack the Hydrierwerke synthetic oil plant at Scholven-Buer, located in the north-western quarter of Gelsenkirchen. A local report detailed three hundred high-explosive bombs hitting the area of the plant, causing fires and inflicting severe damage upon the installations. A further 3,100 bombs fell in other parts of Scholven, causing much residential and industrial destruction and surface buildings at two coal mines were also hit and severely damaged.

Eleven 61 Squadron crews were called to briefing late on the 30th to learn that they were to be part of a 5 Group force of 154 Lancasters and thirteen Mosquitos to attack an enemy supply line at Houffalize in the Ardennes region of Belgium. They departed Skellingthorpe between 02.03 and 02.24 with S/L Horsley the senior pilot on duty and a bomb load each of eleven 1,000 and four 500-pounders. They found the target area to be under five to seven-tenths stratus cloud at 5,000 to 6,000 feet, with another layer of eight-tenths with tops at 9,000 feet, all of which made identification very difficult. The marking was punctual and accurate, but the red TIs were observed only by a proportion of the crews, who chanced upon a gap in the clouds directly over the aiming-point. Seven of the 61 Squadron participants bombed from 9,500 to 11,000 feet between 04.59 and 05.08, but four others were unable to establish the location of the aiming-point after orbiting for up to fifteen minutes and aborted their sorties, F/O Crocombe and crew after losing their port-outer engine. A number of crews in the force descended to below the cloud base and confirmed that the bombing was concentrated around the markers, but it would be deemed necessary to revisit this objective within a short time.

During the course of the month the squadron took part in ten operations and dispatched 147 sorties for the loss of two Lancasters and crews. It had been a long and hard-fought year, which had begun with the Command's morale at its lowest ebb during the dark nights of the Berlin campaign but was ending with the Allied forces sweeping across Europe into the ever-shrinking Reich. The scent of victory was in the air, but much remained to be done before the proud, resolute and tenacious German forces finally laid down their arms and any thoughts that the enemy defences were spent, were badly misplaced. Although the Luftwaffe was stretched beyond its capacity to defend every corner of the Reich, it could and would still occasionally inflict grievous losses on Bomber Command.

January 1945

The final year of the war began with a flourish, as the Luftwaffe launched its ill-conceived and, ultimately, ill-fated Operation Bodenplatte (Baseplate) at first light on New Year's Day. With the intention of destroying the Allied air forces on the ground at the recently liberated airfields in France, Holland and Belgium. The operation was only modestly successful and cost the German day fighter force around 250 aircraft, many of the pilots from which were killed, wounded or fell into Allied hands, and it was a setback from which the Tagjagd would never fully recover. The Allies, on the other hand, could make good their losses within hours from their enormous stockpiles.

5 Group was also active that morning, having roused the crews early from their beds to attend briefings for an attack on the recently repaired Dortmund-Ems Canal near Ladbergen, for which 102 Lancasters and two Mosquitos were made ready. The seven 61 Squadron participants took off between 07.38 and 07.47 with S/L Horsley the senior pilot on duty and headed off to take-up their briefed position in the bomber stream. The 54 Base squadrons from Coningsby and Metheringham fell in line behind 83 Squadron, with the 55 Base squadrons from East Kirkby and Spilsby about three miles further back, and a third section, made up of 53 Base units from Waddington, Skellingthorpe and Bardney some twenty miles to the rear. The last mentioned were allowed to catch up, putting the force two minutes behind schedule at point C over the North Sea, and it was between points C and D that the fighter escort was expected to join them, and, although not immediately apparent, it did eventually put in an appearance. The gaggles held together fairly well, although the controller would complain later that the legs were too short to keep them tight, and some aircraft were seen to break formation. When about eight minutes from the target, smoke from a Mosquito-laid red TI could be seen on the southern tip of the island between the two branches of the canal and crews were able to home in on it without difficulty. A six-gun flak battery greeted their arrival with accurate salvoes, and while this did not inhibit the bombing runs, five 61 Squadron Lancasters sustained damage as they released their loads from 10,000 to 12,500 feet between 11.10 and 11.22, some aiming at the bridge over the River Glane, and the impression was of an effective operation. On return, a number of 55 Base crews complained that the gaggle was too tight and put crews at risk from "friendly" bombs. The use of delay fuses prevented an immediate assessment of the results, but photo-reconnaissance revealed later that the canal had been breached again and the surrounding fields were flooded.

Operations for the day were not yet done for 5 Group, which now had an appointment with the Mittelland Canal at Gravenhorst, for which 152 Lancasters and five Mosquitos were made ready. 61 Squadron's ten Lancasters departed Skellingthorpe between 16.30 and 16.50 with no senior pilot on duty and began their climb-out through fog, all reaching the target area to find that the clear conditions enjoyed during the morning raid nearby had persisted, and so accurate were the initial TIs and illumination, delivered visually or by H2S, that the third flare force was not required and was sent home. The main force was called in ahead of H-Hour at around 19.10, and the 61 Squadron element bombed on red TIs from 9,800 to 12,700 feet between 19.12 and 19.18. One of the perils of operating on New Year's Day was the risk of falling victim to trigger-happy American flak gunners stationed on the front line, who had been spooked by the German raids at dawn and now fired at anything that moved, as a result of which, a number of RAF aircraft and crews would be lost to "friendly fire" incidents. The employment of predominantly delayed-action bombs again prevented an immediate assessment of results, but a highly successful operation was confirmed later by photo-reconnaissance. Two of the 61 Squadron crews landed at Manston and the rest at Banff in Scotland and made their way home on the following morning.

The old enemy of Nuremberg was posted on the 2nd as the first major urban target of the New Year and faced a main force of 445 Lancasters drawn from 1, 3 and 6 Groups with a further sixty-nine Lancasters representing 8 Group to provide the marking and bombing support. 8 Group also contributed twenty-two Lancasters to a simultaneous attack by 351 Halifaxes of 4 and 6 Groups on two I G Farben chemicals plants, one in Ludwigshafen and the other close by in Oppau. Now that mobile Oboe stations had been set up on the Continent, both operations would also benefit from a Mosquito presence, seven for Nuremberg and twenty-two for Ludwigshafen. The two forces followed a similar route until dividing shortly before reaching Ludwigshafen, where the Nuremberg force continued on towards the east for a further 140 miles. The success of the Ludwigshafen operation was confirmed by local reports that five hundred high-explosive bombs had fallen within the confines of the two production plants, along with many thousands of incendiaries. This had put an end to all production of synthetic oil, and adjacent industrial buildings, residential property and railway installations had also been destroyed. Nuremberg was left devastated by the loss of 4,640 houses, a large proportion of them apartment blocks, while more than four hundred industrial units were destroyed and eighteen hundred people killed.

5 Group had remained on the ground during the above and many of its crews were called to briefing on the evening of the 4th to learn of a controversial attack planned against the small French town of Royan in the early hours of the 5th. The raid was in response to requests from Free French forces, which were laying siege to the town because of its location on the eastern bank at the mouth of the Gironde Estuary and in the way of an advance towards the port of Bordeaux. It was occupied by a German garrison, the commander of which had offered the inhabitants an opportunity to evacuate the area, but around two thousand had declined and would suffer the consequences. 1, 5 and 8 Groups put together a force of 347 Lancasters and seven Mosquitos, of which fifteen of the former represented 61 Squadron and departed Skellingthorpe between 00.32 and 01.12 with S/L Horsley the senior pilot on duty, and each sitting on a cookie and sixteen 500-pounders. They were part of the first of two waves heading for the unsuspecting target, separated by one hour, and the clock was approaching 04.00 as they lined up for the bombing run in cloudless skies and excellent visibility. The start of the attack was delayed for two minutes to allow misplaced markers to be corrected, then a red TI went down at 04.01 very close to the aiming point, and another fell in the middle of the town near the beach, at which point, the Master Bomber called in the main force. The 61 Squadron crews carried out their attacks from 6,300 to 9,000 feet between 04.02 and 04.11, mostly with an overshoot as directed by the Master Bomber, and witnessed a yellow oil fire at 04.08, which began to emit volumes of black smoke. This was just one of a number of large explosions created by the first phase of bombing, and the resultant fires acted as a beacon to the 1 Group force following behind. The attack destroyed about 85% of the town, and between five and eight hundred people lost their lives, as events turned out unnecessarily, as the town was not taken, and it would be mid-April before the garrison surrendered.

5 Group was not involved in a major attack on Hannover by more than 650 aircraft on the night of the 5/6th, the first on this northern city since the series in the autumn of 1943. However, a rushed battle order came through to 5 Group stations at 18.30, which would lead to another late briefing and take-off for 131 crews, and it was actually between 00.13 and 01.01 on the 6th that a dozen 61 Squadron crews departed Skellingthorpe bound for a German motorised supply column trapped at

Houffalize in the Belgian Ardennes. F/Ls Burns and Miller were the senior pilots on duty as they made their way south on a clear night above low cloud, which, over the target, formed thin layers of eight to ten-tenths cover between 4,000 and 10,000 feet. The marker force crews were able to identify the aiming-point visually, and the first red Mosquito-laid TIs were seen to go down close together, followed by greens at H-3. They were backed up to leave a compact group of reds and greens visible by their glow through the clouds, and the Master Bomber, who was circling at 10,000 feet, called in the main force to bomb. Nine of the 61 Squadron crews complied from 9,250 to 12,000 feet between 03.00 and 03.10, while two others were among around a third of the force to retain their bombs in accordance with instructions at briefing if they failed to identify the aiming-point. Afterwards, one of the marker crews descended to 3,500 feet between the cloud layers, and observed two large columns of smoke, the source of which could not be identified. Post-raid reconnaissance confirmed that the target had been bombed with great accuracy, and the success had been gained for the loss of just two Lancasters. 61 Squadron's PA165 crashed in the target area killing F/O Sears and all but his rear gunner, who was taken into captivity.

A major operation against Munich was planned for the 7th, and a two-wave force of 645 aircraft drawn from all five of the Lancaster-equipped groups with the 5 Group element of 213 Lancasters and three Mosquitos representing the entire first wave and taking off two hours ahead of the 1, 3, 6 and 8 Group second wave force. The 61 Squadron element of sixteen Lancasters departed Skellingthorpe as dusk was descending over Lincolnshire between 16.33 and 17.09 with W/C Pexton the senior pilot on duty, and set course for Gravesend to begin the sea crossing that would terminate on the French coast near Berck-sur-Mer. A section of the ORB entry is too corrupted to decipher, and one unidentified crew turned back early because of an unserviceable rear turret and F/O Bain and crew were some seventy miles west of Strasbourg when an identical issue ended their interest in proceedings. The others entered Germany south of Strasbourg and encountered broken medium-level cloud at 14,000 feet above the target, with haze or thin cloud below, by which time the Master Bomber had made a visual identification of the aiming-point and sent the first two primary blind marker crews in to deliver their TIs at the same time, thirty seconds ahead of the planned opening of the attack. The flare force went in immediately afterwards and illuminated the city very effectively, allowing ground detail to be identified by the visual marker element and red TIs to be delivered and straddle the River Isar, bracketing the aiming-point. The Master Bomber ordered the backers-up to drop their TIs between the reds, after which, the next batch of flares formed a circle around the aiming-point.

The main force was then called in and the 61 Squadron participants delivered their loads accurately within the specified area with up to a twenty-five-second overshoot from 17,000 to 20,000 feet between 20.31 and 20.36, the lower altitude that of F/L Lipton and crew who dropped fifteen hundred feet to escape the condensation trails. The city was seen to be burning well as the force withdrew, and the glow of fires could be seen from up to 130 miles away. Two hours after the 5 Group attack, in what would become an established pattern, the second wave force arrived to complete the destruction of the central and some industrial districts, and this proved to be the final large-scale attack of the war on Munich. Fourteen Lancasters failed to return, and among them were four belonging to 5 Group.

With the exception of 617 Squadron, 5 Group remained on the ground for the ensuing six days, with snow-clearing providing exercise for all capable of wielding a shovel. The crews were, therefore, no doubt relieved to be called to briefing on the 13th, when they learned that 5 Group would be operating alone against the Wintershall oil refinery at Politz near Stettin. The plant had sustained damage in the previous attack in December, but production had not been halted, and a force of 218 Lancasters and seven Mosquitos was assembled for the return, of which sixteen of the Lancasters were provided by 61 Squadron. Another dusk departure from Skellingthorpe was accomplished between 16.30 and 16.53 with F/Ls Bartlett, Grynkiewicz, Miller and Rawle the senior pilots on duty. F/O Hutchins and crew turned back within the hour after the mid-upper turret let them down, leaving the others to cross the North Sea at 1,500 feet in accordance with instructions to not climb until approaching the Danish coast at 19.30. They arrived in the target area on time to find clear skies with slight haze, by which time the blind marker crews had identified the target by means of H2S and had delivered their green TIs in a line approaching the target shortly after 22.00. The illuminators then dropped their flares, which caused ground detail to stand out, highlighted by the snow on the ground. A blind-bombing attack had been planned, but because of the excellence of the conditions, Mosquitos were able to go in at low level, after which the main force was called in and the 61 Squadron crews bombed from 13,800 to 17,000 feet between 22.15 and 22.28 to help seal the fate of the plant. Photographic reconnaissance confirmed that the site had been severely damaged, and Bomber Command claimed it to be in ruins.

Oil targets would continue to dominate during the remainder of the month, and a two-phase attack was planned for the following night against the I G Farbenindustrie A.G Merseburg-Leuna refinery, which lay some 250 miles from the Dutch frontier and five hundred miles from the bomber bases of eastern England and was one of five similar production sites situated in an arc on the western side of Leipzig from north to south. The first phase would be carried out by 5 Group, which detailed 210 Lancasters and nine Mosquitos, fourteen of the former contributed by 61 Squadron, which departed Skellingthorpe between 16.06 and 16.30 with F/Ls Bartlett, Burns, Lipton and Rawle the senior pilots on duty and headed for the Sussex coast near Brighton to begin the Channel crossing for the southern approach to eastern Germany. F/O Cooksey and crew were tracking across north-eastern France when the rear gunner became unwell and they had to turn back, leaving the others to reach the target area to find clear skies but poor vertical visibility due to a layer of haze. In the event, this was no hindrance to the primary blind markers, whose job was to establish their position over the aiming-point by means of H2S. They delivered their TIs from 18,000 feet, after which, the first element of the flare force went in to light the way for the low-level Mosquito element after the Master Bomber called for ground marking only. By 20.50 he was satisfied and sent the marker aircraft home and called in the main force crews, who produced what appeared to be concentrated bombing, those from 61 Squadron dropping their loads of a cookie and nine 500-pounders each onto red and green TIs from 14,250 to 16,750 feet between 21.03 and 21.12 with a fourteen-second overshoot in accordance with the Master Bomber's instructions.

Returning crews reported explosions and smoke rising upwards as they turned for home, leaving behind them a beacon for the second wave of 363 Lancasters and five Mosquitos of 1, 6 and 8 Groups following three hours behind. They would add to the massive destruction, which effectively put the plant out of action for the remainder of the war. On return at 01.21, 61 Squadron's LM720 flew into a radar mast on Bord Hill near Langham airfield in Norfolk and crashed with fatal consequences for F/O Corewyn and crew.

Feverish activity across the Command on the 16th prepared more than twelve hundred aircraft for action, the majority to participate in four major operations that night, three to target oil refineries and the largest to deliver an area attack on the eastern city of Magdeburg, which also contained the Braunkohle A.G Bergius-process oil (hydrogenation) plant located in the Rothensee district to the north of the city centre. The independent 3 and 5 Groups were handed the refineries at Wanne-

Eickel in the Ruhr and Brüx in north-western Czechoslovakia respectively, leaving 320 Halifaxes of 4 and 6 Groups to take care of Magdeburg and 283 Lancasters of 1 and 6 Groups to ply their trade at Zeitz-Tröglitz, the location of another Braunkohle-Benzin A.G plant, situated some twenty miles south-west of Leipzig. Brüx, now known as Most in the Czech Republic, lay some 140 miles due south of Berlin and it was for this destination that ten 61 Squadron crews were briefed as part of a 5 Group force of 224 Lancasters and six Mosquitos, which would be accompanied by seven 101 Squadron ABC Lancasters for RCM duties. They were each carrying a cookie and nine 500-pounders for what would be a nine-hour round-trip and departed Skellingthorpe between 17.47 and 18.15 with F/Ls Bartlett, Miller and Rawle the senior pilots on duty.

There were ten early returns from the force, but none from among the 61 Squadron contingent, which reached the target area over nine to ten-tenths low cloud with tops at 3,000 feet. This interfered with the low-level marking system, which began with four primary blind markers identifying the target by means of H2S and dropping green TIs, and they were followed by the first illuminators, who also relied on H2S to deliver their flares. It seems that a number of Mosquitos managed to get below the cloud base to put red TIs onto the aiming-point and reported that the greens were among the oil tanks. However, the reds were not generally visible through the clouds and the Master Bomber called for skymarking, while informing flare force 3 that it would not be required. The 61 Squadron participants bombed either on the glow of the red TIs or on the cascading greens from 16,500 to 17,750 feet between 22.31 and 22.41 and observed many explosions and large columns of thick, black smoke emerging through the cloud tops and passing through 8,000 feet. Photo-reconnaissance would confirm that massive damage had been inflicted upon the plant, and a severe setback delivered to the enemy's oil production.

There would be no further operations for 5 Group during the month, although a number would be posted before being cancelled. The squadron spent the period inducting new crews, attending lectures, training, and during the last few days, clearing snow from the runways. A major operation on the 28th involved 602 aircraft from 1, 4, 6 and 8 Groups divided into two forces separated by three hours, each with its own specific target. The first phase, by 226 aircraft, was to be directed at the marshalling yards in the town of Kornwestheim, situated just beyond the northern boundary of Stuttgart, while the second phase would target the Hirth aero-engine factory at Zuffenhausen, some two miles to the south. The attacks were not entirely successful and scattered bombs across much of the city and in open country while causing some useful industrial damage.

During the course of the month the squadron operated on eight occasions and dispatched one hundred sorties for the loss of two Lancasters and crews.

February 1945

The weather at the start of February provided difficult conditions for marking and bombing, particularly for 5 Group, and a number of operations would struggle to achieve their aims in the face of thick, low cloud and strong winds. 5 Group was back in harness immediately at the start of the new month following the long lay-off, and 271 Lancaster and eleven Mosquito crews were called to briefings on all 5 Group stations on the 1st to learn that their target was to be the marshalling yards in the town of Siegen, situated some fifty miles east of Cologne. This was a 5

Group show, and was one of three major operations planned for the night, the others by larger forces taking place at Ludwigshafen and Mainz further into southern Germany. A high wind during the night had helped to clear some of the snow, and the seventeen 61 Squadron Lancasters took off between 15.40 and 16.24 with S/L Horsley the senior pilot on duty and each Lancaster carrying either twelve 1,000-pounders or a cookie and sixteen 500-pounders. As NF912 became airborne the port-outer engine cut out and with great skill, S/L Horsley AFC completed a tight circuit before force-landing on the airfield, where the Lancaster was rent by an explosion and consumed by fire. Only the rear gunner survived with injuries, and among those losing their lives was wireless operator, F/Sgt Chapman CGM, who had gained his award for remaining at his post despite being severely wounded during the Nuremberg disaster at the end of March 1944.

The others reached the target area shortly after 19.00 and encountered ten-tenths cloud at between 3,000 and 7,000 feet, which caused problems for the flare and marker forces, some of which were finding it difficult to obtain a clear H2S image on their screens. Eventually, one of the primary blind marker crews ran in and dropped green TIs at 19.05 from 15,000 feet, and their glow was visible through the clouds. This prompted the first flares, followed by an attempt to mark at low-level with red TIs, which were not visible through the clouds, and when the Master Bomber called for skymarking at 19.10, the remaining illuminators were superfluous to requirements and sent home. The bombing phase was put back by four minutes until 19.20, forcing crews to either orbit or dogleg to waste time if they were still on approach, and then instructions were issued to aim at the skymarkers, which were being driven by the strong wind across the intended aiming-point and beyond the target. The glow of red target indicators was faintly visible through the clouds, but this was most likely a decoy fire site prepared by the Germans. It attracted many bomb loads, perhaps some from the 61 Squadron participants, who bombed from 8,000 to 12,000 feet between 19.19 and 19.27, contributing to what became a widely scattered raid. Much of the bombing fell into open and wooded country, and although the railway station sustained damage, the marshalling yards escaped.

The next briefing revealed the bad news that a tour of operations was to be increased again to thirty-six sorties. Fourteen 61 Squadron crews were in attendance at 15.00 on a drizzly afternoon on the 2nd, to be told further that the night's operation was to be against Karlsruhe in southern Germany. This was to be another 5 Group effort involving 250 Lancasters and eleven Mosquitos and was again only one of three major operations taking place. Wiesbaden was to receive its one and only major raid of the war at the hands of almost five hundred aircraft, while a 320-strong predominantly Halifax force dealt with an oil plant at Wanne-Eickel in the Ruhr. The 61 Squadron element departed Skellingthorpe between 19.36 and 20.08 with pilots of flight lieutenant rank leading the way and headed for the assembly point over Reading, before setting course for the French coast. The winds turned out to be lighter than forecast, and this caused a change in route, which now took the force directly from Reading to the target, straddling the Franco-Belgian frontier all the way into Germany, where they encountered heavy cloud at between 3,000 and 15,000 feet. F/L Lipton and crew were approaching Metz at 6,000 feet when the starboard-outer engine caught fire and could not be extinguished, prompting the abandonment of NG241, which crashed some fifteen miles west-south-west of Metz, while the crew drifted down safely to land in Allied territory.

The flare force arrived over the target at 17,500 to 18,500 feet between 23.03 and 23.28 and tried to perform their assigned tasks in difficult conditions, some with malfunctioning H2S equipment. The Mosquito crews attempted to establish an aiming-point, but the illumination was not getting through to the ground, and even had they dropped red TIs, it is unlikely that they would have been visible. At 23.11 the Master Bomber called for skymarking and sent the Mosquitos and remaining illuminators home as the 61 Squadron crews began their bombing runs to attack the glow of markers from 14,000 to 16,500 feet between 23.20 and 23.25 in accordance with instructions. F/O Cooksey and crew had been delayed by icing and were still five minutes short of the target when the Master Bomber called a halt to bombing, but they were allowed to count the sortie as completed. This final raid of the war on Karlsruhe was a complete failure and cost fourteen Lancasters, four of them from Fulbeck's 189 Squadron.

While the frontier towns of Goch and Cleves were being pounded by the other groups ahead of the advancing British XXX Corps on the night of the 7/8th, 5 Group returned to the Dortmund-Ems Canal at Ladbergen with 177 Lancasters and eleven Mosquitos, the heavy brigade carrying delayed action bombs. 61 Squadron made ready a dozen Lancasters, which departed Skellingthorpe between 20.44 and 21.10 with S/L Fadden the senior pilot on duty and all reached the target area to find seven to ten-tenths cloud at between 6,000 and 9,000 feet. They delivered their fourteen 1,000-pounders each from 9,500 to 11,250 feet between 23.59 and 00.11 onto what were believed to be accurate TIs observed through gaps in the cloud and in accordance with the Master Bomber's instructions. F/O Smith and crew were some twenty miles out over the Channel homebound at 4,000 feet when attacked by jet fighters at 02.10 and claimed two of them as destroyed. It turned out to be a rare unsuccessful attack on this target, photographic reconnaissance revealing that the bombs had fallen into fields and had failed to cause any breach.

Sixteen 61 Squadron crews found themselves at briefing on the following day for another long round-trip to the Wintershall oil refinery at Politz, as part of a 5 Group force of 227 Lancasters and seven Mosquitos. They were to act as the first wave in a two-phase attack, which would be completed two hours later by 248 Lancasters from 1 and 8 Groups and departed Skellingthorpe between 16.34 and 17.35 with pilots of flight lieutenant rank taking the lead and F/O Palmer and crew undertaking their first sortie together. The blind markers and the flare force crews went in at 13,000 to 14,500 feet between 21.03 and 21.15 to carry out their assigned tasks in the face of an ineffective smoke screen, and fierce night-fighter activity was evident to the main force crews as they reached the target area to find clear skies and excellent visibility. The 61 Squadron crews identified ground detail in the light of the illuminating flares before delivering their loads onto red TIs from 9,250 to 12,500 feet between 21.15 and 21.22 with a thirteen second overshoot in accordance with the Master Bomber's instructions. The Palmer crew overshot the aiming point and on return to it at 21.27 were instructed to go home. A number of crews reported up to six explosions and black smoke rising through 7,000 feet as they turned away to the west, confident in the quality of their work. Ten Lancasters failed to arrive back to home airspace, and among them were three belonging to 61 Squadron from which a remarkable fifteen crew members survived to fall into enemy hands. LL911 and PB759 went down in the target area and only the rear gunner in the crew of F/O Collins RAAF in the former lost his life, while F/O Tasker RAAF and three others paid the ultimate price. F/L Bartlett alone of his crew was killed when PB737 crashed in the Berlin defence zone probably when homebound, and the loss also of a 50 Squadron crew made it a sad day for the Skellingthorpe community.

Briefings took place on the 13th for the first round of Operation Thunderclap, the Churchill-inspired offensive against Germany's eastern cities, which was devised partly to act in support of the advancing Russians, and also as a demonstration to Stalin of RAF air power, should he turn against the Allies after the war. The historic and culturally significant city of Dresden was selected to open the offensive in another two-phase affair, with a 5 Group force of 246 Lancasters and nine Mosquitos leading the way, to be followed three hours later by 529 Lancasters of 1, 3, 6 and 8 Groups. It had proved to be a successful policy thus far, with the 5 Group low-level marking system and main force attacks providing a beacon for the second force, and should it be required on this night, 8 Group would provide any necessary marking for phase two from high level. The 61 Squadron contingent of sixteen Lancasters departed Skellingthorpe between 17.53 and 18.09 with S/L Fadden the senior pilot on duty, the crews having absolutely no concept of the ramifications of the operation, both in terms of its outcome on the ground and its hysterical aftermath. To set the record straight, Dresden was Germany's seventh largest city and its largest remaining largely un-bombed built-up area, which, according to American sources, contained more than a hundred factories and fifty thousand workers contributing to the war effort. It was also an important railway hub, to the extent that the marshalling yards had been attacked twice in late 1944 by the USAAF.

The heavy force was two hours out when W/C Maurice Smith of 54 Base, the Master Bomber for the 5 Group attack, lifted off the Woodhall Spa runway at a few minutes before 20.00 hours in Mosquito KB401 AZ-E, a 627 Squadron aircraft, and he was followed away by eight others from 627 Squadron. By this time F/O Edwards and crew had turned back from the midpoint of the Channel crossing after the pilot became unwell and had been followed home by F/O Bain and crew from a position thirty miles south of Abbeville when the rear turret failed. The heavy brigade and the Mosquitos arrived in the target area at the same time to encounter three layers of cloud between 3,000 and 5,000 feet, 6,000 to 8,000 feet and 15,000 to 16,000 feet, but otherwise good visibility. The first primary blind marker crew delivered green TIs from 15,000 feet at 22.03 and was followed in by the flare force, which lit the way for the low-level Mosquitos. The main force Lancasters were carrying eight hundred tons of bombs, mostly in the form either of a cookie and twelve 500-pounders or one 2,000-pounder and fourteen J-Type cluster bombs, which the 61 Squadron crews delivered from 12,000 to 13,000 feet between 22.12 and 22.23 onto the glow of red TIs in accordance with the Master Bomber's instructions, mostly with an overshoot of up to twenty-six seconds. As far as the crews were concerned, this was no different from any other attack, and the fires visible for more than a hundred miles into the return journey nothing out of the ordinary.

By the time that the second force of 1, 3, 6 and 8 Group Lancasters arrived over Dresden three hours after 5 Group, the skies had cleared, and the fires created by the earlier attack provided the expected reference point. A further eighteen hundred tons of bombs rained down onto the historic and beautiful old city, setting off the same chain of events that had devastated parts of Hamburg in July 1943 and a number of other cities since. Dresden's population had been swelled by masses of refugees fleeing from the eastern front, and many were engulfed in the ensuing firestorm, which was still burning on the following morning, when three hundred American bombers carried out a separate attack under the umbrella of a fighter escort and completed the destruction. There were claims that RAF aircraft had strafed the streets and open spaces to increase the level of terror, and such accusations abound in the city to this day. In fact, American fighters were responsible and were trying to add to the general confusion and chaos. Initial propaganda-inspired reports from the Office of the Propaganda Minister, Joseph Goebbels, falsely claimed a death toll of 250,000 people, but an accurate figure of twenty-five thousand has been settled upon since.

The destruction of Dresden has been used by some in this country also as a weapon with which to denigrate Bomber Command and Harris, and label them as war criminals, while, curiously, no accusations have been levelled at the Americans. It should also be understood that Harris had no interest in attacking Dresden and had to be nagged by Chief-of-the-Air-Staff Portal to fulfil Churchill's wishes. The airmen involved simply carried out the job asked of them, and the Dresden raid, though resulting in massive casualties, was no different from any other attack on a city, indeed, the death toll at Hamburg was much higher, and yet there has been no similar outcry. The legacy of this operation served to deny Harris and the men under his Command their due recognition for the massive part they played in the ultimate victory, and only in recent times has a monument been erected in Green Park in London and a campaign clasp awarded, sadly, far too little and far too late for the majority. Churchill, with his eyes set on a peacetime election, betrayed Harris and the Command in a typical politically motivated U-turn, in which he accused Harris of bombing solely for the purpose of inflicting terror. In the post-war honours, Harris was the only commander in the field to be omitted.

Round two of Thunderclap was planned for the following night, when Chemnitz was posted as the target for 717 aircraft drawn from 1, 3, 4, 6 and 8 Groups, while 224 Lancasters and eight Mosquitos of 5 Group targeted the Deutsche Erdöl oil refinery in the small town of Rositz, situated twenty-five miles due south of Leipzig and thirty miles north-west of Chemnitz. Thirteen 61 Squadron Lancasters were made ready, and they departed Skellingthorpe between 16.45 and 17.14 with five pilots of flight lieutenant rank taking the lead, before losing the services of F/O Bain and crew to a rear turret issue after twenty minutes. The others pushed on across Germany to be greeted by six to ten-tenths thin cloud in the target area in two layers, one at 6,000 to 8,000 feet, and the other at 10,000 to 12,000 feet, but the primary blind marker crew made a good run on H2S at 15,000 feet at 20.48 to drop green TIs, and the illuminators followed up between 20.51 and 20.58 from a similar height. The main force crews arriving on time carried out support runs with the marker element, before being called in to bomb at 21.07, those from 61 Squadron crews carrying out their attacks on red and green TIs or on their glow from 7,500 to 14,500 feet between 21.02 and 21.20. Explosions were witnessed and three or four large fires were evident in the oil plant sending black smoke rising through 5,000 feet as the force turned away. It was established afterwards that the southern part of the site had been damaged but it would be necessary to return to finish the job. The Chemnitz raid had been compromised by adverse weather conditions, and it would be March before success was achieved against this target.

W/C Pexton was posted to pastures new on the 16th to be succeeded by W/C C W Scott, but the details of both postings are not included in the Form 540 of the ORB. The new commanding officer presided over his first briefing when the Braunkohle-Benzin (Brabag) oil refinery at Böhlen was posted as the target on the 19th for a 5 Group force of 264 Lancasters and six Mosquitos. It was another of the collection of similar plants in the Leipzig area and some ten miles north of Rositz, for which 61 Squadron dispatched seventeen Lancasters from Skellingthorpe in a late take-off between 23.11 and 23.48 again with pilots of flight lieutenant rank the most senior on duty. They all completed the three-and-a-half-hour flight out and would meet up with the later-departing Mosquito element at the target, which included the Master Bomber for the occasion, 54 Base's former 61 Squadron stalwart, W/C Ed Benjamin DFC and Bar, who was flying the same Mosquito used by W/C Smith at Dresden six nights earlier. They encountered ten-tenths cloud over the target in two layers at 5,000 to 8,000 feet and 10,000 to 14,000 feet, and this would introduce a challenging element to the operation. The illuminators went in at around 15,000 feet between 04.05 and 04.13, and the VHF chatter suggested that a Mosquito had been able to mark a factory building with a red TI, and that it had been backed up. The main force was called in, before W/C Benjamin's VHF was suddenly cut off as his Mosquito was shot down by flak with fatal consequences for the occupants. His Deputy took over and the attack continued, the 61 Squadron crews carrying out their bombing runs in accordance with confusing instructions from 8,000 to 14,000 feet between 04.18 and 04.32, aiming mostly at the glow in the cloud of red and green TIs. Post-raid reconnaissance revealed only superficial damage to the site, which would have to be attacked again.

The following night, the 20th, proved to be a busy one, with more than five hundred Lancasters targeting Dortmund, while 268 Halifaxes from 4 and 6 Groups provided the heavy elements for raids on Rhenania-Ossag oil refineries in Düsseldorf and Monheim. 5 Group, meanwhile, prepared itself for a further attempt on the Mittelland Canal at Gravenhorst, for which ten 61 Squadron crews were briefed as part of an overall force of 154 Lancasters and eleven Mosquitos. They departed Skellingthorpe between 21.44 and 22.10 with fourteen 1,000-pounders in each bomb bay and immediately lost the services of F/O Edwards and crew to the failure of their port-outer engine. The others reached the target area to find ten-tenths cloud between them and the aiming-point, but the primary blind marker crew succeeded in delivering two green TIs by H2S from 12,000 feet at 00.53, and they fell on the starboard side of the canal. After the flare force went in, the Mosquito element descended to 400 feet but could not identify the aiming-point, and just before H-Hour, the Master Bomber sent the markers home, to be followed almost immediately by the main force as he abandoned the operation.

The operation was rescheduled for twenty-four hours later, when Duisburg and Worms were also to be attacked by heavy forces of 362 and 349 aircraft respectively. 5 Group detailed 165 Lancasters and twelve Mosquitos, and among those attending the briefing at Coningsby was G/C Evans-Evans, the station commander, who would be taking the bulk of the 83 Squadron commanding officer's highly experienced crew with him. Evans-Evans was 43 and a larger-than-life character, who had commanded 115 Squadron for a spell earlier in the war during its Wellington era and had never lost the enthusiasm to be "one of the boys" and take part in operations. A number of years of good living had widened his girth, and it must have been a struggle to fit into the cramped confines of a Lancaster cockpit. The ten 61 Squadron participants departed Skellingthorpe between 16.59 and 17.17 with F/Ls Amatt, Burns and Hutchins the senior pilots on duty and reached the target area to find moonlight beaming down from clear skies with some ground haze. One of the primary blind markers was able to deliver his green TIs two minutes late because of a change in the wind, and they fell about a mile south of the aiming-point, quite close to the Wet Triangle meeting point of the Mittelland and Dortmund-Ems Canals. After the flare force had done its job, the Mosquitos delivered their red TIs, which were backed up successfully, before the main force was called in at 20.25.

The 61 Squadron crews released their loads of thirteen 1,000-pounders each from 8,000 to 10,750 feet between 20.35 and 20.41 but could not assess the outcome because of the use of long-delay fuses. The presence of night-fighters was clearly evident by the number of combats taking place, and nine Lancasters failed to return, among them the one belonging to 83 Squadron containing G/C Evans-Evans and seven others. Only the rear gunner survived, and, among those killed was the twenty-two-year-old navigator, S/L Wishart DSO, DFC and Bar, who had completed sixty-one operations in Lancasters with 97 (Straits Settlements) Squadron and eighteen in Mosquitos as navigator to Master Bombers. G/C Ingham was left deeply saddened by the loss of his crew, who had not been scheduled to operate but probably jumped at the opportunity presented by G/C Evans-Evans. They would not be the last highly experienced or tour-expired veterans to chance their arm once too often and succumb to the temptation to do one more.

53 Base was not involved in the 5 Group operation by seventy-four Lancasters to bomb what was believed to be a U-Boot base at Horten in Oslo Fjord on the night of the 23/24th. Whether or not a U-Boot base existed is uncertain, but no shipping was seen by the crews, and a local report described heavy damage in the port area and a shipyard, and the sinking of a tanker and floating crane. Meanwhile, some 770 miles to the south, a force of 366 Lancasters, plus one from the Film Unit, and thirteen Mosquitos drawn from 1, 6 and 8 Groups had been sent against the city of Pforzheim, situated in southern Germany between Karlsruhe to the north-west and Stuttgart to the south-east. This would be the first area raid on the city, which was known as a centre for jewellery and watch manufacture but was believed by the Allies to be involved in the production of precision instruments in support of Germany's war effort. They were greeted by clear skies and bright moonlight in the target area, and the thin veil of ground haze proved to be no impediment as the first red Oboe TIs went down at 19.52, to be followed quickly by illuminator flares and salvoes of concentrated reds and greens. Fires rapidly took hold until the whole town north of the river looked like a sea of flames, and by 20.06, the fires were too dazzling for the TIs to be visible and the Master Bomber ordered the smoke to be bombed. The raid lasted twenty-two minutes, during which 1,825 tons of bombs fell into the built-up area, reducing 83% of it to ruins and setting off a firestorm in which 17,600 people lost their lives. This was the highest death toll to result from a single attack on a German city after Hamburg (40,000) and Dresden (25,000). It was during this operation that the final Victoria Cross was earned by a member of RAF Bomber Command. It went posthumously to the Master Bomber from 582 Squadron, Captain Ed Swales of the South African Air Force, who continued to control the attack in a Lancaster severely damaged by a night-fighter, before sacrificing his life to allow his crew to abandon the stricken aircraft.

A daylight attack on the Dortmund-Ems Canal was planned for the afternoon of the 24th, and involved 166 Lancasters and five Mosquitos, eighteen of the former provided by 617 Squadron with Tallboys on board. 61 Squadron contributed seventeen Lancasters, which departed Skellingthorpe between 13.36 and 14.09 with W/C Scott leading the squadron into battle for the first time. After climbing out the force formed into gaggles and reached the target protected by an 11 Group fighter escort to encounter ten-tenths cloud with tops at between 4,000 and 9,000 feet, at which point the Master Bomber abandoned the operation and sent the force home with its bombs. Once back home at their respective stations, crews complained about the unsatisfactory forming up of Base gaggles, which had been generally chaotic. As RF137 was having its bomb load removed on its dispersal pan at 18.46, an explosion tore the Lancaster apart, killing three armourers and injuring eleven others and damaging SW277 beyond repair.

During the course of the month, the squadron took part in ten operations and dispatched 142 sorties for the loss of six Lancasters and four crews.

March 1945

The new month would see the Command bludgeon its way across Germany, concentrating on oil, rail and road targets, along with the few towns still boasting a built-up area. Mannheim was raided for the last time in numbers by a large force from 1, 6 and 8 Groups on the 1st, while 5 Group remained at home. On the 2nd, Cologne was pounded for the final time, first by a force of seven hundred aircraft, which inflicted huge destruction across the city, particularly west of the Rhine, and later by a 3 Group force, of which only fifteen bombed because of a faulty G-H station in England. The city ceased to function, thereafter, and was still paralyzed when American forces marched in four days later. Just when it seemed that German resistance to air attack might end, March would prove that the defenders were still capable of mounting a challenge, even though they were stretched beyond their capacity to protect every corner of the Reich.

5 Group opened its March account with a return to the Ladbergen aqueduct section of the Dortmund-Ems Canal on the evening of the 3rd, for which 212 Lancasters and ten Mosquitos were made ready. Fifteen 61 Squadron crews attended briefing to learn of their part in the main event and departed Skellingthorpe between 18.23 and 18.52 with W/C Scott the senior pilot on duty and each crew sitting on thirteen 1,000-pounders. They encountered eight to ten-tenths cloud in the target area at between 3,500 and 6,000 feet, and it was noted that the defences had been strengthened since the last attack and were throwing up a curtain of intense light flak as high as 15,000 feet. H2S allowed the two 83 Squadron primary blind marker crews to locate the canal and deliver their green TIs from 14,000 feet at 21.47 and 21.49, and the first illuminators went in a minute later to light the way for the low-level Mosquitos, after which, a large red glow could be seen through the clouds. At 21.59, the Master Bomber called in the main force to bomb on the glow or on actual sight of the TIs through gaps in the thin cloud, and the 61 Squadron crews complied from 8,250 to 10,000 feet between 22.00 and 22.10, contributing to the breaching of both branches, which rendered the waterway unnavigable and, finally, out of action for the remainder of the war.

The Luftwaffe mounted Operation Gisella on this night, sending some two hundred intruders to catch the bombers as they prepared to land, and they succeeded in shooting down twenty, including two from 5 Group, for the loss of three of their own. It was a tactic that could have resulted in many more Bomber Command casualties had Hitler not insisted that it was better for propaganda and morale for the wreckage of Allied bombers to be seen on German rather than English soil.

Eighteen 61 Squadron crews attended briefing on the 5th, to learn that 5 Group would be sending 248 Lancasters and ten Mosquitos back to Böhlen for another crack at the Braunkohle-Benzin synthetic oil refinery. A simultaneous operation by a Thunderclap force of 760 aircraft would attempt to redress the recent failure at Chemnitz, some thirty-five miles to the south. Take-off from Skellingthorpe by the 61 Squadron contingent was accomplished without incident between 16.56 and 17.45 with the recently posted-in S/L Moore the senior pilot on duty and all reached the target area, some after climbing above 15,000 feet to escape icing conditions. Ten-tenths cloud lay over the target in layers between 2,000 and 11,000 feet but the uncertainty of prevailing conditions on arrival had been anticipated and two marking plans prepared, low-level and skymarking. The lead primary blind marker crew made its first run at 14,000 feet to drop green TIs at 21.40 and although they were not observed to burst because of the cloud, it was thought that the illuminator flares were well-placed. Some of the marker crews experienced H2S difficulties and not all were able to pinpoint on Leipzig for the run-in. This meant that they were unsure of their position, and when the Master Bomber called for Wanganui flares at 21.45, they withheld them rather than risk dropping them inaccurately and attracting some of the bombing. A large explosion was witnessed at 21.50, and three minutes later, Wanganui flares were observed by the approaching main force crews. Fifteen of the 61 Squadron participants delivered their cookie and eleven 500-pounders each from 10,750 to 14,000 feet between 21.53 and 22.10, observing another large explosion at 21.57. The crews of F/Os Swales and Roocroft bombed at Chemnitz after being unable to positively identify the correct markers to aim for. The Master Bomber called a halt at 22.10 and sent everyone home leaving evidence of fires and smoke behind them. Post-raid reconnaissance revealed extensive damage to the coal-drying plant and some hits in other areas of the site, but it was still not a knockout blow. Meanwhile, the Thunderclap force had succeeded in inflicting severe fire damage in central and southern districts of Chemnitz.

The target posted on 5 Group stations on the 6th was the town and port area of Sassnitz, located on the Baltic Island of Rügen, about thirty miles north of Peenemünde, a region with memories of heavy casualties sustained by 5 Group in August 1943. The two-fold purpose of the operation was to destroy the port installations and facilities and sink shipping to render it unusable as a refuge for escaping Kriegsmarine units. 150 Lancasters and seven Mosquitos were made ready, ten of the former by 61 Squadron, which departed Skellingthorpe between 18.06 and 18.27 with F/L Amatt the senior pilot on duty. Those reaching the target area found five to nine-tenths drifting cloud with tops in places at 8,000 feet, over which an 83 Squadron blind marker Lancaster made a run at 22.50 to drop green TIs over the port from 12,000 feet. The flare force maintained illumination of the town and outer harbour for the next twenty-five minutes, and apart from a short break when cloud slid across the aiming-point, the markers remained visible to the main force crews. The 61 Squadron element bombed on red TIs from 8,000 to 10,000 feet between 22.59 and 23.11 and were on their way home by the time that bombing activity ceased at H+18, leaving those with bombs still aboard to take them home. Three large ships identified in the harbour were attacked, and, according to post-raid reconnaissance, sunk, and there was also extensive damage in the northern part of the town.

There was a return to the oil campaign for 5 Group on the following night, for an attack on a refinery at Harburg, south of Hamburg, for which a force of 234 Lancasters and seven Mosquitos was made ready. They would not be alone over Germany, however, as more than a thousand other aircraft would be engaged against similar targets at Dessau and Hemmingstedt and in minor and support operations. 61 Squadron provided fifteen Lancasters, which departed Skellingthorpe between 17.30 and 18.23 with S/L Fadden the senior pilot on duty and lost the services of F/O Clarke and crew during the North Sea crossing to an unserviceable compass and mid-upper turret. The others arrived over the target to find eight-tenths thin cloud and red and yellow target indicators clearly visible, which nine 61 Squadron crews bombed in accordance with the Master Bomber's instructions with a seven-second overshoot from 12,250 to 14,000 feet between 21.58 and 22.08. The crews of F/L Boland and F/O Swales were unable to bomb, the former having supported the Path Finders during a first pass and then being forced off track by the defences when attempting a second run. The latter lost time when becoming entangled in the Kiel defence zone and was still approaching the target when the call came from the Master Bomber to cease the attack.

There was consternation at Skellingthorpe when three 61 Squadron Lancasters failed to return, and it would be some time before news of their fate arrived via the Red Cross. NF988 and NG182 were brought down in the target area and only the rear gunner survived from the experienced crew of F/L Miller in the former, which had a second pilot on board. F/O Pearce and his navigator escaped with their lives from the latter to add two more names to the list of crewmen from Skellingthorpe on extended leave in PoW camps. There were no survivors from the crew of F/O Farren RAAF after ME474 crashed into the sea, which eventually gave up the remains of the pilot and flight engineer for burial. Returning crews reported bomb bursts along with explosions and black smoke rising through 10,000 feet, and expressed confidence in the success of the operation. 5 Group crews distinguished themselves on this night by claiming the destruction of seven enemy fighters. Post-raid reconnaissance confirmed further damage to this previously attacked target, with oil storage tanks taking the most hits, and revealed that a rubber factory had also been severely damaged.

An all-time record was set on the 11th, when 1,079 aircraft, the largest Bomber Command force ever for a single target, was assembled to attack Essen for the last time. 5 Group contributed 199 Lancasters and a single Mosquito, 61 Squadron loading fourteen Lancasters with a cookie and sixteen 500-pounders each and dispatching them from Skellingthorpe between 11.47 and 12.26 with W/C Scott and S/L Moore the senior pilots on duty. They found the target city covered by ten-tenths cloud with tops at 6,000 feet, which required the Path Finder element to employ skymarkers in the form of red and blue smoke puffs, and these were bombed by the 61 Squadron crews from 16,000 to 18,800 feet between 15.17 and 15.23. More than 4,600 tons of bombs were dropped into the already ravaged city and former industrial powerhouse and left it with a huge pall of smoke rising through 10,000 feet as the force turned away. It would be still in a state of paralysis when the American ground forces captured it unopposed on the 10th of April. Operations were not yet over for the 11th, as 5 Group sent eleven Lancasters that night to mine the approaches to Oslo harbour in the Onions III garden.

A little over twenty-four hours later, the short-lived record was surpassed by the departure from their stations in the early afternoon of 1,108 aircraft, which had Dortmund as their destination. This time 5 Group provided 211 Lancasters, fifteen of them from 61 Squadron, which departed Skellingthorpe between 13.07 and 13.45 with S/L Moore the senior pilot on duty and a bomb load of a cookie and sixteen 500-pounders in each bomb bay. The spearhead of the bomber stream arrived over the eastern Ruhr to find it still under a blanket of ten-tenths cloud topping out at 6,000 feet, which required the Path Finders to skymark the target with green and blue smoke puffs. The Master Bomber directed the main force crews to aim for the blues, and the 61 Squadron element complied from 15,000 to 17,000 feet between 16.47 and 16.53. Returning crews spoke of brown smoke climbing through the clouds to 8,000 feet from the northern end of the city, and also a ring of smoke encircling the entire area, which was so dense that it remained visible for 120 miles into the return flight. A new record of 4,800 tons of bombs was delivered, and photo-reconnaissance revealed that the central and southern districts of the city had received the greatest weight and had been left in chaos with all industry silenced permanently and railway tracks torn up.

The Group's next objective was the Wintershall oil refinery at Lützkendorf, another site to the west of Leipzig and south-west of Leuna in the Geiseltal. *(Lützkendorf no longer exists on a map of Germany and is now known as either Mücheln or Krumpa)*. The briefing of 244 Lancaster and eleven Mosquito crews took place on the 14th, seventeen of the former representing 61 Squadron, and they departed Skellingthorpe between 16.31 and 17.03 with W/C Scott the senior pilot on duty. They headed out over the Wash and the bulge of East Anglia en-route to the Scheldt Estuary and lost the services of F/O Ainsworth and crew to W/T failure after an hour. The rest crossed Belgium to swing south of Cologne, before pointing their snouts to the east for the long leg to the target, where they were greeted by conditions described variously as ten-tenths cloud, no cloud, thin layer of cloud, thin banks of stratus with tops at 12,000 feet, a little medium cloud, poor visibility and good visibility. Ahead, the primary blind marker aircraft could be seen delivering their green TIs at 21.49, followed by the illuminators immediately afterwards between 21.51 and 22.00 to drop flares and bombs. Finally, the low-level Mosquitos fulfilled their brief to accurately mark the aiming-point before the main force crews were called in and the 61 Squadron participants bombed on red and green TIs in accordance with the Master Bomber's instructions from 8,000 to 9,750 feet between 22.02 and 22.10. Returning crews claimed an accurate attack, reporting explosions and fires and thick black smoke drifting across the plant and ascending through 7,000 feet, which rendered impossible a detailed assessment. Night-fighters were very much in evidence over the target and during the return flight, and a hefty eighteen Lancasters failed to return, 7.4% of those dispatched. Post-raid reconnaissance revealed a partially successful operation, which meant that a further visit would be required.

Sixteen 61 Squadron crews assembled in the briefing room at 14.00 on the 16th, to learn that they were to attack the virgin target of Würzburg, a small city on the River Main, situated some sixty miles south-east of Frankfurt in southern Germany. While this operation was in progress, a similar-sized force drawn from 1 and 8 Groups would be delivering the final attack of the war on Nuremberg, fifty miles to the south-east. A 5 Group force of 225 Lancasters and eleven Mosquitos was made ready for an early-evening take-off, the 61 Squadron element departing Skellingthorpe between 17.24 and 17.52 with seven pilots of flight lieutenant rank leading the way. What a contrast from earlier in the war, when flight lieutenants were thin on the ground, usually two per squadron to act as deputy flight commanders. F/O Edwards and crew turned back from the midpoint of the Channel when an engine issue disabled the rear turret, while the bomber stream continued on and reached the target area to find clear skies with ground haze. The marking and flare forces carried out their assigned tasks between 21.25 and 21.34, leaving the way clear for the main force crews to exploit the favourable bombing conditions, those representing 61 Squadron finding red and yellow target indicators marking the aiming-point. They were in the bomb sights as the Master Bomber called for a twenty-six-second overshoot, and the loads of a cookie and incendiaries went down from 8,000 to 10,000 feet between 21.33 and 21.38.

Returning crews reported a successful operation but had to wait for the reconnaissance photos to discover the extent of the destruction. The bombing had officially lasted just seventeen minutes, during which period 1,127 tons of bombs had fallen into the historic old cathedral city, destroying an estimated 89% of the built-up area and killing four to five thousand people. Among six missing Lancasters was 61 Squadron's RF176, which crashed somewhere in southern Germany with no survivors from the crew of F/L Grynkiewicz, who were approaching the end of their tour. The Nuremberg operation had also been highly destructive, but had cost 1 Group twenty-four Lancasters, thus proving that the enemy defences were not yet spent and were still capable of giving the Command a bloody nose.

There was still business to attend to at the Böhlen oil refinery, and 5 Group prepared a force of 236 Lancasters and eleven Mosquitos on the 20th to deal what was hoped to be the knockout blow. Briefings began at 20.00 and was attended at Skellingthorpe by fifteen 61 Squadron crews with S/L Fadden the most senior pilot present, while out on the dispersals the armourers were loading each Lancaster with a cookie and eleven 500-pounders. They took off between 23.19 and 23.56 and set out on the now familiar path to eastern Germany, arriving at the target early because of stronger-than-forecast winds, to encounter fairly favourable conditions, with three to six-tenths cloud topping out at 6,000 to 8,000 feet. The main force element had to orbit while the first primary blind marker crew delivered green TIs at 03.33, which fell 750 yards south of the plant and were followed at H-16 by a yellow TI bursting two miles short. A cluster of illuminator flares ignited ahead, revealing that a smoke screen had been activated and was generating much smoke to create difficulties for the Mosquito low-level marker crews. Despite the challenges, they deposited red TIs on the button and the main force was called in, a few dummy TIs attracting a number of bomb loads, but the 61 Squadron crews complied with the instructions of the Master Bomber to bomb on specific reds and yellows from 12,000 to 14,000 feet between 03.45 and 03.53. The main weight of the attack was concentrated around the target and numerous explosions were witnessed, as was smoke rising through 5,000 feet as they turned away. The operation put the oil plant out of action, and it was still idle when American forces moved in a few weeks later. The success cost nine Lancasters among which were two belonging to 61 Squadron, NG386 disappearing without trace with the crew of F/O Ainsworth, while RA560 came down in southern Germany with no survivors from the crew of F/O Swales RAAF.

It was after 22.00 on the 21st when 151 Lancaster and eight Mosquito crews of 5 Group were informed that the Deutsche Erdölwerke synthetic oil refinery at Hamburg was to be their target that night. The 53 Base squadrons were not to be involved in this operation, which was attended by thin stratus cloud at around 2,000 feet and resulted in the destruction of twenty storage tanks at a cost of four Lancasters.

After its night off, 61 Squadron was alerted on the 22nd, and fourteen crews attended briefing to learn of their target for that afternoon, which turned out to be a railway bridge at Bremen, while 617 Squadron attended to a similar structure at Nienburg, situated some twenty-five miles to the south-east. A force of eighty-two Lancasters was assembled, and the 61 Squadron crews departed Skellingthorpe between 11.15 and 11.55 with W/C Scott and S/L Moore the senior pilots on duty and fourteen 1,000-pounders in each bomb bay. They began the North Sea crossing at the Norfolk coast near Sheringham and arrived in the target area under clear skies and in good visibility, which enabled them to pick out the River Weser and the bridges spanning its length within the city. The 61 Squadron crews delivered their attacks visually, in accordance with the instructions of the Master Bomber from 15,400 to 17,000 feet between 14.07 and 14.10, some of them having to aim at the smoke that was enveloping the bridge, while dodging the moderate to intense heavy flak. It was impossible to assess the outcome, but photo-reconnaissance would reveal the bridge to be still intact.

The town of Wesel had the misfortune to lie close to the Rhine and in the path of advancing British ground forces. Since the 16th of February it had been systematically reduced to rubble by repeated air attacks, and now had one final onslaught to face, having already endured one by 3 Group earlier in the day. 5 and 8 Groups assembled a force of 195 Lancasters and eleven Mosquitos, of which sixteen of the former were provided by 61 Squadron and departed Skellingthorpe between 19.05 and 19.43 with F/Ls Amatt, Davies, Hutchins and Phillips the senior pilots on duty. F/O Mouritz and crew turned back when fifteen miles south of Eastbourne after the failure of their port-inner engine, while the rest found the target to be under clear skies with slight ground haze and easily identified visually and by the red and green TIs marking out the aiming point. The 61 Squadron crews bombed from 8,000 to 11,800 feet between 22.34 and 22.38 in accordance with the Master Bomber's instructions, noting that, despite the Master Bomber ending the attack at H+8, bombing had continued for some minutes afterwards. Post-raid reconnaissance confirmed the effectiveness of the raid, which left only 3% of Wesel's buildings standing and after the war it would claim justifiably to be the most completely destroyed town in Germany.

The month's final operations for 5 Group took place on the 27th, when twenty Lancasters of 617 Squadron were sent with Tallboys and Grand Slams to the Valentin U-Boot bunker at Farge, a small port on the eastern bank of the Weser, northwest of Bremen. In his classic book, The Dambusters, Paul Brickhill described the target as the largest concrete structure in the world, measuring some 1,450 by 300 yards, which boasted a reinforced-concrete roof twenty-three-feet thick. The massive structure contained a tank large enough for completed U-Boots to be tested under water, but at the time of the attack it was still under construction and was not operational. In fact, Bomber Command had been monitoring progress and had been waiting for the concrete roof to be poured with the intention of attacking it before it had chance to set. A simultaneous operation by ninety-five Lancasters against a nearby underground oil storage facility involved eighteen Lancasters from 61 Squadron, which departed Skellingthorpe between 10.03 and 10.36 with S/L Fadden the senior pilot on duty. They all arrived at the target to find clear skies and good visibility, and identified the aiming-point visually, before bombing from 15,200 to 18,500 feet between 13.00 and 13.04. They were unable to assess the outcome, but three explosions and thick brown smoke suggested a successful attack, and their attention was drawn inevitably to the 617 Squadron activity, where a sheet of flame was observed. The 617 Squadron attack was another masterly display of precision bombing, and photo-reconnaissance confirmed two direct hits by Grand Slams, which had penetrated the partially completed roof and caused a great deal of it to collapse. The structure was still incomplete at the end of hostilities, having never been used, and its enormous bulk remains to this day as a permanent monument to a failed regime.

During the course of the month the squadron took part in twelve operations and dispatched 183 sorties for the loss of six Lancasters and crews. Although the airmen of Bomber Command could not know, fewer than four weeks of operations remained ahead of them before the bombing war finally came to an end.

April 1945

There would be a gentle introduction to April for 5 Group, with no operations until the 4th, when briefings were held to inform crews about that day's operation against what was believed to be a military barracks at Nordhausen, situated in the Harz Mountains between Hannover to the north-west and Leipzig to the south-east. The site was actually a pair of enormous parallel tunnels under the Kohnstein Hill, which had been developed originally by the Badische Anilin-und Sodafabrik (BASF) Company to mine gypsum between 1917 and 1934. Following the destruction of Peenemünde, smaller tunnels had been created as a link between them to form a horizontal ladder effect, and the site turned over to the Mittelwerk GmbH (Gesellschaft mit beschrenkter Haftung, or Limited Company) for the manufacture of V-2 rockets and other secret projects. The "barracks" were part of the Mittelwerk-Dora forced workers camp, where inmates existed under the most horrendous conditions and brutal treatment, while they were starved, worked to death or simply executed by an increasingly desperate regime seeking to change the course of the war.

The site had been attacked with only modest success on the previous day by 1 Group, but the 5 Group operation by 243 Lancasters was to be divided between the barracks and the town, ninety-three to the former and 150 to the latter. The 53 Base squadrons were assigned to the latter and had been given the marshalling yards as the aiming point for their cookie and sixteen 500-pounders each. The nineteen 61 Squadron participants departed Skellingthorpe between 05.46 and 06.30 with a whole host of flight lieutenant pilots leading the way and headed south-east towards the Dutch coast to swing round the south-eastern corner of the Ruhr and then head north to the target. They arrived to encounter five-to-seven-tenths cloud with tops as high as 7,000 feet, through which the 61 Squadron crews were able to establish a visual reference carry out their attacks from 13,000 to 16,700 feet between 09.16 and 09.22 and although some of the early bombing of the town was seen to undershoot, the Master Bomber corrected this by calling for a five-second overshoot. Thereafter, the markers became obscured by smoke, which was a problem also for those assigned to the barracks and some redirected their attention upon the town. Only one aircraft failed to return, a 49 Squadron Lancaster, which must have been the one observed by 61 Squadron's F/O Yarrall and crew to fall in flames over the target, presumably having been hit by bombs from above as there was no opposition. At debriefing, crews were able to report what appeared to be a concentrated attack on both aiming-points, claiming severe damage, but it would the 8th before photo-reconnaissance confirmed that a large part of the town had been left devastated and there was evidence also that the Mittelwerk site had sustained substantial damage. Tragically and inevitably, there would have been casualties among any unfortunate slave workers not protected within the tunnels.

53 Base was called into action on the 6th to attack blockade-runners at the Dutch port of Ijmuiden, and a force of fifty-four Lancasters and a Mosquito was made ready, the nine 61 Squadron Lancasters departing Skellingthorpe between 08.26 and 08.55 with S/L Moore the senior pilot on duty and fourteen 1,000-pounders in each bomb bay. On arrival at the target, a band of cloud was encountered at between 3,000 and 5,500 feet concealing the area, which persuaded the Master Bomber to abandon the operation and send the crews home.

The only sizeable effort on the night of the 7/8th was by 175 Lancasters and eleven Mosquitos of 5 Group, which had a benzol plant at Molbis, near Leipzig, as their target. Situated south of the city, and less than two miles east of Böhlen, it had become a familiar destination for 5 Group via a well-trodden route across Belgium to pass south of Cologne. 61 Squadron made ready seven of its Lancasters, which departed Skellingthorpe between 17.55 and 18.08, four with flight lieutenant pilots, and found themselves delayed by wrongly forecast head winds, which, while not adversely affecting them, it would prevent some others from reaching the target area in time to participate in the attack. Two 83 Squadron primary blind markers formed the tip of the spear and identified Zeitz on H2S, before making the ten-mile north-easterly run from there to the target. Green TIs were released from 15,000 feet at 22.48 and the flare force followed up between 22.50 and 22.57 to enable the low-level Mosquitos to drop red and green TIs among the chimneys of the plant. The approaching main force crews were greeted by clear skies with ground haze, or perhaps, a smoke screen in operation, but the highly accurate and visible marking was an invitation for them to plaster the aiming-point with high explosives. The 61 Squadron crews bombed on red and green TIs from 16,000 to 17,000 feet between 23.01 and 23.07, and returned confident in the quality of their work, which photo-reconnaissance confirmed to have been a complete success that ended all production at the plant. Later in the day, the length of a tour was reduced from thirty-six to thirty-three sorties, handing an unexpected bonus to a lucky few, including 61 Squadron's F/L Burns and crew for whom the above operation had been their thirty-third.

Two major operations were scheduled for the 8th, the larger one involving 440 aircraft from 4, 6 and 8 Groups to be directed against Hamburg's shipyards, where the new Type XXI U-Boots were under construction, while 5 Group took on the Lützkendorf refinery, following a failed attempt on the 4th by 1 and 8 Groups to conclusively end production at the site. A force of 231 Lancasters and eleven Mosquitos was put together, the eleven 61 Squadron participants departing Skellingthorpe between 18.08 and 18.31 with S/L Fadden the senior pilot on duty. They set course for Berck-sur-Mer on the French coast and crossed northern Luxembourg before swinging to the north-east on track for the target, where conditions were as they had been twenty-four hours earlier, with clear skies and either ground haze or generated smoke. The primary blind markers ran in at 14,000 feet at 22.33 to deliver green TIs, and the illuminators followed between 22.35 and 22.42, after which, the main force was called in. The 61 Squadron crews attacked in accordance with the Master Bomber's instructions to bomb the northerly red and yellow TIs and ran in at 11,000 to 14,000 feet between 22.46 and 22.50. All but one then returned safely, confident that it would not be necessary to return to that particular target but absent from the debriefing process was the crew of F/O MacFarlane RCAF and crew in ME385, which was brought down by flak in the target area. The pilot and four others failed to survive, leaving the rear gunner in enemy hands and bomb-aimer evading a similar fate, a remarkable feat so deep inside Germany. Returning crews described their experiences to the intelligence section, reporting many explosions, including a large one at 22.47, which was surpassed in size by another one two minutes later from which flames were said to have reached up to 3,000 feet. The complete destruction of the site was confirmed by photo-reconnaissance, and the plant would remain out of action for the remainder of the war.

Orders were received on 53 Base stations on the 9th to prepare for an attack on the Eurotank oil storage facilities on Finkenwerder Island, situated in the Elbe to the west of Hamburg city centre and the home of the Blohm & Voss shipyards and aircraft factory. A force of forty Lancasters was made ready, ten of them provided by 61 Squadron, which departed Skellingthorpe between 14.28 and 14.52 with F/Ls Greenfield and Rawle the senior pilots on duty. They were greeted at the target by clear skies and good visibility, which enabled them easily to identify the docks area, before bombing visually from 16,400 to 18,000 feet between 17.37 and 17.39. On return, there were reports of concentrated bombing, which produced many fires and much black smoke rising to through 15,000 feet, and a few crews reported flak damage, the presence of jet fighters and at least two Lancasters going down in the target area. Both were from Skellingthorpe, one of them RF121 of 61 Squadron, in which F/L Greenfield DFC RAAF lost his life alongside four of his crew, while the flight engineer and rear gunner ended their war in enemy hands. It was a sad loss of an experienced crew, and with some thirty-two sorties to his credit, F/L Greenfield may well have been on the final operation of his tour.

53 Base squadrons were not called into action on the 10th, when other elements of 5 Group returned to the Leipzig area to hit a railway line at Wahren, situated to the north-west of the city. A larger operation on this night, involving more than three hundred aircraft from 1 and 8 Groups, was to be directed at the Plauen marshalling yards to the south-west of Dresden, and the two forces would adopt a similar route until shortly before reaching Leipzig. 5 Group contributed all seventy-six Lancasters and eleven Mosquitos, with 8 Group providing the other eight Oboe Mosquitos, which, now that mobile Oboe stations had been set up on the Continent, could operate over the whole of Germany. Clear skies over the target provided excellent conditions for bombing, and photo-reconnaissance would confirm serious damage to the eastern half of the targeted stretch of track.

A major attack on Kiel by elements of 3, 6 and 8 Groups was planned for the night of the 13/14th, while 5 Group took advantage of that activity to send eighteen Lancasters to lay mines in the Forget-me-not garden in Kiel harbour. 5 Group was used to being handed the most distant targets, and as the final days of the bombing war approached, it found itself facing three long-range trips on consecutive nights, all to railway targets. The first of these was at Pilsen in Czechoslovakia, for which a force of 222 Lancasters and eleven Mosquitos was made ready on the 16th. The fourteen 61 Squadron Lancasters departed Skellingthorpe between 23.20 and 23.51 with F/Ls Friend, Hamilton and Rawle the senior pilots on duty and W/C F Wild DFC flying as second pilot with the first mentioned to gain up-to-date operational experience before assuming command of 630 Squadron on the 28th. W/O Morrison and crew were within fifty-five miles of their destination when the loss of an engine prevented them from maintaining height above 7,000 feet and forced them to turn back. The others found clear skies in the target area with only slight haze, and ahead, watched the first primary blind marker crew deliver green TIs at 03.38, before the flare forces followed between 03.51 and 03.56. The main force was called in at 03.58, and the 49 Squadron participants bombed from 11,900 to 14,000 feet between 04.00 and 04.06, aiming at the north-westerly red and yellow TIs with an eight-second overshoot in accordance with the Master Bomber's instructions. Returning crews reported a large explosion at 04.00, followed by oily smoke, and it was concluded that the raid had been successful.

There was good news to celebrate on the 17th, when the length of a tour was reduced further to thirty successful sorties, although, as previously mentioned, that may not have been the final word on the matter. That evening, the target posted for ninety 5 Group Lancasters and eleven Mosquitos was the marshalling yards at Cham, on Germany's border with Czechoslovakia. 53 Base was not involved in the operation, which delivered delayed-action bombs and left the crews guessing as to the outcome. Photo-reconnaissance confirmed later that another concentrated and accurate attack by the "Independent Air Force" had left tracks torn up and rolling stock damaged.

5 Group was not involved when a force of over nine hundred aircraft reduced the island of Heligoland to the appearance of a cratered moonscape during the day on the 18th, but 53 Base stations were alerted to another long-range operation that night, for which a force of 113 Lancasters and ten Mosquitos was put together. The target was the railway yards at Komotau (now Chomutov), also in Czechoslovakia, which proved to be the last raid in the communications offensive begun more than a year earlier. 61 Squadron made ready nineteen Lancasters, which departed Skellingthorpe between 23.04 and 23.45 with F/Ls Friend, Hamilton and Rawle the senior pilots on duty and lost the services of F/O Cover and crew to an over-revving port-inner engine. At the target the others found two layers of broken cloud, one at 6,000 feet and the other at between 10,000 and 12,000 feet, the Master Bomber directing the main force crews to descend into the lane of clear air between the two layers and bomb on red and yellow TIs with an eight-second overshoot. The 61 Squadron crews complied from 8,000 to 10,500 feet between 03.58 and 04.02, and post-raid reconnaissance revealed the yards to be heavily cratered with most of the tracks cut and locomotive sheds and workshops severely damaged.

617 Squadron employed Grand Slams and Tallboys to complete the destruction of Heligoland by daylight on the 19th, while the rest of 5 Group remained at home with a sense that it was all coming to an end. It was the 23rd, before orders came through again to prepare for the next operation, which was to be directed at the railway yards and port area of Flensburg on the Baltic side of Schleswig-Holstein. The ten 61 Squadron crews departed Skellingthorpe between 15.03 and 15.24 with F/L Friend the senior pilot on duty, and made their way across the peninsula, while the Master Bomber, S/L Blair of 50 Squadron, contacted his two Deputies for a conference by VHF at H-29. Blair's bomb-aimer identified the target and led him to the start of the bombing run, at which point he ordered an overshoot in the case of cloud obscuring the ground. That was precisely what happened when a layer of ten-tenths cloud with tops at 4,500 feet slid across the area as he began his final approach, and judging it impossible to bomb by any method, issued further orders to maintain the gaggle in the hope of going round again. However, the gaggle had begun to break up, and despite reducing speed to 130 knots for a considerable time, he was unable to rescue the situation and ordered the crews to disperse and go home. His frustration at debriefing was clear, as he made the point that they could have bombed if the formation had remained together.

5 Group operated for the final time on the 25th, with an operation in the morning against the SS barracks at Hitler's Eaglesnest retreat at Berchtesgaden in the Bavarian mountains, which 5 Group supported with eighty-eight Lancasters and a single Mosquito in an overall 1, 5 and 8 Group force of 359 Lancasters and sixteen Mosquitos. 53 Base was not involved in the attack, during which it proved difficult to identify the barracks in the absence of visible markers, but a nearby lake and the town stood out clearly and the bombing took place under clear skies in the minutes either side of 09.00.

The Skellingthorpe squadrons had to wait until mid-evening before embarking on what would prove to be their final offensive operation of the war as part of a 5 Group force of 107 Lancasters and twelve Mosquitos targeting the Vallø Oljeraffineri oil refinery at Tonsberg in southern Norway, situated close to the western shore of Oslo Fjord, a dozen or so miles south of the recently attacked Horten. The purpose of the attack was to cut off fuel supplies from its storage tanks, but as matters turned out, they were largely empty. Fourteen 61 and fifteen 50 Squadron Lancasters took off, the former between 20.04 and 20.32 with S/L Moore the senior pilot on duty and lost the services of the crews of F/Os Cover and Clarke respectively to a port-inner engine issue and the failure of navigational instruments and the bomb sight. The others reached the target to encounter a layer of eight to ten-tenths cloud at between 7,500 and 10,500 feet, which prompted the Master Bomber to call the main force element down to clear air. The 61 Squadron crews complied and bombed on red and yellow TIs from 8,000 to 9,250 between 23.45 and 23.53, but not all could pick out the aiming-point, and F/O Shaw and crew were among a handful to withhold their bombs. Returning crews reported many fires and explosions together with much black smoke, which suggested a successful conclusion to the squadron's and group's offensive activities, but, sadly, some bombs hit civilian housing adjacent to the site and killed fifty-three people. When F/O Scofield and crew touched down at Skellingthorpe at 03.29 on the 26th, they unwittingly had the honour of bringing to an end 61 Squadron's offensive service, although this would not be appreciated for some days, during which further operations were posted but cancelled.

Later on the 26th, the humanitarian Operation Exodus began, the purpose of which was to bring home former PoWs from the Continent, and eight 61 Squadron Lancaster flew to Melsbroek aerodrome at Brussels, followed by a further two to Juvincourt in France on the 30th. A second humanitarian operation, Manna, began on the 30th to drop food to the starving Dutch people still under occupation, and this would continue until the end of hostilities on the 8th of May. During the course of this final month of the bombing war, the squadron took part in nine operations and dispatched 113 sorties for the loss of two Lancasters and crews. 61 Squadron did not take part in Operation Manna but continued Exodus flights, bringing home ninety-six PoWs on the 4th of May, 336 on the 6th, 168 on the 7th and many more as such flights continued into the summer.

61 Squadron ended its war with an impressive record of service, including the fifth highest number of overall operations in Bomber Command, the second highest number of bombing operations in Bomber Command, the third highest number of overall Lancaster operations in Bomber Command, the fifth highest number of Lancaster sorties in Bomber Command, the second highest number of overall operations in 5 Group and the fourth highest number of sorties in 5 Group. It also sustained the fifth highest number of operational losses in Bomber Command and in 5 Group.

Three 61 Squadron Lancasters achieved a century of operations, ED860 reaching the magic figure during an operation to Vitry-la-Francois on the 27/28.6.44 in the hands of F/L Turner and crew. She eventually completed 130 operations before coming to grief as mentioned in the narrative.

EE176, "Mickey the Moocher", survived the war after completing 122 or 128 operations, and JB138 notched up a total of 113 or 123. The wartime record of 61 Squadron bears comparison with any in the Command and it was one of the mainstays of 5 Group and Bomber Command. Its achievements stand as a testimony to the courage, dedication and skill of its members, whether serving in the air or on the ground, and to the quality of those who had the honour to be its commanding officers and flight commanders.

Roll of Honour

Sgt	Charles	ABLETT	03.01.1944.
Sgt	Charles Frederick	ABRAHAM	07.02.1943.
Sgt	Cyril Arthur	ACOMBE-HILL	28.01.1944.
Sgt	Stanley	ADAIR	13.08.1944.
P/O	Reginald	ADCOCK	07.12.1941.
P/O	Patrick James Neil	ADSHEAD	31.07.1941.
F/O	Kenneth William	AINSWORTH	21.03.1945.
F/O	George Frederick	ALDERDICE	26.07.1943.
F/Sgt	Peter Henry	ALDERTON	13.05.1943.
Sgt	Douglas Ronald	ALDOM	13.08.1940.
F/O	Norman Frederick	ALDRED	23.09.1944.
F/L	Richard Sydney Edward	ALDRIDGE	18.04.1941.
Sgt	Alan	ALGAR	05.10.1940.
P/O	John Francis	ALLEN	20.02.1944.
F/O	Eric Robert	ALSTON	25.04.1944.
Sgt	William Flight	ANDERSON	28.06.1940.
P/O	Alexander John	ANDERSON	26.08.1944.
F/O	Richard Bruce	ANDERSON	06.01.1945.
Sgt	Francis Bernard	ANDREWS	17.01.1943.
Sgt	Gordon Arthur	ANGWIN	15.08.1943.
Sgt	Jack	ARCHER	29.08.1941.
F/O	Ronald Earle	ARCHIBALD	04.06.1942.
Sgt	Walter Frederick	ARDRON	03.08.1943.
F/Sgt	Albert Winston	ARMSTRONG	03.06.1942.
F/Sgt	Kenneth	ASHURST	16.02.1942.
Sgt	Earnshaw	ASHWORTH	06.12.1944.
F/Sgt	Harry	ASPINALL	23.04.1944.
P/O	Denis Lowe	ATKINSON	31.01.1942.
F/Sgt	Joseph McKay	ATKINSON	25.08.1942.
Sgt	James	ATKINSON	15.04.1940.
P/O	George Andrew	ATKINSON	13.06.1940
Sgt	Reginald Albert	ATTFIELD	08.12.1940.
F/Sgt	Algernon Early William	AYRE	12.05.1944.
Sgt	Leonard	AYRES	06.12.1944.
P/O	Kenneth Douglas	BABINGTON-BROWNE	08.03.1943.
Sgt	Peter Henry	BAIGENT	08.07.1944.
Sgt	Albert Wallace	BAKER	25.03.1942.
Sgt	Victor Edward	BAKER	09.08.1941.
F/Sgt	John Stanley	BALDWIN	03.01.1944.
F/Sgt	Ronald William Benjamin	BALDWIN	06.01.1945.
Sgt	Charles Arthur	BALSER	08.07.1944.
Sgt	Stanley James	BANTING	23.08.1943.

Rank	Name	Surname	Date
Sgt	Robert Ross	BARBOUR	02.01.1944.
F/O	Percy	BARLOW	17.12.1944.
G/C	John Francis Tufnell	BARRETT	03.09.1941.
Sgt	Eric Edward	BARTHOLMEW	11.11.1942.
F/L	Ronald William	BARTLETT	08.02.1945.
P/O	Cyril McCulloch	BATEMAN	27.06.1941.
F/Sgt	Ronald Charles	BATTERSBY	15.01.1945.
Sgt	William	BEACH	28.01.1944.
Sgt	Herbert William	BEASLEY	26.06.1943.
F/L	George Liddell Carruthers	BEATTIE	04.06.1942.
F/Sgt	Douglas Richard	BEESLEY	11.04.1944.
F/O	Alan Victor	BEETCH	27.01.1944.
F/O	James Rutherford Hutton	BELL	17.06.1943.
Sgt	Frederick George	BELLCHAMBERS	01.10.1942.
Sgt	Wilfred Thomas	BELTON	10.09.1942.
Sgt	Ronald William	BENNETT	17.12.1944.
F/Sgt	Thomas Laidlaw	BENSON	08.03.1945.
Sgt	Jack	BERRY	17.09.1942.
Sgt	John	BESTWICK	12.06.1941.
Sgt	Frank	BESTWICK	09.03.1943.
Sgt	Oliver Percy	BESWICK	03.06.1942.
Sgt	Ronald Stacey	BETTRIDGE	20.02.1944.
Sgt	Thomas Ralph	BEVAN	25.09.1942.
P/O	Raymond Harry	BIRD	03.01.1943.
W/OII	Robert Francis	BIRD	16.01.1943.
Sgt	Jack	BLACKETT	01.09.1943.
F/Sgt	John Lawrence	BLAIR	10.09.1942.
F/Sgt	William Enos	BLAKE	31.03.1944.
F/Sgt	James Higgins	BLANE	19.07.1944.
F/O	Peter Frederick Barlow	BLUETT	31.05.1942.
F/Sgt	Edward James	BOAKES	15.01.1945.
Sgt	Arthur William	BOND	28.04.1943.
Sgt	Herbert Frederick	BORE	25.02.1944.
Sgt	Terence	BOWDEN	28.01.1944.
Sgt	George Patrick	BOYD	15.10.1944.
P/O	John Charles	BRADEY	18.08.1943.
P/O	Robert	BRADLEY	18.08.1943.
Sgt	Sydney Edward	BRADSHAW	23.06.1942.
W/O	Murray Ronald	BRAINES	03.10.1943.
F/O	Raymond	BRAKEWELL	21.03.1945.
F/Sgt	Anthony Phillip	BRANDER	27.01.1944.
F/Sgt	Patrick Joseph	BREENE	12.06.1941.
P/O	Eric	BREMNER	20.02.1944.
Sgt	Kenneth Thomas	BRENTNALL	15.08.1943.
Sgt	David John	BREWER	20.02.1944.
Sgt	Bernard Stanley	BRIDGE	17.06.1943.

Rank	First Names	Surname	Date
Sgt	Arthur	BRIGGS	09.03.1943.
F/Sgt	Cyril	BRIGNELL	06.11.1944.
Sgt	Harry Mayo Richard	BROADHEAD	17.09.1942.
Sgt	Donald Charles	BROCKLEY	26.03.1942.
Sgt	William	BRODERICK	25.03.1944.
Sgt	Alec Albert	BROOKER	13.09.1940.
F/O	Peter Paul	BROSKO	29.07.1944.
Sgt	Jack	BROWN	04.07.1942.
Sgt	Abraham Lawson	BROWN	02.03.1943.
F/Sgt	Cyril Douglas	BROWN	30.07.1943.
Sgt	Douglas	BROWN	08.08.1943.
Sgt	Bromley John William	BROWN	18.08.1943.
Sgt	John William	BROWN	24.02.1944
Sgt	Thomas	BROWN	23.09.1944.
F/Sgt	Edmund William	BROWNE	16.03.1945.
P/O	Alastair William	BUCHAN	25.03.1942.
Sgt	Jack	BUCKLEY	26.03.1942.
F/O	Arthur David	BULL	31.03.1944.
Sgt	Frank Charles	BUNCLARK	11.11.1942.
Sgt	Michael Charles	BURGOINE	21.04.1943.
AC1	Harry Squire	BURKE	12.03.1940.
P/O	Robert William	BURKWOOD	25.06.1944.
Sgt	Robert Horace	BURN	03.08.1943.
LAC	Benjamin	BURNELL	24.02.1945.
Sgt	Ralph	BURNETT	30.06.1940.
F/O	William Stirling	BURNS	23.09.1944.
F/Sgt	John Kean	BURNSIDE	13.08.1944.
Sgt	Edmund Robert John	BURRELL	28.06.1942.
S/L	Thomas Noel Challoner	BURROUGH	31.01.1942.
F/O	Alan Gladstone	BURT	31.01.1942.
Sgt	Herbert Frank	BURTON	13.01.1943.
Sgt	Wilfred	BUTLER	31.07.1941.
F/Sgt	William Charles	BUTLER	02.01.1944.
Sgt	Thomas Arthur	BUTTERWORTH	31.01.1942.
P/O	Reginald Kenneth	BUXTON	18.08.1943.
Sgt	John Jesse	CADD	16.01.1943.
Sgt	Mervyn	CADDY	04.07.1942.
Sgt	Ronald William	CADMAN	01.10.1942.
Sgt	John	CAIRNS	20.02.1944.
F/O	Denis Henry	CALMAN	26.11.1943.
P/O	Paul	CAMPBELL	11.11.1942.
F/O	Ian Melville	CAMPBELL	23.09.1944.
F/Sgt	Philip Stuart	CAMSELL	02.10.1943.
Sgt	William Arthur	CANNON	05.10.1940.
P/O	Leslie	CANNON	18.03.1944.
Sgt	Richard Claud Harold	CANTIN	26.11.1943.

P/O	Denis	CARBUTT	24.03.1944.
P/O	David Stuart	CARNEGIE	20.07.1940.
Sgt	Edward	CARR	08.03.1943.
F/O	Hubert Edward	CARROT	09.10.1943.
F/Sgt	Reginald Walter	CARVER	30.12.1943.
Sgt	Arthur Joseph Patrick	CASEY	17.12.1940.
P/O	Ian Mckenzie	CASSAVETTI	29.03.1942.
Sgt	Ernest West	CATLIN	10.09.1942.
P/O	Frederick Arthur	CAUNTER-JACKSON	12.06.1941.
Sgt	William	CHAMBERS	31.07.1941.
P/O	Harry Mathew	CHAMPION	02.03.1943.
Sgt	Robert Arthur	CHANIN	10.02.1941.
P/O	Colin Deans	CHAPMAN	14.11.1940.
Sgt	Joseph Ernest	CHAPMAN	25.02.1944.
F/Sgt	Leslie	CHAPMAN	01.02.1945.
F/Sgt	John Hamilton	CHARLES	31.05.1942.
P/O	Joseph Frederic	CHEVALIER	29.03.1942.
P/O	Gordon Frederick	CHIPPERFIELD	08.04.1941.
P/O	Verdun James	CHORLEY	22.10.1943.
F/L	Eric Rodger	CHURCH	26.08.1944.
Sgt	William John	CHURCHER	02.01.1944.
P/O	Cecil Stephen	CHURCHILL	29.03.1942.
F/O	Basil Alfred	CLACK	16.06.1944.
P/O	Ralph Edward	CLARK	03.06.1942.
Sgt	Scott	CLARK	26.11.1940.
Sgt	George Ellis	CLARK	26.07.1943.
Sgt	Norman Will Hilton	CLARK	18.08.1943.
Sgt	Bernard	CLARK	27.01.1944.
Sgt	Richard William Tudor	CLARKE	02.03.1941.
Sgt	Arthur George	CLARKE	29.08.1941.
F/O	Roy Leslie	CLARKE	01.09.1943.
F/Sgt	John George	CLELLAND	25.03.1942.
P/O	William Herbert	CLEMERSON	17.10.1940.
F/L	Cyril Herbert	CLEVELAND	02.10.1943.
F/O	Derek Charles Gray	CLINKARD	07.03.1940.
F/O	Fred	CLOUGH	16.08.1943.
Sgt	John	COAKER	18.02.1943.
Sgt	Cyril Hugh	COAKLEY	11.11.1942.
Sgt	Andrew McNab	COCKBURN	20.07.1940.
F/Sgt	Eric John	COE	24.09.1944.
P/O	Charles James Bertram	COGDELL	26.11.1943.
P/O	Cyril George	COLBORNE	29.06.1941.
Sgt	Cedric Nils	COLDICOTT	25.09.1942.
F/Sgt	Ronald Sydney	COLE	01.10.1942.
Sgt	Richard Derrick	COLE	23.09.1944.
Sgt	Ronald Frank	COLEMAN	25.06.1944.

Rank	Name	Surname	Date
W/O	Michael De Beauchamp	COLLENETTE	28.04.1943.
P/O	Alan James	COLLINS	25.02.1944.
F/O	John James	CONDON	23.09.1944.
W/OII	James Francis	COOPER	05.09.1942.
F/L	Frederick Edgar Howard	COOPER	20.12.1940.
Sgt	Kingsley Gerard	COOPER	02.03.1941.
F/O	Herbert Wright	COOPER	19.07.1944.
Sgt	Ernest Humphries	CORBETT	11.11.1942.
F/O	William George	COREWYN	15.01.1945.
Sgt	Alexander McGee	CORMACK	25.09.1942.
S/L	William Duncan	CORR	17.10.1943
Sgt	Eugene Patrick	CORRIGAN	02.03.1941.
P/O	Raymond	COULSON	09.10.1943.
Sgt	Ronald	COURT	14.10.1942
F/Sgt	Leo Martin	COWAN	29.08.1942.
Sgt	George Edward	COWAN	17.12.1940.
Sgt	Alfred Douglas	COX	02.03.1941.
F/O	John Grant	COX	25.03.1944.
Sgt	William	CRAIG	25.02.1944.
F/Sgt	Roy	CRAMP	09.10.1943.
Sgt	Terence	CRAVEN	09.08.1941.
Sgt	James	CRAWFORD	07.12.1941.
Sgt	Charles Gordon	CROSBY	03.01.1944.
Sgt	Gilbert Frederick	CRUMP	12.05.1944.
P/O	Lloyd Wesley	CUMING	27.01.1944.
P/O	Thomas Cedric	CUNDILL	13.08.1940.
F/L	Ronald Percy	CUNNINGHAM	02.01.1944.
Sgt	Robert Nixon	CUNNINGHAM	24.03.1944.
P/O	David Fraser	CURRIE	29.07.1944.
Sgt	Anthony Frederick Phillip	CURSETT-SUTHERLAND	25.08.1942.
F/Sgt	Geoffrey Ernest	DALE	01.10.1942.
W/OII	Charles Francis	DALEY	09.03.1943.
Sgt	Dennis Edward	DALTON	03.08.1943.
Sgt	Leonard William	DANN	31.01.1942.
Sgt	Leonard	DARBEN	31.03.1944.
P/O	Gerald	D'ARCY-WRIGHT	06.10.1940.
Sgt	George Francis	DARE	01.10.1942.
Sgt	Harold	DAUNCEY	28.06.1942.
F/O	George Albert	DAVEY	19.07.1944.
Sgt	Edward Reginald	DAVIDSON	16.04.1943.
Sgt	Malcolm Charles	DAVIES	10.09.1942.
Sgt	Henry Carlton	DAVIES	10.06.1940.
F/L	Richard Edward	DAVIES	01.09.1943.
Sgt	Griffith John	DAVIES	21.01.1944.
Sgt	Anthony John Maxwell	DAVIES	21.03.1945.
F/Sgt	Benjamin John	DAVIS	25.08.1942.

Rank	Name	Surname	Date
Sgt	John	DAVIS	03.01.1943.
Sgt	Thomas	DAVIS	26.07.1943.
Sgt	Raymond	DAWSON	29.03.1942.
F/Sgt	William Waller	DAWSON	17.04.1943.
F/Sgt	Eric John	DAY	16.03.1945.
Sgt	Kenneth Henry	DEAN	18.03.1944.
Sgt	Owen	DEEHAN	08.12.1940.
Sgt	Richard James	DELVE	17.10.1944
F/Sgt	Maurice Hamilton	DENISON	04.06.1942.
F/Sgt	James William	DEVENISH	25.02.1944.
Sgt	Anthony John	DEVERELL	07.03.1945.
Sgt	Richard Cuthbert	DICKINSON	13.09.1940.
P/O	Richard John Robert	DOCKER	18.08.1943.
Sgt	John Gordon	DONNELLY	08.04.1941.
Sgt	Patrick	DONOGHUE	25.06.1944.
P/O	William Harry	DONOVAN	20.09.1942.
Sgt	John	DOUGLAS	15.01.1945.
F/Sgt	James Robert	DOW	26.03.1942.
F/O	Tom	DOWNING	15.08.1943.
F/Sgt	Ernest Edward	DOWSE	03.09.1941.
Sgt	Hugh	DRACASS	29.03.1942.
Sgt	Arthur	DRURY	18.04.1941.
Sgt	John Robert	DRYDEN	23.06.1942.
F/O	Lawrence	DUCKWORTH	03.09.1941.
Sgt	Cecil Thomas Oswald	DUDLEY	17.06.1943.
F/Sgt	Thomas	DUFF	31.03.1944.
F/Sgt	John Alvin	DUFFIELD	25.09.1942.
F/O	Edward Robinson	DURANT	03.08.1944.
F/Sgt	Rex Ronald Boyce	DURTNALL	31.07.1941.
Sgt	Edwin	DYSON	25.09.1942.
P/O	Robert Samuel	DYSON	10.07.1943.
P/O	John	EADIE	08.07.1940.
P/O	Raymond Patrick	EARL	26.09.1940.
Sgt	Peter Richard	EARL	15.01.1945.
Sgt	David	EASTON	18.08.1943.
F/Sgt	Donald Murray	EASTON	21.03.1945.
P/O	Jack Hilton	EASTWOOD	12.05.1944.
P/O	Arthur James Douglas	EAVES	26.11.1943.
Sgt	Owen Glynne	EDWARDS	17.10.1945
P/O	John Frederick	EDWARDS	17.04.1943.
Sgt	Vernon Albert	EDWARDS	09.02.1945.
Sgt	Edward Francis	EDWIN	14.11.1940.
F/L	Johann Walter	EINARSON	25.02.1944.
Sgt	Raymond	EKE	22.11.1944.
Sgt	Harold	EKIN	25.08.1942.
Sgt	Frank	ELLICK	02.10.1943.

Sgt	Victor	EMANUEL	15.04.1940.
F/Sgt	William Young	EMERSLUND	25.09.1942.
P/O	Alexander Campell	ENNIS	30.06.1940.
Sgt	Ronald	ETHERIDGE	15.04.1940.
Sgt	Thomas Alfred	EVANS	31.01.1942.
Sgt	Sidney	EVANS	20.12.1940.
Sgt	Philip Haig	FAIRBANKS	10.09.1942.
F/Sgt	Wendell Wilburn	FAIRBROTHER	16.02.1942.
Sgt	James Traynor	FALLON	23.06.1942.
F/O	Frederick Stanley	FARREN	07.03.1945.
F/Sgt	Robert Gordon	FAWKES	31.05.1942.
Sgt	Graham	FELLOWS	21.04.1943.
Sgt	Eric Parker	FENWICK	26.11.1940.
Sgt	Hugh Henry	FETHERSTON	26.03.1942.
Sgt	Kenneth Marcel	FILLMORE	31.07.1941.
F/O	Eric	FILMER	08.08.1943.
F/Sgt	Keith	FINCH	25.03.1944.
Sgt	John	FITZPATRICK	07.03.1945.
Sgt	Dominick	FLANAGAN	17.10.1940.
F/Sgt	Samuel	FLEET	01.02.1945.
Sgt	Percy John	FOLKER	02.03.1943.
F/Sgt	Douglas	FORBES	08.03.1943.
Sgt	John Reid (Jack)	FORREST	01.09.1943.
F/L	John Augustus	FORREST	25.06.1944.
S/L	Douglas Sinclair	FORSYTH	03.09.1942.
P/O	Alec Leonard	FOSTER	03.09.1942.
Sgt	Roy	FOSTER	30.07.1943.
F/O	Basil John	FOX	03.08.1943.
Sgt	Gordon Victor	FOYLE	16.06.1944.
Sgt	Ernest George	FRANCIS	18.08.1943.
Sgt	John	FRASER	10.06.1940.
Sgt	Edward	FRASER	27.09.1943.
F/O	Desmond Clayton	FREEMAN	24.09.1944.
F/Sgt	Andrew McWilliams	FREW	08.07.1944.
P/O	Jack Ernest Anthony	FRIEND	01.05.1940.
Sgt	Charles	FROST	01.05.1940.
F/L	Walter Eric	FRUTIGER	10.02.1941.
F/Sgt	Kenneth Rosslyn	FULLER	26.11.1943.
Sgt	Christopher George	FURBY	26.03.1942.
Sgt	Ronald Clifford	GAIT	03.01.1943.
F/Sgt	Lloyd George	GALLAWAY	01.10.1942.
F/Sgt	Roy Thomas	GALLOWAY	07.03.1945.
Sgt	Roy Buglar	GANDERTON	02.06.1942.
Sgt	Robert Alfred	GAPP	10.02.1941.
P/O	Donald Edwin	GARDENER	13.08.1940.
F/O	Edwin Charles	GARDNER	17.10.1940.

Sgt	Spencer Arthur Grafton	GARDNER	11.04.1944.
Sgt	Robert Cecil	GARDNER	25.04.1944.
Sgt	Phillip William	GARNHAM	02.03.1943.
F/Sgt	Arthur Thomas	GARRETT	25.02.1944.
F/Sgt	Roy John West	GEATER	31.07.1941.
F/Sgt	Ronald V. George	GEORGE	23.04.1944.
F/O	William	GIBB	09.04.1945.
F/Sgt	Eric William	GIBBS	16.03.1945.
F/L	Clifford Argo	GILES	08.03.1943.
F/Sgt	Reginald Thomas	GILL	25.02.1944.
F/L	David Stapylton	GILLETT	13.01.1943.
F/O	Francis Ormond	GILMORE	03.08.1944.
Sgt	Gerald	GLASSBROOK	03.06.1942.
Sgt	Ronald Philips	GLASSON	07.03.1940.
Sgt	Arthur Frederick	GLEADLE	02.01.1944.
F/O	Douglas Gordon	GLENNIE	08.04.1941.
F/O	Charles William	GLOVER	01.05.1940.
P/O	Laurence Trevor	GLOVER	27.06.1941.
F/O	Harry Drinen	GLOVER	31.03.1944.
F/O	Colin Cortland	GODLEY	03.08.1943.
Sgt	Sydney John	GOLDING	13.06.1940.
P/O	John William	GOLIGHTLY	20.02.1944.
F/L	Hedley Charles Cornick	GOODYEAR	23.04.1944.
P/O	Edmond Jack	GOODYER	16.06.1944.
Sgt	Peter Aubrey Joseph	GORE	26.07.1943.
Sgt	Maurice	GOUGH	02.03.1941.
Sgt	William	GOULDING	13.08.1944.
AC1	Peter Gladstone	GRAHAM	15.04.1940.
Sgt	Thomas	GRAHAM	18.08.1943.
Sgt	William McKinlay	GRANT	03.08.1943.
F/L	William Edwin	GRANTHAM	08.07.1944.
Sgt	David James	GREEN	17.09.1942.
F/Sgt	John Michael	GREEN	18.03.1944.
AC1	John Bell	GREENALL	01.05.1940.
F/Sgt	Charles William	GREENAWAY	25.06.1944.
F/L	Albert Paulton	GREENFIELD	09.04.1945.
F/Sgt	Paul Walter	GREGORY	28.06.1942.
Sgt	James Walter	GREIG	30.06.1940.
Sgt	James John	GRIFFIN	15.08.1943.
F/Sgt	Thomas Charles James	GRIST	21.04.1943.
Sgt	John	GROCOCK	28.06.1942.
F/Sgt	John Victor	GROVES	31.03.1944.
F/Sgt	Ernest George	GRUNDY	25.03.1944.
F/L	Henryk Boleslaw	GRYNKIEWICZ	16.03.1945.
Sgt	Ronald	GUEST	01.02.1941.
F/Sgt	Ernest Harold	GUNDERS	15.08.1943.

P/O	Leslie George	GUNNING	03.01.1943.
P/O	Bernard John	GUNTER	08.03.1943.
F/O	James Reed	GUTHRIE	10.06.1940.
F/Sgt	Gordon Edward	GWALTER	16.03.1945.
P/O	Nathaniel Robert	GYLES	28.04.1943.
F/Sgt	William John	HADDON	09.04.1945.
Sgt	Albert Frederick	HADEN	13.01.1943.
Sgt	Gavin McMurray	HAIR	17.01.1943.
W/O	Hilton Alfred	HALES	17.12.1944.
P/O	Henry	HALKIER	08.08.1943.
Sgt	George	HALL	02.03.1941.
Sgt	Robert Kirby	HALL	02.03.1943.
Sgt	Ernest Alfred	HALL	16.08.1943.
Sgt	Walter Duncan	HAMER	03.09.1941.
Sgt	Richard Stephen Edward	HAMILTON	06.11.1940.
F/L	Gordon	HAMILTON	02.10.1943.
Sgt	Frederick John Lawrence	HANSON	03.06.1942.
F/O	Joseph Edward	HANSON	01.10.1942.
P/O	Eric Hugh Milbourn	HARBOUR	30.07.1943.
Sgt	Terence Edward	HARDY	19.07.1944.
F/Sgt	Thomas Arthur	HARRIS	18.08.1943.
P/O	Hector William	HARRIS	26.11.1943.
F/L	Alan Bruce	HARRISON	03.09.1941.
Sgt	John Reginald	HARRISON	15.08.1943.
F/Sgt	Norman Rhodes	HARTLEY	03.06.1942.
Sgt	John Douglas	HARTLEY	12.03.1940.
F/L	George Henry	HARVEY	30.12.1943.
Sgt	Francis Sydney	HASLEMORE	27.06.1941.
P/O	James Arthur	HASTE	31.03.1944.
P/O	Ronald Henry William	HATT	13.01.1943.
P/O	George Alan	HAWES	01.10.1942.
F/O	Peter	HAWKINS	21.03.1945.
F/Sgt	Ian Archie	HAY	07.03.1945.
P/O	Sydney	HEALD	26.11.1943.
F/O	Lawrence	HEALEY	22.10.1943.
Sgt	Frank Douglas	HEALING	02.03.1941.
Sgt	Gordon Edward	HEASMAN	03.01.1944.
F/Sgt	James Henry Charles	HEASMAN	24.09.1944.
F/O	Derek Cecil	HEATHER	23.09.1944.
P/O	Robert	HEGGIE	25.03.1942.
P/O	William Duncan	HERMON	26.09.1940.
Sgt	Stanley William	HERRING	09.02.1945.
P/O	Eric Iver	HEWETT	07.03.1940.
Sgt	Harold	HEWITT	01.10.1942.
Sgt	William Hutchinson	HEWITT	17.10.1940.
LAC	Claude Henry	HIGGINS	24.02.1945.

Rank	First Names	Surname	Date
Sgt	Gordon Anthony	HILL	10.09.1942.
Sgt	John Edward	HILL	10.02.1941.
F/Sgt	Alfred Frederick	HILL	24.07.1941.
F/Sgt	Ernest	HILL	23.09.1944.
Sgt	John Brown	HILLHOUSE	07.02.1943.
Sgt	John Edwin	HILLS	24.09.1940.
Sgt	George Arthur	HITCHON	18.02.1943.
Sgt	John Norman	HOAD	23.09.1944.
Sgt	Charles Carlile	HOBBS	07.03.1940.
F/Sgt	William John	HOBBS	08.07.1944.
F/Sgt	Frank	HOBSON	10.09.1942.
Sgt	George Austin	HODGES	03.08.1943.
P/O	Frederick William	HOLDEN	18.04.1941.
Sgt	Thomas Arthur	HOLDEN	05.07.1941.
Sgt	Joseph Gerald	HOLDEN	03.01.1944.
P/O	Donald Alfred	HOLDSWORTH	17.04.1943.
F/Sgt	Robert Henry Phillip	HOLLANDER	23.04.1944.
P/O	Tony Angelo	HOLMAN	03.08.1943.
Sgt	William Thomas	HOLMES	31.01.1942.
Sgt	Nevil Temple	HOLMES	10.08.1943.
Sgt	John	HOPKINS	26.11.1940.
F/S	Arthur Anthony	HORN	05.07.1941.
F/O	Albert Keith	HORNIBROOK	23.09.1944.
Sgt	Leslie	HORROCKS	21.01.1944.
S/L	Hugh Wilkinson	HORSLEY	01.02.1945.
Sgt	Ronald William	HORWOOD	23.08.1943.
Sgt	Roland	HOUGHTON BROWN	22.06.1940.
F/L	Douglas James	HOW	13.09.1940.
Sgt	Cyril	HOWARD	08.07.1944.
F/Sgt	Wilfred Geoffrey	HOWITT	09.04.1945.
F/O	John	HOYLAND	02.11.1944.
P/O	John Ralph	HUBBARD	25.03.1942.
F/O	William	HUGHES	18.08.1943.
P/O	Squire Ronald	HUGHES	22.10.1943.
Sgt	John	HUGHES	16.06.1944.
F/Sgt	George James	HULL	18.03.1944.
Sgt	Arthur	HULMES	16.08.1943.
Sgt	Donald Alastair Barham	HUME	29.03.1942.
Sgt	Keith Reginald	HUMPHREY	26.10.1940.
Sgt	Terence Edward	HUNT	08.07.1944.
F/O	Harold Arnold	HUNT	07.03.1945.
F/Sgt	Dwain Nowell	HUNTER	30.07.1943.
Sgt	Douglas	HYDES	09.10.1943.
Sgt	Thomas Joseph	HYNES	20.02.1944.
Sgt	Basil George	IMBER	02.01.1944.
Sgt	George John	INGLIS	03.01.1943.

F/Sgt	John Ogilvie	INGRAM	10.07.1943
Sgt	Richard Spencer Castle	IVATT	22.11.1940.
Sgt	John Leslie	JACKSON	11.11.1942.
Sgt	William John	JACKSON	21.04.1943.
Sgt	Stanley William	JAMES	18.08.1943.
F/Sgt	William Douglas	JAMES	21.01.1944.
Sgt	William Norton	JAMES	31.03.1944.
F/O	Thomas Cecil	JAMES	22.11.1944.
F/Sgt	Sidney Joseph	JAMES	15.01.1945.
F/Sgt	Franciszek	JANISZEWSKI	29.08.1942.
F/O	Herbert Arthur	JEFFREYS	22.11.1944.
Sgt	Thomas Amwyl	JEFFRIES	03.09.1942.
Sgt	Herbert William	JENNINGS	23.09.1944.
Sgt	Douglas Alfred	JOHNSON	05.07.1941.
F/Sgt	Einar	JOHNSON	23.08.1943.
Sgt	Edward Francis	JOHNSON	26.11.1943.
F/Sgt	Anthony Lionel Ely	JOHNSTON	16.02.1942.
Sgt	William Alexander Milne	JOHNSTONE	07.03.1945.
Sgt	Ronald Sidney	JONES	31.01.1942.
F/Sgt	Phillip Llewellyn	JONES	25.02.1944.
Sgt	Ronald Claude Hamilton	JONES	25.04.1944.
F/O	Ernest	JONES	16.06.1944.
Sgt	Richard	JONES	25.06.1944.
F/Sgt	John Lewis	JONES	16.03.1945.
P/O	Peter Clement Vellacott	JOSLIN	05.09.1942.
F/O	Trevor Francis	JOYCE	01.09.1943.
Sgt	Cecil Norman	JUDD	16.01.1943.
F/O	Ronald Peter Nicolas	KAYSER	12.05.1944.
Sgt	Peter John	KEAY	16.04.1943.
W/OII	Robert James	KEE	03.01.1943.
F/Sgt	Edward James	KEMISH	25.06.1944.
F/Sgt	John Topham	KENDALL	10.08.1943.
Sgt	James Stuart	KENNEDY	30.12.1943.
Sgt	Bernard	KENRICK	23.04.1944.
Sgt	Donavan Peter George	KENT	07.04.1942.
F/Sgt	Frank William	KIDSON	10.09.1942.
F/Sgt	James Henry	KINCH	28.06.1942.
F/Sgt	John Robert	KING	09.04.1945.
Sgt	Eric Ronald	KINGMAN	12.05.1944.
F/O	Thomas Hugh Burton	KIRKBY	07.03.1945.
Sgt	Peter	KITCHING	21.03.1945.
Sgt	Eric	KNIGHT	04.07.1942.
Sgt	Charles John	KNIGHT	06.09.1940.
P/O	Frank	KOHUT	26.08.1944.
F/O	Robert Wallace	KOMISKI	04.07.1942.
P/O	Julius	KRAMER	25.06.1944.

F/L	Brian McMenamen	LAING	03.08.1943.
Sgt	Francis Mervyn	LANCASTER	21.03.1945.
P/O	Tom Hwfa Nixon	LANE	13.09.1940.
Sgt	William	LANE	21.03.1945.
P/O	John Graham	LANGFORD	14.11.1940.
P/O	Frank	LANGLEY	27.01.1944.
P/O	Conrad	LARNACH	15.08.1943.
Sgt	Ronald	LARTER	02.06.1942.
Sgt	Peter Alec	LASHLY	10.09.1942.
Sgt	Richard	LAUGHTON	18.08.1943.
F/O	Jean Paul	LAURIN	17.06.1943.
S/L	Leslie Scott	LAWRENCE	10.06.1940.
F/O	Leonard Charles Robert	LEACH	14.10.1942.
Sgt	John Benjamin	LEIGH	07.12.1941.
F/Sgt	Herbert Dalton	LEWIS	07.02.1943.
P/O	James Melford	LEWIS	18.08.1943.
Sgt	Kenneth	LEYSHON	07.04.1942.
Sgt	Lloyd John Holmes	LINCOLN	07.04.1942.
Sgt	Stanley Holmes	LINCOLN	03.06.1942.
F/O	Bryan Spofforth	LITTLE	19.07.1944.
Sgt	Leslie	LITTLEWOOD	11.11.1942.
Sgt	Kenneth	LLOYD	26.06.1943.
Sgt	Horace Cecil	LOADSMAN	26.10.1940.
Sgt	Henry George	LOATES	02.03.1941.
Sgt	Arthur	LOCKETT	08.03.1945.
Sgt	Geoffrey Stewart	LODINGTON	08.08.1941.
F/Sgt	Bernard Ewart	LONGHURST	22.11.1944.
F/Sgt	David	LORIMER	04.06.1942.
Sgt	Edward John	LOVEROCK	18.02.1943.
Sgt	George Frederick	LOWE	25.03.1944.
Sgt	Leonard	LUCAS	18.08.1943.
Sgt	Edward	LUNNISS	02.01.1944.
Sgt	Sydney	LUPTON	13.05.1943.
F/O	Richard	LYON	03.08.1943.
P/O	Wiliam	MacFARLANE	17.04.1943.
F/O	John Alexander	MacFARLANE	09.04.1945.
Sgt	John	MacFIE	25.06.1944.
Sgt	Gordon William	MacKENZIE	03.08.1943.
P/O	John Wallace Allan	MacKIE	29.07.1944.
Sgt	Roderick	MacKINNON	02.03.1941.
F/Sgt	Stephen Joseph	MacLEAN	01.02.1942.
Sgt	William	MacPHEE	17.09.1942.
F/Sgt	William Reddington	MacPHERSON	29.07.1944.
P/O	Hedley Robert	MADGETT	18.08.1943.
F/Sgt	Henry	MAINEY	05.07.1941.
F/Sgt	George	MALCOLM	06.01.1945.

Rank	Name	Surname	Date
P/O	Albert Charles	MANATON	12.03.1940.
Sgt	Geoffrey Herbert	MARSHALL	01.02.1942.
Sgt	Edward Colin	MARSHALL	04.07.1942.
P/O	Virgil Austin	MARTIN	26.11.1943.
Sgt	Tom	MARTIN	21.01.1944.
P/O	Colin	MATHESON	20.06.1940.
P/O	Douglas Spencer	MATTHEWS	09.01.1942.
F/Sgt	Phillip Marcus	MATTHEWS	23.09.1944.
Sgt	Peter John	MAXWELL	20.09.1942.
F/Sgt	Edward Joseph	MAY	05.09.1942.
P/O	John Gilbert	McALPINE	26.11.1943.
Sgt	John	McCABE	23.09.1944.
Sgt	Kenneth William	McCASKILL	03.02.1942.
F/Sgt	Gerard	McCHRYSTAL	07.03.1945.
Sgt	John	McCLEARY	25.08.1942.
Sgt	Joseph	McCREVEY	24.03.1944.
Sgt	George Hugh	McCRORY	05.08.1940.
F/O	William Donald	McCULLOCH	23.06.1942.
Sgt	Henry	McCULLOUGH	09.03.1943.
F/O	Walter Harry	McDOWELL	22.10.1943.
F/O	William	McGILLIVRAY	02.11.1944.
P/O	Andrew	McINTYRE	26.07.1943.
F/Sgt	Alastair Macnab	McKELVIE	03.06.1942.
F/Sgt	Raymond Murdoch	McKENZIE	09.02.1945.
P/O	James Day	McKEOWN	23.06.1942.
P/O	George	McLAUGHLIN	19.07.1944.
Sgt	Donald Tennant	McLEAN	20.09.1942.
F/Sgt	Albert Benjamin	McLELLAN	10.09.1942.
Sgt	William	McMARTH	08.03.1945.
S/L	Ian George Armour	McNAUGHTON	23.06.1942.
Sgt	Joseph Francis	McNEILL	21.04.1943.
P/O	John Aird	McPHEE	16.01.1943.
F/Sgt	William Vincent	McQUAID	30.07.1942.
Sgt	Robert Stanley	MEACHEN	23.09.1944.
Sgt	Alfred Victor	MEADS	26.07.1943.
Sgt	Noel Stephen Joseph	MEEHAN	30.12.1943.
Sgt	David James	MEIKLE	16.04.1942.
F/O	Ernest William Terence	MELLANDER	25.03.1944.
Sgt	Kenneth Francis	MERRIFIELD	19.07.1944.
F/Sgt	Victor Douglas	MERROW	01.02.1945.
F/Sgt	Noel Roy	MEYER	25.08.1942.
W/O	Edward	MIDDLETON	12.05.1944.
Sgt	Leonard George	MILLAR	30.07.1942.
Sgt	Tom	MILLER	16.01.1943.
P/O	James Henry	MILLER	15.08.1943.
F/L	Stanley Edward	MILLER	07.03.1945.

Sgt	Roy Colin	MILLS	31.03.1944.
Sgt	Laurence Dorning	MILLS	21.03.1945.
F/Sgt	Montague John	MILN	23.09.1944.
Sgt	John	MITCHELL	29.03.1942.
P/O	Jeffrey Guy	MITCHELL	22.06.1940.
F/Sgt	George	MITCHELL	08.03.1943.
Sgt	Peter William	MITCHELL	18.08.1943.
F/L	Ernest William	MITCHELL	03.10.1943.
P/O	Reginald Donovan	MIX	28.04.1943.
Sgt	Thomas	MOFFAT	26.08.1944.
F/L	Alexander	MONCRIEFF	14.11.1940.
F/Sgt	James Roland	MOORE	17.10.1947
W/OII	Franklin Guy	MOORE	28.04.1943.
Sgt	Arthur Pugh	MORETON	09.04.1945.
Sgt	Bruce	MORGAN	04.07.1942.
F/Sgt	John Charles	MORGAN	13.01.1943.
F/O	Kenneth Llewellyn	MORGAN	07.02.1943.
F/Sgt	Robert Stinson	MORLEY	17.06.1943.
F/Sgt	James William	MORRIS	24.09.1944.
F/Sgt	Ernest	MORRIS	22.11.1944.
Sgt	Lewis Wilson	MORRISON	25.09.1942.
Sgt	Robert McCrindle	MORRISON	13.08.1940.
W/OII	Claire Keith	MORROW	30.07.1943.
Sgt	Sidney Harold	MORTIMER	03.08.1943.
Sgt	John Walter	MORTON	04.07.1942.
S/L	Edward Henry	MOSS	31.03.1944.
Sgt	Kenneth Leslie	MOWL	07.03.1945.
Sgt	James Inglis	MOYES	06.11.1940.
Sgt	David Thomson	MUIR	17.12.1944.
AC1	Alec	MULLINEUX	12.03.1940.
W/O	Geoffrey Douglas	MUMMERY	07.03.1945.
F/Sgt	George Edward	NASH	08.07.1944.
F/Sgt	William Bonar	NESS	18.08.1943.
P/O	Arthur Francis	NEVIN	13.08.1944.
Sgt	Harold James	NEWEY	20.02.1944.
F/O	Edward Roy	NEWLAND	17.12.1944.
P/O	Charles William Joseph	NEWMAN	25.04.1944.
F/Sgt	Donald Cecil	NEWMAN	25.06.1944.
Sgt	Robert Eastwood	NEWTON	07.04.1942.
Sgt	Thomas Raine	NEWTON	18.02.1943.
Sgt	James Ernest	NICHOLSON	03.09.1941.
F/O	Francis John	NIXON	25.02.1944.
F/Sgt	Eric William	NOBLE	07.04.1942.
Sgt	Lister	NOBLE	17.01.1943.
Sgt	Kenneth	NORGATE	29.08.1942.
Sgt	Jack	NORMAN	28.04.1943.

Rank	First Names	Surname	Date
F/O	John Edward	NORTHEND	13.01.1943.
F/O	Francis Dunsford	NORTON	18.08.1943.
Sgt	Basil	NUTLEY	31.03.1944.
Sgt	Alfred Cecil	NUTTALL	08.08.1941.
Sgt	John	NUTTALL	17.06.1943.
S/L	John Humphrey Ridding	OLDFIELD	06.11.1940.
Sgt	Harold Sewell	OLDFIELD	26.11.1943.
W/O	Aubrey William	OSMAN	17.09.1942.
F/Sgt	Ernest Joseph	OUTRAM	25.04.1944.
Sgt	Robert Rupert Bisgrove	OWEN	20.09.1942.
Sgt	Glyndwr	OWENS	08.07.1941.
Sgt	John Paty	PADLEY	03.08.1943.
F/L	Harry Charles Shaw	PAGE	31.01.1942.
Sgt	Henry William John	PAIN	25.02.1944.
P/O	Stanley George	PALK	18.08.1943.
Sgt	Denis Isiah	PALLETT	26.10.1940.
F/O	John Michael	PALMER	24.03.1944.
F/Sgt	Albert Alfred	PARDOE	20.02.1944.
Sgt	Colin Mellor	PARKER	23.06.1942.
S/L	Edward Donald J.	PARKER	16.01.1943.
Sgt	Alfred Raymond	PARKER	07.02.1943.
Sgt	John Lewis	PARKER	11.04.1944.
F/O	Maurice	PARRY	24.07.1941.
F/Sgt	Edward	PARRY	11.04.1944.
F/O	John Robert Bruno	PARSONS	31.01.1942.
Sgt	Robert Albert	PARSONS	30.07.1942.
Sgt	Frederick Stanley	PARTRIDGE	16.02.1942.
F/Sgt	Leslie James	PARTRIDGE	02.06.1942.
P/O	Alfred George	PASCOE	30.06.1940.
F/O	Reginald Herbert	PASSANT	08.07.1944.
Sgt	Edward Ernest	PATCHETT	03.06.1942.
Sgt	Alan	PATERSON	01.09.1943.
Sgt	Harold Alexander	PATERSON	09.04.1945.
P/O	John Douglas	PATEY	31.05.1942.
Sgt	Henry	PATRICK	02.01.1944.
P/O	William Shearer	PATTINSON	29.08.1942.
Sgt	Neville James	PATTON	07.04.1942.
Sgt	Edward	PEACOCK	25.03.1944.
Sgt	Arthur George Edward	PEARCE	16.02.1942.
Sgt	Nelson	PECKHAM	08.03.1945.
P/O	Herbert Orlando	PEEL	03.09.1942.
Sgt	Rowland	PELHAM	22.11.1940.
W/C	William Mitchell	PENMAN	03.10.1943.
P/O	John Montague	PHILLIPS	30.07.1943.
F/Sgt	Joseph David	PIGEAU	16.08.1943.
F/Sgt	Clifford	PLANT	09.04.1945.

Rank	Name	Surname	Date
P/O	Louis	POCH	10.09.1942.
Sgt	Cyril Arthur	PONDER	21.01.1944.
Sgt	Gerald Harry	POSTINS	29.07.1944.
F/O	Eric Albert	POVEY	03.08.1943.
Sgt	Rex Spurway	POWELL	20.06.1940.
Sgt	Ian Frank	PRATT	04.06.1942.
Sgt	Robert John	PREECE	18.02.1943.
Sgt	Ernest Frederick	PRICE	16.06.1944.
Sgt	Jack	PRITCHARD	04.07.1942.
F/O	Peter Harold Howard	PRITCHARD	12.06.1941.
F/Sgt	Harold William	PRONGER	31.03.1944.
Sgt	Kenneth	PROUTEN	30.12.1943.
P/O	Alan William	PULLAN	17.06.1943.
F/O	John Howard	PULLMAN	23.04.1944.
Sgt	Jack	PUNTER	23.08.1943.
Sgt	Fred	PURSGLOVE	30.06.1940.
W/O	Henry John	PYKE	01.02.1945.
Sgt	Gordon Frederick George	RACKSTRAW	16.02.1942.
Sgt	James Metcalfe	RAINE	04.07.1942.
Sgt	John McFadyen	RAMSEY	01.10.1942.
Sgt	John Victor	RANDALL	07.12.1941.
P/O	Herbert	RANKIN	25.02.1944.
Sgt	Walter Milton	RATCLIFFE	16.03.1945.
Sgt	Walter Benedict	RAYMENT	05.10.1940.
W/OII	Clifford Harold	REED	16.01.1943.
Sgt	Jack Valentine	REES	17.04.1943.
P/O	Edwin	REEVE	17.12.1940.
W/O	William Joseph	REID	13.05.1943.
F/Sgt	Joseph Harvey	RENAUD	26.07.1943.
Sgt	Joseph Albert	RICE	30.07.1942.
F/Sgt	John Edward	RICHARDS	29.08.1942.
F/O	Francis	RICHARDS	08.03.1943.
F/O	William Harold	RICHARDS	15.08.1943.
Sgt	Harrnet Richard	RICHARDSON	17.12.1940.
Sgt	Richard	RICHARDSON	15.01.1945.
Sgt	Herbert	RICHMOND	29.08.1941.
S/L	John Lawrence	RILEY	07.12.1941.
Sgt	William Arthur	ROBERTS	26.03.1942.
Sgt	Edward	ROBERTS	13.01.1943.
Sgt	Tegwyn	ROBERTS	23.09.1944.
Sgt	Andrew	ROBERTSON	06.11.1940.
F/Sgt	Eric Nigel Riddell	ROBERTSON	09.08.1941.
P/O	Ian Ronald	ROBERTSON	28.04.1943.
Sgt	James	ROBERTSON	26.11.1943.
Sgt	Jack Martin	ROBINSON	01.10.1942.
Sgt	Benjamin	ROBINSON	03.08.1943.

Rank	First Names	Surname	Date
P/O	Harry	ROBINSON	18.08.1943.
F/Sgt	Frank	ROE	28.06.1942.
W/O1	James Joseph	ROONEY	02.03.1943.
P/O	Maurice	ROOT-REED	03.10.1943.
F/Sgt	Horace Sydney	ROSHER	24.09.1944.
Sgt	Alexander	ROSS	02.01.1944.
P/O	James Louis	ROSSIGNOL	21.04.1943.
Sgt	William Stanley	ROWCLIFFE	20.06.1940.
P/O	Bernard Lawrence	ROWLAND	03.08.1944.
P/O	William James	RUDDY	28.06.1942.
Sgt	Clarence Edward	RUSSELL	14.11.1940.
F/Sgt	John	RYAN	10.11.1944.
Sgt	Arthur Gladstone	SALE	20.09.1942.
Sgt	Peter Miller Hamilton	SALMOND	16.08.1943.
Sgt	John	SAMSON	04.07.1942.
F/O	Charles Henry	SAUNDERS	21.03.1945.
Sgt	Frederick Arthur	SCALES	23.09.1944.
Sgt	Leslie Harry	SCHOLEY	18.08.1943.
F/Sgt	Robert Alexander Leslie	SCOTT	16.08.1943.
Sgt	William John Ryland	SCOTT	08.02.1945.
P/O	Christopher Charles	SCRIMSHAW	13.08.1944.
F/O	Jack Etherington	SEARS	06.01.1945.
P/O	Elwood Raymond	SEIBOLD	03.06.1942.
F/O	George Edward	SHARPE	02.01.1944.
W/C	George Harcus	SHEENAN	25.08.1942.
P/O	Harry Christie	SHELDON	13.08.1940.
Sgt	Norman Harold	SHERGOLD	25.06.1944.
Sgt	Herbert	SHERLIKER	18.03.1944.
F/Sgt	Arthur Albert	SHERRIFF	01.02.1945.
Sgt	Alan Walton	SHERWOOD	24.03.1944.
F/O	Alfred Vernon	SHIRLEY	02.01.1944.
Sgt	Harold Edgar	SHORT	24.03.1944.
Sgt	William	SIMONS	03.06.1942.
Sgt	Norman Gordon	SIMPSON	22.11.1944.
F/Sgt	Kenneth	SIMS	20.02.1944.
Sgt	Raymond John	SIMS	22.11.1944.
Sgt	Donald	SINCLAIR	26.09.1940.
Sgt	Robert	SINCLAIR	14.11.1940.
Sgt	James	SINCLAIR	08.03.1945.
Sgt	Frederick Walter	SKELCHER	31.03.1944.
Sgt	Kenneth Edward	SLADE	17.01.1943.
Sgt	Robert Edward	SLOAN	13.05.1943.
Sgt	John Eric	SMART	26.03.1942.
F/Sgt	Edmond Rhys	SMART	08.08.1943.
F/O	Albert Stanley	SMITH	20.06.1940.
Sgt	Peter Tristan	SMITH	21.04.1943.

Sgt	William Stanley	SMITH	09.10.1943.
P/O	Cyril Frankham	SMITH	22.10.1943.
Sgt	Eric	SMITH	26.11.1943.
Sgt	John Stuart	SMITH	21.01.1944.
F/Sgt	William	SMITH	08.07.1944.
Sgt	William James	SMITH	29.07.1944.
P/O	Victor Patrick	SMITH	09.04.1945.
F/Sgt	Arthur William	SNELLING	21.03.1945.
P/O	Arthur William Avis	SOUTER	18.08.1943.
Sgt	Charles Philip	SOUTHCOTT	08.08.1943.
Sgt	James	SPENCER	29.08.1941.
Sgt	Arthur Raymond	SPENCER	09.03.1943.
P/O	Joseph Aloysius	SPENCER	23.08.1943.
Sgt	George William Sidney	SPRIGGS	10.08.1943.
P/O	Ronald	STEER	16.08.1943.
Sgt	Albert Henry	STEERS	06.12.1944.
F/O	James Anthony	STEPHENS	26.11.1943.
F/O	Wilbert	STEPHENS	03.08.1944.
P/O	Kenneth John	STEPHENSON	03.10.1943.
P/O	Jack Graham	STEWART	30.07.1942.
F/Sgt	Maurice Wilfred	STOBART	06.01.1945.
Sgt	James	STOCK	03.01.1944.
F/L	Donald Edward Ross	STONE	23.09.1944.
Sgt	Ramon	STONES	18.03.1944.
P/O	Robert Lorne	STOREY	04.07.1942.
F/O	John	STOREY	02.01.1944.
Sgt	Willie	STOVOLD	16.06.1944.
P/O	Andrew Paul Edmund	STRANGE	26.11.1943.
Sgt	Richard	STUART	30.12.1943.
Sgt	Lindsay Snowdon	SUDDICK	31.03.1944.
Sgt	John Elphege	SULLIVAN	30.07.1942.
P/O	Ross Edwin	SUTHERLAND	03.08.1944.
F/O	John Frederick	SWALES	21.03.1945.
F/Sgt	Harold Lewis	SWEET	26.11.1943.
P/O	Maurice Roy	TAGG	20.07.1940.
F/Sgt	John Edward	TALBOT	06.11.1944.
F/Sgt	William Stanley Horace	TANDY	08.03.1945.
F/Sgt	John Lauson	TARRAN	03.06.1942.
F/O	Brian Stanley	TASKER	09.02.1945.
P/O	Raymond Charles	TAYLOR	03.09.1942.
Sgt	William Barrie	TAYLOR	13.08.1940.
Sgt	Robert Arthur	TAYLOR	25.04.1944.
F/O	Gerald McLaughlin	TAYLOR	13.08.1944.
F/Sgt	Ralph	TAYLOR	21.03.1945.
Sgt	David Wilkie	THIRSK	08.08.1943.
Sgt	Lloyd Watson	THOMAS	10.09.1942.

Rank	Name	Surname	Date
Sgt	Percy	THOMAS	02.03.1941.
Sgt	Claude Percival	THOMAS	08.04.1941.
Sgt	John	THOMAS	13.05.1943.
F/O	Ernest Arthur	THOMAS	09.10.1943.
Sgt	Thomas	THOMPSON	20.09.1942.
F/Sgt	Lyle Harold	THOMPSON	18.08.1943.
P/O	Maxwell Hartley	THOMPSON	09.10.1943.
F/O	John Bernard	THOMPSON	19.07.1944.
F/L	Douglas Lindsay	THOMSON	03.10.1943.
P/O	Harold David	THOMSON	03.08.1944.
Sgt	Charles Maxwell	THORN	17.09.1942.
Sgt	Charles Edward	THROWER	13.08.1940.
F/O	Harold John Robert	TICKLE	03.01.1943.
Sgt	Charles Reginald	TINGLE	21.01.1944.
Sgt	John	TITTERINGTON	02.06.1942.
F/O	Gordon Leslie	TOFIELD	02.06.1942.
Sgt	Wilfred	TOOLE	29.08.1942.
W/OII	John Blackstock	TOOMBS	26.11.1943.
Sgt	Thomas	TORNEY	21.03.1945.
F/Sgt	Ronald	TOWNDROW	08.07.1944.
F/Sgt	John Frederick	TROTTER	18.08.1943.
Sgt	Herbert Alfred	TUCK	17.12.1944.
F/O	George Arthur	TULL	03.01.1944.
F/Sgt	John Olmstead	TULLER	20.09.1942.
F/Sgt	Harry Edward	TURNER	31.01.1942.
Sgt	Harry Victor	TURTON	04.07.1942.
F/Sgt	George	TWYNEHAM	23.09.1944.
P/O	John Bennett	UNDERWOOD	31.05.1942.
P/O	Charles Frederick Walter	UNDERWOOD	03.09.1942.
F/O	Hubert Gregory	UNDERWOOD	07.03.1945.
F/Sgt	Peter George	UREN	08.07.1944.
F/Sgt	Robert	URQUHART	18.08.1943.
P/O	Benson	USHER	31.05.1942.
W/C	George Engebret	VALENTINE	03.09.1941.
F/Sgt	Brian Henry	VAREY	26.11.1943.
P/O	Alfred Newton	VIDLER	18.08.1943.
Sgt	Eric	VINE	26.11.1943.
P/O	John James	WAKEFIELD	18.08.1943.
F/Sgt	John Edward	WALDEN	15.08.1943.
Sgt	George Henry	WALKER	07.04.1942.
Sgt	Jack Lewis	WALLIS	04.06.1942.
F/O	Hubert	WALLIS	20.02.1944.
P/O	Samuel Partington	WALSH	02.06.1942.
Sgt	Frank Douglas	WALTER	26.10.1940.
Sgt	Francis Llewellyn D'Oyly	WALTERS	09.03.1943.
Sgt	Frederic Stanley	WALTHO	20.07.1940.

Rank	Name	Surname	Date
Sgt	Joseph Frank	WALTON	08.07.1941.
Sgt	Richard Charles	WALTON	18.08.1943.
Sgt	William	WARBURTON	27.01.1944.
F/Sgt	Wilfred	WARD	13.08.1940.
P/O	Edward Noel	WARD	20.12.1940.
W/OII	Thomas Herbert	WARNE	18.02.1943.
Sgt	Jack Arthur	WATERS	08.12.1940.
Sgt	Thomas Frank	WATKINS	23.08.1943.
Sgt	John Knox	WATSON	01.09.1943.
Sgt	Ronald	WAUDBY	17.01.1943.
Sgt	Ivan Fenton	WAUGH	24.07.1941.
F/O	Kenneth Gordon	WEBB	27.06.1941.
Sgt	Cyril Stanley	WEBB	19.10.1944.
F/Sgt	Peter Henry George	WEBSTER	16.02.1942.
P/O	John Colin	WEBSTER	17.10.1946
Sgt	Charles Norman	WEBSTER	22.06.1940.
Sgt	Henry Francis	WEBSTER	16.08.1943.
S/L	Dennis Crosby	WELLBURN	01.09.1943.
Sgt	Cyril Leslie	WELLS	07.12.1941.
S/L	Peter Wynn Mason	WEST	04.07.1942.
Sgt	Frank Edward	WEST	08.08.1943.
F/O	Robert Alexander	WEST	28.01.1944.
S/L	George Ernest	WESTON	01.10.1942.
Sgt	James Alexander	WESTON	26.11.1943.
Sgt	Reginald Thomas	WEVILL	31.03.1944.
Sgt	Nathaniel John Edward	WHEELER	02.10.1943.
F/O	Rihard Arthur	WHITAKER	31.03.1944.
Sgt	Albert Edward George	WHITE	30.07.1943.
F/O	David Conway	WHITE	26.11.1943.
F/Sgt	James Standley	WHITECROSS	22.10.1943.
Sgt	Charles Douglas	WHITEHALL	13.05.1943.
Sgt	James Milton	WHITEHEAD	18.02.1943.
F/Sgt	Samuel Vernon	WICKLAND	23.09.1944.
F/L	Douglas Arthur Clarence	WILKINSON	03.10.1943.
F/O	Ernest Arthur Chenery	WILLARD	02.01.1944.
Sgt	James Clough	WILLIAMS	26.09.1940.
Sgt	Howard Llewellyn	WILLIAMS	07.02.1943.
F/O	Cyril Frederick	WILLIAMS	16.04.1943.
Sgt	Mervyn Stephen	WILLIAMS	02.01.1944.
F/O	Eric Albert	WILLIAMS	11.04.1944.
Sgt	Leslie Alexander	WILLIAMS	06.01.1945.
Sgt	Anthony	WILLIAMSON	31.05.1942.
F/Sgt	Harry Robert	WILLIAMSON	01.10.1942.
Sgt	Frederick George	WILLIAMSON	26.11.1940.
F/Sgt	George John Anstey	WILLIS	17.10.1948
P/O	Thomas Ivor Ravenhill	WILSON	09.01.1942.

F/Sgt	John	WILSON	07.12.1941.
LAC	Henry George	WILSON	24.02.1945.
Sgt	Henry	WINDLE	02.03.1941.
P/O	George Peter	WISE	24.07.1941.
LAC	Winston Kitchener	WOOD	07.03.1940.
F/O	Julian Vernon Orison	WOOD	13.05.1943.
P/O	James Rankin Stratton	WOOD	25.06.1944.
Sgt	Thomas Charles	WOODHOUSE	17.09.1942.
F/Sgt	Frank	WOODRUFF	27.06.1941.
Sgt	Arthur Bradley	WOODVINE	11.04.1944.
F/Sgt	John	WOODWARD	27.06.1941.
P/O	James	WOOLFORD	17.01.1943.
F/Sgt	James Harold Boston	WOOLGAR	10.09.1942.
F/Sgt	Raymond	WORDSWORTH	08.07.1941.
Sgt	John Henry	WORROW	17.01.1943.
Sgt	Maurice Leonard	WORTH	25.02.1944.
P/O	James Allister	WRIGHT	29.08.1942.
Sgt	Joseph	WRIGHT	03.09.1942.
Sgt	Robert	WRIGHTSON	02.03.1943.
F/O	George Michael	WYATT	30.06.1940.
Sgt	Harold	WYRILL	18.03.1944.
F/Sgt	Albert Cranston	YATES	10.09.1942.
Sgt	George Edward	YOUNG	07.02.1943.
P/O	Gerald Arthur	YOUNG	09.03.1943.
F/O	Myron	YOWNEY	20.02.1944.

61 Squadron

MOTTO **PER PURUM TONANTES** (Thundering through the clear sky)　　　Code **QR**

Stations

HEMSWELL	08.03.37. to 17.07.41.
NORTH LUFFENHAM	17.07.41. to 05.05.42.
WOOLFOX LODGE (Conversion Flight)	16.10.41. to 05.05.42.
SYERSTON	05.05.42. to 15.11.43.
St EVAL (Detachment)	16.07.42. to 22.08.42.
SKELLINGTHORPE	15.11.43. to 01.02.44.
CONINGSBY	01.02.44. to 15.04.44.
SKELLINGTHORPE	15.04.44. to 16.06.45.

Commanding Officers

WING COMMANDER C H BRILL	22.03.37. to 26.09.39
WING COMMANDER C M De CRESPIGNY	26.09.39. to 28.01.40.
WING COMMANDER F M DENNY	28.01.40. to 19.05.40.
WING COMMANDER G H SHEEN DSO	19.05.40. to 11.10.40.
WING COMMANDER G E VALENTINE DSO	11.10.40. to 03.09.41.
WING COMMANDER C T WEIR DFC	05.09.41. to 19.06.42.
WING COMMANDER C M COAD AFC	19.06.42. to 11.02.43.
WING COMMANDER W M PENMAN DFC AFC	11.02.43. to 04.10.43.
WING COMMANDER R N STIDOLPH DFC	04.10.43. to 22.04.44.
WING COMMANDER A W DOUBLEDAY DSO DFC	22.04.44. to 25.09.44.
WING COMMANDER W D PEXTON DFC AFC	25.09.44. to 16.02.45.
WING COMMANDER C W SCOTT AFC	16.02.45. to 12.06.45.

Aircraft

HAMPDEN	02.39. to	10.41.
MANCHESTER	03.41. to	06.42.
LANCASTER I/III	06.42. to	05.46.
LANCASTER II	10.42. to	03.43.

Operational Record

OPERATIONS	SORTIES	AIRCRAFT LOSSES	% LOSSES
704	6082	156	2.6

CATEGORY OF OPERATIONS

BOMBING	MINING	OTHER
613	85	6

HAMPDEN

OPERATIONS	SORTIES	AIRCRAFT LOSSES	% LOSSES
283	1339	28	2.1

CATEGORY OF OPERATIONS

BOMBING	MINING	OTHER
229	49	5

MANCHESTER

OPERATIONS	SORTIES	AIRCRAFT LOSSES	% LOSSES
44	197	12	6.1

CATEGORY OF OPERATIONS

BOMBING	MINING
33	11

LANCASTER

OPERATIONS	SORTIES	AIRCRAFT LOSSES	% LOSSES
377	4546	116	2.6

CATEGORY OF OPERATIONS

BOMBING	MINING	OTHER
351	25	1

Aircraft Histories

HAMPDEN.   **To October 1941.**

L4103	To 106 Squadron.
L4104	To 83 Squadron.
L4105	To 16 Operational Training Unit.
L4106	To 83 Squadron.
L4108	To 144 Squadron.
L4109	To 14 Operational Training Unit.
L4110	To 14 Operational Training Unit.
L4111	Crashed on approach to Digby on return from patrol 8.3.40.
L4112	FTR from a mining sortie 27/28.6.40.
L4113	FTR from a mining sortie 14/15.4.40.
L4115	To 44 Squadron.
L4116	Crashed on landing at Hemswell while training 17.4.40.
L4117	To 14 Operational Training Unit.
L4119	Crashed in Leicestershire on return from Aalborg 1.5.40
L4120	To 106 Squadron.
L4146 QR-R	From 76 Squadron. FTR from rail targets in Germany 23/24.5.40.
P1170	Crashed on landing at Doncaster while training 14.10.39.
P1171	To 83 Squadron.
P1253	From 106 Squadron. Crashed in Suffolk on return from Cologne 2.3.41.
P1323	To 49 Squadron.
P2082	FTR from mining sortie 5/6.11.40.
P2088	To 14 Operational Training Unit.
P2089	Crash-landed in Dorset on return from Bordeaux 19/20.8.40.
P2090 QR-R	FTR Kiel 26/27.9.40.
P2144	Force-landed on approach to Bircham Newton on return from Düsseldorf 3.6.41.
P4298	To 25 Operational Training Unit.
P4324 QR-P	FTR Merseburg 26/27.8.40.
P4335	FTR Salzbergen 12/13.8.40.
P4336	FTR from rail targets in the Ruhr 9/10.6.40.
P4337	To 5 Operational Training Unit.
P4338	To 144 Squadron.
P4339 QR-H	Collided with Hampden L4138 (16 Operational Training Unit) seconds after take-off from Cottesmore 13.6.40.
P4341	FTR Geestacht 29/30.6.40.
P4342	To 25 Operational Training Unit.
P4343	FTR from mining sortie 20/21.7.40.
P4344	FTR from mining sortie 20/21.7.40.
P4346	FTR Schwerte 21/22.6.40.
P4349	Crash-landed in Norfolk on return from Hanover 7/8.6.40.
P4355	FTR from rail targets in Germany 20/21.6.40.
P4356	FTR Geestacht 29/30.6.40.

P4357	Ditched off Yorkshire coast during training 5.8.40.
P4358	FTR from mining sortie 20/21.7.40.
P4379	FTR Salzbergen 12/13.8.40.
P4390	FTR Dortmund-Ems Canal 7/8.7.40.
P4396	FTR Hamburg 13/14.11.40.
P4397	Damaged at Hemswell in collision with X2911 (61 Squadron) during take-off for Calais 24.9.40.
P4398	To 83 Squadron.
P4399	Crashed in Kent on return from Cologne 31.7.41.
P4400	To 25 Operational Training Unit.
P4401	Converted for use as torpedo bomber.
P4405	Crashed in Norfolk on return from Wilhelmshaven 10.2.41.
P4418	To 14 Operational Training Unit.
X2893	To Aeroplane and Armaments Experimental Establishment.
X2894	Crashed in Norfolk on return from Stettin 5/6.9.40.
X2906	To 25 Operational Training Unit.
X2911	Collided with P4397 (61 Squadron) on take-off from Hemswell when bound for Calais 24.9.40.
X2912	To 49 Squadron.
X2920	Crashed in Yorkshire on return from mining sortie 5/6.10.40.
X2922	FTR Boulogne 13/14.9.40.
X2967	FTR Berlin 14/15.11.40.
X2971	FTR Kiel 25/26.10.40.
X2975	FTR Düsseldorf 8/9.12.40.
X2979	Crashed in Norfolk on return from Merseburg 17.10.40.
X2980	To 16 Operational Training Unit.
X2981	Exploded in the air during trials of Imp Mine 20.12.40.
X2987	Crashed while landing at Hemswell on return from Duisburg 22.11.40.
X2989	To 408 (Goose) Squadron RCAF.
X3005	Abandoned over Yorkshire on return from Kiel 24.3.41.
X3006	Crashed on take-off from Hemswell when bound for Hamburg 14.11.40.
X3058	To 106 Squadron.
X3064	Crashed in Lincolnshire on return from Kiel 26.11.40.
X3120	FTR Düsseldorf 2/3.6.41.
X3126	Crashed on approach to Hemswell on return from abortive operation to Bremen 3.1.41.
X3127	FTR Kiel 8/9.8.41.
X3128	FTR Mannheim 16/17.12.40.
X3138	To 5 Air Observers School.
X3140	To 408 (Goose) Squadron RCAF.
X3147	Crashed in Norfolk on return from Cologne 2.3.41.
AD723	Crashed in Lincolnshire on return from Cologne 2.3.41.
AD725	Crashed on landing at Hemswell during training 1.2.41.
AD727	From 44 Squadron. FTR from mining sortie 11/12.6.41.
AD732	FTR Cherbourg 18.4.41.
AD752	To 144 Squadron.
AD754	From 144 Squadron. To 408 (Goose) Squadron RCAF.
AD804	To 144 Squadron.

AD806	FTR Osnabrück 5/6.7.41.
AD825	Abandoned near Swindon on return from Brest 18.4.41.
AD826	To 455 Squadron RAAF.
AD827	FTR Kiel 8/9.4.41.
AD868	To 44 Squadron.
AD937	FTR Mönchengladbach 7/8.7.41.
AD963	To 408 (Goose) Squadron RCAF.
AD974	To 49 Squadron.
AE135	To 455 Squadron RAAF.
AE186	From 207 Squadron. To 44 Squadron.
AE189 QR-G	FTR Kiel 24/25.7.41.
AE200	To 144 Squadron.
AE202	To 44 Squadron.
AE219	From 207 Squadron. To 408 (Goose) Squadron RCAF.
AE235	To 144 Squadron.
AE247	From 207 Squadron. FTR Frankfurt 29/30.8.41.
AE256	To 455 Squadron RAAF.
AE259	Crashed in Lincolnshire on return from Kiel 9.8.41.
AE263	FTR Kiel 8/9.8.41.
AE266	Crashed on landing at Upwood on return from Cologne 31.7.41.
AE286	To 408 (Goose) Squadron RCAF.
AE288	To 408 (Goose) Squadron RCAF.
AE289	To 408 (Goose) Squadron RCAF.
AE290	To 44 Squadron.
AE308	To 455 Squadron RAAF.
AE352	To 455 Squadron RAAF.
MANCHESTER.	**From June 1941 to June 1942.**
L7276	From Aeroplane and Armaments Experimental Establishment. No operations. To 25 Operational Training Unit.
L7284	From 207 Squadron. No operations. To 39 Maintenance Unit.
L7288	From 97 (Straits Settlements) Squadron. No operations. To 1654 Conversion Unit.
L7292	From 97 (Straits Settlements) Squadron. No operations. To Torpedo Development Unit.
L7293	From 49 Squadron. To 207 Squadron.
L7304	From 207 Squadron. FTR Kiel 26/27.6.41.
L7307	No operations. To 97 (Straits Settlements) Squadron.
L7315	From 97 (Straits Settlements) Squadron. Crashed in Lincolnshire while training 29.6.41.
L7388	FTR Berlin 2/3.9.41.
L7395	Abandoned near Wittering following abortive sortie to Cologne 13/14.3.42.
L7396	FTR Brest 31.1/1.2.42.
L7401	From 44 (Rhodesia) Squadron. To 50 Squadron.
L7415	From 44 (Rhodesia) Squadron. To 50 Squadron.
L7419	From 207 Squadron. To 50 Squadron.

L7422	From 207 Squadron. Ultimate fate unknown.
L7425	From 44 (Rhodesia) Squadron. To 1661 Conversion Unit.
L7426	To 83 Squadron.
L7433	FTR from mining sortie 16/17.2.42.
L7453	From 44 (Rhodesia) Squadron. To 49 Squadron.
L7454	From 207 Squadron. FTR from mining sortie 29/30.3.42
L7458 QR-A	To 1660 Conversion Unit.
L7464	To 50 Squadron.
L7470	FTR Essen 6/7.4.42.
L7471	To 50 Squadron.
L7472	FTR Brest 31.1/1.2.42.
L7473	From 97 (Straits Settlements) Squadron. To 1485 Flight.
L7475 QR-D	From 97 (Staits Settlements) Squadron. To 50 Squadron.
L7477 QR-N	From 44 (Rhodesia) Squadron. To 1661 Conversion Unit.
L7486	From 207 Squadron. Returned to 207 Squadron.
L7494	FTR Boulogne 7/8.12.41.
L7495	Abandoned over Lincolnshire on return from Hamburg 16.1.42.
L7496	To 207 Squadron.
L7497	FTR Essen 25/26.3.42.
L7516 QR-F	To 50 Squadron.
L7518 QR-O	FTR Essen 25/26.3.42.
L7519	To 50 Squadron.
L7520	No operations. Crashed in Bedfordshire during training 2.11.41.
L7521	To 50 Squadron.
R5784	To 50 Squadron.
R5785 QR-M	FTR Le Havre 10/11.4.42.
R5786	To 50 Squadron.
R5787 QR-M	FTR Brest 31.1/1.2.42.
R5789	Crashed in Wiltshire following aborted sortie to Cherbourg 9.1.42.
R5796	To 207 Squadron.
R5832	To 1660 Conversion Unit.
R5834	Force-landed in Norfolk on return from Brest 10.2.42.
LANCASTER.	**From April 1942.**
L7532	From 97 (Straits Settlements) Conversion Flight. To 50 Sqn via 61 Squadron Conversion Flight.
L7539	From 44 (Rhodesia) Squadron. Training only. To 50 Squadron Conversion Flight.
L7571 QR-S	From 97 (Straits Settlements) Squadron. To 207 Squadron.
R5488 QR-F	From 97 (Straits Settlements) Squadron. FTR from mining sortie 3/4.7.42.
R5491	From 44 (Rhodesia) Squadron. To 1656 Conversion Unit via 61 Squadron Conversion Flight.
R5505	From 207 Squadron. Training only. To Empire Central Flying School.
R5511	Completed 21 operations. To 1654 Conversion Unit.
R5517	FTR Emden 22/23.6.42.
R5540	To 1661 Conversion Unit via 44 (Rhodesia) Squadron Conversion Flight.
R5541	From 207 Squadron. To 97 (Straits Settlements) Squadron.

R5543	FTR from Atlantic Patrol 20.8.42.
R5544	FTR Essen 1/2.6.42.
R5545	No operations. Crashed while landing at North Luffenham during training 1.5.42.
R5560	To 1654 Conversion Unit.
R5561	FTR Cologne 30/31.5.42. (Operation Millennium).
R5562	FTR Essen 2/3.6.42.
R5563	FTR from attack on SS Corunna off the Spanish coast 19.8.42.
R5565 QR-S	From 83 Sqn via Navigation Training Unit. FTR Magdeburg 21/22.1.44.
R5605	FTR from attack on SS Corunna off the Spanish coast 19.8.42.
R5613 QR-B	FTR Essen 2/3.6.42.
R5615 QR-H	FTR Bremen 27/28.6.42.
R5618 QR-H	To 1654 Conversion Unit.
R5627	FTR Bremen 3/4.6.42.
R5660	From Aeroplane &Armaments Experimental Establishment. To 1654 Conversion Unit via 50 Squadron Conversion Flight.
R5661	FTR from attack on SS Corunna off the Spanish coast 19.8.42.
R5662 QR-A	FTR Frankfurt 24/25.8.42.
R5663 QR-B	FTR from mining sortie 3/4.7.42.
R5679 QR-O	FTR from mining sortie 24/25.9.42.
R5682 QR-R	FTR Bremen 4/5.9.42.
R5699 QR-H	Completed 34 operations. Crashed while landing at Syerston following early return from Munich 21.12.42.
R5703 QR-D	Crashed soon after take-off from Syerston when bound for Wismar 1.10.42.
R5724 QR-F	Crash-landed at Wittering on return from mining sortie 25.9.42.
R5734 QR-V	From 1654 Conversion Unit. FTR Nuremberg 30/31.3.44.
R5737	FTR Saarbrücken 29/30.7.42.
R5742	From 106 Squadron. FTR Nuremberg 28/29.8.42.
R5757	From 156 Squadron. To 1661 Conversion Unit.
R5759	FTR Wismar 1/2.10.42.
R5842	From A.V.Roe. To 44 (Rhodesia) Squadron 3.42.
R5843	To 1654 Conversion Unit via 50 Squadron Conversion Flight.
R5844	To 106 Sqn via 50 Squadron Conversion Flight.
R5845	To 1660 Conversion Unit via 97 (Straits Settlements) Conversion Flight.
R5846	To 44 (Rhodesia) Squadron.
R5853	From 97 (Straits Settlements) Squadron. To 576 Sqn via 1660 Conversion Unit.
R5856 QR-Q/U	From 83 Squadron via 1660 Conversion Unit. FTR St Leu d'Esserent 7/8.7.44.
R5859 QR-G	To 61 Squadron Conversion Flight. Crash-landed on approach to Bodney on return from Mannheim 7.12.42.
R5864 QR-X	From 106 Sqn and back. Returned to 61 Squadron. Destroyed at Syerston when bomb load detonated 8.12.42.
R5866	To 1654 Conversion Unit.
R5888	FTR Düsseldorf 10/11.9.42.
R5910	From 106 Squadron. Returned to 106 Squadron.
W4111	FTR Düsseldorf 10/11.9.42.

W4136	From 44 (Rhodesia) Squadron Conversion Flight. FTR Karlsruhe 2/3.9.42.
W4166	FTR Munich 19/20.9.42.
W4168	Completed 21 operations. Crashed on landing at Swinderby on return from Turin 10.12.42.
W4173	FTR Essen 16/17.9.42.
W4192 QR-E	FTR Essen 12/13.1.43.
W4198 QR-L/H	FTR Berlin 26/27.11.43.
W4233	Crashed in Yorkshire on return from Kiel 14.10.42.
W4236 QR-K	FTR Mannheim 9/10.8.43.
W4244 QR-F	Crashed on approach to Exeter on return from mining sortie 10/11.11.42.
W4257	FTR St Nazaire 2/3.4.43.
W4269 QR-G	FTR Duisburg 12/13.5.43.
W4270	Crashed in Bottesford circuit while training 18.2.43.
W4272	Conversion Flight only. To 15 Squadron via 1654 Conversion Unit.
W4279 QR-S/Z	FTR Kassel 3/4.10.43.
W4301	To 460 Squadron RAAF.
W4315 QR-Q	From 50 Squadron. Ditched on return from Berlin 27/28.1.44.
W4317 QR-R	FTR Pilsen 16/17.4.43.
W4357 QR-A	FTR Kassel 22/23.10.43.
W4381	From 106 Squadron. To 1661 Conversion Unit.
W4762	To 50 Squadron.
W4763	FTR Gelsenkirchen 9/10.7.43.
W4766 QR-J	From 57 Squadron. FTR Peenemünde 17/18.8.43.
W4767 QR-J	FTR Berlin 17/18.1.43.
W4769 QR-V	Completed 18 operations. FTR Essen 3/4.1.43.
W4774	FTR Montchanin 17.10.42.
W4789	From 12 Squadron. FTR Cologne 16/17.6.43.
W4795	From 207 Squadron. FTR Stettin 20/21.4.43.
W4798	From 207 Squadron. Ultimate fate unclear in records.
W4830 QR-E	Abandoned over Lincolnshire on return from Gelsenkirchen 26.6.43.
W4884	From 5 Lancaster Finishing School.
W4898	FTR from a mining sortie 28/29.4.43.
W4899	To 1668 Conversion Unit.
W4900 QR-Q	To 1669 Conversion Unit.
W4903 QR-P	FTR Nuremberg 8/9.3.43.
W4920 QR-O	FTR Berlin 1/2.3.43.
W4929	To 617 Squadron.
W4934 QR-S	FTR Peenemünde 17/18.8.43.
W4950 QR-L	From 156 Squadron. To 6 Lancaster Finishing School.
W4957	From 83 Sqn via Navigation Training Unit. To 46 Maintenance Unit.
W5000 QR-B	FTR Hamburg 2/3.8.43.
W5002 QR-L	FTR Milan 15/16.8.43.
DS603	Hercules-powered Mk II. No operations. To 115 Squadron.
DS604 QR-W	Hercules-powered Mk II. No operations. To 115 Squadron.
DS605 QR-X	Hercules-powered Mk II. No operations. To 115 Squadron.
DS607 QR-N	Hercules-powered Mk II. To 115 Squadron.
DS608 QR-O	Hercules-powered Mk II. To 115 Squadron.

DS609 QR-R	Hercules-powered Mk II. To 115 Squadron.
DS610 QR-S	Hercules-powered Mk II. To 115 Squadron.
DS612	Hercules-powered Mk II. To 115 Squadron.
DS613	Hercules-powered Mk II. To 115 Squadron.
DS621	Hercules-powered Mk II. To 115 Squadron.
DV186	FTR Milan 15/16.8.43.
DV228	FTR Leverkusen 22/23.8.43.
DV232 QR-K	Crashed near Nottingham on return from Mannheim 6.9.43.
DV239 QR-V	FTR Hannover 8/9.10.43.
DV294 QR-K	FTR Augsburg 25/26.2.44.
DV297 QR-O	From 106 Squadron. FTR Berlin 26/27.11.43.
DV304 QR-V	From 101 Squadron. FTR Revigny 18/19.7.44.
DV311 QR-P	FTR Nuremberg 30/31.3.44.
DV312 QR-Z	To 207 Squadron.
DV339 QR-W	From 106 Squadron. FTR Berlin 26/27.11.43.
DV344 QR-Z/V	From 106 Squadron. FTR Berlin 1/2.1.44.
DV397 QR-N/W	FTR Berlin 24/25.3.44.
DV399 QR-R	FTR Berlin 29/30.12.43.
DV400 QR-Y	FTR Berlin 27/28.1.44.
DV401 QR-Z	FTR Berlin 2/3.1.44.
ED314 QR-Y	From 44 (Rhodesia) Squadron. FTR Hannover 27/28.9.43.
ED332 QR-D	FTR Berlin 16/17.1.43.
ED359 QR-F	FTR Lorient 7/8.2.43.
ED470 QR-W	From 50 Squadron. FTR Münster 24.9.44.
ED613	FTR Essen 25/26.7.43.
ED630 QR-C-	FTR Kassel 22/23.10.43.
ED661	From Vickers Armstrong. FTR Peenemünde 17/18.8.43.
ED703	FTR Munich 9/10.3.43.
ED717 QR-S	Ditched off Isles of Scilly on return from La Spezia 14.4.43.
ED718 QR-P	FTR Munich 2/3.10.43.
ED722 QR-B	FTR Milan 15/16.8.43.
ED782	FTR Hamburg 29/30.7.43.
ED826	From 1654 Conversion Unit. To 15 Squadron via 1654 Conversion Unit.
ED860 QR-N	From 156 Squadron. Crashed on take-off from Skellingthorpe when bound for Bergen 28.10.44.
EE176 QR-M	From 97 (Straits Settlements) Squadron. To 1653 Conversion Unit. Completed 122 operations
EE186 QR-D	From 106 Squadron. FTR St Leu d'Esserent 4/5.7.44.
EE190 QR-M	Crash-landed in North Africa following a raid on Italy 16.7.43.
HK538 QR-F	FTR Leipzig 19/20.2.44.
JA695 QR-W	From 57 Squadron via 5 Maintenance Unit. FTR Aachen 11/12.4.44.
JA872 QR-K	From 630 Squadron. To 46 Maintenance Unit.
JA873	FTR Hamburg 2/3.8.43.
JA874 QR-E	To 617 Squadron.
JA900	FTR Peenemünde 17/18.8.43.
JB116 QR-R	To 9 Squadron.
JB129 QR-G	FTR Berlin 24/25.3.44.

JB132	Crashed in Nottinghamshire after collision with Lancaster R5698 (1654 Conversion Unit) on return from Berlin 1.9.43.
JB137	To 5 Lancaster Finishing School.
JB138 QR-J	Completed 113 operations. To 5 Lancaster Finishing School.
JB351	From 83 Squadron. Damaged beyond repair during operation to Scholven 22.6.44.
JB532 QR-A	To 630 Squadron.
JB534	To 106 Squadron.
JB546	To 57 Squadron.
JB561	To 630 Squadron.
JB565	To 57 Squadron.
JB597	To 630 Squadron.
LL775 QR-O	FTR Augsburg 25/26.2.44.
LL777 QR-S	Crash-landed in Belgium on return from Giessen 6/7.12.44.
LL843	From 467 Squadron RAAF. To 1659 Conversion Unit.
LL911 QR-X	FTR Politz (99th operation) 8/9.2.45.
LL918	From 460 Squadron RAAF.
LM274 QR-F	Completed 69 operations.
LM310 QR-E	From 106 Squadron. FTR Schweinfurt 24/25.2.44.
LM339	FTR Milan 7/8.8.43.
LM359 QR-B	FTR Munich 24/25.4.44.
LM360 QR-O	Aircraft in which F/L Bill Reid won a VC during an operation to Düsseldorf 3/4.11.43. To 50 Squadron.
LM377 QR-F	From 106 Squadron. FTR Berlin 1/2.1.44.
LM452 QR-T	FTR Stuttgart 28/29.7.44.
LM454 QR-Z	FTR Bourg Leopold 11/12.5.44.
LM476 QR-E	FTR Braunschweig 22/23.4.44.
LM478	Crashed on landing at Skellingthorpe on return from Bourg-Leopold 12.5.44.
LM481	To 1653 Conversion Unit.
LM483 QR-Y	Struck off Charge 17.3.45.
LM518 QR-C	FTR Prouville 24/25.6.44.
LM590	To 1669 Conversion Unit 12.44.
LM718 QR-K	FTR Dortmund Ems Canal at Ladbergen 23/24.9.44.
LM720	Crashed in Norfolk on return from Leuna 14/15.1.45.
LM729 QR-V	FTR Munich 17/18.12.44.
ME373	
ME385 QR-O	FTR Lützkendorf 8/9.4.45.
ME430	
ME439	
ME443 QR-N	
ME474 QR-V	FTR Harburg 7/8.3.45.
ME481	
ME493	
ME591 QR-C	FTR Leipzig 19/20.2.44.
ME595 QR-R/Y	FTR Brunswick 14/15.10.44.
ME596 QR-H	FTR Rüsselsheim 12/13.8.44.
ME719	To 1661 Conversion Unit.

ME725 QR-G	FTR Giessen 6/7.12.44.	
ME732 QR-P	FTR Dortmund Ems Canal at Ladbergen 23/24.9.44.	
ME783 QR-E	FTR Chatellerault 15/16.6.44.	
ND509	From 57 Squadron.	
ND727 QR-C	FTR Frankfurt 18/19.3.44.	
ND865	From 83 Squadron. To 5 Lancaster Finishing School.	
ND867 QR-V	FTR St-Leu-d'Esserent 7/8.7.44.	
ND896	To 5 Lancaster Finishing School.	
ND902 QR-R	Damaged beyond repair during operation to Bergen 28/29.10.44.	
ND987 QR-B	FTR Prouville 24/25.6.44.	
ND988 QR-E	FTR Dortmund Ems Canal at Ladbergen 23/24.9.44.	
NF912	Crashed at Skellingthorpe soon after take-off for Siegen 1.2.45.	
NF914 QR-T	FTR Calais 24.9.44.	
NF988 QR-T	FTR Harburg 7/8.3.45.	
NF997		
NG178		
NG179 QR-C	FTR Trondheim 22/23.11.44.	
NG182 QR-K	FTR Harburg 7/8.3.45.	
NG220		
NG231		
NG241 QR-Y	FTR Karlsruhe 2/3.2.45.	
NG367		
NG380		
NG386 QR-P	From 1669 Conversion Unit. FTR Böhlen 20/21.3.45.	
NG490		
PA162 QR-L	FTR Trossy-St-Maximin 3.8.44.	
PA165 QR-V	FTR Houffalize 5/6.1.45.	
PA329 QR-R		
PA998 QR-O	FTR Darmstadt 27/28.8.44.	
PB342 QR-B	To 617 Squadron.	
PB434 QR-R	Crashed on landing at Skellingthorpe on return from the Mittelland Canal at Gravenhorst 6/7.11.44.	
PB436 QR-D	FTR Königsberg 29/30.8.44.	
PB596	From 9 Squadron.	
PB649	To 227 Squadron.	
PB666	To 227 Squadron.	
PB725 QR-E	FTR Mittelland Canal at Gravenhorst 6/7.11.44.	
PB727		
PB737 QR-E	FTR Politz 8/9.2.45.	
PB759 QR-N	FTR Politz 8/9.2.45.	
PD199 QR-C	FTR Düsseldorf 2/3.11.44.	
PD266		
RA560 QR-K	FTR Böhlen. 20/21.3.45.	
RA561		
RA593		
RF121 QR-J	FTR Hamburg 9.4.45.	
RF123		
RF137 QR-E	Blew up on the ground at Skellingthorpe 24.2.45.	

RF160
RF176 QR-T	FTR Würzburg 16/17.3.45.
RF201 QR-C
SW277	From 9 Squadron. Destroyed when RF137 blew up at Skellingthorpe 24.2.45.

HEAVIEST SINGLE LOSS

17/18.08.43. Peenemünde. 4 Lancasters FTR.